MERGERS AND ACQUISITIONS

Patrick A. Gaughan
Fairleigh Dickinson University

HarperCollins*Publishers*

Sponsoring Editor: Suzy Spivey
Project Editor: Ellen MacElree
Design Supervisor: Heather A. Ziegler
Cover Design: Eugene M. Smith, Jr.
Cover Photo: © Roy F. Hillstrom, Jr., Hillstrom Stock Photo, Inc.
Production Assistant: Jeffrey Taub
Compositor: Ruttle, Shaw & Wetherill
Printer and Binder: R. R. Donnelley & Sons Company
Cover Printer: New England Book Components, Inc.

Mergers and Acquisitions

Library of Congress Cataloging-in-Publication Data
Gaughan, Patrick A.
    Mergers and acquisitions / Patrick A. Gaughan.
       p.   cm.
    Includes bibliographical references and index.
    ISBN 0-06-042452-4
    1. Consolidation and merger of corporations—United States.
  I. Title.
  HD2346.5.G38   1991
  658.1'6—dc20   91-2238
                                                        CIP

91 92 93 94 9 8 7 6 5 4 3 2 1

To Claudia with Love

Special Dedication to Margaret M. Gaughan

Contents

CHAPTER 6   MERGER TACTICS   223

CHAPTER 7   LEVERAGED BUYOUTS   269

CHAPTER 8   JUNK BONDS   336

CHAPTER 9   EMPLOYEE STOCK OWNERSHIP PLANS   399

CHAPTER 10   CASE STUDIES IN LEVERAGED BUYOUTS   420

CHAPTER 11   CORPORATE RESTRUCTURING   459

Foreword

Mergers and acquisitions have become indispensable tools in building a new generation of companies with the power and resources to compete on a global basis. While mergers have actually been around since the 1890s, they have in recent years dramatically transformed and redefined the business landscape.

When done for the right reasons and in the right way, mergers and acquisitions can indeed be beneficial. They can increase overall efficiency and profitability in our economy by creating new value in the combined companies. The merged entities themselves stand to reap significant rewards in terms of more efficient production, enhanced market coverage, technological advances, and better use of physical resources.

Unfortunately, mergers have gotten a bad name as a result of the increasing prominence of corporate raiders and hostile takeover attempts. Beginning in the late 1970s, a new lexicon came into existence, featuring such terms as *poison pills, golden parachutes, greenmail*, and *equity carve-outs*. With disturbing suddenness, we had entered the age of the leveraged buyout. Fueled by a reinvigorated junk bond market capable of raising astonishing sums of capital, corporate raiders were able to finance once unimaginable takeover bids.

The corporate raiders played the game to the hilt. Sometimes referred to as takeover artists, the raiders were in truth speculators whose activities were aimed not at building stronger, more efficiently managed companies, as they proclaimed, but at making mountains of quick money for themselves by breaking up and liquidating companies.

Whatever the raiders' motives, managing American businesses rapidly became infinitely more complex and risky. Takeover offensives and defensive counterstrategies reached creative—and at times absurd—new heights. Restructuring became the corporate watchword for the 1980s. New conflicts arose concerning the roles of federal and state governments in providing protection for companies that were the targets of unwanted takeover attempts. The field of mergers and acquisitions became elevated—some might say reduced—to a science. And corporate managers and business leaders who ignored these changes and did not learn to play by the new rules did so at their own peril.

Mergers and Acquisitions by Patrick Gaughan goes a long way toward providing the vital information managers need. It addresses its subject from a pragmatic and comprehensive standpoint, making generous use of the latest research and case studies in the field. In painstaking detail, Gaughan describes the issues, methods, motives, and techniques that shape the modern-day world of mergers and acquisitions. He delves, for example, into the intricate web of state and federal laws and regulations that affect mergers and acquisitions. The book also discusses the tax issues that must be carefully evaluated in the course of any merger, acquisition, or leveraged buyout. Another area that Gaughan puts into sharp focus is the financial analysis that both the acquiring and target companies should rigorously conduct prior to sealing any deal.

Today, running a business successfully often means understanding and being able to harness the complexities of mergers and acquisitions. The record shows that as many as two out of every three transactions fail to live up to initial projections of their value. Even for managers experienced in the art of mergers and acquisitions, this book offers fresh insights into a demanding and difficult field. There is much that all of us can learn about handling mergers and acquisitions.

Mergers and Acquisitions can help business managers capitalize on the opportunities inherent in mergers and acquisitions transactions—while avoiding the numerous pitfalls. It is a timely addition to our corporate knowledge base.

E. L. Hennessy, Jr.
Chairman of the Board
Allied-Signals Inc.

Preface

The field of mergers and acquisitions underwent rapid and dramatic changes over the past decade, a period that witnessed the development of the fourth and most unusual merger wave in U.S. economic history. Large-scale megamergers became commonplace. Hostile deals captured media headlines on a regular basis. Huge leveraged buyouts became unremarkable. The deal making reached its peak in 1988 with the blockbuster $25 billion leveraged buyout of RJR Nabisco.

Financial markets responded to the demand for these deals by creating a new form of high-risk finance—the original issue junk bond. Armed with an access to billions of dollars of debt capital, raiders proceeded to assault some of the larger, most well established American companies. These firms then responded by developing a powerful array of defensive measures to help thwart the aggressive maneuvers being used by the raiders. The field of mergers and acquisitions thus became increasingly more sophisticated and intricate as the stakes involved rose through the 1980s.

Mergers and leveraged buyouts also became a major source of controversy. Critics contended that the leveraging of corporate America was cause for concern. Policymakers pushed for legislative changes that would impede the growth of takeovers. Incumbent management of the Fortune 500, concerned that they would become the next target, were in the forefront of this effort.

As suddenly as it rose, however, the merger wave slowed, mainly due to the collapse of the junk bond market as well as other factors. The start of the 1990s features a new world of mergers and acquisitions that continues, but in a transformed state. Highly leveraged deals have been replaced partly by more conservatively financed transactions. The volume of deals has declined, yet large-scale acquisitions still continue. It is clear that mergers and acquisitions are a permanent and essential part of the world of corporate finance.

* * *

The focus of this book is decidedly pragmatic. I have attempted to write in a manner that will be useful for both the business student as well as the practitioner. Since the world of mergers and acquisitions is clearly interdisciplinary, material from the fields of law and economics is presented along with corporate finance, which is the primary emphasis of the book. The work of finance practitioners has been integrated with that of the academic world of finance. For example, three chapters are devoted to the valuation of businesses including the valuation of privately held firms. This is an important topic that is usually ignored by traditional finance textbooks. Much of the finance literature tends to be divided into two camps: practitioners and academicians. Clearly, both groups have made valuable contributions to the field of mergers and acquisitions. This book attempts to weave together these contributions into one comprehensible format.

The increase in merger and acquisition activity has given rise to the growth of academic research in this field. This book attempts to synthesize some of the more important and relevant research studies and to present their results in a straightforward and pragmatic manner. I do not attempt to cover all of the voluminous research in the field. Instead, the findings of the more important studies are highlighted. Issues such as the shareholder wealth effects of antitakeover measures have important meaning to investors who are concerned about how the value of their investment will be affected by defensive actions of corporations. This is a good example of where the academic research literature has made important pragmatic contributions which have served to shed light on important policy issues.

I have avoided incorporating some theoretical articles that have less relevance to those seeking a pragmatic treatment of mergers and acquisitions. On the other hand, some theoretical analyses, such as agency theory, can be helpful in explaining some of the incentives for managers to pursue a management buyout. Material from the field of portfolio theory can help explain some of the risk reduction benefits junk bond investors can derive through diversification. These more theoretical discussions, along with others, are presented because they have important relevance to the real world of mergers and acquisitions.

The rapidly evolving nature of mergers and acquisitions requires constant updating. Every effort has been made to include important recent developments occurring just prior to the publication date. Therefore, I feel that this text provides one of the most current presentations of the ever evolving world of acquisitions.

I would like to thank the reviewers of the manuscript for their constructive comments. They include Carolyn Kay Brancato; Kenneth Davidson, Esq., Federal Trade Commission; A. C. Edwards, Western Michigan University; Gershon Mandelker, University of Pittsburgh; and George E. Pinches, University of Kansas. I am very grateful to Professor Michael Grossman for his long-term support and friendship. Finally, special thanks are due to Professor Elizabeth Bogan and Dean Frederick Kelly for their support during the writing of this book.

Patrick A. Gaughan

Chapter
1

Introduction to Mergers and Acquisitions

T he 1980s represented one of the most intense periods of merger activity in U.S. economic history. This period witnessed the fourth merger wave of the twentieth century and specifically featured the hostile raid and the corporate raider. In addition, the junk bond market grew into a tool of high finance whereby bidders for corporations obtained access to billions of dollars to finance raids on some of the largest, most established corporations in the United States. This access to capital markets allowed *megamerger* deals to become a reality.

Not only did the volume of mergers and acquisitions reach an all-time high in the 1980s (Table 1.1), but also the average price of each acquisition increased steadily (Table 1.2). Prior to the 1980s, larger U.S. companies had little need to worry about preserving their independence. With the advent of the hostile raid, however, they erected formidable defenses against takeovers and increasingly called on state governments to pass laws to make hostile acquisitions more difficult.

The 1980s also featured the rapid growth and decline of the leveraged buyout (LBO)—the use of debt capital to finance a buyout of the firm's stock. In an LBO, a public company goes private by purchasing its publicly outstanding shares. This financing technique was popular in the mid-1980s but became a less viable alternative toward the end of the decade as the number of good LBO targets declined. The end of the decade also signaled a dramatic decline in the junk bond market,

1

Table 1.1   NET MERGER-ACQUISITION ANNOUNCEMENTS, 1963–1989

Year	Number	Year to Year Percentage Change
1963	1,361	
1964	1,950	+43%
1965	2,125	+ 9%
1966	2,377	+12%
1967	2,975	+25%
1968	4,462	+50%
1969	6,107	+37%
1970	5,152	−16%
1971	4,608	−11%
1972	4,801	+ 4%
1973	4,040	−16%
1974	2,861	−29%
1975	2,297	−20%
1976	2,276	− 1%
1977	2,224	− 2%
1978	2,106	− 5%
1979	2,128	+ 1%
1980	1,889	−11%
1981	2,395	+27%
1982	2,346	− 2%
1983	2,533	+ 8%
1984	2,543	−
1985	3,001	+18%
1986	3,336	+11%
1987	2,032	−39%
1988	2,258	+11%
1989	2,366	+ 4.8%

Source: Merrill Lynch Business Brokerage and Valuation, *Mergerstat Review,* 1990.

as raiders and LBO firms lost some of their access to the financing necessary to complete leveraged transactions (see Figure 1.1).

This book describes the growth and development of the art of mergers and acquisitions as of the beginning of the 1990s through both a historical focus and a review of the laws or rules that govern the game of mergers and acquisitions. In addition, we examine the motives that inspire mergers and acquisitions. We also discuss the offensive and defensive techniques of hostile acquisitions through analysis of the different methods that can be deployed to bring about a hostile take-over. The vast array of defenses that can be implemented to thwart a hostile bid are then reviewed. We explore offensive and defensive methods from the viewpoints of both management and shareholder.

Table 1.2   AVERAGE AND MEDIAN PURCHASE PRICE, 1968–1989
            (millions of dollars)

Year	Total Dollar Value Paid	Base*	Total**	Number of Transactions Valued at $100MM or More	$1000MM or More	Average Price	Median Price
1968	43,609.0	1,514	4,462	46		28.8	NA
1969	23,710.9	2,300	6,107	24		10.3	NA
1970	16,414.9	1,671	5,152	10	1	9.8	NA
1971	12,619.3	1,707	4,608	7		7.4	NA
1972	16,680.5	1,930	4,801	15		8.6	2.8
1973	16,664.5	1,574	4,040	28		10.6	3.4
1974	12,465.6	995	2,861	15		12.5	3.6
1975	11,796.4	848	2,297	14	1	13.9	4.3
1976	20,029.5	998	2,276	39	1	20.1	5.1
1977	21,937.1	1,032	2,224	41		21.3	6.6
1978	34,180.4	1,071	2,106	80	1	31.9	8.1
1979	43,535.1	1,047	2,128	83	3	41.6	8.5
1980	44,345.7	890	1,889	94	4	49.8	9.3
1981	82,617.6	1,126	2,395	113	12	73.4	9.0
1982	53,754.5	930	2,346	116	6	57.8	10.5
1983	73,080.5	1,077	2,533	138	11	67.9	16.5
1984	122,223.7	1,084	2,543	200	18	112.8	20.1
1985	179,767.5	1,320	3,001	270	36	136.2	21.1
1986	173,136.9	1,468	3,336	346	27	117.9	24.9
1987	163,686.3	972	2,032	301	36	168.4	51.3
1988	246,875.1	1,149	2,258	369	45	215.1	56.9
1989	221,085.1	1,092	2,366	328	35	202.5	36.6
Total	1,634,216.1	27,795	67,761	2,677	237		

*Base: The number of transactions which disclosed a purchase price.
**Total: Net merger-acquisition announcements.
Source: Merrill Lynch Business Brokerage and Valuation, *Mergerstat Review,* 1990.

The impact on the shareholder is examined through a review of the wealth effects of these different offensive and defensive tactics.

Also analyzed in detail are the technique of leveraged buyouts; the junk market, which is one of the main sources of LBO financing; and employee stock ownership plans, an important financing technique of leveraged buyouts. Examples of leveraged buyouts are considered through case studies that cover some of the leading leveraged buyouts.

Leveraged transactions often rely on the utilization of tax benefits. Therefore, we discuss the various tax issues involved in both leveraged and nonleveraged transactions and, in addition, corporate restructuring that involves a contraction, as opposed to acquisition-related expansion.

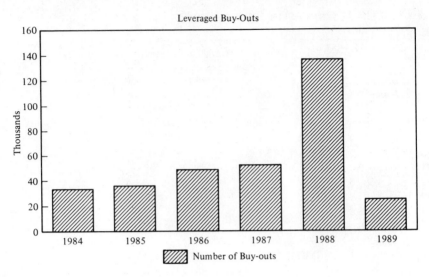

Figure 1.1 *Source:* IDD Information Services.

The process of valuation for mergers and acquisitions is covered in three parts; (1) a review of financial analysis to ensure that the reader has a common body of financial knowledge with which to approach the valuation process; (2) an application of this financial analysis to valuing publicly held firms; and (3) an analysis of the methods of valuing privately held businesses.

Throughout this book, we present the material from both a pragmatic and an academic viewpoint. The pragmatic focus utilizes a how-to approach as well as a detailed description of the real world of mergers and acquisitions rather than a theoretical treatment. This approach is complemented by a more traditional academic analysis of the relevant research literature in each of the areas described above. Research that lacks pragmatic value is not reviewed. This dual pragmatic/academic approach will give the reader the benefits of the practitioner's experience as well as the researchers' work on the frontier of the field.

TERMINOLOGY OF MERGERS AND ACQUISITIONS

A *merger* is a combination of two corporations in which only one corporation survives and the merged corporation goes out of existence. In a merger, the acquiring company assumes the assets and liabilities of the merged company. Sometimes, the term *statutory merger* is used to refer to this type of business transaction. A statutory merger differs from a *subsidiary merger* which is a merger of two companies where the target company becomes a subsidiary of the parent company. The acquisition of Electronic Data Systems by General Motors is an example of a subsidiary merger.

A merger differs from a *consolidation*, which is a business combination whereby two or more companies join to form an entirely new company. For example, in 1986 the computer manufacturers Burroughs and Sperry combined to form UNISYS. In a consolidation, the original companies cease to exist, and their stockholders become stockholders in the new company. Despite the differences between them, the terms *merger* and *consolidation*, as is true of many of the terms in the mergers and acquisitions field, are sometimes used interchangeably. In general, when the combining firms are approximately the same size, the term *consolidation* applies; when the two firms differ significantly by size, *merger* is the more appropriate term. In practice, however, this distinction is often blurred, with the term *merger* being broadly applied to combinations involving firms of both different and similar sizes.

Another term that is broadly used to refer to various types of transactions is *takeover*. We find that this term sometimes refers only to hostile transactions and at other times to both friendly and unfriendly mergers.

THE MERGER APPROVAL PROCESS

Most mergers and acquisitions are negotiated in a friendly environment. The process usually begins when the management of one firm contacts the target company's management, often through the investment bankers of each firm. The management of both firms keeps the board of directors up to date on the progress of the negotiations inasmuch as mergers usually require the board's approval. Upon reaching agreeable terms and receiving board approval, the deal is taken before the shareholders for their approval. This approval is granted through a vote. The exact percentage necessary for stockholder approval depends on the articles of incorporation, which, in turn, are regulated by the prevailing state corporation laws. Following approval, each firm files the necessary documents with the state authorities in which each firm is incorporated. Once this step is completed and the compensation has changed hands, the deal is completed.

THE SHORT FORM MERGER

A short form merger may take place in situations where the stockholder approval process is not necessary. Stockholder approval may be bypassed when the corporation's stock is concentrated in the hands of a small group, such as management, which is advocating the merger. Some state laws may allow this group to approve the transaction on their own without soliciting the approval of the other stockholders. The merger is simply approved by a resolution by the board of directors.

A short form merger can occur only when the stockholdings of insiders are beyond a certain threshold stipulated in the prevailing state corporation laws. In Delaware the percentage is 90 percent, and in New York it is 95 percent.[1]

FREEZEOUTS AND THE TREATMENT OF MINORITY SHAREHOLDERS

A majority of shareholders must approve before a merger can be completed. A two-thirds percentage is a common majority threshold. When this majority approves the deal, minority shareholders are required to tender their shares, even though they did not vote in favor of the deal. Minority shareholders are said to be *frozen out* of their positions. This majority approval requirement is designed to prevent a *holdout problem* which may occur when a small minority attempts to hold up the completion of a transaction unless they receive compensation over and above the acquisition stock price.

This is not to say that dissenting shareholders are without rights. Those shareholders who believe that their shares are worth significantly more than what the terms of the merger are offering can go to court to pursue their *shareholder appraisal rights*. There they can demand a cash settlement for the "fair value" of their shares. Of course, corporations resist these maneuvers since the payment of cash for the value of shares will raise problems relating to the positions of other stockholders. Such suits are very difficult for dissenting shareholders to win.

PURCHASE OF ASSETS COMPARED TO PURCHASE OF STOCK

The most common form of merger or acquisition involves purchasing the stock of the merged or acquired concern. An alternative to the stock acquisition is to purchase the target company's assets. In doing so, the acquiring company can limit its acquisitions to those parts of the firm that coincide with the acquirer's needs. When a significant part of the target remains after the asset acquisition, the transaction is

---

[1]Martin Lipton and Erica H. Steinberger, *Takeovers and Freezeouts* (New York: Law Journal Seminars Press, 1987), pp. 9–13.

only a partial acquisition of the target. When all the target's assets are purchased, the target becomes a corporate shell with only the cash or securities that it received from the acquisition as assets. In these situations, the corporation may choose to pay stockholders a liquidating dividend and dissolve the company. Alternatively, the firm may use its liquid assets to purchase other assets or another company.

ASSUMPTION OF THE SELLER'S LIABILITIES

If the acquirer buys all the target's stock, it assumes the seller's liabilities. The change in stock ownership does not free the new owners of the stock from the seller's liabilities. Most state laws provide this protection, which is sometimes referred to as *successor liability*. One way the acquirer can avoid assuming the seller's liabilities is to buy only the assets rather than the stock of the target. In cases where a buyer purchases a substantial portion of the target's assets, the courts have ruled that the buyer is responsible for the seller's liabilities. This is known as the *trust funds doctrine*. The court may also rule that the transaction is a *de facto merger*—a merger that occurs when the buyer purchases the assets of the target, and, for all intents and purposes, the transaction is treated as a merger.

The issue of successor liability may also apply to other commitments of the firm, such as union contracts. The National Labor Relations Board's position on this issue is that collective bargaining agreements are still in effect after acquisitions.

ASSET SELLOFFS

When a corporation chooses to sell off *all* its assets to another company, it becomes a corporate shell with cash and/or securities as its sole assets. The firm may then decide to distribute the cash to its stockholders as a liquidating dividend and go out of existence. The proceeds of the assets sale can also be distributed through a *cash repurchase tender offer*. That is, the firm makes a tender offer for its own shares using the proceeds of the asset sale to pay for shares. The firm may also choose to continue to do business and use its liquid assets to purchase other assets or companies. Laws are in force which regulate the distribution of proceeds where outstanding assets exist.

Firms that choose to remain in existence without assets are subject to the Investment Company Act of 1940. This law, one of a series of securities laws passed in the wake of the Great Depression and the associated stock market crash of 1929, applies when 100 or more stockholders remain after the sale of the assets. It requires that investment companies register with the Securities and Exchange Commission and adhere to its regulations applying to investment companies. The law also establishes standards that regulate investment companies. Specifically, it covers:

- Promotion of the investment company's activities.
- Reporting requirements.
- Pricing of securities for sale to the public.
- Issuance of prospectuses for sales of securities.
- Allocation of assets within the investment company's portfolio.

If a company that sells off all its assets chooses to invest the proceeds of the asset sale in Treasury Bills, these investments are not regulated by the act.

There are two kinds of investment companies: *open end investment companies* and *closed end investment companies*. The first, commonly referred to as mutual funds, issue shares that are equal to the value of the fund divided by the number of shares that are bought, after taking into account the costs of running the fund. The number of shares in a mutual fund increases or decreases depending on the number of new shares sold or the redemption of shares already issued.

Closed end investment companies generally do not issue new shares after the initial issuance. The value of these shares is determined by the value of the investments that are made using the proceeds of the initial share offering.[2]

ALTERNATIVE TO MERGERS OR ACQUISITIONS: HOLDING COMPANIES

Rather than a merger or an acquisition, the acquiring company may choose to purchase only a portion of the target's stock and act as a *holding company*, which is a company that owns sufficient stock to have a controlling interest in the target. The company that acquires the controlling interest is called the *parent company*, and the target is then treated as a subsidiary of the parent. If an acquirer buys 100 percent of the target, the company is known as a *wholly owned subsidiary*.

A 51 percent interest may not be necessary to allow a buyer to control a target. For companies with a widely distributed equity base, effective working control can be established with as little as 10 to 20 percent of the outstanding common stock.

---

[2]Ben Branch, *Investments*, 2nd ed. (Chicago: Longman Financial Services, 1989).

Advantages of the Holding Company Alternative

1. *Lower cost.* With a holding company structure, an acquirer can attain control of a target for a much smaller investment than would be necessary in a 100 percent stock acquisition. Obviously, a smaller number of shares to be purchased permits a lower total purchase price to be set. In addition, since fewer shares are demanded in the market, there is less upward price pressure on the firm's stock and the cost per share may be lower. The acquirer can attempt to minimize the upward price pressure by buying shares gradually over an extended period of time.

2. *No control premium.* Since 51 percent of the shares were not purchased, the control premium that is normally associated with 51 to 100 percent stock acquisitions would not have to be paid. As is discussed elsewhere in this book, the premium in friendly acquisitions can be significant, and it is even greater in hostile deals.

Disadvantages of the Holding Company Alternative

The holding company structure adds another layer to the corporate structure. Normally, stockholder income is subject to double taxation. Income is taxed at the corporate level, and some of the remaining income may then be distributed to stockholders in the form of dividends. Stockholders are then taxed on this dividend income at the individual level.

Holding companies receive dividend income from a company that has already been taxed at the corporate level. This income is then taxed at the holding company level before it is distributed to stockholders. This amounts to *triple taxation* of corporate income. According to the tax laws, only 15 percent of the dividend paid by a subsidiary is subject to taxation. If the corporate tax rate, for example, is 34 percent, this subsidiary income is taxed first at the 34 percent level and then at the 15 percent holding company level. For $100 of income that is received at the subsidiary level, and $66 is left to be paid to stockholders, including the holding company. This income is then taxed at a 15 percent rate, which implies a combined rate of

$$0.34 + (1 - 0.34).15 = 0.439$$
$$43.9\%$$

The income distributed to stockholders is then taxed at their individual level. If a holding company owns 80 percent or more of a subsidiary's stock, then the dividend income paid by a subsidiary is not subject to taxation.

Chapter
2

History of Mergers

*F*our periods of high merger activity, often called merger waves, have taken place in the history of the United States. These periods were characterized by cyclic activity: that is, high levels of mergers followed by periods of relatively fewer mergers. The four waves occurred between 1897 and 1904; 1916 and 1929; 1965 and 1969; and 1981 to the present. These activities provoked major changes in the structure of American business. They were instrumental in transforming American industry from a collection of small and medium-sized businesses to the current form of multinational corporations. Each merger wave developed for different reasons and produced different results.

In this chapter, our discussion focuses on the later merger periods because they are, of course, more relevant to recent trends in the world of mergers. By examining recent periods, we can more closely approximate the present and the foreseeable future. We also examine some of the precedent-setting mergers of the 1970s.

THE FIRST WAVE, 1897–1904

The first merger wave set in after the Depression of 1883, peaking between 1898 and 1902 and ending in 1904. Although these mergers affected all major mining and manufacturing industries, certain industries clearly demonstrated a higher incidence of merger activity. According to a National Bureau of Economic Research study by Professor

Table 2.1   MERGERS, 1897–1904

Year	Number of Mergers
1897	69
1898	303
1899	1,208
1900	340
1901	423
1902	379
1903	142
1904	79

Ralph Nelson, eight industries experienced the greatest merger activity: primary metals, food products, petroleum products, chemicals, transportation equipment, fabricated metal products, machinery, and bituminous coal.[1] These industries accounted for approximately two-thirds of all mergers during this period.

The many horizontal mergers and industry consolidations of this era often resulted in a near monopolistic market structure. For this reason, this merger period is known for its role in creating large monopolies. This period is also associated with the first billion dollar megamerger deal when U.S. Steel was formed when Carnegie Steel combined with its major rivals. The resulting steel giant combined 785 separate firms. Some of today's great industrial giants originated in the first merger wave: Du Pont Inc., Standard Oil, General Electric, Eastman Kodak, American Tobacco Inc., Navistar International (formerly International Harvester), and USX Corporation (formerly U.S. Steel).

In the first merger movement, there were 300 major combinations covering many industrial areas and controlling 40 percent of the nation's manufacturing capital. The pace of merger activity is shown in Table 2.1.

By 1909, the 100 largest industrial corporations controlled nearly 18 percent of the assets of all industrial corporations. Even the enactment of the Sherman Antitrust Act (1890) did not impede this period of intense activity. The Justice Department was largely responsible for the limited effect of the Sherman Antitrust Act. During the period of major consolidation of the early 1900s, the Justice Department, charged with enforcing the act, was understaffed and unable to aggressively pursue antitrust enforcement. The agency's activities were directed

---

[1] Ralph Nelson, *Merger Movements in American Industry: 1895–1956* (Princeton, N.J.: Princeton University Press, 1959).

more toward labor unions. Therefore, the pace of horizontal mergers and industry consolidations continued without any meaningful antitrust restrictions.

By the end of the first great merger wave, a marked increase in the degree of concentration was evident in American industry. There was a dramatic decline in the number of firms in some industries, such as the steel industry, and in some areas, all but one firm survived. It is ironic that monopolistic industries formed in light of the passage of the Sherman Antitrust Act in 1890. However, an act is only as strong as the courts' willingness to enforce it, and this willingness, in turn, is dependent on the interpretation the courts apply. The Sherman Antitrust Act was not interpreted as being directed at the formation of monopolies through mergers. Rather, it focused on regulating stockholder trusts, in which investors would invest funds in a firm and entrust their stock certificates with directors who would ensure that they received dividends for their "trust certificates." For this reason, the law was not applied to hinder the formation of monopolies in several industries in the first merger wave.

In addition to lax enforcement of federal antitrust laws, other legal reasons explain why the first merger wave thrived. For example, state corporation laws were gradually relaxed. In particular, corporations became better able to secure capital, hold stock in other corporations, and expand their lines of business operations, thereby creating a fertile environment for firms to contemplate mergers. Greater access to capital made it easier for firms to raise the necessary financing to carry out an acquisition, and relaxed rules controlling the stockholdings of corporations allowed firms to acquire the stock in other firms with the purpose of acquiring them.

Not all states liberalized corporate laws. As a result, the pace of mergers and acquisitions was greater in some states than in others. New Jersey, in which the passage of the New Jersey Holding Company Act of 1888 helped liberalize state corporation laws, was the leading state in mergers and acquisitions, followed by New York and Delaware. This act pressured other states to enact similar legislation rather than see firms move to reincorporate in New Jersey. Many firms, however, did choose to incorporate in New Jersey, which explains the wide variety of New Jersey firms that participated in the first merger wave. This trend declined dramatically by 1915 when the differences in state corporation laws became less significant.

The development of the U.S. transportation system was one of the major factors that initiated the first merger wave. Following the Civil War, the establishment of a major railway system created national rather than regional markets which firms could potentially serve. Many firms, no longer viewing market potential as being limited by narrowly defined market boundaries, expanded to take advantage of a now broader based market. Many firms, now facing competition from distant rivals, chose to merge with local competitors in order to maintain their market share. Changes in the national transportation system made supplying distant markets both easier and less expensive. The cost of rail freight transportation fell at an average rate of 3.7 percent per year during the 1882–1900 period.[2] In the early 1900s, transportation costs increased very little, despite a rising demand for transportation services.

Several other structural changes helped firms access national markets. For example, the invention of the Bonsack continuous process cigarette machine enabled the American Tobacco Company to supply the nation's cigarette market with a relatively small number of machines.[3]

As firms expanded, they exploited economies of scale in production and distribution. For example, the Standard Oil Trust controlled 40 percent of the world oil production by using only three refineries. The Trust eliminated unnecessary plants and thereby achieved greater efficiency.[4]

As noted, the first merger wave did not start until 1897, but the first great takeover battle began much earlier—in 1868. While the term *takeover battle* is commonly used today in describing the sometimes acerbic conflicts among firms in takeovers, it can be more literally applied to the conflicts that occurred in early corporate mergers. One such takeover contest involved an attempt to take control of the Erie Railroad in 1868. The takeover attempt pitted Cornelius Vanderbilt against Daniel Drew, Jim Fisk, and Jay Gould. As one of their major takeover defenses, the defenders of the Erie Railroad issued themselves large quantities of stock, even though they lacked the authorization to do so. At that time, bribery of judges and elected officials was common, and so legal remedies for violating corporate laws were particularly weak. The battle for control of the railroad took a violent turn when the target corporation hired guards, equipped with firearms and cannons, to guard their headquarters. The takeover attempt ended when Vanderbilt abandoned his assault on the Erie Railroad and turned his attention to weaker targets.

In the late nineteenth century, as a result of such takeover contests,

---

[2]Ibid.

[3]Alfred D. Chandler, *The Visible Hand: The Managerial Revolution in American Business* (Cambridge, Mass.: Belknap Press, 1977), p. 249.

[4]Alfred D. Chandler, "The Coming of Oligopoly and Its Meaning for AntiTrust," in *National Competition Policy: Historian's Perspective on Antitrust and Government Business Relationships in the United States*, Federal Trade Commission Publication, August 1981, p. 72.

the public became increasingly concerned about unethical business practices. Corporate laws were not particularly effective during the 1890s. Not until the passage of antitrust legislation in the late 1800s and early 1900s, and tougher securities laws after the Great Depression, did the legal system attain the necessary power to discourage unethical takeover tactics.

Lacking adequate legal restraints, the banking and business community adopted its own voluntary code of ethical behavior. This code was enforced by an unwritten agreement among investment bankers, who agreed to do business only with firms that adhered to their higher ethical standards. Today, Great Britain relies on such a voluntary code. Although these informal standards did not preclude all improper activities in the pursuit of takeovers, they did set the stage for reasonable behavior during the first takeover wave.

Financial factors rather than legal restrictions forced the end of the first merger wave. First, the shipbuilding trust collapse in the early 1900s brought to the fore the dangers of fraudulent financing. Second, and most important, the stock market crash of 1904, followed by the Banking Panic of 1907, closed many of the nation's banks and ultimately paved the way for the Federal Reserve System. As a result of a declining stock market and a weak banking system, the basic financial ingredients for fueling takeovers were absent. Without these, the first great takeover period came to a halt.

THE SECOND WAVE, 1916–1929

George Stigler, the Nobel Prize-winning economist and professor at the University of Chicago, has contrasted the first and second merger waves as "merging for monopoly" versus "merging for oligopoly." During the second merger wave several industries were consolidated. Rather than monopolies, the result was often an oligopolistic industry structure. The consolidation pattern established in the first merger period continued into the second. During this second period, the American economy continued to evolve and develop, owing primarily to the post–World War I economic boom, which provided much investment capital for eagerly waiting securities markets. The availability of capital, which was fueled by favorable economic conditions and lax margin requirements, set the stage for the stock market crash of 1929.

The antitrust environment of the 1920s was stricter than that which had prevailed before the first merger wave. By 1910, Congress had become concerned about the abuses of the market and the power wielded by monopolies. It had also become clear that the Sherman Antitrust Act was not an effective deterrent to monopoly. As a result, Congress passed the Clayton Act in 1914, a law that reinforced the antimonopoly provisions of the Sherman Act. (For a detailed discussion of the Clayton Act see Chapter 3.) As the economy and the banking system rebounded in the late 1900s, this antitrust law became a more important deterrent to monopoly. The more stringent antitrust environment produced fewer monopolies in the second wave and more oligopolies and many vertical mergers. In addition, many companies in unrelated industries merged. This was the first large-scale formation of conglomerates. However, while these business combinations involved firms that did not directly produce the same products, they often had similar product lines.

ALLIED CHEMICAL CORPORATION

Allied Chemical Corporation, one of the conglomerates formed in this period, consolidated control over five different companies: General Chemical, Barrett, Solvay Process, Semet-Solvay, and National Aniline and Chemical. Although these firms clearly had different product lines, they operated in related business areas: General Chemical was a combination of 12 producers of sulfuric acid; Barrett sold byproducts of ammonia as well as coal tar products; Solvay Process was the country's largest producer of ash; Semet sold coal tar products; and National Aniline and Chemical Company was the nation's largest seller of dye-stuffs. Consolidated under the single aegis of the Allied Chemical Corporation, these various different production processes united under a single management structure. Thus, Allied was able to exploit the various economies that existed across these production processes and their related marketing activities.[5]

Between 1926 and 1930, a total of 4,600 mergers took place, and in the 1919–1930 period, 12,000 manufacturing, mining, public utility, and banking firms disappeared. According to Earl Kintner, "During 1921–1933, assets of $13 billion were acquired by merger representing 17.5% of the nations total manufacturing assets."[6] The continued de-

[5]Jesse Markham, "Survey of the Evidence and Findings on Mergers," in *Business Concentration and Public Policy* (Princeton, N.J.: Princeton University Press, 1955). See comments by George W. Stocking, pp. 208–209.

[6]Earl W. Kintner, *Primer on the Law of Mergers* (New York: Macmillan Publishing Co., 1973), p. 9.

velopment of a nationwide rail transportation system, combined with the growth of motor vehicle transportation, continued to transform local markets into national markets. Competition among firms was enhanced by the proliferation of radios in homes as a major form of entertainment. This led to the increased use of advertising as a form of product differentiation. Marketers took advantage of this new advertising medium to start national brand advertising. The era of mass merchandising had begun.

The public utility industry in particular experienced marked concentration. Many of these mergers involved public utility holding companies that were controlled by a relatively small number of stockholders. These utilities were often organized with a pyramidal corporate structure to provide profits for these stockholders and, according to the Federal Trade Commission, did not serve the public interest. The utility trusts were eventually regulated by the Public Utility Holding Company Act (PUHCA) of 1935. This law, designed to curb abuses, empowered the Securities and Exchange Commission (SEC) to regulate the corporate structure and voting rights of public utility stockholders. The act also gave the SEC the right to regulate the issuance of securities by utilities as well as their acquisition of assets or securities of other firms. Since the utilities' abuses of corporate power and fiduciary responsibilities were far more common at that time than they are today, the PUHCA essentially serves little purpose today.

While mergers affected industries across the board, the following experienced a disproportionate number of mergers:

- Primary metals.
- Petroleum products.
- Food products.
- Chemicals.
- Transportation equipment.

Mergers were facilitated not only by the limited enforcement of antitrust laws, but also by the federal government's encouragement of the formation of business cooperatives as part of the war effort. The government encouraged businesses to work together to enhance the nation's productivity. Rather than compete with each other during a time of war, the nation's firms, particularly those in manufacturing and mining, were urged to help maximize the war effort. Even after the war ended, however, the government maintained these policies through the 1920s.

The second merger wave ended with the stock market crash on October 24, 1929. "Black Thursday" would mark the largest stock market drop in history until the crash of October 1987. Although this collapse was not per se the cause of the Great Depression, it played a large role in it, for in contributing to a dramatic drop in business and investment confidence, business and consumer spending was further curtailed, thereby worsening the depression. After the crash, the number of corporate mergers declined dramatically. No longer focusing on expansion, firms sought merely to maintain solvency amid the rapid and widespread reduction in demand.

Investment bankers played key roles in the first two merger periods, exercising considerable influence among business leaders. They often vetoed a merger by withholding finances from the firm when they felt that the merger was against the investment bank's policies or ethical interests. The investment banks easily achieved controlling influence since a small number of them controlled the majority of the capital available for financing mergers and acquisitions. The investment banking industry was more concentrated in those years than it is today. The bulk of their capital was controlled by a small group who tended not to compete with each other. For example, one investment banker generally did not attempt to solicit business from another; each banker had his own clients, and those relationships tended not to change. This sharply contrasts with the high degree of competition that exists in the industry today.

The number of mergers that took place during the first two waves demonstrates that investment banks generally supported merger activities. However, in the third merger period—the conglomerate era—the financial impetus for mergers would come from sources other than investment banks.

THE 1940s

Before we proceed to a discussion of the third merger period, we will briefly examine the mergers of the 1940s. During this decade, larger firms acquired smaller, privately held companies for motives of tax relief. In this period of high estate taxes, the transfer of businesses within families was very expensive, and so it was that the incentive to sell out to other firms arose. These mergers did not result in increased concentration because most of them did not represent a significant percentage of the total industry's assets. Most of the family business combinations involved smaller companies.

The 1940s did not feature any major technological changes or dramatic development in the nation's infrastructure. Thus, the increase in the number of mergers was relatively small. Nonetheless, their numbers were still a concern to Congress, which reacted by passing the

Celler–Kefauver Act. This law strengthened Section 7 of the Clayton
Act. (For further details on the Clayton Act, see the following section
and Chapter 3.)

THE THIRD WAVE, 1965–1969

The third merger wave featured a historically high level of merger
activity. This was brought about, in part, by a booming economy.
During this wave, often known as the conglomerate merger period,
relatively smaller firms targeted larger firms for acquisition. In contrast,
during the two earlier waves, the majority of the target firms were
significantly smaller than the acquiring firms. Peter Steiner reports that
the "acquisition of companies with assets over $100 million, which
averaged only 1.3 per year from 1948 to 1960, and 5 per year from
1961 to 1966, rose to 24 in 1967, 31 in 1968, 20 in 1969, 12 in 1970
before falling to 5 each year in 1971 and 1972."[7]

The number of mergers and acquisitions during the 1960s is listed
in Figure 2.1. These data were compiled by W. T. Grimm and Company
which began recording mergers and acquisition announcements on
January 1, 1963.

The conglomerates formed during this period were more than
merely diversified in their product lines. The term *diversified firms* is
generally applied to firms that have some subsidiaries in other industries but a majority of their production within one industry category. A
good example of a diversified firm is General Motors, an automobile
manufacturer with subsidiaries in related industries such as the Electronic Data Systems, a computer company. Unlike the diversified firms,
conglomerates conduct a large percentage of their business activities in
different industries. Good examples are LTV, Litton Industries, and
ITT. In the 1960s, ITT acquired such diverse businesses as restaurant
chains, consumer credit agencies, hotels, home building, and airport
parking firms.

As firms with the necessary financial resources sought to expand,
they came up against tougher antitrust enforcement. The heightened
antitrust atmosphere of the 1960s was an outgrowth of the Celler–
Kefauver Act of 1950 which had strengthened the antimerger provisions
of the Clayton Act of 1914. The Clayton Act made the acquisition of
other firms' stock illegal when the acquisition resulted in a merger that
significantly reduced the degree of competition within an industry.

---

[7]Peter O. Steiner, *Mergers: Motives, Effects and Policies* (Ann Arbor: University of
Michigan Press, 1975).

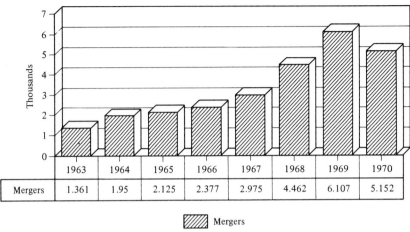

Third Merger Wave
Merger Acquisition Announcements
1963–1970

	1963	1964	1965	1966	1967	1968	1969	1970
Mergers	1.361	1.95	2.125	2.377	2.975	4.462	6.107	5.152

Mergers

Figure 2.1 The third merger wave peaked in 1969. The decline in the stock market coupled with tax reforms reduced the incentive to merge.

However, the law had an important loophole: it did not preclude the anticompetitive acquisition of a firm's assets. The Celler–Kefauver Act closed this loophole. Armed with tougher laws, the federal government adopted a stronger antitrust stance, coming down hard on both horizontal and vertical mergers. Expansion-minded firms found that their only available alternative was to form conglomerates.

The more intense antitrust enforcement of horizontal mergers was partially motivated by the political environment of the 1960s. During this decade Washington, emphasizing the potential for abuses of monopoly power, worked through the Federal Trade Commission and the Justice Department to curb corporate expansion, which created the potential for monopolistic abuses. A prime advocate of this tougher antitrust enforcement was Assistant Attorney General Richard Mc-Lauren, the main architect of the federal government's antitrust efforts during the 1960s. Harold Geneen, then chief executive of ITT, one of the leading conglomerates of that era, has described the difficulty his firm had in acquiring companies when McLauren was in office.[8] McLauren opposed conglomerate acquisitions based on his fears of "potential reciprocity." This would occur, for example, if ITT and its other subsidiaries gave Hartford Insurance, a company ITT acquired, a competitive edge over other insurance companies. ITT was forced to

---

[8]Harold Geneen, *Managing* (New York: Avon Books, 1989), pp. 228–229.

compromise its plans to add Hartford to its conglomerate empire. It was able to proceed with the acquisition only after agreeing to divest itself of other divisions with the same combined size of Hartford Insurance and to not acquiring another large insurance company, for another 10 years, without prior Justice Department approval.

With the election of Richard M. Nixon toward the end of the decade, Washington advocated a freer market orientation. Nixon supported this policy through his four new appointees to the U.S. Supreme Court who espoused a broader interpretation of concepts such as market share. For example, they based their interpretation of market share on a definition of the entire market as an international rather than a national market. Consequently, if as a result of a merger a firm had a large percentage of the U.S. market but a small percentage of the international market, it could be judged to lack significant monopolistic characteristics.

The rapid growth of management science accelerated the conglomerate movement. Schools of management began to attain widespread acceptability among prominent schools of higher education, and the master's of business administration became a valued credential for the corporate executive. Management science developed methodologies that facilitate organizational management and that could theoretically be applied to a wide variety of organizations, including corporations, government, educational institutions, and even the military. As these management principles gained wider acceptance, graduates of this movement felt they possessed the broad-based skills necessary to manage a wide variety of organizational structures. Such managers reasonably believed that they could manage a corporate organization that spanned several industry categories. The belief that the conglomerate could become a manageable and successful corporate entity started to become a reality.

Because most of the mergers involved the formation of conglomerates, rather than vertical or horizontal mergers, they did not increase industrial concentration. For this reason, the degree of competition in different industries did not change appreciably, despite the large number of mergers. Some 6,000 mergers entailing the disappearance of 25,000 firms took place; nonetheless, competition or market concentration in the U.S. economy was not greatly reduced.

The Price–Earnings Game and the Incentive to Merge

As mentioned earlier, investment bankers did not finance most of the mergers in the 1960s, as they had in the two previous merger waves. Tight credit markets and high interest rates were the concomitants of the higher credit demands of an expanding economy. As the demand for loanable funds rose, both the price of these funds and interest rates increased. In addition, the booming stock market prices provided financing for many of the conglomerate takeovers.

The bull market of the 1960s bid stock prices higher and higher. The Dow Jones Industrial Average, 618 in 1960, rose to 906 in 1968. As their stock prices skyrocketed, investors were especially interested in growth stocks. Potential bidders soon learned that acquisitions, financed by stocks, could be an excellent, "pain-free" way to raise earnings per share without incurring higher tax liabilities. Mergers financed through stock transactions may not be taxable. For this reason, stock-financed acquisitions had an advantage over cash transactions which were subject to taxation.

Companies played the price-earnings ratio game to justify their expansionist activities. The *price–earnings ratio (P/E ratio)* is the ratio of the market price of a firm's stock divided by the earnings available to common stockholders on a per share basis. The higher the P/E ratio, the more investors are willing to pay for a firm's stock given their expectations about the firm's future earnings. High P/E ratios for the majority of stocks in the market indicate widespread investor optimism; such was the case in the bull market of the 1960s. The high stock values finance the third merger wave. We can illustrate mergers inspired by the P/E ratio as follows.

Let's assume that the acquiring firm is larger than the target firm it is considering merging with. Let's further assume that the larger firm has a P/E ratio of 25:1 and annual earnings of $1 million, with 1 million shares outstanding. Each share sells for $25. The target firm has a lower P/E ratio of 10:1, with annual earnings of $100,000 and 100,000 shares outstanding. This firm's stock sells for $10. The larger firm offers the smaller firm a premium on its stock to entice its stockholders to sell. This premium comes in the form of a stock-for-stock offer in which one share of the larger firm, worth $25, is offered for two shares of the smaller firm, worth a total of $20. The large firm issues 50,000 shares to finance the purchase.

This acquisition causes the earnings per share (EPS) of the higher P/E firm to rise.

$$\text{EPS} = \frac{\text{Earnings available to common stockholders}}{\text{Number of common shares outstanding}}$$

$$= \frac{\$1.1 \text{ million}}{1.050 \text{ million shares}}$$

$$= \$1.05$$

The earnings per share of the higher P/E firm has risen to $1.05 from $1.00. We can see the effect on the price of the larger firm's stock if we make the crucial assumption that the P/E ratio stays the same. We also assume that the market will continue to value this firm's future earnings in a similar manner as it did prior to the acquisition. We will examine the validity of this type of assumption in greater detail in later chapters.

If we assume that the P/E ratio of the combined firm remains at $25, then the stock price will rise to $26.25 (25 × $1.05). We can see that the larger firm can offer the smaller firm a significant premium, while its EPS and stock price rises. This process can continue with other acquisitions, which also result in further increases in the firm's stock price. This process will end if the market decides not to apply the same P/E ratio. A bull market, such as occurred in the 1960s, helped promote high P/E values. When the market falls, however, as it did at the end of the 1960s, this process is not feasible.

The process of acquisitions, based on P/E reasoning, becomes increasingly untenable as a firm seeks to apply it to successively larger firms. The crucial assumption in creating the expectation that stock prices will rise is that the P/E ratio of the high P/E firm will apply to the combined firm. However, as the targets become larger and larger firms, the target becomes a more important percentage of the combined firm's earning power. As the combined firm incorporates several relatively lower P/E firms, the market becomes reluctant to apply the

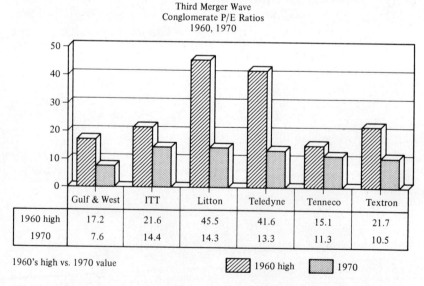

Third Merger Wave
Conglomerate P/E Ratios
1960, 1970

1960's high vs. 1970 value	Gulf & West	ITT	Litton	Teledyne	Tenneco	Textron
1960 high	17.2	21.6	45.5	41.6	15.1	21.7
1970	7.6	14.4	14.3	13.3	11.3	10.5

1960 high   1970

Figure 2.2 The end of the third merger wave was signaled by the dramatic decline in the P/E ratios of some of that era's leading conglomerates.

Table 2.2   CONGLOMERATE P/E RATIOS IN THE 1960s

Corporation	High	1970 Value
Gulf & Western	17.2	7.6
ITT	21.6	14.4
Litton Industries	45.5	14.3
Teledyne	41.6	13.3
Tenneco	15.1	11.3
Textron	21.7	10.5

Source: Peter O. Steiner, Mergers: Motives, Effects, Policies (Ann Arbor: University of Michigan Press, 1975), p. 104.

original higher P/E ratio. Therefore, it becomes more difficult to find target firms that will not decrease the acquirer's stock price. As the number of suitable acquisition candidates declines, the merger wave slows down. Therefore, a merger wave based on such "finance gimickry" can last only a limited time period before it exhausts itself, as this one did.

With the bull market growth and the formation of huge conglomerates, the term *the Go Go Years* was applied to the 1960s. When the stock market fell in 1969, it affected the pace of acquisitions by reducing P/E ratios. Figure 2.2 and Table 2.2 demonstrate how this decline affected some of the larger conglomerates.

Accounting Manipulations and the Incentive to Merge

Various accounting manipulations that allowed firms to realize "paper gains" on their financial statements also helped create an incentive for firms to merge in the 1960s. The result, in turn, was a temporary inflation in their stock prices. The two methods of accounting for mergers are *pooling of interests* and *purchase accounting*. However, prior to changes in the accounting rules, each method gave the firm an opportunity to incur paper gains while consummating mergers.

The pooling of interests method, which is discussed in greater detail in Chapter 12, assumes that the transaction between stockholders is just an exchange of equity securities. Therefore, the capital stock of the target firm is eliminated, and the acquirer issues new stock to replace it. The two firms' assets and liabilities are combined at their historical book values as of the acquisition date.[9] With the purchase method,

---

[9]Joseph H. Marren, *Mergers and Acquisitions* (Homewood, Ill.: Dow Jones Irwin, 1985), p. 210.

assets and liabilities are entered on the merged firm's books at their values as of the acquisition date. This accounting valuation method is based on the idea that the resulting values, recorded on the firm's books, should reflect the values generated in the bargaining process. This process should result in a fairer representation of the valuation of these assets. Through the pooling of interests method, the acquiring firm can generate additional paper earnings if it acquires "undervalued assets." The acquiring company can generate earnings whenever it likes by selling these assets at their actual market values. To illustrate this accounting manipulation, A. J. Briloff recounts how Gulf and Western generated earnings in 1967 by selling off the films of Paramount Pictures, acquired in 1966.[10] The bulk of Paramount's assets were in the form of feature films which it listed on its books at a value significantly less than their market value. In 1967, Gulf and Western sold 32 of the films of its Paramount subsidiary. This generated significant income for Gulf and Western in 1967 which succeeded in supporting Gulf and Western's stock price.

Peter O. Steiner states that these accounting manipulations made fire and casualty insurance companies popular takeover targets during this period.[11] He hypothesizes that conglomerates found their large portfolios of undervalued assets to be particularly attractive in light of the impact of a subsequent sale of these assets on the conglomerate's future earnings. Even the very large Hartford Insurance Company, which had assets of nearly $2 billion in 1968, had assets that were clearly undervalued. ITT capitalized on this undervaluation when it acquired Hartford Insurance. Many analysts believe that the purchase accounting method would eliminate these accounting manipulations because these assets would be valued at market values at the time of exchange. Unfortunately, there is some opportunity for deception such as in the case of the valuation of goodwill and its treatment as an amortizable asset. The acquiring firm could retain this goodwill (such as in the case of a firm's name) even after its assets were sold.

Another artificial incentive that encouraged conglomerate acquisitions involved securities, which were used to finance acquisitions. Acquiring firms would issue convertible debentures in exchange for common stock of the target firm. Convertible debentures are debt securities that can be converted into a specific amount of common stock. In such a situation the target's earnings are added without an increase in common stock outstanding. If the stock price rose, however, the value of

---

[10]A. J. Briloff, "Accounting Practices and the Merger Movement," *Notre Dame Lawyer* 45, no. 4 (Summer 1970): 604–628.

[11]Steiner, *Mergers*, p. 116.

the convertible debentures would also rise since their conversion values rise. When convertible debentures are used to finance acquisitions, the earnings of the two firms are added together, but the stock of the target has been replaced by debt. Earnings per share rise since the target earnings are added to the acquiring firm but the total shares outstanding remain the same. If the same P/E ratio is applied to the merged firm, the stock price rises, thereby yielding a profit for the convertible debenture holders.

Several laws enacted toward the end of the 1960s helped to end the third merger wave. In 1968, the Williams Act placed limits on the aggressiveness of tender offers and takeover attempts. Still a very influential piece of takeover regulation, the Williams Act will be discussed in detail, along with tender offers, in Chapter 3. Although the act limited some abusive takeover tactics, it did not stop hostile takeovers; it may unintentionally actually have facilitated some of them.

In 1969, passage of the Tax Reform Act ended some of the manipulative accounting abuses that created paper earnings that temporarily support stock prices. Specifically, it limited the use of convertible debt to finance acquisitions. Before this law, debtholders were willing to accept very low rates in exchange for the future capital gains on the sale of the convertible debentures. The low debt rates did not increase the riskiness of the corporation's capital structure since the associated fixed payments were low. The 1969 Tax Reform Act ended the use of low-rate convertible debt to finance acquisitions by stipulating that the low-rate convertible debt would be treated as common stock. Consequently, earnings per share would not enjoy a paper increase because, for the purpose of its calculation, common stock had in effect risen. This law also placed limits on the valuation of undervalued assets of targets which were to be sold at higher values to generate increased earnings.

The changing regulatory atmosphere at the end of the 1960s set the stage for a slowdown in this merger wave. When the stock market fell in 1969, the P/E game could no longer be played. Indeed, many analysts felt that the conglomerate mergers helped collapse this market inasmuch as when securities attain values far in excess of the underlying economic basis for their valuation, a collapse is sure to follow. This would be one lesson of the stock market crash of October 1987.

Market Efficiency and Artificial Manipulations of Stock Prices

Many conglomerate mergers of this period were inspired by financial manipulations that would create the appearance that the combined firms were in better financial condition than their underlying economic earning power would imply. Should stock prices have risen in response to these financial manipulations? The finance literature questions the efficacy of such manipulations in an efficient market. However, many believe that these manipulations were, in part, the basis for the third merger wave.

Market efficiency refers to the ability of market prices to reflect all available information. An efficient market, which quickly assimilates all relevant and available information, should not be fooled by purely artificial manipulations of financial statements. Many studies have been documented which test the efficiency of markets in response to various events such as announcements of earnings, stock splits, or world events. A number of studies examine the influence of accounting changes on stock prices.[12] Stock prices should not respond to accounting changes that do not reflect the firms' changed economic value. Altered entries on its books or variations in "reported earnings" do not affect the firm's earning capacity. T. Ross Archibald has examined the reaction of stock prices to changes in the method of depreciation from accelerated depreciation to straight-line depreciation for financial statement purposes.[13] As a result of these changes, 65 of the firms that Archibald examined experienced an increase in reported profits without any change in their underlying economic earning power. Archibald notes that price changes following the announcements tended to be negative. This implies that investors saw through the reported profits changes and evaluated the stocks in terms of their true investment potential.

Other studies have supported the efficient markets view that firms should not be able to easily fool the market by making accounting changes designed to present a false picture of economic viability. As Robert Kaplan and Richard Roll show, a firm's stock price eventually fell, even though the firm engaged in accounting changes that presented a more favorable appearance while having a poor performance.[14] However, Kaplan and Roll observed that the stock prices of these firms did

---

[12]E. F. Fama, L. Fisher, M. Jensen, and R. Roll, "The Adjustment of Stock Prices to New Information," *International Economic Review* 10, no. 1 (February 1969): 1–21. Philip Brown and Ray Ball, "An Empirical Evaluation of Accounting Income Numbers," *Journal of Accounting Research* 6, no. 2 (Autumn 1963): 159–178; Frank Rielly and Eugene Drzyminski, "Tests of Stock Market Efficiency Following World Events," *Journal of Business Research* 1, no. 2 (Summer 1973): 57–72.

[13]T. Ross Archibald, "Stock Market Reaction to the Depreciation Switch-Back," *Accounting Review* 47, no. 1 (January 1972): 22–30.

[14]Robert S. Kaplan and Richard Roll, "Investor Evaluation of Accounting Information: Some Empirical Evidence," *Journal of Business* 45, no. 2 (April 1972): 225–257.

experience some temporary benefits. These studies on the efficiency of securities markets are consistent with the experiences of the conglomerate era in the history of mergers. In the long term the market is relatively efficient in processing information. However, there is evidence of short-term inefficiency.

The conglomerate firms achieved temporary gains through financial manipulations. The more exaggerated these gains, however, the more certain the market will eventually respond with a more accurate evaluation. This occurred when the market turned against the conglomerates and marked the end of the third merger wave.

THE TREND-SETTING MERGERS OF THE 1970s

The number of merger and acquisition announcements in the 1970s fell dramatically as shown in Table 2.3. (See also Figure 2.3.).

Even so, the decade played a major role in merger history. Several pathbreaking mergers changed the types of acceptable takeover behavior in the years to follow. The first of these mergers was the INCO versus ESB merger.

INCO Versus ESB Merger

After the third merger wave, an historic merger paved the way for a type that would be pervasive in the fourth wave: the hostile takeover by major, established companies.

In 1974, the Philadelphia-based ESB (formerly known as the Elec-

Table 2.3   MERGER AND ACQUISITION ANNOUNCEMENTS, 1969–1980

Year	Announcements
1969	6,107
1970	5,152
1971	4,608
1972	4,801
1973	4,040
1974	2,861
1975	2,297
1976	2,276
1977	2,224
1978	2,106
1979	2,128
1980	1,889

Source: Merrill Lynch Business Brokerage and Valuation, *Mergerstat Review,* 1989.

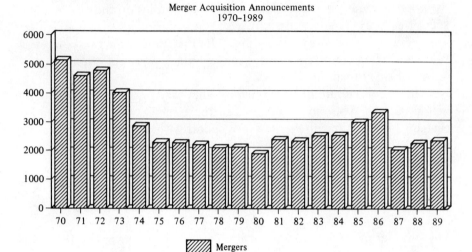

Figure 2.3

tric Storage Battery Company) was the largest battery maker in the world, specializing in automobile batteries, under the Willard and Exide brand names as well as other consumer batteries under the Ray-O-Vac brand name. Its 1974 sales were more than $400 million. Although the firm's profits had been rising, its stock prices had fallen in response to a generally declining stock market. Several companies had expressed an interest in acquiring ESB, but all these efforts were rebuffed. On July 18, 1974, International Nickel Company (INCO) announced a tender offer to acquire all outstanding shares of ESB for $28 per share or a total of $157 million. The Toronto-based INCO controlled approximately 40 percent of the world's nickel market and was, by far, the largest representative of this industry. Competition in the nickel industry had increased in the previous 10 years while demand proved to be increasingly volatile. In an effort to smooth their cash flows, INCO sought an acquisition target that was less cyclical.

INCO ultimately selected ESB as the appropriate target for several reasons. As part of the energy industry, it was attractive in light of the high oil prices; the possibility of a battery-driven car made a battery producer all the more appealing. INCO saw ESB's declining stock price as an inexpensive way to enter the booming energy field while at the same time helping smooth out the volatility of its own sales. Unfortunately, the acquisition of ESB did not prove to be a wise move for INCO. Although the battery business did have great potential, ESB was not a technological leader in the industry. It specialized mainly in lead–acid batteries used in automobiles. However, long-life dry cell batteries, such as those marketed by Duracell and Eveready, were the growth part of the business. Even in the car battery market, ESB was losing out to maintenance-free batteries such as Sears' low-maintenance alternative. Since the takeover was an unfriendly acquisition, INCO was unable to make an accurate study of the firm from the inside. Before INCO acquired ESB, major, reputable corporations did not participate in unfriendly takeovers; only smaller firms and less re-spected speculators engaged in such activity. If a major firm's takeover overtures were rebuffed, the acquisition was discontinued. Moreover, most large investment banks refused to finance hostile takeovers.

At this time, the level of competition that existed in investment banking was putting pressure on the profits of Morgan Stanley, INCO's investment banker. While seeking additional sources of profits, Morgan Stanley was also concerned that by refusing to aid INCO in its bid for ESB, it might lose a long-term client. Morgan Stanley, long known as a conservative investment bank, reluctantly began to change posture as it saw its market share erode owing to the increasingly aggressive advance of its rivals in the investment banking business. Underwriting, which had constituted 95 percent of its business until 1965, had become less profitable as other investment banks challenged the traditional relationships of the underwriting business by making competitive bids when securities were being underwritten.[15] Many banks, seeking other areas of profitability, expanded their trading operations. By the 1980s, trading would displace underwriting as the investment bank's key profit center.[16] This situation would change once again toward the end of the 1980s as fees related to mergers and acquisitions became an increasingly important part of some investment banks' revenues.

ESB found itself unprepared for a hostile takeover given the novelty of this type of action. INCO gave it only a three-hour warning of its "take it or leave it offer." ESB had installed some antitakeover defenses, but they proved most ineffective. It sought help from the investment bank of Goldman Sachs which tried to arrange a friendly takeover by United Aircraft, but by September 1974 INCO's hostile takeover of ESB was completed.[17] The takeover of ESB proved to be a poor in-vestment primarily because INCO was not given a free hand to manage the company owing to legal actions associated with antitrust consider-ations. Not until 39 months after it had completed the acquisition did

[15]John Brooks, *The Takeover Game* (New York: E. P. Dutton, 1987), p. 4.

[16]Ken Auletta, *Greed and Glory on Wall Street: The Fall of the House of Lehman* (New York: Random House, 1986). Auletta provides a good discussion of this trend at the investment bank of Lehman Brothers.

[17]For an excellent discussion of this merger, see Jeff Madrick, *Taking America* (New York: Bantam Books, 1987), pp. 1–59.

it attain the right to exercise free control over the company. Moreover, as noted earlier, ESB's competitors were already aggressively marketing superior products. By 1981, ESB was reporting operating losses; INCO eventually sold it in four separate parts.

Although the acquisition was not financially successful, it was precedent-setting. It set the stage for hostile takeovers by respected companies in the second half of the 1970s and through the fourth merger wave of the 1980s. This previously unacceptable action—the hostile takeover by a major industrial firm with the support of a leading investment banker—now gained legitimacy. The word *hostile* now became part of the vocabulary of mergers and acquisitions. "ESB is aware that a hostile tender offer is being made by a foreign company for all of ESB's shares', said F. J. Port, ESB's president. 'Hostile' thus entered the mergers and acquisitions lexicon."[18]

Morgan Stanley received a $250,000 fee for its advisory services. This fee, which did not involve the outright risk of the firm's capital and was considered attractive at the time, pales by comparison to today's merger advisory fees. For example, in 1989, Morgan Stanley and three other investment banks received $25 million in advisory fees from Kohlberg Kravis and Roberts in the $25.08 billion leveraged buyout of Nabisco.

United Technologies Versus Otis Elevator

As suggested earlier, following INCO's hostile takeover of ESB, other reputable firms began to consider unfriendly acquisitions. Firms and their chief executives, who had inclined to be raiders but had been inhibited by public censure from the business community, now became unrestrained. United Technologies was one such firm.

In 1975, United Technologies had recently changed its name from United Aircraft through the efforts of its chairman, Harry Gray, and president, Edward Hennessy, who were transforming the company into a growing conglomerate. They were quite familiar with the INCO–ESB acquisition, having participated in the bidding war for ESB as the white knight that Goldman Sachs had solicited. By mid-1975, Otis Elevator's common stock was selling for $32 per share, with earnings of $43.5 million on sales of $1.1 billion. Otis Elevator was an attractive target, with a book value of $38 per share and a stock price that was as high as $48 per share in 1973. Before its takeover of Otis Elevator, United Technologies had never participated in a hostile takeover.

---

[18]"Hostility Breeds Contempt in Takeovers, 1974," *Wall Street Journal*, October 25, 1989.

At that time the growth of the elevator manufacturing business was slowing down, and its sales patterns were cyclical inasmuch as it was heavily dependent on the construction industry. Nonetheless, this target was extremely attractive. One-third of Otis's revenues came from servicing elevators, revenues that tend to be much more stable than those from elevator construction. That Otis was a well-managed company made it all the more appealing to United Technologies. Moreover, 60 percent of Otis's revenues were from international customers, a detail that fit well with United Technologies' plans to increase its international presence.

Initially, United attempted friendly overtures toward Otis which were not accepted. On October 15, 1975, United Technologies bid $42 per share for a controlling interest in Otis Elevator, an offer that precipitated a heated battle between the two firms. Otis sought the aid of a white knight, the Dana Corporation, while filing several lawsuits to enjoin United from completing its takeover. A bidding war that ensued between United Technologies and the Dana Corporation ended with United winning with a bid of $44 per share. Unlike the INCO–ESB takeover, the takeover of Otis proved an excellent investment of United's excess cash. Otis went on to enjoy greater than expected success, particularly in international markets.

United's takeover of Otis was a groundbreaking acquisition: not only was it a hostile takeover by an established firm, but it was also a successful venture. Hostile takeovers were now an avenue through which established firms could profitably expand. The larger U.S. companies began considering hostile takeovers as ways to enhance future profitability. The financial community now felt the competitive pressures to provide the requisite financing needed for these unfriendly takeover bids. The takeover business was quickly changing.

Colt Industries Versus Garlock Industries

Colt Industries' takeover of Garlock Industries was yet another precedent-setting acquisition, moving hostile takeovers to a sharply higher level of hostility. The other two hostile takeovers by major firms had amounted to heated bidding wars but were mild in comparison to the aggressive tactics used in this takeover.

In 1964, the Fairbanks Whitney Company changed its name to Colt Industries, which it had acquired in 1955. During the 1970s, the company was almost totally restructured, with Chairman George Strichman and President David Margolis divesting the firm of many of its poorly performing businesses. The management wanted to use the cash from these sales to acquire higher growth industrial businesses. By 1975, Colt Industries was a successful conglomerate with sales of $1 billion.

Its target, Garlock Industries, manufactured packing and sealing products and had sales of approximately $160 million, with a rising earnings per share. At the time of Colt's offer, Garlock's common stock was selling for $20 per share and its book value exceeded $21 per share.

Having abandoned the option of a friendly takeover bid, Colt planned a surprise attack on Garlock. At that time, a surprise attack was feasible because the Williams Act allowed a shorter waiting period for tender offers. Garlock had already initiated antitakeover defenses, such as staggered elections of directors and acquisitions that would absorb excess cash. Garlock also filed several lawsuits designed to thwart Colt's bid. They filed suit in federal court, for example, alleging that Colt Industries had failed to abide by federal securities disclosure laws. Their legal actions also alleged that the proposed Colt Industries–Garlock merger would violate antitrust laws. One of Garlock's most acerbic defenses was its use of public relations as an antitakeover defensive strategy. Garlock had employed the public relations firm of Hill and Knowlton, widely regarded as one of the leading public relations firms. The firm played on the Colt Industries name by placing advertisements in the *New York Times* and the *Wall Street Journal* in which it asserted that the sudden Colt tender offer, which it termed a "Saturday Night Special," was not in the stockholders' interests.

In the end the public relations defense, as well as all other defenses, proved ineffectual. Garlock accepted Colt's bid, and the Saturday Night Special became a most effective takeover tactic. The Colt–Garlock battle brought the level of bellicosity of takeover battles to an all-time high, and in the years that followed, this aggressive behavior would only increase. Potential takeover targets now realized that no existing antitakeover defense could protect them from hostile bids; *all* companies were now vulnerable to such moves. In addition, the gloves were off in the battles to take over targets. Companies now began scrambling to erect yet stronger defenses. Playing on these fears, investment bankers offered to sell their defensive skills to worried potential targets, and many were put on retainers as specialists in antitakeover defenses. The game had changed, and the hostile takeover was now an acceptable part of the world of modern corporate finance.

THE FOURTH WAVE, 1981–

The downward trend that characterized mergers and acquisitions in the 1970s through 1980 reversed itself in 1981. Table 2.4 shows the dominant pattern for the 1970–1989 period. Here we merely highlight the major trends that differentiate this wave from the other three; the

Table 2.4   MERGER AND ACQUISITION
            TRANSACTIONS, 1970–1989

Year	Number
1970	5,152
1971	4,608
1972	4,801
1973	4,040
1974	2,861
1975	2,297
1976	2,276
1977	2,224
1978	2,106
1979	2,128
1980	1,889
1981	2,395
1982	2,346
1983	2,533
1984	2,543
1985	3,001
1986	3,336
1987	2,032
1988	2,258
1989	2,366

Source: Merrill Lynch Business Brokerage and
Valuation, *Mergerstat Review,* 1990.

characteristics unique to each wave are discussed separately and in detail in various chapters of this book. The unique characteristic of the fourth wave is the predominant role of hostile mergers. As noted earlier, by 1980 hostile mergers had become an acceptable form of corporate expansion, and the corporate raid had gained status as a highly profitable speculative activity. Consequently, corporations and speculative partnerships played the takeover game as a means of enjoying very high profits in a short time period. Whether takeovers are considered friendly or hostile is generally determined by the reaction of the target company's board of directors. If the board approves the takeover, it is considered friendly; if the board is opposed, the takeover is deemed hostile.

Although the absolute number of hostile takeovers is not high in respect to the total number of takeovers, the relative percentage of hostile takeovers in the total value of takeovers is large. Table 2.5 reflects the absolute number of tender offers for publicly traded companies as compared to the total number of mergers and acquisitions. See also Figure 2.4.

Table 2.5 MERGERS AND HOSTILE TENDER OFFERS, 1974–1989

Year	Merger–Acquisition Announcements	Tender Offers	Contested Tender Offers
1974	2,861	76	12
1975	2,297	58	20
1976	2,276	70	18
1977	2,224	69	10
1978	2,106	90	18
1979	2,128	106	26
1980	1,889	53	12
1981	2,395	75	28
1982	2,346	68	29
1983	2,533	37	11
1984	2,543	79	18
1985	3,001	84	32
1986	3,336	150	40
1987	2,032	116	31
1988	2,258	217	46
1989	2,366	132	28

Source: Merrill Lynch Business Brokerage and Valuation, *Mergerstat Review,* 1990.

At first glance, the total number of hostile mergers would indicate that hostile mergers were relatively unimportant in the fourth wave. But this conclusion would be misleading. We can put the total overall number of mergers into perspective by comparing the dollar size of hostile mergers with the total dollar value of all mergers. Table 2.6 shows these data for those companies that reported their transactions.

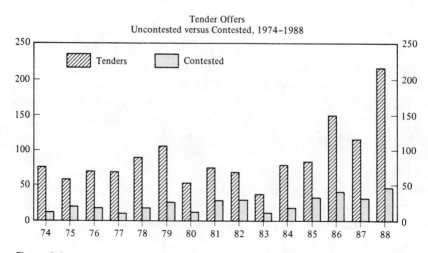

Tender Offers
Uncontested versus Contested, 1974–1988

Figure 2.4

Table 2.6   DOLLAR VALUE OF MERGERS AND HOSTILE TENDER OFFERS, 1982–1986
(million $)

Year	Dollar Value of Reported Transactions	Tender Offers for Publicly Traded Companies	Contested Tender Offers
1982	$53,754	$27,342	$9,901
1983	73,080	9,755	4,683
1984	122,224	58,665	11,332
1985	179,767	79,764	41,622
1986	173,136	NA	34,044

Source: Carolyn Kay Brancato and Jan E. Christopher, "Merger and Acquisition Activity: The Level of Hostile Mergers," Congressional Research Service, Library of Congress, Washington, D.C.

The fourth merger period can also be distinguished from the other three waves by the size and prominence of the merger and acquisition targets. Some of the nation's largest firms became the target of acquisitions during the 1980s. The fourth wave became the wave of the megamergers. The total dollar value paid in acquisitions rose sharply during this decade. Table 2.7 shows how the average and median price paid has risen since 1970. (See also Figure 2.5.)

In addition to the rise in the dollar value of mergers, the average size of the typical transaction increased significantly. The number of $100 million transactions increased more than 23 times from 1974 to 1986. This was a major difference from the conglomerate era of the

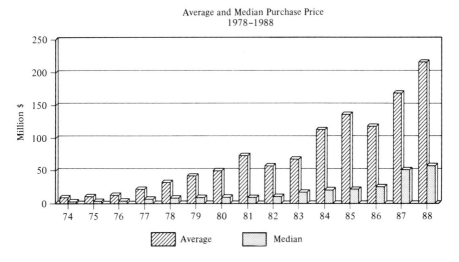

Average and Median Purchase Price
1978–1988

Figure 2.5

Table 2.7   AVERAGE AND MEDIAN PURCHASE PRICE, 1970–1989
            (million $)

Year	Average Price	Median Price
1970	$28.8	NA
1971	10.3	NA
1972	9.8	NA
1973	7.4	NA
1974	8.6	$2.8
1975	10.6	3.4
1976	12.5	3.6
1977	21.3	6.6
1978	31.9	8.1
1979	41.6	8.5
1980	49.8	9.3
1981	73.4	9.0
1982	57.8	10.5
1983	67.9	16.5
1984	112.8	20.1
1985	136.2	21.1
1986	117.9	24.9
1987	168.4	51.3
1988	215.1	56.9
1989	202.5	36.6

Source: Merrill Lynch Business Brokerage and Valuation, Mergerstat Review, 1990, p. 7.

1960s in which the acquisition of small and medium-sized businesses predominated. The 1980s became the period of the billion dollar mergers and acquisitions.

Table 2.8 indicates the rising importance of the larger merger and acquisition announcements among the total number of such announcements. As shown in this table, the higher dollar categories were responsible for an increasingly greater percentage of the total merger and acquisition transactions between 1976 and 1986. Inflationary influences were not the sole explanation of this trend. The size of merger and acquisition targets rose significantly during this period. The sizes of some of the larger mergers and acquisitions are shown in Table 2.9, and the 10 largest for the 1981–1988 period are listed in Table 2.10.

Not all industries experienced a rapid growth in mergers in the 1980s. The oil industry, for example, experienced more than its share of mergers, which resulted in a greater degree of concentration within that industry. The oil and gas industry accounted for 21.6 percent of the total dollar value of mergers and acquisitions in the 1981–1985 time

Table 2.8   NUMBER OF NET MERGER-ACQUISITION ANNOUNCEMENTS BY
PURCHASE-PRICE DISTRIBUTION, 1976–1989

	$0.5 - 5.0 MM	$5.1 - 25.0 MM	$25.1 - 99.9 MM	$100.0 - 499.9 MM	$500.0 - 999.9 MM	Over 999.9 MM	Base
1976	498(50%)	344(34%)	117(12%)	35(4%)	3	1	998
1977	451(44%)	377(36%)	163(16%)	39(4%)	2		1,032
1978	417(39%)	404(38%)	170(16%)	76(7%)	3	1	1,071
1979	387(36%)	393(38%)	184(18%)	69(7%)	11(1%)	3	1,047
1980	306(35%)	324(36%)	166(19%)	80(9%)	10(1%)	4	890
1981	388(35%)	433(38%)	192(17%)	86(8%)	15(1%)	12(1%)	1,126
1982	296(32%)	338(36%)	180(20%)	96(10%)	14(2%)	6	930
1983	321(30%)	380(35%)	238(22%)	104(10%)	23(2%)	11(1%)	1,077
1984	270(25%)	361(33%)	253(23%)	166(15%)	16(2%)	18(2%)	1,084
1985	296(23%)	454(34%)	300(23%)	204(15%)	30(2%)	36(3%)	1,320
1986	219(15%)	519(35%)	384(26%)	260(18%)	59(4%)	27(2%)	1,468
1987	92(10%)	294(30%)	285(29%)	218(22%)	47(5%)	36(4%)	972
1988	101(9%)	320(28%)	359(31%)	267(23%)	57(5%)	45(4%)	1,149
1989	127(12%)	321(29%)	316(29%)	250(23%)	43(4%)	35(3%)	1,092

*Base: Number of transactions disclosing a purchase price.

Source: Merrill Lynch Business Brokerage and Valuation, *Mergerstat Review,* 1990, p. 8.

Table 2.9   ILLUSTRATIVE LARGER MERGERS

Companies		Combined Market Value (billion $)
Nabisco	Standard Brands	$2.0
Dart Industries	Kraft	2.4
Schering	Plough	1.4

Source: J. Fred Weston and Thomas E. Copeland, *Managerial Finance* (Chicago: Dryden Press, 1986), p. 902.

period. Table 2.11, which was compiled by the Congressional Research Service based on data supplied by W. T. Grimm, ranks the industry classifications by order of dollar value paid.

One reason why some industries experienced a disproportionate number of mergers and acquisitions as compared to other industries was deregulation. When the airline industry was deregulated, for example, airfares became subject to greater competition, leading the competitive position of some air carriers to deteriorate since they could no longer compete effectively. The result was numerous acquisitions in this industry. The banking and petroleum industries experienced a similar pattern of competitively inspired mergers and acquisitions.

Table 2.10 TEN LARGEST ACQUISITIONS, 1981–1988

Year	Buyer	Target	Price (billion $)
1988	Kohlberg Kravis	R. J. R. Nabisco	$25.07
1984	Chevron	Gulf Oil	$13.3
1988	Philip Morris	Kraft	$13.1
1984	Texaco	Getty Oil	$10.1
1981	Du Pont	Conoco	$8.0
1987	British Petroleum	Standard Oil of Ohio	$7.8
1981	U.S. Steel	Marathon Oil	$6.6
1986	Kohlberg Kravis	Beatrice	$6.2
1985	General Electric	RCA	$6.0
1984	Mobil	Superior Oil	$5.7

Source: Wall Street Journal, November 1988. Reprinted by permission of the Wall Street Journal, copyright © Dow Jones & Company, Inc. All rights reserved.

Table 2.11 VALUE OF MERGERS AND ACQUISITIONS RANKED BY INDUSTRY, 1981–1985

Industry Classification	Dollar Value Paid	Percent
Oil and gas	$110,304.8	21.6
Banking and finance	43,321.2	8.5
Conglomerate	30,812.6	6.0
Food processing	26,971.4	5.3
Broadcasting	22,529.0	4.4
Insurance	22,246.3	4.3
Retail	21,984.0	4.3
Drugs, medical supplies	15,102.1	3.0
Mining and minerals	14,854.3	2.9
Chemicals and paints	14,545.6	2.8
Leisure and entertainment	13,250.9	2.6
Transportation	10,925.0	2.1
Other	164,596.6	32.2

Source: Julius Allen, "Corporate Takeovers: A Survey of Recent Developments and Issues," Congressional Research Service, Report No. 87-726E, August 6, 1987.

Role of the Corporate Raider

In the fourth wave the *corporate raider* made an initial appearance. The corporate raider's main source of income is the proceeds from takeover attempts. The word *attempts* is the curious part of this definition since the raider frequently earns handsome profits from acquisition attempts without ever taking ownership of the targeted corporation. The corporate raider Paul Bilzerian, for example, participated in numerous raids prior to his acquisition of the Singer Corporation in 1988. Although he earned significant profits from these raids, he did not complete a single major acquisition until Singer.

Many of the takeover attempts by raiders were designed ultimately to sell the target shares at a higher price than what the raider originally paid. The ability of raiders to receive *greenmail payments* (or some of the target's valued assets) in exchange for the stock that the raider had already acquired made hostile takeover attempts quite profitable. Even if the target refused to participate in such transactions, the raider may have succeeded in putting the company "in play." When a target goes into play, the stock tends to be concentrated in the hands of arbitragers, who readily sell to the highest bidder. This process often results in a company eventually being taken over, though not necessarily by the original bidder.

Although arbitrage is a well-established practice, the role of arbitragers in the takeover process did not become highly refined until the fourth merger wave. Arbitragers, such as the infamous Ivan Boesky, would gamble on the likelihood of a merger being consummated. They would buy the stock of the target in anticipation of a bid being made for the company. Arbitragers became a very important part of the takeover process during the 1980s. Their involvement changed the strategy of takeovers. Moreover, the development of this "industry" helped facilitate the rising number of hostile takeovers that occurred in those years.

Other Unique Characteristics of the Fourth Wave

The aggressiveness of investment bankers in pursuing mergers and acquisitions was crucial to the growth of the fourth wave. In turn, mergers were a great source of virtually risk-free advisory fees for investment bankers. The magnitude of these fees reached unprecedented proportions during this period. Merger specialists at both investment banks and law firms developed many innovative products and techniques designed to facilitate or prevent takeovers. They pressured both potential targets and acquirers into hiring them, either to bring about or to prevent takeovers. To help finance takeovers, the investment bank of Drexel Burnham Lambert pioneered the development of the junk bond market. These previously lowly regarded securities became an important investment vehicle for financing many takeovers. Junk bond financing enabled expansionist firms and raiders to raise the requisite capital necessary to contemplate acquisitions or raids on some of the more prominent corporations.

The fourth merger wave featured innovative acquisition techniques and investment vehicles. Offensive and defensive strategies became highly intricate. In addition, companies undertook various forms of corporate restructuring at unprecedented levels. One such strategy, the leveraged buyout, combined the use of debt financing to acquire companies. Management often resorted to this technique to bring their corporations private. While public corporations had been brought private before the fourth wave, this type of transaction became much more prominent during the 1980s.

The fourth wave provoked new conflicts between the federal and state governments. Besieged corporations increasingly looked to their state governments for protection against unwanted acquisition offers. They were often able to persuade the local legislatures to pass antitakeover legislation. The passage of antitakeover state laws brought the federal and state governments into direct conflict. Some representatives of the federal government, such as the Securities and Exchange Commission, felt that these laws were an infringement of interstate commerce. For their part, some state governments believed that such laws were based on their right to exercise constitutionally granted state rights. It also made some state governments protectors of indigenous corporations.

Various stockholder groups have strongly criticized this role of state government. Boone Pickens, the spokesperson of the United Shareholders Association, views these laws as an infringement of shareholders' rights. He cites the decline of stock prices in states that passed such laws as evidence that the market opposes antitakeover legislation. Target corporations, on the other hand, have stated that the raids that occurred during the fourth merger wave were disruptive to the growth of corporate America. The impact of specific antitakeover measures on shareholder wealth will be explored in detail in Chapter 5.

BUSINESS CYCLES AND MERGERS

Studies of the relationship between periods of merger activity and business cycles suggest a relationship between the two phenomena. A review of merger activity between 1897 and 1954 by Ralph Nelson showed that merger periods were a procyclical time series with peaks of merger activity usually preceding the peaks in the business cycle.[19] In addition, merger peaks preceded stock market peaks by an average of one month. Merger troughs preceded troughs in stock prices by an average of three months. Nelson's studies also showed that periods of

---

[19]Nelson, *Merger Movements in American Industry.*

low merger activity seemed to be more closely correlated with variations in macroeconomic aggregates, such as industrial production, than stock prices. In periods of heightened merger activity, however, mergers were more positively correlated with stock prices than with macroeconomic aggregates. The association between periods of merger activity and stock prices was supported by subsequent research. Melicher, Ledolter, and D'Antonio found that stock price increases (decreases) preceded increases (decreases) in merger activity.[20] Although the lead and lag relationships are different from those in the Nelson study, the fact that the two time series co-vary was supported. The Melicher study also showed that merger periods were inversely related to changes in bond yields.

The association between merger periods, stock prices, and macroeconomic aggregates, such as industrial production, is not surprising. Economic expansion is the product of expansion of the individual microeconomic components of the economy such as individual firms. The expansion of firms helps fuel economic growth. Other businesses may respond to this growth by also expanding. One form of corporate expansion is mergers and acquisitions. The association between stock prices and merger periods is also expected. A period of increased merger and acquisition activity means that stockholders are receiving merger premiums. As a result, investors may conclude that the probability of their receiving similar premiums on their equity holdings is also higher and so a rise in stock prices may take place.

SUMMARY

This chapter has described the ebb and flow development of corporate mergers and acquisitions in the United States. It is characterized by four main periods of intense merger activity called merger waves. The earlier merger waves were greatly influenced by the United States' technological growth into a major industrial economy. The last merger wave, which has yet to end, is unique in that it featured the appearance of the corporate raider. While corporate raiders had existed prior to the 1980s, the fourth wave brought forth a raider armed with a larger arsenal of junk bond financing that was used to attack some of America's largest corporations. In doing so, the raider permanently changed the outlook of corporate management which had not previously been exposed to such formidable outside threats.

---

[20]R. W. Melicher, J. Ledolter, and L. D'Antonio, "A Time Series Analysis of Aggregate Merger Activity," *Review of Economics and Statistics* 65 (August 1983): 423–430.

The remainder of this book more fully describes the recent developments of the world of mergers and acquisitions. The different dimensions of merger activity are explored in depth so that the reader will obtain a more complete understanding of the intricacies of this continually evolving field.

REFERENCES

Allen, Julius. "Corporate Takeovers: A Survey of Recent Developments and Issues." Congressional Research Service.

Archibald, T. Ross. "Stock Market Reaction to the Depreciation Switch-Back." *Accounting Review* 47, no. 1 (January 1972): 22–30.

Auletta, Ken. *Greed and Glory on Wall Street: The Fall of the House of Lehman*. New York: Random House, 1986.

Brancato, Carolyn Kay, and Jan E. Christopher. "Merger and Acquisition Activity: The Level of Hostile Mergers." Congressional Research Service, Library of Congress, Washington, D.C.

Briloff, A. J. "Accounting Practices and the Merger Movement." *Notre Dame Lawyer* 45, no. 4 (Summer 1970).

Brooks, John. *The Takeover Game*. New York: E. P. Dutton, 1987.

Brown, Philip, and Ray Ball. "An Empirical Evaluation of Accounting Income Numbers." *Journal of Accounting Research* 6, no. 2 (Autumn 1963):159–178.

Brown, Stanley. *Ling*. New York: Atheneum, 1972.

Chandler, Alfred D. *The Visible Hand: The Managerial Revolution in American Business*. Cambridge, Mass.: Belknap Press, 1977.

Chandler, Alfred D. "The Coming of Oligopoly and Its Meaning for AntiTrust." In *National Competition Policy: Historian's Perspective on Antitrust and Government Business Relationships in the United States*. Federal Trade Commission Publication, August 1981.

Fama, E. F., L. Fisher, M. Jensen, and R. Roll. "The Adjustment of Stock Prices to New Information." *International Economic Review* 10, no. 1 (February 1969): 1–21.

Geneen, Harold. *Managing*. New York: Avon Publishing Co., 1984.

"Hostile Corporate Takeovers: Investment Advisor Fees." Report No. 87–217E by Kevin F. Winch. Congressional Research Service, Library of Congress, Washington, D.C.

"Hostility Breeds Contempt in Takeovers, 1974." *Wall Street Journal*, October 25, 1989.

Kaplan, Robert S., and Richard Roll. "Investor Evaluation of Accounting Information: Some Empirical Evidence." *Journal of Business* 45, no. 2 (April 1972).

Kinter, Earl W. *Primer on the Law of Mergers*. New York: Macmillan Publishing Co., 1973.

Madrick, Jeff. *Taking America*. New York: Bantam Books, 1987.

Markham, Jesse. "Survey of the Evidence and Findings on Mergers." In *Business Concentration and Public Policy*. Princeton N.J.: Princeton University Press, 1955.

Marren, Joseph H. *Mergers and Acquisition*. Homewood Ill.: Dow Jones Irwin, 1985.

Melicher, R. W., J. Ledolter, and L. D'Antonio. "A Time Series Analysis of Aggregate Merger Activity." *Review of Economics and Statistics* 65 (August 1983): 423–430.

Mergerstat Review. New York: Merrill Lynch Business Brokerage and Valuation.

Nelson, Ralph. *Merger Movements in American Industry: 1895–1956*. Princeton, N.J.: Princeton University Press, 1959.

Rielly, Frank, and Eugene Drzyminski. "Tests of Stock Market Efficiency Following World Events." *Journal of Business Research* 1, no. 1 (Summer 1973): 57–72.

Steiner, Peter O. *Mergers: Motives, Effects, Policies*. Ann Arbor: University of Michigan Press, 1975.

Weston, J. Fred, and Thomas E. Copeland. *Managerial Finance*. Chicago: Dryden Press, 1986.

Chapter
3

The Legal Framework of Mergers

Several laws regulate the field of mergers and acquisitions. Because target companies use some of these laws as a defensive tactic when contemplating a takeover, an acquiring firm must take careful note of legal considerations. The three main groups of laws are securities laws, antitrust laws, and state corporation laws.

SECURITIES LAWS

The Williams Act, passed in 1968, is one of the most important pieces of securities legislation in the field of mergers and acquisitions. It had a pronounced impact on merger activity in the 1970s and 1980s. Prior to its passage, the tender offers were largely unregulated, a situation that was not a major concern before 1960 since few tender offers were made. In the 1960s, however, the tender offer became a more popular means of taking control of corporations and ousting an entrenched management.

In tender offers that used securities as the consideration, the disclosure requirement of the Securities Act of 1933 provided some regulation. In cash offers, however, there was no such regulation. As a result, the Securities and Exchange Commission (SEC) sought to fill this gap in the law, and Senator Harrison Williams, as chairman of the Senate Banking Committee, proposed legislation for that purpose in 1967. The bill won congressional approval in July 1968.

The Williams Act provided an amendment to the Securities and Exchange Act of 1934, a legal cornerstone of securities regulations. This act, together with the Securities Act of 1933, was inspired by the government's concern for greater regulation of securities markets. Both have helped eliminate some of the abuses that many believed contributed to the stock market crash of October 1929.

Specifically, these laws provide for greater disclosure of information by firms when they issue securities. In addition, the Securities and Exchange Act of 1934 proscribed certain activities of the securities industry, including wash sales and churning of customer accounts. It also provided an enforcement agency, the Securities and Exchange Commission, which was established to enforce federal securities laws.

The Williams Act had four major objectives.

1. *To regulate tender offers.* Before the Williams Act was passed, stockholders of target companies were often stampeded into tendering their shares quickly to avoid receiving less advantageous terms.
2. *To provide procedures and disclosure requirements for acquisitions.* Through greater disclosure, stockholders could make more enlightened decisions regarding the value of a takeover offer. Disclosure would enable target shareholders to gain more complete knowledge of the potential acquiring company. In a stock-for-stock exchange, the target company stockholders would become stockholders in the acquiring firm. A proper valuation of the acquiring firm's shares depends on the availability of detailed financial data.
3. *To provide shareholders with time to make informed decisions regarding tender offers.* Even though the necessary information might be available to target company stockholders, they still need time to analyze these data. The Williams Act allows them to make more informed decisions.
4. *To increase confidence in securities markets.* By increasing investor confidence, securities markets can attract more capital. Investors will be less worried about being placed in a position of incurring losses when making decisions based on limited information.

Section 13d of the Williams Act

Section 13d of the Williams Act provides an early warning system for stockholders and target management, alerting them to the possibility that a threat for control may soon occur. This section provides for disclosure of a buyer's stockholdings, when these holdings reach 5 percent of the target firm's total common stock outstanding. When the law was first passed, this threshold level was 10 percent; this percentage was later considered too high, and the more conservative 5 percent was adopted.

The disclosure of the necessary information, pursuant to the rules of Section 13d, is necessary even where there is no tender offer. The buyer who intends to take control of a corporation must disclose the necessary information following the attainment of a 5 percent holding in the target. The buyer makes this disclosure by filing a Schedule 13D.

A filing may be necessary even though no one individual or firm actually owns 5 percent of another firm's stock. If a group of investors act in concert, under this law their combined stockholdings are considered as one *group*. Specifically, the law states that:

> When two or more persons act as a partnership, limited partnership, syndicate or other group for the purpose of acquiring, holding or disposing of securities of an issuer, such a syndicate or group shall be deemed a person for the purpose of this subsection.

When the individual members of a group reach an agreement to attempt to take control of a company, they must make the required disclosure within the stipulated time frame. The stockholdings of each individual member of the group become the holdings of this new legal entity, as far as this section of the law is concerned. The group filing requirement also applies to management, which might act in concert to defeat a tender offer. When stockholding managers and/or directors act together, they are subject to the same 13d filing requirements as outside investors.[1]

The definition of a group attracted a great deal of attention in the late 1980s in association with the alleged *stock parking* scandal involving Ivan Boesky. Stock parking occurs when bidders hide their purchases by having another investor buy the target company's stock for them. Brokerage firms are obviously in a good position to buy stock in this manner, since they regularly purchase stock in many companies for various clients. When a brokerage firm is merely concealing the true ownership of the stock, however, the transaction can be a violation of the Williams Act. Some have asserted that Boesky's brokers, Jeffries and Company, amassed holdings of stock for Boesky, while being aware of Boesky's intent to attempt a takeover. It was asserted that this constituted a group in the eyes of the Williams Act, and that both parties should therefore have made proper disclosure.

There is, of course, a great economic incentive to illegally pursue

---

[1]*Warner Communications, Inc.* v. *Murdoch*, 581 F. Supp. 1482 (D. Del., March 16, 1984).

a stock parking arrangement with another party. Once disclosure is made, the marketplace becomes aware of the acquiring firm's intentions. The market is also aware that the stock of a target company tends to rise significantly in takeover attempts. Thus, other speculators, such as arbitragers, seek to profit by buying the target firm's stock, hoping to sell their stock at higher prices to those who will eventually bid for control of the company. This type of speculating is an example of one form of *risk arbitrage.*

Schedule 13D

Section 13d provides for the filing of a Schedule 13D. Firms are required to file six copies of this schedule with the Securities and Exchange Commission within 10 days of acquiring 5 percent of another firm's outstanding stock. In addition, a copy must be sent to the executive offices of the issuer of the securities by registered or certified mail. Another copy must be sent in the same manner to each organized exchange on which the stock is traded. Figure 3.1 presents a copy of Schedule 13D.

Schedule 13D requires the disclosure of the following information.[2]

1. The name and address of the issuing firm and the type of securities to be acquired. For example, a company may have more than one class of securities. In this instance, the acquiring firm must indicate the class of securities of which it has acquired at least 5 percent.
2. Detailed information on the background of the individual filing the information, including any past criminal violations.
3. The number of shares actually owned.
4. The purpose of the transaction. At this point the acquiring firm must indicate whether it intends to take control of the company or is merely buying the securities for investment purposes.
5. The source of the funds used to finance the acquisition of the firm's stock. The extent of the reliance on debt, for example, must be disclosed. Written statements from financial institutions documenting the bidder's ability to procure the requisite financing may be required to be appended to the schedule.

Schedule 13G

The SEC makes special provisions for those investors who acquire 5 percent or more of a company's shares, and who did not acquire more

---

[2]Bryon E. Fox and Eleanor M. Fox, *Corporate Acquisitions and Mergers*, Vol. 2 (New York: Matthew Bender Publishing Co., 1987), p. 27.

OMB APPROVAL
OMB Number: 3235-0145 Expires: September 30, 1988

SECURITIES AND EXCHANGE COMMISSION
Washington, D.C. 20549

SCHEDULE 13D

Under the Securities Exchange Act of 1934
(Amendment No. ________)*

____
(Name of Issuer)

____
(Title of Class of Securities)

____
(CUSIP Number)

____
(Name, Address and Telephone Number of Person Authorized to Receive Notices and Communications)

____
(Date of Event which Requires Filing of this Statement)

If the filing person has previously filed a statement on Schedule 13G to report the acquisition which is the subject of this Schedule 13D, and is filing this schedule because of Rule 13d-1(b)(3) or (4), check the following box ☐.

Check the following box if a fee is being paid with the statement ☐. (A fee is not required only if the reporting person: (1) has a previous statement on file reporting beneficial ownership of more than five percent of the class of securities described in Item 1; and (2) has filed no amendment subsequent thereto reporting beneficial ownership of five percent or less of such class.) (See Rule 13d-7.)

Note: Six copies of this statement, including all exhibits, should be filed with the Commission. See Rule 13d-1(a) for other parties to whom copies are to be sent.

*The remainder of this cover page shall be filled out for a reporting person's initial filing on this form with respect to the subject class of securities, and for any subsequent amendment containing information which would alter disclosures provided in a prior cover page.

The information required on the remainder of this cover page shall not be deemed to be "filed" for the purpose of Section 18 of the Securities Exchange Act of 1934 ("Act") or otherwise subject to the liabilities of that section of the Act but shall be subject to all other provisions of the Act (however, see the Notes).

SEC 1746 (2-87)

Figure 3.1

SCHEDULE 13D

CUSIP No. _____		Page _____ of _____ Pages

1	NAME OF REPORTING PERSON S.S. OR I.R.S. IDENTIFICATION NO. OF ABOVE PERSON

2	CHECK THE APPROPRIATE BOX IF A MEMBER OF A GROUP*	(a) ☐ (b) ☐

3	SEC USE ONLY —

4	SOURCE OF FUNDS*

5	CHECK BOX IF DISCLOSURE OF LEGAL PROCEEDINGS IS REQUIRED PURSUANT TO ITEMS 2(d) or 2(E)	☐

6	CITIZENSHIP OR PLACE OF ORGANIZATION

NUMBER OF SHARES BENEFICIALLY OWNED BY EACH REPORTING PERSON WITH	**7**	SOLE VOTING POWER
	8	SHARED VOTING POWER
	9	SOLE DISPOSITIVE POWER
	10	SHARED DISPOSITIVE POWER

11	AGGREGATE AMOUNT BENEFICIALLY OWNED BY EACH REPORTING PERSON	
12	CHECK BOX IF THE AGGREGATE AMOUNT IN ROW (11) EXCLUDES CERTAIN SHARES*	☐
13	PERCENT OF CLASS REPRESENTED BY AMOUNT IN ROW (11)	
14	TYPE OF REPORTING PERSON*	

*SEE INSTRUCTIONS BEFORE FILLING OUT!

Figure 3.1 *(continued)*

than 2 percent of those shares in the last 12 months, but who have no interest in taking control of the firm. Such investors are required to file the much less detailed Schedule 13G. Schedule 13G must be filed on February 14 of each year. These share owners are sometimes called *5% beneficial owners.*

Section 14d

The Williams Act also provides for disclosure of various information in tender offers, principally through Section 14d.

To Whom Should Disclosure Be Made   The disclosure must come in the form of a Schedule 14D1 and be submitted to those parties indicated under this section of the law. Ten copies of this schedule must be sent to the SEC, and another must be hand delivered to the executive offices of the target company. A copy must also be hand delivered to other bidders, if any. In addition, the acquiring firm must not only telephone each of the exchanges on which the target company's stock is traded to notify them of the tender offer, but also mail a copy of the Schedule 14D1 to them. If the target stock is traded on the over-the-counter market, similar notice must be provided to the National Association of Securities Dealers. Figure 3.2 shows the front page of Campeau Corporation's Schedule 14D1 pursuant to its tender offer for Federated Stores.

Information Requested on Schedule 14D1   Figure 3.3 shows the first two pages of a 14D1. A partial list of this schedule's more notable supplemental information requirements is listed below, according to the item number as it appears on the filing instructions of the schedule: (As the numbering system, based on the numbers on the actual schedules, shows, this is a partial listing.)

Item 1   The name of the target company and the class of securities involved.

Item 2   The identity of the person, partnership, syndicate, or corporation that is filing. Additional background information on the corporate officers, including past criminal violations, should also be included.

Item 3   Any past contracts between the bidder and the target company.

Item 4   The source of the funds that will be used to carry out the tender offer. This item has often been the source of considerable debate in hostile takeover attempts. The target firm frequently

SECURITIES AND EXCHANGE COMMISSION
WASHINGTON, D.C. 20549

SCHEDULE 14D-1

Tender Offer Statement
Pursuant to Section 14(d)(1)
of the Securities Exchange Act of 1934

SC 14D1

88 01 2414

Federated Department Stores, Inc.
(Name of Subject Company)

CRTF Corporation
(Bidder)

Common Stock, $1.25 par value
(Title of Class of Securities)

314099 3 10 2
(CUSIP Number of Class of Securities)

JAN 27 1988

Bechtel Information Services
Gaithersburg, Maryland

Patrick H. Bowen, Esq.
CRTF Corporation
1114 Avenue of the Americas
24th Floor
New York, New York 10036
(212) 764-2538
(Name, Address and Telephone Number
of Person Authorized to Receive Notices
and Communications on Behalf of Bidder)

RECD S.E.
JAN 25 1988
FEB

Copies to:

Robert A. Kindler, Esq.
Cravath, Swaine & Moore
One Chase Manhattan Plaza
New York, New York 10005
(212) 428-1640

CALCULATION OF FILING FEE

Transaction Valuation*	Amount of Filing Fee
$4,251,681,100*	$850,336.22*

* For purposes of calculating fee only. This amount assumes the purchase of 90,461,300 shares of Common Stock of Federated Department Stores, Inc. ("Federated"), including the associated Preferred Stock Purchase Rights issued pursuant to the Rights Agreement dated as of January 23, 1986, as amended, between Federated and Manufacturers Hanover Trust Company, as Rights Agent, at $47 per share net. Such number of shares represents all shares reported to be outstanding as of November 28, 1987, and assumes the exercise of all stock options appearing to be outstanding as of January 31, 1987.

☐ Check box if any part of the fee is offset as provided by Rule 0-11(a)(2) and identify the filing with which the offsetting fee was previously paid. Identify the previous filing by registration statement number, or the form or schedule and the date of its filing.

Amount Previously Paid:	N/A	Filing Party:	N/A
Form or Registration No:	N/A	Date Filed:	N/A

Figure 3.2

OMB APPROVAL
OMB Number: 3235-0102
Expires: January 31, 1990

SECURITIES AND EXCHANGE COMMISSION
Washington, D.C. 20549

SCHEDULE 14D-1

Tender offer statement pursuant to section 14(d)(1) of the Securities Exchange Act of 1934.

(Amendment No.)*

____

(Name of Subject Company [Issuer])

____

(Bidder)

____

(Title of Class of Securities)

____

(CUSIP Number of Class of Securities)

____

(Name, Address and Telephone Numbers of Person Authorized to Receive Notices and Communications on Behalf of Bidder)

Calculation of Filing Fee

Transaction valuation*	Amount of filing fee

*Set forth the amount on which the filing fee is calculated and state how it was determined.

☐ Check box if any part of the fee is offset as provided by Rule 0-11(a)(2) and identify the filing with which the offsetting fee was previously paid. Identify the previous filing by registration statement number, or the Form or Schedule and the date of its filing.

Amount Previously Paid: ______________________________

Form or Registration No.: ______________________________

Filing Party: ______________________________

Date Filed: ______________________________

Note: The remainder of this cover page is only to be completed if this Schedule 14D-1 (or amendment thereto) is being filed, inter alia, to satisfy the reporting requirements of section 13(d) of the Securities Exchange Act of 1934. See General Instructions D, E and F to Schedule 14D-1.

* The remainder of this cover page shall be filled out for a reporting person's initial filing on this form with respect to the subject class of securities, and for any subsequent amendment containing information which would alter the disclosure provided in a prior cover page.

The information required in the remainder of this cover page shall not be deemed to be "filed" for the purpose of Section 18 of the Securities Exchange Age of 1934 ("Act") or otherwise subject to the liabilities of that section of the Act but shall be subject to all other provisions of the Act (however, see the Notes).

SEC 1747 (5-87)

Figure 3.3

1)' Names of Reporting Persons S.S. or I.R.S. Identification Nos. of Above Person ————————

2) Check the Appropriate Box if a Member of a Group (See Instructions)
   ☐ (a) ————————————————————
   ☐ (b) ————————————————————

3) SEC Use Only ————————————————————

4) Sources of Funds (See Instructions) ————————————————

5) ☐ Check if Disclosure of Legal Proceedings is Required Pursuant to Items 2(e) or 2(f).

6) Citizenship or Place of Organization ————————————————

7) Aggregate Amount Beneficially Owned by Each Reporting Person ———————

8) ☐ Check if the Aggregate Amount in Row 7 Excludes Certain Shares (See Instructions).

9) Percent of Class Represented by Amount in Row 7 —————————————

10) Type of Reporting Person (See Instructions) ——————————————

2

Figure 3.3 *(continued)*

contends that the financing of the acquiring firm is insufficient to complete the takeover. This issue has been the focus of much litigation.

Item 5   The purpose of the tender offer. The company must reveal any plans it may have to change the target company. For example, the company must fully disclose if it plans to sell off any assets, or change the board of directors, the dividend policy, or the target's capital structure.

Item 9   The bidder's financial statements. Once again this item has often proved to be a major point of contention. Many targets of unwelcomed bids contend that the bidder has not made adequate disclosure of its true financial condition. Targets in hostile bids may argue that, pursuant to Item 9, the financial data and financing terms indicate that the resulting combined firm may be significantly riskier.

Item 10   Information material to the transaction, including information such as any antitrust conflicts or current litigation that the bidder may be involved in. Here again, acquiring firms and target firms have had varying interpretations of this item. Target firms often claim that acquiring firms have not made complete disclosure pursuant to Item 10.

Item 11   Any exhibits relevant to the schedule, such as copies of loan agreements for financing the acquisition, or any relevant written opinions of professionals hired by the acquiring firm. For example, opinion related to the fairness of the offer price or the tax consequences of the transaction should be appended.

Commencement of the Offer

The time period of the tender offer can be crucially important in a contested takeover battle. Therefore, the date on which the offer is initially made is important. According to Rule 14d–2, the tender offer will begin on 12:01 A.M. on the date that any one of the following occurs:

1. Publication of the tender offer.
2. Advertisement of the tender offer.
3. Submittal of the tender offer materials to the target.

Position of the Target Corporation

Originally, the Williams Act only required the bidder to file a disclosure statement. In 1980, the act was amended to require the target to comply with disclosure requirements. The target company must now respond to the tender offer by filing a Schedule 14D9 within 10 days after the commencement date, indicating whether or not it recommends acceptance or rejection of the offer. If the target contends that it maintains no position on the offer, it must state its reasons.

In addition to filing with the SEC, the target must send copies of the Schedule 14D9 to each of the organized exchanges on which the target's stock is traded. If the stock is traded on the over-the-counter market, the National Association of Securities Dealers must also be sent a copy of this schedule.

Time Periods of the Williams Act

Minimum Offer Period   According to the Williams Act, a tender offer must be kept open for a minimum of 20 business days during which the acquiring firm must accept all shares that are tendered. However, it cannot actually buy any of these shares until the end of the offer period. The minimum offer period was added to discourage shareholders from being pressured into tendering their shares rather than risk losing out on the offer. With a minimum time period, shareholders can take their time to consider this offer and compare the terms of the offer with that of other offers. The offering firm can get an extension on the 20-day offer period, if, for example, it believes there is a better chance of getting the shares it needs. The acquiring firm must purchase the shares tendered (at least on a pro rata basis) at the offer price, unless the firm does not receive the total number of shares it requested in the terms of the tender offer. The acquirer may, however, still choose to purchase the tendered shares.

The tender offer may be worded to contain other escape clauses. For example, when antitrust considerations are an issue, the offer may be contingent on attaining the regulatory agencies' approval. Therefore, the offer might be so worded to state that the bidder is not bound to buy, if the Justice Department or the Federal Trade Commission objects to the merger. The mere presence of an investigation by the regulatory authorities might allow a bidder to refuse to purchase the tendered shares.

Withdrawal Rights   The Williams Act has been amended several times to enhance shareholders' rights to withdraw their shares from participation in the offer. In its original form, Section 14d–5 of the Williams Act granted stockholders the right to withdraw their tendered shares up to seven calendar days, after the dissemination of the tender offer materials. This section of the law also allows the shares to be withdrawn at any time after 60 days, following the distribution of the tender offer materials. This later time period is relevant for offers that may have been extended.

Rule 14d–7 originally established that the withdrawal rights period could be extended until 15 business days after the date of the commencement of the offer, or until the expiration of 10 business days after commencement of a competing offer.[3] This time period started after the competing tender offer materials had been distributed. This rule was amended in 1986 and changed the seven-day withdrawal rights period. *Under the amended rule, the withdrawal rights period is extended to cover the entire time that the offer remains open.* The withdrawal rights period extension allows stockholders sufficient time to consider alternative offers.

Proration Periods

In many instances tender offers are oversubscribed. For example, an offer to purchase 51 percent of a target company's stock may receive 80 percent of the total shares outstanding. According to the earlier wording of the law, under Rule 14d–6, in a partial tender offer that is oversubscribed, the bidder must accept the securities tendered within the first 10 calendar days following the dissemination of the tender offer materials, or within 10 calendar days after a notice of an increase in the consideration in an offer has been distributed.[4] Based on this proration period, approximately five-eighths of each share submitted would be accepted if all 80 percent of the shares were tendered during the first 10 days of an offer to purchase 51 percent of the outstanding stock. If an additional 10 percent were submitted after the tenth calendar day of the offer, these shares would not be accepted, unless the acquiring company decided to accept more shares than what were stipulated in the 51 percent offer.

At first, the proration period frustrated the 20-day offer period. In the case of partial tender offers, stockholders had an incentive to rush to tender within the first 10 days of the offer, thus avoiding being closed out of even pro rata appearance if the offer were oversubscribed. Many stockholders would tender early to take advantage of the proration period while reserving the right to withdraw their shares until the end of the withdrawal rights periods.

The proration period rules were changed in 1982, when the SEC adopted Rule 14d–8. This rule requires a bidder in a partial tender

---

[3]Martin Lipton and Erica H. Steinberger, *Takeovers and Freezeouts* (New York: Law Journal Seminars Press, 1987), p. 2.05[1].

[4]Ibid., p. 2.05[3].

offer to accept all shares tendered during the entire offer period, on a pro rata basis. Therefore, when offers are extended, the proration period is automatically extended. The proration period is not, however, automatically extended by the extension of the withdrawal rights period. Rule 14d–8 ties the proration period to the offer period. The offer period, however, is not extended when the withdrawal rights period is extended. The SEC felt that a longer proration period was necessary to help small investors who may need more than the first 10 days of the offer period to make an informed decision. The SEC's amendment reduced the significance of the proration period.

Method of Tendering Shares

Stockholders tender their shares through an intermediary, such as a commercial bank, which is referred to as the *paying agent*. As stockholders seek to participate in the tender offer, they submit their shares to the paying agent in exchange for cash or securities, in accordance with the terms of the offer. Attached to their shares must be a letter of transmittal (see Figure 3.4). The agent accumulates the shares but does not pay the stockholders until the offer expires. In the event that the offer is extended, the paying agent holds the shares until the new offer expires, unless instructed otherwise by the individual stockholders.

The bidder can extend an undersubscribed tender. In fact, it is not unusual for an offer to be extended several times, as the bidder tries to get enough shares to assure control. For example, an October 1988 tender offer by Coniston Partners for T. W. Services, a diversified food and medical services company, was repeatedly extended through the following expiration dates as T. W. Services fought to remain independent:

February 2, 1989

February 9, 1989

February 16, 1989

February 23, 1989

March 9, 1989

March 21, 1989

April 4, 1989

April 18, 1989

May 2, 1989

May 16, 1989

LETTER OF TRANSMITTAL
To Tender Shares of Common Stock
(Including the Associated Preferred Share Purchase Rights)
of

Texas Eastern Corporation

Pursuant to the Offer to Purchase dated January 17, 1989
of

Colorado Interstate Corporation
a wholly owned subsidiary of

The Coastal Corporation

THE OFFER AND WITHDRAWAL RIGHTS WILL EXPIRE AT 12:00 MIDNIGHT, NEW YORK
CITY TIME, ON MONDAY, FEBRUARY 13, 1989, UNLESS THE OFFER IS EXTENDED.

The Depositary:
CITIBANK, N.A.

By Courier:
CITIBANK, N.A.
c/o Citicorp Data Distribution, Inc.
404 Sette Drive
Paramus, New Jersey 07653

By Mail:	*Facsimile Copy Number:*	*By Hand:*
CITIBANK, N.A.	(201) 262-7521	CITIBANK, N.A.
c/o Citicorp Data Distribution, Inc.	*Telex Number:*	111 Wall Street
P.O. Box 7072	TWX 7109904964	Mergers & Acquisitions Window
Paramus, New Jersey 07653	CDDI-PARA (answer back)	5th Floor
		New York, New York

To confirm receipt:
(201) 262-4743
(Call collect)

Delivery of this instrument to an address other than as set forth above, or transmission of instructions via a facsimile or telex number other than as set forth above, will not constitute a valid delivery.

This Letter of Transmittal is to be used either if certificates for Shares (as defined below) and/or Rights (as defined below) are to be forwarded herewith or if tender of Shares and/or Rights, if available, is to be made by book-entry transfer to the account maintained by the Depositary at The Depository Trust Company, the Midwest Securities Trust Company or the Philadelphia Depository Trust Company (each a "Book-Entry Transfer Facility") pursuant to the procedures set forth in Section 3 of the Offer to Purchase (as defined below). Stockholders who tender Shares and/or Rights, if available, by book-entry transfer are referred to herein as "Book-Entry Stockholders" and other stockholders are referred to herein as "Certificate Stockholders." Delivery of documents to a Book-Entry Transfer Facility does not constitute delivery to the Depositary. **Unless the Rights are redeemed or the Purchaser (as defined below) determines they are invalid, stockholders are required to tender one Right for each Share tendered to effect a valid tender of Shares.**

Stockholders whose certificates are not immediately available, or who cannot deliver their certificates (or who cannot comply with the book-entry transfer procedures on a timely basis) and all other documents required hereby to the Depositary on or prior to the Expiration Date (as defined in the Offer to Purchase) must tender their Shares and/or Rights according to the guaranteed delivery procedure set forth in Section 3 of the Offer to Purchase. See Instruction 2.

NOTE: SIGNATURES MUST BE PROVIDED BELOW.
PLEASE READ THE ACCOMPANYING INSTRUCTIONS CAREFULLY.

☐ **CHECK HERE IF TENDERED SHARES ARE BEING DELIVERED BY BOOK-ENTRY TRANSFER MADE TO THE ACCOUNT MAINTAINED BY THE DEPOSITARY WITH A BOOK-ENTRY TRANSFER FACILITY AND COMPLETE THE FOLLOWING:**

Name of Tendering Institution_____
Check Box of applicable Book-Entry Transfer Facility:
☐ The Depository Trust Company
☐ Midwest Securities Trust Company
☐ Philadelphia Depository Trust Company
Account Number_____
Transaction Code Number_____

☐ **CHECK HERE IF TENDERED SHARES ARE BEING DELIVERED PURSUANT TO A NOTICE OF GUARANTEED DELIVERY PREVIOUSLY SENT TO THE DEPOSITARY AND COMPLETE THE FOLLOWING:**

Name(s) of Registered Holder(s) _____
Window Ticket Number (if any) _____
Date of Execution of Notice of Guaranteed Delivery _____
Name of Institution which guaranteed delivery _____
If Delivered by Book-Entry Transfer, Check Box of Applicable Book-Entry Transfer Facility:
☐ The Depository Trust Company
☐ Midwest Securities Trust Company
☐ Philadelphia Depository Trust Company
Account Number _____
Transaction Code Number _____

Figure 3.4 Texas Eastern Corporation, 1989 Letter of Transmittal. (Reprinted by permission of Texas Eastern Corporation.)

☐ **CHECK HERE IF TENDERED RIGHTS ARE BEING DELIVERED BY BOOK-ENTRY TRANSFER MADE TO THE ACCOUNT MAINTAINED BY THE DEPOSITARY WITH A BOOK-ENTRY TRANSFER FACILITY AND COMPLETE THE FOLLOWING:**

Name of Tendering Institution _____

Check Box of applicable Book-Entry Transfer Facility:

☐ The Depository Trust Company

☐ Midwest Securities Trust Company

☐ Philadelphia Depository Trust Company

Account Number _____

Transaction Code Number _____

☐ **CHECK HERE IF TENDERED RIGHTS ARE BEING DELIVERED PURSUANT TO A NOTICE OF GUARANTEED DELIVERY PREVIOUSLY SENT TO THE DEPOSITARY AND COMPLETE THE FOLLOWING:**

Name(s) of Registered Holder(s) _____

Window Ticket Number (if any) _____

Date of Execution of Notice of Guaranteed Delivery _____

Name of Institution which guaranteed delivery _____

If Delivery by Book-Entry Transfer, Check Box of Applicable Book-Entry Transfer Facility:

☐ The Depository Trust Company

☐ Midwest Securities Trust Company

☐ Philadelphia Depository Trust Company

Account Number _____

Transaction Code Number _____

DESCRIPTION OF SHARES TENDERED			
Name(s) and Address(es) of Registered Holder(s) (Please fill in, if blank)	Certificate(s) Tendered (Attach additional signed list if necessary)		
	Certificate Number(s)*	Total Number of Shares Evidenced by Certificate(s)*	Number of Shares Tendered**
	Total Shares		

*Need not be completed by Book-Entry Stockholders.

**Unless otherwise indicated, it will be assumed that all Shares evidenced by any certificate(s) delivered to the Depositary are being tendered. See Instruction 4.

DESCRIPTION OF RIGHTS TENDERED*			
Name(s) and Address(es) of Registered Holder(s) (Please fill in, if blank)	Certificate(s) Tendered (Attach additional signed list if necessary)		
	Certificate Number(s)**	Total Number of Rights Evidenced by Certificate(s)**	Number of Rights Tendered***
	Total Rights		

*If the tendered Rights are represented by separate certificates, complete using the certificate numbers of such Rights certificates. If the tendered Rights are not represented by separate certificates, or if such certificates have not been distributed, complete using the certificate numbers of the Shares with respect to which the Rights were issued. Stockholders tendering Rights which are not represented by separate certificates should retain a copy of this description in order to accurately complete a supplementing Letter of Transmittal if certificates for Rights are received.

**Need not be completed by Book-Entry Stockholders.

***Unless otherwise indicated, it will be assumed that all Rights evidenced by any certificate(s) delivered to the Depositary are being tendered. See Instruction 4.

The name and address of the registered holders should be printed, if not already printed above, exactly as they appear on the certificates representing Shares and/or Rights tendered hereby. The certificates and the number of Shares and/or Rights that the undersigned wishes to tender should be indicated in the appropriate boxes.

Figure 3.4 *(continued)*

Later, in June 1989, Coniston raised its bid to $34 from $29 and took over T. W. Services.

If the stockholder wishes to withdraw shares, he or she must submit a *letter of withdrawal.* Stockholders may want to withdraw in order to take advantage of another, more attractive offer. In this case, the originator of the other competing offer may attempt to facilitate this process by sending stockholders a letter urging them to withdraw and providing them a letter of withdrawal form. This letter of withdrawal must be accompanied by a *signature guarantee,* verifying that the signature is authentic. A formal letter of withdrawal form, however, is not required to withdraw the shares. Although such a form is often used, any slip of paper is acceptable, if it indicates the stockholder's intention to withdraw the shares and is accompanied by the appropriate signature guarantee.

Stockholders, as well as brokers acting on behalf of stockholders, may wait until the last minute before tendering their shares in the hope that a better offer will materialize. As the expiration date approaches, a broker may still take advantage of the offer by submitting a *letter of guaranteed delivery* (see Figure 3.5). This guarantees that the broker will send the shares within five New York Stock Exchange days. Based on this written guarantee, these shares will be included in the offer. The letter of guarantee can be offered only by brokers, not individuals. An individual, however, can take advantage of this option by asking a broker to submit the guarantee.

Throughout the process, a stockholder can obtain up-to-date information on the offer from the paying agent or through a special *information agent.* An information agent is usually a proxy firm, such as D. F. King, which is hired by the bidder as a source of information on the offer.

Changes in the Tender Offer

The Williams Act allows a modification in the offer period if there is a material change in the terms of the offer. The length of the extension in the offer period depends on the significance of the change, which is generally considered a *new offer.* A new offer gives the stockholders an additional 20-day period to consider the offer. A higher price might be considered such a significant change. A less significant change results in an *amended offer,* which provides a 10-day extension in the offer period. An increase in the number of shares to be purchased might be considered an amended offer.

Best Price Rule

Under Section 14d–7, if the bidder increases the consideration offered, the bidder must pay this increased consideration to all those who have already tendered their shares.

Payment Following Completion of the Offer

The law provides that the tendered shares must either be paid for promptly after the offer is terminated or returned to the shareholders. This prompt payment may be frustrated by other regulatory requirements, such as the Hart–Scott–Rodino Act. The bidder may postpone payment if other regulatory approvals must still be obtained after the Williams Act offer period expires.

Competing Tender Offers

An initial tender offer often attracts rival tender offers in takeover battles. Since the law was designed to give stockholders time to carefully consider all relevant alternatives, an extension of the offer period is possible when there is a competing offer. The Williams Act states that, in the event of a new tender offer, stockholders in the target company must have at least 10 business days to consider the new offer. In effect, this 10-day consideration period can extend the original offer period. Consider, for example, that we are 16 days into the first offer, when a new bidder makes a tender offer for the target firm; then target shareholders have at least 10 days to decide on the original offer. As a result, the original offer period is extended 6 more days, or a total of 26 days. If, on the other hand, the new offer occurred on the fourth day of the first offer period, there would not be an extension of the original offer period.

Williams Act Merger Tactics

Although most securities laws offer protection to stockholders, they often give the participants in a takeover battle opportunities for tactical maneuvering. The *two-tiered tender offer* is a tactical tool used by the acquiring firm to offset the influence of the Williams Act. In a two-tiered offer, the bidder offers a higher price or better terms for an initial percentage of the target which might give the bidder control. The second tier tends to receive less advantageous terms.

The two-tiered offer gives stockholders an incentive to rush to

NOTICE OF GUARANTEED DELIVERY
for
Tender of 13 7/8% Senior Subordinated
Notes due 1999
of
THE BIBB COMPANY

As set forth in the "The Exchange Offer and Solicitation--Guaranteed Delivery Procedures" of the Prospectus and Consent Solicitation dated May 11, 1990 (the "Prospectus") of The Bibb Company (the "Company"), this form or one substantially equivalent hereto must be used to accept the Company's offer (the "Exchange Offer") to exchange $992.50 principal amount of the Company's 14% Senior Subordinated Notes due 1999 (the "New Notes") for each $1,000 principal amount of the Company's outstanding 13 7/8% Senior Subordinated Notes due 1999 (the "Old Notes") if certificate(s) representing the Old Notes are not immediately available or if the procedure for book entry transfer cannot be completed on a timely basis or time will not permit all required documents to reach the Exchange Agent prior to 5:00 P.M., New York City Time, on June 14, 1990, unless extended (the "Expiration Date"). Such form may be delivered by hand or transmitted by telegram, facsimile transmission, mail or hand delivery to the Exchange Agent.

To: CITIBANK, N.A.
Exchange Agent

By Hand:	*By Overnight Courier:*	*By Mail:*
Citibank, N.A.	Citibank, N.A.	Citibank, N.A.
Corporate Trust Window	c/o Citicorp Data Distribution, Inc.	c/o Citicorp Data Distribution, Inc.
111 Wall Street	404 Sette Drive	P.O. Box 7002
5th Floor	Paramus, NJ 07652	Paramus, NJ 07653
New York, NY		

By Facsimile:	*For Confirmation of Receipt:*	*By TWX:*	*Answer Back:*
(201) 262-3240	(201) 262-4743	7109904964	CDDI PARA

Delivery of this instrument to an address or transmission of instructions via facsimile other than as set forth above does not constitute a valid delivery.

This form is not to be used to guarantee signatures. If a signature or a Consent and Letter of Transmittal is required to be guaranteed by an "Eligible Institution" under the instructions thereto, such signature guarantee must appear in the applicable space provided in the signature box on the Consent and Letter of Transmittal.

Figure 3.5 Reprinted by permission of the Bibb Company.

LADIES AND GENTLEMEN:

The undersigned hereby tenders to The Bibb Company upon the terms and subject to the conditions set forth in the Prospectus, and any supplements or amendments thereto, and the related Consent and Letter of Transmittal, receipt of which is hereby acknowledged, $_____ principal amount of Old Notes pursuant to the guaranteed delivery procedure set forth in "The Exchange Offer And Solicitation--Guaranteed Delivery Procedures" of the Prospectus. This tender is accompanied by delivery of a properly completed and duly executed Consent and Letter of Transmittal (or facsimile thereof) and any other documents required therein.

Signature(s):_____   Address:_____

_____   _____

Name(s) of Record Holder(s):_____   Area Code and Tel. No.:_____

_____   If Old Notes will be delivered by
                                          book entry transfer, check trust company
                                          below:

Certificate No.(s) of Old Notes   ___ The Depository Trust Company
(if available):_____   ___ Midwest Securities Trust Company
                                          ___ Philadelphia Depository Trust Company
Dated:_____   Depository Account No. _____

GUARANTEE
(Not to be used for signature guarantee)

The undersigned, a member firm of a registered national securities exchange or of the National Association of Securities Dealers, Inc., or a correspondent in the United States, hereby (a) represents that the above named person(s) "own(s)" the Old Notes tendered hereby within the meaning of Rule 10b-4 under the Securities Exchange Act of 1934, as amended, (b) represents that such tender of Old Notes complies with Rule 10b-4 and (c) guarantees delivery to the Exchange Agent of certificates for the Old Notes tendered hereby, in proper form for transfer, or delivery to the Exchange Agent of such Old Notes pursuant to the procedure for book entry transfer within two business days after the Expiration Date.

Name of Firm:_____   _____
                                          Authorized Signature

Address: _____   Name:_____

_____   Title:_____

Area Code and Tel. No.:_____   Dated:_____

Figure 3.5 *(continued)*

tender, even though the Williams Act allows them a 20-day waiting period. Recognizing that two-tiered offers would counteract the effectiveness of the Williams Act waiting period, in 1982 the SEC ruled that the proration period for two-tiered tender offers would be 20 days. Therefore, stockholders would be guaranteed participation in the first tier and would not have an incentive to rush their decision. This ruling reduced the popularity of two-tiered tender offers among hostile bidders.

Proposals to Change the Williams Act

Several legislative efforts have been made to amend the Williams Act, most of them centering on closing various perceived loopholes in the law. One such proposal involves closing the *10-day window*—the 10-day period between when the bidding corporation acquires 5 percent of the target's stock and when it is required to file a Schedule 13D. Because of the length of this time period, the acquiring firm may be able to buy a controlling interest in the target before it has to reveal its acquisition through the filing of Schedule 13D. The bidding firm may be able to keep its stock acquisition secret from stockholders during this intervening time period. If stockholders find out that a bidder is actively seeking control, they may not sell at the market price, but may instead hold out for the premium that is normally associated with attempts to gain control of a target.

Another proposal that addresses this issue involves lowering the 5 percent threshold to 2 percent. Thus, the acquirer will not be able to acquire as significant a percentage of the target without providing full disclosure of its activities. Other proposals suggest combining both changes and informing stockholders that offers to buy their stock are part of a general effort to gain control of the target. Stockholders can then be alerted to that fact that their shares may be able to command a control premium. As a result, shareholders may be reluctant to sell their shares unless they receive some premium.

Comparison with Foreign Takeover Rules: Case of Great Britain

The United States' takeover laws differ considerably from those of other nations. British takeover regulation, for example, is a form of self-regulation by the corporate sector and the securities industry. This regulation is based on the Code of Takeovers and Mergers, a collection of standards and regulations on takeovers and mergers, and is enforced by the Panel on Takeovers and Mergers. This panel is composed of members of the Bank of England, the London Stock Exchange, and various other financial leaders. Its chief responsibility is to make sure there is a "level playing field," that is, that all investors have equal access to information on takeover offers. The panel also attempts to prevent target firms from adopting antitakeover measures without prior shareholder approval. Some of the more important provisions of the British code are as follows:

1. Investors acquiring 30 percent or more of a company's shares must bid for the remaining shares at the highest price paid for the shares already acquired.
2. Substantial partial offers for a target must gain the approval of the target and the panel.
3. Antitakeover measures, such as supermajority provisions or the issuance of options to be given to friendly parties, must be approved by the target's shareholders.

The unique aspect of the British system is that compliance is voluntary; the panel's rulings are not binding by law. Its rulings are considered most influential, however, and are almost always adopted.[5]

ANTITRUST LAWS

The ability to merge with or acquire other firms is limited by antitrust legislation. Various antitrust laws are designed to prevent firms from reducing competition through mergers. Many mergers are never attempted, simply because of the likelihood of governmental intervention on antitrust grounds. Other mergers are halted when it becomes apparent that the government will likely oppose the merger.

The government has changed its stance on the antitrust ramifications of mergers several times since 1890. As noted earlier, in recent years, the government's attitude has been evolving toward a freer market view, which favors a more limited government role in the marketplace. Although many horizontal mergers were opposed during the 1980s, many others proceeded unopposed. This is in sharp contrast to the government's earlier position in the 1960s. During that period, mergers and acquisitions involving businesses only remotely similar to the acquiring firm's business were often opposed on antitrust grounds.

---

[5]John Brooks, *The Takeover Game* (New York: E. P. Dutton, 1987).

This situation encouraged large numbers of conglomerate mergers, which were generally not opposed.

The Sherman Antitrust Act

The Sherman Antitrust Act, originally passed in 1890, is the cornerstone of all U.S. antitrust laws. The first two sections of the law contain its most important provisions:

Section 1. This section prohibits all contracts, combinations, and conspiracies in restraint of trade.

Section 2. This section prohibits any attempts or conspiracies to monopolize a particular industry.

This act made the formation of monopolies, and other attempts to restrain trade, unlawful and criminal offenses punishable under federal law. The government or the injured party can file suit under this law, and the court can then decide the appropriate punishment, which can range from an injunction to more severe penalties, including triple damages and imprisonment.

These first two sections of the Sherman Act make it immediately clear that it is written broadly enough to cover almost all types of anticompetitive activities. Surprisingly, however, the first great merger wave took place following the passage of the bill. This first merger wave, which took place between 1897 and 1904, was characterized by the formation of monopolies. The resulting increased concentration in many industries, combined with the formation of many powerful monopolies, revealed that the act was not performing the functions its first two sections implied.

The apparent ineffectiveness of the Sherman Act was partly the fault of the law's wording. Specifically, it stated that all contracts which restrained trade were illegal. In its early interpretations, however, the court reasonably refused to enforce this part of the law on the basis that this rule implies that almost all contracts could be considered illegal. The court had difficulty finding an effective substitute. These court rulings made the law a dead letter for more than a decade after its passage. The lack of government resources also made it difficult for the government to enforce the law. The law started to have more of an impact on the business community under the pressure of trust busting President Teddy Roosevelt. In an effort to correct the deficiencies associated with the wording of the law and the lack of an enforcement agency, the government decided to make a more explicit statement of its antitrust position. This effort came with the passage of the Clayton Act.

The Clayton Act

The goal of the Clayton Act was to strengthen the Sherman Act while also specifically proscribing certain business practices. Its main provisions are as follows:

Section 2 Price discrimination among customers was prohibited except when it could be justified by cost economies.

Section 3 Tying contracts were prohibited. An example of a tying contract would be if a firm refused to sell certain essential products to a customer unless that customer bought other products from the seller.

Section 7 The acquisition of stock in competing corporations was prohibited if the effect was to lessen competition.

Section 8 Interlocking directorates were prohibited when the directors were on the boards of competing firms.

As we can readily see, the Clayton Act did not prohibit any activities that were not already illegal under a broad interpretation of the Sherman Act. The Clayton Act, however, clarified which business practices unfairly restrain trade and reduce competition. The bill did not address the problem of the lack of an enforcement agency charged with the specific responsibility for enforcing the antitrust laws. With the passage of the Federal Trade Commission Act in 1914, the Federal Trade Commission (FTC) was established to address this problem. The FTC was charged specifically with enforcing antitrust laws, such as the Clayton Act and the Federal Trade Commission Act. The FTC was also given the power to issue cease and desist orders to firms engaging in unfair trade practices.

Section 7 is particularly relevant to mergers and acquisitions: "No corporation shall *acquire* the whole or any part of the stock, or the whole or any part of the assets, of another corporation where in any *line of commerce* in any *section of the country* the effect of such an acquisition may be to substantially lessen competition or tend to create a *monopoly* [italics in original]. This section reflects four main aspects of the Clayton Act.

1. *Acquisition.* Originally, the Clayton Act prohibited only the acquisition of stock in a corporation if the effect was to lessen competition. However, the marketplace quickly exposed a loophole in the wording of the section. The loophole involved the acquisition of the assets of a target company. This was later amended, with the law covering both stock and asset acquisitions.

2. *Line of commerce.* Through the use of the terms *line of commerce* the act adopted a broader focus than just a particular industry. This broader focus allows antitrust agencies to consider the competitive effects of a full range of a firm's business activities.

3. *Section of the country.* The act can be applied on a regional rather than a national basis. Through this provision, the antitrust authorities can look at regional market shares rather than national market shares. Therefore, a firm that dominated a regional market, and enjoyed a monopoly in that section of the country, could be found in violation of this law. The antitrust authorities often require the violating firm to divest the operations in the affected region in order to diminish their market power in that area.

4. *Tendency to lessen competition.* The working of this part of Section 7 is quite vague. It states that a firm *may* lessen competition or *tend* to create a monopoly. This vague wording is intentionally designed to take into account the possibility that the effect on competition may not be immediate. This wording gives the antitrust authorities the power to act if there is only a reasonable probability that competition will be lessened. This almost assumes that, if a firm has the power to limit competition, it will do so. Therefore, the law seeks to prevent these activities before they occur. This view of business behavior changed considerably in the 1980s.

The Federal Trade Commission Act of 1914

One weakness of the Sherman Antitrust Act was that it didn't give the government an effective enforcement agency to investigate and pursue antitrust violations. At that time, the Justice Department did not possess the resources to be an effective antitrust deterrent. In an effort to address this problem, the Federal Trade Commission Act, passed in 1914, established the Federal Trade Commission (FTC). The FTC was charged with enforcing both the Federal Trade Commission Act and the Clayton Act. In particular, it was passed with the intention of creating an enforcement arm for the Clayton Act. This independent agency was given the power to initiate antitrust lawsuits. The commission was not given a role in the criminal enforcement of antitrust violations. The act also broadened the range of illegal business activities beyond those mentioned in the Clayton Act.

The Celler–Kefauver Act of 1950

Section 7 of the Clayton Act was written broadly enough to give the antitrust authorities broad latitude in defining an antitrust violation. However, through a loophole in the Clayton Act, corporations were engaging in acquisitions even when these acquisitions represented a clear lessening of competition.

As noted above, the Clayton Act was originally worded to prohibit the acquisition of another corporation's stock where the effect was to lessen competition. However, historically, corporations and raiders have continually found loopholes in the law. Many firms were able to complete acquisitions by purchasing a target firm's assets rather than its stock. Under the original wording of the Clayton Act, this would not be a violation of the law. This loophole was eliminated by the passage of the Celler–Kefauver Act of 1950 which prohibited the acquisition of assets of a target firm where the effect was to lessen competition. The Celler–Kefauver Act also prohibited vertical mergers and conglomerate mergers when they were shown to reduce competition. The previous antitrust laws were aimed at horizontal mergers, which are combinations of firms producing the same product. This law set the stage for the aggressive antitrust enforcement of the 1960s.

The Hart–Scott–Rodino Antitrust Improvements Act of 1976

This bill requires that the FTC and the Justice Department be given the opportunity to review proposed mergers and acquisitions in advance. According to the Hart–Scott–Rodino Act, an acquisition or merger cannot be consummated until these authorities have reviewed the transaction. These two authorities must decide which of the two will investigate the particular transaction. This law prevents consummation of a merger until the end of the specified waiting periods. Failure to file in a timely manner can delay completion of the transaction.

The Hart–Scott–Rodino Act was passed to prevent the consummation of transactions that would ultimately be judged to be anticompetitive. Thus, the Justice Department would be able to avoid disassembling a company that had been formed, in part, through an anticompetitive merger or acquisition. The law became necessary because of the government's inability to halt transactions through the granting of injunctive relief while it attempted to rule on the competitive effects of the business combination. When injunctive relief was not obtainable, mandated divestiture, designed to restore competition, might not take place for many years after the original acquisition or merger. The Hart–Scott–Rodino Act was written to prevent these problems before they occurred.

Type of Information to be Filed   The law requires the filing of a 16-page form. (See Figure 3.6, which shows page 1 of that form.) Business data describing the business activities and revenues of the acquiring and the target firms' operations must be provided according to Standard Industrial Classification (SIC) Codes. Most firms already have this information since it has to be submitted to the U.S. Bureau of the Census. In addition, when filing, the acquiring firm must attach certain reports it has compiled to analyze the competitive effects of this transaction. This presents an interesting conflict. When a transaction is first being proposed within the acquiring firm, its proponents may tend to exaggerate its benefits. If this exaggeration comes in the form of presenting a higher market share than what might be more realistic, the firm's ability to attain antitrust approval can be hindered. For this reason, when the firm is preparing its premerger reports, it must keep the antitrust approval in mind.

The Antitrust Pre-Merger Review Time Periods

All-Cash Offers   The time periods for review vary depending on whether the offer is an all-cash offer or whether it includes securities in the compensation package. In an all-cash offer, the regulatory authorities have 15 days in which to review the filing. However, the agency may decide that it needs additional information before it can make a judgment on the antitrust ramifications of the merger or acquisition. It may therefore take another 10 days before it decides whether or not to challenge a transaction. The request for additional information usually indicates that the deal will not receive antitrust approval. In cash offers, the waiting period begins when the acquirer files the required forms.

Securities Offers   In offers that include securities in the compensation package, the initial review period is 30 days. If the regulatory authorities request additional information, they may take an additional 20 days to complete the review. For offers that are not cash offers, the waiting period starts when *both* firms have filed the necessary forms.

16 C.F.R. Part 803 - Appendix

NOTIFICATION AND REPORT FORM FOR CERTAIN MERGERS AND ACQUISITIONS

THE INFORMATION REQUIRED TO BE SUPPLIED ON THESE ANSWER SHEETS IS SPECIFIED IN THE INSTRUCTIONS

➡ Attach the Affidavit required by § 803.5 to this page.

FOR OFFICE USE ONLY
TRANSACTION NUMBER

☐ CTO   ☐ ETR

Is this Acquisition a CASH TENDER OFFER?   ☐ YES   ☐ NO

Do you request Early Termination of the Waiting Period?   ☐ YES   ☐ NO
(Grants of early termination are published in the Federal Register.)

ITEM 1

(a) NAME AND HEADQUARTERS ADDRESS OF PERSON FILING NOTIFICATION *(ultimate parent entity)*

(b) PERSON FILING NOTIFICATION IS

☐ an acquiring person   ☐ an acquired person   ☐ both

(c) LIST NAMES OF ULTIMATE PARENT ENTITIES OF ALL ACQUIRING PERSONS | LIST NAMES OF ULTIMATE PARENT ENTITIES OF ALL ACQUIRED PERSONS

(d) THIS ACQUISITION IS *(put an X in all the boxes that apply)*

☐ an acquisition of assets   ☐ a consolidation (see § 801.2)

☐ a merger (see § 801.2)   ☐ an acquisition of voting securities

☐ an acquisition subject to § 801.2(e)   ☐ a secondary acquisition

☐ formation of a joint venture or other corporation (see § 801.40)   ☐ an acquisition subject to § 801.31

☐ an acquisition subject to § 801.30 *(specify type)*: _____

☐ other *(specify)* _____

(e) INDICATE HIGHEST NOTIFICATION THRESHOLD IN § 801.1(h) FOR WHICH THIS FORM IS BEING FILED *(acquiring person only)*

☐ $ 15 million   ☐ 15%   ☐ 25%   ☐ 50%

(f) VALUE OF VOTING SECURITIES | VALUE OF ASSETS

(g) PUT AN X IN THE APPROPRIATE BOX TO DESCRIBE ENTITY FILING NOTIFICATION

☐ corporation   ☐ partnership   ☐ other *(specify)* _____

(h) DATA FURNISHED BY

☐ calendar year   ☐ fiscal year *(specify period)*: _____ *(month/day)* to _____ *(month/day)*

(i) PUT AN X IN THE APPROPRIATE BOX AND GIVE THE NAME AND ADDRESS OF THE ENTITY FILING NOTIFICATION *(if other than ultimate parent entity)*

☐ NA   ☐ This report is being filed on behalf of a foreign person pursuant to § 803.4.   ☐ This report is being filed on behalf of the ultimate parent entity by another entity within the same person authorized by it to file pursuant to § 803.2(a).

NAME OF ENTITY FILING NOTIFICATION | ADDRESS

THIS FORM IS REQUIRED BY LAW and must be filed separately by each person which, by reason of a merger, consolidation or acquisition, is subject to § 7A of the Clayton Act, 15 U.S.C. § 18a, as added by Section 201 of the Hart-Scott-Rodino Antitrust Improvements Act of 1976, Pub. L. No. 94-435, 90 Stat. 1390, and rules promulgated thereunder (hereinafter referred to as "the rules" or by section number). The statute and rules are set forth in the *Federal Register* at 43 FR 33450; the rules may also be found at 16 CFR Parts 801-03. Failure to file this Notific.tion and Report Form, and to observe the required waiting period before consummating the acquisition, in accordance with the applicable provisions of 15 U.S.C. § 18a and the rules, subjects any "person," as defined in the rules, or any individuals responsible for noncompliance, to liability for a penalty of not more than $10,000 for each day during which such person is in violation of 15 U.S.C. § 18a.

All information and documentary material filed in or with this Form is confidential. It is exempt from disclosure under the Freedom of Information Act, and may be made public only in an administrative or judicial proceeding, or disclosed to Congress or to a duly authorized committee or subcommittee of Congress.

Complete and return *two* notarized copies (with *one set* of documentary attachments) of this Notification and Report Form to Premerger Notification Office, Bureau of Competition, Room 303, Federal Trade Commission, Washington, D.C. 20580, and *three* notarized copies (with *one set* of documentary attachments) to Director of Operations, Antitrust Division, Room 3218, Department of Justice, Washington, D.C. 20530. The central office for information and assistance with respect to matters in connection with this Notification and Report Form is Room 303, Federal Trade Commission, Washington, D.C. 20580, phone (202) 326-3100.

Figure 3.6

A bidding firm can request an early termination of the waiting period if it feels that the transaction does not create any antitrust conflicts. Early terminations have been much more common in recent years. An early termination, however, is totally up to the discretion of the regulatory agencies.

The waiting period is designed to provide the antitrust agency with an opportunity to identify those transactions that might reduce competition. The reasoning is that it is far easier to prevent a deal from occurring than to disassemble a combined firm after the merger has been completed. If the antitrust agencies determine that there is an antitrust problem, they normally file suit to prevent the merger. Target firms can use the waiting period as a defensive tactic. Targets of hostile bids may be purposefully slow to report the required information. On the other hand, firms that receive favorable, friendly bids may choose to expedite the selling process by responding quickly.

Who Must File   The original wording of the Hart–Scott–Rodino Act is somewhat vague, leading some to believe that it did not apply to certain business entities such as partnerships. The act requires that *persons* or *corporations* must file if they fulfill one of the following two criteria:

- An entity buys at least $15 million of another entity's voting securities or assets.
- An entity buys at least 50 percent of another entity's voting securities. This criterion applies only if the acquired entity has total assets or annual sales in excess of $25 million.

Deadlines for Filing   A bidder must file under Hart–Scott–Rodino as soon as it announces a tender offer or any other offer. The target is then required to respond. This response comes in the form of the target's filing, which must take place 15 days after the bidder has filed.

Exemptions to the Hart–Scott–Rodino Act   Certain acquisitions supervised by governmental agencies, as well certain foreign acquisitions, are exempt from the requirements of the Hart–Scott–Rodino Act. The *investment exception* is one that tends to attract much attention in tender offers since it is in many ways a grey area.

The investment exception.   The investment exception applies to the filing requirement associated with the purchase of $15 million worth of voting securities. It permits an individual to acquire up to 10 percent of an issuer's voting securities as long as the acquisition is "solely for the purposes of investment."[6] The investment exception is designed to exempt those buyers of securities who are passive investors and have no interest in control. It allows investors to buy a large dollar amount of voting securities in a particular company without having to adhere to the Hart–Scott–Rodino filing requirement.

Tender offers have been a source of problems for the enforcement authorities. Clearly, a tender offer is designed to take control of a target corporation. However, the investment exception may cover the *initial* purchases of stock. If the purchasing company does not file, relying on the applicability of the investment exception, then its motives may be subsequently questioned if it later initiates a tender offer. The regulatory authorities may find it difficult to prove that, in cases where the stock has been accumulated over an extended time period, the initial purchases were part of an overall plan to take control of the target. The classic challenge to the investment exception was the unsuccessful takeover attempt of Houston Natural Gas by the Coastal Corporation. Prior to its takeover attempt, Coastal held $15 million worth of shares in Houston Natural Gas. On January 19, 1984, Coastal bought 75,500 shares of Houston Natural Gas but did not file under the Hart–Scott–Rodino Act. Coastal relied on the applicability investment exception. On January 27, 1984, Coastal announced a tender offer for Houston Natural Gas. The Department of Justice sued Coastal, contending that it had purposefully evaded the requirements of the Hart–Scott–Rodino Act which it felt were binding in this case. Coastal agreed to a settlement and paid a fine equal to $230,000, which was based on a maximum fine of $10,000 per day for each day between January 19 and February 11 (when it eventually did file).

The convertible securities exception. Securities that are convertible into voting securities are exempt from the filing requirements of the Hart–Scott–Rodino Act, as are options and warrants. Before these securities are converted, or before these options and warrants are exercised, the holders must file under Hart–Scott–Rodino.

Raiders may try to evade the filing requirements of the Hart–Scott–Rodino Act by purchasing *call options*. A call option gives the holder the right to purchase a particular security at a particular price during a certain period of time. For this right the purchaser pays the issuer, who is usually a securities firm, a fee called the *option's premium.* Under the convertible securities exemption of the Hart–Scott–Rodino Act, a raider could postpone announcing his or her intentions by purchasing options. The raider could then exercise the option at an advan-

---

[6]Ralph Ferrara, Meredith Brown, and John Hall, *Takeovers: Attack and Survival* (Stoneham, Mass.: Butterworth Legal Publishers, 1987), p. 151.

tageous time. Although the wording of the law may seem to allow this loophole, such purchases of options have been challenged. These challenges have come as a surprise to those raiders who felt they were relying on the explicit wording of the law.

The government's position on this issue was evident in the recent government lawsuit against Donald Trump. Donald Trump purchased call options on the stock of the Holiday Corporation and the Bally Manufacturing Corporation in August 1986. The government later filed a civil suit charging that Trump was in violation of the Hart–Scott–Rodino Act.[7] The government contended that before purchasing the call options Trump should have filed a notification with the FTC. Trump settled the suit in April 1988 without admitting any wrongdoing. He agreed to pay a $750,000 fine in return for the FTC dropping the legal action.

Use of acquisition vehicles.   A legal entity, such as a corporation, developed specifically for the purpose of facilitating a takeover may not be bound by the filing requirements of the Hart–Scott–Rodino Act. These corporations are often newly formed subsidiaries of the acquiring company. They usually receive an infusion of funds from the parent corporation which is used to purchase the target's securities. These acquisition vehicles may escape the regulatory scope of the Hart–Scott–Rodino Act through the size requirements dictated by the wording of the law. The enforcement criteria indicate that, in order for the filing requirements to apply, the corporation must be of a certain size as indicated by its last balance sheet. However, the last balance sheet may never have been assembled since the entity was recently formed.

The regulatory authorities have held that acquisition vehicles expressly formed for the purpose of evading the Hart–Scott–Rodino Act are illegal. Many raiders simply formed partnerships which, in their opinion, were not covered under the act. They may try to use three partnerships with no one partnership holding as much as 50 percent of the target's stock. Since they would not have to file, they could keep their activities secret until they were in a sufficiently strong position to mount a successful takeover.[8]

On May 28, 1987, the Justice Department and the FTC announced the closing of the partnership loophole. Effective July 5, 1987, any partnership controlled by an investor that buys more than $15 million of a corporation's stock must file with the government. Pursuant to this

---

[7]*Wall Street Journal*, April 6, 1988.

[8]This discussion refers solely to the filing requirements associated with the Hart–Scott–Rodino Act, and not disclosure laws such as the Williams Act.

filing, they must receive advance clearance of the takeover from the regulatory agencies. The closing of the partnership loophole somewhat limited the ability of raiders to mount a strong offensive without the knowledge of investors. However, the megamergers that followed in 1988 showed that, while this new regulation was an inconvenience, it would not slow the pace of takeovers.

Purchases by brokerage firms   The takeover market provides great financial rewards for its participants who are able to buy the stock of targets before the market is aware the firm is a takeover target. This provides a strong incentive to find ways around the laws and regulations governing mergers and acquisitions. One approach which acquiring firms and raiders have taken to avoid compliance with the Hart–Scott–Rodino Act is through stock purchases by brokerage firms. Ostensibly, these purchases will not be in the name of the acquiring firm that has not openly declared its intentions to acquire the target. At a predetermined time, the acquiring firm will announce its intentions, and shares in the target will be transferred from the name of the brokerage firm to that of the acquiring firm.

This type of evasive maneuver occurred in March 1986 when the First City Financial Corporation had its broker, Bear Stearns, acquire stock in Ashland Oil. The Justice Department and the FTC alleged that First City had Bear Stearns and Company buy the stock while providing First City with the option of subsequently transferring the stock to First City's account.[9] Ultimately, First City agreed to pay a fine of $400,000 without admitting to any wrongdoing. Through this action, the Justice Department and the FTC put all potential bidders on notice that the use of brokerage firms to avoid the disclosure requirements of the Hart–Scott–Rodino Act would not be tolerated.

CHANGING PATTERNS OF ANTITRUST ENFORCEMENT IN THE UNITED STATES

The courts have adopted varying positions on antitrust enforcement throughout the twentieth century. These positions are reflected in the various court decisions that have established legal precedents on which the courts have subsequently relied. The discussion below briefly outlines some of the more notable antitrust decisions in order to give the reader an understanding of how the U.S. courts' views on what is illegal monopolistic behavior by firms have developed over the century.

---

[9]*Wall Street Journal*, April 4, 1988.

1911: U.S. v. Standard Oil of New Jersey et al.

In this case,[10] the Supreme Court found that Standard Oil of New Jersey illegally monopolized the petroleum refining industry. The Rockefellers originally organized Standard Oil as an Ohio corporation by consolidating many oil companies into one large trust. Upon encountering difficulties with the Ohio antitrust laws, the Rockefellers decided to move to New Jersey which had a more pro-business environment. This landmark case was heard before the widespread proliferation of the horseless carriage. Therefore, the issue was not monopolization of the gasoline refining market. Rather, Standard Oil was found guilty of monopolizing the market for kerosene and lubricating oil through its 90 percent market share. The court found that Standard Oil engaged in various anticompetitive actions, including:

1. Acquiring 120 rivals.
2. Securing discriminatory rail and freight rates.
3. Foreclosing crude supplies to competitors by buying up pipelines.
4. Conducting business espionage.
5. Using predatory pricing to drive rivals out of business. (This later point was strongly disputed by Standard Oil.)[11]

This decision led to the court's definition of illegal monopolization. The court found that Standard Oil was guilty because (1) it had acquired a monopoly position; and (2) it had clear intent to acquire such a monopoly position and exclude rivals.

The court's solution to the problem of Standard Oil's monopolization of this market was to rule that the company would have to be dissolved. Standard Oil was split into 33 geographically dispersed subsidiaries which, it was hoped, would compete with each other. Unfortunately, at first this did not happen because the Rockefeller family held significant stock positions in most of these subsidies. Eventually, however, the shareholdings became more dispersed and competition did begin.

1911: U.S. v. American Tobacco Company

In this case,[12] the Supreme Court found American Tobacco guilty of monopolizing the cigarette trade through illegal business practices, including:

---

[10]*U.S. v. Standard Oil of New Jersey et al*, 221 U.S. 1, 76 (1911).

[11]Frederick M. Scherer, "Industrial Market Structure and Economic Performance," 2nd ed. (Boston: Houghton Mifflin, 1980). This section on the court's evolving position on antitrust enforcement draws heavily on his seminal work.

[12]*U.S. v. American Tobacco Company*, 221 U.S. 106 (1911).

1. Excluding rivals from having access to wholesalers.
2. Buying 250 former rivals.
3. Buying supplies of leaf tobacco.
4. Establishing "fighting brands" in local markets. These brands were sold below cost in order to drive out the local competitors.[13]

The court found that these activities were a clear effort by American Tobacco to monopolize the cigarette business. As its solution, the court decided to split American Tobacco into 16 separate companies, including American Tobacco, Liggett and Myers, Lorillard, Reynolds, and the American Snuff Company. The court's position and solution in the American Tobacco case was very similar to the Standard Oil decision. It ruled that the purposeful establishment of a monopoly position through the use of illegal business practices should be remedied by dissolving the monopoly.

1920: U.S. v. U.S. Steel Corporation et al.

As noted in Chapter 2, U.S. Steel was formed in 1901 in the first billion dollar megamerger. As a result, U.S. Steel consolidated control of 65 percent of the domestic steel and iron output. It was alleged that, over a series of four dinners orchestrated by U.S. Steel chairman Judge E. H. Gary, U.S. Steel colluded with rival steel producers to establish prices in the steel industry and to limit competition.

On the District Court level, the court ruled in favor of U.S. Steel. The Justice Department appealed, and the case went to the U.S. Supreme Court which ruled in favor of U.S. Steel.[14] In applying the Rule of Reason, the Court found that U.S. Steel did not have monopoly power. Indeed, the Court cited the fact that U.S. Steel's market share had declined from a high of 65 percent in 1901 to 52 percent in 1915. It also found that U.S. Steel did not attempt to engage in unfair competition and did not use its position as a price leader to drive out rivals. The Court almost seemed to imply that the orderly establishment of prices lent stability to the steel market and did not adversely affect rival producers. This position was supported by the testimony of rival steel producers.

The Rule of Reason marked a movement away from strict antitrust enforcement. The overall effect on the defendant and its impact on the market were considered in evaluating whether the alleged illegal activity or monopoly position had resulted in significant adverse effects. In the U.S. Steel case, the Court found that even if U.S. Steel had

---

[13]Scherer, "Industrial Market Structure."

[14]In *U.S. v. U.S. Steel Corporation et al.*, 223 Fed 55 (1915), 251 U.S. 417 (1920).

monopoly power there was no evidence that it used this power to reduce competition. By employing the Rule of Reason, the Court stated that not every contract that restrains trade is illegal. The alleged violator would have to restrain trade *unreasonably*; size alone could not make a firm guilty of antitrust violations.

This position was also consistent with the Supreme Court's ruling in the International Harvester case of 1927 when the Court found that price leadership alone was not per se illegal.[15] In these two decisions the court found it reasonable for smaller firms to follow the pricing policies of their larger rivals.

1945: U.S. v. Aluminum Company of America et al.

The Alcoa case[16] grew out of the complaints of competitors who found it very difficult to enter the aluminum industry because Alcoa owned a large percentage of the total available high-grade bauxite reserves. The Justice Department charged Alcoa with monopolization in 1937, and the Supreme Court found the firm guilty in 1945. In his now famous ruling, Judge Learned Hand found that Alcoa had built up its supply of bauxite reserves with the intent to monopolize the aluminum industry. He stated that Alcoa had increased its supply by an amount that was far greater than what was needed to satisfy demand. Through its efforts, Alcoa had amassed 90 percent of the aluminum ingot supply according to one of three definitions of the market that the Court considered. The Court's solution required that Alcoa sell some of its facilities to Reynolds Metals and Kaiser Aluminum. In addition, Alcoa was barred from building new plants for a period of time. This decision signaled the movement back to stronger antitrust enforcement.

The decision in the Alcoa case contrasts with the Supreme Court's position in the U.S. Steel case. The Alcoa decision implied that an industry could be judged by its structure. Given the fact that Alcoa had amassed such large bauxite reserves, it had achieved a monopoly position. Under the *structure argument*, such a firm is guilty of monopolization through the implication that a monopolistic structure will cause a firm to behave like a monopolist. The *behavior argument* is consistent with the U.S. Steel decision. Under this view, an industry can have a monopolistic structure but not exhibit the negative characteristics normally associated with monopoly. For example, a firm can have a large market share but not use its size and the benefits that derive from size, such as the ability to buy on favorable terms, to drive out smaller competitors.

---

[15]*U.S. v. International Harvester Company*, U.S. 693 (1927).

[16]*U.S. v. Aluminum Company of America et al.*, 148 F. 2d 416, 424 (1945).

1946: U.S. v. New York Great Atlantic and Pacific Tea Company et al.

The Alcoa decision was followed by the Atlantic and Pacific (A&P) Tea decision, which also adopted a position of strict antitrust enforcement.[17] The court found several executives of A&P guilty of criminal activity by trying to monopolize the retail food business. A&P was found guilty of using its position as a dominant buyer to extract special discounts from suppliers; of threatening suppliers with setting up internal sources of supply unless suppliers capitulated to A&P's demands; and of implementing aggressive price competition in regional markets where it encountered greater competition. Some critics of the A&P decision maintained that A&P was merely engaging in aggressive competition that should permit buying at the best possible prices. Extracting cash discounts from suppliers could be interpreted as a good business practice that allowed consumers to benefit in the form of lower prices, particularly in those cities where A&P used more competitive pricing.

The Alcoa and A&P decisions marked the heyday of antitrust enforcement in the United States. In these decisions the Supreme Court adopted a position that a company could be found guilty of antitrust violations without proof of illegal business practices (such as in Alcoa).

The 1950s to 1960s

In the 1950s, many firms, concerned by the precedent established by the Alcoa and A&P decisions, agreed to consent decrees allowing the defendant in an antitrust action to take remedial action without actually admitting guilt. In 1954, Eastman Kodak, for example, agreed to reduce its share of the film processing market by *unbundling* (i.e., including the processing fees in the price of the film). Kodak also agreed to reduce its market share to less than 50 percent in seven years.

In this period, companies sought to compromise with the Justice Department and were reluctant to go to court and risk an adverse ruling. The precedent set in the decisions of the late 1940s also made firms reluctant to engage in horizontal mergers. Moreover, the passage of the Celler–Kefauver Act in 1950 made firms leery of engaging in vertical combinations, a feeling reinforced by the Supreme Court's decision in the Du Pont–General Motors case in 1949 in which Du Pont was forced to divest itself of its interest in General Motors (23 percent) because the Court believed that Du Pont's relationship with GM would preclude other paint manufacturers from marketing to the automobile

---

[17]*U.S.* v. *New York Great Atlantic and Pacific Tea Company et al.*, 67 F. Supp. 626 (1946), 173 F. 2d (1949).

manufacturer. The intense antitrust environment established in the late 1940s was one factor that led to the conglomerate merger wave in the late 1960s.

Between the 1940s and the 1960s, the courts exhibited a clear tendency to rule in favor of the government agencies initiating the antitrust actions. This tendency put companies on the defensive and enhanced the Justice Department's proclivity for aggressive antitrust enforcement.

DEFINING MARKET SHARE

1968 Justice Department Merger Guidelines

One key factor which the Court has relied on in deciding antitrust cases has been the market share of the alleged violator of antitrust laws. In 1968, the Justice Department issued merger guidelines that set forth the types of merger that the government would oppose. Through these guidelines, used to help interpret the Sherman and Clayton acts, the Justice Department presented its definitions, in terms of specific market share percentages, of highly concentrated and less highly concentrated industries. The guidelines were expressed in terms of concentration ratios, which are the market shares of the top four or top eight firms in the industry.

Under the 1968 guidelines, an industry was considered to be highly concentrated if the four largest firms held at least 75 percent of the total market.

The guidelines for horizontal acquisitions indicated that a challenge could ordinarily be expected if the market shares of the parties were as follows:

Market	Acquiring Company	Acquired Company
Highly	4%	4% or more
Concentrated	10%	2% or more
	15%	1% or more
Less Highly	5%	5% or more
Concentrated	10%	4% or more
	15%	3% or more
	20%	2% or more
	25%	1% or more[18]

---

[18]Charles A. Scharf, Edward E. Shea, and George C. Beck, *Acquisitions, Mergers, Sales, Buyouts and Takeovers*, 3rd ed., (Englewood Cliffs, N.J.: Prentice-Hall Publishing Co., 1985), p. 138.

The issuance of these guidelines made antitrust enforcement more mechanistic. Companies considering a merger with another firm could be better able to ascertain in advance the Justice Department's position on the merger. Moreover, the Justice Department used these guidelines to determine its enforcement policies.

1982 Justice Department Guidelines

The limitations of such a rigid antitrust policy began to be felt in the 1970s; a policy that allowed more flexibility was clearly needed. Such a policy was instituted in 1982 through the work of William Baxter, head of the antitrust division of the Justice Department. Baxter was both a lawyer and an economist. Using his economics training, he introduced the *Herfindahl–Hirschman (HH) Index* to American antitrust policy. The Herfindahl–Hirschman Index is the sum of the squares of the market shares of each firm in the industry.

$$HH = \sum_{i=1}^{n} = s_i^2$$

where: s_i = the market share of the ith firm

Using this index rather than simple market shares of the top four or top eight firms in the industry provides a more precise measure of the impact of increased concentration that would be brought on by a merger of two competitors.

Properties of the Herfindahl–Hirschman Index

1. The index increases with the number of firms in the industry.
2. The index sums the squares of the firms in the industry. In doing so, it weights larger firms more heavily than smaller firms. Squaring a larger number will have a disproportionately larger impact on the index than squaring a smaller number. Moreover, a merger that increases the size differences between firms will result in a larger increase in the index than what would have been reflected using simple concentration ratios.
3. Since larger firms have greater impact on the index, the index can provide useful results even if there is incomplete information on the size of the smaller firms in the industry.

Example of the Herfindahl–Hirschman Index

Consider an industry composed of eight firms, each of which has a 12.5 percent market share. The Herfindahl–Hirschman Index then is equal to:

$$HH = \sum_{1=1}^{8} [(12.5^2)]$$
$$= 1,250$$

If two of these equal-sized firms merge, then the index is computed to be:

$$HH = \sum_{1=1}^{6} (12.5)^2 + 625$$
$$= 1,562.5$$

Just as in the 1968 merger guidelines, the Justice Department established a threshold level for concentration in the industry. Instead of the concentration ratios used in the 1968 guidelines, the 1982 guidelines were set in terms of HH Index values.[19]

HH > 1,800   Highly concentrated
HH > 1,000   Moderately concentrated
HH < 1,000   Unconcentrated

1984 Justice Department Guidelines

On June 14, 1984, the Justice Department again revised its merger guidelines in an attempt to further refine its antitrust enforcement policies. The department recognized that its prior guidelines, including the more accurate Herfindahl–Hirschman Index, were too mechanistic and inflexible. In an attempt to enhance the flexibility of its policies, the department allowed the consideration of *qualitative information* in addition to the quantitative measures it had been employing. This qualitative information would include factors such as the efficiency of firms in the industry, the financial viability of potential merger candidates, and the ability of U.S. firms to compete in foreign markets.

The 1984 merger guidelines also introduced the 5 *percent test*. This test requires the Justice Department to make a judgment on the effects of a potential 5 percent increase in the price of each product of each merging firm. This test is based on the assumption that there may be an increase in market power resulting from the merger. If so, the merged firms may have the ability to increase prices. The test attempts to examine the potential effects of this increase on competitors and consumers.

One microeconomic measure that provides an indication of the

---

[19]Ibid. p. 139.

responsiveness of consumers and competitors is the concept of *elasticity*. The price elasticity of demand provides an indication of the consumers' responsiveness to a change in the price of a product. It is measured as follows:

$$e = \frac{\% \text{ Change in quantity}}{\% \text{ Change in price}} =$$

$e > 1$ Demand is elastic. This percentage change in quantity is more than the percentage change in price.

$e = 1$ Unitary elasticity. The percentage change in quantity is equal to the percentage change in price.

$e < 1$ Inelastic demand. The percentage change in quality is less than the percentage change in price.

If demand is inelastic, in the price range indicated by the 5 percent price change, this implies greater market power for the merged firms. If, however, demand is elastic, consumers are not as adversely affected by the merger.

STATE ANTITAKEOVER LAWS

Many non-Americans are confused and dismayed by the sometimes conflicting combination of federal laws and state laws that characterizes the U.S. legal system. Indeed, under current federal and state takeover laws, it is possible that conforming to some aspects of the federal laws means being in violation of certain state laws. The line of demarcation between federal takeover laws and their state counterparts has to do with the focus of each. Federal laws tend to be directed at securities regulation, tender offers, and antitrust considerations, whereas state laws govern corporate charters and their bylaws.

There currently exists a broad array of inconsistent state laws across the United States. Many of these laws were passed in response to pressure by particular corporations who found themselves the object of interest by potential acquirers. The usual scenario is that a local firm petitions the state legislature to pass an antitakeover law or amend the current one in order to make it more difficult for a local corporation to be taken over. The political pressure that is brought to bear on the state legislatures comes in the form of allegations that a takeover by a "foreign raider" will mean a significant loss of jobs as well as other forms of community support such as charitable donations by the local corporation.

Some antitakeover regulations are clearly necessary, for the actions of certain speculators have, in some instances, gotten out of hand. It does not seem to make sense, however, to have a variety of different antitakeover laws throughout the United States. Some critics of state antitakeover laws regard this situation as an infringement of interstate commerce and are urging the federal government to establish greater uniformity in order to facilitate interstate commerce. On the other hand, given the federal versus state rights division, states have traditionally been given the right to regulate areas such as corporate charters. This issue will probably not be resolved in the near future.

Genesis of State Antitakeover Laws

State antitakeover laws were first developed in the late 1960s and early 1970s. These statutes typically required that disclosure materials be filed following the initiation of the bid. The problem with these "first-generation" state antitakeover laws was that they applied to firms that did only a small amount of business in that state. This seemed unfair to bidding corporations. Thus, the stage was set for a legal challenge.

Edgar* v. *MITE The constitutionality of these first-generation antitakeover laws was successfully challenged in 1982 in the famous *Edgar* v. *MITE* decision.[20] In this decision, the U.S. Supreme Court ruled that the Illinois Business Takeover Act was unconstitutional. The Illinois law permitted the state to block a nationwide tender offer for a state-affiliated target corporation if the bidder failed to comply with Illinois' disclosure laws. The challenge to the Illinois law caused states with similar laws to question their constitutionality and redevelop their provisions. The states still wanted to inhibit takeovers, which they felt were not in the best interest of their states. Now they had to adopt a different approach which came in the form of the "second-generation" laws.

The second-generation state antitakeover laws had a narrower focus than the first-generation. They tended to apply only to those firms that were incorporated within the state or that conducted a substantial part of their business activities within state boundaries. They were not directed at regulating disclosure in tender offers as the first-generation laws were. Rather, they focused on issues of corporate governance, which are traditionally the domain of state corporation laws.

---

[20]*Edgar* v. *MITE Corporation,* 102 S Ct 2629 (1982).

Components of Second-Generation Laws

Most second-generation laws incorporate some or all of the following provisions:[21]

- Fair price provision.
- Business combination provision.
- Control share provision.
- Cash out statute.

Fair Price Provision   A fair price provision requires that, in a successful tender offer, all shareholders who do not decide to sell will receive the same price as shareholders who do accept the offer. These provisions are designed to prevent the abuses that can occur in two-tiered tender offers. With two-tiered bids, a high price is offered to the first-tier tenders, whereas a lower price or less advantageous terms (such as securities of uncertain value instead of cash) are offered to the members of the second tier. The following states have fair price statutes: Connecticut, Florida, Georgia, Illinois, Louisiana, Mississippi, Pennsylvania, Washington, and Wisconsin.[22]

Business Combination Provision   This provision prevents business agreements between the target company and the bidding company for a certain time period. For example, the wording of a business combination provision may rule out the sales of the target's assets by the bidding company. These provisions are designed to prevent leveraged acquisitions. When an acquiring company assumes a large amount of debt to finance a takeover, it may be relying on the sales of assets by the target to pay the high interest payments required by the debt. The law is designed to prevent the transformation of local firms, with a low-risk capital structure, into riskier leveraged companies. The following states have business combination statutes: Arizona, Connecticut, Delaware, Georgia, Idaho, Indiana, Kansas, Kentucky, Maine, Maryland, Massachusetts, Michigan, Minnesota, Missouri, Nebraska, New Jersey,

---

[21]For an excellent and more detailed discussion of these and other provisions of second-generation laws, see Robert Winter, Robert Rosenbaum, Mark Stumpf, and L. Stevenson Parker, *State Takeover Statutes and Poison Pills* (Clifton, N.J.: Prentice-Hall Law and Business, 1988).

[22]Robert Winter, Robert Rosenbaum, Mark Stumpf, and L. Stevenson Parker, *State Takeover Statutes and Poison Pills*.

New York, Pennsylvania, South Carolina, Tennessee, Virginia, Washington, and Wisconsin.[23]

Control Share Provision   A control share provision requires that acquiring firms obtain prior approval of current target stockholders before the purchases are allowed. Typically, these provisions apply to stock purchases beyond a certain percentage of the outstanding stock. They are particularly effective if the current share ownership includes large blocks of stock that are held by groups generally supportive of management such as an employee stockholder. The following states have control share provisions: Arizona, Florida, Hawaii, Idaho, Indiana, Kansas, Louisiana, Maryland, Massachusetts, Michigan, Minnesota, Missouri, Nebraska, Nevada, North Carolina, Ohio, Oklahoma, Oregon, South Carolina, Tennessee, Utah, and Virginia.[24]

Cash Out Statute   This provision, like the fair price requirement, is designed to limit tender offers. It typically requires that, if a bidder buys a certain percentage of stock in a target firm, the bidder is then required to purchase all the remaining outstanding shares at the same terms given to the initial purchase. This provision limits acquiring firms that lack the financial resources for a 100 percent stock acquisition. It also limits leveraged acquisitions since it may require the bidder to assume an even greater amount of debt with the associated high debt service. Bidders might, therefore, be discouraged because of their inability to obtain financing for a 100 percent purchase or simply because they do not believe their cash flow will service the increased debt. The following states have cash out statutes: Maine, Pennsylvania, and Utah.[25]

CTS* v. *Dynamics   The *Edgar* v. *MITE* decision, delivered a severe blow to the first-generation laws. Many opponents of antitakeover legislation attacked the second-generation laws, which they felt were also unconstitutional. These legal actions resulted in the *CTS* v. *Dynamics* decision of April 1987.[26] In this case, the CTS Corporation used the Indiana law to fight off a takeover by the Dynamics Corporation. Dynamics challenged the law contending that it was unconstitutional. In

---

[23]Ibid.

[24]Ibid.

[25]Ibid.

[26]*Dynamics Corporation of America* v. *CTS Corporation*, 637 F. Supp. 406 (N.D. Ill. 1986).

CTS v. *Dynamics*, the U.S. Supreme Court ruled that the Indiana antitakeover law was constitutional. This law allows stockholders to vote on whether or not a buyer of controlling interest can exercise his or her voting rights. The CTS decision gave the Supreme Court's approval to the second-generation state takeover laws. Since the April 1987 *CTS* decision, 13 states have adopted antitakeover laws. In all, 29 states have some kind of law regulating takeovers.

Amanda Acquisition Corporation v. *Universal Foods Corporation*
In November 1989, the Supreme Court refused to hear a challenge to the Wisconsin antitakeover law. The Court's unwillingness to hear this challenge further buttressed the legal viability of state antitakeover laws. The Wisconsin law requires a bidder that acquires 10 percent or more of a target company's stock to receive the approval of the other target shareholders or wait three years to complete the merger. The three-year waiting period makes heavily leveraged buyouts, which were typical of the fourth merger wave, prohibitively expensive.

The Supreme Court decision arose out of a legal challenge by the Amanda Acquisition Corporation, which is a subsidiary of the Boston-based High Voltage Engineering Corporation. Amanda challenged the Wisconsin law that prevented it from proceeding with a tender offer for the Milwaukee-based Universal Foods Corporation. The directors of Universal Foods opposed the takeover. Amanda Acquisition Corporation charged that the Wisconsin law was an interference with interstate commerce and harmful to shareholders. The Supreme Court failed to agree and refused to hear the challenge to the law. The Supreme Court's position in this case reaffirms the *CTS* v. *Dynamics* decision which upheld the constitutionality of the Indiana antitakeover law in 1987. Based on the *CTS* v. *Dynamics* decision, as well as the Supreme Court's position in the *Amanda Acquisition Corporation* v. *Universal Foods Corporation* case, state antitakeover laws appear to be safe from challenge and may well be a permanent fixture in the laws of mergers.

Delaware Antitakeover Law   The Delaware antitakeover law is probably the most important of all the state antitakeover laws because more corporations are incorporated in Delaware than in any other state.[27] The popularity of Delaware as the preferred state of incorporation is due to its advantageous corporation laws and highly specialized

---

[27]This overview is based on the state laws as of 1989. These laws often are changed by amendments. In the interest of completeness, this section repeats some material discussed earlier in this chapter.

court system. The state's Fortune 500 companies, such as General Motors, Mobil, Rockwell International, and Dow Chemical, are among the 180,000 companies that have incorporated in Delaware. One-half of all New York Stock Exchange companies are incorporated there, along with 56 percent of the Fortune 500.

The Delaware antitakeover law was passed in 1988 but was made retroactive to December 23, 1987, the date before corporate raider Carl Icahn acquired 15 percent of Texaco Corporation. The law was passed in response to an intense lobbying effort by companies seeking to adopt a protective statute. They threatened that if such a protective statute was not passed they would reincorporate in states that did have antitakeover laws. The choice of the effective date testifies to the power of this lobbying effort.

The law stipulates that an unwanted bidder who buys more than 15 percent of a target company's stock cannot complete the takeover for three years except under the following conditions:[28]

1. If the buyer buys 85 percent or more of the target company's stock. This 85 percent figure may not include the stock held by directors or the stock held in employee stock ownership plans.
2. If two-thirds of the stockholders approve the acquisition.
3. If the board of directors and the stockholders decide to waive the antitakeover provisions of this law.

The law is designed to limit takeovers financed by debt. Raiders who have financed their takeovers by large amounts of debt often need to sell off company assets and divisions in order to pay off the debt. The need to pay off the debt quickly becomes significant in the case of the billion dollar takeover, as in the 1980s when interest payments were as much as half a million dollars per day.

Although the Delaware law might discourage some debt-financed takeovers, it is not that effective against cash offers. Moreover, even debt-financed offers at a very attractive price can be sufficiently appealing for stockholders to waive the antitakeover provisions of the law.

Pennsylvania Antitakeover Law   In April 1990, the Pennsylvania State Legislature approved the strongest antitakeover law in the United States. This law, sometimes referred to as the disgorgement statute, was designed to deal with the changes that took place in the hostile takeover market during the late 1980s. These changes included the increased use of proxy fights as an alternative to a hostile tender offer.

---

[28]Section 203 of the Delaware General Corporation Law.

As the junk bond market declined, many raiders lacked the requisite financing to make credible tender offers. Some then resorted to proxy fights to initiate hostile bids. In addition, those that were able to finance hostile tender offers or to extract greenmail under the threats of a takeover enjoyed great financial gains at the expense of the target. The new Pennsylvania statute is directed at reducing the incentive to engage in these activities.

The law restricts the voting rights of any investor or group that purchases 20 percent or more of a target's stock.[29] In addition, the statute allows Pennsylvania corporations to sue a "controlling person or group," which is defined as a 20 percent voting interest, to seek disgorgement of all profits of short-term investors who disposed of their shares within 18 months of the acquisition of the controlling position.[30] The law, which does not distinguish between friendly and unfriendly takeovers, applies not only to those that actually acquire a controlling interest but also to those that declare an intent or otherwise seek to acquire such an interest. The statute can also be applied to those who solicit proxies unless they satisfy certain restrictive conditions such as if the proxy votes are not given in exchange for consideration. The statute can be deactivated by the board of directors.

Protection was given to labor contracts, and severance pay was guaranteed for cases of successful hostile bids. Labor contracts can be enforced, and severance pay can be guaranteed in the case of a successful hostile bid.

The latest disgorgement statute is added to the other statutes, which together make up the strictest antitakeover laws of any state. The prior antitakeover statutes in Pennsylvania had already included a cash out provision, a business combination rule, and a control share provision. Combined with the disgorgement statute, this boldest set of antitakeover measures, which, some have labeled "fat-cat protectionism" or "corporate Stalinism," is sure to be challenged in the early 1990s. Many of the largest Pennsylvania firm's, such as Westinghouse Electric Corp., H.J. Heinz Co., and Sun Co. decided that they did not want to be covered by some of the strong provisions of the new Pennsylvania law. Other firms, such as Mellon Bank Corp. and PNC Financial decided to completely exempt themselves from the law.[31]

---

[29]Diana B. Henriques, "A Paradoxical Antitakeover Bill," *New York Times*, April 8, 1990, p. 15.

[30]Robert D. Rosenbaum and L. Stevenson Parker, *The Pennsylvania Takeover Act of 1990* (Englewood Cliffs, N.J.: Prentice–Hall Law & Business, 1990).

[31]Vindu Goel, "Many Pennsylvania Firms Opt Out of Provisions in State Anti-Takeover Law," *Wall Street Journal*, July 27, 1990, p. A5B.

State Antitrust Actions   Many states have their own antitrust laws. The wording of these laws is often similar to that of the Federal laws. In addition, the states have the power, under federal law, to take action in federal court and to block mergers they feel are anticompetitive, even when the Justice Department or the Federal Trade Commission fails to challenge the merger. The states' ability to do so was greatly enhanced by a 9 to 0 U.S. Supreme Court ruling in April 1990.[32] The ruling came as a result of California officials' challenge to the $2.5 billion takeover of Lucky Stores, Inc. by American Stores Company in June 1988. The ruling, written by Justice John Paul Stevens, overturned a 1989 U.S. Court of Appeals Ninth Circuit ruling in 1989 which held that the Clayton Act did not permit California to block the Lucky Stores and American Stores merger. California obtained a stay of the ruling from Justice Sandra Day O'Connor in August 1989.[33] This prevented combining the operations of Lucky Stores, the state's largest supermarket chain, with Alpha Beta, owned by American Stores and the state's fourth largest, until the matter was finally adjudicated. California's argument that the merger would cost the California consumers $440 million per year in grocery bills was found to be compelling by the U.S. Supreme Court.[34] This ruling opens the door for states to be active in opposing mergers on antitrust grounds when the federal government decides to adopt a pro-business stance and to limit its antitrust enforcement. This also makes antitrust enforcement less sensitive to the political makeup of the executive branch of the federal government.

REGULATION OF INSIDER TRADING

The Securities and Exchange Commission (SEC) rules specify remedies for shareholders who incur losses resulting from insider trading. Insiders are bound by SEC Rule 10b–5 which states that insiders must "disclose or abstain" from trading the firm's securities. Illegal insider trading can occur, for example, if insiders, acting on information unavailable to other investors, sell the firm's securities prior to an announcement of poor performance. Other investors, unaware of the upcoming bad news, may pay a higher price for the firm's securities. The opposite might be the case if insiders bought the firm's stock or

---

[32]Stephen Wermiel, "Supreme Court Raises the Risks During Mergers," *Wall Street Journal*, May 1, 1990, p. A3.

[33]Linda Greenhouse, "High Court Reinforces States in Fighting Business Mergers," *New York Times*, May 1, 1990, p. 1.

[34]*California v. American Stores Co.*, No. 89-258.

call options prior to the announcement of a bid from another firm. Stockholders might not have sold the shares to the insiders if they knew of the upcoming bid and its associated premium.

Insiders can be defined more broadly than the management of a company. They may include outsiders such as attorneys, investment bankers, financial printers, or consultants who can be considered "temporary insiders." Under Rule 10b–5, however, the U.S. Supreme Court held that outside parties who trade profitably based on their acquired information did not have to disclose their inside information. This was the case in the 1980 *Chiarella* v. *United States* in which a financial printer acquired information on an upcoming tender offer by reviewing documents in his print shop.[35] On the other hand, if an individual misappropriates confidential information on a merger or acquisition and uses it as the basis for trade, Rule 10b–5 will apply. The rule is applicable only to SEC enforcement proceedings or criminal actions, but not to civil actions, under the Insider Trading Sanctions Act of 1984, which permits the recovery of treble damages on the profits earned or the loss avoided.[36]

A classic example of illegal insider trading was the famous Texas Gulf Sulphur case.[37] In 1963, Texas Gulf Sulphur discovered certain valuable mineral deposits that it did not disclose for several months; actually, the firm publicly denied the discovery in a false press release. Meanwhile, officers and directors bought undervalued shares based on their inside information. The SEC successfully brought a suit against the insiders.

Insider Trading Scandals of the 1980s

The world of mergers and acquisitions has recently been plagued with several notorious insider trading scandals in which some of the field's leading participants were convicted of insider trading violations. Each of the major cases provided information that led to the subsequent conviction of other violators.

In June 1986, Dennis Levine, an investment banker at Drexel Burnham Lambert, pleaded guilty to securities fraud, tax evasion, and perjury. He had acquired information on upcoming merger deals through payments to other investment bankers. Levine was an impor-

---

[35]*Chiarella* v. *United States*, 445 U.S. 222, 100 S. Ct. 1108, 63 L. Ed. 2d, 348 (1980).

[36]*SEC* v. *Materia*, CCH Fed. Sec. L. Rep., 99, 526 (S.D.N.Y. 1983), aff'd 745 F. 2d. 197, cert. denied.

[37]*SEC* v. *Texas Gulf Sulphur Company*, 401 F. 2d 833, 852 (2nd Cir. 1968), cert. denied 394 U.S. 976 (1969).

tant link in the conviction of arbitrager Ivan Boesky, a leading risk arbitrager on Wall Street.[38] Boesky would, for example, purchase the securities of firms that he anticipated would be taken over. If he bought these securities before any increase in the target's price, he could realize significant profits. Boesky had illegally acquired insider information from investment bankers on deals prior to a public announcement of a merger or acquisition.

Information provided in turn by Boesky and others, such as Boyd Jeffries, a broker at Jeffries and Company (who had already pleaded guilty in April 1987 of breaking securities laws), led to Michael Milken's guilty plea to six felony counts in 1990.[39] Milken was later fined and sentenced to a ten-year prison term. Milken, the leading figure in the junk bond market, was the government's most significant conviction in its campaign to stamp out insider trading. His legal problems were one of the major factors leading to the collapse of Drexel Burnham Lambert and the junk bond market.

A COMPANY'S OBLIGATIONS TO DISCLOSE MERGER NEGOTIATIONS

Firms are not obligated to disclose merger negotiations until a final agreement has been reached,[40] which is acknowledged as that point when both parties agree on price and financial structure. If both elements are not in place, a firm may not be bound to make any disclosures. The courts have even found that a press release issued by Heublein executives denying that they knew of any factors that would explain the increased trading volume in Heublein stock on the New York Stock Exchange was not misleading. The Supreme Court later disagreed with Greenfield's court's position on this matter.

In 1988, the Supreme Court, in a 6-0 ruling, took the position that the issuance of misleading information on the status of merger negotiations was illegal. This was the case in the 1978 acquisition of Basic, Inc. by Combustion Engineering, Inc. Basic stockholders sued because Basic's management made misleading statements in denying that merger talks were underway.[41] Although management denied the ex-

---

[38]Ivan Boesky, *Merger Mania* (New York: Holt, Rinehart and Winston, 1985).

[39]Ellen Joan Pollock and Ann Hagedorn, "Milken Faces Myriad Civil Suits," *Wall Street Journal*, April 26, 1990, p. A2.

[40]Lipton and Steinberger, *Takeovers and Freezeouts*, p. 2–86. *Greenfield v. Heublein, Inc.*, 742 F. 2nd. 751 (3rd Cir. 1974), cert. denied 105 St. Ct. 1189 (1985).

[41]*Levinson v. Basic, Inc.*, CCH Fed. Sec. L. Rep. 91, 801 (N.D. Ohio 1984).

istence of merger negotiations, the two firms had been working on a deal for more than a year. In reaching its decision, the Supreme Court endorsed the efficient market view of securities pricing, which implies that securities markets reflect all available information.[42] Shareholders, relying on management's misleading statements, sold shares at a lower price than the market would have paid had the information on the merger negotiations been available. The Supreme Court ruled that shareholders could sue even if they did not explicitly rely on management's statements when making their trades.

REFERENCES

Bebchuk, Lucian A. "The Case for Facilitating Competing Tender Offers: A Reply and an Extension." *Stanford Law Review* 35 (1982): 23–50.

Boesky, Ivan. *Merger Mania*. New York: Holt, Rinehart and Winston, 1985.

Breit, William, and Kenneth G. Elzinga. *The Antitrust Book*. 2nd ed. Chicago: Dryden Press, 1989.

Brooks, John. *The Takeover Game*. New York: E. P. Dutton, 1987.

Chiarella v. *United States*, 445 U.S. 222, 100 S. Ct. 1108, 63 L. Ed. 2d, 348 (1980).

Coffee, John C., Jr. "Regulating the Market for Corporate Control: A Critical Assessment for the Tender Offer's Role in Corporate Governance." *Columbia Law Review* 84 (1984): 1145–1296.

DeBondt, Werner F.M., and Harold E. Thompson. "The Williams Act: Bane or Boon to the Market for Corporate Control?" Working Paper, University of Wisconsin-Madison, October 1989.

Delaware General Corporation Law, Section 203.

Dynamics Corp. of America v. *CTS Corp.*, 637 F. Supp. 406 (N.D. Ill. 1986), *Edgar vs. MITE Corporation*, 102 S Ct 2629 (1982).

Ferrara, Ralph, Meredith Brown, and John Hall. *Takeovers: Attack and Survival*. Stoneham, Mass.: Butterworth Legal Publishers, 1987.

Fox, Bryon E., and Eleanor M. Fox. *Corporate Acquisitions and Mergers*, Vol. 2. New York: Matthew Bender Publishing Co., 1987.

---

[42]Stephen Wermiel and Thomas Ricks, "Supreme Court Decision Eases Filing of Suits Over False Merger Talks Data," *Wall Street Journal*, March 8, 1988.

Gilson, Ronald J. *The Law and Finance of Corporate Acquisitions.* Mineola, N.Y.: Foundation Press, 1986.

Goel, Vindu. "Many Pennsylvania Firms Opt Out of Provisions in State Anti-Takeover Law." *Wall Street Journal,* July 27, 1990, p. A5B.

Greenfield v. *Heublein, Inc.,* 742 F. 2nd. 751 (3rd Cir. 1974), cert. denied 105 St. Ct. 1189 (1985).

Levinson v. *Basic, Inc.,* CCH Fed. Sec. L. Rep. 91, 801 (N.D. Ohio 1984).

Lipton, Martin, and Erica H. Steinberger. *Takeovers and Freezeouts.* New York: Law Journal Seminars Press, 1987, p. 2.05[1].

Pollack, Ellen Joan, and Ann Hagedorn. "Milken Faces Myriad Civil Suits." *Wall Street Journal,* April 26, 1990, p. A2.

Scharf, Charles A., Edward E. Shea, and George C. Beck. *Acquisitions, Mergers, Sales, Buyouts and Takeovers.* 3rd ed. Englewood Cliffs, N.J.: Prentice-Hall Publishing Co., 1985.

Scherer, Frederick M. *Industrial Market Structure and Economic Performance.* 2nd ed. Boston: Houghton Mifflin, 1980.

SEC v. *Materia,* CCII Fed. Sec. L. Rep., 99, 526 (S.D.N.Y. 1983), aff'd 745 F. 2d. 197, cert. denied.

SEC v. *Texas Gulf Sulphur Company,* 401 F. 2d 833, 852 (2nd Cir. 1968), cert. denied 394 U.S. 976 (1969).

Smiley, Robert. "The Effect of the Williams Amendment and Other Factors on Transaction Costs in Tender Offers." *Industrial Organization Review* 3 (1975): 138–145.

Smiley, Robert. "The Effect of State Securities Statutes on Tender Offer Activity." *Economic Inquiry* 19 (1985); 426–435.

U.S. v. *Aluminum Company of America et al.,* 148 F. 2d 416, 424 (1945).

U.S. v. *American Tobacco Company,* 221 U.S. 106 (1911).

U.S. v. *International Harvester Company,* U.S. 693 (1927).

U.S. v. *New York Great Atlantic and Pacific Tea Company et al.,* 67 F. Supp. 626 (1946), 173 F. 2d (1949).

U.S. v. *Standard Oil of New Jersey et al.,* 221 U. S. 1, 76, (1911).

U.S. v. *U.S. Steel Corporation et al.,* 223 Fed 55 (1915), 251 U.S. 417 (1920).

Warner Communications Inc. v. *Murdoch,* 581 F. Supp. 1482, (D. Del. March 16, 1984).

Wermiel, Stephen, and Thomas Ricks. "Supreme Court Decision Eases Filing of Suits Over False Merger Talks Data." *Wall Street Journal,* March 8, 1988.

Winter, Robert, Robert Rosenbaum, Mark Stumpf, and L. Stevenson Parker. *State Takeover Statutes and Poison Pills*. Clifton, N.J.: Prentice-Hall Law and Business, 1988.

APPENDIX

This section describes some of the major state antitakeover laws in greater detail. The reader should be mindful of the fact that these laws are often amended and tend to vary over time.

ARIZONA

Arizona's strict antitakeover law is modeled on the Indiana law. It contains a control share provision that requires the approval of a majority of voting shares excluding interested shareholders. Interested shareholders refer to the acquiring entity as well as officers and directors of the target.

A business combination provision is also included, which prohibits the acquirer from selling the target's assets for five years. In addition, an anti-greenmail provision is part of the law and prohibits the company from paying a premium for more than 5 percent of the outstanding shares.

CONNECTICUT

This law includes a fair price provision, which requires all shareholders to receive the same compensation and terms.

DELAWARE

The law stipulates that an unwanted bidder who buys more than 15 percent of a target company's stock cannot complete the takeover for three years except under the following conditions:

1. If the buyer buys 85 percent or more of the target company's stock. This 85 percent figure may not include the stock held by directors or the stock held in employee stock ownership plans.
2. If two-thirds of the stockholders approve the acquisition.

3. If the board of directors and the stockholders decide to waive the antitakeover provisions of this law.

FLORIDA

The Florida antitakeover law contains a fair price provision that is effective unless waived by a majority of the disinterested directors or two-thirds of the outstanding disinterested stockholders. The law also contains a control share provision that requires the approval of disinterested shareholders before the acquirer's voting rights can be exercised. The law applies to any company that has more than 100 shareholders. To be protected by this law a company does not have to be incorporated in Florida.

GEORGIA

The Georgia antitakeover law entails a fair price requirement similar to the requirements referred to above.

HAWAII

The Hawaii law contains a control share provision.

ILLINOIS

The Illinois law contains a fair price provision similar to those outlined above. It also contains a *nonmonetary factors provision* which allows the board of directors and company officers to consider other, nonmonetary factors such as the effects of a merger on employees as well as on the local community.

INDIANA

The Indiana law contains a control share provision whereby the stockholders can decide whether an acquirer can exercise his or her voting rights. It also includes a business combination provision prohibiting any combination between a 20 percent shareholder and the target company for five years after the 20 percent acquisition.

KENTUCKY

The Kentucky law contains both fair price and business combination provisions.

LOUISIANA

The Louisiana law contains both a fair price provision and a control share acquisition clause. The law can be applied to companies that are not incorporated within the state of Louisiana.

MAINE

The Maine law contains a cash out provision, as well as a nonmonetary factors clause similar to the Illinois law.

MARYLAND

Maryland was the first state to adopt a fair price provision. The price to be paid is the highest of the following three amounts:

1. The highest price paid for the company's shares within the past two years.
2. The market value of a share of the company's stock on the date the acquisition was announced.
3. The value of No. 2 multiplied by the highest price paid in the previous two years divided by the market value of the stock on the date shares were first acquired.

MASSACHUSETTS

The Massachusetts law, copied from the Indiana law, was adopted in response to the political pressure created by the attempted takeover of Gilette by Revlon and its CEO Ronald Pearlman.

In addition, the Indiana law applies to firms that are not incorporated in Massachusetts. The majority of the employees must reside within the state. However, the law is not applicable for firms that are not incorporated within Massachusetts if the target firm resides in a state that has a control share acquisition law.

MICHIGAN

The Michigan law contains a fair price statute.

MINNESOTA

The Minnesota law, a very strict antitakeover law, was adopted in response to the Dart Group's attempted takeover of the Dayton Hudson Corporation.

Most provisions of the law are copied from the Indiana law. It contains an anti-greenmail provision that prohibits companies from paying a premium for more than 5 percent of their outstanding shares; it also prohibits the negotiation of golden parachutes once an offer has been made; and it contains a nonmonetary factors clause. (Golden parachutes are explained in Chapter 5.)

MISSISSIPPI

The Mississippi law is mainly a fair price law.

MISSOURI

The Missouri law contains both a fair price and a business combination provision.

NEVADA

Nevada's antitakeover law is a control share acquisition statute.

NEW JERSEY

The New Jersey Shareholders Protection Act is a business combination law forbidding acquirers of more than 10 percent of a company's voting stock from buying the rest of the corporation for five years unless the board of directors approves the acquisition. After five years, a bidder still needs to receive the approval of two-thirds of the stockholders or to offer a "fair price" before it can take control of the firm's assets.

NEW YORK

The New York law contains a business combination provision, as well as an anti-greenmail provision similar to the Minnesota law.

NORTH CAROLINA

The North Carolina law was the first of a series of antitakeover laws enacted after the Indiana decision. It was prompted after the attempted takeover of Burlington Industries by Asher Edelman. The law contains both a control share and a fair price provision, and it applies to corporations that may be incorporated in other states. The law is relatively strict in that it requires the approval of 95 percent of the voting shares for mergers between a target company and a 20 percent stockholder. This virtually guarantees defeat of the merger if company insiders are opposed to it.

OHIO

This law is very similar to the Indiana law except that it contains a nonmonetary factors provision and prohibits the transfer of control shares before a stockholder vote, as opposed to allowing the transfer of shares but prohibiting the exercise of their voting rights.

OKLAHOMA

The Oklahoma law is mainly a control share acquisition statute.

OREGON

The Oregon law is primarily a control share acquisition statute.

PENNSYLVANIA

The Pennsylvania law contains both fair price and cash out provisions. Short-term takeover profits can be seized. In addition, voting rights of buyers of 20 percent or more of a Pennsylvania firm's stock are restricted. Labor contracts can be enforced, and severance pay can be guaranteed in the event of successful hostile bids.

The new Pennsylvania law that was recently enacted restricts the *voting rights* of buyers of 20 percent or more of a Pennsylvania firm's stock. It also provides security for labor contracts, guarantees severance pay, and allows short-term profits from unsuccessful tender offers to be seized.

UTAH

The Utah statute contains both control share and cash out provisions.

VIRGINIA

The Virginia antitakeover statute is a fair price law.

WASHINGTON

Washington was the first state to adopt an antitakeover law that did not resemble the Indiana law. It was developed in response to Boone Pickens' intention to acquire a stake in Boeing and Company. Though incorporated in Delaware, Boeing is a major employer in Washington. The law therefore applies to companies that are not incorporated in Washington but that have a majority of their assets or that employ more than 20,000 employees there. The law contains both fair price and business combination provisions.

WISCONSIN

The Wisconsin law is modeled on the Indiana law, although it contains additional provisions. It contains fair price, business combination, anti-greenmail, and control share provisions. The control share provision is somewhat different from other such provisions. The voting power of 20 percent shareholders is limited after that threshold is reached. The voting power of shares beyond that threshold can be voting only at 20 percent of their original voting rights. In other words, for each share beyond the 20 percent threshold the voting power is now one-fifth.

Chapter
4

Motives and Determinants of Mergers

 T his chapter focuses on the major determinants of mergers and acquisitions. Among the motives and determinants considered are the following.

1. Synergy
   a. Operating Synergy
      i. Economies of Scale
      ii. Economies of Scope
   b. Financial Synergy
2. Diversification
3. Economic Motives
   a. Horizontal Integration and Market Power
   b. Vertical Integration
4. Hubris Hypothesis
5. Improved Management
6. Tax Motives

SYNERGY

The term *synergy* is more often associated with the physical sciences rather than with economics or finance. It refers to the type of reactions that occur when two substances or factors combine to produce a greater effect together than what the sum of the two operating independently could account for. For example, a synergistic reaction occurs in chemistry when two chemicals combine to produce a more potent total reaction than the sum of their separate effects. Simply stated, synergy refers to the phenomenon of $2 + 2 = 5$. It refers to the ability of a corporate combination to be more profitable than the individual profits of the firms that were combined.

Some analysts do not feel comfortable with the above definition as it applies to mergers. They feel that it is too vague and implies that factors, such as the elimination of duplicate facilities, will automatically result in increased profitability.

> I do not like that definition. It is too facile and too deceptive. In a poorly conceived merger and its aftermath, a corporation might borrow heavily to buy a company, slam it together with its existing business, and eliminate a lot of the costs at the top. Everyone starts calling that synergy. . . .
>
> I define synergy as an acquirer being able to use its significant strengths to improve the performance of the acquired company, or taking one of the acquired company's strengths to bolster a weakness of its own.
>
> Two strengths or two weaknesses combined do not make synergy. Synergy is much more than eliminating some duplication at the top. Synergy is taking a company that is selling $50 million a year in the United States, putting it through an acquirer's distribution system, and selling $100 million worldwide.[1]

What is to be included in the area of synergistic effects? Some researchers, such as Paul Asquith and Michael Bradley, view synergy broadly and include the elimination of inefficient management by installing the more capable management of the acquiring firm.[2] Although it is reasonable to define synergy in this manner, this chapter will define the term more narrowly and treat management-induced gains separately. In doing so, synergy will be treated much as Mike Jensen and Richard Ruback do when they exclude the inefficient management gains and focus on operating synergy.[3]

The two main types of synergy are operating and financial. Operating synergy refers to the efficiency gains or operating economies that

[1]J. Tracy O'Rourke, "Postmerger Integration," in Richard S. Bibler, ed., *The Arthur Young Management Guide to Mergers and Acquisitions* (New York: John Wiley & Sons, 1989), pp. 227–228.

[2]Paul Asquith, "Merger Bids, Uncertainty and Stockholder Returns," *Journal of Financial Economics*, 11, no. 1–4 (April 1983): 51–83; Michael Bradley, Anand Desai, and E. Han Kim, "The Rationale Behind Interfirm Tender Offers: Information or Synergy," *Journal of Financial Economics* 11, no. 1–4 (April 1983): 183–206.

[3]Michael Jensen and Richard Ruback, "The Market for Corporate Control: The Scientific Evidence," *Journal of Financial Economics* 11, no. 1–4 (April 1983): 5–50.

are derived in horizontal or vertical mergers. Financial synergy refers to the possibility that the cost of capital can be lowered by combining one or more companies.

Operating Synergy

One of the main sources of operating synergy is the cost reductions that occur as a result of a corporate combination. These cost reductions may come as a result of *economies of scale*—decreases in per unit costs that result from an increase in the size or scale of a company's operations.

Manufacturing firms typically operate at high per unit costs for low levels of output. This is because the fixed costs of operating their manufacturing facilities are spread out over relatively low levels of output. As the output levels rise, the per unit costs decline. This is sometimes referred to as spreading overhead. Some of the other sources of these gains arise from increased specialization of labor and management as well as the more efficient use of capital equipment which might not be possible at low output levels. This phenomenon continues for a certain range of output, after which per unit costs rise as the firm experiences diseconomies of scale. Diseconomies of scale may arise as the firm experiences the higher costs and other problems associated with coordinating a larger scale operation. The extent to which diseconomies of scale exist is a topic of dispute to many economists. Some cite as evidence the continued growth of large, multinational companies, such as Exxon, General Motors, and AT&T. These firms have exhibited extended periods of growth while still paying stockholders an acceptable return on equity. Others contend that such firms would be able to provide stockholders a higher rate of return if they were a smaller, more efficient company.

The graph presented in Figure 4.1 depicts scale economies and diseconomies. It shows that there is an optimal output level where per unit costs are a minimum. This implies that an expansion through the horizontal acquisition of a competitor may increase the size of the acquiring firm's operation and lower per unit costs.

One example of the economies of scale was the proposed acquisition of Harcourt Brace Jovanovich by Harper and Row. Although the merger failed to materialize, the initial motivation for the takeover came from significant economies of scale that might have been possible following the merger. The reasoning contained many convincing elements. Both Harper & Row (now HarperCollins) and Harcourt Brace Jovanovich are major publishers of college textbooks. If the two firms had merged, a significant elimination of duplicate resources could have been accomplished. For example, both companies employ a sales force that calls

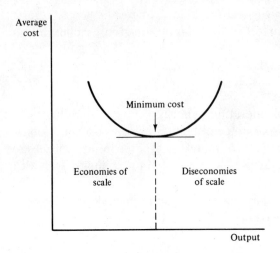

Figure 4.1 Economies and diseconomies of scale.

on many of the same college departments to promote their line of textbooks. The duplication in the sales force could have been eliminated by having only one salesperson, instead of two, call on each campus.

Other duplicate facilities could have been eliminated by having just one distribution department and one billing department. Through such cost reductions, the combined Harper and Row and Harcourt Brace Jovanovich could have expanded its product line and sales while not experiencing a proportionate increase in costs. This could be done far more quickly than through internal expansion. In addition, the strengths in the product lines of one company would have made up for the weaknesses in the other firm's product line.

Another example of the scale economies that may be achieved through mergers and acquisitions can be found in the brewing industry. Through mergers Heilmans, Strohs and Pabst put together a national distribution network with production at regional centers.[4] Scale economies were achieved in production, distribution, and advertising. Further economic advantages were achieved when Strohs merged with Schaffer and later with Schlitz.

Another concept that is closely related to and sometimes confused with economies of scale is *economies of scope*. This is the ability of a firm to utilize one set of inputs to provide a broader range of products and services. A good example of scope economies arises in the banking industry. Scope economies, rather than economies of scale, are often seen as the main benefits banks derive by merging.[5]

---

[4]Jerry A. Viscone and Gordon S. Roberts, *Contemporary Financial Management* (Columbus, Ohio: Merrill Publishing Co., 1987), p. 704.

When financial institutions merge, they can share inputs to offer a broader range of services such as a trust department or an investment counselor. Smaller banks might not be able to afford the costs of these departments. Inputs such as a computer system can be shared to process a wide variety of loans and deposit accounts. Whether these benefits are either the true reason or a sufficient reason for the increased number of banking mergers that have taken place in the recent period of deregulation is a very different issue.[6] The recent banking merger movement has given rise to a new breed of bank in the industry—the superregional bank. The acquisition of other regional banks largely accounts for the growth of the superregionals. Some superregionals, such as the Bank One Corporation of Columbus, Ohio, or Barnett Bank of Florida, have grown to the point where they are competitive with the larger money center banks in the provision of many services. Others, such as The Bank of New England, have expanded too rapidly through acquisitions and have endangered their future viability.

An example of anticipated synergistic benefits that were expected to derive from expected economies of scale and economies of slope, but which never materialized, is described in the Case Study of the Allegis Corporation.

Financial Synergy

Financial synergy refers to the impact of a corporate merger or acquisition on the costs of capital to the acquiring firm or the merging partners. If financial synergy exists in a corporate combination, the costs of capital should be lowered. Whether financial synergy actually exists, however, is a matter of dispute within corporate finance.

As noted above, the combination of two firms can reduce risk if the firms' cash flow streams are not perfectly correlated. If the acquisitions or merger lowers the volatility of the cash flows, then suppliers of capital may consider the firm less risky. The risk of bankruptcy would presumably be less given the fact that wide swings, up and down, in the combined firm's cash flows would be less likely. This implies that it is less likely that cash flows would fall so low that the firm could become technically insolvent. Technical insolvency occurs when a firm

[5]Loretta J. Mester, "Efficient Product of Financial Services: Scale and Scope Economies," *Review,* Federal Reserve Bank of Philadelphia, January/February 1987, pp. 15–25.

[6]Patrick A. Gaughan, "Financial Deregulation, Banking Mergers and the Impact on Regional Businesses," Proceedings of the Pacific Northwest Regional Economic Conference, University of Washington, Spring 1988.

CASE STUDY: *ALLEGIS: SYNERGY THAT NEVER MATERIALIZED*

The case of the Allegis Corporation is a classic example of synergistic benefits that had every reason to occur but failed to materialize. The concept of Allegis was the brainchild of chairman Richard Ferris, CEO of the Allegis Corporation. Ferris had risen through the ranks of the firm's precursor, United Airlines, which had been the world's largest investor-owned airline.

Ferris's dream was to form a diversified travel services company that would be able to provide customers with a complete package of air travel, hotel, and car rental services. Accordingly, United Airlines bought Hertz Car Rental from RCA in June 1985. United paid $587 million—a price that was considered to be a premium. In addition to buying Pan American Airways Pacific routes, Ferris bought the Hilton International Hotel chain from the Transworld Corporation for $980 million. The Hilton International purchase on March 31, 1987, was also considered to be expensive. United Airlines had already acquired the Westin International hotel chain in 1970 for only $52 million.

On February 18, 1987, United Airlines changed its name to the Allegis Corporation. The change of name underscored the management's efforts to have the company perceived as a diversified travel services company. The concept was supposed to allow customers the ability to do "one-stop" travel shopping. With one phone call they could book their air travel, hotel reservations, and car rental within the same corporate umbrella. Allegis hoped to weave the network together through a combination of cross discounts, bonus miles, and other promotional savings and the introduction of a new computer system called Easy Saver. Through Easy Saver, customers could check prices and book reservations through the Allegis network. All travel services could be charged on Allegis's credit card. Travel agents using United Airlines' Apollo computer reservation system, the largest in the airline industry, would pull up Allegis's air, hotel, and car services before any other competitor's products.

Despite the concept's appeal, the market failed to respond.

Whatever the long-term outlook of Allegis's much vaunted effort to package car-rental, hotel and air travel services might have been, consumers just haven't seen much benefit. And the system has posed some early snarls for travel agents.

"Consumers just don't believe in the value of synergies that Allegis says exist between airlines, rental cars and hotels," says Daniel T. Smith, director of consumer affairs at the International Airline Passengers Association, a consumers group with about 10,000 members.[a]

Investors joined the public in failing to respond to the full travel service concept. At a time when the stock market was providing handsome returns to investors, the Allegis stock price fell; in February 1987, its stock price was in the low to mid-$50 range. The market did respond, however, when Coniston

[a]Robert Johnson, "Full Service Just Didn't Fly with Public, Travel Agents," *Wall Street Journal*, June 11, 1987, p. 22.

TABLE 4.1   CEO RICHARD FERRIS AND THE ALLEGIS CORPORATION
Ferris's Bumpy Ride at Allegis

1962   Bachelor's degree from Cornell University in hotel management. Later that year joins Western International Hotels, Westin's predecessor, as staff planner.

1971   Joins UAL as president of its food services division.

1979   Named chief executive officer of UAL and quickly faces industrywide crisis of confidence in the DC-10 following a disastrous American Airlines crash in Chicago; Mr. Ferris grounds United's entire fleet of DC10s.

1982   Becomes UAL's chairman and president. Air traffic controllers' strike, fare wars and recession thrust UAL's results deep into the red.

May 1985   Mr. Ferris's demand that United pilots accept a two-tier wage system triggers a 29-day walkout by 5,000 United pilots. UAL blames the strike for a $91-million second-quarter loss.

June 1985   In the biggest step so far toward implementing Mr. Ferris's broad travel-services strategy, UAL agrees to acquire RCA Corp.'s Hertz unit, prompting speculation that other airlines will follow its expansion into travel services.

October 1985   UAL acquires Pan American World Airways's Pacific operations for $750 million.

August 1986   Labor strife wrecks United's plan to acquire Frontier Airlines.

December 1986   UAL agrees to buy Transworld Corp.'s Hilton International Co. unit in a transaction valued at $980 million.

April 1987   The union representing United pilots launches a $4.5 billion takeover bid for the airline; Allegis management rejects the offer as "grossly inadequate" and grants golden parachutes to Mr. Ferris and seven other top officials.

May 12, 1987   Boeing Co. enters an unusual anti-takeover aircraft-financing arrangement with Allegis.

May 26, 1987   Coniston Partners, a New York investment firm that holds a 13% Allegis stake, announces it will seek to gain control of the Allegis board.

May 28, 1987   Allegis directors proposes a plan to distribute $60 a share to stockholders and keep the company intact in a last-ditch effort to forestall a takeover.

June 4, 1987   United pilots propose a restructuring plan that would break up the company and pay holders $70 a share. Allegis stock soars as a result, heightening pressure on management to sweeten its offer.

June 9, 1987   Mr. Ferris, under pressure from directors, employees and shareholders, resigns his post.

Source: *Wall Street Journal* (June 11, 1987), p. 22.

Partners, a New York investment firm, accumulated a 13 percent stake in the travel company. Coniston planned to sell off the various parts of the Allegis travel network and distribute the proceeds to the stockholders. Allegis responded on April 1, 1987, with a large recapitalization plan proposal that would have resulted in the company assuming $3 billion worth of additional debt to finance a $60 special dividend. The recapitalization plan was supposed to support the stock price while instilling stockholder support for Allegis and away from the Coniston proposal. The United Airlines Pilots Union followed Allegis's recapitalization plan proposal with its own offer to buy the airline and sell off the nonairline parts. Their offer would have paid $70 to stockholders.

The pressure on CEO Ferris continued to mount, leading up to a pivotal board of directors meeting.

> *According to Charles Luce (Chairman of the Board), the board, watching the company's stock rise, "thought the market was saying that Allegis was worth more broken up and that the current strategy should be abandoned." Although the outside directors had supported Ferris during the company's acquisition program, they now decided that Ferris was an obstacle to restructuring the company. "There comes a point," says Luce, "when no board can impose its own beliefs over the opposition of the people who elected it." Ferris was replaced by Frank A. Olsen, chairman of Allegis's Hertz subsidiary.*[b]

See Table 4.1 for a listing of events leading to Ferris's downfall. Following Ferris's resignation, Allegis sold off Hertz and Hilton International.

[b]Arthur Fleisher, Jr., Geoffrey C. Hazard, Jr., and Miriam Z. Klipper, *Board Games: The Changing Shape of Corporate America* (Boston: Little, Brown, 1988), p. 192.

cannot meet its current obligations as they come due. Technical insolvency can occur even when total assets exceed total liabilities. Another more serious form of business failure occurs when total liabilities exceed total assets and the net worth of the firm is negative. Even though technical insolvency may be less serious than this form of bankruptcy, it may be sufficient to result in a fall in the firm's credit rating, which may cause the cost of capital to rise.

Higgins and Schall explain this effect in terms of *debt-coinsurance.*[7] If the correlation of the income streams of two firms is less than perfectly positively correlated, the bankruptcy risk associated with the combination of the two firms may be reduced. Under certain circumstances one of the firms could experience conditions forcing it into bankruptcy. It is difficult to know in advance which one of two possible firms would succumb to this fate. In the event one of the firms goes under, creditors may suffer a loss. If the two firms were combined in advance of these financial problems, however, the cash flows of the solvent firm, which are in excess of its debt service needs, would cushion the decline in the other firm's cash flows. The offsetting earnings of the firm in good condition might be sufficient to prevent the combined firm from falling into bankruptcy and causing creditors to suffer losses.

The problem with the debt-coinsurance effect is that the benefits accrue to debtholders at the expense of equity holders. Debtholders gain by holding debt in a less risky firm. Higgins and Schall observe

[7]Robert C. Higgins and Lawrence C. Schall, "Corporate Bankruptcy and Conglomerate Mergers," *Journal of Finance* 30 (March 1975): 93–113.

that these gains come at the expense of stockholders who lose in the acquisition. These researchers assume that total returns that can be provided by the combined firm are constant (R_T). If more of these returns are provided to bondholders (R_B), they must come at the expense of stockholders (R_S).

$$R_T = R_S + R_B$$

In other words, Higgins and Schall maintain that the debt-coinsurance effect does not create any new value but merely redistributes gains among the providers of capital to the firm. There is no general agreement on this result. Lewellen, for example, has concluded that stockholders gain from these types of combinations.[8] Other studies, however, fail to indicate that the debt-related motives are more relevant for conglomerate than for nonconglomerate acquisitions.[9]

Higgins and Schall show that the stockholders' losses can be offset by issuing new debt after the merger. The stockholders will then gain through the tax savings on the debt interest payments. Galais and Masulis have demonstrated this result.[10] The additional debt would increase the debt/equity ratio of the post-merger firm to a level that stockholders must have found desirable or, at least, acceptable, before the merger. With the higher debt/equity ratio, the firm becomes a higher risk/higher return investment.

As noted above, a company can experience economies of scale through acquisitions. These economies are usually thought to come from production cost decreases by operating at higher capacity levels or through a reduced sales force or a shared distribution system. As a result of acquisitions, financial economies of scale are also possible in the form of lower flotation and transaction costs.[11]

A larger company has certain advantages in financial markets which may lower the cost of capital to the firm. It enjoys better access to financial markets, and it tends to experience lower costs of raising capital, presumably because it is considered to be less risky than a smaller firm. Therefore, the costs of borrowing by issuing bonds are lower since a larger firm would probably be able to issue bonds offering

---

[8]W. G. Lewellen, "A Pure Rationale for the Conglomerate Merger," *Journal of Finance* (May 1971).

[9]P. Elgers and J. Clark, "Merger Types and Shareholder Returns," *Financial Management* (Summer 1980): 66–72.

[10]D. Galais and R. W. Masulis, "The Option Pricing Model and the Risk Factor of Stock," *Journal of Financial Economics* (January/March 1976): 53–82.

[11]Haim Levy and Marshall Sarnat, "Diversification, Portfolio Analysis and the Uneasy Case for Conglomerate Mergers," *Journal of Finance* (September 1970): 795–802.

a lower interest rate than a smaller firm. In addition, there are certain fixed costs in the issuance of securities, such as SEC registration costs, legal fees, and printing costs. These costs would be spread out over a greater dollar volume of securities since the larger company would probably borrow more capital with each issue of bonds.

The analysis is similar in the case of equity securities. Flotation costs per dollar raised would be lower for larger issues than for smaller issues. In addition, the selling effort required may be greater for riskier issues than for less risky larger firms. It is assumed in this discussion that larger firms are less risky and bear a lower probability of bankruptcy and financial failure. We should be aware, however, that if a larger firm, which might result from a combination of several other firms, is so inefficient that profits start to fall, the larger combination of companies could have a greater risk of financial failure.

Levy and Sarnat have developed a model showing the diversification effect that occurs when two or more imperfectly correlated income streams combine to lower the probability of default. This lower risk level induces capital holders to provide capital to the combined firm or conglomerate at lower costs than they would have provided to the individual, pre-merger components. Their analysis presents the financial synergistic benefits as an economic gain that results from mergers.

DIVERSIFICATION

Diversification played a major role in the acquisitions and mergers that took place in the third merger wave—the conglomerate era. During the late 1960s, firms often sought to expand by buying other firms rather than through internal expansion. This outward expansion was often facilitated by some creative financial techniques which temporarily caused the acquiring firm's stock price to rise while adding little real value through the exchange. The legacy of the conglomerates has drawn poor, or at least mixed, reviews. Indeed, many of the firms that grew into conglomerates in the 1960s were disassembled through various spinoffs and divestitures in the 1970s and 1980s. This process of deconglomerization raises serious doubts as to the value of diversification based on expansion.

Although many companies have regretted their attempts at diversification, others have claimed to have gained significantly. One such firm is General Electric. Contrary to what the name would imply, GE is no longer merely an electronics company. Through a pattern of acquisitions and divestitures, the firm has become a diversified conglomerate with operations in insurance, television stations, plastics, medical equipment, and so on. Table 4.2 chronicles some of GE's acquisitions and divestitures. As of 1987, the firm was well diversified into several different industry groups. Figure 4.2 shows the major components of the firm's business.

During the 1980s, at a time when the firm was acquiring and divesting itself of various companies, earnings rose dramatically (see Figure 4.3). On the other hand, earnings, as a percentage of stockholder equity, have not shown the same upward pattern (Figure 4.4).

By expanding through the acquisition of other firms, the acquiring corporation may attempt to achieve some of the benefits that investors receive by diversifying their portfolio of assets. The portfolio theory research literature in finance has attempted to quantify some of the risk-reduction benefits that an investor may enjoy through diversification. This research clearly supports the intuitive belief of investors that

TABLE 4.2   GENERAL ELECTRIC'S ACQUISITIONS AND DIVESTITURES, 1984–1988
             GE's Strategic Moves

Recent acquisitions and divestitures of $100 million or more

Acquisitions

1964   Buys Employers Reinsurance for $1.1 billion

1966   Buys RCA for $6.3 billion
           Buys 80% of Kidder Peabody for about $600 million

1967   Buys Miami television station for $270 million
           Buys D&K Financial for $100 million
           Buys the medical equipment business of Thomson S.A. of France in exchange for GE consumer electronics business
           Buys Gelco Corp. for $250 million

1968   Buys Montgomery Ward's credit card operation for $1 billion and assumption of $1.8 billion in debt
           Buys Roper Corp. for $510 million
           Agrees to buy Borg-Warner's plastics business for $2.3 billion

Divestitures

1963   Sells housewares division to Black & Decker for about $300 million

1964   Sells Utah International for $2.4 billion
           Sells GE Credit's second-mortgage unit for $600 million

1965   Sells interest in Australian coal fields for $390 million

1967   Sells North American Co. for Life & Health for $200 million
           Sells consumer electronics business to Thomson S.A. in exchange for Thomson's medical equipment business and cash

1968   Sells RCA Global Communications for $160 million
           Sells five radio stations for $122 million

The Conglomerate that Jack Welch Built

GE's Chairman has Refashioned the Company. . .
1987 lines of business based on revenues in billions of dollars

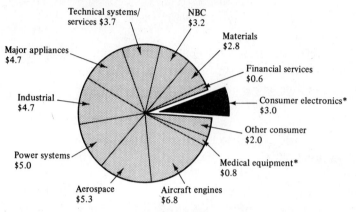

Technical systems/ services $3.7
NBC $3.2
Materials $2.8
Major appliances $4.7
Financial services $0.6
Industrial $4.7
Consumer electronics* $3.0
Other consumer $2.0
Power systems $5.0
Medical equipment* $0.8
Aerospace $5.3
Aircraft engines $6.8

Figure 4.2 General Electric is a highly diversified conglomerate which derives its revenues from a broad range of businesses. It has exhibited increased earnings partly as a result of greater efficiency and cost cutbacks through workforce reductions. Nonetheless, the stock market failed to reflect this diversified firm's performance. (*Source:* Reprinted by permission of the Wall Street Journal, August 4, 1988, p. 1. Copyright © 1988 Dow Jones & Company, Inc. All Rights Reserved Worldwide.)

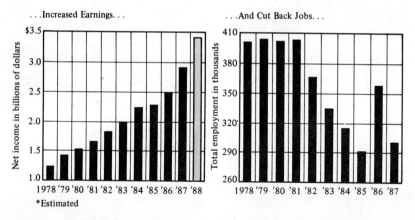

. . .Increased Earnings. . .   . . .And Cut Back Jobs. . .

*Estimated

Figure 4.3 General Electric: Net income and total employment. (*Source:* Reprinted by permission of the Wall Street Journal, August 4, 1988, p. 1. Copyright © 1988 Dow Jones & Company, Inc. All Rights Reserved Worldwide.)

"putting all one's eggs in one basket" is not a wise decision. On the other hand, when this strategy is applied to capital assets and whole corporations, it loses some of its appeal.

A company will often pursue diversification outside its own industry when management is displeased by the current volatile level of earn-

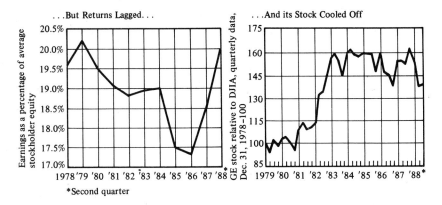

Figure 4.4 General Electric: Earnings and stock, December 31, 1988. (*Source:* Reprinted by permission of the Wall Street Journal, August 4, 1988, p. 1. Copyright © 1988 Dow Jones & Company, Inc. All Rights Reserved Worldwide.)

ings. A volatile income stream makes it more difficult to pay regular dividends and creates an unstable environment for long-term planning. Financial markets may interpret a fall-off in earnings that results in a reduction or cancellation of a quarterly dividend as a negative sign.

Empirical Evidence on Acquisition Programs

General Electric's program of acquisitions resulted in a diversified corporate structure and increased earnings. The example of General Electric contrasts with the popular belief that, generally, conglomerate acquisitions such as those that occurred in the third merger wave had few beneficial effects. This company's experience, however, is consistent with some empirical research in this area.

Katherine Schipper and Rex Thompson have analyzed the wealth effects of firms that announced acquisition programs.[12] Specifically, they considered what impact an announcement of an acquisitions program had on the value of the acquiring firm. They examined announcements of such programs prior to the 1967–1970 period because regulatory changes such as the Williams Act and the Tax Reform Act of 1969 took place in these years. These regulatory changes created certain impediments to the types of acquisition activities that occurred in the 1960s.

Schipper and Thompson found that during this period acquisition programs were capitalized as positive net present value programs. Figure 4.5 shows that cumulative abnormal returns for the acquiring firm's

---

[12]Katherine Schipper and Rex Thompson, "The Value of Merger Activity," *Journal of Financial Economics* 11, no. 1–4 (April 1983): 85–119.

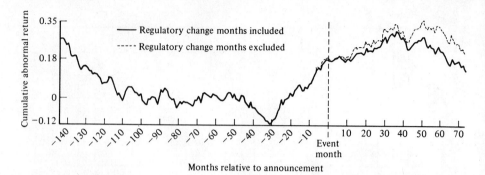

Figure 4.5 Cumulative abnormal returns relative to acquisition programs of acquiring firms. [*Source:* Katherine Schipper and Rex Thompson, "Evidence on the Capitalized Value of Merger Activity for Acquiring Firms," *Journal of Financial Economics* (April 1983): 100.]

stock responded positively to the acquisition program announcement. (Cumulative abnormal returns is explained in Chapter 6.) These results indicate that, at least prior to the regulatory changes of the late 1960s, the market had a positive view of acquisition programs, many of which involved substantial diversification.

Diversification to Enter More Profitable Industries

One reason why management may opt for diversified expansion is its desire to enter industries that are more profitable than the industry that the acquiring firm is currently in. It could be that the parent company's industry has reached the mature stage or that the competitive pressures within that industry preclude the possibility of raising prices to a level where extranormal profits can be enjoyed.

One problem which some firms may encounter when they seek to expand by entering industries offering better profit opportunities is the lack of an assurance that those profit opportunities will persist for an extended time in the future. Competitive pressures may work, in the long run, to equalize the rates of return in many industries.

No one can quarrel with a decision to exploit a profitable opportunity. The difficulty lies in the fact that industries that are highly profitable do not stay so indefinitely; there are strong competitive pressures in the direction of the long run equalization of rates of return among industries. This is not to say there has been a trend towards equalization of rates of return, for there are also forces that generate dispersion (namely the development of new industries and unpredictable shifts in supply and demand). The point is, however, that different industries are profitable at different points in time. The tendency for above-average rates of return to move towards the average is strongest in industries that are relatively easy to enter. In short, industries into which it is relatively easy to diversify are least likely to have persistent above-normal rates of return, for it is precisely the ease of entry that, with time, brings profits to the average level.[13]

Diversification and Dividend Stability

The market interprets dividends as a signal of the firm's financial condition. The announcement that a firm has decided to cancel a dividend or to lower the current quarterly dividend below the previous quarter's dividend may be interpreted as a sign of financial weakness. Stephen Ross has shown that a firm's increase in dividends is regarded as an unambiguous sign that the firm's financial position has improved.[14] Ross established various conditions in which the dividend signal would provide valuable information.

A volatile earnings stream might make it more difficult for a firm to pay a dependable flow of dividends to stockholders. It is important to note that a major school of thought in the academic world of finance does not place great value on the role of a firm's dividend policy in determining stock prices. This school of thought, led by such Nobel prize winners as Merton Miller of the University of Chicago and Franco Modigliani of the Massachusetts Institute of Technology, places little value on such factors as the *clientele effect*. This factor asserts that different groups of investors are investing in equities for the dividend income they would receive. Such investors might be those who inherited stock and use the dividends as a source of income. Other large institutional investors, such as certain pension funds, must adhere to restrictions that prohibit them from investing in equities that do not pay dividends. According to the clientele effect, if a company changes its dividend policy from one that pays regular and predictable dividends to one that does not pay dividends and pays them in an unpredictable manner, certain investors will seek to sell the stock and the price of the stock will fall in the market. Based on certain restrictions that do not apply in the real world of finance, the Miller–Modigliani school of thought would contend that investors can make adjustments that will cause them to be indifferent to the firm's dividend policy.[15] In this

---

[13]Michael Gort, "Diversification, Mergers and Profits," in *The Corporate Merger* (Chicago: University of Chicago Press, 1974), p. 38.

[14]Stephen Ross, "The Determination of Financial Structure: The Incentive Signaling Approach," *Bell Journal of Economics* (Spring 1977): 23–40.

[15]Merton H. Miller and Franco Modigliani, "Dividend Policy, Growth and the Valuation of Shares," *Journal of Business* 34 (October 1961): 411–433.

perspective the dividend policy is an irrelevant detail and does not affect the wealth of stockholders.

According to the Miller–Modigliani view, the value of a company is determined by the earning power of the firm's assets and its investment policy. The distribution of the earnings stream between dividends and retained earnings does not affect the value of the firm. If, for example, the dividend policy was not to their liking, investors could simply manufacture their own dividends by selling off part of their portfolios.[16]

Some academicians are impressed with the mathematical logic of the Miller–Modigliani model and conclusions. In contrast, many finance practitioners feel that the Miller–Modigliani position is not well grounded in the practicalities of real world finance.

The issue of dividend stability, in the face of volatile earnings flows, is more important for smaller firms than larger ones. The larger, more well-established companies tend to have certain options available that smaller firms may not. These include lines of credit and retained earnings from previous quarters. These additional sources of contingency funding enable larger firms to pay a stable flow of dividends even when earnings are erratic. An erratic or declining trend in dividends can make a firm vulnerable to a takeover. Falling dividends are often associated with a decline in the firm's stock price. The falling stock price makes it less expensive to acquire the firm. The firm is particularly vulnerable to a takeover when the value of its assets remains at the same level while the stock price declines. Even when they can take measures to enable them to pay dividends each quarter, larger firms with volatile earnings may prefer to stabilize their flow of income. This stability is often attempted by diversifying through the purchase of other firms.

The attempted takeover of ITT by an investment group led by Jay Pritzger and Philip Anschutz provides an example of the relationship between the failure to maintain dividends at their previous levels and the resulting vulnerability to a takeover. (See Case Study.)

By diversification outside its industry, a corporation acquires an income stream that may vary in response to factors other than those that cause the acquirer's income to fluctuate. The risk-reduction benefits can be statistically measured by considering the covariances and correlation coefficients between the cash flows of the acquirer and the target. If, for example, both the target and the acquirer were steel

---

[16]For an excellent discussion of this view, see James C. Van Horne, *Financial Management and Policy* (Englewood Cliffs, N.J.: Prentice-Hall, 1989), pp. 327–338.

CASE STUDY: *ITT: DIVIDEND POLICY AND THE VULNERABILITY TO A TAKEOVER*

During the early 1980s, ITT was a conglomerate undergoing a major restructuring.[a] The successful and highly diversified conglomerate that Harold Geneen had built had begun to show signs of wear. The 1980s were a period of deconglomerization where large, diversified companies were selling off divisions in an attempt to increase earnings and lift stock prices as conglomerates fell into disfavor.

ITT had been increasing its common stock dividend every year until the fall of 1983. The company was paying out approximately $450 million per year in dividends. Between 1979 and 1983, much of the dividends paid out were financed by asset sales. The proceeds of asset sales in the company's restructuring program could not be used to revitalize the company since earnings were not sufficient to meet the expected dividend payments.

In the summer of 1983, ITT announced that it would cut its $2.76 quarterly dividend to $1.00. Investors reacted to the dividend cut, and the stock price fell. ITT common stock was priced at approximately $35 prior to the dividend cut and fell to a low of $20 after the announcement.

The full impact of the dividend cut was partially offset by the Pritzger group's stock purchases. The Pritzger group, led by financier Jay Pritzger, had been purchasing ITT common stock as a prelude to an eventual bid to take control of ITT in a leveraged buyout. The dividend cut enabled them to acquire a toe-hold interest in the company at a less expensive price. The fall in the stock price made the takeover bid all the more feasible.

The Pritzger bid was partially dependent on management support. The deal contained various financial incentives, which Rand Araskog terms a *bribe* for management to support the bid. Management strongly opposed the takeover. After a protracted struggle, the bid was withdrawn and ITT remained independent.

[a]Rand Araskog, *ITT Wars* (New York: Henry Holt Publishers, 1989).

---

firms, then the cash flows would likely exhibit a high positive correlation.

The covariance and the correlation between two variables are two ways of measuring how the variables move together. In corporate finance we are often interested in variables like earnings streams and cash flows. The covariance and the correlation coefficient provide us with a quantitative way to measure the extent to which the cash flows of an acquiring firm and its target move together. The covariance and correlation coefficient provide much the same information. The mathematical representations of these two measures are shown below.

$$\text{Cov}_{i,j} = \frac{\{[CF_{i,t} - E(CF_i)] \times [CF_{j,t} - E(CF_j)]\}}{N}$$

$$\text{Corr}_{i,j} = \frac{\text{Cov}_{i,j}}{SD_i \times SD_j}$$

where: Cov_{ij} = the covariance between cash flows i and j
$\quad\quad CF_i$ = the ith cash flow
$\quad E(CF_i)$ = the expected value of the ith cash flow
$\quad\quad\quad N$ = the number of cash flow observations
$\quad \text{Corr}_{ij}$ = the correlation coefficient between cash flows i and j
$\quad\quad SD_i$ = the standard deviation of the ith cash flow

The mathematical representations are useful as a point of reference to see how the covariance and the correlation coefficients are specifically related to each other. For the purposes of this discussion, however, we can obtain a sufficient understanding through an intuitive understanding of the basic relationship between the two measures.[17]

The correlation coefficient varies between a range of -1 and $+1$. A correlation coefficient for the cash flows of two firms of -1 means there is a perfect, one-for-one, inverse relationship between the cash flows. It is here that the greatest risk-reduction benefits are found. The more diversified two firms are, and the more lines of business each has, the more difficult it is for a high negative correlation to be found. A $+1$ correlation coefficient implies that there are no risk-reduction benefits. A high positive correlation might be found if one steel company acquired another steel company. A zero correlation implies that there is no observable relationship between the cash flows of the two firms.

An example of the acquisition of a company whose earnings have a negative correlation with the acquiring company would be that of a cyclical and a countercyclical company. If the acquiring company has a cyclical earnings stream, its earnings may be highly responsive to cyclical fluctuations in the economy. The term *business cycles* is actually a misnomer. *Cycles* implies a regular and repetitive pattern that is not indicative of the actual fluctuations in the economy. The ups and downs of the U.S. and the world economy occur unpredictably and nonrepetitively.

Figure 4.6 depicts the sales of a firm which are highly responsive to fluctuations in the economy. Such a firm is said to be procyclical. An

---

[17]For a more detailed discussion of the application of these two statistical concepts to portfolio theory, see Robert Kolb, *Principles of Finance* (Glenview, Ill.: Scott Foresman Publishing Co., 1988), pp. 293–340.

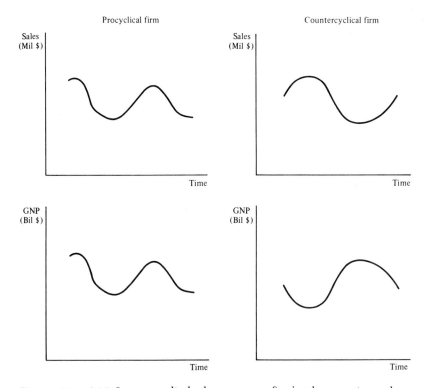

Figures 4.6 and 4.7 In a procyclical sales pattern, a firm's sales may rise as the economy rises. In a countercyclical sales pattern, a firm's sales may move opposite the market. This is a less common occurrence.

example of such a firm is a steel company or an automobile company. A firm that has procyclical sales and earnings may want to attenuate the amplitude of its "cycles" by acquiring a noncyclical or even a countercyclical firm. A countercyclical firm is one whose revenues vary opposite to the movements of the economy. An example of counter-cyclical revenues is shown in Figure 4.7.

It is difficult to find a purely countercyclical firm; it is easier to find targets whose revenues and earnings are less responsive to fluctuations in the economy. Typically, manufacturers of capital goods and consumer durables tend to be hit the hardest by economic downturns. The construction industry is particularly vulnerable to recessions. Nondurable industries, on the other hand, tend to be less volatile relative to the economy as a whole. The downside risk of such cyclical firms tends to be offset by the fact that capital goods manufacturers and construction industry firms tend to expand more in good times than most other businesses. A firm that already has a cyclical sales and earnings pattern, ver, may not be sufficiently attracted by a target's positive performance in good times which comes at the cost of sharp downturns in poorer times. Therefore, the cyclical firm, interested in lowering its level of risk, may choose to acquire a noncyclical target.

Corporate Finance Theory and Diversification

Many firms have pursued diversification as a means of becoming less volatile. The INCO acquisition of ESB is a clear example of a volatile, commodity-based firm seeking to acquire a firm with a more stable pattern of earnings. The large conglomerates that rose up in the 1960s, such as Tenneco, Gulf and Western, ITT, Teledyne, and LTV, were highly diversified corporations.

Corporate finance theory takes a dim view of acquisitions in which diversification is the main motive.[18] The main reason why is that the acquiring company is providing a service to stockholders that they can accomplish better themselves. Let us consider, for example, a steel company that has a typical pattern of cyclical sales and is considering acquiring a pharmaceutical company exhibiting a recession-resistant sales pattern. Financial theory states that the managers of the steel company are doing their stockholders a disservice through the acquisition of other companies. If stockholders in the steel company wanted to be stockholders in the pharmaceutical firm, they could easily adjust their portfolio to add shares of the pharmaceutical firm or another company with a noncyclical earnings pattern. Stockholders can accomplish such transactions in a far less costly manner than through a corporate acquisition. Moreover, the fact that stockholders in the steel company allocated that part of their portfolio to a company that clearly had a pattern of cyclical earnings indicates that they were willing to accept the downturns in earnings—presumably because of the upside potential.

Another disadvantage of mergers that are motivated by diversification is the tendency to stretch the acquiring company's management skills. The ability to successfully manage a firm in one industry does not necessarily extend to other businesses. The history of American business is replete with instances of firms that have diversified into areas beyond their managerial expertise. A classic example would be the acquisition by a regulated company, such as a public utility, of a firm in an unrelated industry which is dependent on intensive market-

[18]Haim Levy and Marshall Sarnat, "Diversification, Portfolio Analysis and the Uneasy Case for Conglomerate Mergers," *Journal of Finance* 25 (September 1970): 795–802.

ing and quick reactions. The managers of a power utility may desire to be in the hotel or restaurant industry but may lack the necessary expertise to manage such a business.

Stock Market Performance of Diversified Companies

One way of testing the implications of corporate finance theory for diversified companies is to compare the performance of the highly diversified conglomerates that expanded through widespread acquisitions in the 1960s with that of nondiversified firms. Frederick Scherer and David Ravenscraft compared the performance of the stocks of the 13 leading conglomerates in the 1960s with that of the market as a whole.[19] They assumed that a hypothetical investor would make a $1,000 investment in the common stock of each conglomerate in 1965 (before the conglomerate stock market boom) or in 1968 (at the peak of the conglomerate stock market boom). (See Table 4.3.) They accounted for such factors as stock splits and assumed that all dividends would be reinvested. Scherer and Ravenscraft showed that, if investors were sufficiently prescient to invest in the conglomerate prior to the conglomerate boom, they would have performed 3.6 times better than the Standard and Poor's (S&P) 500 by 1968. By 1983, this portfolio would have been 2.7 times the value of the S&P 500. On the other hand, those investors whose timing was not so fortuitous, and who bought the conglomerate stocks at the peak and thereby paid a premium for their investment, did not fare nearly as well. This portfolio failed to keep pace with the S&P 500.

Scherer and Ravenscraft's results confirm the belief of corporate finance theory which implies that diversified firms are not providing investors a benefit when they diversify. This result is reflected in the market performance of diversified firms (see Table 4.3). We can see that the distribution of stock value growth for diversified firms was highly skewed. Six of the conglomerates fall below the S&P 425, while three are slightly better and three others are significantly better. Scherer and Ravenscraft show that one conglomerate, Teledyne, performed sixteen times better than the S&P 425. They point out that this type of distribution would have been what one would have expected if the investments were made in individual high tech firms as opposed to diversified, and supposedly, less risky conglomerates.

Market timing determines whether conglomerates provide positive

---

[19]David Ravenscraft and Frederick Scherer, "Mergers and Managerial Performance," in *Knights, Raiders and Targets*, edited by John Coffee, Louis Lowenstein, and Susan Rose Ackerman (New York: Oxford University Press, 1988), pp. 194–210.

TABLE 4.3   1983 VALUE OF A $1,000 1965 INVESTMENT IN EACH OF 13 LEADING
             CONGLOMERATES OR THE S&P INDUSTRIALS

Rank	Company	1983 Value
1	Teledyne	$65,463
2	Whittaker	24,025
3	Gulf & Western	16,287
4	U.S. Industries	7,152
5	Textron	4,947
6	Walter Kidde	4,813
7	Chromalloy-American	4,672
	S&P 425 industrials	4,106
8	Beatrice	3,992
9	Consolidated Foods	3,820
10	ITT	3,625
11	Litton Industries	2,691
12	W. R. Grace	2,587
13	Genesco	408

Source: John C. Coffee, Jr., Louis Lowenstein, and Susan Rose-Ackerman, ed., *Knights, Raiders and Targets* (New York: Oxford University Press, Inc., 1988).

returns just like any other investment. The fact that a firm is a conglomerate does not improve its probability of yielding higher than normal returns. Although this notion does not conclusively refute corporate finance theory's view of the drawbacks of diversified corporations, it clearly fails to provide support.

Perhaps the strongest indictment of large-scale diversification, as practiced by the sizable conglomerates of the 1960s, is the dismantling of many of them through selloffs. Many of the leveraged buyouts that occurred in the late 1970s and 1980s were the result of divestiture efforts by diversified firms. These firms made a decision that the company could be better managed and achieve greater profits if its operations were concentrated in fewer areas.

CONGLOMERATES AND RETURNS TO ACQUIRED FIRM'S STOCKHOLDERS

The Scherer and Ravenscraft study seems to downplay the risk-reduction benefits of conglomerates. It is important to note, however, that other research studies cast the wealth effects of conglomerates in a better light. For example, research studies have shown that returns to stockholders in conglomerate acquisitions are greater than in non con-glomerate acquisitions.[20]

A study by Pieter Elgers and John Clark of 337 mergers between 1957 and 1975 found that conglomerate mergers provided superior gains relative to nonconglomerate mergers. They reported these gains for both buyer and seller firms, with substantial gains registered by stock-holders of seller firms and moderate gains for buying company stock-holders. This finding was confirmed by James Wansley, William Lane, and Ho Yang in a study of 52 nonconglomerate and 151 conglomerate mergers. They also found that returns to shareholders were larger in horizontal and vertical acquisitions than in conglomerate acquisitions.[21]

The poor performance of National Intergroup, which was reflected in the fact that the firm experienced losses in six of the eight fiscal years prior to 1990, made the firm vulnerable to a takeover. The mar-ket's reaction to this poor performance is reflected in the pattern of declining stock prices shown in Figure 4.8. The New York-based in-vestment group, Centour Partners L.P., took advantage of this situation and bought a 16.5 percent interest in the firm. Centour waged a proxy battle in 1990 to restructure the company. National Intergroup re-sponded to this pressure with its own plan to sell off the Ben Franklin Stores and Permian Oil, which was then referred to as Permian Part-ners. The plan also called for the eventual shedding of all units with the exception of its Fox Meyer drug distribution chain and the resig-nation of embattled chairman Howard Love.

ECONOMIC MOTIVES FOR MERGERS AND ACQUISITIONS

In addition to economies of scale and diversification benefits, there are two other economic motives for mergers and acquisitions: (1) the in-crease in market share and market power that results from horizontal integration and (2) the various other benefits that result from vertical integration.

---

[20]P. Elgers and J. Clark, "Merger Types and Shareholder Returns," *Financial Manage-ment* (Summer 1980): 66–72.

[21]James Wansley, William Lane, and Ho Yang, "Abnormal Returns to Acquired Firms by Type of Acquisition and Method of Payment," *Financial Management* (Autumn 1983): 16–22.

CASE STUDY *NATIONAL INTERGROUP: A STUDY OF DIVERSIFICATION GONE SOUR*

In 1980, National Steel was the sixth largest steel company in the United States. Howard Love had just become president, and one of his goals was to make the firm a diversified corporation that would be somewhat insulated from the cyclical nature of the steel industry. His program of diversification involved the sale of some steel assets and the use of the proceeds to acquire other nonsteel businesses. National Steel sold one steel mill to employees of the company and a 50 percent share in three other mills to NKK Corporation of Tokyo.

As part of the firm's efforts to deemphasize the role of steel in the firm's future, National Steel changed its name to National Intergroup in 1983. This name change coincided with the firm's effort to diversify its operations by acquiring thrift institutions. The firm had previously purchased one of the nation's largest and best managed thrift institutions, First Nationwide Financial Corporation. This business was eventually sold for $426 million, even though it was doing well.

It is ironic that Love had commissioned a study by the management consulting firm of Bain and Company. He requested the firm to find other fields for National Intergroup's expansion. *Business Week* reports that the Bain report indicated that the management consulting firm recommended to Love that National Intergroup build closely on its expertise in wholesale steel distribution. Nonetheless, National Intergroup continued to expand outside the steel industry.

In 1985, National Steel acquired the Permian Corporation, a supplier of crude oil. The acquisition cost 3 million shares of National Steel common stock, $88 million in cash, and the assumption of $234 million worth of debt. In 1986, National Steel acquired Fox Meyer, Inc. Based in Dallas, Fox Meyer was the third largest wholesaler in the drug industry. The cost of $343 million was approximately double the market value of the company. The acquisition was 100 percent financed by debt. Although National paid a high price for the company, Fox Meyer did have several appealing attributes. The drug industry is generally noncyclical. It is not capital intensive, and it does not tend to need large infusions of cash. Labor is relatively cheap compared to that for the steel industry. Given the overall growth of the health care industry, the move into the pharmaceutical wholesaling industry could be considered a move into a growth area. In 1986, Fox Meyer, through its subsidiary, bought Ben Franklin Stores, a large 5 and 10 cents chain, and Lawrence Pharmaceuticals, a regional drug distributor. Both firms were purchased at a premium: The combined cost of the two was $62 million in cash as well as the assumption of $57 million in debt.

In retrospect, National Steel's diversification efforts have not proved to be successful. Following the acquisition of Permian Oil, oil prices declined, and as a result Permian went into the red. Moving from a cyclical industry, such as the steel industry, into an inherently volatile commodity-based industry, such as the oil industry, provided few anticyclical benefits. Initially, the Fox Meyer acquisition also looked attractive, but it never fulfilled its expectations. The division experienced higher than anticipated costs in a project to sell supplies to hospitals. It was also forced to abandon an ambitious program to sell computer services to druggists. In addition, not long after Fox Meyer was acquired, an industry price war developed and cut sharply into Fox Meyer's profit margins.

National Intergroup thought that the Ben Franklin Stores chain would blend well with the Fox Meyer operation. Moreover, National Intergroup's management felt that Fox Meyer's computer inventory system could be applied to Ben Franklin's operations. The continued efforts to implement the computerization of Ben Franklin Stores drained Fox Meyer's cash reserves and management resources. The computer-based problems at Ben Franklin caused the company to be unable to fill orders and sales fell. The 5 and 10 cent chain was forced to close 43 stores by mid-1988. Part of the problem was that National Intergroup did not understand the trends in that part of the retail industry. Five and 10 cents stores were having a difficult time remaining competitive with the more attractive, innovative chains such as K-Mart and Wall-Mart. On the surface it appeared that Ben Franklin would have certain synergies with Fox Meyer, but those gains never materialized.

The acquisition spree left National Intergroup with over $440 million worth of long-term debt. In 1988, debt and long-term liabilities were double the value of equity. The acquisitions were purchased at a premium, and most performed poorly. Although the steel industry, beset with all the problems that the domestic steel industry faced along with its overall cyclical nature, was an unglamorous business, the acquisitions which National Intergroup added proved to be worse. National Intergroup expanded out of areas in which it had expertise into areas in which it had little to offer. In addition, the high prices paid for many of the targets put pressure on management to show even greater gains than the previous management had. Because the firm was out of its element, these additional gains failed to materialize. In June 1990 the firm announced that it planned to sell all units except for Fox Mayer. Its embattled chairman, Howard Love, agreed to step down. Following the sales, the company would be renamed Fox Mayer.

Sources: Company reports; Ernest Beazley, "Steelmaker Suffers from a Case of Diversification Blues," *Wall Street Journal*; "National Intergroup: How Pete Went Wrong," *Business Week*, March 6, 1989, pp. 56–57; "Last Chance for Love?", *Business Week*, April 24, 1989, p. 31; "National Intergroup Chairman to Resign After Firm Sheds All Units But Fox Meyer," *Wall Street Journal*, June 6, 1990, p. A3; and "Intergroup Sees Profits in Drugs," *New York Times*, June 11, 1990, p. D8.

Horizontal Integration

Horizontal integration involves the mergers of firms selling a similar product or service. If, for example, one airline buys another airline, this is an example of horizontal integration. The result of this process is that the industry is more *concentrated*. Concentration may be defined as the percentage of total industry activity, measured by total revenues, that is controlled by the largest companies in the industry. The greater

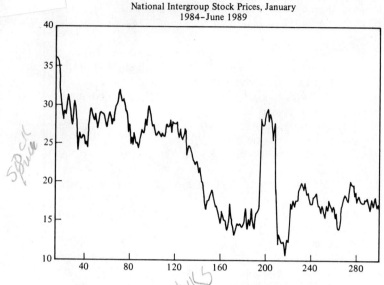

Figure 4.8 The failure of National Intergroup's diversification strategy was reflected in a decline in the firm's stock price.

the amount controlled by a smaller number of companies, the more concentrated the industry.

An aggregate concentration is the overall concentration over time in American industry. Some critics of the current mergers and acquisitions movement contend that this activity is creating an American economy that is becoming more concentrated, stifling competition and the ability of smaller firms to compete. Indeed, critics of capitalism predicted this trend as far back as Karl Marx, who warned that big businesses would tend to acquire other, smaller firms until a few large companies dominated the capitalistic economy.[22] Although Marx's prognostications on the future of the capitalist economy have proven inaccurate, some critics of the current mergers and acquisitions movement have offered arguments somewhat similar to the Marxian criticisms.

An obvious advantage of horizontal integration is the efficiency gains associated with synergy and economies of scale. (These benefits are discussed above.) An example of the various benefits obtainable was the combination of LTV's Jones and Laughlin Steel operation with the Youngstown Steel and Tube Company. Scherer and Ravenscraft report

[22]Karl Marx, *Capital*, Vol. 1, 1912.

that the merger brought the infusion of "competent and highly motivated management that cracked production bottlenecks, instituted better production scheduling, and began a drive to improve badly eroded labor relations."[23] Jones and Laughlin and Youngstown Steel and Tube combination produced yet more valuable gains. The Youngstown headquarters was closed, and the field sales force was reduced. Scherer and Ravenscraft also report significant savings related to iron and coke procurement.

Another benefit that can be derived from horizontal combinations is an increase in monopoly power—the ability to command higher prices for a company's products and services without fear of lost sales owing to price competition. Monopoly power does not imply, however, that the company can simultaneously set both its price and the quantity that consumers will buy. This is contrary to popularly held beliefs about the extent of monopoly power. In order to explain this result, we need to consider the microeconomics of monopolistic firms.

The two main economic models in the theory of the firm are pure competition and monopoly, the two extreme forms of market structure. Between these two cases are other possibilities including oligopoly, which is an industry characterized by few firms, and monopolistic competition, which is an industry structure characterized by many small firms producing a somewhat differentiated product.

Pure competition (Figure 4.9) is characterized by many small firms, each of which is a price taker. That is, the total output of each is so small compared to the market output that variations in the amount of the firm's output has no effect on market price. The products are totally undifferentiated and homogeneous. Price is set in the market through the interaction of the market demand and market supply. If the competitive firm increases its price, its sales will fall to zero. Given the large numbers of buyers and sellers that exist in the competitive industry model, buyers would have no reason to purchase from a higher priced seller. This is a major point of difference with the monopolist.

It is often erroneously believed that a monopolist has market power which enables the firm to establish a higher price while simultaneously maintaining the same high volume of sales. Being a monopolist does *not* remove the firm from the influences of market demand as reflected by the demand curve that prevails for the product. The downward-sloping nature of the demand curve assures that, when price increases, the quantity demanded will fall. The true power of the monopolist is

---

[23]David J. Ravenscraft and Frederick M. Scherer, *Mergers, Sell-Offs and Economic Efficiency*, (Washington D.C.: Brookings Institution, 1987), p. 151.

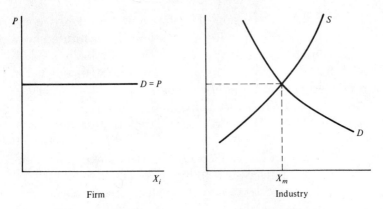

Figure 4.9 In pure competition the price is set in the market and each firm is a price taker. Therefore, the demand curve for the competitive firm is perfectly elastic and is the same as the price line.

the ability to select the price–output combination that will maximize profits. For the monopolist, this means a point on the elastic part of the demand curve (Figure 4.10).

The profit-maximizing part of the demand curve is determined in the same manner for all firms—the intersection of the marginal revenue and marginal cost functions. For the competitive firm, the marginal revenue and the price line are the same since the firm is a price taker and all units sold bring in the same revenue—the market price. The monopolist, on the other hand, is the market and, therefore, faces the market demand curve. Each additional unit sold decreases the market price as the firm moves down the demand curve. The profit-maximizing output level for the monopolist that results from the intersection of the marginal revenues and marginal cost occurs at the price–output combination $(X_m - P_m)$. (See Figure 4.11.) At this output level, profits are determined by the difference between price and average costs.

$$\text{Profit} = (X_m - AC_m)\, P_m$$

The microeconomic theory of the firm shows that a monopolist has the opportunity to earn extranormal returns; this is the essence of the market power that a monopolist enjoys. Normal returns are those that are just equal to the opportunity costs incurred by the firm. For example, competitive firms, such as a small farm, may show an accounting profit of $40,000. Economic returns, or what we generally call economic rent, however, may be zero inasmuch as the farmer may incur an opportunity cost of $40,000 if this is the prevailing wage rate in the market for an individual with his skills.

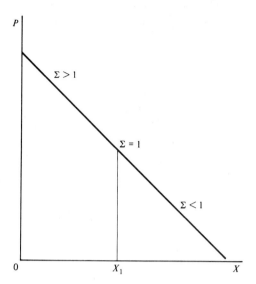

Figure 4.10 The price elasticity of demand increases as you move up the demand curve. The lower half of the straight line demand curve is the inelastic range while the upper half is the elastic range.

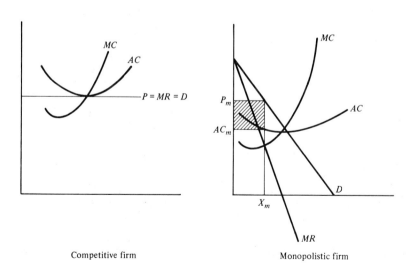

Figure 4.11 The competitive firm earns zero economic profits in the long run with price equaling average cost. This is not the case in a monopoly where the monopolist earns economic profits equal to $(P_m - AC_m)\ X_m$. This is highlighted in the shaded region of the monopoly graph.

Microeconomics implies that if the competitive firm is able to earn extranormal returns in the short run, such as $90,000 for the farmer in the above example, new entrants into the industry will bring down prices and revenues so that the long-run equilibrium of the industry has each of the producers earning a normal return.

One difference between the pure competition model and monopoly is the existence of barriers to entry. Such barriers might come in the form of patents, trade secrets, or high capital requirements. The monopolist can theoretically earn extranormal returns without the worry that new entrants can enter and drive the market price down. Of course, the situation also depends on how long a time horizon is adopted. If the monopoly profits are very high, barriers to entry, such as very high capital requirements, will eventually be overcome. The ability to set the price–output combination does not mean that the monopolist will definitely earn profits. Surely, the manufacturers of the Edsel had a monopoly on the production of this product, but that did not insulate them from the workings of the market system and a demand curve for the product that was insufficient to ensure a profit.

Few industries correspond to either the extreme pure competition or the monopoly model described above. The models are not without value, however. Their value comes when a market structure exists which closely approximates either of the two models. It is then that we would expect the conclusions that prevailed in the extreme case to be relevant to the actual market structure.

Most horizontal combinations do not result in an outright monopoly but rather in increased concentration in the industry and an oligopolistic market structure. Many theoretical models describe oligopoly in a similar manner as monopoly and pure competition.[24] Unfortunately, although the models present interesting theoretical exercises, the additional cost of reviewing them here exceeds the benefits to be derived from their application to the field of mergers and acquisitions.

The formation of a larger firm through the horizontal combination of competitors may provide benefits by lowering costs through scale economies and lowering risk through diversification. Monopoly power is not usually enjoyed in a more concentrated industry. As the industry becomes more concentrated, several larger competitors arise, each of whom may have lower economic and financial costs. In this case each may be better able to compete with larger rivals. On the other hand,

---

[24]See Donald McClosky, *The Applied Theory of Price* (New York: Macmillan Publishing Co., 1982), pp. 434–461; and A. Koutsoyianis, *Modern Microeconomics* (New York: John Wiley & Sons, 1975), pp. 216–254.

if the concentration results in one large firm that competes against many small rivals, then the large firm may enjoy a clear competitive advantage. This is generally not the case, however. As the industry moves to increased concentration, smaller firms have an incentive to combine so that they can maintain their ability to compete.

The Social Cost of Increased Concentration

The costs to society which result from increased concentration are a function of the state of competition that exists after the horizontal mergers. If the industry structure formed approximates monopoly, then the social costs can be significant. This can be seen by the fact that in pure competition each firm is a price taker, and competitive firms produce an output where price equals marginal costs. In monopoly, a firm maximizes profits by setting marginal revenue equal to marginal costs. The rule is the same for the competitive firm, but in the instance of monopoly, marginal revenue is less than price. The end result is that a competitive industry has lower prices and higher output levels than a monopolized industry.

This can be seen in Figure 4.12. If a competitive pricing rule is used ($P = MC$), then an output level equal to X_C results, with price equal to P_C. On the other hand, if such an industry were to become so concentrated that a monopoly resulted, then a lower output level equal to X_m and a higher price equal to P_m would result. The end result is that consumers would pay higher prices in the monopolized industry and have a lower total output available.

One way to see the effect on society is to consider a concept which economists call deadweight loss or welfare loss—that is, the loss of *consumer and producer surplus.* Consumer surplus is the difference between the price paid and the height up to the demand curve for all units bought by consumers. The height up to the demand reflects the maximum that consumers would be willing to pay for each unit. This maximum declines as consumers purchase more units. Producer surplus is the difference between the supply curve and the price that producers receive for each unit. The supply curve reflects the producers' cost conditions. In a competitive market, the supply curve is the horizontal summation of the individual marginal cost curves of each producer above the average cost curve. In such a market, the height up to the supply curve reflects the additional costs of producing units. Producers should not accept less than the marginal costs of producing each additional unit. The upward-sloping shape of the supply curve reflects diminishing returns in production.

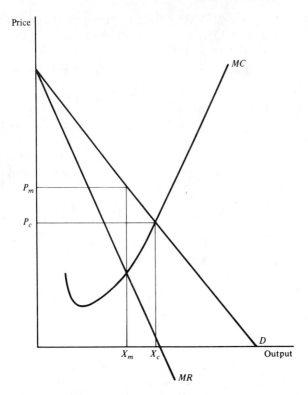

Figure 4.12 Consumers benefit more from a competitive market. They buy more output (X_c) than in a monopolized market (X_m) and pay less $(P_c < P_m)$.

Gains from trade occur to both parties since consumers pay less than the maximum they would have been willing to pay for all units up to X_e. Producers gain from trading with consumers since they receive a price greater than the additional costs of producing each unit for all units up to X_e. The total gains from trade are depicted in Figure 4.13, and the combined total of the two shaded triangular areas depict consumer surplus (CS) and producer surplus (PS).

The welfare loss in monopoly occurs because fewer units are sold and each is sold for a higher price than in competition. Given that trading ends at an output level of X_m instead of X_c, a loss of consumer and producer surplus results. The combined loss of consumer and producer surplus is the deadweight or welfare loss. In Figure 4.14 the upper triangle refers to the loss of consumer surplus, and the lower shaded triangle shows the loss of producer surplus.

The obvious practical question that arises is whether horizontal mergers result in a welfare loss to society. Economists have written

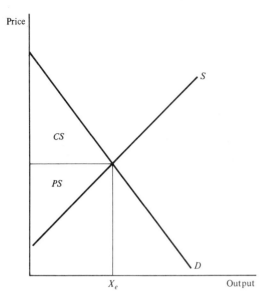

Figure 4.13 A free market system brings about an exchange between suppliers and demanders in which the gains from trade are maximized. Consumer gains are denoted by consumer surplus (CS) and supplier gains are denoted by producer surplus (PS).

many theoretical papers that purport to measure the welfare loss.[25] In reality, these are interesting exercises, but they have failed to provide a convincing measure of the deadweight loss in the extreme case of monopoly. Neither do they provide guidance for the intermediate cases of oligopoly which are more relevant to the horizontal mergers that have occurred throughout the world.

There is no real basis for assuming that a deadweight loss occurs when firms combine horizontally. The mere fact that a more concentrated industry structure results does not imply that competition has declined. The final outcome might be a number of strong competitors who engage in a heightened state of competition characterized by competitively determined prices and differentiated products. If so, then the argument for a deadweight loss resulting from increased concentration is weakened. The existence of a welfare loss resulting from the formation of oligopolies needs to be considered on an individual, industry-by industry, basis.

---

[25]See Arnold C. Harberger, "Three Basic Postulates for Applied Welfare Economics," *Journal of Economic Literature* 9, no. 3 (September 1971): 785–797.

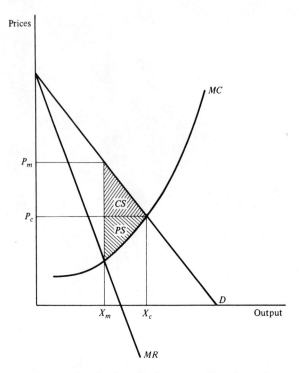

Figure 4.14 The deadweight loss or welfare loss of monopoly derives from the loss of the gains from trade. The loss of the consumer and producer surplus is shown in the shaded region. X_m units are traded instead of X_c. The marketplace loses the gains from trade (CS and PS) on the units that are not traded.

Efficiency Gains from Horizontal Mergers   As demonstrated above, increased concentration may well lead to an increase in monopoly power, which might result in a deadweight loss for society. It is also possible that the development of more formidable competitors could enhance competition and that horizontal acquisitions could provide overall efficiency gains even in the presence of initial deadweight losses. This may occur when realizable cost reductions follow the horizontal acquisitions. Oliver Williamson has presented a theoretical framework showing the possibility of efficiency gains that might outweigh the deadweight loss. His model makes certain simplifying assumptions that facilitate the ease of exposition. One such assumption is constant average and marginal costs. The Williamson model is depicted in Figure 4.15.[26]

---

[26]Oliver E. Williamson, "Economies As an Antitrust Defense," *American Economic Review* (March 1968):

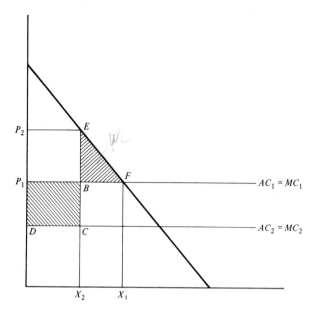

Figure 4.15 Williamson's model helps demonstrate the trade-off between the potential efficiency gains of horizontal mergers and the deadweight or welfare loss that can occur. Less units are traded ($X_2 < X_1$) so there is a loss of the gains from the trade but there may be a cost saving on these units that are traded (P, B C D).

The deadweight loss or welfare loss is shown in the triangle labeled WL. This occurs when a merger occurs and the price increases to P_2 from P_1 and output declines from X_1 to X_2. Williamson states, however, that cost reductions such as those that could arise from synergy could produce cost savings that might more than offset the welfare loss. In Figure 4.15, a welfare loss arises when firms merge and prices increase from P_1 to P_2. This results in the welfare loss shown by the shaded triangle (EBF). Williamson contends that cost savings may occur, as reflected in the decline in the average and marginal cost curves from AC_1 to AC_2. This results in a cost savings equal to the shaded rectangular area (P_1DCB).

Williamson states that these savings could be greater than the welfare loss. The conclusion that the net economic loss will be positive is dependent on the economic conditions set forth in the expression below.

$$\frac{\Delta(AC)}{AC} - \frac{1}{2}\eta \frac{Q_1}{Q_2}\left(\frac{\Delta P}{P_1}\right)^2 > 0$$

If the above inequality shows that the left side of the equation is

TABLE 4.4   COST SAVINGS NECESSARY TO OFFSET MERGER PRICE INCREASES

η $(\Delta P/P) \times 100$	2	1	1/2
5	0.26	0.12	0.06
10	1.05	0.50	0.24
20	4.40	2.00	0.95
30	10.35	4.50	2.10

Source: Oliver E. Williamson, *Antitrust Economics* (Oxford, UK: Basil Blackwell, 1987), p. 8.

greater than zero, then there are positive net economic benefits. If it is zero or negative, there are either no gains or a positive net welfare loss. Williamson includes a table that shows the cost decrease necessary to offset the price increases that occur after a post-merger increase in market power. (See Table 4.4.) The table shows the cost savings that would result from applying the formula, assuming different possible elasticities and price increases. For example, if prices rise 30 percent and the price elasticity of demand is 1, then a 5 percent cost decrease is needed to neutralize the price effect.

Based on his assumptions, Williamson's formula provides some handy guidelines. The obvious drawbacks of a pragmatic application is that it is largely dependent on the accuracy of these assumptions. For example, if a merger is approved based on anticipated price increases that turn out to be too low or when the price elasticity of demand is inaccurately estimated, welfare losses may occur when a net cost savings was anticipated. The other major problem with the model is that it focuses on societal gains. It is the merged firm that experiences the gains, whereas the costs are incurred by the consumers. Some feel that, although the companies may gain more than consumers, this result is nonetheless inequitable and unfair.

Empirical Evidence on the Monopoly Hypothesis

We have little empirical evidence that firms combine to increase their monopoly power. Much of the evidence that elucidates this question is indirect. A Ph.D. dissertation by Robert S. Stillman in 1983 showed that competitors failed to react when other firms in the same industry announced a combination.[27] Stillman's analysis considered the value of the stock of firms in the affected industry when events took place that increased the probability of mergers in that industry. He also considered

---

[27]Robert S. Stillman, "Examining Antitrust Policy Towards Mergers," Ph.D. Dissertation, University of California at Los Angeles, 1983. This dissertation was later published in the *Journal of Financial Economics* 11, no. 1 (April 1983): 225–240.

the fact that product prices might rise after horizontal mergers, bene-fiting other firms in the industry. With higher product prices, resulting from a more concentrated industry, the equity values of the firms in the industry should also rise.

Stillman examined a small sample of 11 mergers that were chal-lenged on antitrust grounds under Section 7 of the Clayton Act. He found no statistically significant abnormal returns for 9 of the 11 merg-ers. Of the other two, one showed positive abnormal returns and the other showed ambiguous results. These results fail to support the view that firms merge in an effort to seek monopoly power.

A similar study, also based on a doctoral thesis, was conducted by B. Epsen Eckbo on a larger sample of 126 horizontal and vertical mergers in the manufacturing and mining industries.[28] Approximately half of Eckbo's sample were horizontal mergers. An average of 15 rival firms existed in each industry category. If the market power hypothesis delineated above was valid, negative abnormal returns would be ob-served for firms in industries that had announced mergers that were challenged on antitrust grounds. The reasoning is that the merger is less likely when there is an antitrust challenge. When challenges take place, negative abnormal returns should be associated with the an-nouncement of the challenge. Eckbo found statistically insignificant abnormal returns. He also showed that firms initially showed positive and statistically significant abnormal returns when the mergers were first announced but failed to show a negative response after the com-plaint was filed.

Like Stillman's results, Eckbo's research does not support the belief that firms merge to enjoy increases in market power. Curiously, Eckbo's results reveal that "stockholders of bidder and target firms in challenged (horizontal) mergers earn larger abnormal returns than do the corre-sponding firms in unchallenged mergers."[29] Eckbo concludes that the gains found in mergers are not related to increases in market power, but rather are motivated by factors such as efficiency gains.

Vertical Integration

Vertical integration involves the acquisition of firms that are closer to the source of supply or to the ultimate consumer. An example of a movement toward the source of supply was Chevron's acquisition of Gulf Oil in 1984. Chevron bought Gulf primarily to augment its reserves,

---

[28]B. Epsen Eckbo, "Horizontal Mergers, Collusion and Stockholder Wealth," *Journal of Financial Economics* 11, no. 1 (April 1983): 241–273.
[29]Ibid.

a motive termed *backward integration*. In the same year, Mobil bought Superior Oil for similar reasons. Mobil was strong in refining and marketing but low on reserves, whereas Superior had large oil and gas reserves but lacked refining and marketing operations. An example of *forward integration* would be if a firm with large reserves bought another company that had a strong marketing and retail capability.

Another example, in the securities industry, occurred when Shearson Lehman Brothers bought E. F. Hutton. Shearson was attracted by E. F. Hutton's strong network of retail brokers. This vertical combination was motivated by a movement toward the consumer. It is also an example of a previously vertically integrated firm that wanted to expand its access to the consumer. Before the merger, Shearson Lehman had a large network of retail brokers. After the merger, however, it acquired a retail capacity to rival all competitors including Merrill Lynch.

It is popularly believed that when a company acquires a supplier it is obtaining a cost advantage over its rivals. The thinking is that it will not have to pay the profit to suppliers that it was previously paying when it was buying the inputs from independent suppliers. This raises the question: What is the appropriate *internal transfer price*? This is the price carried on the company's books when it acquires its supplies or inputs from a supplier that it now controls and who may be a subsidiary. If the price for these inputs is less than the prevailing market price, then the parent company will appear to be more profitable than it really is. The reason is that the lower costs and higher profits for the parent company come at the cost of lower profitability for the subsidiary. This is a paper transfer, however, and does not mean increased value to the combined firm.

Consider the case of an automobile manufacturer that purchases tires from a tire manufacturing company at a unit price of $50, which we will assume is a competitive price for this type of tire. The cost to the automobile manufacturer may contain a $5 profit to the tire maker. If the car company then buys a tire manufacturer, which it operates as a subsidiary, it should still record the tire cost at $50. The car company would be fooling itself if it thought that it was saving $5 per tire by buying the tire maker. To purchase the tire company, the car company is investing capital for which it is earning no return but which allows the parent company to earn a higher return. On the other hand, if the subsidiary is allowed to earn a $5 profit by charging the parent the full $50 market price, then the investment in the tire manufacturer will show a positive return while the automobile manufacturer's return should remain at the pre-acquisition level. The transaction is merely a paper transfer and does not result in increased value.

Another interesting example of vertical integration occurs in the marketing of automobiles. Automobile manufacturers have long realized that they may need to provide potential buyers with financial assistance in the form of cheaper and more readily available credit in order to sell more cars. For this reason, General Motors formed General Motors Acceptance Corporation (GMAC). GMAC provides low-cost credit to many car buyers who might not have been able to get the financing necessary to buy a new car. Financing incentives have become a regular part of the competition among automakers. Firms may lower the financing costs well below the cost of capital in order to sell certain car models that are experiencing slow sales. GMAC will sell commercial paper at money market rates that may be above the financing costs it charges customers. These costs have sometimes gone as low as 0 percent.

One advantage of keeping GMAC as an independent subsidiary is that the high debt levels generated by the aggressive procurement of capital by GMAC does not affect the debt/equity ratio of the parent company. General Motors does not suffer a lower debt and credit rating that would increase its cost of capital. One of the main advantages a firm experiences when it engages in backward integration is the enhanced access to dependable sources of supply. Through relationships with the supplier, it can gain priority access to inputs that are built to parent company specifications. In addition, it can reduce the probability of being cut off from access. The subsidiary should give the parent company first priority in deliveries. Although this policy may raise some interesting antitrust issues, it is clearly an advantage to the parent company.

Vertical Integration and the Competitive Advantage   Vertical integration can be used to reinforce a supplier's competitive position. Michael Porter relates how metal producers used forward integration to create a pull-through demand for substitute products. In the 1970s and early 1980s, steel and aluminum manufacturers actively competed for the can market. Each group of manufacturers tried to enhance any competitive advantage.

> A strategy practiced successfully by the aluminum industry, among others, is to forward integrate selectively into downstream products to create pull-through demand for a substitute. A related strategy is to induce end users to backward integrate into the intermediate industry to get around intermediate producers who are unwilling to substitute. By integrating forward and creating demand with end users, a firm can sometimes force recalcitrant intermediate buyers to bear the switching costs of substitution.

Forward integration can also demonstrate the performance of the substitute, and be a means for developing procedures for its use and for lowering switching costs.[30]

Vertical integration proved to be a successful tool in the can industry. The end users, the beverage companies, incurred few costs in switching to aluminum cans. The problem for the aluminum manufacturers was that, to reach the end users, the aluminum companies had to go through the can makers. Can makers, on the other hand, face considerable costs related to the investment in capital equipment to switch. The aluminum manufacturers' strategy was very successful; by the late 1980s, they totally dominated the can market. By 1989, 99.9 percent of all beer cans and 96 percent of all beverage cans were made of aluminum.[31]

Forward integration can help overcome the reluctance to incur the increased switching costs since the aluminum manufacturers ultimately make that decision. The outcome of this process is that vertical integration can enable firms to be better able to compete. To the extent that this occurs, consumers are better off. Vertical integration can also result in lower prices to consumers, which we can demonstrate by making more extensive use of economic analysis.[32]

A basic relationship exists between marginal revenue and price. Marginal revenue is the change in total revenue that results from the sale of additional units. Marginal revenue equals price times the change in price that results from the sale of additional units times the number of additional units sold. This relationship is shown below.

$$MR = P + \frac{\Delta P}{\Delta Q}Q \tag{4.1}$$

Let us consider the case of the gasoline market and the relationship between retailers and refiners or wholesalers. Each of these parts of the market will have its own marginal revenues functions.

$$MR_R = P_R + \frac{\Delta P_R}{\Delta Q}Q \tag{4.2}$$

$$MR_W = P_W + \frac{\Delta P_W}{\Delta Q}Q \tag{4.3}$$

---

[30]Michael Porter, *Competitive Advantage* (New York: Free Press, 1985), pp. 308–309.

[31]"BevPak Brings Back the Shine to Steel Cans," *Wall Street Journal*, June 8, 1989.

[32]This example draws on an example developed by Charles Baird in *Intermediate Microeconomics* (Minneapolis, Minn.: West Publishing Co., 1975), pp. 250–253.

where: MR_R = the marginal revenue of gasoline retailers
MR_W = the marginal revenue of gasoline wholesalers
P_W = the wholesale price of gasoline
P_R = the retail price of gasoline
Q = the quantity of gasoline sold

$$\frac{\Delta P_R}{\Delta Q} = \text{the slope of the retail gasoline demand curve} \qquad (4.4)$$

$$\frac{\Delta P_W}{\Delta Q} = \text{the slope of the wholesale gasoline demand curve} \qquad (4.5)$$

If we subtract Equation 4.3 from Equation 4.2, we get:

$$MR_R - MR_W = (P_R - P_W) + \frac{\Delta P_R}{(\Delta Q} - \frac{\Delta P_W}{\Delta Q)}Q \qquad (4.6)$$

Equation 4.6 shows that the difference between the marginal revenue of the wholesaler and that of the retailer equals the difference between the retail price and the wholesale price plus the second term on the right side of the equation. If we assume that the slope of the wholesale demand curve and the slope of the retail demand curve are equal, this term becomes zero.

When the wholesale demand curve is steeper than the retail demand curve, this term is greater than zero. This can be seen if we remember that both slopes are negative.

Figure 4.16 shows the demand and supply curves for retail gasoline. D_R shows the price of retail gasoline for each quantity, and S_R shows the supply price of retail gasoline. This supply curve reflects all the costs of the gasoline retailer other than the wholesale price that must be paid to the retailer. If the retail market for gasoline is competitive, then S_R equals all the costs that a gasoline retailer normally incurs such as rent and labor plus a normal return equal to the opportunity cost that the retailer incurs. The difference between D_R and D_W is equal to S_R. S_W is what is added to the wholesale price of gasoline by the retailer. In other words, it is the retailer markup.

Let us assume that a single refiner monopolistically controls the refining market. The refiner maximizes profits by equating marginal revenue and marginal cost. This occurs at q^*. To determine the wholesale and retail prices that prevail at this output level, we need to go straight up to both demand curves at that quantity level. In doing so we get P_R and P_W.

A total of q^* gallons of gasoline reach the market. Wholesalers are

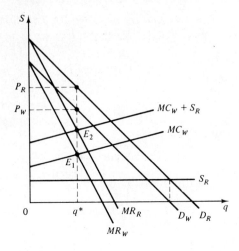

Figure 4.16 Baird's model shows some potential price effects of vertical mergers. [*Source:* Charles W. Baird, *Prices and Markets: Intermediate Microeconomics* (St. Paul, MN: West Publishing Co., 1982), p. 252.]

charged P_W which retailers mark up by an amount equal to S_R and quote P_R at the pump.

Let us now assume that the monopolist refiner buys out all the independent gasoline retailers. The operative demand curve and the marginal revenue curve for the refiner now become D_R and M_R, respectively. The profit-maximizing refiner sets M (not M_W) equal to $M_W + S_R$. This is based on the assumption that costs do not change at the retail level after the acquisition of the retailers. It is possible, however, that cost economies and heightened managerial expertise might lower cost, in which case a lower combined marginal cost curve would prevail. Let us assume that this is not the case.

Given the slopes of the relevant curves, the optimum quantity and output clearly does not change after the acquisition. The two demand curves are parallel since the vertical distance between the two is merely S_R for every output level. This is also the vertical distance between the two marginal revenue curves. The vertical distance between the two marginal cost functions is also S_R. Since the distance between the two marginal cost and the two marginal revenue curves is S_R, it follows that q^* must be the same before and after the merger. MR_W and MC_W are the relevant pre-merger marginal revenue and marginal cost curves that determine the pre-merger optimal output for the refiner. MR_R and MC_R are the post-merger relevant marginal revenue and marginal cost costs for the refiner who is now also the retailer. If the vertical distance between both the two marginal revenue and the marginal cost curves is S_R, it follows that the optimal price and quantity combination is unchanged. In effect, both curves shift up by an equal amount for the refiner after the merger. One clear result from this process is that consumers should be indifferent given that the prices and quantity of gasoline on the market remain the same before and after the merger. Clearly, this type of market process does not hurt consumers.

The situation differs if we assume that S_R is positively sloped. In the original example it was assumed that S_R was constant. Since S_R is the vertical distance between the two demand curves, D_R will be flatter than D_W as S_R rises as output increases. MR_R, the post-merger marginal revenue, will also be flatter than MR_W—the pre-merger marginal revenue. The post-merger marginal revenue is higher than the pre-merger marginal revenue by an amount greater than the difference between P_R and P_W. In other words, the difference between the two marginal revenue curves is greater than S_R. At the pre-merger optimum quantity Q^*, MR_R will be above $MC_W + S_R$. Given that the post-merger optimum quantity must occur at the intersection of MR_R and $MC_W + S_R$, the optimum quantity must be to the right, or greater than, Q^*. The post-merger quantity must be greater, and, therefore, the post-merger price must be lower.

When the S_R rises with a high volume of output, the consumer is better off if the monopolist refiner engages in forward integration and acquires all the refiners and monopolizes this stage of production as well. Consumers are charged lower prices per gallon and consume a greater quantity of gasoline. To apply this result to any market, we would have to consider the marginal costs in providing the product at the retail level. If the retailer can expand without any significant increases in cost, then the result is applicable. If not, then it will not experience these gains. The importance of this result is that it challenges the "knee jerk" response of some merger critics who state that vertical mergers increase market power and hurt consumer welfare. This result need not necessarily follow. Each market and its relevant cost conditions may dictate the result.

Vertical Integration As a Threat to Competition   Having pointed out that vertical integration can facilitate competition, it must be noted that a vertically integrated company can move to foreclose competition in ways that would not be available to a nonvertically integrated company. A classic example of this effect occurred in the airline industry.[33]

An extended battle took place in the early 1980s resulting from actions brought by the Civil Aeronautics Board and the Department of Justice regarding Airline Computer Reservation Systems (CRS) and

---

[33]This example is based on material in Margaret E. Guerin–Calvert, "Airline Computer Reservation Systems" in *The Antitrust Revolution* (Glenview, Ill.: Scott, Foresman and Co., 1989), pp. 338–363.

competition among airlines. Certain airlines complained that the hold that the leading airlines had on the industry through their CRS outlets established at travel agencies restrained their ability to compete. Certain airlines had engaged in forward integration by expanding their operations to include the provision of airline reservation systems in travel agencies.

Table 4.5 shows that the computer reservation systems of American Airlines, United, and TWA accounted for 80 percent of the total travel agency revenues in the industry. American and United accounted for 70 percent by themselves. This is important since travel agencies are responsible for approximately 70 percent of all airline tickets sold.

Airlines that did not have major CRS systems contended that they were unable to compete with those airlines that had these systems. The non-CRS airlines pointed out that the CRS displays were biased in that they first showed the CRS provider's own airline's flights even if they were less convenient for the traveler.

Airlines such as Air Florida, New York Air, and Midway airlines contended that, in addition to bias in providing information to travel agencies, they were charged higher booking fees than other airlines. These higher fees, which were unrelated to the actual costs of adding an airline to the system, were held to be discriminatory pricing and a means whereby established airlines created barriers to entry, making it more expensive for new airlines to enter the industry and be competitive.

The non-CRS airlines maintained that the goal of this form of forward integration by certain airlines was to foreclose competition. The

TABLE 4.5   CRS MARKET SHARES

Airline	CRS	Domestic Travel Agency Revenues (million $)	Percent of Total
American	Sabre	$ 6,376.3	43
United	Apollo	$ 4,040.90	27
TWA	PARS	$ 1,561.1	10
Eastern	SODA	$ 605.3	4
Delta	Datas II	$ 259.8	2
—	Mars Plus	$ 281.9	2
—	Unautomated	$ 1,822.5	12
Total		$14,947.8	100

Source: Margaret E. Guerin-Calvert, "Airline Computer Reservation Systems," in *The Antitrust Revolution* (Glenview, Ill.: Scott, Foresman and Co., 1989), pp. 338–363.

Justice Department agreed with this position and urged the Civil Aeronautics Board (CAB) to enact changes that would correct the problems of bias in the computer reservation systems and the pricing of the system itself. CAB was particularly concerned that these practices would undermine the gains that had been made in enhancing industry competition through deregulation.

CAB instituted new rules in July 1984 which sought to correct the problems. Specifically, it disallowed the bias and discriminatory pricing policies. Some air carriers believe that although these new rules did not totally correct the problems they went a long way toward correcting the anticompetitive practices made possible by forward integration.

THE HUBRIS HYPOTHESIS OF TAKEOVERS

An interesting hypothesis regarding takeover motives has been proposed by Richard Roll.[34] He considers the role that hubris, or the pride of the managers in the acquiring firm, may play in explaining takeovers. The hubris hypothesis implies that managers seek to acquire firms for their own personal motives and that the pure economic gains to the acquiring firm are not the sole or even the primary motivation in the acquisition.

Roll uses this hypothesis to explain why managers might pay a premium for a firm that the market has already correctly valued. Managers, he states, have superimposed their own valuation over that of an objectively determined market valuation. Roll's position is that the pride of management allows them to believe that their valuation is superior to that of the market. Implicit in this theory is an underlying conviction that the market is efficient and can provide the best indicator of the value of a firm. Many would dispute this point. As evidence, Roll draws on a wide body of research studies. This evidence is described in the following section.

Empirical Evidence of the Hubris Hypothesis

Roll states that if the hubris hypothesis explains takeovers, then the following should occur for those takeovers motivated by hubris:

1. The stock price of the acquiring firm should fall after the market becomes aware of the takeover bid. This should occur since the

---

[34]Richard Roll, "The Hubris Hypothesis of Corporate Takeovers," *Journal of Business*, 59, no. 2 (April 1986): 197–216.

takeover is not in the best interests of the acquiring firm's stock-holders and does not represent an efficient allocation of their wealth.

2. The stock price of the target firm should increase with the bid for control. This should occur since, not only is the acquiring firm going to pay a premium, but also the acquirer may pay a premium in excess of the value of the target.

3. The combined effect of the rising value of the target and the falling value of the acquiring firm should be negative. This takes into account the costs of completing the takeover process.

A number of studies show that the acquiring firm's announcement of the takeover results in a decline in the value of the acquirer's stock. Dodd found statistically significant negative returns to the acquirer following the announcement of the planned takeover.[35] Other studies have demonstrated similar findings.[36] Not all studies support this con-clusion, however. Paul Asquith failed to find a consistent pattern of declining stock prices following the announcement of a takeover.[37]

There is more widespread agreement on the positive price effects for target stockholders who have been found to experience wealth gains following takeovers. Bradley, Desai, and Kim show that tender offers result in gains for target firm stockholders.[38] Admittedly, the hostile nature of tender offers should produce greater changes in the stock price than in friendly takeover offers. Most studies, however, show that target stockholders gain following both friendly and hostile takeover bids.

The research on the combined effect of the upward movement of the target's stock and the downward movement of the acquirer's stock does not seem to provide strong support for the hubris hypothesis. Malatesta examined the combined effects and found that "the evidence indicates that the long-run sequence of events culminating in merger has no net impact on combined shareholder wealth."[39] It could be

[35]P. Dodd, "Merger Proposals, Managerial Discretion and Stockholder Wealth," *Journal of Financial Economics* 8 (June 1980): 105, 138.

[36]C. E. Eger, "An Empirical Test of the Redistribution Effect of Mergers," *Journal of Financial and Quantitative Analysis* 18 (December 1983): 547–572.

[37]Paul Asquith. "Merger Bids, Uncertainty and Stockholder Returns," *Journal of Financial Economics* 11 (April 1983): 51–83.

[38]Michael Bradley, Anand Desai, and E. Han Kim, "The Rationale Behind Interfirm Tender Offers: Information or Synergy," *Journal of Financial Economics* 11, no. 1 (April 1983): 183–206.

[39]Paul Malatesta, "Wealth Effects of Merger Activity," *Journal of Financial Economics* 11, no. 1 (April 1983): 178–179.

countered, however, that Malatesta's failure to find positive combined returns does support the hubris hypothesis.

Roll did not intend the hubris hypothesis to explain all takeovers. He merely proposed that an important human element enters takeovers when individuals are interacting and negotiating the purchase of a company. Management's acquisition of a target may be motivated purely by a desire to maximize stockholder wealth. However, other motives may include a desire to enter a target's industry or to become "the largest firm in the business." The extent to which these motives may play a role will vary from takeover to takeover. It is therefore of some interest that much evidence does support the hubris hypothesis. Surely the questionably high premiums paid for some firms, such as Federated Stores and R.J.R. Nabisco, imply some element of hubris. The fact that Campeau Corporation was forced to declare bankruptcy not long after the acquisition of Federated lends support to the view that it overpaid in the highly leveraged deal.

IMPROVED MANAGEMENT HYPOTHESIS

Some takeovers are motivated by a belief that the acquiring firm's management can better manage the target's resources. The bidder may feel that its management skills are such that the value of the target would rise under its control. This leads the acquirer to pay a value for the target in excess of the target's current stock price.

The improved management argument may have particular validity in cases of large companies making offers for smaller, growing companies. The smaller companies, often led by entrepreneurs, may offer a unique product or service that has sold well and facilitated the rapid growth of the target. As the target grows, however, it requires a very different set of management skills than what proved necessary when it was a smaller business.

The growing enterprise may find that it needs to oversee a much larger distribution network and may have to adopt a very different marketing philosophy. Many of the decisions that a larger firm has to make require a vastly different set of managerial skills than those that resulted in the dramatic growth of the smaller company. The lack of managerial expertise may be a stumbling block in the growing company and may limit its ability to compete in the broader marketplace. These managerial resources are an asset which the larger firm can offer the target.

Little empirical research has been conducted on the importance of this motive. The difficulty is determining which takeovers are motivated solely by this motive. Improved management is usually one of several

---

CASE STUDY: *AMES DEPARTMENT STORES: IMPROVED MANAGEMENT THAT FAILED TO IMPROVE ITS TARGET*

In October 1988, Ames Department Stores acquired the Zayre discount chain of nearly 400 stores for $778 million. Ames, whose operations were concentrated mainly in the New England area, was the nation's fourth largest discount retailer behind K Mart, Wal-Mart, and Target. Ames's management felt it possessed the expertise necessary to turn around the Zayre chain which had been experiencing sagging sales prior to the acquisition. This optimistic belief was based, in part, on Ames's continued growth in sales and profits prior to 1989. Given the seeming similarity of the two chains, it was believed that much of the managerial expertise at Ames would readily transfer to Zayre.

Upon completing the takeover, Ames instituted a number of major changes that included renaming all the Zayre stores Ames and changing the Zayre pricing and advertising policies. For example, Ames reduced the number of weekly circulars that Zayre had previously used for its direct mail marketing. Fashionable clothing, a staple at Zayre's, was replaced by more basic apparel. The strategy failed miserably. What had worked for Ames failed to apply to the Zayre stores. The sales at the acquired stores declined 16 percent after the takeover.[a] The poor performance was also reflected in a reported $228 million loss for the combined firm for the fiscal year ending January 27, 1990 (Figure 4.17). The board of directors suspended the firm's 2 1/2 cent per share dividend which, in turn, was followed by a decline in the stock price. Industry analysts reported that, in addition to the managerial errors cited above, Ames tried to merge the Ames and Zayre computer systems too rapidly. This error resulted in technical problems that caused suppliers to be paid late. Alienated suppliers then refused to sell on credit and demanded cash in advance. This created a liquidity crisis at Ames. The liquidity problems crisis came at a time when Ames was reporting large losses. Firms with large losses are not generally considered to be ideal credit risks by lenders. As of the middle of 1990, Ames was forced to file for bankruptcy protection.

[a]Eric Berg, "Ames Rocky Retailing Marriage," *Wall Street Journal*, April 11, 1990. p. D1.

---

factors in the acquirer's decision to make a bid. It is quite difficult to isolate improved management and to explain its role in the bidding process.

The argument that takeover offers by large companies for smaller, growing companies are motivated, in part, by managerial gains may be reasonable. For large public firms, a takeover may be the most cost efficient way of bringing about a management change. Proxy contests may enable dissident stockholders to oust incumbent management whom they may feel is incompetent. One problem with this process is that corporate democracy is not very egalitarian. It is very costly to use

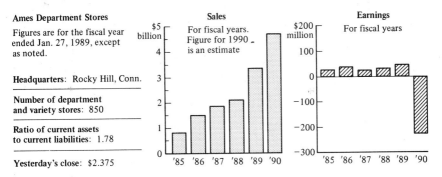

Ames Department Stores Financial Performance

Figure **4.17** Steady sales and sudden losses. (*Source:* The *New York Times*, April 11, 1990, p. D1. Copyright © 1990 by The New York Times Company. Reprinted by permission.)

a proxy fight to replace an incumbent management team. The process is biased in favor of management who may also occupy seats on the board of directors. It is, therefore, very difficult to win a proxy battle. The proxy process will be explained in detail in Chapter 6.

Given that the proxy process is a costly method of replacing management, the hostile tender offer, in certain circumstances, becomes a more reasonable tool of effecting a management change. In other words, if displeased stockholders cannot accomplish a change in management that will increase the value of their investment from within the firm, then it may be more efficient to attempt such a change from outside the company. Failed proxy fights by Coniston Partners seeking to replace the management of Gillette and the proxy battle by Carl Icahn to take over Texaco are examples of the weaknesses of the proxy tool as a way of changing management. If the current management is causing the reduction in stockholder wealth, then a takeover, rather than an internal change, may be the only way to implement a management change. One problem, however, particularly in the examples cited above, is the existence of antitakeover laws that make changes in control more difficult. Another problem occurs when the capital necessary to implement a successful tender offer is not available. In these instances, the proxy fight becomes a more effective alternative.

Tax gains can be important motives for certain takeovers. A target can become more valuable, for example, if it has transferable tax losses that an acquirer can use to offset income. Other sources of gains can be investment tax credits which can also be used to offset income. The area of taxation is so important and detailed that a separate chapter in this book (Chapter 11) is devoted to the tax issues that play a role in takeovers.

SUMMARY

We have seen that there are a wide variety of motives and determinants of mergers and acquisitions. Firms can acquire another firm in hopes of experiencing economic gains. These economic gains may come as a result of economies of scale or scope economies. Some of these gains are reported as motives for horizontal and vertical acquisitions. Other gains may come in the form of financial benefits when a larger firm that resulted from the combination of two or more smaller firms has better access to capital markets. This better access could come in the form of a lower cost of capital. This latter motive has been the subject of much debate in finance. Its importance is still much in dispute.

Another motivation for mergers and acquisitions can take the form of improved management. A bidding firm may be able to pay a premium for a target because of the anticipated gains it will experience when it applies its superior management to the target's business. The bidder, on the other hand, may falsely believe that it can extract higher returns than what the market believes are possible from the target. Hubris, rather than objective analysis, may motivate a takeover. These last two motives are examples of the ever-present human element that permeates takeovers. Sound analysis should not be replaced by the individual motivations of managers. The human element cannot be discounted as an important part of the world of mergers and acquisitions.

REFERENCES

Asquith, Paul. "Merger Bids, Uncertainty and Stockholder Returns." *Journal of Financial Economics 11* (April 1983): 51–83.

Baird, Charles. *Intermediate Microeconomics*. Minneapolis, Minn.: West Publishing Co., 1975.

"BevPak Brings Back the Shine to Steel Cans." *Wall Street Journal*, June 8, 1989.

Bradley, Michael, Anand Desai, and E. Han Kim. "The Rationale Behind Interfirm Tender Offers: Information or Synergy." *Journal of Financial Economics* 11, no. 1 (April 1983): 183–206.

Dodd, P. "Merger Proposals, Managerial Discretion and Stockholder Wealth." *Journal of Financial Economics* 8 (June 1980): 105–138.

Eckbo, Epsen B. "Horizontal Mergers, Collusion and Stockholder Wealth." *Journal of Financial Economics* 11, no. 1 (April 1983): 241–273.

Eger, C. E. "An Empirical Test of the Redistribution Effect of Mergers." *Journal of Financial and Quantitative Analysis* 18 (December 1983): 547–572.

Elger, P., and J. Clark. "Merger Types and Shareholder Returns." *Financial Management* (Summer 1980): 66–72.

Fleisher, Arthur, Jr., Geoffrey C. Hazard, Jr., and Miriam Z. Klipper. *Board Games: The Changing Shape of Corporate America*. Boston: Little, Brown, 1988.

Galais, D., and R.. W. Masulis. "The Option Pricing Model and the Risk Factor of Stock." *Journal of Financial Economics* (January/ March 1976): 53–82.

Gaughan, Patrick A. "Financial Deregulation, Banking Mergers and the Impact on Regional Businesses." Proceedings of the Pacific Northwest Regional Economic Conference, University of Washington, Spring 1988.

Gort, Michael. "Diversification, Mergers and Profits." In *The Corporate Merger*. Chicago: University of Chicago Press, 1974.

Guerin-Calvert, Margaret E. "Airline Computer Reservation Systems." In *The Antitrust Revolution*. Glenview, Ill.: Scott, Foresman and Co., 1989, pp. 338–363.

Harberger, Arnold C. "Three Basic Postulates for Applied Welfare Economics." *Journal of Economic Literature* 9, no. 3 (September 1971): 785–797.

Higgins, Robert C., and Lawrence C. Schall. "Corporate Bankruptcy and Conglomerate Mergers." *Journal of Finance* 30 (March 1975): 93–113.

"Intergroup Sees Profits in Drugs." *New York Times*, June 11, 1990, p. D8.

Jensen, Michael, and Richard Ruback. "The Market for Corporate Control: The Scientific Evidence." *Journal of Financial Economics* 11, no. 1-4 (April 1983): 5–50.

Johnson, Robert. "Full Service Just Didn't Fly with Public, Travel Agents." *Wall Street Journal*, June 11, 1987, p. 22.

Kolb, Robert. *Principles of Finance*. Glenview, Ill.: Scott, Foresman and Co., 1988.

Koutsoyianis, A. *Modern Microeconomics*. New York: John Wiley and Sons, 1975.

Levy, Haim, and Marshall Sarnat. "Diversification, Portfolio Analysis and the Uneasy Case for Conglomerate Mergers." *Journal of Finance* 25 (September 1970): 795–802.

Lewellen, W. G. "A Pure Rationale for the Conglomerate Merger." *Journal of Finance* (May 1971).

McClosky, Donald M. *The Applied Theory of Price*. New York: Macmillan Publishing Co., 1982.

Malatesta, Paul. "Wealth Effects of Merger Activity." *Journal of Financial Economics* 11, no. 1 (April 1983): 178–179.

Mester, Loretta J. "Efficient Product of Financial Services: Scale and Scope Economies." Federal Reserve Bank of Philadelphia, January/February 1987, pp. 15–25.

Miller, Morton, and Franco Modigliani. "Dividend Policy, Growth and the Valuation of Shares." *Journal of Business* 34 (October 1961): 411–433.

Morch, Randall, Andrei Shleifer, and Robert W. Vishny. "Do Managerial Objectives Drive Bad Acquisitions?" *Journal of Finance* 45, no. 1 (March 1990): 31–48.

"National Intergroup Chairman to Resign After Firm Sheds All Units But Fox Meyer." *Wall Street Journal*, June 6, 1990, p. A3.

O'Rourke, Tracy. "Postmerger Integration." In Richard S. Bibler, ed. *The Arthur Young Management Guide to Mergers and Acquisitions*. New York: John Wiley and Sons, 1989, pp. 227–228.

Porter, Michael. *Competitive Advantage*. New York: Free Press, 1985.

Ravenscraft, David J., and Frederick M. Scherer. "Mergers and Managerial Performance." In *Knights, Raiders and Targets*, edited by John Coffee, Louis Lowenstein, and Susan Rose Ackerman. New York: Oxford University Press, pp. 194–210.

Ravenscraft, David J., and Frederick M. Scherer. *Mergers, Sell-Offs and Economic Efficiency*. Washington D.C.: Brookings Institution, 1987, p. 151.

Roll, Richard. "The Hubris Hypothesis of Corporate Takeovers." *Journal of Business* 59, no. 2 (April 1986): 197–216.

Ross, Stephen. "The Determination of Financial Structure: The Incentive Signaling Approach." *Bell Journal of Economics* (Spring 1977): 23–40.

Schipper, Katherine, and Rex Thompson. "The Value of Merger Activity." *Journal of Financial Economics* 11, no. 1–4 (April 1983): 85–119.

Stillman, R. S. "Examining Antitrust Policy Towards Mergers." *Journal of Financial Economics* 11, no. 1 (April 1983): 225–240.

Van Horne, James C. *Financial Management and Policy*. Englewood Cliffs, N.J.: Prentice-Hall, 1989, pp. 327–338.

Viscone, Jerry A., and Gordon S. Roberts. *Contemporary Financial Management*. Columbus, Ohio: Merrill Publishing Co., 1987.

Wansley, James, William Lane, and Ho Yang. "Abnormal Returns to Acquired Firms by Type of Acquisition and Method of Payment." *Financial Management* (Autumn 1983): 16–22.

Williamson, Oliver E. *Antitrust Economics*. Oxford: Basil Blackwell, 1987.

Williamson, Oliver E. "Economies As an Antitrust Defense." *American Economic Review* (March 1968).

Chapter
5

Antitakeover Measures

Corporate takeovers reached new levels of hostility during the 1980s. This heightened bellicosity was accompanied by many innovations in the art of corporate takeovers. Although hostile takeover tactics advanced, the methods of corporate defense were slower to develop. As a result of the increased application of financial resources by threatened corporations, however, antitakeover defenses became quite elaborate and more difficult to penetrate. By the end of the 1980s, the art of antitakeover defenses became very sophisticated. Major investment banks organized teams of defense specialists who worked with managements of larger corporations to erect formidable defenses that might counter the increasingly aggressive raiders of the fourth merger wave. One investment bank, Goldman Sachs, specialized in defense. After installing the various defenses, teams of investment bankers, along with their law firm counterparts, stood ready to be dispatched in the heat of battle to advise the target's management on the proper actions to take to thwart the bidder.

The array of antitakeover defenses can be divided into two categories: preventative and active measures. Preventative measures are designed to reduce the likelihood of a financially successful hostile takeover, whereas active measures are employed after a hostile bid has been attempted.

This chapter describes the more frequently used categories of defenses. The impact of these measures on shareholder wealth, a highly controversial topic, is explored in detail. Opponents of these measures contend that they entrench management and reduce the value of stockholders' investment. They see the activities of raiders as an element that seeks to keep management "honest." Managers who feel threatened by raiders, they contend, will manage the firm more effectively which will, in turn, result in higher stock values. Proponents of the use of antitakeover defenses contend that they prevent the actions of the hostile raiders who have no long-term interest in the value of the corporation, but merely are speculators seeking to extract a short-term gain while sacrificing the future of the company that may have taken decades to build. They are not reluctant to take actions that will reduce the rights of such short-term shareholders since they feel that they are not equal, in their eyes, to long-term shareholders and other *stakeholders*, such as employees and local communities. The evidence on the shareholder wealth effects does not, however, provide a consensus view, leaving the issue somewhat unresolved. Some studies purport to show clear adverse shareholder wealth effects, while others fail to detect an adverse impact on the shareholders' position. The reader will be presented with the results of most of the major studies in this field and can make an independent judgment.

PREVENTATIVE ANTITAKEOVER MEASURES

Preventative antitakeover measures are becoming an increasingly important part of corporate America. Most Fortune 500 companies have considered and developed a plan of defense in the event the company should become the target of a hostile bid. Most of these plans are directed at reducing the value that a bidder can find in the firm. The value-enhancing characteristics of a target are outlined in Chapter 14. These include characteristics such as high and steady cash flows, low debt levels, and low stock price relative to the value of the firm's assets. The presence of these factors may make a firm vulnerable to a takeover. Therefore, many preventative measures are designed to alter these characteristics of the firm in advance, or upon completion of a hostile takeover, so that the financial incentive a raider might have to acquire the target is significantly reduced. In effect, the installation of preventative measures is an exercise in wall building. Higher and more resistant walls need to be continually designed and installed since the raiders, and their investment banking and legal advisers, devote their energies to designing ways of scaling these defenses.

Among the preventative measures that are discussed in this chapter are:

Poison pills: These are securities issued by a potential target to make the firm less valuable in the eyes of a hostile bidder. Both flip-over and flip-in poison pills are described.

Corporate charter amendments: The target corporation can enact various amendments in its corporate charter which will make it more difficult for a hostile acquirer to bring about a change in managerial control of the target. These corporate charter changes are sometimes referred to as *shark repellents*. Some of the amendments which are discussed are supermajority provisions; staggered boards; fair price provisions; and dual capitalizations.

Golden parachutes: The attractive severance agreements sometimes offered to top management can be used as a preventative anti-takeover measure. Alone, they will not prevent a takeover. However, they may help enhance the effect of some of the above and create a disincentive to acquire the target.

Brown Foreman Versus Lenox Corporation— First-Generation Poison Pills

Poison pills were invented by the famous takeover lawyer, Martin Lipton, who used them in 1982 to defend El Paso Electric against General American Oil and again in 1983 during the Brown Foreman versus Lenox takeover contest. Brown Foreman was the fourth largest distiller in the United States, marketing such name brands as Jack Daniels whiskey, Martel cognac, and Korbel champagne and generating annual sales of $900 million. Lenox was a major producer of china. Lenox's shares were trading at around $60 per share on the New York Stock Exchange. Brown Foreman believed that Lenox's stock was undervalued and offered $87 a share for each share of Lenox. This price was more than 20 times the previous year's per share earnings of $4.13. Such an attractive offer is very difficult to defeat.

Martin Lipton suggested that Lenox offer each stockholder preferred shares which would be convertible into 40 shares of Brown Foreman stock if Brown Foreman took over Lenox. These convertible shares would be an effective antitakeover device because, if converted, they would seriously dilute the Brown family's 60 percent share ownership position. These first-generation poison pills, however, involved a number of problems. First, they were more difficult to redeem than their modern counterparts, and so they were more cumbersome to use. Second, they had an immediate, adverse impact on the balance sheet.

Second-Generation Poison Pills—FLIP-OVER Rights

Poison pills did not become popular until late 1985 when their developer, Lipton, perfected them. The new pills did not involve the issuance of preferred stock so that, by being easier to use, the pills would be more effective. They would also eliminate any adverse impact which an issue of preferred stock might have on the balance sheet. Preferred stock is considered to be fixed income security by financial analysts. An increase in the amount of preferred stock would be generally interpreted as increased financial leverage and risk.

The perfected pills came in the form of rights offerings that allowed the holders to buy stock in the acquiring firm at a low price. *Rights* are a form of call option issued by the corporation, entitling the holders to purchase a certain amount of stock for a particular price during a specified time period. The rights certificates used in modern poison pills are distributed after a triggering event. A typical triggering event would be one of the following:

1. An acquisition of 20 percent of the outstanding stock by any individual, partnership, or corporation.
2. A tender offer for 30 percent or more of the target corporation's outstanding stock.

The board of directors can usually disarm the rights by redeeming them for a small fee. A typical right has a lifetime of 10 years. They cannot trade independently, which leaves open the possibility of friendly mergers. Flip-over poison pills seemed to be a most potent defense until they were effectively overcome in the takeover of the Crown Zellerbach Corporation by the Anglo-French financier Sir James Goldsmith.

Goldsmith Versus Crown Zellerbach Corporation

Crown Zellerbach was a San Francisco-based forest products company with substantial holdings of forest-related assets. James Goldsmith saw great value in Crown Zellerbach's assets at a time when the market failed to reflect its worth. "I do believe in forests. I do believe in forest lands. Everybody says they are a disaster. But they're still making profits. And forest lands will one day be as valuable as they were."[1]

Crown Zellerbach's chairman, William T. Creason, concerned about

---

[1] Moira Johnston, *Takeover* (New York: Penguin Books, 1986), p. 55.

the company's vulnerability to a takeover from a raider such as Goldsmith, adopted an elaborate set of antitakeover defenses designed to maintain the company's independence. These measures were as follows. (Use of the antitakeover measures, other than poison pills, will be described separately later in this chapter.)

1. *Formation of a defensive team.* Crown Zellerbach formed a well-rounded defensive team that included the prestigious investment bank Salomon Brothers as well as attorney Martin Lipton. Crown Zellerbach also included the publicist Gershon Kekst, which highlights the important role public relations can play in takeover contests.

2. *Updating of the stockholders lists.* The corporation updated its stockholders lists so that if a takeover battle ensued, it would be in a position to quickly contact important institutional and individual investors.

3. *Staggering the board of directors.* The board of directors elections were staggered to make it more difficult to take control of the board.

4. *Enactment of the anti-greenmail amendment.* An anti-greenmail amendment was enacted in Crown Zellerbach's corporate charter to preempt the possibility that a raider would make a bid in the hope of attracting greenmail compensation.

5. *Addition of a supermajority provision.* This alteration of the corporate charter required a two-thirds majority vote on future bylaw changes.

6. *Issuance of a poison pill.* Crown Zellerbach's poison pill allowed stockholders to buy $200 worth of stock in the merged concern for $100. This significant discount for current Crown Zellerbach stockholders would make the company less valuable. As noted above, the pill was issued in the form of rights that were activated when either (1) an acquirer bought 20 percent of Crown Zellerbach's stock; or (2) an acquirer made a tender offer for 30 percent of Crown Zellerbach stock. The rights became *exercisable* after a bidder bought 100 percent of the company's stock.

The rights were thought to be such a formidable obstacle to a raider that no bidder would trigger them. Because of the large financial incentives involved, however, the market developed a means of evading the effects of the defenses. This innovative tactic was first developed by the team representing Sir James Goldsmith.

Designed to enable Crown to still do a deal with a favored suitor, the rights, trading independently of the shares, could be redeemed or cancelled by the board by buying them back from shareholders for 50 cents each. But once a raider had acquired 20 percent of Crown's stock, the rights could no longer be redeemed and would not expire for 10 years.

The pill's consequences were so devastating, it was hoped he would hold short of 20 percent. But what if he kept buying? Would the pill be any defense against his gaining control on the open market? Marty Lipton warned: "The plan wouldn't prevent takeovers; it would have no effect on a raider who was willing to acquire control and not obtain 100 percent ownership until after the rights expired."[2]

Goldsmith's tactic entailed buying just over 50 percent of Crown Zellerbach stock. He bought this stock gradually but stopped purchasing once he had a controlling interest in the company. The rights were issued when Goldsmith bought more than 20 percent, but they never became exercisable since he didn't buy 100 percent.

The ironic part of this takeover was that Goldsmith used Crown Zellerbach's poison pill against Crown Zellerbach. After the rights were issued, the company found it more difficult to pursue other options such as a friendly bidder, sometimes referred to as a white knight. The fact that these wealth-reducing rights were outstanding lowered the interest of potential white knights. Ironically, this made Crown Zellerbach more vulnerable. Crown Zellerbach's management, after a protracted but futile struggle, was forced to agree to a takeover by Goldsmith.

Household International and the Legality of Poison Pills

Various legal challenges have been made to the modern versions of poison pills. One such challenge involved the poison pills issued by Household International Corporation. A lawsuit was brought by a dissident director of Household International, and he was represented by the famous takeover lawyer, Joseph Flom. Household International had been able to ward off a takeover bid through the use of a poison pill defense. In a November 1985 ruling in the Delaware Supreme Court, however, the court upheld the legality of poison pills. The court's position was that the pills did not necessarily keep bidders away; rather, they gave target corporations the opportunity to seek higher bids.

Having been upheld in the courts, 200 large corporations rushed to adopt their own poison pill defenses. In contrast, there had been

---

[2] Ibid., p. 121.

CASE STUDY: *DYSON–KISSNER–MORAN VERSUS HOUSEHOLD INTERNATIONAL*

Household International Inc. was a large financial services company located in Prospect Heights, Illinois. While its main operations were in the financial services industry, it possessed diversified holdings that included Household Finance, National Car Rental as well as a retail food business. John Moran, one of the largest shareholders as well as director of Household, planned to make a bid to take over Household through his New York-based investment company, Dyson–Kissner–Moran.

Dyson–Kissner–Moran was estimated to be 1 percent the size of the larger Household International. It never made a hostile bid for Household, but it did engage in negotiations to buy the company. The other directors, unwilling to allow Household International to be acquired by Moran's investment company, decided to try to prevent the acquisition by adopting a poison pill that would be activated when a bidder bought more than 20 percent of Household. Moran felt that management and the directors adopted the pill to preserve their own positions. He therefore sued Household on August 17, 1984, in a Delaware court where Household was incorporated. He lost at the Chancery Court level but appealed to the Delaware Supreme Court. In November 1985, however, the Delaware Supreme Court upheld the legality of Household's poison pill.

The Household decision is extremely important because it helps establish the legality of poison pills as an antitakeover defense. Since so many corporations are incorporated in Delaware, this decision has had great impact.[a]

[a] Moira Johnston, *Takeover* (New York: Penguin Books, 1986), p. 55.

---

only 37 new pills in 1985. By the end of 1986, approximately 400 corporations had adopted poison pills, and by January 1988, 30 percent of the Fortune 500 companies had adopted them.

Flip-in Poison Pills

Flip-in poison pills were an innovation designed to deal with the problem of a bidder that was not trying to take 100 percent control of the target. With the flip-over provisions, a bidder could avoid the impact of the pill simply by not buying 100 percent of the target.

Flip-in provisions allow holders of rights to acquire stock in the target as opposed to *flip-over* rights, which allow holders to acquire stock in the acquirer. The flip-in rights were designed to dilute the target company regardless of whether the bidder merged the target into his company. They can be effective in dealing with raiders who seek to acquire a controlling influence in a target while not even acquiring majority control. Controlling ownership can often be achieved with stockholdings less than 51 percent. This is particularly true of widely held corporations where most stockholders have a small percentage of the outstanding stock. The presence of flip-in rights makes such controlling acquisitions very expensive.

Recent Court Rulings Limiting the Use of Poison Pills

Recent court rulings have limited the effectiveness of poison pills as an antitakeover defense. These rulings are described below.

1. *Maxwell* v. *Macmillan, 1988*.   British publisher Robert Maxwell successfully challenged Macmillan's poison pill defense. A Delaware court ruled that Macmillan's poison pill defense unfairly discriminated against Maxwell's offer for the New York publishing firm. The court ruled that the poison pill should be used to promote an *auction*. Macmillan's pill, the court ruled, prevented an effective auction.[3]

2. *Rales* v. *Interco, 1988*.   A Delaware court reached a similar decision when it ruled that Interco's poison pill unfairly favored Interco's own recapitalization plan while discriminating against Rales tender offer. (This case is discussed later in this chapter.)[4]

3. *Bank of New York* v. *Irving Trust, 1988*.   A New York State court ruled that Irving Trust's poison pill unfairly discriminated against the Bank of New York's bid for Irving. The ruling didn't totally strike down Irving's pill, but only those provisions that did not allow the Bank of New York, which held 4.9 percent of Irving at the time of ruling, also to buy Irving shares at a discounted price in the event an acquirer bought a 20 percent stake. The court ruled that, if other shareholders could buy shares at half price, so could the Bank of New York.[5]

Poison Puts

Poison puts are a unique variation on the poison pill theme. They involve an issuance of bonds that contain a *put option* exercisable only in the event an unfriendly takeover occurs. A put option allows the

---

[3] "Maxwell of Britain Wins a Ruling in Battle to Take Over Macmillan," *New York Times*, July 1988.

[4] "Interco Defense Against Rales Is Struck Down," *Wall Street Journal*, November 2, 1988.

[5] "The Poison Pill Takes a Beating," *Wall Street Journal*, November 14, 1988, p. D2.

holder to sell a particular security to another individual or firm during a certain time period and for a specific price.

The issuing firm hopes that the holders' cashing of the bonds, by creating large cash demands for the merged firm, will make the takeover prospect most unattractive. If the acquiring firm can convince bond-holders, however, not to redeem their bonds, these bond sales can be avoided. In addition, if the bonds are offered at higher than prevailing interest rates, the likelihood of redemption will not be as high. The existence of poison puts does not insure that a firm will not be a target of an unwanted bid. The July 1990 offer of $410 million by Ratners Group P.L.C., the world's largest jewelry chain, for Kay Jewelers, Inc. is an example.[6] Under the terms of the offer, Ratners would pay Kay $17 per share, which was a $6 per share premium. The bid, however, was made contingent on Kay's bondholders accepting 75 cents on the dollar for their bonds. This is ironic in light of the fact that Kay's bondholders had the right to put their bonds back to the company at 100 cents on the dollar. Ratners rationalized the bond component of their offer by pointing out that, at the time of the bid, the bonds were trading at 70 cents on the dollar and they had earlier traded as low as 45 cents on the dollar. Therefore, Ratners felt that bondholders were receiving a "premium." Bondholders, on the other hand, were dissatisfied and felt they were only being offered 75 percent of the amount they had lent the firm.

Impact on Stock Prices

Several studies have examined the impact of poison pill provisions on stock prices. A study by Paul Malatesta and Ralph Walking considered what effect the announcement of the adoption of a poison pill had on 132 firms between 1982 and 1986.[7] They found that poison pill defenses appeared to reduce stockholder wealth and that, on the average, the firm that announced poison pill defenses received abnormal negative stock returns on the announcement date. When these firms abandoned their poison pill plans, they showed abnormal positive returns.

The findings of Malatesta and Walking were confirmed by Michael Ryngaert in his study of 380 firms that had adopted poison pill defen-

---

[6] Anise Wallace, "Bid for Kay Stirs Bondholders Ire," *New York Times*, July 12, 1990, p. D2.

[7] Paul H. Malatesta and Ralph A. Walking, "Poison Pills Securities: Stockholder Wealth, Profitability and Ownership Structure," *Journal of Financial Economics* 20, no. 1/2 (January/March 1988): 347–376.

ses.[8] He found significant stock price declines from firms that adopted pill defenses and that were perceived as takeover targets. Ryngaert also analyzed the impact on the target firm's stock of legal challenges to the pill defense. He noted negative excess stock returns in 15 of 18 pro-management court decisions (upholding the legality of the pill) and positive excess returns in 6 of 11 pro-acquirer decisions (invalidating the pill). Ryngaert's research also touched on the effectiveness of poison pills as an antitakeover defense. He found that hostile bids are more likely to be defeated by firms that have a poison pill in place. Thirty-one percent of the pill-protected firms remained independent after receiving unsolicited bids, compared to 15.78 percent for a control group of nonpill-protected firms that also received unsolicited bids. Moreover, in 51.8 percent of the unsolicited bids, pill-protected firms received increased bids, which Ryngaert attributes to the presence of the pill defense. Another study, conducted by the Securities and Exchange Commission, reported negative returns equal to -1 percent for 37 pill plans.[9] A privately conducted study by the investment bank of Kidder Peabody failed to find that poison pill adoptions had an impact on stock prices.[10] The methodology of the Kidder, Peabody study, however, has been criticized and its findings are not considered reliable.

The consensus of the research is that poison pill defenses tend to be associated with negative excess returns to the target's stock. We must remember, however, that these studies focus on a narrow time period around the date when the adoption of the pill plan was announced. Pill-protected firms that ultimately get acquired may exhibit higher returns as a result of the pill defense. These higher premiums were not reflected in this body of research.

Impact of Poison Pills on Takeover Premiums   One of the more frequently cited studies concerning the impact of poison pills on takeover premiums is the study by Georgeson and Company, a large proxy solicitation firm. In a study released in March 1988, the firm showed that companies protected by poison pills received 69 percent higher premiums in takeover contests than unprotected companies. The study

---

[8] Michael Ryngaert, "The Effects of Poison Pill Securities on Stockholder Wealth" 20 (January/March 1988): 377–417.

[9] Securities and Exchange Commission, Office of the Chief Economist, "The Economics of Poison Pills," March 1986.

[10] Kidder, Peabody and Company, "The Impact of the Adoption of Stockholder Rights Plans on Stock Prices," June 1986.

compared the premiums paid to pill-protected companies with those without this protection. Protected corporations in the Georgeson sample received premiums that were 78.5 percent above where the company's stock was trading six months before the contest. Nonprotected corporations received 56.7 percent premiums.

The Georgeson study contradicts the widely held belief that poison pills are bad for stockholders. Some of the studies cited above have demonstrated that poison pills cause stock prices to decline, presumably because they are more difficult takeover targets. Therefore, there is a lower likelihood that they will be the object of a takeover bid. On the other hand, the Georgeson study implies that, in the event of a bid, the premium will be higher.

Corporate Charter Amendments

Changes in the corporate charter are common antitakeover devices. The extent to which they can be implemented depends on state laws, which vary among states. Corporate charter changes generally require shareholder approval. The vast majority of antitakeover charter amendments are approved. Only in extreme cases of poor management performance do stockholders actively resist antitakeover amendments. In part, this is a result of the fact that management is generally much more organized in its lobbying efforts than those shareholders who may oppose the proposed charter changes. Another important reason why shareholders tend to approve these amendments is that the majority of shareholders in large U.S. corporations are institutions which have, in the past, been known to side with management. There is evidence that this tendency is starting to change somewhat. Moreover, institutions as a whole are not unified in their support of management. Brickley, Lease, and Smith point out that certain types of institutional investors, such as banks, insurance companies, and trusts, are more likely to vote in favor of management's proposals than other institutions, such as mutual funds, public pension funds, endowments, and foundations.[11] They feel that the latter category of investors is more independent of management in that they do not generally derive income from the lines of business controlled by management. When the charter amendment proposal clearly reduces shareholder wealth, institutions in general are more clearly found to be in opposition to the amendment. The process

---

[11] James Brickley, Ronald Lease, and Clifford Smith, "Ownership Structure and Voting on Antitakeover Amendments," *Journal of Financial Economics* 20, no. 1/2 (January/March 1988):267–292.

of proxy approval of shareholder amendments will be discussed in detail in Chapter 6.

Some of the more common antitakeover corporate charter changes are:

1. Staggered terms of the board of directors.
2. Supermajority provisions.
3. Fair price provisions.
4. Dual capitalizations.

Staggered Terms of the Board of Directors   The board of directors is a body of individuals who have been elected by the stockholders to oversee the actions of management as well as to recommend actions to stockholders. They are part-time positions that provide compensation for the members in the form of either an annual stipend or a fee for each meeting attended. Most large corporations have boards composed of notable figures who may be CEOs of other large corporations. For many directors, the position is considered prestigious and is not accepted merely for its monetary compensation. Many directors of Fortune 500 companies have annual incomes far greater than the income they receive from their directorships.

The board of directors appoints management who, in turn, manage the day-to-day operations of the corporation. The directors are generally not aware of the minutiae of the company's daily workings and tend to rely on management for this information. They often provide an overall direction to the corporation and decide on major issues and proposed changes. Many boards are composed of the inside board and the outside board. The inside board is made up of members of management, whereas the outside board members are those directors who do not have direct managerial responsibilities for the corporation's day-to-day operations. One study showed that, on average, boards of public companies contain 13 directors, 9 of whom are outside directors.[12]

Many issues, such as a bid to buy the corporation, are usually required to be brought by management before the board of directors. The board sets forth requirements and may recommend that the particular issue be taken to the stockholders for voting approval. In some instances stockholders have sued the corporation to require the board of directors to bring all bids before stockholders for their consideration. This occurred, for example, when several Gillette stockholders sued Gillette in 1987.

---

[12] Jay W. Lorsch, *Pawns or Potentates* (Boston: Harvard Business School Press, 1989), p. 19.

If stockholders want to change the management of a corporation, they may have to change the board of directors. For example, if a hostile bidder takes control of a company, he may want to replace management with others who would run the company in the manner he sees fit. The bidder may want to make himself chief executive of the target corporation. If he has the requisite number of votes and is not impeded by any antitakeover defenses that limit his ability to hold elections and vote in new directors, he may elect new directors. These new directors will appoint new management according to the bidder's preferences. Normally, the managers are selected by means of a majority vote of the board of directors.

Some common stock have cumulative voting rights associated with ownership. That is, a share of stock comes with one vote for each director position available. Cumulative voting allows stockholders the right to pool their votes so that all the votes that could have been used to vote for each director in the election can be applied to one or a few of the director seats. This provides significant stockholders with the power to place their representatives on the board to advocate their positions. Most sizable, publicly held companies that are traded on the large organized exchanges, however, do not have cumulative voting. Bhagat and Brickley reported in their 1984 study that 24 percent of the 383 New York Stock Exchange firms in their sample had cumulative voting.[13]

It is also not considered unusual to have a corporation give membership on the board of directors to a union or bank in return for wage concessions or an easement of the provisions of a loan agreement. The policy of conceding seats on the board took an unusual turn in 1988 when, in return for voting in favor of management in their proxy fight with Carl Icahn, the Texaco Corporation was reported to have reserved a seat on Texaco's board for a representative of institutional investors. The votes of institutional investors played a critical role in deciding the proxy fight defeating Icahn in the proxy contest.

The staggered board defense staggers the terms of the board of directors so that only a few of the directors can be elected during any given year. This is very important in a takeover battle since the incumbent board may be made up of members who are sympathetic to current management. Indeed, they may also contain members of management. Director approval is desirable because directors may recommend the merger to stockholders, or they may decide that the offer is not worthy

---

[13] S. Bhagat and J. A. Brickley, "Cumulative Voting: The Value of Minority Shareholder Rights," *Journal of Law and Economics* 27 (October 1984):339–366.

of a stockholder vote. When a bidder has already bought majority control, the staggered board may prevent him from electing managers who will pursue his goals for the corporation such as the sale of assets to pay down the debt he may have incurred in the acquisition process.

Typical Staggered Board Provision   A staggered board provision comes in the form of an amendment of the corporate charter. The ability to amend the corporate charter is dictated by the prevailing state laws. A typical staggered board provision provides for one-third of the board to be elected each year for a three-year term. This type of board is sometimes referred to as a *classified board*. In contrast, every member of the nonclassified board comes up for election at each annual meeting. A good analogy to these boards is the United States legislature. Senate elections are similar to a classified board in that all U.S. senators are not elected each year; the House of Representatives is similar to a nonclassified board.

Staggered elections extend the amount of time a bidder will have to wait before she can attain majority representation on the board. This reduces the bidder's ability to enact important changes in the direction of the corporation. Given the time cost of money, an acquirer may decide that she may not want to wait two years to get control of a target.

The Delaware Law and the Removal of Directors   As discussed in Chapter 3, the laws of the state of Delaware are probably the most important of all state laws, given the large number of corporations that have incorporated in this state. The Delaware law stipulates the necessary conditions for removing directors. These conditions vary depending on whether the board is a classified or nonclassified board. According to the Delaware law, classified board members cannot be removed before their term expires. Nonclassified board members, however, can be removed at any time by a majority stockholder vote.

Staggered Board Research   In DeAngelo and Rice's study of the impact of antitakeover amendments on stockholder wealth, the sample chosen consisted of 100 different firms, of which 53 included staggered boards.[14] This study demonstrated that the passage of antitakeover charter amendments yielded negative returns. While their analysis

---

[14] Harry DeAngelo and Eugene Rice, "Antitakeover Charter Amendments, and Stockholder Wealth," *Journal of Financial Economics* 11 (1983):329–360.

applied to other forms of antitakeover amendments, staggered boards made up a significant percentage of the amendments considered.

One drawback of the DeAngelo and Rice study is that their results showed relatively low *t*-statistics. The *t*-statistic allows the analyst using regression analysis to test whether certain explanatory variables influence the dependent variable to make a judgment regarding whether there is a certain degree of confidence in the functional relationship found in the analysis. Low *t*-statistics imply that we may not be very confident of the strength of the functional relationship analyzed.

Richard Ruback also failed to find a statistically significant relationship between a negative stock price effect and staggered board provisions.[15] Although his research showed a negative 1 percent decline in stock prices resulting from passage of staggered board provisions, these results were not statistically significant. The conclusion we must draw from this research is that there may be a negative impact on stock prices and stockholder wealth from the passage of staggered board provisions. Insofar as this relationship might exist, however, it seems to be relatively weak.

Supermajority Provisions A corporation's charter dictates the number of voting shares needed to amend the corporate charter or to approve important issues such as mergers. Other transactions that may require stockholder approval are corporate liquidation, lease of important assets, sale of the company, or transactions with interested parties or substantial shareholders. The definition of a substantial shareholder may vary, but it most often means a stockholder with more than 5 to 10 percent of the company's outstanding shares.

A supermajority provision provides for a higher than majority vote to approve a merger—typically, 80 percent or two-thirds approval. The more extreme versions of these provisions require a 95 percent majority. These provisions can be most effective when management, or other groups that tend to be very supportive of management on issues such as mergers, hold a sufficient amount of stock to make approval of a merger difficult. For example, if management and an employee stock ownership plan hold 22 percent of the outstanding stock and the corporation's charter requires 80 percent approval for mergers, then it will be very difficult to complete a merger if the 22 percent do not approve.

Supermajority provisions generally contain escape clauses which allow the corporation to waive or cancel the supermajority provision. The most common escape clause provides that the supermajority pro-

---
[15] Richard Ruback, "An Overview of Takeover Defenses," In *Mergers and Acquisitions*, edited by Alan J. Auerbach (Chicago: National Bureau of Economic Research, University of Chicago Press, 1987), pp. 49–67.

visions do not affect mergers that are approved by the board of directors or mergers with a subsidiary. Most of these escape clauses are carefully worded so that the members of the board of directors who are interested parties cannot vote with the rest of the board on related issues. An example of the interested party qualification would be the raider who holds 12 percent of a target company's stock which has allowed him to command one or more seats on the board of directors. The escape clause would prevent this raider from exercising his votes on issues of approving a merger offer.

The state corporation laws determine the ability of the corporation to implement supermajority provisions. States vary in the extent to which they allow corporations to enact supermajority provisions. The states that allow these provisions are discussed in Chapter 3. Supermajority provisions are most frequently used in conjunction with other antitakeover corporate charter changes. Corporations commonly enact supermajority provisions after they have put other antitakeover charter amendments into place. If the supermajority provisions require a supermajority to amend the corporate charter, it is more difficult for a raider to erase the other antitakeover provisions once the supermajority provision is in place. Supermajority provisions are a more effective defense against partial offers. Offers for 100 percent of the target tend to negate the effects of most supermajority provisions. Exceptions can occur when certain groups loyal to the target hold a percentage greater than the difference between 100 percent and the supermajority threshold.

Supermajority Provision Research   Several major studies of antitakeover amendments have included supermajority provisions. The DeAngelo and Rice study[16] and the Linn and McConnell study,[17] both conducted in 1983, failed to find significant negative price effects for the various antitakeover amendments considered. These results are somewhat contradicted, however, by a study by Gregg Jarrell and Annette Poulson (1986) who point out that these other studies considered only the earlier versions of supermajority provisions which do not include an escape clause.[18] They found that the later supermajority

---

[16] DeAngelo and Rice, "Antitakeover Charter Amendments and Stockholder Wealth," pp. 275–300.

[17] Scott C. Linn and John J. McConnell, "An Empirical Investigation of the Impact of Antitakeover Amendments on Common Stock Prices," *Journal of Financial Economics* 11 (April 1983): 361–399.

[18] Gregg A. Jarrell and Annette B. Poulson, "Shark Repellents and Stock Prices: The Effects of Antitakeover Amendments Since 1980," *Journal of Financial Economics*, 19, no. 1 (September 1987).

provisions, which included such escape clauses, were associated with a statistically significant negative 5 percent return. On the other hand, those supermajority provisions without escape clauses did not show significant negative returns.

A study by John Pound shed light on the effectiveness of classified boards and supermajority provisions. He examined two samples of 100 firms each; one group had supermajority provisions and classified boards while the control group had neither. His results showed that the frequency of takeovers was 28 percent for the group with the antitakeover amendments in place but 38 percent for the nonprotected control group.[19]

Fair Price Provisions   A fair price provision is a modification of a corporation's charter which requires the acquirer to pay minority shareholders at least a fair market price for the company's stock. This can be stated in the form of a certain price or in terms of the company's price–earnings ratio. That is, it can be expressed as a multiple of the company's earnings per share. The P/E multiple chosen is usually derived from the firm's historical P/E ratio or is based on a combination of the firm's and the industry's P/E ratio. Fair price provisions are usually activated when a bidder makes an offer. When the fair price provision is expressed in terms of a specific price, it usually states that stockholders must receive at least the maximum price paid by the acquirer when he bought his holdings.

Many state corporation laws already include fair price provisions. Fair price amendments to a corporation's charter augment the fair price provisions of the state's laws. In states where fair price provisions exist, corporate fair price provisions usually provide for higher prices for stockholders in merger offers. The target corporation can waive most fair price provisions. For the fair price provision to be rendered not applicable, it is usually necessary that there be a 95 percent majority and approval of the board of directors. Fair price provisions are not as common as some of the other antitakeover charter amendments, such as supermajority provisions and staggered boards. Approximately 35 percent of the firms that have implemented antitakeover charter amendments have fair price provisions.

Fair Price Provisions and Two-Tiered Tender Offers   Fair price provisions are most useful when the target firm is the object of a two-

---

[19] John Pound, "The Effectiveness of Antitakeover Amendments on Takeover Activity," *Journal of Law and Economics* 30 (October 1987):353–367.

tiered tender offer. In such an offer, a bidder has made an offer for 51 percent of the target at one price and with one set of conditions such as all cash. (While it may make most sense to establish clear control through a 51 percent purchase offer, not all two-tiered bids include a 51 percent first-step purchase offer.) The purchase of 51 percent of the first tier establishes control. The second tier is less valuable. This bidder, therefore, will often offer a lower price for these shares as well as less attractive terms such as compensation in the form of securities whose value may be open to interpretation.

The two-tiered offer is designed to give the target company stockholders an incentive to tender early so as to be part of the first tier. Stockholders may tender and have their stock accepted on a pro rata basis. This means they would receive a blended combination of the first and second tier prices and terms. A fair price provision could force the bidder to provide those in the second tier with the same prices and terms as those in the first tier. The existence of a fair price provision is a disincentive for a bidder to initiate a two-tiered offer. This is one reason why the two-tiered offer has become less popular.

Although the fair price provision is an impediment to a raider, it is not considered a potent defense. It primarily causes a bidder to pay a blended price which is usually higher. These high prices alone did not slow down the pace of acquisitions in the fourth merger wave when abundant debt financing was available.

Fair price provisions may provide for higher prices in completed acquisitions, but they are not necessarily in the best interests of stockholders. The existence of fair price provisions may cause some stockholders to fail to receive takeover premiums owing to the fact that the existence of these provisions might prevent some deals. The extent to which this occurs depends on the effectiveness of the antitakeover efforts.

Fair Price Research   Research on the impact of fair price provisions on stockholder wealth has thus far failed to show a significant relationship between fair price amendments and stock prices. Jarrell and Poulson reported an insignificant −0.65 percent change in stock prices in response to the implementation of fair price amendments.[20] The main effort seems to be a restructuring of the offer with a blended price as opposed to a two-tiered structure.

Jarrell and Poulson's results were contradicted by later research. A study by V. B. McWilliams of 763 antitakeover amendments by 325 New York and American Stock Exchange firms considered 231 fair price

---

[20] Jarrell and Poulson, "Shark Repellents and Stock Prices," p. 127.

amendments as well as 158 staggered board provisions, 29 supermajority voting provisions, 111 special voting rights provisions, 108 provisions that limited the power of shareholders to act at meetings, and 126 provisions allowing director removal only for cause.[21] Her research failed to show a significant difference in share price effects among the different types of chapter amendments. McWilliams reported a positive stock price effect for all the amendment categories she considered. Her results differed from those of the Jarrell and Poulson study, which had considered a total of 649 amendments. Jarrell and Poulson reported an average abnormal return of 3.0 percent for the non-fair price provisions, which included a combination of supermajority provisions, classified board provisions, and the authorization of preferred stock.

Dual Capitalizations   Dual capitalization is a restructuring of equity into two classes of stock with different voting rights. Its purpose is to give a group of stockholders who might be sympathetic to management's view greater voting power. Management often increases its voting power directly in a dual capitalization by acquiring stock with greater voting rights. A typical dual capitalization involves the issuance of another class of stock that has superior voting rights to the current outstanding stock. The stock with the superior voting rights might have 10 or 100 votes for each share of stock. This stock is usually distributed by the issuance of superior voting rights stock to all stockholders. Stockholders are then given the right to exchange this stock for ordinary stock. Most stockholders choose to exchange the super voting rights stock for ordinary stock because the super usually lacks marketability or pays low dividends. However, management, who may also be shareholders, may not exchange their super voting rights stock for ordinary stock. This results in management increasing its voting control of the corporation.

The effectiveness of dual capitalization was dealt a blow in July 1988 when the Securities and Exchange Commission ruled that public corporations were prohibited from issuing new classes of stock that would diminish the voting power of existing stockholders.[22] Following this vote, organized exchanges and the National Association of Securities Dealers are prohibited from listing or trading shares of stock of any company that issued shares carrying more than one vote per share. Companies can, however, issue stock with less than one vote per share.

---

[21] V. B. McWilliams, "The Stock Price Effects of Antitakeover Amendment Provisions," unpublished paper, Northeastern University, September 1988.

[22] "Share Vote Proposal Approved," *New York Times*, July 8, 1988, pp. D1 and D5.

CASE STUDY: *TRUMP VERSUS GRIFFIN*

A classic battle for control involving superior voting rights stock was waged in 1988 between real estate tycoon, Donald Trump, and television star, Merv Griffin. Griffin, fresh with cash from the sale of the "Wheel of Fortune" and "Jeopardy" television shows to Coca-Cola for $250 million, set his sights on Donald Trump's Resorts casino. The Resorts Corporation was originally the Mary Carter Paint Company, changing its name to Resorts in 1968. It is a diversified business including a helicopter and plane airline, a hotel in the Bahamas, as well as the 700-room Resorts International hotel and casino. Resorts was Atlantic City's first casino hotel.

Donald Trump, in addition to owning a significant stake in Resorts, also owns the Trump Plaza and the Trump's Castle casinos. In 1990 he constructed the 1,260-room Taj Mahal casino which cost an estimated $1 billion. Because casino licensing regulations provide that an individual can hold only three casino licenses, Trump decided that Resorts was the most likely candidate for sale.

Resorts had two classes of stock: Class A and Class B. Class A shares only had 1/100 votes per share, while each Class B share had one vote for each share. Class A shares sold for as much as $75 in 1986, while Class B shares were not traded on an organized exchange. Trump had 88 percent of the voting shares in Resorts. Although he did have effective voting control of Resorts, he was under pressure to divest himself of one casino. Griffin, aware of Trump's position, made a bid for Resorts at $35 per share. Given his superior voting rights stock, Trump remained in control of Resorts. He could not have been compelled to sell, although he had to face the choice of selling one casino in order to take ownership of the Taj Mahal. Trump eventually sold his interest in Resorts and tendered his superior voting rights stock to Merv Griffin.

The Resorts deal was played out vividly in the media, given the notoriety of the two protagonists. The acquisition proved to be a disaster for Merv Griffin who discovered that Resorts needed a greater than anticipated level of capital investment. Resorts was forced to file Chapter 11 not long after the acquisition.[a]

[a] Pauline Yoshihashi and Neil Barsky, "Merv Griffin's Plunge into Casino Gambling Could Prove a Loser," *Wall Street Journal,* February 10, 1989, p. A1.

In addition, the ruling contained a grandfather clause that allowed companies with existing unequal voting rights to continue trading.

Dual Capitalization Research In 1987, Megan Partch, in a study of 44 companies that had instituted dual capitalizations between 1962 and 1984, did not observe a significant relationship between stock prices and dual capitalizations.[23] Partch reported a positive excess return of

---

[23] Megan Partch, "The Creation of a Class of Limited Voting Common Stock and Shareholder Wealth," *Journal of Financial Economics* 18, no. 2 (June 1987): 313.

1.2 percent on the announcement of the dual capitalization. On the other hand, she found as many increases as decreases in stock prices. When the longer time period that started with the initial announcement of the dual capitalization and the date of the shareholders meeting is considered, the results fail to show statistical significance. In addition, many of the firms in her study had a high degree of managerial ownership—on the average, 49 percent. Thus, these firms are very atypical of the larger New York Stock Exchange firms which are the more active users of antitakeover devices. Given the large proportion of managerial ownership, these firms would not be likely takeover targets.

In another study of dual capitalizations, Gregg Jarrell and Annette Poulsen examined 94 firms that recapitalized with dual classes of stock that had different voting rights between 1976 and 1987.[24] Forty of the firms were listed on the New York Stock Exchange, with 26 on the American Stock Exchange and 31 traded over-the-counter. The study found significant abnormal negative returns equal to 0.82 percent for a narrow time period around the announcement of the dual capitalization. Jarrell and Poulsen also reported that the greatest negative effects were observed for firms that had high concentrations of stock held by insiders (30 to 50 percent insider holdings). Dual capitalizations will be more effective in consolidating control in the hands of management when management already owns a significant percentage of the firm's stock. The fact that negative returns were higher when management already held more shares implies that when management entrenchment was more likely (which in turn implies that the potential for a successful bid was lower) the market responded by devaluing the shares.

The dual capitalization plan is subject to shareholder approval, and, following its approval, shareholders voluntarily exchange their low voting rights shares they have been given for dividend paying stock. They may do this even though the approval and exchange may mean that the subsequent value of their holdings may be lower owing to the reduced likelihood of a takeover premium when insiders attain veto power over mergers and acquisitions. Some researchers believe that shareholders willingly accept these offers because the managers in these firms are already able to block takeovers.[25] This may not be a satisfactory explanation, however, since it does not tell us why managers would go to the expense and trouble to acquire control they supposedly already possess. Because they seek to enhance their control, we can conclude

---

[24] Gregg Jarrell and Annette Poulsen, "Dual Class Recapitalizations As Antitakeover Mechanisms," *Journal of Financial Economics* 20 (January/March 1988):129–152.

[25] Richard Ruback, "Coercive Dual-Class Exchange Offers," *Journal of Financial Economics* 20 (January/March 1988):153–173.

that they are not convinced they are in a position to block takeovers without dual classes of stock.

Unbundled Units   In December 1988, Shearson Lehman Hutton introduced an innovative stock restructuring package that was intended to revitalize the market for a company's equity. This innovation involved the exchange of a share of a company's stock for a package of three other securities the company would issue.[26] Under the Shearson plan, the company would offer stockholders a package that included a 30-year bond, a share of preferred stock, and an equity appreciation certificate. Together these three component securities would have the characteristics of the original equity. The 30-year bond would pay as interest what the firm was previously paying as dividends. This would provide the company the tax benefits associated with interest payments. The preferred stock would pay as preferred stock dividends any increases in the firm's underlying common stock dividend over the 30-year life of the security. It would liquidate at a token price such as $250. The equity appreciation certificate would entitle the holder to any rise in the price of the firm's common stock over the next 30 years. Under this plan, the issuing firm would still have its original common stock outstanding, but stockholders would be given the option to exchange their shares of common stock for the package of these three securities. This plan has additional antitakeover benefits for the issuing firm. The package of new securities does not contain voting rights. Thus, the total voting power of the corporation becomes more concentrated in the hands of fewer stockholders, thereby increasing the voting power of management which would presumably not opt for the exchange.

Shearson first introduced this plan by announcing that four corporations, American Express, Pfizer, Inc., Dow Chemical and Sara Lee, were offering unbundled units to stockholders. The initial market reception was mixed. However, on March 28, 1989, Shearson announced the withdrawal of the offering, citing the SEC's insistence that the unbundled stock units (USU) be treated as outstanding shares for the purchase of computing earnings per share. In addition, subsequent analysis has revealed that the original terms of exchange offered for some of the USU's were not advantageous for shareholders.[27]

Golden Parachutes

Golden parachutes are special compensation agreements that the company provides to upper management and can be considered both a preventative and an active antitakeover defense. They can be used in

---

[26] "Package Deal: Some Firms, Seeking to Raise the Value of Their Shares, Plan to Offer New Securities Units," *Wall Street Journal,* December 6, 1988, p. A18.

[27] Raaj Sah and Navendu Vasavada, "Unbundled Stock Units: What Went Wrong?," *Financial Management Collection* 5, no. 2 (Summer 1990): 1.

advance of a hostile bid to make the target less desirable, but they can also be used in the midst of a takeover battle.

Many CEOs of corporations feel that golden parachutes are a vital course of action in a takeover contest. One problem corporations face during a takeover battle is that of retaining management employees. When a takeover has been made, a corporation's management is often besieged by calls from recruiters. Managers, insecure about their positions, are quick to consider other attractive offers. Therefore, some corporations adopt golden parachutes to alleviate their employees' concerns about job security. For example, Dorman Commons, former chairman of Natomas Inc., a San Francisco-based oil company, believes that golden parachutes protect shareholders because they "permit key officers to respond objectively to a threat and negotiate without fear for their personal futures."[28]

A typical golden parachute agreement provides for lump-sum payments to certain senior management upon either voluntary or involuntary termination of their employment. This agreement is usually effective if termination occurs within one year after the change in control. Monies to fund golden parachutes are sometimes put aside in separate accounts referred to as *rabbi trusts*. The amount of compensation is usually determined by the employee's annual compensation and years of service.

Golden parachutes are usually triggered by some predetermined ownership of stock by an outside entity. Richard Lambert and David Larker found that the trigger control percentage of stocks acquired by a bidder was an average 26.6 percent for the firms they studied.[29] They also showed that the participants in golden parachutes plans are narrowly defined. In their sample, golden parachute agreements covered only 9.7 percent of the executives. These agreements are extended to executives who do not have employment contracts. They are effective even if the managers leave the corporations voluntarily after a change in control.

Golden parachutes are not usually applied broadly. One unusual exception is what are known as *silver parachutes*, compensation agreements given to most employees in the firm including lower level employees. The most common type of silver parachute is a one-year severance pay agreement.

Golden parachutes have been challenged in court by stockholders who contend that these agreements violate management's fiduciary

---

[28] Dorman L. Commons, *Tender Offer* (New York: Penguin Books, 1985), p. 112.

[29] Richard A. Lambert and David F. Larker, "Golden Parachutes, Executive Decision Making and Stockholder Wealth," *Journal of Accounting Economics* 7 (1985): 179–203.

responsibilities. The problem arises because golden parachutes generally do not have to be approved by a stockholder vote prior to implementation. In several major lawsuits the courts have ruled against stockholders. The Gulf Resources and Chemicals, Sunbeam, and Esmark cases have failed to provide support to the stockholders' position. The courts have ruled that the Business Judgment Rule applies here. This rule holds that management's actions are valid as long as they are enacted while management is acting in the stockholder's best interests. The fact that management's action may not maximize stockholder wealth, in retrospect, is irrelevant according to this rule.

Many analysts believe that golden parachutes are a burden on both corporation and stockholders. Some stockholder advocates consider them to be a form of self-dealing on the part of management and one of the more flagrant abuses of the modern takeover era. The magnitude of these compensation packages, they state, is clearly excessive. The golden parachute given Michael Bergerac, former chairman of Revlon Corporation, following his resignation at the end of the unsuccessful defense against corporate raider Ronald Pearlman, was estimated to have provided Bergerac with a compensation package in excess of $35 million. This package included stock options worth $15 million.

The excessiveness of golden parachute agreements has given rise to the term *golden handcuffs*, which reflects the belief that golden parachutes serve only to entrench management at the expense of stockholders. This belies their role as an antitakeover device. If the compensation package is very large, some raiders might be put off from making a bid for the company. Although large golden parachute agreements can be a mild deterrent, they are not considered an effective antitakeover tool. In conjunction with other, stronger devices, however, they can be a more effective deterrent.

CHANGING THE STATE OF INCORPORATION

Because many states have enacted different antitakeover laws, some companies have found it beneficial to reincorporate in states that provide takeover protection. When a firm incorporated in Delaware threatened to reincorporate in another state with strong antitakeover laws, the Delaware legislature decided to pass its own antitakeover law in 1987. The provisions of this law are reviewed in Chapter 3. Many large corporations have found Delaware to be the preferred state to incorporate in because, among other reasons, the Delaware corporation laws allow management and directors considerable leeway to take actions they judge to be in the shareholder's best interest. For example, in

CASE STUDY: *BORDEN'S PEOPLE PILL*

The Borden Corporation developed an innovative antitakeover defense when it instituted the so-called *people pill.* In January 1989, Borden revealed that its top 25 executives had signed a contract to quit the company if the firm were to be taken over by a raider who did not give stockholders a "fair" value for their investment and if a single member of the management team was demoted or fired. Both conditions must be met for the people pill to be activated.

Borden's board of directors approved the people pill out of concern that the firm might become a takeover target. The board felt that the plan would help insure that, in the event of an unwanted bid, the stockholders of the food company would receive a fair return on their investment. The fair stock price was determined to be a cash offer for 100 percent of the stock's value as determined by an opinion by the firm's investment bankers (a friendly opinion) plus a premium of at least 50 percent of the firm's profits that an acquirer would reasonably be expected to make from asset sales or other synergies. The pill would be activated by an offer for 85 percent of the firm's shares which were not already in the acquirer's hands.

As of 1990, this innovative antitakeover defense contributed to initiating the firm's independence. However, it is difficult to say how effective this defense really is. At a time when asset sales and the breakup value of the firm are the most important factors, from a heavily leveraged raider's viewpoint, the loss of management might not be as important. Many feel that the present market has a surplus of management talent, and so the loss of some executives might not be all that troublesome. Some raiders, with an eye on enacting a change in management, might consider a mass resignation a benefit.[a]

[a] Alix Freedman, "Borden Officials Link Jobs in New Antitakeover Plan," *Wall Street Journal,* January 1989.

1985, the Delaware court ruled that an exclusionary self-tender offer by Unocal, in its battle with Mesa Petroleum, fell within the nebulous limits of the Business Judgment Rule.[30] This flexibility, combined with a highly developed and predictable court system, led many companies to incorporate in Delaware rather than other states.

Reincorporating in a state with strong antitakeover laws will not ensure a firm's independence. Singer moved its state of incorporation from Connecticut to New Jersey, a state with a strong antitakeover law; the move did not prevent Singer from ultimately being taken over by raider Paul Bilzerian. Nonetheless, reincorporating does make a takeover more difficult for the raider. This stronger bargaining position may help the target get a better price for the shareholders.

[30] *Unocal v. Mesa Petroleum,* 493 A 2d. 946 (Del 1985).

Incorporation Research

Jeffrey Netter and Annette Poulson examined the shareholder wealth effects of reincorporation announcements for 36 firms in 1986 and 1987.[31] They divided their sample into two groups: 19 firms that reincorporated from California and the remaining 17 firms. They point out that California is a shareholder rights state whose corporation laws protect shareholder interests. Among the rights provided are mandatory cumulative voting, a prohibition against classified boards, and other shareholder rights such as the ability to remove directors without cause or to call special meetings. Netter and Poulson reason that, if there were a stock price effect, it would be greater in reincorporations from California to Delaware. Their results failed to reveal any shareholder wealth effects either from the 36 reincorporations in their sample or the California subsample. On the basis of their study, we can conclude that the greater flexibility provided to management by incorporating in Delaware will not reduce shareholder wealth.

ACTIVE ANTITAKEOVER DEFENSES

Installing the various preventative antitakeover defenses will not prevent a company from being a target of a hostile bid. It will, however, make the takeover more difficult and costly. Some bidders may decide to bypass a well-defended target in favor of other firms that have not installed formidable defenses. Nonetheless, even those firms that have taken all the preventative actions described above may need to actively resist raiders when they become targets of a hostile bid. The second half of this chapter describes some of the various actions a target can take after it receives an unwanted bid. The various actions discussed in the second half of this chapter are described below.

> *Greenmail:* Share repurchases of the bidder's stock at a premium.
>
> *Standstill agreements:* These usually accompany a greenmail payment. Here the bidder agrees not to buy additional shares in exchange for a fee.
>
> *White knight:* The target may seek out a friendly bidder, or white knight, as an alternative to the hostile acquirer.
>
> *White squire:* The target may place shares or assets in the hands of

---

[31] Jeffrey Netter and Annette Poulson, "State Corporation Laws and Shareholders: The Recent Experience," *Financial Management* 18, no. 3 (Autumn 1989): 29–40.

a friendly firm or investor. These entities are referred to as white squires.

Capital structure changes: Targets can take various actions that will alter capital structure. Through a *recapitalization,* the firm can assume more debt while it pays shareholders a larger dividend. The target can also simply assume more debt without using the proceeds to pay shareholders a dividend. Both alternatives make the firm more heavily levered and less valuable to the bidder. Targets can also alter the capital structure by changing the total number of shares outstanding. This can be done through a new offering of stock, placement of shares in the hands of a white squire, or an employee stock ownership plan. Instead of issuing more shares, some targets buy back shares to ensure they are not purchased by the hostile bidder.

Litigation: Targets commonly sue the bidder, and the bidder often responds with a countersuit.

Pac-Man defense: One of the more extreme defenses occurs when the target makes a counteroffer for the bidder.

The coverage of these active antitakeover defenses will be similar to our coverage of the preventative measures. The use of each is described along with the research on the shareholder wealth effects. The reader should bear in mind that a target may choose to use several of these defenses together as opposed to merely selecting one. It is, therefore, difficult for research studies to isolate the shareholder wealth effects. In addition, some of the research, using different data sets drawn from different time periods, reach conflicting conclusions. As the market changes and adapts to the various defenses, their effectiveness and, therefore, their impact on stock prices, also varies. These problems were also apparent in the research studies on the preventative measures. Once again, the reader will have to draw his or her own conclusions on the impact on stockholders and other shareholders.

Greenmail

The term *greenmail* refers to the payment of a substantial premium for a significant stockholder's stock in return for the stockholder's agreement that he or she will not initiate a bid for control of the company. Greenmail is sometimes also called *targeted share repurchases,* although this term also applies to other purchases of stock from specific groups of stockholders who may not ever contemplate a raid on the company.

One of the earlier reported instances of greenmail occurred in July 1979 when Carl Icahn bought 9.9 percent of Saxon Industries stock for approximately $7.21 per share. Saxon repurchased Icahn's shares for $10.50 per share on February 13, 1980.[32] This stock buyback helped launch Icahn on a career as a successful corporate raider. Ichan was not the first greenmailer, however. That distinction may belong to Charles Bluhdorn, chairman of Gulf and Western Industries, "who was an early practitioner when Cannon Mills in 1976 bought back a Gulf & Western holding."[33]

Icahn Versus Hammermill Paper Corporation   One classic example of greenmail occurred following the announcement by the famous corporate raider, Carl Icahn, that he owned more than 10 percent of Hammermill Paper Corporation's common stock. Hammermill was a high-quality manufacturer of paper products for over 80 years.[34] During late 1979, Hammermill stock was valued at approximately $25 per share, a low valuation since the stock's book value was approximately $37 per share. Analysts felt that even this valuation was too low inasmuch as many of Hammermill's assets, such as its timberlands, were carried on the firm's books below their actual value. Icahn suggested that Hammermill be liquidated because its per share liquidation value would exceed the cost of a share of stock. Hammermill's management, busily engaged in rejuvenating the company, vehemently opposed liquidation. Ultimately, both parties filed suit against each other while they pursued a proxy contest. Icahn lost the proxy battle and Hammermill eventually paid Icahn $36 per share for each of his 865,000 shares. Jeff Madrick reports that Icahn made a $9 million profit on an investment of $20 million.

The payment of greenmail raises certain ethical issues regarding the fiduciary responsibilities of management and directors, both of whom are charged with maximizing the value of stockholder wealth. Many claim, however, that they use tools such as greenmail to pursue their own goals which may conflict with the goal of maximizing stockholder wealth.

Managerial Entrenchment Hypothesis Versus Stockholder Interest Hypothesis   The *management entrenchment hypothesis* proposes that nonparticipating stockholders experience reduced wealth when

---

[32] "Icahn Gets Green As Others Envy Him," *Wall Street Journal*, November 13, 1989, p. B–1.

[33] Ibid.

[34] Jeff Madrick, *Taking America* (New York: Bantam Books, 1987), pp. 242–243.

management takes actions to deter attempts to take control of the corporation. This theory asserts that managers of a corporation seek to maintain their positions by actions such as greenmail or the installation of other active and preventative corporate defenses. According to this view, stockholder wealth declines in response to a reevaluation of this firm's stock by the market.

The *stockholder interest hypothesis* implies that stockholder wealth rises because there are fewer competitors for control of the corporation. The fact that management does not need to devote resources to preventing takeover attempts is considered a cost saving. Such cost savings might come in the form of management time savings, reduced expenditures in proxy fights, and a smaller investor relations department.

The Legality of Differential Payments to Large-Block Shareholders

The courts have ruled that differential payments to large-block shareholders are legal as long as they are made for valid business reasons.[35] However, the term *valid business reasons* is so broad that it gives management considerable latitude to take actions that may favor management more than stockholders. Managers can claim that, in order to fulfill their plans for the corporation's future growth, they need to prevent a takeover of the corporation by any entity that would possibly change the company's direction.

The interpretation of legitimate business purposes can involve a difference in business philosophies between the incumbent management and a bidder. It can also simply be that managers are seeking to preserve the continuity of their business strategies. Although many feel that the court's broad views on this matter may serve to entrench management, others see the court's position as one that helps preserve management's ability to conduct long-term strategic planning. Many corporate managers believe that the court's position allows them to enact the necessary defenses to fend off takeovers by hostile bidders who might acquire the corporation simply to sell off assets and achieve short-term returns. Considerable debate surrounds the issue of short-term versus long-term motives of corporate bidders.

The legality of greenmail itself was upheld in a legal challenge in the Texaco greenmail payment to the Bass Brothers. The Delaware Chancery court found that the payment of a 3 percent premium to the

---

[35] C. M. Nathan and M. Sobel, "Corporate Stock Repurchases in the Context of Unsolicited Takeover Bids," *Business Lawyer* (July 1980): 1545–1566.

Bass Brothers was a reasonable price to pay for eliminating the potentially disruptive effects that the Bass Group might have posed for Texaco in the future.[36] The Delaware Chancery Court's approval of the greenmail payment and dismissal of a shareholder class action were upheld by the Delaware Supreme Court. The important decision clearly established a precedent for the legality of greenmail in the all-important Delaware court system.

Greenmail Research

Much of the research on the impact of antitakeover measures on shareholder wealth uses the market model. This model calculates the abnormal returns to common stockholders, or what are sometimes referred to as *prediction errors*, attributable to the particular antitakeover measure being studied. One of the leading studies on the effects of greenmail payments on stockholder wealth was conducted by Bradley and Wakeman. Their study considered 86 repurchases from insiders or individuals who were unaffiliated with the firms during 1974–1980. They looked at the impact of repurchases on abnormal returns based on the following market model:

$$R_{jt} = a_j + B_j R_{mt} + e_{jt}$$

where: R_{jt} = the dividend inclusive return of security j on day t
R_{mt} = the dividend inclusive return of the market on day t

Abnormal returns were defined as

$$AR_{jt} = R_{jt} - (a_j + B_j R_{jt})$$

The Bradley and Wakeman study showed that privately negotiated purchases of a single block of stock from stockholders who were unaffiliated with the company reduced the wealth of nonparticipating stockholders.[37] Repurchases from insiders, however, were associated with increases in shareholder wealth. Bradley and Wakeman's research therefore supports the management entrenchment hypothesis. In revealing that stockholders lose money as a result of targeted share repurchases from outsiders, the study implies that these target share repurchases are not in the stockholder's best interest. It further implies that, by engaging in these repurchases, management is doing stockholders a disservice.

---

[36] *Good* v. *Texaco, Inc.*, No. 7501 (Del. Ch. Feb. 19, 1985), aff.d sub nom. *Polk* v. *Good*, 507 A. 2d 531 (Del 1986).

[37] Michael Bradley and L. MacDonald Wakeman, "The Wealth Effects of Targeted Share Repurchases," *Journal of Financial Economics* 11 (April 1983): 301–328.

Another major study on the topic of greenmail and targeted share repurchases was conducted by Wayne Mikkelson and Richard Ruback in 1986.[38] This analysis considered 111 repurchases and found that only 5 percent occurred after the announcement of a takeover attempt. One-third of the repurchases took place after less overt attempts to change control such as formulation of preliminary plans for acquisitions or proxy fights. Almost two-thirds of them occurred without any overt indication of an impending takeover. Interestingly, the Mikkelson and Ruback study showed that the downward impact of the targeted share repurchases was more than offset by the stock price *increases* caused by purchasing the stock. Mikkelson and Ruback found a combined overall impact on stock prices of +7 percent! Their study supports the stockholder interest hypothesis in that it finds that the target share repurchases actually benefit incumbent stockholders. It therefore conflicts with the Bradley and Wakeman results and so has added more fuel to this debate. Mikkelson and Ruback's analysis also showed that the payment of greenmail was not associated with a lower probability of a change in control. They showed that the frequency of control changes following targeted share repurchases was three times higher than a control sample of firms that did not engage in such repurchases.

Raiders or Saviors?   Raiders have been much maligned in the media. As noted earlier, critics have contended that they are short-term speculators who have no long-term interest in the future of the company. They feel that the payment of greenmail to such short-term speculators can only injure the firm's future viability. This view, however, has been challenged by the results of a study by Holderness and Sheehan. They analyzed the activities of six popular raiders, Carl Icahn, Irwin Jacobs, Carl Lintner, David Murdock, Victor Posner, and Charles Bluhdorn, over the time period 1977 and 1982.[39] Their analysis showed that stock prices rose significantly after the announcement that they had first purchased shares in a target firm. They found that the traditional view of "raiding" was not supported by the activities of these investors over a two-year time period that had followed each purchase. Holderness and Sheehan define raiders as those who would use their position as significant shareholders to try to expropriate assets from the firm. They

---

[38] Wayne Mikkelson and Richard Ruback, "Targeted Share Repurchases and Common Stock Returns," Working Paper No. 1707–86, Massachusetts Institute of Technology, Sloan School of Management, June 1986.

[39] Clifford G. Holderness and Dennis P. Sheehan, "Raiders or Saviors? The Evidence of Six Controversial Raiders," *Journal of Financial Economics* 14, no. 4 (December 1985): 555–581.

contend that if this was the case, then share prices would have declined following the initial share repurchase. Instead, the market responded with an increase in its valuation of the firm. This implies that the market does not view these investors as expropriating raiders. Their analysis of instances when these raiders were the recipients of repurchase offers by the target shows that the announcement of the repurchases yielded negative returns. Similar to Mikkelson and Ruback, however, when the aggregate effects of the initial stock purchase, intermediate events, and the eventual share repurchase are combined, the overall effects are positive and statistically significant.

Holderness and Sheehan see part of the reason for the positive stock price effect on the announcement of share repurchases as partially the result of an improved management effect. They believe that the market may anticipate that these raiders will either play a direct role in the management of the firm or will seek to change management. Indeed, in 10 of the 73 targets studied, they found that the raiders played a direct role in the management of the firm.

One final conclusion that Holderness and Sheehan draw from their analysis is that these six investors managed to purchase undervalued stocks. They attribute this "superior security analyst's acumen" either to the possession of nonpublic information or to a greater ability to analyze public information. They see the positive stock price effects around the initial announcement of the purchases as support for this view of raiders.

Standstill Agreements

A standstill agreement occurs when the target corporation reaches a contractual agreement with a potential acquirer whereby the would-be acquirer agrees not to increase its holdings in the target during a particular time period. Such an agreement takes place when the acquiring firm has established sufficient stockholdings so as to be able to create a threat to mount a takeover battle for the target. Many standstill agreements are accompanied by the target's agreement to give the acquirer the right of first refusal in the event the acquirer decides to sell the shares it currently owns. This agreement is designed to prevent these shares from falling into the hands of another bidder who would force the target to pay them standstill compensation or, even worse, to attempt to take over the target. Another version of a standstill agreement occurs when the acquirer agrees not to increase its holdings beyond a certain percentage. In other words, the target establishes a ceiling above which the acquirer cannot increase its holdings. The acquiring firm agrees to these various restrictions for a fee.

CASE STUDY: *TYPICAL STANDSTILL AGREEMENT*

In August 1980, the NVF Company reached an agreement with City Investing in which NVF agreed not to acquire any more than 21 percent of City Investing stock for a period of five years. The agreement required that NVF not take any steps to take control of City Investing. Thus, in return for financial compensation, NVF gave up its right to pursue a proxy fight or a tender offer for City Investing stock.

City Invested was given the right of first refusal in the event NVF decided to liquidate its holdings in City Investing. City Investing was thereby protected against the shares falling into the hands of another firm that might seek to take control of the company. NVF was given similar protection in the event another firm sought to take control of City Investing. The agreement with the two firms stipulated that if another company made a bid for more than 21 percent of City Investing, then NVF would also be able to bid for more than 21 percent.[a]

[a] This account is based on Dunn and DeAngelo, "Standstill Agreements and Privately Negotiated Stock Repurchases," *Journal of Financial Economics* 11 (1983): 275–300. "Posner Can Buy Up to 21% Stake in City Investing," *Wall Street Journal,* August 6, 1980, p. 3.

Like greenmail, standstill agreements provide compensation for an acquirer not to threaten to take control of the target. In fact, standstill agreements are often accompanied by greenmail.

The same debate between the management entrenchment hypothesis and the stockholder interest hypothesis that applied to greenmail also applies to standstill agreements. Those who prefer one theory over the other with respect to greenmail generally hold the same views for standstill agreements.

Standstill Research   In one of the more reputable studies on the topic of standstill agreements, Larry Dann and Harry DeAngelo examined 81 standstill agreements between 1977 and 1980.[40] They found that standstill agreements and negotiated stock purchases at a premium were associated with negative average returns to nonparticipating stockholders. On the average, stock prices fell 4 percent. The Dann and DeAngeleo study supports the management entrenchment hypothesis and, as such, is inconsistent with the stockholder interest hypothesis with respect to nonparticipating stockholders.

---

[40] Dann and DeAngelo, "Standstill Agreements and Privately Negotiated Stock Repurchases," pp. 275–300.

The Mikkelson and Ruback study considered the impact of green-mail payments that were accompanied by standstill agreements.[41] They found that when negative returns associated with targeted share repurchases they were much greater when these purchases were accompanied by standstill agreements. We may therefore conclude that these two antitakeover devices tend to have a complementary negative impact on stock prices that is greater than the negative effect we would expect if just one of them were implemented.

White Knights

When a corporation is the target of an unwanted bid or the threat of a bid from a potential acquirer, it may seek the aid of a *white knight*—that is, another company that would be a more acceptable suitor for the target. The white knight will then make an offer to buy all or part of the target company on more favorable terms than the original bidder. These favorable terms may be a higher price, but management may also look for a white knight that will promise not to disassemble the target or lay off management or other employees. It is sometimes difficult to find a willing bidder who will agree to such restrictive terms. Often, the target has to bargain for the best deal possible to stay out of the first bidder's hands.

The incumbent managers of the target maintain control by reaching an agreement with the white knight to allow them to retain their current positions. They can also do so by selling the white knight certain assets and keeping control of the remainder of the target.

Boone Pickens and Mesa Petroleum Versus Cities Service

In June 1982 Boone Pickens, the CEO of Mesa Petroleum, made a bid for Cities Service Oil Company. Although not part of the Seven Sisters, the seven largest oil companies in the United States, Cities Service was about 20 times as large as Mesa Petroleum. Mesa had been carrying an investment in Cities Service since 1979 and had chosen this time to make a bid for the larger oil company. Pickens felt that Cities Service possessed valuable assets but was badly managed.

> Cities Service was a case study of what was wrong with Big Oil's management. Based in Tulsa, Oklahoma, Cities was a large company. By 1982, it ranked 38th in the Fortune 500 and was the nineteenth largest oil company

---

[41] Mikkelson and Ruback, "Targeted Share Repurchases."

CASE STUDY: *GILLETTE: STANDSTILL AGREEMENTS AND GREENMAIL*

In 1986, Gillette was being pursued by Ronald Pearlman who had previously taken over the Revlon Corporation. When it appeared that he was about to make a tender offer for Gillette, Gillette responded by paying Revlon $558 million in return for Revlon agreeing not to make a $65 tender offer to stockholders. One unique aspect of this deal was that Gillette even paid greenmail to the investment bank that represented Revlon. Gillette paid Drexel Burnham Lambert $1.75 million in return for an agreement not to be involved in an acquisition or attempted acquisition of Gillette for a period of three years. This is testimony to the activist role that investment banks play in takeovers. Gillette was worried that, having seen Gillette's vulnerability, Drexel Burnham would approach another potential suitor.

The payment of greenmail seems to be only a temporary fix, as is confirmed by the fact that another bidder, Coniston Partners, initiated an attempt to take control of Gillette by means of a proxy fight. During the legal proceedings that followed the acerbic proxy fight between Gillette and Coniston, it was revealed that Gillette had entered into standstill agreements with *10* different companies:

Colgate Palmolive
Ralston Purina
Anheuser-Busch
Pepsico
Metromedia
Citicorp Industrial Corporation (They do LBOs and asset-based lendings)
Salomon Brothers (acting on its own behalf)
Kidder, Peabody
Kohlberg Kravis Roberts
Forstmann Little[a]

Gillette eventually reached a settlement with Coniston in which Coniston conceded to a standstill agreement in return for Gillette's agreement to buy back shares from Coniston and other shareholders. A total of 16 million shares were purchased at a price that was above the market price at that time of $45.[b] The Gillette case study is an example of some of the benefits of raiders that Holderness and Sheehan reported. Gillette had been the target of several raiders including Revlon's CEO Ronald Pearlman. He had agreed to a standstill agreement with Gillette after an aborted takeover attempt in November 1986. Although Pearlman had a standstill agreement with Gillette, he renewed his interest in acquiring the firm in late 1987 when it appeared that other bidders were showing interest in the razor manufacturer. The constant pressure that Gillette was under appeared to have shown beneficial effects. Gillette responded to the various takeover threats by cutting costs and thinning out its

---

[a] "Trial Discusses Identity of 10 Firms Gillette Company Contacted as White Knights," *Wall Street Journal,* June 27, 1988, p. 16.
[b] Alison Leigh Cowan, "Gillette and Coniston Drop Suits," *New York Times,* August 2, 1988, p. D1.

workforce. Gillette also enacted various restructuring measures, which included reducing and eliminating weak operations within the firm.[c] By 1990, the firm had laid off a total of 2,400 workers and had sold several weak businesses. Gillette's common stock responded to the increased efficiencies by showing a 50 percent total return in 1989, up from the 24 percent average annual return the firm's stock yielded during the prior 10 years.[d] At least in the case of Gillette, the Holderness and Sheehan hypothesis on the beneficial effects of raiders seems to be borne out.

[c] "How Ron Pearlman Scared Gillette into Shape," *Business Week,* October 12, 1987, p. 40.
[d] Anthony Ramirez, "A Radical New Style for Stodgy Old Gillette," *New York Times,* February 25, 1990, p. 5.

in the country. It was unusually sluggish, even by the less demanding standards of the oil industry, and had been for fifty years. Its refineries and chemical plants were losers, and although it has 307 million barrels of oil and 3.1 trillion cubic feet of gas reserves, it had been depleting its gas reserves for at least ten years. While it had leases on ten million acres, it was finding practically no new oil and gas. Cities' problems were hidden by its cash flow, which continued in tandem with OPEC price increases. The stock, however, reflecting management's record, sold at about a third of the value of its underlying assets. The management didn't understand the problem or didn't care; either condition is terminal.[42]

Mesa Petroleum made a $50 per share bid for Cities Service. Cities Service responded with a Pac-Man defense in which it made a $17 per share bid for the smaller Mesa Petroleum. The Cities Service offer was not a serious one since Mesa's stock had been trading at $16.75 prior to the Cities offer which, therefore, did not contain a premium. Cities asked Gulf Oil to be its white knight. Pickens, a critic of the major oil companies, was equally critical of Gulf Oil. Gulf made a $63 per share bid for Cities Service. Cities saw Gulf as a similar type of oil company and one that would be much friendlier to Cities management than Gulf. At that time Gulf was the third largest oil company in the United States. Cities accepted Gulf's bid. Mesa ended up selling its shares back to Cities for $55 per share, which resulted in an $11 per share profit for Mesa or a total of $40 million. However, Gulf had second thoughts about the Cities acquisition: Gulf would have taken on a significant amount of debt if it had gone through with the merger. In addition,

[42] T. Boone Pickens, *Boone* (Boston: Houghton Mifflin Co., 1987), p. 150.

Gulf was concerned that the FTC might challenge the merger on anti-trust grounds. Much to Cities Service surprise and chagrin, Gulf dropped its offer for Cities. Cities Service stock dropped to $30 a share following the announcement of Gulf's pullout. Cities Service management was highly critical of Gulf and stated that its action was reprehensible.

Cities Service then had to look for another white knight. Occidental Petroleum, led by the well-known Armand Hammer, made an initial offer of $50 per share in cash for the first 49 percent of Cities stock and securities of somewhat uncertain value for the remaining shares. Cities rejected this bid as inadequate, and Occidental upped its offer to $55 in cash for the front end and better quality securities for the back end. Cities Service then agreed to sell out to its second white knight.

Eaton Corporation versus Carborundum Corporation

The Mesa Petroleum versus Cities Service takeover attempt is somewhat atypical of white knights in that what appeared to be the white knight failed to materialize and the target was forced to seek another white knight in the heat of the takeover contest. A more typical white knight scenario occurred in the attempted takeover of Carborundum Corporation by the Eaton Corporation.

The Eaton Corporation, a Cleveland-based automobile and truck parts company, had 120 plants and 46,000 employees. It made transmissions, truck parts, and materials-handling equipment. Its 1976 sales were $1.8 billion, which yielded a profit of $90 million. Carborundum was a company in Niagara Falls which produced abrasives for industrial users as well as manufacturing insulating materials and pollution control products. It was a highly innovative company with an excellent research and development record. Eaton wanted Carborundum for its innovative development of ceramic parts for engines. These parts had impressive performance characteristics at high temperatures. Eaton, being an automobile manufacturer, found this attribute most appealing. Eaton with the assistance of its investment banker Shearson Lehman Brothers made a friendly offer for Carborundum in 1977. This bid was quickly rejected. Eaton then responded with a tender offer of $47 per share. This offer seemed low, given the fact that Carborundum's book value was $49 per share.

Carborundum approached Kennecott Corporation to be its white knight. Kennecott responded with a $66 a share offer that was 40 percent higher than the Eaton bid. Carborundum, sensing that its days as an independent company were limited, decided to accept Kennecott's higher offer.

White Squire Defense

The white squire defense is similar to the white knight defense. In the white squire defense the target company seeks to implement a strategy that will preserve the target company's independence. A *white squire* is a firm that consents to purchase a large block of the target company's stock. The white squire is typically not interested in acquiring control of the target. From the target's viewpoint the appeal is that a large amount of the voting stock in the target will be placed in the hands of a company or investor who will not sell out a hostile bidder. A good example of a white squire defense was Carter Hawley Hale's sale of convertible preferred stock to the General Cinema Corporation in 1984. The stock sold to General Cinema had voting power equal to 22 percent of Carter Hawley Hale's outstanding votes. Carter Hawley Hale felt this was necessary to prevent a takeover by the Limited Corporation in 1984. Carter Hawley Hale accompanied this white squire defense with a stock repurchase program that increased the voting power of General Cinema's stock to 33 percent of Carter Hawley Hale's voting shares.

Another version of the white squire defense combines it with the white knight defense. Here the target places a block of stock or options to buy voting shares in the hands of a white knight. This strategy is designed to give the white knight an advantage over the original bidder. Such was the result in the Ampco-Pittsburg's hostile bid for the Buffalo Forge Company in 1983. Buffalo Forge entered into an agreement to sell to a white knight, Ogden Corporation. As part of this agreement it sold Ogden 425,000 shares of treasury stock and gave Ogden the option to purchase an additional 143,000 shares at the same $32.75 price.[43] These so-called *leg-up stock options* were held to be legal in court.[44] (They are called *leg-up stock options* because they give one party a leg-up advantage over the other in the bidding process.)

Warren Buffett is a legendary white squire. Through his company, Berkshire Hathaway, he has reportedly invested $2 billion in white squire stock positions in companies such as Gillette, Coca-Cola, U.S. Air, and Champion International Corporation.[45] In 1989, for example,

---

[43] Dennis Block, Nancy E. Barton, and Stephen A. Radin, *Business Judgment Rule* (Englewood Cliffs, N.J.: Prentice–Hall Law and Business Publishers, 1988), p. 94.

[44] *Buffalo Forge Co.* v. *Ogden Corp.*, 717 F. 2d (2nd Cir.), attd 555 F. Supp. 892 (W.D.N.Y.).

[45] James White, "White Squires Step into Breach As Debt-Driven Investing Falters," *Wall Street Journal*, February 21, 1990, p. C1.

he bought $600 million in Gillette preferred stock which are convertible into 11 percent of Gillette's common stock.[46]

As the leveraged buyout boom slowed in the late 1980s, some investment firms, such as Forstmann Little and Company, attempted to start *white squire funds*. In 1990, Theodore Forstmann sought to raise $2 billion to buy 15 percent or greater stakes in other companies.[47] These equity investments are appealing to pension funds and other institutional investors who seek a good return on their invested capital. The investments are also attractive to cash-hungry companies that receive not only the takeover protection that white square investments can provide, but also an infusion of additional liquidity. Forstmann had to abandon his initial attempt at assembling a white squire fund, due to insufficient interest. The concept, however, may eventually become more popular in the 1990s.

Lockup Transactions

Lockup transactions are similar to a white squire defense. In the case of lockups, the target is selling assets to another party instead of stock. Sometimes the term *lockup transaction* is also used more generally to refer to the sale of assets as well as the sale of stock to a friendly third party. In a lockup transaction the target company sells assets to a third party and thus tries to make the target less attractive to the bidder. Often the target sells those assets it judges the acquirer wants most. This can also come in the form of *lockup options*, which are options to buy certain assets in the event of a change in control. These options can be written so that they become effective even if a bidder acquires less than 51 percent of the target.

In some instances, lockup options have been held to be invalid. The court's position has been that, in limiting the desirability of the target to the original bidder, they effectively preempt the bargaining process that might result during the 20-day waiting period for tender offers required by the Williams Act. An example of such an invalid option was Marathon Oil's option that it gave to U.S. Steel in 1981 to buy its Yates Oil Field at a fixed price in an attempt to avoid a takeover by Mobil Oil Corporation. This option would be exercisable in the event Marathon was taken over. It would have an important impact on future bidding contests since it was one of Marathon's most valued

---

[46] Ramirez, "A Radical New Style for Stodgy Old Gillette," p. 5.

[47] James White, "Forstmann Tries to Turn a Profit from Prophecies," *Wall Street Journal*, February 21, 1990, p. C1.

CASE STUDY: *REVLON VERSUS PANTRY PRIDE*

In 1985, Ronald Pearlman, chief executive of Pantry Pride, made an offer for Revlon Inc. MacAndrews and Forbes Holdings, the parent company of Pantry Pride, had built a diversified company with acquisitions between 1978 and 1984 that included a jewelry company, a cigar company, a candy manufacturer as well as Pantry Pride—the popular retail chain. Charles Revson had built Revlon into one of the nation's largest cosmetics companies. Revson's successor, Michael Bergerac, a former head of the conglomerate ITT and protege of Harold Geneen, expanded Revlon considerably through large acquisitions in the health care field. In terms of its revenues, Bergerac's Revlon was more of a health care company than a cosmetics company.

Revlon's acquisition strategy had not fared well for Bergerac, and Revlon's earnings had been declining. Pearlman decided to make a bid for Revlon, his goal being to sell off the health care components and keep the well-known cosmetics business. Pantry Pride made a cash tender of $53 a share. Revlon's board of directors had approved a leveraged buyout plan by Forstmann Little at $56 cash per share. When Pantry Pride increased its offer to $56.25, Revlon was able to get Forstmann Little to increase its offer to $57.25 by giving Forstmann Little a lockup option to purchase two Revlon divisions for $525 million. This was reported by Revlon's investment banker to be $75 million below these divisions' actual value.[a] This option would be activated if a bidder acquired 40 percent of Revlon's shares.

Delaware's Chancery Court ruled that in agreeing to this lockup agreement the board of directors had breached its fiduciary responsibility. The court felt that this option effectively ended the bidding process and gave an unfair advantage to Forstmann Little's LBO. However, in their ruling, the court did not declare lockup options illegal. It stated that the options can play a constructive role in the bargaining process and thus increase bids and shareholder wealth.

[a] Block, Barton, and Radin, *Business Judgment Rule,* p. 101.

assets. The court invalidated this option on the basis that it opposed the spirit of the Williams Act. An appeals court later affirmed this ruling. U.S. Steel ended up acquiring Marathon Oil when Mobil's bid was stopped on antitrust grounds.

An example of the legal viability of lockup options came in subsequent takeover battles involving lockup options that were partially fought in the same Delaware Chancery Court. In the 1988 takeover contest between J. P. Stevens and West Point–Pepperell, both textile manufacturers, the court ruled that the financial enticements which J. P. Stevens offered another bidder, Odyssey Partners, were legal. The enticements included $17 million toward Odyssey's expenses and an additional $8 million if the bidding prices rose significantly. These enticements can be considered small compared to the $1.2 billion offer for J. P. Stevens. The key to the court's thinking is whether the lockup option or the financial incentives given to one bidder and not the other help facilitate the bidding process or limit it. The belief is that the bidding process will bring about higher bids and thereby maximize stockholder wealth. Chancellor Allen of the Delaware Chancery Court wrote in his opinion, "The Board may tilt the playing field if, but only if it is in the stockholders interest to do so."[48]

Although the J. P. Stevens–West Point–Pepperell decision outlined the legally legitimate uses of lockup agreements, a subsequent decision in the Delaware Supreme Court further underscored the illegitimate uses of these agreements. The court ruled that a lockup agreement between Macmillan Inc. and Kohlberg, Kravis, and Roberts (KKR), which allowed KKR to buy certain valuable Macmillan assets even if the agreement between KKR and Macmillan fell through, was merely designed to end the auction process and to preempt bidding, which would maximize the value of stockholder wealth. The court stated that a lockup could be used only if it maximized stockholder wealth. In this case, the lockup was used to drive away an unwanted suitor, Maxwell Communications Corporation. The court's position remains that a lockup can be used only to promote, not inhibit, the auction process.[49]

Capital Structure Changes

A target corporation can initiate various changes in its capital structure in an attempt to ward off a hostile bidder. These defensive capital structure changes are utilized in four main ways.

1. Recapitalize.
2. Assume more debt.
   a. More bonds
   b. Bank loan
3. Issue more shares.
   a. General issue
   b. White squire
   c. Employee stock ownership plan
4. Buy back shares.
   a. Self-tender
   b. Open market purchases
   c. Targeted share repurchases

---

[48] "When Targets Tilt Playing Fields," *New York Times*, April 21, 1988, p. D2.

[49] "Delaware High Court Rules a Company Can't Use 'Lockup' Just to Stop a Suitor," *Wall Street Journal*, May 8, 1989.

Recapitalize Recapitalization has become a more popular, albeit drastic, antitakeover defense. Following a recapitalization, the corporation is in dramatically different financial condition than it was before it. A recapitalization plan often involves paying a superdividend to stockholders which is usually financed through assumption of considerable debt. For this reason they are sometimes known as *leveraged recapitalizations*. When a company is recapitalized, it substitutes most of its equity for debt while paying stockholders a large dividend. In addition to the stock dividend, stockholders receive a stock certificate called a *stub* which represents their new share of ownership in the company.

Recapitalization as an antitakeover defense was pioneered in 1985 by the Multimedia Corporation. Multimedia, a Greenville, South Carolina, broadcasting company, initiated a recapitalization plan after the original founding family members received unsolicited bids for the company in response to their leveraged buyout offer. In addition to a cash payout, Multimedia stockholders saw the value of their stub increase from an original value of $8.31 to $52.25 within two years.[50] The success of the Multimedia deal led to several other recapitalizations, several of which were completed in the following two years. They are as follows:[51]

Company	Year
Metromedia	May 2, 1985
FMC Corporation	April 28, 1986
Colt Industries	July 21, 1986
Owens-Corning	August 28, 1986
Caesar's World	May 18, 1987
Harcourt Brace Jovanovich	May 26, 1987
Allegis Corporation	May 28, 1987

One attraction of a recapitalization plan is that it allows the corporation to act as its own white knight. Many companies in similar situations would either seek out an outside entity to serve as a white knight or attempt a leveraged buyout. The recapitalization plan is an alternative to both. In addition, the large increase in the company's debt, as reflected in the examples shown in Table 5.1, makes the firm less attractive to subsequent bidders. A recapitalization may defeat a hostile bid because stockholders receive a value for their shares, which is usually significantly in excess of historical stock prices. This amount is designed to be superior to the offer from the hostile bidder.

---

[50] "The New Way to Halt Raiders," *New York Times*, May 29, 1988, p. D4.

[51] *New York Times*, May 29, 1988, p. D4.

Table 5.1 COMPARATIVE EFFECTS OF RECAPITALIZATION[a]

		Before Recapitalization	After Recapitalization
Multimedia	Long-term debt	73.2	877.7
	Net worth	248.7	d576.4[b]
	Book value/share	14.91	d52.4
FMC Corporation	Long-term debt	303.2	1787.3
	Net worth	1123.1	d506.6
	Book value/share	7.54	d11.25
Colt Industries	Long-term debt	342.4	1643.1
	Net worth	414.3	d1078
	Book value/share	2.55	d36.91
Owens-Corning	Long-term debt	543.0	1645.2
	Net worth	944.7	d1025
	Book value/share	31.70	d25.94
Holiday Corporation	Long-term debt	992.5	2500
	Net worth	638.7	d850
	Book value/share	27.07	d31.15
Harcourt Brace Jovanovich	Long-term debt	790.3	2550
	Net worth	531.5	d1050
	Book value/share	13.48	d21.00

[a] This table includes only those six companies that actually completed the leveraged recapitalization.

[b] d denotes deficit.

Source: Robert Kleinman, "The Shareholder Gains from Leveraged Cash Outs: Some Preliminary Evidence," *Journal of Applied Corporate Finance* 1, no. 1 (Spring 1988): 50.

Another feature of recapitalization that is most attractive to the target company's management is that it may give management a greater voting control in the target following the recapitalization. The target company can issue several shares of common stock to an employee stock ownership plan.[52] It can also create other security options that may give management enhanced voting power. Other stockholders, however, will receive only one share in the recapitalized company (the stub) as well as whatever combination of debt and cash has been offered. The company is required to make sure that all nonmanagement stockholders receive at least a comparable monetary value for their common stockholdings as did management. The increase in concentration of shares in the hands of insiders that occurred in some of the largest recapitalizations is shown in Table 5.2.

---

[52] Ralph C. Ferrara, Meredith M. Brown, and John Hall, *Takeovers: Attack and Survival* (Salem, N.C.: Butterworth Legal Publishers, 1987), p. 425.

Table 5.2   CHANGES IN SHARE OWNERSHIP OF INSIDERS

Firm	Before Recapitalization	After Recapitalization
1. Multimedia	13%	43%
2. FMC Corporation	19%	40%
3. Colt Industries	7%	38%
4. Owens-Corning	1%	16.2%
5. Holiday Corporation	1.5%	10%
6. Harcourt Brace Jovanovich	7%	30%
7. Caesar's World	1.5%	1.5%[a]
8. Allegis	1%	1%[a]
Means[a]	6.4%	29.5%

[a] Note that the percentage ownership of insiders for Caesar's World and Allegis does not change. In the case of Caesar's World, the New Jersey Casino Control Commission rejected the leveraged recapitalization after it had been approved by stockholders. In the case of Allegis, the leveraged recapitalization was subsequently canceled in favor of restructuring. Hence, the mean value for the "after recapitalization" column excludes these two companies.

Sources: Proxy statements and the Value Line Investment Survey; Robert Kleinman, "The Shareholder Gains from Leveraged Cash Outs: Some Preliminary Evidence," *Journal of Applied Corporate Finance* 1, no. 1 (Spring 1988): 50.

Many recapitalizations may require stockholder approval before they can be implemented, depending on the prevailing state laws and the corporation's own charter. When presenting a recapitalization plan to stockholders, corporations often seek approval for a variety of other antitakeover measures that are proposed as part of a joint antitakeover plan. Some of the other measures discussed earlier such as fair price provisions or staggered boards might be included here.

In addition to possible restrictions in the company charter and state laws, companies may be limited from using the recapitalization defense by restrictive covenants in prior debt agreements. The corporation enters into these legal agreements when it borrows from a bank or from investors through the issuance of corporate bonds. Such agreements place limitations on the firm's future options so as to provide greater assurance for the lenders that the debt will be repaid. The language of these restrictive covenants might prevent the company from taking on additional debt, which might increase the probability that the company could be forced into receivership.

Comparison Between Recapitalization Plans and Leverage Buyouts   There are a number of similarities between leveraged buyouts and recapitalization plans. Some of these are shown below.

1. *Tax advantages of debt.* In a recapitalization plan, the firm assumes a considerable amount of debt and thereby substitutes tax deductible interest payments for taxable dividend payments. Dividend payments are often suspended following the payout of a larger initial dividend. The effect of a leveraged buyout is similar. Firms taken private in a leveraged buyout have assumed considerable debt to finance the LBO. This has the effect of sheltering operating income for the time period in which the debt is being paid.

2. *Concentration of ownership in management's hands.* In an LBO, management usually receives a percentage of ownership as part of the LBO process. When the debt is repaid, this ownership position can become quite valuable, even after warrants held by debtholders are exercised. In a recapitalization plan, management often receives new shares instead of the cash payout that stockholders receive. Managers of firms involved in defensive recapitalization prefer this arrangement because the concentration of ownership in their hands helps prevent a takeover.

Robert Kleinman points out that in view of the similarities between leveraged buyouts and recapitalizations, it is not surprising that good LBO and recapitalization candidates have much in common, such as:

1. A stable earnings stream that can be used to service debt.
2. Low pre-LBO or pre-recapitalization plan debt levels. A low level of debt on the balance sheet gives the firm greater ability to assume more debt.
3. A strong market position.
4. A product line that is not vulnerable to a high risk of obsolescence.
5. A business that does not need high levels of research and development expenditures.
6. A high borrowing capacity as reflected by the collateral value of the firm's assets.
7. Assets and/or divisions that can be readily sold to help pay the debt.
8. Experienced management with a proven track record, an important characteristic since the added pressure of the high debt service does not leave a high margin for error.[53]

---

[53] Kleinman, "The Sharcholder Gains from Leveraged Cash Outs," pp. 47–48.

Sante Fe Versus Henley

In 1989, the Santa Fe Corporation used the largest recapitalization plan ever implemented as a defensive tactic to prevent a takeover by the Henley Group. Henley was a conglomeration of assorted companies spun off from the Allied Signal merger. They were managed by Michael Dingman who prides himself in bringing poorly performing companies to profitability. The term *Dingman's Dogs* is sometimes used to describe these poor performers.[54] In February 1988, following the Henley Group's extended attempt to take over Santa Fe, as well as overtures from other would-be bidders such as Olympia and York, Santa Fe announced a major recapitalization plan. The plan featured the payout of a $4.7 billion dividend to stockholders, which was to be financed through the selloff of assets as well as the assumption of considerable debt. Santa Fe agreed to pay a $25 dividend to stockholders combined with a $5 subordinated debenture for each of its 156.5 million shares. The cash portion of this payout came to $4 billion. The debentures had a face value of $783 million and a 16 percent coupon rate. The repayment structure on the debentures was structured so that no payments would be made for five years. This requirement was designed to reduce the demands on Santa Fe's already stretched cash flows.

Santa Fe raised approximately $2.25 billion from assets sales. These included the Southern Pacific Railroad, pipelines, timberlands, and other real estate as well as other subsidiaries. In addition, Santa Fe borrowed $1.9 billion. Santa Fe's financial leverage increased dramatically. The debt to total capital ratio rose from 26 to 87 percent following the recapitalization plan. This higher financial leverage represents a greater degree of risk for the corporation. The higher amount of fixed payments that Santa Fe is forced to make may present a problem for the firm in the event that its revenues decline in response to an economic downturn. However, Santa Fe feels that, given the increased stability that it now sees in some of its businesses, it will be able to sustain the payments even in tougher economic conditions.

Use of Recapitalization Plans Protected by Poison Pills

The recapitalization plan is the company's own offer which is presented to stockholders as an alternative to a hostile raider's offer. Before 1988, companies used poison pills to try to counteract the bidder's tender offer while presenting their own unencumbered recapitalization plan.

---

[54] *Business Week*, February 15, 1988, p. 28.

In November 1988, a Delaware Chancery Court struck down the combined use of these defenses.[55]

Interco, a St. Louis based retailer, had been the object of a tender offer from the Rales Brothers in 1988. Interco is a diversified manufacturer of such well-known products as London Fog rainwear, Florsheim shoes, and Converse athletic shoes, as well as furniture under the names of Broyhill and Ethan Allen. The Rales Brothers, relatively little known investors from Washington, D.C., had made a $2.73 billion tender offer for Interco. When Interco responded with a recapitalization plan combined with its poison pill defense, the Rales Brothers sued. They contended, and the Delaware court agreed, that Interco's recapitalization offer was unfair to stockholders since the poison pill was directed against the Rales's tender offer while Interco's recapitalization plan was not affected by the poison pill. The court agreed that the combined use of these two defenses was an abuse of the Business Judgment Rule. Given the presence of the poison pill, stockholders could not consider both offers on an equal footing.

By taking away the poison pill shield, the recapitalization plan loses some of its original advantage as an antitakeover defense. In the wake of the Interco decision, a recapitalization plan must be financially better for stockholders to be effective. This may be difficult since tender offers can be all cash, whereas some recapitalization plans can be more difficult to evaluate since they involve a combination of cash and securities.

Assume More Debt   While the assumption of more debt occurs in a recapitalization plan, the firm can also directly add debt without resorting to a recapitalization in an effort to prevent a takeover. A low level of debt relative to equity can make a company vulnerable to a takeover. A hostile bidder can utilize the target's borrowing capacity to help finance the acquisition of the target. Although some may interpret a low level of debt to be beneficial to the corporation by lowering its risk, this can also increase the company's vulnerability to a takeover. Additional debt can also make the target riskier because of the higher debt service relative to the target's cash flow. Presumably some level of debt would outweigh the positive effect of adding the target's cash flows to that of the acquirers. This is something of a *scorched earth defense* since preventing the acquisition by assuming additional debt may result in the target's future bankruptcy. (See Interco case study.)

The target can acquire the additional debt in two ways: (1) it can borrow directly from a bank or other lender, or (2) it can issue bonds.

---

[55] "Interco Defense Against Rales Is Struck Down," *Wall Street Journal*, November 2, 1988, p. 83.

CASE STUDY: *INTERCO: A CASE STUDY IN THE PROBLEMS WITH RECAPITALIZATION*

In the fall of 1988, St. Louis-based Interco found itself the object of a hostile bid from the Rales Brothers. Steven and Michael Rales had offered $74 per share in a $2.73 billion all-cash tender offer. Interco responded with a recapitalization plan defense. This defense was coupled with a poison pill, however. As is explained elsewhere in this chapter, the use of a poison pill to shield a recapitalization plan was found by a Delaware Chancery Court to be illegal. Nonetheless, the recapitalization plan proved sufficient to counter the Rales Brothers' offer. While the recapitalization plan ensured Interco's independence, it did so at a drastic price. The plan, in part developed by merger strategists Bruce Wasserstein and Joe Perella, increased Interco's debt service obligations beyond the firm's ability to pay. The result was a cash flow crisis that culminated in the firm's eventual default on June 15, 1990. Holders of junk bonds issued in the recapitalization process eventually had to accept equity in exchange for their bonds in order to avoid further losses that would result from bankruptcy.[a]

The expected success of the Interco recapitalization plan was contingent on the accuracy of the forecasts developed for assets sales and revenues from the company's operations. This plan, labeled Project Imperial, was reported by the *Wall Street Journal* to have been developed by "a few number crunching financial people with very little oversight from top officials at either Interco or Wasserstein–Perella."[b] The *Journal* reported that 10-year projections of cash flows and earnings were made by a team of financial analysts, one of whom was only one and a half years out of college, without the benefit of much basic research. While several scenarios were considered, the worst case showed a 20 percent annual return following the recapitalization.

The firm of Wasserstein–Perella earned $5.5 million for its work in the antitakeover defense of Interco. The plan it developed called for the sale of divisions such as the Ethan Allen furniture chain for approximately $500 million. However, the eventual sale price proved to be only $388 million. The Central Hardware division was valued at $312 million in the recapitalization plan but brought only $245 million when it was sold. Record annual profits of $70 million were forecasted for divisions such as Converse shoes, while fiscal 1990 profits proved to be only $11 million. Given the volatile and competitive nature of the athletic shoe industry, the continual generation of increasing profit levels would be a most difficult task for any company in this industry. (See Figure 5.1.)

The fate of the Interco recapitalization plan is symbolic of much of what went wrong in the world of leveraged mergers during the late 1980s. Seemingly sophisticated financial analysis could be developed to make risky leveraged deals appear attractive. The art of financial valuation, as practiced by some, has therefore fallen into much criticism.[c]

[a]Michael Quint, Interco Pact Includes Conversion of Bonds to Stock, New York Times, August 1, 1990, p. D22.
[b] George Anders and Francine Schwadel, "Wall Streeters Helped Interco Defeat Raiders—But at a Heavy Price," *Wall Street Journal,* July 11, 1990, p. 1.
[c] Data for this case study were drawn from research by George Anders and Francine Schwadel of the *Wall Street Journal.*

INTERCO's Tale of Woe

It Sold Off Businesses...
Contribution to sales

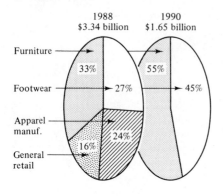

Proceeds Were Disappointing...
Projected versus actual sales, in millions of dollars

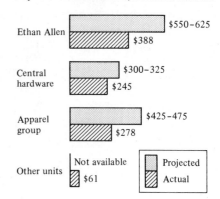

Leaving a Heavy Debt Load...
Long-term debt (including current maturities and debentures issued in recap) in billions of dollars

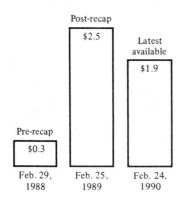

As the Stock Fails to Recover
Interco's stock price, monthly close

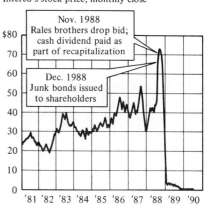

Figure 5.1 INTERCO's recapitalization problems. (*Source:* George Anders and Francine Schwadel, "Wall Streeters Helped Interco Defeat Raiders—But at a Heavy Price," *Wall Street Journal,* July 11, 1990, p. A7. Reprinted by permission of the *Wall Street Journal,* copyright © 1990 Dow Jones & Company, Inc. All Rights Reserved Worldwide.)

If the target has to wait for SEC approval for the bonds to be issued, it might be taken over before the debt issuance is completed. Companies with this defense in mind can prepare for it by obtaining prior SEC approval to issue bonds and taking advantage of Rule 415 which is called the *shelf registration rule*. This rule allows the corporation to register with the SEC all those securities offerings it intends to make within the upcoming two years.

Liability Restructuring Research

The assumption of additional debt is a way the corporation alters its balance sheet by increasing its liabilities. Dann and DeAngeleo analyzed the impact that an increase in a company's liabilities would have on its stock prices.[56] They reported an average stock price decline following liability restructurings of −2%. This implies that there is a measurable reduction in stockholder wealth following these restructurings.

Issue More Shares   Another antitakeover option available to the target company would be to issue more shares. This would change the company's capital structure since it increases equity while maintaining the current level of debt. By issuing more shares the target company makes it more difficult and costly to acquire a majority of the stock in the target. The notion of increasing the number of shares to make it more difficult for a raider to obtain control has been around for some time. Matthew Josephson, in his book *The Robber Barons*, points out how this tactic was used to prevent Cornelius Vanderbilt from obtaining control of the Erie Railroad: "This explains how the 'Erie Gang' or the Erie Lackawanna Railroad successfully prevented the New York Central Railroad and Cornelius Vanderbilt from taking control of Erie. Every time Vanderbilt came close to getting a majority Erie would issue more shares."[57]

On the negative side, issuing more shares dilutes stockholder equity. It is reasonable to expect the company's stock price to decline in the face of this stock issuance. This downward movement in the company's stock price is the market's reflection of the costs of this issuance. In the presence of these clear costs to stockholders, many states require that corporations receive adequate compensation in return for the newly issued shares. When the shares are issued and not given to a particular group or company, they are called a *general issue*. However, since these shares might fall into hostile bidders' hands, the target often issues these shares directly into friendly hands. Such is the case in a white squire defense where the target both increases the number of shares

---

[56] Larry Y. Dann and Eugene DeAngelo, "Corporate Financial Policy and Corporate Control: A Study in Defensive Adjustments in Asset and Ownership Structure." Working Paper 86-11, Managerial Economics Research Center of the University of Rochester, August 1986.

[57] Matthew Josephson, *The Robber Barons* (New York: Harcourt Brace & Co., 1934).

necessary to obtain control and makes sure that these newly issued shares will not fall into the hostile bidder's hands. The white squire is presumably interested in the stock only for investment purposes and not in order to take control of the company.

Share Issuance and ESOPs Another option which the target can seek out is to issue the stock to the *employee stock ownership plan* (ESOP). In order to make it easy for the ESOP to purchase these shares, the ESOP may borrow using the corporation's guarantee. The company can also make tax deductible contributions into the ESOP which can then be used to repay the loan. ESOPs are discussed in greater detail in Chapter 7.

In light of the passage of the Delaware antitakeover law, leveraged "bust-up" acquisitions can be impeded by placing 15 percent of a firm's outstanding shares in an employee stock ownership plan. In December 1989, Chevron Corporation, in a defensive measure to prevent a takeover by cash-rich Penzoil Corporation, issued 14.1 million shares to create an ESOP. Chevron borrowed $1 billion to repurchase the newly issued shares.[58] Prior to the issuance of these shares, employees had held 11 percent of Chevron's outstanding shares through a profit-sharing program. In an effort to offset the dilution effects of the share issuance, Chevron announced a program of stock repurchases in 1990.

Shamrock Holdings Inc. Versus Polaroid Corporation In 1988, when Polaroid was the target of a unwanted takeover offer from Shamrock Holdings Inc., it utilized the ESOP stock issuance defense. Shamrock Holdings Inc. is a Burbank, California, television and radio company owned by the Roy Disney family. It bought 6.9 percent of Polaroid and expressed interest in acquiring control of the company. Polaroid created an employee stock ownership plan for the purpose of avoiding this takeover. It then placed 10 million newly issued shares, which constituted 14 percent of the outstanding stock of Polaroid, into the ESOP.

Polaroid considered this an effective defense since the ESOP would likely exercise its voting power to oppose an acquisition by Shamrock and to maintain current management. Polaroid, a Delaware-based corporation, had its defense bolstered by the ESOP stock issuance inasmuch as a bidder must buy 85 percent of a Delaware incorporated target in order to be able to take control and sell off assets. (See Chapter

---

[58] "Chevron Purchasing Shares to Replace Stock Used for ESOP," *Wall Street Journal*, February 13, 1990, p. A5.

3.) With the ESOP stock issuance only 86 percent of the outstanding stock remains in public hands.

Impact of ESOPs on Share Prices   Following Polaroid's successful use of the ESOP defense, more companies began to adopt ESOPs. A recent study by Analysis Group, Inc., a consulting firm in Belmont, Massachusetts, showed that the formation of defensive ESOPs had a depressing effect on stock prices. Defensive ESOPs are those employee stock ownership plans that are formed as a takeover defense. The Analysis Group study also showed that, in a group of 21 firms forming ESOPs after the Polaroid ESOP was upheld in a Delaware court, the stock prices of 11 of these firms declined significantly following the announcement of the formation of the ESOP. For those firms that showed a decline, the average change was −5.1 percent (see Table 5.3).[59]

Buy Back Shares   Another way to prevent a takeover is for the target to buy back its own shares. Such share repurchases can have several advantages for a target corporation, namely:

1. Share repurchases can divert shares away from a hostile bidder. Once the target has acquired certain shares, these shares are no longer available for the bidder to purchase.
2. Share repurchases can also divert shares away from the hands of arbitragers. Arbitragers can be of great assistance to a hostile bidder since they acquire shares with the explicit purpose of earning high returns by selling them to the highest bidder. This is often the hostile acquiring corporation. By preventing some of the target's shares from falling into the hostile bidder's hands, the target can make the acquisition process more difficult.
3. The acquisition of the target's own shares can allow the corporation to use up its own resources. The target can use these resources to finance the target's own acquisition. For example, if the target uses some of its excess cash reserves to acquire its own shares, the acquirer cannot use this cash to pay off some of the debt incurred in the acquisition.
4. Similar reasoning can be applied to share repurchases by the target which are financed through debt. By borrowing, the target is using up its own borrowing capacity which could have been

---

[59] "Use of ESOPs Against Bids Lowers Stock," *Wall Street Journal,* June 6, 1989, p. C1.

TABLE 5.3   ESOPs AND STOCK PRICES

Company	Takeover Rumors	Price Change (pct.)
Boise Cascade	No	1.1
Dunkin Donuts	Yes	−4.9
Fairchild Industries	Yes	−1.7
ITT Corporation	No	−2.1
Lockheed Corporation	Yes	−6.2
Tribune Corporation	Yes	−9.8
Horn & Hardart	Yes	−12.1
Average		5.1

Source: Analysis Group, Inc., *Wall Street Journal,* June 6, 1989, p. C1. Reprinted by permission of the *Wall Street Journal,* copyright © 1989 Dow Jones & Company, Inc. All Rights Reserved Worldwide.

used to finance some of the acquisition. This can be effective in deterring bids by raiders who are relying on the heavy use of leverage.

5. The acquisition of shares can be a necessary first step in implementing a white squire defense. If the target has enough SEC-authorized shares available it must first acquire them through share repurchases.

Although share repurchases have several clear advantages for a target corporation, they are not without drawbacks. Share repurchases may be an instinctive first reaction by an embattled target CEO who is striving to maintain his company's independence. However, by repurchasing his company's shares, he is withdrawing outstanding shares from the market. With fewer shares outstanding, it may be easier for the acquirer to obtain control since the bidder has to buy fewer shares to acquire 51 percent of the target. One solution to this dilemma is to use targeted share repurchases. This takes shares out of the hands of those who would most likely sell them to the hostile bidder. If at the same time these shares are placed in friendly hands, the strategy can be successful. When Carter Hawley Hale combined a buyback of 17.5 million shares in 1984 with a sale of stock to General Cinema Corporation, it was implementing a similar strategy to prevent The Limited from obtaining control of Carter Hawley Hale.

A target can implement a share repurchase plan in three ways:

1. General, nontargeted purchases.
2. Targeted share repurchases.
3. Self-tender offer.

General, nontargeted purchases simply buy back a certain number of shares without regard to their ownership. Targeted share repurchases, on the other hand, are designed to take shares out of the hands of stockholders who may sell their shares to the hostile bidder. A self-tender occurs when the target makes a tender offer for its own securities. Regulations governing self-tenders are different from those that apply to tender offers by an outside party. Self-tenders are regulated by Section 13e of the Securities and Exchange Act of 1934. A company engaging in a self-tender has two main sets of filing requirements. According to Rule 13e-1, the target cannot buy its own securities following a tender offer by a hostile bidder unless it first files with the SEC and announces its intentions. The target firm must disclose the following:

1. Name and class of securities.
2. Identity of purchaser.
3. Markets and exchanges that will be used for the purchases.
4. Purpose of the repurchase.
5. Intended disposition of the repurchased shares.[60]

The target corporation is also bound by Rule 14d–9 which requires that it file a Schedule 14D–9 with the SEC within 10 days of the commencement of the tender offer. The 14d–9 filing, which is also required in the case of a hostile bid, requires management to indicate its position on the self-tender.

Discriminatory Self-Tenders: Unocal Versus Mesa

In February 1985, Boone Pickens announced a bid from his investor group, Mesa Partners II, for Unocal Corporation.[61] Mesa had just purchased 8 percent of the larger Los Angeles-based oil company. Pickens' company, Mesa Petroleum, was flush with cash from successful prior offers for Gulf and Phillips Petroleum. Pickens made $800 million on his bid for Gulf and $90 million on the offer for Phillips.[62] Pickens has stated that these gains were not greenmail, based on his long-held position of refusing to accept a higher payment for his shares unless other shareholders could participate in the buyout by the target.

Pickens increased the pressure on Phillips by increasing his holdings to 13 percent of Unocal's outstanding shares. He found Unocal an attractive target because of its low debt level and significant size (revenues of $11.5 billion). Mesa increased its credibility by amassing a war

---

[60] Ferrara, Brown, and Hall, *Takeovers*, p. 78.

[61] *Unocal v. Mesa*, 493 A. 2d 949 (Del 1985).

[62] Madrick, *Taking America*, p. 282.

chest of $4 billion in financing through the help of its investment banker Drexel Burnham Lambert. In April 1985, Pickens bid for just over 50 percent of Unocal at $54 per share. Unocal, led by chairman Fred Hartley, responded with a discriminatory self-tender offer for 29 percent of Unocal's outstanding shares. Hartley wanted to defeat the Pickens bid but did not want to give his foe greenmail. His self-tender offer, therefore, contained a provision that Mesa Partners II could not participate in Unocal's offer. Pickens appealed to the Delaware Chancery Court to rule on what he felt was a clearly unfair offer by Unocal. The Delaware Chancery Court agreed that Unocal's offer was illegal, a ruling that was later reversed by the Delaware Supreme Court. The Delaware Supreme Court concluded on May 17, 1985 that Unocal's offer was within the board of directors' rights according to the Business Judgment Rule. The court found that Mesa's offer was a "grossly inadequate two-tiered coercive tender offer coupled with the threat of greenmail." The higher court held that Unocal's response to this type of offer was within its rights as provided by the vague Business Judgment Rule. The Delaware Supreme Court ruling forced Pickens to capitulate: he agreed to a standstill agreement. Ironically, this ruling led to the SEC's review of discriminatory self-tenders, which eventually resulted in a change in tender offer rules making such discriminatory self-tenders illegal.

Market Reaction to the Unocal Decision   Kamma, Weintrop, and Weir analyzed the market reaction to the Delaware Supreme Court decision expanding the board of directors' authority to take a broad range of actions to keep a company independent.[63] The market responded by lowering the probability of a potential target receiving a takeover premium in a successful hostile bid. Kamma, Weintrop, and Weir examined a sample of 124 firms that were targets of stock purchases that warranted Schedule 13D filings on May 10 and May 24, 1985. They divided these firms into two groups: 24 that were clearly targets of hostile bids and the remaining 100 that were not. These subsamples were further subdivided into Delaware and non-Delaware firms. The study results revealed that the 14 "hostile Delaware firms" earned abnormal negative returns of 1.51 percent. The other group of firms failed to show a statistically significant abnormal performance. Kamma, Weintrop, and Weir's results support the subsequent SEC action that made discriminatory repurchases illegal and show that such discriminatory repurchases result in a decline in stockholder wealth.

---

[63] Sreenivas Kamma, Joseph Weintrop, and Peggy Weir, "Investors' Perceptions of the Delaware Supreme Court Decision in *Unocal v. Mesa," Journal of Financial Economics* 20 (January/March 1988): 419–430.

CASE STUDY: *POLAROID'S $1.1 BILLION STOCK BUYOUT*

In 1988, the Polaroid Corporation found itself the object of a unwanted bid from Roy E. Disney and his company, Shamrock Holdings, Inc. Polaroid had rejected Disney's overtures and instituted various defenses including the placement of stock into an employee stock ownership plan. However, Disney did not give up his bid to take over the camera manufacturer.

In January 1989, Polaroid announced a plan to buy back $1.1 billion worth of stock. Ironically, the stock repurchase would be financed by the sale of a large block of stock to a private investor group. The private investor group's ownership in Polaroid will rise from 8½ percent to 13 percent due to the combined effect of both the increased number of shares as well as the fact that there are fewer shares outstanding as a result of the buyback. The group would pay $300 million for Polaroid preferred stock, which would be convertible into common stock at $50 per share. This would give the group, which included institutional investors such as the California State Teachers Retirement System, 8 million new shares. "If Polaroid bought back stock at its current level, it could buy 27 million shares, reducing the 71.6 million shares outstanding to 44.6 million."[a]

Polaroid used the combination of a stock sale and a stock repurchase to take shares off the market where they might fall into a raider's hands as well as to place more shares into friendly hands. The combined effect was to make a takeover by Disney or any other raider more difficult.

[a] $1.1 Billion Polaroid Buyback," *New York Times,* January 31, 1989, p. D1.

The Walt Disney Company's Acquisition of Arvida

In 1984, the Walt Disney Company became the target of a hostile bid by Saul Steinberg and Reliance Group Holdings. Financed by Drexel Burnham Lambert, Steinberg made a credible offer to take over the venerable motion picture company. In an effort to ward off this hostile bid, Walt Disney sought to acquire other firms by offering Disney stock in exchange for the target's stock. In May 1984 Disney began negotiation to purchase the Arvida Corporation from the Bass Brothers. The Bass Brothers had bought this real estate concern in a leveraged buyout from the bankrupt Penn Central Corporation in 1978. Disney felt that Arvida was a natural fit since it was a real estate development firm. Disney owned extensive real estate in Florida, much of which was undeveloped. Disney, lacking the expertise to develop its real estate assets, sought this expertise in Arvida. Moreover, the acquisition of Arvida, financed by Disney stock, reduced Steinberg's holdings from 12.1 to 11.1 percent.[64]

---

[64] John Taylor, *Storming the Magic Kingdom* (New York: Ballantine Books, 1987), p. 89.

One of the problems with defensive acquisitions financed by the issuance of stock is that the acquiring company may be concentrating shares in the hands of other substantial shareholders. As a result of this stock purchase, the Bass Brothers owned 5.9 percent of Disney stock. This problem can be alleviated if the new stockholders will sign a standstill agreement and promise to support management's position in future stockholder votes. In this particular case, the Basses refused to sign such an agreement.

Corporate Restructuring

Corporate restructuring is another of the more drastic antitakeover defenses. It may involve selling off major parts of the target or even engaging in major acquisitions. Such defensive restructuring has been criticized as a case of "Do Unto Yourself As Others Would Do Unto You." Defensive corporate restructuring can be both a preventative and an active antitakeover defensive. If a firm believes it may become a takeover target, it may restructure in order to prevent this occurrence. Takeovers also occur in the midst of a takeover battle when the target feels that only drastic actions will prevent a takeover.

It is often difficult for an incumbent management to justify restructuring to prevent an acquisition. It involves the management taking considerable liberty with stockholders' resources. Management should be able to convince stockholders that such drastic changes in the nature of the target's business coupled with the rejection of the bidder's proposed premium are both in their best interests.

Defensive restructuring can take the following forms:

1. Take the corporation private—leveraged buyout.
2. Sell off valued assets.
3. Acquire other companies.
4. Liquidate the company.

Going private is often the reaction of a management that does not want to give up control of the corporation. Going private and leveraged buyouts are discussed in detail in Chapter 7. They can be justified from the stockholder's point of view when they result in higher premiums than rival bids.

The sale of valued assets to prevent a takeover is a highly controversial defensive action. The idea is that the target will sell off the assets the acquirer wants, and so the target will become less desirable in the eyes of the hostile bidder. As a result the bidder may withdraw its offer. This is essentially a lockup transaction. Stockholders have often strongly opposed these actions and have sometimes successfully sued to prevent the completion of these transactions.

There are several reasons why a target may acquire another company to prevent its own takeover. First, it may seek to create an antitrust conflict for the acquirer. This will then involve the acquisition of a company in one of the bidder's main lines of business. This tactic was somewhat more effective when the Justice Department exercised stricter antitrust enforcement. However, even if there is a reasonable likelihood that the takeover will be opposed on antitrust grounds, this defense can be deactivated by the sale of the acquired business following the acquirer's acquisition of the target. In its filings with the Justice Department and the FTC, the acquirer can clearly state its intentions to sell the target's new acquisitions. This will likely result in an approval of the acquisition pending the acquirer's ability to sell off the necessary parts of the target. A classic case of acquisitions designed to ward off bidders by creating antitrust conflicts occurred when Marshall Field and Company made a series of acquisitions in 1980 in areas where potential bidders were present. These acquisitions were usually motivated not by any economic factor but only to keep Marshall Field independent. The outcome of these acquisitions was a financially weaker Marshall Field and Company.

The target might want to acquire another concern to reduce its appeal in the eyes of the acquirer. If the target is a highly profitable, streamlined company, this state of financial well-being can be quickly changed by acquiring less profitable businesses in areas the acquirer does not want to be in. If these acquisitions involve the assumption of greater debt, this increased leverage can also make the target less appealing.

One final restructuring option available for the target company is liquidation. In liquidation the target sells all the target's assets and uses the proceeds to pay a liquidating dividend to stockholders. The payment of the dividend is restricted by a variety of legal constraints that protect the rights of the firm's creditors. Therefore, the liquidating dividend needs to be calculated after financial adjustments have been made to take into account outstanding obligations that have to be satisfied. In the best interests of stockholders, this dividend payment has to exceed the offer of the hostile bidder. However, this can be possible in instances where the target feels that, perhaps because of inordinately low securities market prices, the premium above market price offered by the bidder is below that of the liquidation value of the company.

Litigation As an Antitakeover Defense Litigation is one of the more common antitakeover defenses. In the early stages of the hostile takeover era (the mid-1970s), it was an effective means of preventing a takeover. However, its power in this area has somewhat diminished. Today litigation is only one of an array of defensive actions a target will take in hopes of preventing a takeover. A major goal of this type of litigation is to have the court grant an injunction that will prevent the takeover process from continuing. Such an injunction coupled with a restraining order might bar the hostile bidder from purchasing additional stock until the bidder can satisfy the court that the target's charges are without merit.

The temporary halting of a takeover can delay the acquisition, giving the target time to mount more effective defenses. The additional time can also allow the target to seek out a white knight. Litigation and the grant of injunctive relief may provide the necessary time to allow a bidding process to develop. Other bidders will now have time to properly consider the benefits of making an offer for the target. The bidding process should result in higher offers for the target. Another major benefit of litigation is to give the bidder time to raise the offer price. The target might indirectly give the bidder the impression that if the offer price and terms were improved it would drop the litigation.

The more common forms of defensive litigation are the following:

1. *Antitrust violations.* This type of litigation was more effective during the 1960s and 1970s when the Justice Department practiced stricter enforcement of the antitrust laws. However, given the department's pro-business stance under the Nixon and Reagan administrations, it became much more difficult to establish an antitrust violation. The Justice Department has become slightly more active in antitrust enforcement under the Bush administration.

2. *Inadequate disclosure.* This type of lawsuit often contends that the bidder has not provided complete and full disclosure as required under the Williams Act. The target might argue that, in not providing full and complete disclosure, the acquirer has either not given stockholders adequate information or has provided information that presents an inaccurate picture of the acquirer or the acquirer's intention. The target in these types of lawsuits commonly maintains that the bidder did not convincingly state how he would raise the requisite capital to complete the purchase of all the stock bid for. The bidder usually contends that the disclosure is more than adequate or agrees to supplement his filings.

3. *Fraud.* This is a more serious charge and is more difficult to prove. Except in more extreme circumstances, it cannot be relied on to play a major role in the target's defense.

Litigation Research   The seminal piece of research in this area of antitakeover defenses is the 1985 study by Gregg Jarrell.[65] In his study of attempted and completed takeovers that involved litigation between 1962 and 1980, Jarrell found that litigation occurred in one-third of all tender offers. As noted earlier, litigation can be beneficial for the target shareholders even when it does not result in the acquirer's retraction of the bid. Litigation can result in a bid being delayed as well as forcing the bidder to raise his offer.

Jarrell found that 62 percent of the offers that had litigation had competing bids, whereas only 11 percent of those that did not have litigation had competing offers. He also found that, although it seems reasonable that ligitation would cause bidders to raise their offer price in order to get the target to drop the litigation and avoid the legal expenses as well as the possibility that the bid might be permanently halted, there was no evidence of a significant price effect. On the average, a stock price decline took place when litigation was initiated. This decline occurred both for firms that were eventually acquired and for those that remained independent. However, unacquired stock returns fell −3.4 percent, whereas acquired returns declined slightly more than −1 percent.

Jarrell also found that when an auction for the firm resulted following the initiation of litigation, there was an additional 17 percent premium above the first offer relative to nonauctioned firms. When litigation results in the bidder withdrawing its offer, however, target company stockholders suffer major losses. They incur both the loss of a premium that averaged 32 percent for Jarrell's sample of firms as well as the costs of litigation. We can conclude that litigation brings clear benefits for targets, but if the bid is withdrawn, it may also result in significant losses for target stockholders.

Anderson Clayton Versus Gerber Products

In 1977, Anderson Clayton, a Houston-based food company, sought to expand by acquiring other companies. It had diversified operations ranging from processing soybeans to a coffee business to a life insurance company.[66] Anderson Clayton made a friendly offer for Stokley Van Camp, a major food processor. When Stokely Van Camp rejected Anderson Clayton's offer, Anderson Clayton set its eyes on other game.

---

[65] Gregg Jarrell, "Wealth Effects of Litigating by Targets: Do Interests Diverge in a Merge," *Journal of Law and Economics* 28 (April 1985): 151–177.

[66] Madrick, *Taking America*, pp. 160–164.

Its gaze finally settled on Gerber Products, a company in Fremont, Michigan, famous for its line of baby foods. Anderson Clayton made friendly overtures toward Gerber Products but was immediately rebuffed. The management of Anderson Clayton decided it would go ahead with an offer for Gerber, even if this meant making an unfriendly tender offer. Anderson Clayton made a $40 bid, which amounted to a P/E multiple of 14. Gerber reacted by mounting an all-out, no-holds-barred defense. A central component of Gerber's defense was its use of litigation.

Gerber Products filed suit against Anderson Clayton in federal court in Grand Rapids, Michigan. Its suit charged that Anderson Clayton's acquisition offer would constitute an antitrust conflict. This charge would seem surprising by today's antitrust enforcement standards since Anderson Clayton and Gerber Products did not market any of the same products. However, Gerber's antitrust charges were based on the antitrust view that persisted in the 1960s and part of the 1970s, which stated that not just actual antitrust conflicts were relevant, but also potential conflicts had to be prevented. Gerber contended that Anderson Clayton could develop a baby products business in the future; therefore, it should be prevented from acquiring a potential competitor. In its suit Gerber also stated that it had been contemplating entering the salad oil market, in which Anderson Clayton had already established its presence.

Gerber's lawsuit also charged that Anderson Clayton did not make full and sufficient disclosure in its tender offer filings of $2.1 million in questionable payments which it had made overseas. This part of the lawsuit was designed not only to put another legal roadblock in front of Anderson Clayton, but also to embarrass the bidder by generating additional adverse publicity on an issue on which Anderson Clayton wanted to adopt a low profile.

Gerber felt that it had additional protection under Michigan's antitakeover law which would delay the tender offer for 60 days. This additional time allowed Gerber Products to seek out an acceptable white knight. Gerber took this opportunity to begin discussions with Europe's Unilever. Gerber also contended in its suit that Anderson Clayton did not make sufficient disclosure of its financing arrangements in its tender offer filing materials. This is also required under Michigan's antitakeover law. Anderson Clayton's response was to try the friendly approach once again. It attempted to convince Gerber's board of directors that the offer should be presented to shareholders. These overtures were also rebuffed. Next, Anderson Clayton filed suit contending that Gerber had made insufficient disclosures. In addition, in order to ensure compliance with Michigan's antitakeover law, Anderson Clayton secured a financing agreement from several New York banks.

In July 1977, at its annual meeting, Gerber disclosed that second-quarter earnings had fallen 33 percent. This was the third quarter in a row that Gerber had declared fallen earnings. Anderson Clayton felt that Gerber was deliberately understating its earnings merely to dissuade potential bidders from making an offer for the company. Anderson Clayton's response to the earnings announcement was to lower its offer from $40 to $37. This action immediately put pressure on Gerber's board of directors since stockholders could now state that the rejection of the first $40 offer cost them $3 per share.

Anderson Clayton felt that Gerber had an advantage because Gerber's lawsuits were filed in Michigan. Indeed, a series of rulings by Judge Fox were all favorable to Gerber. Anderson Clayton faced the prospect of a trial on the securities charges in September 1977, followed by another trial in which the antitrust charges would then be decided. Anderson Clayton believed that the series of legal issues that needed to be decided would not be settled until as late as 1979. Even if Anderson Clayton won, Unilever or some other bidder might materialize and then escalate Gerber's price.

In light of the uncertainties of the extended legal battle, Anderson Clayton decided to withdraw its offer. The Gerber Products legal defense was credited with warding off Anderson Clayton's offer. Gerber Products' stock prices fell from $34.375 to $28.25 in one day in response to this announcement. Arbitragers, who had gambled that Gerber would be bought by some company, experienced large losses. Litigation was now recognized as a potent defense that must be carefully considered when evaluating a takeover contest.

Pac-Man Defense

The *Pac-Man defense*, so-named after the popular video game in which characters try to eat each other before they are eaten themselves, is one of the more colorful defenses employed by target companies. It occurs when the target makes an offer to buy the raider in response to the raider's bid for the target. One of the more famous uses of this defense came when the Martin Marietta Corporation made an offer to buy Bendix following Bendix's unwanted $43 tender offer for Martin Marietta in the summer of 1982.

The Pac-Man defense is often threatened, but it is seldom used. Prior to the Bendix–Martin Marietta takeover battle, two companies had used it in a vain effort to maintain their independence. NLT Corporation ended up merging with its bidder—American General Corporation. As stated earlier, Cities Service tried the Pac-Man defense in response to Boone Pickens' bid from Mesa Petroleum. Although the defense halted Mesa's bid and helped to get Mesa to accept greenmail, nonetheless Cities Service was put in play and ended up selling out to Occidental Petroleum.

In another early use of the Pac-Man defense, in 1984 Houston Natural Gas Corporation (now Enron Corporation) used a bid for the raider to try to fend off the Coastal Corporation. It was not successful since Houston Natural Gas ended up selling off nearly half its assets to maintain its independence. On the other hand, Heublein Corporation threatened to use the Pac-Man defense when it was confronted by General Cinema Corporation and was able to scare away General Cinema.

EII Holdings Versus American Brands   Another of the few successful uses of the Pac-Man defense occurred in January 1988 when EII Holdings made an offer for American Brand Corporation.[67] In January 1988, Donald Kelly, chairman of EII Holdings, announced a $6 billion bid for American Brands, a firm in Old Greenwich, Connecticut. By 1988, megamerger offers in the billions of dollars were not unusual. Kelly took this occasion as an opportunity to announce a 4.6 percent stake in American Brands. He indicated plans to dismantle American Brands following the takeover. Kelly had previously taken EII holdings private through a leveraged buyout in which he was aided by Kohlberg, Kravis, and Roberts.

EII Holdings was a diverse consumer products group of companies formed from the spinoff of 15 companies following the acquisition of Beatrice. It had lost $1.2 billion for nine months prior to the offer for American Brands. A total of $132 million of this loss came from interest costs, and $147.5 million was a result of the October 1987 stock market crash. EII Holdings was heavily leveraged and to buy American Brands, EII would have to incur significant debt.

American Brands' main businesses were tobacco, spirits, office products, and financial services. Among its popular brand names are Master Locks, Jim Beam bourbon, Titleist golf equipment, and Pall Mall cigarettes. Its financial condition was in sharp contrast to that of EII Holdings. It had strong credit lines compared to the debt-laden EII Holdings. Its chairman, William J. Alley, had been fine tuning the company into good financial condition by selling off businesses that were not in the categories outlined above. American Brands had re-

---

[67] "Takeovers Are Back But Now the Frenzy Is Gone," *Business Week*, February 9, 1988, p. 24; Pamela Sebastian, "American Brands Offer to Buy Debt at E-II Holdings Gets Tepid Response," *Wall Street Journal*, February 24, 1988, p. 8; Stephen Lebaton, "American Brands Set to Buy E-II," *New York Times*, February 1, 1988, p. 1.

cently showed record sales of $9.2 billion, which provided an income of $1.1 billion. This was an increase of 26 percent and 33 percent, respectively.

Many people speculated that Kelly was gambling and that Alley would respond with a Pac-Man defense. Kelly was rumored to have been looking for a buyer to purchase EII Holdings. One way to get such a buyer would be to force an unwilling buyer's hand. Alley responded with an offer for EII Holdings of $2.7 billion. The acquisition was completed, and American Brands took ownership. In the months that followed, American Brands began to disassemble EII by selling off product lines such as Samsonite luggage and Culligan water-treatment operations. American Brands indicated that it only planned to keep five or six of the companies it acquired.

"Just Say No"

In the most basic form of antitakeover defense, the target refuses to be taken over, simply hiding behind its poison pills and other defenses and stating that it will not deactivate them and will not bring the offer before the shareholders. In the "just say no defense," the target can refuse to take any measures, even providing more cash to shareholders, by stating that it has more optimistic plans for the future of the company.

The Universal Foods Corporation, a manufacturer of products such as french fries and cheese, used the just say no defense in 1989 when it turned down an offer from the High Voltage Engineering Corporation. When High Voltage Engineering offered $38 per share, Universal responded that its investment banker, Goldman Sachs, had determined that this offer was inadequate. Universal's board of directors decided that profits were rising and that this was not the time to sell the company. Martin Lipton, the originator of the just say no defense, advised his client, Universal Foods, to reject the offer and not take any other action. Universal compromised by raising its dividend from 18 cents per share to 22 cents.[68] The company's defense, especially its poison pill, was challenged in court. In March 1989, a federal court judge in Wisconsin ruled that if the company's executives believed that the offer was inadequate, then they were in a position to determine an accurate value for the company.

The just say no defense, however, can be challenged by higher offers that will counter the board of directors' position that the future

---

[68] Floyd Norris, "Universal Foods Takeover Defense," *Wall Street Journal*, March 31, 1989, p. D8.

value of the company is worth more to stockholders than the offer price. There will always be some price that will leave the board of directors with no choice but to approve the offer.

Other Less Common Defenses

Pension Parachutes *Pension parachutes* are similar to golden parachutes and can also be considered both an active and a preventative takeover defense. They occur when the target attempts to put a large amount of corporate assets in the company pension plan. It can so be planned that they occur only in the event an outside party buys a certain percentage of the target's stock. An example was the attempted takeover of Union Carbide by the GAF Corporation. When confronted with the GAF bid, Union Carbide tried to amend the company's retirement plan in order to vest an excessive amount of funds in the event of a change in control. GAF challenged this attempt in court, and it was ruled legal.

Overfunded Pension Plans Overfunded pension plans can be a valuable asset to a company; they can also be used to help pay for an acquisition. Asher Edelman, a well-known corporate raider, attempted to use the overfunded pension liabilities of the Fruehauf Corporation to finance the acquisition of Fruehauf. In an attempt to reduce the attractiveness of this asset, Fruehauf amended the company's pension plan so that $70 to $100 million in overfunding would not be available for use in the event any outside entity bought more than 40 percent of Fruehauf. This maneuver was also challenged legally with the court ruling it illegal. The use of pension fund assets by companies has been the focus of much congressional debate. As yet, substantive laws have not resulted.

Golden Handcuffs *Golden handcuffs*, as mentioned earlier, occur when the target is able to negotiate certain conditions for an acquisition which will be favorable for the target. The ability to negotiate favorable conditions implies a certain degree of bargaining power for the target. This probably results from the effectiveness of the target's defenses. Golden handcuffs place limits on what the acquirer can do with the target after the target is acquired. These limitations vary among takeovers and can place restrictions on employee layoffs, require the acquirer to retain management, or prohibit the breakup of the target.

A proposed golden handcuff occurred when Getty Oil was confronted by various attempts by Gordon Getty, a holder of 40 percent of

Getty stock, to take control of the firm. The management proposed that Getty Oil buy back enough stock to make Gordon Getty a holder of 51 percent of the stock and give him control. In return for voting control of Getty Oil, Gordon Getty would have to agree to let someone else run Getty Oil as well as to consent to an outside board of directors.[69] Gordon Getty declined to agree to such restrictive conditions. He ended up supporting an offer to sell the firm to Texaco.

THE INFORMATION CONTENT OF TAKEOVER RESISTANCE

John Pound of Harvard University has studied the information content of takeover bids and the resistance of the target to the takeover.[70] Pound used consensus earnings forecasts as a proxy for the market's expected value of the targets as standalone entities. The effect of different types of takeover contests and defenses on the market's value of the target was assessed by considering whether the consensus changed. These tests were conducted for three samples: targets of friendly bids; targets of hostile bids that were ultimately acquired; and targets of hostile bids that remained independent. Pound observed that the consensus forecasts were unchanged after the initial takeover bid. He therefore concluded that the bids themselves do not convey important information. It also implies that the bid did not reveal to the marketplace a previously undiscovered case of undervaluation.

Pound found the resistance to a takeover to be associated with a downward revision of the average earnings forecasts of approximately 10 percent. This was the case both for firms that were acquired and for those that remained independent. Pound concluded that the market interprets the resistance as a negative signal about future performance.

REFERENCES

Bhagat, S., and J. A. Brickley. "Cumulative Voting: The Value of Minority Shareholder Rights," *Journal of Law and Economics* 27 (October 1984): 339–366.

Block, Dennis, Nancy E. Barton, and Stephen A. Radin. *Business*

---

[69] Steve Coll, *The Taking of Getty Oil* (New York: Atheneum Publishers, 1987).

[70] John Pound, "The Information Effects of Takeover Bids and Resistance," *Journal of Financial Economics* 22, no. 2 (December 1988): 207–227.

Judgement Rule. Englewood Cliffs, N.J.: Prentice-Hall Law and Business Publishers, 1988.

Bradley, Michael, and L. Macdonald Wakeman. "The Wealth Effects of Targeted Share Repurchases." *Journal of Financial Economics* 11 (April 1983): 301–328.

Brickley, James, Ronald Lease, and Clifford Smith. "Ownership Structure and Voting on Antitakeover Amendments." *Journal of Financial Economics* 20, no. 1/2 (January/March 1988): 267–292.

Coll, Steve. *The Taking of Getty Oil*. New York: Atheneum Publishers, 1987.

Commons, Dorman L. *Tender Offer*. New York: Penguin Books, 1985.

Dann, Larry Y., and Harry DeAngelo. "Corporate Financial Policy and Corporate Control: A Study in Defensive Adjustments in Asset and Ownership Structure." Working Paper 86–11, Managerial Economics Research Center of the University of Rochester, August 1986.

Dann, Larry, and Harry DeAngelo. "Standstill Agreements and Privately Negotiated Stock Repurchases and the Market for Corporate Control." *Journal of Financial Economics* 11 (1983).

DeAngelo, Harry, and Eugene Rice. "Antitakeover Charter Amendments and Stockholder Wealth." *Journal of Financial Economics* 11 (April 1983).

Ferrara, Ralph C., Meredith M. Brown, and John Hall. *Takeovers: Attack and Survival*. Austin, TX: Butterworth Legal Publishers, 1987.

Good vs. *Texaco, Inc.*, 507 A. 2d, Delaware Supreme Court.

Herzel, Leo, and Richard Shepio. *Bidders and Targets*. Cambridge: Basil Blackwell, Inc., 1990.

"High Court Rules a Company Can't Use 'Lockup' Just to Stop a Suitor." *Wall Street Journal*, May 8, 1989.

Ho, Michael J. "Share Rights Plans: Poison Pill, Placebo or Suicide Table?" Master's Thesis, Massachusetts Institute of Technology, Sloan School of Management.

"Icahn Gets Green As Others Envy Him." *Wall Street Journal*, November 13, 1989, p. B–1.

"Interco Defense Against Rales Is Struck Down." *Wall Street Journal*, November 2, 1988.

Jarrell, Gregg. "Wealth Effects of Litigating by Targets: Do Interests Diverge in a Merge." *Journal of Law and Economics* 28 (April 1985).

Jarrell, Gregg A., and Annette B. Poulson. "Shark Repellents and Stock

Prices: The Effects of Antitakeover Amendments Since 1980." Mimeograph, August 1986.

Johnston, Moira. *Takeover*. Arbor House Publishers, 1986.

Josephson, Matthew. *The Robber Barons*. New York: Harcourt Brace & Co., 1931.

Kidder, Peabody and Company. "The Impact of the Adoption of Stockholder Rights Plans on Stock Prices." June 1986.

Lambert, Richard A., and David F. Larker. "Golden Parachutes, Executive Decision Making and Stockholder Wealth." *Journal of Accounting Economics* 7 (1985).

Lebaton, Stephen. "American Brands Set to Buy E-II." *New York Times*, February 1, 1988, p. D1.

Linn, Scott C., and John J. McConnell. "An Empirical Investigation of the Impact of Antitakeover Amendments on Common Stock Prices," *Journal of Financial Economics* 11 (April 1983).

Lorsch, Jay W. *Pawns or Potentates*. Boston: Harvard Business School Press, 1989.

Madrick, Jeff. *Taking America*. New York: Bantam Books, 1987.

Malatesta, Paul H., and Ralph A. Walking. "The Impact of Poison Pill Securities on Stockholder Wealth." Working Paper, University of Washington, July 1985.

"Maxwell of Britian Wins a Ruling in Battle to Take Over Macmillan." *New York Times*, July 1988.

Mikkelson, Wayne, and Richard Ruback. "Targeted Share Repurchases and Common Stock Returns." Working Paper No. 1707–86, Massachusetts Institute of Technology, Sloan School of Management, June 1986.

Nathan, C. M., and M. Sobel. "Corporate Stock Repurchases in the Contest of Unsolicited Takeover Bids." *Business Lawyer*, July 1980.

"The New Way to Halt Raiders." *New York Times*, May 29, 1988, p. D4.

"$1.1 Billion Polaroid Buyback." *New York Times*, January 31, 1989, p. D1.

"Package Deal: Some Firms, Seeking to Raise the Value of Their Shares, Plan to Offer New Securities Units." *Wall Street Journal*, December 6, 1988, p. A18.

Partch, Megan. "The Creation of a Class of Limited Voting Common Stock and Shareholder Wealth." University of Oregon Working Paper, May 1986.

Pickens, T. *Boone*. Boston: Houghton Mifflin Co., 1987.

"The Poison Pill Takes a Beating." *Wall Street Journal*, November 14, 1988, p. D2.

Pound, John. "The Effectiveness of Antitakeover Amendments on Take-over Activity." *Journal of Law and Economics* 30 (October 1987): 353–367.

Pound, John. "The Information Effects of Takeover Bids and Resistance." *Journal of Financial Economics* 22, no. 2 (December 1988).

Ruback, Richard. "An Overview of Takeover Defenses." In *Mergers and Acquisitions*, edited by Alan J. Auerbach. Chicago: National Bureau of Economic Research, University of Chicago Press, 1987.

Sah, Raaj, and Navendu Vasavada. "Unbundled Stock Units: What Went Wrong?" *Financial Management Collection* 5, no. 2 (Summer 1990): 1.

Sebastian, Pamela. "American Brands Offer to Buy Debt at E-II Holdings Gets Tepid Response." *Wall Street Journal*, February 24, 1988, p. 8.

Securities and Exchange Commission, Office of the Chief Economist. "The Economics of Poison Pills." March 1986.

"Share Vote Proposal Approved." *New York Times*, July 8, 1988, pp. D1 and D5.

"Takeovers Are Back But Now the Frenzy Is Gone." *Business Week*, February 8, 1988, p. 24.

Taylor, John. *Storming the Magic Kingdom*. New York: Ballantine Books, 1987.

"Trial Discusses Identity of 10 Firms Gillette Company Contacted as White Knights." *Wall Street Journal*, June 27, 1988, p. 16.

"When Targets Tilt Playing Fields." *New York Times*, April 21, 1988, p. D2.

Chapter
6

Takeover Tactics

In the late 1980s, increasingly powerful takeover tactics were required to complete hostile acquisitions because potential targets erected ever stronger antitakeover defenses. In the years preceding the fourth merger wave, comparatively simple tactics had been sufficient to force a usually surprised and bewildered target into submission. As hostile takeovers reached new heights of intensity, targets became more wary, and bidders were required to advance the sophistication of their takeover tactics.

This chapter analyzes the evolution of takeover tactics employed in the 1980s and discusses the effectiveness and use of these tactics. The reader must bear in mind that, as is true for much of the material in this book, the area of takeover tactics is continually evolving. The great financial gains available to the investment bankers and attorneys representing bidders has created great incentives to devise new tactics to overcome defenses. Investment bankers regularly seek new ways to circumvent an effective defense while lawyers representing bidders seek ways to have the courts strike down certain defenses. In addition, the availability of capital may dictate the effectiveness of certain tactics. For example, the effectiveness of tender offers was greatly diminished when the junk bond market declined in the late 1980s. This made bidders rethink alternative takeover strategies such as proxy fights.

This chapter discusses the use of the tender offer in detail. The laws regulating tender offers, discussed fully in Chapter 3, are here approached from the viewpoint of the impact of takeover rules on the hostile bidder's tactics. For example, we will describe under what circumstances a bidder has actually made a legal tender offer and thereby become bound by the filing requirements of the Williams Act. It will be shown that such factors may determine the success of the bid. The legal environment determines the rules within which a bidder must structure a tender offer. The ways these rules affect the tender offer tactics are discussed from a strategic viewpoint.

The tender offer process, along with different variations such as two-tiered tender offers and partial tenders, are also described in this chapter. We also consider the shareholder wealth effects of the different types of tender offers and other takeover tactics, just as in Chapter 5, where the impact of the various antitakeover measures on shareholder wealth was discussed.

The other broad category of takeover tactics covered in this chapter is proxy fights. This tactic is discussed in a similar manner to tender offers. The corporate election process through which proxy fights are waged is considered in detail. The different types of proxy fights, such as battles for seats of the board of directors as opposed to contests that seek to produce a managerial change in the corporation, are described. While this chapter is directed mainly at the tactics a hostile bidder may employ, an effort is also made to show the proxy fight process from the target's point of view, with a discussion of management's options. Once again, the shareholder wealth effects of this takeover tactic are analyzed through a review of the research literature in this field.

The start of the 1990s witnessed the increasing use of proxy fights as a way of enhancing the effectiveness of tender offers. This tactic became necessary when the availability of junk bond financing, on which many tender offers relied in the fourth merger wave, dramatically declined. At the beginning of the 1990s, bidders found that they could not circumvent the increasingly effective target defenses by increasing the offer price of their all-cash tender offers. They rediscovered the proxy fight as another tool that would increase the effectiveness of their budget-constrained tender offer.

TENDER OFFERS

Since the Williams Act is the key piece of federal legislation regulating tender offers, it is ironic that the law does not even define the term. Instead, an exact definition has been left to the courts to formulate. This ambiguity has naturally led to some confusion regarding what constitutes a tender offer. In some instances, bidders, believing that their actions were not a tender offer, have failed to follow the rules and procedures of the Williams Act. This occurred in the landmark case involving the Sun Company's bid for the Becton Dickinson Company.

In late 1977, the Sun Company structured a deal with Fairleigh S. Dickinson, founder of the New Jersey private college of the same name, to purchase shares which Dickinson, his family, and other related parties held. Because the company did not file the proper disclosure statements at the time this agreement was reached, the court ruled that it had violated the Williams Act under the definition of a group as offered by the law. In deciding the case, the federal district court ruled that the establishment of an agreement between Dickinson and the Sun Company to sell shares to Sun and to have Dickinson become chairman of Becton Dickinson following its acquisition by the Sun Company warranted a disclosure filing. In arriving at its decision, the court established a definition of a tender offer,[1] naming eight factors that are characteristic of a tender offer. These factors, which the SEC sometimes refers to as the Eight Factor Test or the Wellman Test, are as follows:

1. Active and widespread solicitation of public shareholders for the shares of an issuer.
2. Solicitation made for the substantial percentage of an issuer's stock.
3. Offer to purchase made at a premium over the prevailing market price.
4. Terms of the offer are firm rather than negotiated.
5. Offer contingent on the tender of a fixed number of shares, often subject to a fixed maximum number to be purchased.
6. Offer open only a limited period of time.
7. Offeree subject to pressure to sell his stock.
8. Public announcements of a purchasing program concerning the target company precede or accompany rapid accumulation of larger amounts of the target company's securities.[2]

The eighth point was not relevant to the *Wellman* v. *Dickinson* case and was not discussed in this ruling. It is derived from an earlier ruling. Not all eight factors need be present for an offer to be judged a tender offer. The court did not want the eight factors to constitute an automatic litmus test for tender offers. Rather, in deciding whether the circumstances of a given stock purchase constitutes a tender offer, the eight factors are considered together, along with any other relevant factors.

---

[1] *Wellman* v. *Dickinson*, 475 F. Supp. 783 (S.D.N.Y. 1979).

[2] Larry D. Soderquist, *Understanding Securities Laws* (New York: Practicing Law Institute, July 1987), p. 236.

Open Market Purchases

The courts have generally found that open market purchases do not by themselves represent a tender offer. They do require that the purchaser file according to Section 13D of the Williams Act, but they do not mandate the additional extensive filings associated with a tender offer. One version of open market purchases is a creeping tender offer. This is the process of gradually acquiring shares in the market or through private transactions. While these purchases may require a Schedule 13D filing, the courts generally do not regard such purchases as a legal tender offer. The courts have repeatedly found that the purchase of stock from sophisticated institutional investors is not under the domain of the Williams Act.[3] However, the courts have maintained that a publicly announced intention to acquire control of a company followed by a rapid accumulation of that firm's stock is a tender offer.[4]

Recent History of the Tender Offer

The tender offer was the most frequently used tool of hostile takeovers in the 1980s, whereas the proxy fight was the weapon of choice in earlier years. Tender offers were first recognized as a powerful means of taking control of large corporations in INCO's acquisition of the ESB Corporation in 1973 (see Chapter 2). INCO employed its tender offer strategy with the help of its investment banker, Morgan Stanley and Company. As noted in Chapter 2, this takeover was the first hostile takeover by a major, reputable corporation, and the fact that a major corporation and the leading investment bank chose to launch a hostile takeover helped give legitimacy and acceptability to hostile takeovers.

Even before the ESB acquisition, however, tender offers had been used. As early as the 1960s, there was much concern that less reputable businessmen would use tender offers to wrest control of companies from their legitimate owners. Tender offers were not considered acceptable practice within the corporate community. Moreover, banking institutions, including both investment banks and commercial banks,

---

[3] *Stromfeld* v. *Great Atlantic & Pacific Tea Company,* 484 F. Supp. 1264 (S.D.N.Y. 1980), Affirmed 6464 F. 2nd 563 (2nd Cir. 1980). *Kennecott Cooper Corp.* v. *Curtiss Wright Corp.,* 584 F 2nd. 1195 (2nd Cir. 1978).

[4] *S-G Securities, Inc.* v. *Fuqua Investment Company,* 466 F. Supp. 1114 (D. Mass. 1978).

CASE STUDY: *THE SUN COMPANY VERSUS BECTON DICKINSON*

The Becton Dickinson Corporation is a health care company with headquarters in Bergen County, New Jersey. Until 1973 the company was run by Fairleigh S. Dickinson, Jr., the son of the founder of the company. At that time he stepped aside as president of the company, leaving the day-to-day management of the firm to Wesley Howe and Marvin Asne. Even so, he directly intervened in conflicts when he felt management's actions were not in the best interests of the company that he and his family had built into a major U.S. health care company. For example, Dickinson overruled management on the removal of a division head and strongly opposed the acquisition of another company. A series of conflicts for control of the company came to a head when Asne and Howe proposed acquiring National Medical Care, a Boston-based medical care company. Dickinson opposed the deal which was so structured that his share of ownership would drop after the acquisition. Following his opposition, the deal fell through. Asne and Howe called for Dickinson's ouster from his position as chairman, a recommendation which the board of directors approved.[a]

Fairleigh Dickinson contacted the Sun Oil Company through his investment banker, Salomon Brothers, which also represented Sun Oil. Sun Oil, a large oil company based in Philadelphia, had embarked on an expansion campaign with the goal of acquiring nonoil companies. It was most interested in Becton Dickinson. An understanding was reached between Sun Oil's chairman Robert Sharbaugh and Fairleigh Dickinson who held 5 percent of Becton Dickinson's outstanding stock. Sun Oil's strategy was to buy approximately 20 to 25 percent of Becton Dickinson's outstanding stock that was concentrated in the hands of institutions. Salomon obtained a commitment from 33 financial institutions, which accounted for approximately 20 percent of Becton Dickinson's outstanding stock.[b] Under the advice of the noted takeover lawyer, Martin Lipton, couriers were sent to those institutions that had previously committed themselves to the deal in order to collect the shares of stock. This was done rapidly and was completed in one day. Following the collection of the shares, Sun Oil informed the New York Stock Exchange and Becton Dickinson.

One unique aspect of its tactics was that Sun Oil did not file a Schedule 14D-1 which the Williams Act required for tender offers. Sun Oil did, however, file a 13D since it had acquired more than 5 percent of Becton Dickinson's stock. Becton Dickinson argued, however, that the Schedule 13D should have been filed earlier based upon the date that Fairleigh Dickinson and Sun Oil reached an understanding and thus had formed a "group." Its legal defense,

---

[a] This account is partially based on Richard Phalon, *The Takeover Barons of Wall Street* (New York: Putnam Publishing Co., 1981).

[b] Jeff Madrick, *Taking America* (New York: Bantam Books, 1987), p. 152.

led by the other great takeover lawyer, Joe Flom of the firm Skadden Arps, hinged on the argument that the purchase of shares from a small number of investors constituted a tender offer. Sun Oil's law firm, Wachtell Lipton, countered that these selected purchases were not a public tender offer. The court ruled that Sun Oil should have filed a 14D-1 and that its rapid selective purchase strategy was designed to evade the requirements of the Williams Act. Although Sun Oil appealed, the lower court's ruling was upheld. In arriving at its decision the court set forth the definition of a tender offer that is described in the first part of this chapter.

generally did not provide financing for tender offers. Nonetheless, the effectiveness of the tender offer was more and more being recognized, and in the late 1960s their use began to increase. Tender offers also proliferated outside the United States and represented an important hostile takeover method in Great Britain, for example. In response to the corporate and financial community's fear that the use of tender offers was growing out of control, the New York Stock Exchange and the American Stock Exchange imposed certain limitations on them. Even so, the figures kept rising: from 8 in 1960 to 45 in 1965.[5]

As their use proliferated, a swell of opposition developed on Capitol Hill. Spearheaded by Senator Harrison Williams, the Williams Act was passed in 1968 (see Chapter 3). Initially, this law had a dampening effect on the number of tender offers: the number declined from 115 in 1968 to 34 in 1970. Eventually, the market adjusted to the regulations of the new law, and the number rose to 205 in 1981. One reason for the strong rebound following the passage of the Williams Act may have been that, although the law made abusive tender offer practices illegal, it also gave a certain legitimacy to the method by providing rules regulating their use. The clear implication was that if tender offers were made in accordance with federal laws, they were a reasonable business practice. The Williams Act also helped increase the premium associated with tender offers. The 1985 Economic Report of the President stated that the premium was the result of the increased regulations of the law. The average cash takeover premium paid to target stockholders had increased from 32 percent prior to the passage of the law to 53 percent following its enactment.

Overall, the Williams Act facilitated the development of the art of

---

[5] Ibid., p. 21.

takeover defenses. Before this legislation, tender offers could be so structured that stockholders could be forced to make a quick decision on them. The Williams Act provided management with an extended offer period before the bidder could purchase the shares, giving the targets time to mount increasingly effective takeover defenses.

Reason for Using a Tender Offer

A company resorts to a tender offer when a friendly, negotiated transaction does not appear to be a viable alternative. The costs associated with a tender offer, such as legal filing fees and publication costs, make the tender offer a more expensive alternative than a negotiated deal. The initiation of a tender offer usually means that the company will be taken over, though not necessarily by the firm that initiated the tender offer. The tender offer may put the company "in play," which may cause it to be taken over by another firm that may seek to enter the bidding contest for the target. The action process may significantly increase the cost of using a tender offer.

Success Rate of Tender Offers

Based on experience in the years 1975–1988, tender offers for publicly traded companies have a success rate of 77 percent.[6] This high rate of success is attributable to the fact that 73 percent of the tender offers recorded by *Mergerstat Review* were not contested. The success rate for uncontested offers is 88 percent, whereas the success rate for contested offers is only 48 percent.

White knights play an important role in unsuccessful, contested tender offers. For example, there were 19 unsuccessful tender offers in 1988, 6 of which remained independent and 13 were acquired by a white knight.[7] The historical experience between 1976 and 1988 shows that more companies that are targets of unsuccessful tender offers are taken over by white knights than those that remain independent.

Cash Versus Securities Tender Offers

The acquiring firm that is initiating a tender offer can go with an all-cash tender offer or can use securities as part or all of the consideration

---

[6] *Mergerstat Review: 1988*, p. 85.

[7] Ibid., p. 86.

used for the offer. Securities may be more attractive to some of the target stockholders since, under certain circumstances, the transaction may be considered tax free. (The tax aspects of mergers are discussed in Chapter 11.) The bidding firm may create a more flexible structure for target shareholders by using a double barreled offer. This is an offer where the target shareholders are given the option of receiving cash or securities in exchange for their shares. If securities are used in the transaction, they must be registered with the SEC under the Securities Act of 1933. The securities must also be issued in compliance with the relevant state's Blue Sky Laws which regulate the issuance and transfer of securities. (For a fuller discussion of the valuation of stock for stock offers, see Chapter 14.)

The SEC review process may also slow down the tender offer. The acquiring firm is encumbered by the waiting periods of the Williams Act and the Hart–Scott–Rodino Act (see Chapter 3). The use of securities may add another waiting period while the firm awaits the SEC review. The SEC's Division of Corporate Finance has designed a system of selective review whereby it responds to repeat issuers more expeditiously.[8] This system permits only brief review of firms that may have already gone through a thorough review process for prior issues of securities. In these cases, the securities registration and review process may present little or no additional delays beyond the Williams Act and Hart–Scott–Rodino waiting periods.

Ten-Day Window of the Williams Act

As noted in Chapter 3, the Williams Act requires that purchasers of 5 percent of the outstanding shares of a company's stock register with the SEC within 10 days by filing a Schedule 13D. The filing of this schedule notifies the market of the purchaser's intentions and alerts stockholders to an impending tender offer. It is in the bidder's interest to purchase shares as quickly as possible during the 10-day period after the acquirer reaches the 10 percent threshold. If the bidder is able to purchase securities during this period, the stock price may be lower than following the notification to the market of the bidder's intentions. The filing gives the stockholders notice that a bidder may be about to make a bid. This implies a dramatic increase in the demand for the securities and makes them more valuable. Stockholders will demand a higher price to part with their stock, knowing that an upcoming bid

---

[8] Martin Lipton and Erica H. Steinberger, *Takeovers and Freezeouts* (New York: Law Journal Seminar Press, 1987), pp. 1–12.

and its associated premium may be forthcoming. The 10-day window gives the bidder an opportunity to purchase a larger amount of stock without having to pay the post-filing premium—assuming, however, that rumors have not already anticipated the content of the filing. It is difficult to purchase larger amounts of stock and keep the purchaser secret.

The 10-day window can be turned into a 12-day window if the initial purchases are made on a Wednesday. This would require the purchaser to file on a Saturday. The SEC usually allows the purchaser to file on the next business day, which would be two days later on Monday.

Bear Hugs

A bidder will sometimes try to pressure the management of the target prior to initiating a tender offer. This can be done by contacting the board of directors with an expression of interest in acquiring the target and the implied intent to go directly to stockholders with a tender offer if these overtures are not favorably received. This strategy—known as the *bear hug*—can also be accompanied by a public announcement of the bidder's intent to make a tender offer. The bear hug forces the target's management to take a public position on the possible takeover by this bidder.

A stronger version of the standard bear hug occurs when one bidder offers a specific price[9] in order, among other reasons, to establish a range for damages in possible stockholder lawsuits that might follow the target management's rejection of the bid. This tactic increases the pressure on the target's board which might be the object of the lawsuits. The typical response of an unreceptive target board is to acquire a fairness opinion from an investment bank that will say that the offer is inadequate. This gives the board of directors a "legitimate" reason to reject the offer. If the bidder makes a public announcement while engaging in a bear hug, the bidder is bound to file pursuant to Rule 14D–2 of the Williams Act and to disseminate tender offer materials or abandon the offer within five days. If, on the other hand, the target discloses the offer, the bidder is not required to file.

From a strategic point of view, if the bidder sees a realistic possibility of a negotiated transaction, the bear hug can be an attractive alternative to a tender offer. It is a less expensive and time-consuming way to conduct a "hostile" acquisition. It may also reduce the adverse consequences sometimes associated with hostile deals, such as the loss

---

[9] Ibid., p. 1.04[2].

of key target employees and a deterioration of employee morale following the acquisition. If the bidder strongly opposes the acquisition, the bear hug may have little value since a tender offer may eventually be necessary.

Response of the Target Management

How should the target company respond to a tender offer? Target company stockholders often view tender offers as a favorable development since they tend to bring high offer premiums. The appropriate response of the target company management, which will maximize the stock offer premium, is not always clear. The debate centers around whether an active resistance to a tender offer will increase the offer premium. Martin Lipton argues that hostile tender offers may not be in the target stockholder's best interests, for they may not maximize stockholder value. Lipton cites evidence that the premium should not be a strong inducement to sell. In the cases he considered, the stock price most often rose above the premium-inclusive offer price.[10] According to Lipton, stockholders were better off in over 50 percent of certain tender offers he considered between the years 1974 and 1979. His analysis did not, however, adjust for the present value of the offer prices that occurred in different years. Lipton's view is that the market price of stocks is usually undervalued and does not reflect the value of a controlling interest in a company. This explanation is reasonable since the price quoted in the marketplace reflects a small-quantity purchase and does not include a control premium. Lipton presents evidence that the market prices are between 50 and 66⅔ percent of the value to someone acquiring control.

Given the lack of a sufficient control premium, Lipton concludes that the board of directors should not be bound to accept a tender offer. Indeed, the board's ability to reject an offer it considers undervalued is protected by the Business Judgment Rule. Lipton's view is underscored in the case of *Panter* v. *Marshall Field & Co.* in which the court upheld the legality of the board of directors of Marshall Field and Company using defensive measures to thwart a tender offer from Carter Hawley Hale which they considered undervalued. Stockholders sued Marshall Field and Company when the firm used corporate resources to make defensive acquisitions that would create an antitrust conflict for potential bidders and make the company less attractive. Marshall

---

[10] Martin Lipton, "Takeover Bids in the Target's Boardroom," *Business Lawyer* 35 (November 1979): 101–133.

Field had become a target because its performance lagged behind that of similar department store chains. Carter Hawley Hale offered more than a 100 percent premium to Marshall Field in its tender offer, but the board of directors resisted the bid. These measures were successful, and Carter Hawley Hale was forced to abandon its tender offer. The court reasoned as follows:

> Directors of publicly owned corporations do not act outside the law when they, in good faith, decide that it is in the best interest of the company, and its shareholders, that it remain an independent business entity. Having so determined, they can authorize management to oppose offers which, in their best judgment, are detrimental to the company and its shareholders.[11]

Lipton goes further in citing the evils of tender offers. He believes that tender offers are not in the long-term best interest of corporate America and the competitive position of the U.S. economy. The interests of speculators, who use tender offers to reap bountiful profits, he states, should not be held above the "nation's corporate system." Unfortunately, rather than citing significant quantitative evidence, Lipton relies more heavily on his position as one of the leading takeover attorneys in the United States.

Many analysts disagree with Lipton, two of his most vocal academic critics being Professors Frank Easterbrook and Daniel Fischel.[12] Neither sees much stockholder wealth-maximizing benefits from defensive antitakeover measures. They contend that opposition to a takeover decreases stockholder welfare and that stockholders are better off when the target does not offer resistance to hostile bids. They base their argument on an efficient markets view of securities prices. They see securities markets as being efficient and, therefore, as allowing little deviation between the stock price and its intrinsic value. Their reliance on the accuracy of stock prices is based on the belief that if there were a deviation between price and value, investors would "reap windfall gains." Investors would buy underpriced securities and sell overpriced ones, a process which, in their perspective, would result in accurately valued securities.

If we accept the notion that the market accurately values stock

---

[11] *Panter v. Marshall Field & Co.*, 486 F. Supp. 1168, N.D. Ill. 1980, as cited in Martin Lipton, "Takeover Bids in the Target's Boardroom: An Update After One Year," *Business Lawyer* 36 (April 1981): 1017–1028.

[12] Frank H. Easterbrook and Daniel R. Fischel, "The Proper Role of a Target's Management in Responding to a Tender Offer," *Harvard Law Review* 94, no. 6 (April 1981): 1161–1202.

prices, a significant premium above the market price represents a potential increase in wealth for stockholders. Easterbrook and Fischel believe that takeover defenses deprive stockholders of this increased value. They therefore, oppose the court's deference to the Business Judgment Rule in allowing boards of directors to use takeover defenses to defeat tender offers. Easterbrook and Fischel took issue with the application of the Business Judgment Rule in the *Panter* v. *Marshall Field* decision.

> The Marshall Field case is an ideal vehicle for comparing our approach with Lipton's. Lipton argues, using the Marshall Field case as an example, that shareholder wealth is maximized if managers are allowed to pursue a policy of independence. But how are stockholders benefited by a legal rule that allows the managers of a target corporation to spend huge sums of stockholder's money (in lawsuits, defensive actions, hiring professionals etc.) for the purpose of preventing them from more than doubling the value of their investment? And why should the business judgment rule, a doctrine designed to prevent second guessing of business decisions by directors, shield this type of conduct from judicial review?[13]

Some argue that takeover defenses can be used to maximize stockholder wealth if they force the bidder to increase the premium but do not defeat the tender offer. Defensive measures can lead to an auction process whereby the premium is bid up to a higher level than the original offer. Easterbrook and Fischel, however, contend that stockholders do not necessarily benefit from this use of defensive measures. They consider the potential for an even higher premium being offered in the future. The defensive measures, they state, may prevent such a bid from being initiated. The target may then be settling for a lower premium than what might ultimately be offered in the absence of any defensive measures. They believe that merely looking at the premium that resulted from an auction process does not fully capture all the wealth effects of defensive measures. Defensive measures may depress pre-offer stock prices which makes the premium resulting from an auction process less attractive.

Tender Offers and Keeping Management Honest

Supporters of hostile tender offers view them as a monitoring mechanism that keeps management honest. Without the possibility of a hostile tender offer, managers might be free to take actions that would maxi-

---

[13] Frank H. Easterbrook and Daniel R. Fischel, "Takeover Bids, Defensive Tactics and Shareholders Welfare," *The Business Lawyer* 36 (July 1981): 1733–1750.

mize their own welfare but that would fail to produce stock prices maximizing the wealth of equity holders. Knowledge that tender offers can be an effective means of taking control may keep management wary and conscious of the value of the firm's stock. The effectiveness of tender offers makes the possibility of a successful hostile bid most real. In this way, tender offers help to deal with the agency problem of corporations. (See Chapter 7.)

Individual stockholders have neither the incentive nor the resources to launch a tender offer. A hostile bidder, on the other hand, may have both resources and incentive. The bidder may compare the value of the company under its management and may decide that it exceeds the company's current market value by a sufficient margin to be able to offer stockholders a significant premium and still profit from the take-over.

Creation of a Tender Offer Team

The bidding firm assembles its team of essential players and coordinates its actions throughout the tender offer process. The team may be composed of the following members outside of the corporation's own management and in-house counsel.

1. *Investment bank.* The investment bank will play a key role in providing the requisite financing and advisory services through the tender offer. The investment bank may provide *bridge financing*, which will allow the bidder to "buy now and pay later." The investment bank may ultimately finance the bid by issuing securities such as junk bonds or loan agreements. The investment bank's merger expertise is most important in cases of actively fought hostile acquisitions where the target employs more sophisticated defensive maneuvers.

2. *Legal advisers.* Lawyers, knowledgeable in the tactics and defenses employed to evade tender offers, can be an invaluable source of advice for the bidder. In many major takeover battles each side may retain one of the major mergers law firms such as: Wachtell Lipton or Skadden, Arps Slate, Meager and Flom. These firms, led by mergers specialists Martin Lipton and Joseph Flom, respectively, have garnered a significant portion of the total legal business related to tender offers.

3. *Information agent.* The information agent is typically one of the major proxy soliciting firms such as Georgeson and Company, D. F. King and Company, or the Carter Organization. The information agent is responsible for forwarding tender offer materials to stockholders. Proxy firms may also actively solicit the

participation of stockholders in tender offers by means of a telephone and mail campaign.

4. *Depository bank.*   The depository bank handles the receipt of
   the tender offers and the payment for the shares tendered. The
   bank makes sure that shares have been properly tendered. An
   on-going tabulation is kept for the bidder, allowing the probability of success to be determined throughout the tender offer.

5. *Forwarding agent.*   The bidder may decide to retain a forwarding agent in addition to the depository bank. The forwarding
   agent enhances the resources of the depository bank and trans-
   mits tenders received to the depository bank. A forwarding agent
   is particularly useful when there is a concentration of shares in
   a given area that is not well serviced by the depository bank.

The Two-Tiered Tender Offer

A two-tiered tender offer is sometimes referred to by the term "front-
end loaded" tender offer. It provides for superior compensation for a
first-step purchase, followed by inferior compensation for the second
tier or the "back-end" of the transaction. The technique is designed to
exert pressure on stockholders who are concerned that they may become part of a second tier and that they may receive inferior compensation if they do not tender early enough to become part of the first
tier. If sufficient shares are tendered in the first tier and if the merger
or acquisition is approved, the remaining shareholders can get "frozen
out" of their positions and may have to tender their shares for the
inferior compensation. The compensation for the two tiers may be
broken down into a first-tier, all-cash offer at a higher price for 51
percent of the target and a second-tier offer at a lower price and may
provide noncash compensation such as debentures. The two-tiered
pricing strategy is coercive to stockholders, for it attempts to stampede
them into becoming part of the first tier.

The aggressive bidder has to choose between two strong alternatives: an all-cash bid for "any-and-all" shares tendered and a two-tiered
offer. During the early 1980s, the two-tiered offer was the hostile
bidder's favorite weapon. Since then, hostile bidders, having gained
access to large amounts of capital through the junk bond market, have
found that the all-cash, any-and-all offer is the more effective offensive
strategy. The target's board of directors finds it difficult to resist the
appeal of the all-cash offer. For their part the directors find it difficult
to justify why they should turn down an all-cash offer at a fixed price
that includes a significant premium. With the access to junk bond funds,
bidders have better justification for higher all-cash premiums. This

situation changed towards the end of the 1980s when the junk bond market declined. All cash offers then had to be financed by more equity and less high-risk debt. This made it more difficult for smaller bidders to participate in major mega-deals.

Bidders who do not have access to larger amounts of capital sometimes use the two-tiered offer. They then choose to use their relatively limited capital where it will have the greatest effect. They can concentrate the cash reserves on the first tier of a two-tiered offer while offering securities for the second tier. Mesa Petroleum used such a financing technique in 1982 when it acquired the Great American Oil Company. Mesa borrowed $500 million to make a $40 per share offer for one-half of Great American. This gave Mesa control of Great American and facilitated the merger of the two companies. Mesa's offer provided for the issuance of securities, equity, and subordinated debentures issued by the combined firm. The value of the securities came to less than $40 per share.[14]

Those who oppose the two-tiered bid maintain that it is too coercive and unfair to shareholders in the second tier who are entitled to equal treatment under the Williams Act. In the past stockholders have sued, seeking appraisal rights and equal compensation to that which first-tier shareholders received. The courts have ruled, however, that the two-tiered structure is not per se illegal.

The majority shareholder who acquires control through the purchase of shares tendered in the first tier must be mindful of the remaining stockholders' interests. They are entitled to fair treatment under the law. The majority shareholder may not force out the minority stockholders in a manner that leaves them with less than a fair value for their shares. The courts have held that stockholders must be dealt with in a fair manner.[15] These rulings, together with the increased access of bidders to junk bond finance and the increased number of fair price provisions in corporate charters, have made the two-tiered offers less popular. Jarrell and Poulson have reported a dramatic rise in the adoption of fair price provisions in corporate charters in response to the increased use of front-end loaded offers.[16] They found that 354 adoptions of fair price amendments took place between 1983 and 1984, which is in sharp contrast to the total of 38 amendments passed between 1979 and 1982. Jarrell and Poulson attribute this increase to the greater incidence of two-tiered bids in the early 1980s. These amendments, however, have reduced the effectiveness of two-tiered bids.

---

[14] Lipton and Steinberger, *Takeovers and Freezeouts*, pp. 1–85.

[15] *Weinberger* v. *U.O.P.*, 457 A. 2d 701 (Del. 1983).

[16] Greg Jarrell and Annette Poulson, "Shark Repellents and Stock Prices: The Effects of Antitakeover Amendments Since 1980," *Journal of Financial Economics* 19, no. 1 (September 1987): 127–168.

Effect of Two-Tiered Tender Offers on Stockholder Wealth

The charge that two-tiered tender offers are coercive and cause decreases in stockholder wealth remains unproven. A study by Robert Comment and Greg Jarrell failed to detect such a decline in stockholder wealth resulting from two-tiered bids.[17] They examined 210 cash tender offers between 1981 and 1984 and found far fewer two-tiered offers than any-and-all offers. Their results also showed that stockholders do as well when confronted with a front-end load bid than when they have an any-and-all offer. Comment and Jarrell attribute this finding to management's ability to enter into a negotiated transaction with the bidder and achieve equal gains in stockholder wealth when offered two-tiered bids as compared to receiving any-and-all offers. Interestingly, the Comment and Jarrell results were not caused by fair price provisions as only 14 of the 210 tender offers in their sample were for firms that had fair price amendments in place. Their sample period predates the passage of many of the fair price amendments. They conclude that there is no need for regulatory changes that prohibit two-tiered bids since they do not appear to have had an adverse impact on shareholder wealth.

Any-and-All Versus Partial Tender Offers

Prior to initiating a tender offer, the bidder must decide whether to make an offer for any-and-all shares tendered or to structure the offer so that only a certain percentage of the outstanding shares are bid for. Generally, the any-and-all offer is considered a more effective takeover tactic and is, therefore, more difficult to defend against. Partial offers are not considered as valuable because of the risk of oversubscription. In an oversubscribed offer, shares are accepted on a pro rata basis. Stockholders incur the risk that they will not receive the full premium for all the shares they would like to tender. This is not the case for an any-and-all offer.

A partial offer that is designed to take control of the target without a second-step close-out transaction is less attractive to stockholders since they may be left holding shares that have a reduced value after the partial buyout is completed. If some or all of their shares are not included in the shares purchased by the bidder, their price may decline

---

[17] Robert Comment and Greg Jarrell, "Two-Tiered and Negotiated Tender Offers," *Journal of Financial Economics* 19, no. 2 (December 1987): 283–310.

as the market assesses the likelihood of an eventual second-step transaction. If a second-step transaction does eventually occur, it may not contain the same premium as the first step since the first step contained a control premium. After the first step is completed, control is usually established, and the remaining shares may be less valuable to the bidder. First-step transactions are often for cash, which has a clear, fixed value, whereas second-step transactions use debt or equity securities as consideration. The debt securities may be highly risky inasmuch as the bidder may have incurred considerable debt to finance the all-cash first step. Stockholders may differ with the bidder on the value of the debt securities in the second-step offer. The bidder sometimes tries to ameliorate these concerns by so structuring the all-securities second-step transaction that it constitutes a tax-free exchange. This advantage for the second-step shareholders may partially offset the higher premium that the first-step shareholders received.

Second-step shareholders also have to be concerned about the bidder's ability to purchase the remaining shares in the second tier. The bidder may be straining his or her financial resources to take control through the first-step transaction and may later be unable to complete the purchase of the remaining shares. For example, William Farley ran out of money after purchasing 95 percent of West Point–Pepperell. He had expected to complete the $2.5 billion takeover of West Point–Pepperell through the issuance of junk bonds by his investment banker Drexel Burnham Lambert, but Drexel Burnham Lambert's financial difficulties coupled with the decline of the junk bond market prevented it. Farley proved unable to service the debt he held as a result of the 95 percent share purchase. He realized a lower than expected price for a division of West Point–Pepperell, Cluett, Peabody & Co. ($350 million plus a $60 million note from the buyer).[18] The combined effect of these developments was his eventual default in March 1990.

Transactions are sometimes structured in three steps. A bidder utilizing a three-step transaction is sometimes referred to as a *three-piece suitor*. The general process for such transactions involves the bidder making an initial stock purchased followed by a second-step tender offer. Once control is established and a majority of the shareholders have tendered their shares in the tender offer, a third-step freeze-out purchase of the minority shareholders who have not tendered their shares is conducted.

---

[18] Robert Johnson, "William Farley's Quest for Status Threatens to Topple His Empire," *Wall Street Journal*, April 30, 1990, p. A1.

Empirical Evidence on the Effects of Tender Offers

The debate between Lipton and Easterbrook and Fischel has helped define and crystallize the issues. Neither side, however, presents substantive quantitative evidence that measures the purported gains and losses. One study that addresses this issue in a quantitative manner was conducted by Harvard University Professor Paul Asquith as an outgrowth of his Ph.D. dissertation at the University of Chicago.[19] Asquith examined successful and unsuccessful merger bids between 1962 and 1976, and he considered the impact of the bids on daily excess returns to stockholders in the affected companies. Daily excess returns are measures developed by Professor Myron Scholes of Stanford University and are calculated as follows:

$$ER_{it} = R_{it} - E(R_{it}) \tag{6.1}$$

where: ER_{it} = excess return for asset i for day t
t = the day under consideration
R_{it} = return on asset i on day t
$E(R_{it})$ = the expected return to asset i on day t

The expected return is estimated by adjusting for the risk level of the firm's stock through application of the beta for that security. (The derivation of beta is explained in Chapter 14.)

Asquith's results indicate a strong positive cumulative excess return for targets of successful bids when considering a 60-day window before and after the offer. Interestingly, the market was efficient in anticipating the offer, as reflected by the fact that most of the nearly 20 percent cumulative excess return was reached before the announcement date (press day). Unsuccessful targets lose most of their almost 10 percent gains by the end of the 60-day period after the announcement.

According to Asquith, acquiring firms in successful bids experience relatively small gains that persist 60 days after the takeover. Those potential acquirers in unsuccessful takeovers display a -5 percent cumulative excess return 60 days following the attempted takeover (see Figures 6.1 and 6.2).

The Wealth Effects of Unsuccessful Tender Offers

Although the premium associated with a successful bid may increase the target shareholder's wealth, there is a question as to whether the increase in a target share caused by the announcement of a bid persists when the bid fails. Michael Bradley, Anand Desai, and E. Han Kim

---

[19] Paul Asquith, "Merger Bids and Stock Returns," *Journal of Financial Economics* 11, no. 1 (April 1983): 51–83.

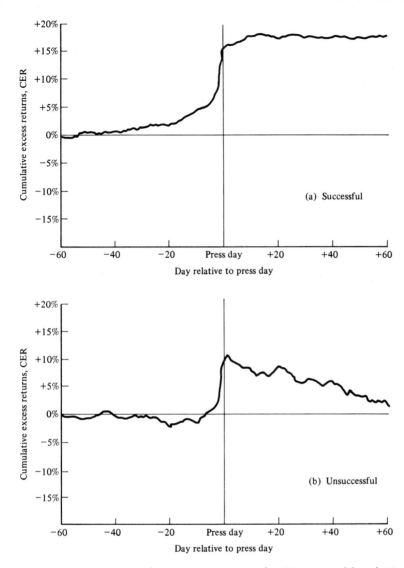

Figure 6.1 Average cumulative excess returns for 211 successful and 91 unsuccessful target firms from 60 days before until 60 days after the merger day in the period 1962–1976. (*Source:* Paul Asquith, "Merger Bids and Stock Returns," *Journal of Financial Economics* 11, nos. 1–4 (April 1983): 70.

analyzed the returns to stockholders by firms that either received or made unsuccessful control-oriented tender offers between 1963 and 1980.[20] They defined a control-oriented tender offer as one in which

_____

[20] Michael Bradley, Anand Desai, and E. Han Kim, "The Rationale Behind Interfirm Tender Offers: Information or Synergy," *Journal of Financial Economics* 11 (April 1983): 183–206.

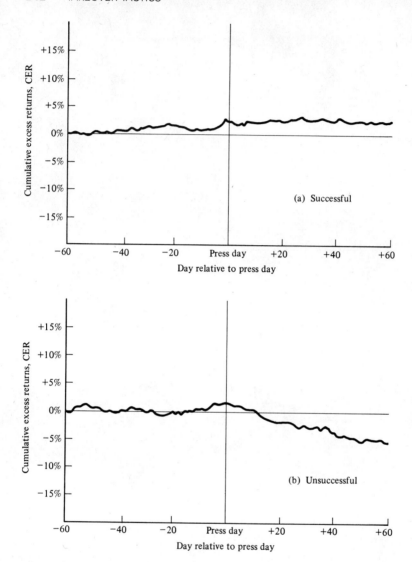

Figure 6.2 Average cumulative excess returns for 196 successful and 89 unsuccessful bidding firms from 60 days before until 60 days after the merger day in the period 1962–1976. (*Source:* Paul Asquith, "Merger Bids and Stock Returns," *Journal of Financial Economics* 11, nos. 1–4 (April 1983): 71.

the bidding firm holds less than 70 percent of the target's shares and is attempting to increase its holdings by at least 15 percent. They considered a total of 697 tender offers. The Bradley study measured the impact of the tender offers by examining the cumulative abnormal returns to both the target and the bidding firm. *Abnormal returns* are those that cannot be fully explained by market movements. Cumulative abnormal returns are defined as follows:

$$R_{it} = a_i + B_{mt} R_{mit} + e_{it} \tag{6.2}$$

where: R_{it} = the cumulative dividend monthly stock return for the ith firm in month t

R_{mit} = the return on an equally weighted market portfolio month t relative to the announcement of offer

a, B = the regression parameters

e_{it} = a stochastic error term with a mean of zero

One goal of the study was to ascertain whether there were permanent wealth effects from tender offers on the target and the acquiring firm separately, as follows.

The Target   The results show that target shareholders realize positive abnormal returns surrounding the month of the announcement of the tender offer. The cumulative abnormal returns "show a positive revaluation of the target shares which does not dissipate subsequent to the rejection of the offer."[21] In their total sample of unsuccessful tender offers 76.8 percent of the firms were taken over and 23.2 percent were not. The data in Figure 6.2 are consistent with the study's hypothesis—that the gains that persist following an unsuccessful change in control will eventually take place. When this change in control does not take place, the gains disappear.

The Bidder   The Bradley study reveals interesting results regarding the impact of tender offers on acquiring firms. As Figure 6.3 shows, the cumulative abnormal returns for bidding firms remain nonnegative when the target is independent, and there is no change in control. When the target is acquired by another bidder and the bidder in question loses the tender offer, the value of the bidding firm falls significantly. Bradley et al. interpret this effect as the market's perception that the bidding firm has lost an opportunity to acquire a valuable resource. This effect is sometimes caused by competitors acquiring resources that will provide a competitive advantage over the firm that lost the bid.

The Bradley study traced out the time frame for the wealth effects on unsuccessful bidders and found that, for their sample of tender offers between 1963 and 1980, the average gap between the announcement of the unsuccessful bid and the subsequent successful tender offer was

---

[21] Ibid., p. 192.

60.6 days. Almost all the decline in the value of a portfolio of unsuccessful bidding firms had occurred by the twenty-first day. The value of the portfolio declined 2.84 percent by the twenty-first day.

Are "Bad Bidders" More Likely to Become Targets?

The impact of poor acquisitions was discussed in Chapter 4 in the context of conglomerate or diversification mergers that performed poorly. It was also discussed in Chapter 2 in the context of the acquisitions that occurred in the third merger wave. The issue of how a firm is affected by a poor acquisition is of interest to stockholders in the bidding firm as they consider whether they should favor a certain acquisition.

In 1988, Mark L. Mitchell and Kenneth Lehn of the SEC analyzed the effects of poor acquisitions on acquiring firms.[22] They found that the probability of becoming a takeover target was inversely related to the cumulative average returns associated with the firm's acquisitions. They used a logistic regression, which is an econometric regression model in which the dependent variable can vary between 0 and 1. In this case, the 0 or 1 represented whether or not a firm became a target. Some studies of the impact of acquisitions on acquiring firms show a zero or negative impact while providing clear benefits for the target firm. Mitchell and Lehn contend that the market differentiates between good and bad acquiring firms. Although they found returns to acquirers to be approximately zero, they observed that subsamples of good acquirers outperformed acquiring firms that pursued failed acquisition strategies, or what Mitchell and Lehn refer to as *bad bidders*. They revealed that bad bidders are themselves more likely to become takeover targets. They see the resulting acquisition of these bad bidders as a partial cause of the current takeover movement.

STREET SWEEPS

A hostile bidder may accumulate stock in the target prior to making a tender offer. As noted above, the purchaser should keep these initial purchases secret so as to put as little upward pressure as possible on the target's stock price. To do so, the acquisitions are often made

---

[22] Mark L. Mitchell and Kenneth Lehn, "Do Bad Bidders Become Good Targets," *Journal of Applied Corporate Finance* 3(2), Summer 1990, pp 60–69.

through various shell corporations and partnerships whose names do not convey the true identity of the ultimate purchaser.

Upon reaching the 5 percent threshold, the purchaser has 10 days before having to make a public disclosure. This time period can be used to augment the holding. The larger the purchaser position in the target, the more leverage the firm has over the target. This leverage may enable the bidder to launch a tender offer that has a high probability of success, given the stockholdings the bidder already possesses. The bidder is also in a better position to make a credible threat of a proxy fight owing to the number of votes it already controls. Even if it fails to take control of the board of directors, it may be able to place its representatives on the board. This could make operations more difficult for management.

Significant stockholdings accumulated through open market purchases may be sufficient to offset defenses such as supermajority voting provisions. They may also be used as a negotiating tool to get the target to agree to a "friendly tender offer" and to discourage potential white knights from making a bid for the target. The would-be white knight knows that it will have to deal with an unwanted substantial stockholder even if it succeeds in obtaining majority control of the target. The hostile bidder may not want to relinquish its stockholding without receiving a high premium, which may be tantamount to greenmail. The white knight is then faced with the unappealing prospect of paying a premium to the other target shareholders and greenmail to the hostile bidder.

The open market purchase of stock may be a precursor to a tender offer, but it may also be an effective alternative to the tender offer. When a hostile bidder concludes that the tender offer may not be successful, it may decide not to initiate one. The result may be large-scale open market purchases of stock. The goal of these purchases may be to try to acquire enough stock to take control of the target. The hostile bidder's investment bank assists the bidder by providing the necessary financing for these purchases and by assembling large blocks of stock to be bought. The use of a "naked street sweep," which is a hostile open market purchase of shares in lieu of a tender offer, is not as effective. The legal problems that a bidder will incur when making large-scale open market purchases without announcing a tender offer were underscored in the attempted acquisition of Becton Dickinson by Sun Oil. In this case, the court ruled that Sun Oil came too close to the legal boundary of the Williams Act and that its purchase of approximately 34% of the stock of Becton Dickinson was actually a tender offer. "Naked street sweeps are now also interdicted by the Hart-Scott-

Rodino Antitrust Improvements Act of 1976 which the FTC has recently invigorated by adding anti-evasion regulations."[23]

The use of *street sweeps* as an effective takeover tactic was pioneered in 1985 by Hanson Trust PLC. In that year Hanson terminated its tender offer for SCM Corporation and immediately bought 25 percent of SCM's outstanding stock from arbitragers. The 25 percent holding was accumulated in just six transactions. This block of stock, which brought Hanson Trust's holdings up to 34.1 percent, was purchased in response to SCM's defensive leveraged buyout proposal. The buyout was prevented by Hanson Trust's stock acquisition since, under New York law (where SCM was incorporated), major transactions such as leveraged buyouts must be approved by a two-thirds majority. Hanson Trust PLC took advantage of the fact that in a takeover contest larger blocks of stock begin to be concentrated in the hands of arbitragers. This creates an attractive alternative to a tender offer. An astute investment bank advising a bidder knows that a larger holding can be amassed through a small number of transactions.

The Hanson Trust street sweep was challenged in court.[24] The court of appeals ruled that Hanson Trust's open market purchase of stock after its cancellation of its tender offer was not bound by the requirements of the Williams Act. This ruling established a precedent that made street sweeps legal and not in violation of the Williams Act (see Case Study: Campeau v. Allied Stores).

ADVANTAGES OF TENDER OFFERS OVER OPEN MARKET PURCHASES

Open market purchases may at first seem to provide many advantages over tender offers. For example, they do not involve the complicated legal requirements and costs associated with tender offers. (The bidder must be concerned that the open market purchases will be legally interpreted as a tender offer.) The costs of a tender offer can be far higher than the brokerage fees incurred in attempting to take control through open market purchases of the target's stock. As noted above, Robert Smiley estimated that the total cost of tender offers averaged

---

[23] Dale Oesterle, "The Rise and Fall of Street Sweep Takeovers," *Duke Law Journal*, 1989, pp. 202–255.

[24] *Hanson Trust PLC* v. *SCM Corp.*, 774 F. 2d 47 (2d Cir. 1985).

approximately 13 percent of the post-tender offer market price of the target's shares.[25]

Open market purchases also have clear drawbacks that are not associated with tender offers. A bidder who purchases shares in the open market is not guaranteed that he will be able to accumulate sufficient shares to acquire clear control. If 51 percent clear control is not achieved, the bidder may become stuck in an undesirable minority position. One advantage of a tender offer is that the bidder is not bound to purchase the tendered shares unless the desired number of shares has been tendered. The bidder who becomes mired in a minority position faces the following alternatives:

- Do a tender offer. In this case the bidder incurs the tender offer expenses in addition to the costs of the open market purchasing program.
- Begin a proxy fight. This is another costly means of acquiring control, but the bidder is now in a stronger position to launch a proxy fight after having already acquired a large voting position.
- Sell the minority stock position. These sales would place significant downward pressure on the stock price and would likely involve significant losses.

Large-scale open market purchases are also difficult to keep secret. Market participants regard the stock purchases as a signal that a bidder may be attempting to make a raid on the target. This then may change the shape of the target's supply curve for its stock by making it more vertical above some price.[26] This threshold price may be quickly reached as the available supply of shares on the market, which may be relatively small compared to the total shares outstanding, becomes exhausted. As stockholders come to believe that a bid may be forthcoming, they have an incentive to *hold out* for a higher premium. The holdout problem does not exist in tender offers since the bidder is not obligated to purchase any shares unless the amount requested has been tendered. If the requested amount has not been tendered at the end

[25] Robert Smiley, "Tender Offers, Transactions Costs and the Theory of the Firm," *Review of Economics and Statistics* 58 (1976): 22–32.

[26] Lloyd R. Cohen, "Why Tender Offers? The Efficient Markets Hypothesis, the Supply of Stock, and Signaling," *Journal of Legal Studies* 19, no. 1 (January 1990): 113–143.

CASE STUDY: *CAMPEAU CORPORATION VERSUS ALLIED STORES: A CASE STUDY IN THE EFFECTIVENESS OF STREET SWEEPS*

One notable example of the effectiveness of street sweeps occurred in 1986 when Campeau Corporation, a real estate concern in Toronto, abandoned its tender offer for Allied Stores and immediately purchased 48 percent of Allied's stock on the open market. Robert Campeau, chairman of the Campeau Corporation, had gotten into a bidding war with Edward J. DeBartolo who runs a closely held corporation with real estate interests in more than 50 shopping malls, hotels, condominiums, and office buildings.[a] DeBartolo had entered into a partnership with raider Paul Bilzerian, and together they made a $3.56 billion tender offer at $67 per share for Allied. This offer topped Campeau's $66 per share offer. Realizing that his tender offer would not be successful, Campeau canceled the offer and, within 30 minutes of the cancellation, bought 25.8 millions shares of Allied or 48 percent of the outstanding stock.[b] The stock acquisition was made possible by the work of Jefferies Group, Inc., the brokerage firm that assembled the block of stock. Lipton and Steinberger report that the Jefferies Group had offered the block to the competing bidders before selling it to Campeau.[c]

The street sweep was challenged by the SEC which argued that the 48 percent stock purchase was a continuation of Campeau's tender offer. A settlement was reached, and the legal challenge to the street sweep was abandoned.

[a] Ann Hagedorn, "Allied Stores Receives $3.56 Billion Offer for DeBartolo Corp., Paul Bilzerian," *Wall Street Journal,* October 9, 1989, p. 3.
[b] Bruce Ingersoll, "Campeau's Purchase of 48% of Allied Was Illegal, SEC Will Argue in Court," *Wall Street Journal,* October 30, 1986, p. 8.
[c] Lipton and Steinberger, *Takeover and Freezeouts,* pp. 1–43.

of the expiration date of the offer, the bidder may cancel the offer or extend it.

PROXY FIGHTS

A *proxy fight* is an attempt by a single shareholder or a group of shareholders to take control or bring about other changes in a company through use of the proxy mechanism of corporate voting. In a proxy fight, a bidder may attempt to use his or her voting rights and garner support from other shareholders to oust the incumbent board and/or management. In order to understand how this device may be used to take control of a target company, we need a basic understanding of the workings of the corporate election process.

Corporate Elections

Corporate elections for seats on the board of directors are typically held once a year at the annual stockholders' meeting. The board of directors is particularly important to the corporation since the board selects the management who, in turn, run the corporation on a day-to-day basis. The date and time of the stockholders' meeting is stipulated in the company's articles of incorporation. The date is usually chosen so as to coincide with the end of the company's fiscal year when the annual report and the summary of the firm's financial results are available for the stockholders' review. SEC rules require that the annual report be sent to stockholders before the annual meeting. Since it takes time to produce the annual report, the annual meeting is usually held four to five months following the close of the firm's fiscal year.[27]

Shareholder Apathy

Shareholder elections tend to be characterized by considerable voter apathy. Easterbrook and Fischel contend that shareholders who supply capital to corporations should not necessarily have an interest in managing the company's affairs.[28] They assert that shareholders can adopt the easier route of voting with their feet and selling their shares when the firm and its management do not perform up to expectations. In their view, the sale of the shares is a far less expensive option than a collective action to alter the course of the company or to take control away from management. Easterbrook and Fischel believe that the federal proxy laws requiring extensive disclosure add further burdensome costs to disssenting groups, which create a disincentive to engage in a proxy fight.

Smaller, individual shareholders are naturally apathetic given their share of ownership in the company, but, surprisingly, larger institutional shareholders often display similar apathy. Institutional shareholders are increasingly dominating equity markets and now account for over 42.7

---

[27] Herbert A. Einhorn and J. William Robinson, *Shareholder Meetings* (New York: Practicing Law Institute, 1984), p. 27.

[28] Frank Easterbrook and Daniel Fischel, "Voting in Corporate Law," *Journal of Law and Economics* 23 (1983): 395–427.

percent of the total equity holdings in the United States.[29] Although they are an important factor in equity markets, they have historically been passive investors and do not tend to take an active role in the control of the companies they invest in.[30]

The traditionally passive role of institutionalized shareholders is starting to change, as in celebrated instances such as the public battle in 1985 between Ross Perot and Roger Smith, CEO of General Motors.[31] Additional evidence of institutional shareholders' activism came in the 1989 proxy fight between Carl Icahn and Texaco. One of the United States' largest pension fund, the California Public Employees Retirement System, sided with management and against Icahn. In return, the $56 billion pension fund was rewarded with a director being named from their list of candidates.[32] One impediment to such activism is the fear that the corporations will pressure institutions such as pension funds to vote with management.[33] That pressure may come from a CEO who gives his pension fund managers explicit instructions to vote with management in proxy contests.

> Take the case of Avon Products, whose CEO, Hicks Waldron, is an outstanding hawk on proxy voting. In a speech to institutional investors last year, Waldron said that when his company's managers intend to vote against management, "they must have my approval. Then we instruct the investment managers how to vote." And in an interview with this magazine last Spring for an article on shareholder activism (May 1987), Waldron said that during the previous proxy season he had ordered his managers to reverse all their antimanagement votes.[34]

Although institutions may be becoming more active, the evidence still indicates that, despite their ability to collectively wield considerable power and control proxy contests, they do not often choose to use this power. Considering that the institutional money managers primary goal is to maximize the value of their portfolio, it is not surprising that

---

[29] Carolyn K. Brancato and Patrick A. Gaughan, *Institutional Investors and Their Role in Capital Markets*, Columbia University Center for Law and Economics Monograph, 1988.

[30] Robert Monks and Nell Minow, Institutional Shareholder Services. "The Employee Benefit Research Institute Report on Proxy Voting," Washington, D.C.

[31] Doron P. Levin, *Irreconciliable Differences*. Boston: Little Brown, 1989).

[32] James White, "Calpers' Hanson Gains Respect for Institutional Shareholders," *Wall Street Journal*, April 3, 1990, p. C1.

[33] Speech at the United Shareholders' Meeting by Nell Minow, Institutional Shareholders Services, Washington, D.C.

[34] Hilary Rosenberg, "The Proxy Voting Crackdown," *Pensions* (April 1988): 105–110.

they show little interest in the day-to-day running of the companies they invest in. Not until the firm's performance flags do they look to divest their holdings.

The sale of an institution's large holdings can depress the stock price. In such an event, the institution may be locked into its position and thereby create an incentive for great activism by institutions. The active monitoring of individual companies by institutions, however, is hampered by the fact that it may hold equity in hundreds of companies. The large number of firms held in an institution's portfolio precludes micromanagement of their holdings. The fact that institutions may be somewhat temporarily locked into some of their positions and the difficulties in micro-management of their portfolios helps explain why institutions are not active investors.

Voting by Proxy

Approximately 80 percent of annual shareholder meetings are held in the spring at a site selected by management. Not all interested stockholders find it possible to attend the stockholders' meeting to execute their votes, simply because they have other commitments or because they are scattered throughout the world. The voting process has been made easier through the use of proxies. Under the proxy system, shareholders can authorize another person to vote for them and to act as their "proxy." Most corporate voting is done by proxies.

Calling a Stockholders' Meeting   The ability to call a stockholders' meeting is very important to a bidder who is also a stockholder in the target. Upon establishing an equity position in the target, the hostile bidder may want to attempt to remove the board of directors and put a board in place that is favorable to the bidder. Such a board may then approve a business combination or other relationship with the bidding firm. The meeting can also be used to have the stockholders approve certain corporate actions, such as the deactivation of antitakeover defenses or the sale of certain assets and the payment of a dividend from the proceeds of this sale. If the next annual meeting is not scheduled for several months, the bidder may want to call a meeting sooner. The ability to call a special meeting, at which the issue of a merger or a new election may be considered, is determined by the articles of incorporation which are governed by the prevailing state corporation laws.

Record Date   The corporation must notify all *stockholders of record* of an election. Only those stockholders recorded on the stock transfer books as owners of the firm's stock on the *record date* may vote at the election. The record date is used for other purposes as well, such as to decide who will receive dividends or notice of a particular meeting. The record date is important because the firm's stock may trade actively with the owners changing continually. The record date is usually no more than 60 days but no less than 10 days from the meeting date. As the owners of stock change, the record date specifies which stockholders will be able to vote. Stockholders who buy the stock before the meeting, but after the meeting date, do not receive notice of the meeting. If the stock is held under a "street name," such as a brokerage firm, the stockholder relinquishes the right to receive notice of events such as meetings.

A stock price will often fall after the record date in a proxy contest.[35] This reflects the fact that the market considers a stock less valuable when it does not carry the right to participate in an upcoming proxy contest. Presumably, this reflects some of the value of the right of voting participation in proxy fights.

Stock can be held in street names for a variety of reasons. Stockholders who turn their portfolios over often may keep their stocks in their brokerage firm's name so as to expedite the registration of their securities. Many stockholders decide they do not want to be bothered with keeping their share certificates and simply leave their shares with the broker who keeps them in the firm's name. A stockholder may be required to leave the purchased shares with the stockbroker if they were used as collateral in a margin purchase. The shareholdings are left with the broker in case the value of the collateral, the shares, falls. The stockholder will then get a margin call, and the shares might be sold if the shareholder cannot provide more collateral.

Bidders who are considering taking control of a company may want to keep the shares in the name of their brokerage firm so as to conceal the true identity of the owner of the shares. If the market anticipates an upcoming bid, the share price can rise. Readers should keep in mind that under the Williams Act, bidders have to make sure that they register their cumulative holdings with the SEC, should they rise to the 5 percent level.

Approximately 70 percent of all corporate stock is held in street names, 30 percent of which is held in the name of brokerage firms and the remaining 70 percent in bank nominee names.[36]

---

[35] Ronald C. Lease, John J. McConnell, and Wayne E. Mikkelson, "The Market Value of Control in Publicly Held Corporations," *Journal of Financial Economics* 11 (1983): 439–472.

[36] James Heard and Howard Sherman, *Conflicts of Interest in the Proxy System* (Washington, D.C.: Investor Responsibility Research Center, 1987), p. 74.

The physical exchange of shares is not the modus operandum of stock sales and purchases. Most brokerage firms do not hold the shares entrusted to them at the brokerage firm; instead, they keep them at a *depository*. One of the largest depositories in the United States is the Depository Trust Company located in New York City. When the shares are held in a depository, they are usually in the depository's name. Although the issuing corporation can obtain the names of the owners of the shares from the depository, this list may not be all that helpful. The depository will show the street names for those shares held by brokerage firms. This may not indicate who the real beneficial owners are. Efforts have been made in recent years to have the depository list reflect the true owners of the firm's stock.

Proxy Contests

Typically, there are two main forms of proxy contests.

1. *Contests for seats on the Board of Directors*. An insurgent group of stockholders may use this means to replace management. If the opposing slate of directors is elected, it may then use its authority to remove management and replace them with a new management team.

2. *Contests about management proposals*. These proposals concern the approval of a merger or acquisition. Management may oppose the merger, and the insurgent group of stockholders may be in favor. Other relevant proposals might be the passage of antitakeover amendments in the company's charter. Management might be in favor, while the insurgent group might be opposed, believing that their opposition will cause the stock price to fall and/or reduce the likelihood of a takeover.

Proxy Contests: From the Insurgents' Viewpoint

In a proxy contest, an insurgent group attempts to wrest control of the target by gathering enough supporting votes to replace the current board with board members of their choosing. The following characteristics increase the likelihood that a proxy fight will be successful.

1. *Insufficient voting support for management*. Management can normally count on a certain percentage of votes to support its position. Some of these votes might be through management's own stockholdings. Without a strong block of clear support for management among the voting shareholders, management and the incumbent board may be vulnerable to a proxy fight.

2. *Poor operating performance.* The worse the firm's recent track record, the more likely other stockholders will vote for a change in control. Stockholders in a firm that has had a track record of declining earnings and a poor dividend record are more likely to support an insurgent group advocating changes in the way the firm is managed.

3. *Sound alternative operating plan.* The insurgents must be able to propose changes that other stockholders believe will reverse the downward direction of the firm. These changes might come in the form of asset sales with the proceeds paid to stockholders by means of higher dividends. Another possibility could be a plan that provides for the removal of antitakeover barriers and a receptive approach to outside offers for the sale of the firm.

Effectiveness of Shareholder Activism

In 1989, John Pound conducted a study of the effectiveness of shareholder activism by examining various countersolicitations by shareholders who opposed management's antitakeover proposals. Pound analyzed a sample of 16 countersolicitation proxy fights by shareholder groups that occurred in the 1980s. He reported the following results:[37]

1. Countersolicitations were unsuccessful more often than they were successful. Dissidents in Pound's sample were successful only 25 percent of the time.

2. When shareholders approved the contested provisions, the net-of-market share values of the company dropped an average of 6 percent. The range of stock price reactions was between -3 percent and -30 percent. Pound found that when the amendments were defeated, stock prices rose.

3. The majority of the countersolicitations that Pound examined were preceded by a direct attempt to take control. In 8 of 16 countersolicitations in his sample, the dissidents had made an outright offer to take control of the company. In another seven cases, the dissidents had purchased a large stake in the firm. In only 1 of the 16 cases was there no attempt to take control.

The Proxy Fight Process

Step 1. *Starting the Proxy Fight.* A proxy fight for control of a company may begin when a bidder, who is also stockholder,

---

[37] John Pound, "Shareholder Activism and Share Values," *Journal of Law and Economics* (October 1989): 357–379.

CASE STUDY: *TORCHMARK VS AMERICAN GENERAL*

Insurgents can lose a proxy fight and still achieve some of their objectives. A hotly contested battle for control may set in motion a process that may bring about major changes in the way the firm is managed or even the sale of the firm. The 1990 proxy battle for American General is a case in point. Torchmark Corporation had attempted to place five new members on American General's 15-member board of directors. Torchmark, a small insurance company in Birmingham, Alabama, was approximately one-sixth the size of the larger insurance company. Torchmark criticized what it felt was the poor performance of American General compared to Torchmark's. As is typical of proxy fights, Torchmark conducted this critical campaign through full-page advertisements in the major financial media. The advertisement placed in the *New York Times* cited the relatively higher growth in dividends, stock prices, earnings per share, and return on equity of Torchmark.

American General won its proxy battle with Torchmark which had sought to take over American General. Their success can be partially attributed to support from institutional investors who controlled approximately 70 percent of American General's shares.[a] Institutions, however, were disappointed with American General's relatively poor performance. In response to criticism, American General's management announced an increase in its quarterly dividend from $0.39 to $0.80 per share. In addition, at their victorious annual meeting in May 1990, CEO Harold Hook announced that the company, which was vulnerable to a hostile takeover resulting from its lagging stock price of approximately $40 per share prior to the meeting, would be put up for sale.[b]

[a] Michael Allen and Randall Smith, "Sale of American General Sought in Spite of Vote," *Wall Street Journal,* May 3, 1990, p. A3.
[b] Ibid.

decides to attempt to change control at the upcoming stock-holders' meeting. An insurgent group of stockholders may have the right to call a special meeting where the replacement of management can be formally considered. A proxy fight might also come as a result of a management proposal for a major change such as the sale of the firm or the installation of certain antitakeover defenses.

Step 2. *The Solicitation Process.* In advance of the stockholders' meeting, the insurgent stockholder group attempts to contact other stockholders to convince them to vote against management's candidates for the board of directors or to vote for an acquisition or against certain antitakeover amendments. The process of contacting stockholders is usually handled by the proxy solicitor hired by the insurgent group. Management may have a proxy firm on retainer and may choose to hire other proxy firms if the proxy battle is particularly contentious. These proxy firms, which may have their own lists of stockholders, compiled from various sources, may use a staff of workers to repeatedly call stockholders to convince them of the merits of their client's position. Materials are then distributed to the beneficial owners of the stock. The depositories will submit a list of shareholders and their holdings to the issuing corporation. The issuing corporation will try to deal directly with the beneficial owners of the shares. An insurgent group can sue to have the issuing corporation share this information with the insurgent stockholders so as to have the interested parties on a more equal footing. When the shares are registered in the names of banks and trust companies, these institutions may or may not have voting authority for these shares. The banks may have voting authority to vote on all, some, or no issues. This voting authority may be such that the bank can vote on minor issues but must consult the beneficial owners on major issues such as a merger. When the shares are held in a brokerage firm's name, the broker may or may not have the authority to vote the shares. Stock exchange rules and SEC regulations determine whether the broker can do so. If the broker is not a trustee, the broker must contact the shareholder for advice. Normally, if the broker does not hear from the stockholder at least 15 days before the meeting, he or she may vote the shares (assuming he has attempted to contact the shareholder at least 25 days before the meeting). In a contest for control, or where there is a rival insurgent group with counterproposals or candidates, however, the broker may not vote even if he or she has not received instructions from the beneficial owner. A beneficial owner is a broad definition of the legal owners of a security. The beneficial owner has the ultimate power to dispose of the holding. This is generally the party listed on the stock transfer sheets as the owner on the record date. To expedite the process, the brokerage firm will tabulate the votes from its various proxies and submit its own summary master proxies reflecting the combined votes of its various clients.

Step 3. *The Voting Process.* Upon receiving the proxies, stockholders may then forward their votes to the designated collector such as a brokerage firm. The votes are sent to the proxy clerks at the brokerage firms that tabulate them.

The brokerage firm or bank usually keeps a running total of the votes as they are received and submits the vote results shortly before the corporation meeting. When the votes are submitted to the issuing corporation, tabulators appointed by the company count them. Voting inspectors are often used to oversee the tabulation process and help ensure its accuracy. The process takes place in an area that is sometimes referred to as the "snake pit." In a proxy fight both the issuing corporation and the dissident group frequently have their own proxy solicitors present throughout the voting tabulation process to help ensure that their client's interests are dealt with fairly. Proxy solicitors are alert to any questionable proxies, which they will then challenge. A proxy might be challenged if the same shares are voted more than once or if it was not signed by the party with voting authority. In cases where more than one vote has been submitted, the one with the latest date is usually selected. Major discrepancies in the voting process are usually followed by legal actions in which the losing party sues to invalidate the election.

THE ROLE OF THE INDEPENDENT ELECTION CORPORATION OF AMERICA

A broker may hire the Independent Election Corporation of America to carry out most of its proxy-related functions. The Independent Election Corporation of America (IECA) helps ensure that stockholders interested in exercising their votes receive their proxy materials in time to participate in the election. The IECA receives the list of the beneficial owners of the shares from the brokerage firms in advance of the election. The IECA then notifies the issuing company that it will be contacting the shareholders and asks the issuing company to forward a specific number of proxy materials to the IECA. Upon receipt of the proxy materials, the IECA forwards them to the beneficial owners in a timely manner. "Upon receipt of the issuer's proxy materials, IECA sends them, along with an IECA shareholder vote authorization form (VAF), to the beneficial owners of shares registered in the names of the IECA clients. The VAF is basically a request for voting instructions from the beneficial owners. It is analogous to the voting instruction request sent by a broker to its clients when the broker runs the proxy department."[38] The IECA then totals the votes and sends the results to the issuing company. The accuracy of its tabulations process is usually subject to oversight from a major accounting firm.

Voting Analysis

The votes of stockholders can be grouped into the following categories.[39]

1. *Shares controlled by insurgents and shareholder groups unfriendly to management.* This is the core of the insurgents' support. The greater the number of shares which this group commands, the more likely the proxy fight will be successful.

2. *Shares controlled by directors, officers, and ESOPs.* This category tends to represent the core of management's support. Directors and officers will surely vote with management. Shares held in ESOPs also tend to vote with management since workers may be concerned that a change in control may mean layoffs. In the 1990 proxy battle between Harold Simmons of NL Industries and the Lockheed Corporation, Simmons attributed his defeat in part to the 18.91 percent of the outstanding shares of Lockheed that were held in the firm's ESOP which was formed in 1989.[40]

3. *Shares controlled by institutions.* Large institutions control equity markets; they are by far the largest category of stockholders. As noted earlier, institutions have historically tended to be passive shareholders and have usually voted with management. This situation is starting to change as institutions are becoming more outspoken and are putting more pressure on management to maximize the value of their shareholdings. If the institutions can be convinced that a change in control may greatly increase value, they may vote in favor of the insurgent's position.

4. *Shares controlled by brokerage firms.* Certain stock exchange rules, such as those instituted by the New York Stock Exchange

---

[38] James E. Heard and Howard Sherman, *Conflicts of Interest in the Proxy Voting System* (Washington, D.C.: Investor Responsibility Research Center, 1987), p. 83.

[39] This section is adapted from a presentation by Morris J. Kramer, "Corporate Control Techniques: Insurgent Considerations," in James W. Robinson, ed., *Shareholders Meetings and Shareholder Control in Today's Securities Markets* (New York: Practicing Law Institute, 1985).

[40] Rick Wartzman and Karen Blumenthal, "Lockheed Wins Proxy Battle With Simmons," *Wall Street Journal*, April 11, 1990, p. A3.

and the American Stock Exchange, do not allow brokerage firms to vote the shares held in their name on behalf of clients, without receiving voting instructions from the owners of the shares. Voting instructions tend to be required for issues such as mergers or antitakeover amendments. Large amounts of shares tend to be held in street names. Brokerage firms, however, are generally not active voters in proxy fights. The reason can be traced to the problems of securing voting instructions, coupled with the fact that one of the brokerage firm's goals is to maximize its commissions and the value of its portfolios. Voting in proxy fights may not pay a return in the foreseeable future. The corporation sends voting materials to the brokerage firms which, in turn, are supposed to forward these materials to the "beneficial owners" of the shares. As of 1986, the issuing corporation has been able to send the materials directly to the beneficial owners by asking the brokerage firm for the names and addresses of the owners. These are supplied unless the shareholders have asked that they not be given out.

5. *Shares controlled by individuals.*   Given the larger equity base of many public corporations, this group of stockholders may not constitute a large percentage of the votes. In some cases, however, they may be important. Individual stockholders tend to vote with management. In some instances, major individual shareholders can be the focal point of the tender offer. For example, Kamal Adham, a major stockholder in Financial General Bankshares, Inc., solicited shareholder support for a proxy fight in favor of the approval of an acquisition of Financial General by a company owned by Adham and others.[41] Adham lost the proxy fight, but a plan for the serious consideration of a merger was later adopted.

The Costs of a Proxy Fight

A proxy fight may be a less expensive alternative to a tender offer. Tender offers are costly since they are offers to buy up to 100 percent of the outstanding stock at a premium that may be as high as 50 percent. In a tender offer, the bidder usually has certain stockholdings that can be sold off in the event the tender offer is unsuccessful. The bidder

---

[41] "NLT Holders Reject by 5–3 Margin a Plan to Create Group to Study Acquisition Bids," *Wall Street Journal*, May 13, 1982, p. 6.

may take a loss unless there is an available buyer such as a rival bidder or the target corporation. The stock sales, however, can be a way for the bidder to recapture some of the costs of the tender offer. While a proxy fight does not involve the large capital outlays that trade offers require, they are not without significant costs. The losers in a proxy fight do not have a way to recapture their losses. If the proxy fight is unsuccessful, the costs of the proxy battle are usually not recoverable. In a minority of circumstances, the insurgents can recover their costs from the corporation.

The major cost categories of a proxy fight are as follows:

1. *Professional fees.* A team of professionals is necessary to carry out a successful proxy fight. This team usually includes proxy solicitors, investment banks, and attorneys.

2. *Printing, mailing costs, and "communications costs."* The proxy materials must be printed and distributed to stockholders. A staff may be assembled by the proxy solicitation firm to contact stockholders directly by telephone. This may be supplemented through full-page advertisements in the *Wall Street Journal* such as the one placed by Lockheed's CEO citing the board of directors' opposition to Harold Simmon's proxy fight (see facing page). Brokerage firms must be compensated for the costs of forwarding the proxy materials to stockholders. Major proxy battles such as the 1990 Lockheed–NL Industries contest can bring firms like D. F. King and Company, which represented NL Industries or Georgeson and Company, which represented Lockheed, in excess of $1 million.[42]

3. *Litigation costs.* Proxy fights, like tender offers, tend to be actively litigated. Both parties incur significant legal fees. For example, the insurgent group may have to sue for access to the stockholder list. The corporation pays management's legal fees, whereas the insurgent group must pay its own legal expenses. Management has the advantage in this area too.

4. *Other fees.* Various other expenses such as tabulation fees are associated with the voting process. The tabulation may be done by the issuing company, the company's transfer agent, or a firm that specializes in tabulation work for corporate elections.

---

[42] Richard Hylton, "Advisors in Forefront of New Proxy Wars," *New York Times*, March 30, 1990, p. D1.

⚛️ Lockheed Shareholders:

IMPORTANT INFORMATION ABOUT YOUR INVESTMENT
(Part One)

Harold Simmons is a Texas investor who to our knowledge has no experience in the management of an aerospace company. NL Industries, Inc., a company he controls, has launched a proxy fight to replace your Board of Directors with its nominees, including Mr. Simmons. NL Industries is seeking to take control of your company without making an offer to acquire it or announcing any specific plans. Your Board of Directors opposes the election of Harold Simmons and his slate to Lockheed's Board because we believe it would be contrary to the interests of Lockheed shareholders.

Your Board of Directors is committed to taking any and all steps necessary to protect and enhance the value of all shareholders' investment in Lockheed.

We will be communicating with you shortly with additional information about Mr. Simmons and his associates as well as about your company's plans and progress, and we will be providing you with a revised **BLUE Proxy Card**. We urge you not to sign any proxy card you may receive from Mr. Simmons and his associates. Please sign, date, and return your new **BLUE Proxy Card** when you receive it!

We think it important, however, for you to be immediately aware of a few facts about Mr. Simmons and his associates:

- Many of those NL Industries has named to its slate have been promised $20,000 each if they are not elected and they are, we believe, personal friends or business associates of Mr. Simmons. None of these nominees has any direct personal investment in Lockheed.

- According to his 13D filings with the Securities and Exchange Commission, Mr. Simmons, who was found by a court to have violated his fiduciary duties under Federal Retirement Law (ERISA) and has been enjoined from further violations until 1992, is currently under investigation by the Securities and Exchange Commission regarding trading in the securities of Lockheed and another company.

- NL Industries has indicated that it intends to propose a shareholder resolution recommending that the Board terminate the company's Shareholder Rights Plan. According to Simmons' public filings, NL's indicated interest in making this proposal is so that it can continue buying Lockheed stock in excess of 20%. The Rights Plan, while restricting certain changes in control without Board approval, is designed in part to protect against the acquisition of control in the marketplace by any shareholder without paying a full and fair price for that right. We oppose NL's proposal because we believe that control of the company rests with ALL the shareholders and that you should reap an economic benefit from any transfer of control through stock acquisitions by anyone. Accordingly, your Board of Directors strongly recommends that you vote **AGAINST** any proposal NL Industries may make to recommend termination of the Rights Plan.

You, our shareholders, are the owners of Lockheed. We are keenly aware of our fiduciary obligations to you.

1989 was a transition year for Lockheed and your Board of Directors and management are moving aggressively to maximize shareholder value. We will continue to keep you informed of significant developments concerning your investment in Lockheed.

On behalf of your Board of Directors,

Daniel M. Tellep

Daniel M. Tellep
*Chairman of the Board
and Chief Executive Officer*

━━━━━━━━━━ **IMPORTANT** ━━━━━━━━━━

If your shares are held in "Street-Name," only your broker or banker can vote your shares and only upon receipt of your specific instructions. Please contact the person responsible for your account and instruct that individual to vote the new **BLUE Proxy Card** on your behalf in accordance with your Board's recommendations.

If you have any questions or need further assistance, please call our proxy solicitor, *GEORGESON & COMPANY INC.*, at 1-800-223-2064.

Reprinted by permission of the Lockheed Corporation.

The Wealth Effects of Proxy Contests

Peter Dodd and Jerrold Warner conducted a study of 96 proxy contests for seats on the boards of directors of companies on the New York and American Stock Exchanges.[43] Their research revealed a number of interesting findings relating the incidence of proxy contests to the value of stockholders' investments in these firms. They showed that a positive stock price effect is associated with proxy contests. In a 40-day period prior to and including the announcement of the proxy contest, a positive, abnormal stock price performance of 0.105 was registered. Based on these results, they concluded that proxy contests result in an increase in value inasmuch as they help facilitate the transfer of resources to more valuable uses.

The value of shareholders' votes was also examined in this study. Dodd and Warner attempted to test the hypothesis originally proposed by Henry Manne which stated that a positive stock price effect in proxy fights is associated with the increased value of the votes held by shareholders.[44] This value is perceived by participants in the contest who lobby for the support of shareholders. If their efforts are responsible for some of the increased value of shares, then the value should decline after the record date. Shares purchased after the record date can only be voted under restricted and limited circumstances. For the 42 contests in which they had the specific record date, Dodd and Warner found negative results, which seems to support the Manne vote–value hypothesis.

COMBINATION OF A PROXY FIGHT AND A TENDER OFFER

A proxy fight is sometimes used in conjunction with an offer to buy the target. For example, on May 1, 1986, Asher Edelman made an offer to buy Fruehauf. Edelman had bought 5 percent of Fruehauf and wanted to acquire the entire corporation. He proposed the acquisition to the Fruehauf board of directors, which rejected the offer. Edelman responded by increasing his shareholdings to 9.5 percent and the bid price to $42 per share.[45] Edelman engaged in a proxy fight at the annual meeting. He proposed his own slate of directors who would, of course,

---

[43] Peter Dodd and Jerrold Warner, "On Corporate Governance: A Study of Proxy Contests," *Journal of Financial Economics* 11, no. 1–4 (April 1983): 401–438.

[44] Henry Manne, "The Higher Criticism of the Modern Corporation," *Columbia Law Review* 62 (1962): 399–432.

[45] John Bussey, "Edelman Plans $44-a-Share Bid for Fruehauf," *Wall Street Journal*, June 12, 1986, p. 12.

be in favor of approving the bid. Edelman lost the proxy fight but followed with a formal tender offer at $44 per share.

A proxy fight can be an effective ancillary tool when coupled with a tender offer. The hostile bidder can use the proxy fight to have a shareholder proposal approved that would dismantle the target's anti-takeover defenses. For example, a bidder could use a proxy fight to have the target dismantle its poison pill or other antitakeover defenses. This would then be followed by a more effective tender offer. Another option available to the bidder/insurgent is to have the target agree to elect not to be bound by the prevailing state antitakeover laws.

PROXY FIGHTS AND TAKEOVERS IN THE 1990s

The collapse of the junk bond market, and the associated fall of the leading junk bond investment bank, Drexel Burnham Lambert, reduced the effectiveness of tender offers. With a shrunken junk bond market, the large amounts of cash that had made tender offers such an effective hostile takeover tool were not available. This limited the options of less well-financed bidders who had traditionally relied on the junk bond market for the financing necessary to pressure a board of directors or to entice shareholders to accept the bid. These bidders then began to look to proxy fights as an alternative. Unfortunately, proxy battles have a lower probability of achieving success than the junk bond financed tender offers that were typical of the mid-1980s.

One such example was the battle for Lockheed cited earlier when Harold Simmons, through his company NL Industries, launched a proxy battle for control of Lockheed Corporation. Houston-based NL Industries, which owned 19 percent of Lockheed, he nominated its own slate of directors and submitted a proposal to shareholders to eliminate some antitakeover defenses such as Lockheed's poison pill. This poison pill becomes effective when a shareholder acquires more than 20 percent.[46] In this instance, however, Simmons failed to convince enough institutional owners of the firm's stock that they should vote for his directors and proposal. As a conciliatory gesture to the insurgents on shareholder rights issues, however, management agreed to take steps to have Lockheed elect to be exempt from the antitakeover provisions of the Delaware antitakeover law. In addition, management, in response to pressure from institutional investors, agreed to allow confidential shareholder voting.[47]

---

[46] Randall Smith and David Hilder, "Raiders Shorn of Junk Gird for Proxy Fights," *Wall Street Journal*, March 7, 1990, p. C1.

[47] Wartzman and Blumenthal, "Lockheed Wins Proxy Battle with Simmons," p. A3.

Table 6.1   1990 MAJOR PROXY BATTLES

Company/ Challenger	Situation	Outcome
American General/ Torchmark Corp.	Torchmark wanted American General to consider a $6.3 billion bid	American General won vote; but put itself up for sale anyway
UAL Corp./ Coniston Partners	Coniston wanted UAL to accept $4 billion bid from union group	UAL agreed to accept higher $4.38 billion union bid
Great Northern Nekoosa/ Georgia-Pacific	Georgia-Pacific wanted Great Northern to take $3.6 billion bid	Great Northern agreed to be acquired by Georgia-Pacific
Norton Co./ BTR PLC	BTR wanted to force Norton to accept $1.6 billion bid	Norton accepted $1.9 billion bid from Cie. de Saint-Gobain
USX Corp./ Carl Icahn	Icahn wanted USX to spin off steel business; no bid	USX holders rejected Icahn referendum
Lockheed Corp./ Harold Simmons	Simmons, with 19%, sought to oust board; no bid	Simmons lost vote, but Lockheed promised board seats to others
Avon Products/ Chartwell Associates	Fishers, Getty, Mary Kay Corp. sought 4 board seats; no bid	Dissidents got two board seats to settle fight before vote
National Intergroup/ Centaur Partners	Centaur, with 16.5%, seeks board majority; no bid	Centaur expected to get strong vote at July 25 meeting
Amstrong World Industries/ Belzbergs	Belzbergs, with 10%, sought 4 board seats; no bid	Belzbergs appear to have won one seat on board
Pic 'n' Save Corp./ David Batchelder	Batchelder seeks 4 board seats; says might make bid	Batchelder using consent solicitation similar to proxy tilt
Xtra Corp./ Robert Gintel	Group, with 21.6%, tried to oust board, charging mismanagement; no bid	Gintel group won vote, replaced management

Table 6.1 highlights some of the major proxy fights that took place in early 1990. Many were created as an alternative to a hostile takeover.

SUMMARY

This chapter discusses the two main alternatives available to a hostile bidder: a tender offer and a proxy fight. Several variations of a tender offer exist—for example, the all-cash tender offer and the two-tiered tender offer. The effectiveness of tender offers has varied over time as firms developed better defenses and as the availability of financing changed. The regulatory environment has also greatly affected the use of this takeover tool. Laws regulating tender offers not only set forth the rules within which an offer must be structured, but they also provide strategic opportunities for both the bidder and the target. The use of tender offers grew significantly in both size and number during the 1980s. Large corporations that once thought themselves invulnerable to takeover succumbed to the junk bond-financed tender offers. When the junk bond market declined in the late 1980s, hostile bidders were forced to look elsewhere. Proxy fights, which work through the corporate election proxy, became a viable tool once again. Proxy contests can bring about a change in control or seek more modest goals, such as the enactment of shareholder provisions in the company's corporate charter.

This chapter describes the process of conducting a proxy fight. Bidders have discovered that a successful proxy battle can be a less expensive alternative to a tender offer, while unsuccessful insurgents have little to show at the end of the contest. Bidders have also found that the combined use of a proxy fight in conjunction with tender offers presents additional opportunities. Proxy fights, for example, can be used to dismantle the target's defenses, making it more vulnerable to a less-well-financed tender offer.

Just as with antitakeover defenses, takeover tactics are continually evolving. Bidders are forced to adapt to the increasingly effective defenses that targets have erected. There is every reason to believe that this evolutionary process will continue through the 1990s.

REFERENCES

Asquith, Paul. "Merger Bids and Stock Returns." *Journal of Financial Economics* 11, no. 1–4 (April 1983): 51–83.

Bradley, Michael, Anand Desai, and E. Han Kim. "The Rationale Behind Interfirm Tender Offers: Information or Synergy." *Journal of Financial Economics* 11 (April 1983): 183–206.

Brancato, Carolyn K., and Patrick A. Gaughan. *Institutional Investors and Their Role in Capital Markets*. Columbia University Center for Law and Economics Monograph, 1988.

Bussey, John. "Edelman Plans $44-a-Share Bid for Fruehauf." *Wall Street Journal*, June 12, 1986, p. 12.

Comment, Robert, and Greg Jarrell. "Two-Tiered and Negotiated Tender Offers." *Journal of Financial Economics* 19, no. 2 (December 1987): 283–310.

Peter Dodd and Jerrold Warner, "On Corporate Government: A Study of Proxy Contests," *Journal of Financial Economics*, 11, no. 1–4 (April 1983):401–438.

Easterbrook, Frank H., and Daniel R. Fischel. "The Proper Role of a Target's Management in Responding to a Tender Offer." *Harvard Law Review* 94, no. 6 (April 1981): 1161–1202.

Easterbrook, Frank H., and Daniel R. Fischel. "Takeover Bids, Defensive Tactics and Shareholders Welfare." *The Business Lawyer* 36 (July 1981): 1733–1750.

Easterbrook, Frank H., and Daniel R. Fischel. "Voting in Corporate Law." *Journal of Law and Economics* 23 (1983): 395–427.

Einhorn, Herbert A., and J. William Robinson. *Shareholder Meetings*. New York: Practicing Law Institute, 1984.

Hagedorn, Ann. "Allied Stores Receives $3.56 Billion Offer for De-Bartolo Corp., Paul Bilzerian." *Wall Street Journal*, October 9, 1989, p. 3.

Hanson Trust PLC v. *SCM Corp.*, 774 F. 2d 47 (2d Cir. 1985).

Heard, James, and Howard Sherman. *Conflicts of Interest in the Proxy System*. Washington, D.C.: Investor Responsibility Research Center, 1987, p. 74.

Hylton, Richard. "Advisers in Forefront of New Proxy Wars." *New York Times*, March 30, 1990, p. D1.

Ingersoll, Bruce. "Campeau's Purchase of 48% of Allied Was Illegal, SEC Will Argue in Court." *Wall Street Journal*, October 30, 1986, p. 8.

Jarrell, Greg, and Annette Poulson. "Shark Repellents and Stock Prices: The Effects of Antitakeover Amendments Since 1980." *Journal of Financial Economics* 19, no. 1 (September 1987): 127–168.

Johnson, Robert. "William Farley's Quest for Status Threatens to Topple His Empire." *Wall Street Journal*, April 30, 1990, p. A1.

Kennecott Cooper Corp. v. *Curtiss Wright Corp.*, 584 F 2nd. 1195 (2nd Cir. 1978).

Kramer, Morris J. "Corporate Control Techniques: Insurgent Considerations." In James W. Robinson, ed., *Shareholders Meetings and Shareholder Control in Today's Securities Markets*. New York: Practicing Law Institute, 1985.

Lease, Ronald C., John J. McConnell, and Wayne E. Mikkelson. "The

Market Value of Control in Publicly Held Corporations." *Journal of Financial Economics* 11 (1983): 439–472.

Levin, Doron P. *Irreconcilable Differences*. Boston: Little, Brown, 1989.

Lipton, Martin. "Takeover Bids in the Target's Boardroom." *Business Lawyer* 35 (November 1979): 101–133.

Lipton, Martin, and Erica H. Steinberger. *Takeovers and Freeze-outs*. Washington, D.C.: Law Journal Seminar Press, 1987, pp. 1–12.

Madrick, Jeff. *Taking America*. New York: Bantam Books, p. 152.

Manne, Henry. "The Higher Criticism of the Corporation," *Columbia Law Review*, 62, (1962):399–432.

Mergerstat Review: 1988. Merrill Lynch.

Mitchell, Mark L., and Kenneth Lehn. "Do Bad Bidders Become Good Targets?" *Journal of Applied Corporate Finance* 3(2), Summer 1990, pp 60–69.

Monks, Robert, and Nell Minow. "Article on the Employee Benefit Research Institute Report on Proxy Voting." Institutional Shareholder Services, Washington, D.C.

"NLT Holders Reject by 5–3 Margin a Plan to Create Group to Study Acquisition Bids." *Wall Street Journal*, May 13, 1982, p. 6.

Oesterle, Dale. "The Rise and Fall of Street Sweep Takeovers," *Duke Law Journal*, 1989, pp 202–227.

Panter v. *Marshall Field* & *Company*, 486 F. Supp. 1168, N.D. Ill. 1980. as cited in: Martin Lipton, "Takeover Bids in the Target's Boardroom: An Update After One Year." *Business Lawyer* 36 (April 1981): 1017–1028.

Phalon, Richard. *The Takeover Barons of Wall Street*. New York: Putnam Publishing Co., 1981.

Pound, John. "Shareholder Activism and Share Values." *Journal of Law and Economics* (October 1989): 357–379.

Rosenberg, Hilary. "The Proxy Voting Crackdown." *Pensions* (April 1988): 105–110.

S-G Securities, Inc. v. *Fuqua Investment Company*, 466 F. Supp. 1114 (D. Mass., 1978).

Smith, Randall, and David Hilder. "Raiders Shorn of Junk Gird for Proxy Fights," *Wall Street Journal*, March 7, 1990, p. C1.

Soderquist, Larry D. *Understanding Securities Laws*. New York: Practicing Law Institute, July 1987, p. 236.

Speech at the United Shareholders Meeting by Nell Minow. Institutional Shareholders Services, Washington, D.C.

Stromfeld v. *Great Atlantic* & *Pacific Tea Company,* 484 F. Supp. 1264 (S.D.N.Y. 1980), Affirmed 6464 F. 2nd 563 (2nd Cir. 1980).

Wartzman, Rick, and Karen Blumenthal. "Lockheed Wins Proxy Battle with Simmons," *Wall Street Journal,* April 11, 1990, p. A3.

Weinberger v. *U.O.P.* 457 A. 2d 701 (Del. 1983).

Wellman v. *Dickinson,* 475 F. Supp. 783 (S.D.N.Y. 1979).

Chapter
7

Leveraged Buyouts

A leveraged buyout (LBO) is a financing technique used by a variety of groups, including the management of a corporation, or outside groups such as other corporations, partnerships, individuals, or investment groups. Specifically, it is the use of debt to purchase the stock of a corporation, and frequently it involves taking a public company private.

The number of large leveraged buyouts increased dramatically in the 1980s, but they first began to occur with some frequency in the 1970s, as an outgrowth of the 1960s bull market. Many private corporations took advantage of the high stock prices and chose this time to go public, thereby allowing many entrepreneurs to enjoy windfall gains. Even though many of these firms were not high quality, their stock was quickly absorbed by the insatiable bull market. When the stock market turned down in the 1970s, the prices of some of these lower quality companies fell dramatically. The bulk of this fall-off in prices occurred between 1972 and 1974 when the Dow Jones Industrial Average fell from 1036 in 1972 to 578 in 1974. In 1974, the average price–earnings ratio was 6, which is quite low even by current post-crash standards.

When the opportunity presented itself, managers of the companies that went public in the 1960s chose to take their companies private. In addition, many conglomerates that had been built up in the 1960s through large-scale acquisitions began to become partially disassembled through selloffs, a process that is called *deconglomeration*. Part of this process took place through the sale of divisions of conglomerates through leveraged buyouts. This process was ongoing through the 1980s

269

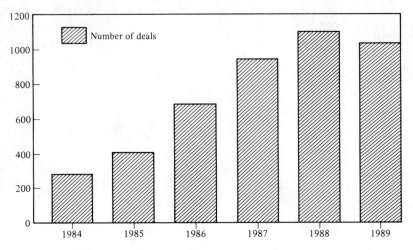

Figure 7.1 Divestitures, 1984–1989. (*Source:* IDD Information Services.)

and is partially responsible for the rising trend in divestitures depicted in Figure 7.1.

LBO DATA

By the mid-1980s, larger companies were starting to become the target of leveraged buyouts; the average LBO transaction increased from $39.42 million in 1981 to $137.45 million in 1987 (see Figure 7.2). The

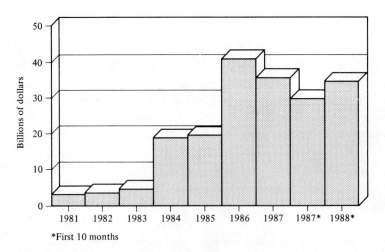

Figure 7.2 Mergers and LBOs, 1981–1988. (*Source:* Prepared by Carol Brancato.)

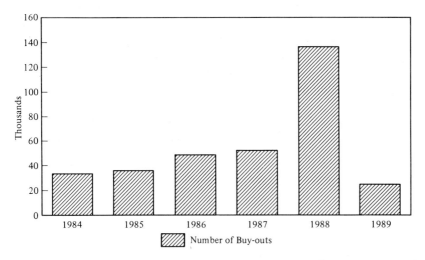

Figure 7.3 Leveraged buy-outs, 1984–1989. (*Source:* IDD Information Services.)

majority of the completed LBO transactions—7 percent—were divest-itures.

Although leveraged buyouts have attracted a great deal of attention in recent years, they are still small in both number and dollar value compared to mergers. In 1987, there were 3,701 mergers but only 259 leveraged buyouts. LBOs accounted for only 7 percent of the total number of transactions. In terms of total value, LBOs accounted for a higher percentage of the total value of transactions. In 1987, LBOs made up 21.3 percent of the total value of transactions, which shows that the typical LBO tends to have a larger dollar value than the typical merger. Figure 7.3 shows that the number of LBOs fell dramatically in 1989. This decrease coincided with the decline in the junk bond market that started in late 1988.

COSTS OF BEING A PUBLIC COMPANY

Many costs and inconveniences are associated with being a public company. First, federal securities laws mandate periodic filings with the SEC; for small firms these filings can be a burden in both money and management time. They may help explain why small and medium-sized firms may want to go private, though not why large firms go private.[1]

---

[1] Victor Brudney and Marvin A. Chirelstein, "A Restatement of Corporate Freezeouts," *Yale Law Journal* 87 (June 1978): 1136–1137.

According to DeAngelo, DeAngelo, and Rice, one of the corporations they examined in 1976, Barbara Lynn Stores, had estimated public ownership costs of $100,000 per year. This cost was large compared to the total market value of the company's stock of $1.38 million.[2] If this $100,000 cost is capitalized at a 13 percent rate of return, which was the rate of return on long-term corporate bonds during the 1980s, it results in a value of $769,231. If a higher capitalization rate is used, such as the rate of return on equities during the 1980s, 17.5 percent, an even lower value results—$571,429.[3] These capitalized values are small relative to the average cost of a leveraged buyout. Robert Kieschnick reports an average buyout cost of approximately $102 million.[4] (This value is somewhat skewed by the large dollar value LBOs that occurred in the 1980s.) This implies that the elimination of the direct costs of being a public company cannot be important for buyouts of large companies.

When stock prices fall significantly (as they did in the 1970s), managers of the recently public companies may seize this opportunity to take their firm private. When stockholders are offered a premium for their stock at a time when the market is declining, they often jump at the opportunity. These going private transactions are frequently financed with debt. Hence, the leveraged buyout started to become increasingly commonplace as the number of LBOs grew in the 1970s.

Public companies are accountable to public stockholders for their actions, but many entrepreneurs do not carefully consider accountability when they decide to take their company public. Instead, they focus on the sizable gains they can enjoy by going public. This is a particular problem for individualistic entrepreneurs. They may be unwilling to answer to the needs of public shareholders. This can become a problem when the stockholders want management to move in a different direction than what management's policies have been pursuing.

TYPES OF LBO CANDIDATES

Premium Companies

Premium companies are high-quality firms with many of the desirable characteristics lenders prefer, including quality assets that can be used

---

[2] H. DeAngelo, L. DeAngelo, and E. Rice, "Going Private: Minority Freezeouts and Stockholder Wealth," *Journal of Law and Economics* (October 1984): 367–402.

[3] *Stocks, Bills, Bonds and Inflation: 1990 Yearbook* (Chicago: Ibbotson Associates).

[4] Robert L. Kieschnick, "Management Buyouts of Public Corporations: An Analysis of Prior Characteristics," in Yakov Amihud, ed., *Leveraged Management Buyouts* (Homewood, Ill.: Dow Jones Irwin, 1989), pp. 35–68.

as collateral, significant and stable cash flows, experienced and successful management, and quality products with large market shares. Not surprisingly, such firms command high premiums in the market. In the early 1980s, LBO premiums were not far above book value. However, the intensified pace of mergers in the later 1980s brought premiums well above book values.[5]

Second-Tier Companies

Second-tier companies are firms whose valuable characteristics are somewhat offset by other deficiencies. For example, such a company may possess valuable assets but have erratic cash flows. This, coupled with a volatile industry, may give the lender cause for concern. Premiums for this type firm are naturally lower. Lenders may require the seller to participate in financing the buyout.

Troubled Companies

Troubled companies are often plagued by the large debts they are servicing and as such are not good LBO candidates. Buyers are often in a much stronger bargaining position, and high premiums for these companies are rare. The buyer's stronger bargaining position is often reflected in a demand for a management change before completing financing agreements.

Many potential buyers in the 1980s discovered that a less expensive way to buy a troubled firm was to buy its *busted bonds* after a Chapter 11 filing. These are the bonds of firms that have filed for bankruptcy protection. They often sell at a deep discount, which may enable the bondholders to use their position as members of the reorganization creditors committee to acquire an equity stake in the troubled concern. Although this route is less certain than a pre-bankruptcy LBO, it is far less expensive.

PLAYERS IN THE LBO PROCESS

Sellers

As in most business transactions, the LBO process features two groups of players: buyers and sellers. The sellers may include entrepreneurial and privately held firms in which the owner is seeking to "cash out." Their reasons for cashing out are varied and include retirement, health

---

[5] J. Terrance Greve, "Management Buyouts and LBO's" in Milton Rask, ed., *Mergers and Acquisitions* (New York: McGraw-Hill, 1987), pp. 345–355.

problems, and divorce. For these entrepreneurs who may have the bulk of their wealth invested in the firm, the LBO may provide the opportunity to reap windfall gains. However, this type of sale can sometimes present problems for the selling corporation. Often they must be kept secret from employees who may experience loss of morale in pondering the uncertainties which a change in control may mean for their employment opportunities. Supplier and customer relationships may also be affected by the new owners.[6]

Buyers, on the other hand, have to be wary of buying a firm in which the entrepreneur is cashing out. If the entrepreneur's skills, contacts, business relationships, and name are crucial to the continuing success of the company, then the business may be considerably less valuable if the entrepreneur decides to leave. In such cases, the buyer often requires that he or she stay on in some capacity for a defined period of time.

A public company may also become a seller when it seeks to divest itself of a particular division that no longer plays a role in the company's future plans. The majority of leveraged buyouts are of this type. Management often makes an offer to buy the division which may have been their source of employment for a long time. The company may sometimes take an active role in facilitating the transaction by working with its investment banker so as to minimize the adverse publicity and ill will that such a divestiture might generate. Complete public companies can also be sellers in leveraged buyouts, which in the 1980s often took place in both hostile and friendly transactions. Public companies can be good targets of a hostile leveraged buyout since LBOs depend on borrowing for their financing and it is easier to determine the collateral value of assets when the company is public. These firms become even more attractive LBO candidates in bear markets, which may cause the value of the outstanding equity to fall below the underlying value of the firm's assets. The leveraged buyouts of complete public companies attract much media attention, but they are far less common than the sale or divestitures of a division of a public firm. The many reasons for this form of corporate restructuring are discussed in Chapter 12.

Buyers

Individuals who are buyers in LBOs are typically the managers of public companies that had gone public in the past. Many of these individuals

---

[6] See Gary B. Anderson, "Defining the Board Game," in Stephen C. Diamond, ed., *Leveraged Buyouts* (Homewood, Ill.: Dow Jones Irwin & Co., 1985), pp. 11–39.

are motivated by the desire not to be answerable to a group of public stockholders as well as the desire to achieve financial gains. The availability of large amounts of debt capital in the late 1980s enabled entrepreneurial managers to pursue the dream of owning their own firm. Corporations, both public and private, can also be buyers in an LBO transaction. The motivation of the small corporation may be similar to that of individuals, whereas larger companies can have varied motives for buying companies through a leveraged buyout. For example, a large corporation could use an LBO as a way of pursuing a diversification strategy. Using an LBO, a corporation would assume debt to buy the publicly owned shares of a target corporation. The availability of the debt capital in the late 1980s enabled these corporations to use another form of currency other than stock. In using debt, the firm may be able to increase earnings per share since the target's earnings are added without an increase in outstanding shares. Employee groups, through employee stock ownership plans (ESOPs), have also become buyers of companies through leveraged buyouts. ESOPs are discussed in detail in Chapter 9.

Investment groups that specialize in raising the necessary capital to complete an LBO are often hired to facilitate the buyout process. Kohlberg, Kravis and Roberts is by far the largest LBO firm followed by Forstmann, Little.

MANAGEMENT BUYOUTS

Management buyouts (MBOs), a special case of leveraged buyouts, occur when the management of a company decides it wants to take its publicly held company private. Because of large sums necessary to complete the purchase, management usually has to rely on borrowing to accomplish this objective. In order to convince stockholders to sell, managers have to be able to offer them a premium above the current market price. Thus, management may have to make the firm even more profitable as a private company than it was as a publicly held concern. The theoretical basis for this type of reasoning is found in the area of financial research known as *agency theory*—the belief that a public corporation is characterized by certain agency costs.[7] These costs are incurred by stockholders, the true owners of the corporation who have

---

[7] Michael Jensen and William Meckling, "Theory of the Firm: Managerial Behavior, Agency Costs and Ownership Structure," *Journal of Financial Economics* 3 (October 1976): 305–360.

to rely on agents, the managers of the company, to manage the company in a way that will maximize their returns. Managers, however, have their own set of objectives which may not coincide with those of the stockholders. For example, managers may want to devote more resources to the perks of office, such as more luxuriously decorated and spacious offices and company jets, than are really necessary.

An extreme version of the agency problem occurs when management fraudulently takes corporate resources for their own without the stockholders' approval. A classic example is the Equity Funding Scandal of 1973 in which management committed fraud and hid it from stockholders for nine years, reporting nonexistent profits and assets during all those years. As a result, stockholders lost several hundred million dollars. The fraud was eventually detected, and the president of the corporation along with 18 other managers and employees were arrested and sentenced to jail. Not all agency costs that a firm experiences are as dramatic as these, but they can still be significant to the firm's owners. One of the more common ways such costs are thought to manifest themselves is by having larger companies than what would be economically efficient. If we assume that the stockholders' goal is to maximize profits, we can determine the optimal output level, as can be shown through the use of marginal analysis. The profit-maximizing output level is shown in Figure 7.4 as X^*—the point where marginal revenue and marginal costs are equal. At this point profit reaches its maximum level of π_{max}. Beyond X^* further sales will generate more additional costs than additional revenues. A profit-maximizing firm would not produce output beyond this level.

The managers of the firm may decide that they could more easily justify higher salaries and other perks if the company were larger. Additional compensation might also come in the form of psychic gratification which comes with being the CEO of one of the larger companies in that industry. The increased size may come through acquisitions of other companies. Managers, however, are somewhat constrained by the fact that they must provide stockholders with a certain level of profitability and dividends. The range between the profit-maximizing level of profitability π_{max} and π_2 may be significant (see Figure 7.5). Mueller, for example, hypothesized that the compensation that managers of larger firms derived is a motive for conglomerate acquisitions. In Mueller's view, managers will even accept a lower rate of return or hurdle rate, so as to be able to complete acquisitions that will lead to greater compensation.[8] If profits fall too low (such as to π_1), stockholders might

---

[8] Dennis Mueller, "A Theory of Conglomerate Mergers." *Quarterly Journal of Economics* 83 (1969): 643–659.

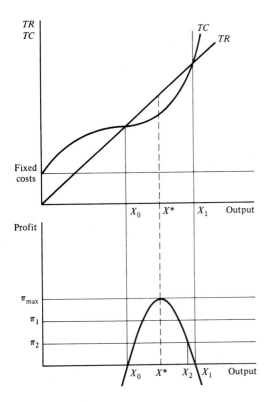

Figures 7.4 and 7.5

have an incentive for incurring the costs involved in forcing a change in management. The process of removing directors and management may sometimes require a proxy fight that can be very costly with uncertain results.

In an effort to deal with the managers' potentially conflicting goals, owners may take various actions to ensure that management's actions will be more consistent with their own objectives. One such set of actions involves establishing a set of monitoring systems that will keep track of management's performance.[9] The board of directors helps fulfill this control mission for stockholders. However, when the board is composed of many members of management, this process may not work as efficiently. One way to ensure that the board will fulfill its policing mission is to have a greater percentage of outside directors—those who

---

[9] Eugene Fama and Michael Jensen, "Separation of Ownership and Control," *Journal of Law and Economics* 26 (1983): 301–325.

do not have management positions with the firm. (Inside directors are managers of the company.) Given the fact that many outside directors are suggested and recommended by the chairman and other inside board members, there are serious concerns that today's corporate boards really perform this function.

Owners can also help ensure that the agents will pursue owners' goals by creating profit incentives for managers through profit-sharing plans or stock options.[10] While this approach may reduce agency costs, it is an imperfect solution to the problem. Seldom can a manager gain more by sacrificing direct gains in the form of bonuses, perks, and a higher expense account in return for a share of the higher profits that may result from all managers making similar sacrifices. The *free rider problem* tends to prevail: that is, one manager attempts to keep his or her perks and expenses high while hoping that other managers lower theirs.

It is difficult to determine the optimal level of profitability for each company. One important guide is the profitability of similar-size firms in this industry. Several measures can be utilized such as average industry profits or the industry average rate of return on equity. If the firm falls too far below the industry average, then questions will be raised regarding the cause of this decline. If management can demonstrate that its profitability is consistent with that of the industry, then it may be able to avoid pressure from stockholders. If stockholders are able to enjoy the industry rate of return on equity, and if this rate of return is consistent with historical performance, then management may be free from significant stockholder pressure.

If the firm is earning minimum profits to satisfy stockholders (π_{min}), considerable gains can be made, providing the agency problem can be eliminated (see Figure 7.6). Going private can help eliminate this problem by making the agents and the owners one. While this makes clear sense in theory, there may be a great difference between theoretical gains and the actual gains derived from attempting to eliminate agency costs.

THE LEVERAGED BUYOUT PROCESS

As stated above, leveraged buyouts are acquisitions financed primarily with debt. They are usually cash transactions in which the cash is borrowed by the acquiring firm. Much of the debt may be secured by

---

[10] Eugene Fama, "Agency Problems and the Theory of the Firm," *Journal of Political Economy* (April 1980): 288–307.

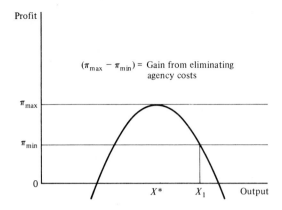

$(\pi_{max} - \pi_{min}) = $ Gain from eliminating agency costs

π_{max}

π_{min}

X^* X_1 Output

Figure 7.6

the assets of the corporation being taken private. This section provides an overview of the LBO process. The financing of the LBO is discussed in greater detail later in this chapter.

The target company's assets are often used to provide collateral for the debt that is going to be incurred to finance the acquisition. Thus, the collateral value of these assets needs to be assessed. This type of lending is often called *asset-based lending*. Firms with assets that have a high collateral value can more easily obtain such loans, and so LBOs are often easier to finalize in capital-intensive industries—firms that usually have more assets that can be used as collateral than noncapital-intensive firms. It is not surprising, therefore, that Waite and Fridson found that LBO activity was more predominant in manufacturing than in nonmanufacturing industries.[11] Still LBOs are possible for firms that do not have an abundance of assets which can be used as collateral. Service industries are one example. They tend not to have as high asset values, but they may be good LBO candidates because their cash flows are high enough to service the interest payments on the debt that will arise when the buyout is completed.

Following is a step-by-step process of a hypothetical leveraged buyout in which a division of a firm is taken private through a management buyout:

Step 1. *The decision to divest is made.* The management of Diversified Industries (DI) has observed that the chemicals

---

[11] S. Waite and M. Fridson, "The Credit Quality of Leveraged Buyouts," *High Performance*, January 1989, New York: Morgan Stanley.

division is performing poorly and has become a drain on the whole company. It is decided at a board of directors meeting that DI will divest itself of the chemicals division. The company does not want to be in the chemicals industry and would rather focus its resources on areas that show more promise. DI's managers are concerned about the welfare of the chemical division's employees. They inform the management of the chemicals division of their plans and express their interest in remaining with the division after divestiture.

Step 2.   *Management of the division makes the decision to purchase the division.*   After much deliberation, the managers of the chemicals division decide to attempt a buyout. They then determine the financial resources they can devote toward its purchase. The management of the overall company, as well as the management of the division, approach DI's investment bank to obtain an assessment of the availability of financing for the LBO.

Step 3.   *A financial analysis of the division is conducted.*   A financial analysis of the chemicals division is conducted. The main focus of this analysis is to determine whether the division, on its own, is sufficiently creditworthy to support the assumption of the debt levels needed to finance the buyout. Several financial measures are often used to facilitate this assessment. Most of them are discussed in Chapters 14–16; however, three of the more frequently used measures for LBOs need to be highlighted here.

Division's book value of assets.   This measure indicates the value of the division's assets carried on the firm's books. It may or may not accurately reflect the value of the division's assets.

Replacement value of assets.   This is the cost to a purchaser of replacing the assets. It is a more accurate reflection of the true value of the division's assets since it provides a better indication of the value the market places on these assets.

Liquidation value of assets.   This measure indicates what a lender might receive if the assets were liquidated such as in the case of a bankruptcy. It is one measure of the lender's protection in the event the division fails as an independent company. It is an imperfect measure, however, since assets sometimes sell at fire sale prices in liquidation proceedings.

Step 4. *The purchase price is determined.* Diversified Industries agrees on a sale price that is in excess of the value of the division's liquidation value of assets. This value should be considered a floor value because, presumably, DI could sell off the chemical division's assets for at least this amount. How much above the liquidation value depends on the relative bargaining abilities of the groups involved in the transaction as well as the intensity of DI's desire to rid itself of the chemical division. A firm may sometimes feel an obligation to the employees of the division and will allow them to buy the division at a price that is not too far above what would be considered a giveaway of company assets. However, in the 1980s the LBO sector sometimes featured intense bidding contests for LBO targets. Such an atmosphere puts pressure on the management of the parent company to seek out the maximum value attainable.

Step 5. *Investment by the division's management is determined.* Once the purchase price has been determined, the managers of the division have to decide the extent of their own capital investment in the transaction. This is often required as a condition of the lenders since managers who have a personal, financial stake in the future of the company will presumably help ensure the company's financial well-being and thereby protect the lenders' interests. Lenders sometimes call this *hurt money.* Although the amount of this investment may be small compared to the total capital raised, it may constitute a significant part of the total wealth of the managers.

Step 6. *The lending group is assembled.* At this point in the process, the investment banker puts together the lending group—the group of lenders who will supply the capital that is borrowed to pay for the LBO. Small transactions sometimes involve just one lender. In larger transactions, however, one lender may not want to commit to the full amount. Lenders seek protection against the risks of default by diversifying their assets. The effort to spread out the exposure to this particular LBO among several lenders is part of that process. LBO funds are an example of investors who wish to partake in the high returns available by investing in LBOs while retaining the protection provided by diversification. These investors pool together their resources to invest in a diversified group of leveraged buyouts. (LBO funds are discussed further later in this chapter.) The process of assembling the debt capital can become more complicated for larger transactions. Commitments for different types of secured or unsecured debt may have to be obtained in advance. This process is also explained later in this chapter.

Step 7. *External equity investment is acquired.* The investment banker, in conjunction with the parties to the transaction, determines whether an additional outside equity investment is necessary. This may be necessary if there is not sufficient debt available in the market for this type of transaction. It may also be a requirement of the lenders who may feel that the risk level of the transaction does not warrant the high percentage of debt relative to equity that would be necessary without outside equity investors. Step 7 is performed in conjunction with steps 5, 6, and 8 since the results of this analysis will affect the investors' willingness to support the transaction.

Step 8. *Cash flow analysis is conducted.* Once the relative components of debt and equity have been tentatively assessed, a cash flow analysis is conducted to determine whether the division's cash flow will be sufficient to service the interest payments on the debt. This is usually done by assuming restrictive budgets for the time period necessary to pay off the debt. These restrictions may come in the form of lower research and development expenditures or a scaled-back building program. Often the cash flow analysis will be redone under different assumptions which will alter the financial structure of the deal, thereby requiring steps 5–7 to be repeated. Several repetitions of this iterative process may occur before the financial structure is agreed to.

Step 9. *Financing is agreed to.* If the cash flows are sufficient to service the debt, within a reasonable range for error, the financing is agreed to and the deal is consummated.

The above scenario was explained within the framework of a management buyout. However, the process is similar when the LBO is conducted by an outside entity such as a corporation. Key to the process are the sources of debt financing and the target's ability to service the interest payments on the debt.

FINANCING FOR LEVERAGED BUYOUTS

Two general categories of debt are used in leveraged buyouts—secured and unsecured debt—and both are often used together.[12] Secured debt, sometimes called *asset-based lending,* may contain two types of debt: senior debt and intermediate-term debt. In some smaller buyouts these two categories are considered one. In larger deals there may be several layers of secured debt, and they vary according to the term of the debt and the types of assets used as security. Unsecured debt, sometimes known as *subordinated debt* and *junior subordinated debt,* lacks the protection of secured debt but generally carries a higher return to offset this additional risk.

Secured LBO Financing

Senior Debt   Senior debt comprises loans secured by liens on particular assets of the company. The collateral provides the downside risk protection required by lenders. It includes physical assets such as land, plant and equipment, accounts receivable, and inventories. The lender projects the level of accounts receivable which the firm would average during the period of the loan. This projection is usually based on the amount of accounts receivable the firm has on its books at the time the loan is closed as well as the historical level of accounts receivable.

The firm will commonly advance 85 percent of the value of the accounts receivable and 50 percent of the value of the target's inventories, excluding the work in progress.[13] Accounts receivable, which are normally collected in short time periods such as 30 days, are more valuable than those of longer periods. The lender has to make a judgment on the value of the accounts receivable; similar judgments have to be made as to the marketability of inventories. The process of determining the collateral value of the LBO candidate's assets is sometimes called qualifying the assets. Assets that do not have collateral value, such as accounts receivable which cannot be collected, are called unqualified assets.

---

[12] For an excellent discussion of the use of secured and unsecured debt in leveraged buyouts, see Stephen C. Diamond, ed., *Leveraged Buyouts* (Homewood, Ill.: Dow Jones Irwin, 1985), pp. 41–57.

[13] Michael R. Dabney, "Asset Based Financing" in Milton Rock, ed., *Mergers and Acquisitions* (New York: McGraw-Hill, 1987), pp. 393–399.

Intermediate-Term Debt Intermediate-term debt is usually subordinate to the senior debt. It is often backed up by fixed assets such as land and plant and equipment. The collateral value of these assets is usually based on their liquidation value. Debt backed up by equipment usually has a term of six months to one year.[14] Loans backed up by real estate tend to have a one- to two-year term. The relationship between the loan amounts and the appraised value of the assets tends to vary depending on the circumstances of the buyout. Generally, debt tends to be 80 percent of the appraised value of equipment and 50 percent of the value of real estate. However, these percentages will vary depending on the area of the country and the conditions of the real estate market. The collateral value of assets, such as equipment and real estate, is based on the auction value of these assets, not the value that they carry on the firm's books. When the auction value is greater than the book value of the assets, the firm's borrowing capacity is greater than what its balance sheet would reflect.

Lenders look for certain desirable characteristics in borrowers even when the borrower has valuable collateral. Some of these factors are as follows.

Desirable Characteristics of Secured LBO Candidates

1. *Stable and experienced management.* Stability is often judged by the length of time management is in place. Lenders feel more secure when management is experienced and has been with the firm for a reasonable period of time. This may imply that there is a greater likelihood that such a management will stay on after the deal is completed. Creditors often judge the ability of management to handle a LBO by the cash flows that were generated by the firms they managed in the past. If their prior management experience was with firms that had significant liquidity problems, then lenders will be much more cautious about participating in the buyout.

2. *Room for significant cost reductions.* Assuming additional debt to finance an LBO usually imposes additional financial pressures on the target. These pressures can be somewhat alleviated if the target can significantly cut costs in some areas, such as fewer employees, reduced capital expenditures, elimination of redundant facilities, and tighter controls on operating expenses. Frank Lichtenberg and Donald Siegel showed that LBO employee cutbacks were concentrated at the administrative layers of em-

---

[14] Ibid.

ployment with an average administrative workforce reduction of 16 percent, while there tended to be minimal cutbacks at the manufacturing level.[15]

3. *Projected stability of costs.* The stability of future costs will greatly influence the success of the LBO. If labor relations are poor, there may be higher labor costs in the future or, even worse, work interruptions resulting from strikes. If the sources of materials are uncertain, their costs may also be difficult to estimate. Such factors reduce the confidence an analyst can have in the projected cash flow analysis.

4. *Equity interest of owners.* The collateral value of assets provides downside risk protection to lenders. The equity investment of the managers or buyers and outside parties also acts as a cushion to protect lenders. The greater the equity cushion, the more likely secured lenders will not have to liquidate the assets. The greater the managers' equity investment, the more likely they will stay with the firm if the going gets tough. LBO lenders in the 1990s demand a much greater equity cushion than the heavy debt deals they financed in the mid-1980s.

Costs of Secured Debt   The costs of senior debt vary depending on market conditions. Senior debt rates are often quoted in relation to other interest rates such as the prime rate. They often range between two and five points above the prime rate for a quality borrower with quality assets. The *prime rate* is the rate that banks charge their best customers. Less creditworthy borrowers will have to pay more. Interest rates, in turn, are determined by many economywide factors such as the Federal Reserve's monetary policy or the demand for loanable funds. Therefore, rates on secured LBO financing will be as volatile as other interest rates in the marketplace. However, these rates will also be influenced by the lenders' demand for participation in this type of financing. Inasmuch as this varies, secured LBO rates may fluctuate even more than other rates in the economy.

Sources of Secured Financing   Secured LBO financing is often obtained through the asset-based lending subsidiary of a major New York or other money center bank. Three of the more active New York commercial banks in LBO funding are Citibank, Manufacturers Hano-

---

[15] Frank Lichtenberg and Donald Siegel, "The Effects of Takeovers on Employment and Wages of Central Office and Other Personnel," Columbia Graduate School Working Paper #FB-89-05, 1989.

ver Trust, and Bankers Trust. The number and types of lenders participating in this type of lending grew significantly during the mid-1980s as the rates of return rose. The size of this group contracted sharply by 1990.

Financing Gap   LBO lenders are quite partial to buyouts in which the target company has significant assets that can be used as collateral. However, even then their value may not be sufficient to cover the total purchase cost of the target. In this case a *financing gap* exists—that is, the financing needs of the leveraged buyout exceed the collateral coverage. At this point, the investment bank must seek other sources of financing. These sources can be covered by equity, subordinated debt, or a loan that exceeds the collateral value of the assets.

Equity involves giving an ownership interest in the target to outside investors in exchange for financing. *Subordinated debt* is debt that has a secondary claim on the assets used for collateral. As a result of this inferior claim on assets, this debt usually has higher interest costs. Loans beyond the collateral value of the target's assets are usually motivated by less tangible forms of security for the lender, such as the existence of dependable cash flows, which make it more likely that the debt payments will be met.

Unsecured LBO Financing

LBOs are usually financed by a combination of secured and unsecured debt. The unsecured debt, sometimes referred to as subordinated and junior subordinated debt, is debt that has a secondary claim of the assets of the LBO target—hence the term *subordinated*. The term *mezzanine layer financing* is often applied to this type of capital inasmuch as this form of debt has both debt and equity characteristics. While it is clearly debt, it is equity-like in that lenders typically receive warrants that may be converted into equity in the target. *Warrants* are options that, unlike the options offered by securities firms, are offered by the corporation itself. They allow the warrant holder to buy stock in the corporation at a certain price for a defined time period. Unlike call options, which are offered by brokerage firms, when warrants are exercised the corporation either issues new stock or satisfies the warrant holder's demands by offering treasury stock.

When the warrants are exercised, the share of ownership of the previous equity holders is diluted. This dilution often occurs just at the time the target is becoming profitable. It is then that the warrants become valuable. In a management buyout, for example, managers may have held a very high percentage of ownership in the company. If the target becomes profitable in the future, management might have its share of ownership dramatically diluted by exercising the warrants by the junior subordinated lenders. Although such forms of debt may have undesirable characteristics for management, they may be necessary to convince lenders to participate in the LBO without the security of collateral.

In the discussion above, mezzanine layer financing was used in conjunction with senior debt to cover the financing gap. However, some leveraged buyouts can be financed solely through unsecured financing. This type of LBO lending is not as desirable to some lenders because it lacks the downside risk protection that marketable collateral provides. Most deals include both secured and unsecured lending.

The risk that a lender incurs when a loan is made is that the interest and principal payments may not be met. Collateral can be a source of protection in the event these payments are not made. Dependable cash flows, however, can also be an invaluable source of protection. The more regular the cash flows, the more assurance the lender has that the loan payments will be made.

Unsecured leveraged buyouts are sometimes called *cash flow LBOs*. These deals tend to have a more long-term focus, with a maturity of 10 to 15 years. In contrast, the secured LBOs might have a financing maturity of only up to five years. Cash flow LBOs allow firms that are not in capital-intensive industries to be LBO candidates. This is most important in the U.S. economy since the United States is increasingly becoming a more service-oriented economy. Many service industries, such as advertising, lack significant physical assets relative to their total revenue but have large cash flows. Cash flow LBOs are generally considered riskier for lenders. In return for the burden of assuming additional risk, lenders of unsecured financing typically require a higher interest rate as well as an *equity kicker*. This equity interest often comes in the form of warrants or direct shares in the target. The percentage of ownership can be as little as 10 percent or as high as 80 percent of the companies' shares. The percentage is higher when the lender perceives greater risk.

Just because the loan is not collateralized does not mean that the lenders are not protected by the firm's assets. Unsecured lenders are entitled to receive the proceeds of the sale of the secured assets after full payment has been made to the secured lenders. Unsecured leveraged buyouts started to become more common in the mid-1980s when the demand for mergers and acquisitions and leveraged buyouts drove up the premiums paid for targets. As premiums rose above the value of the target's assets, lenders were increasingly being requested to lend beyond the limits of the target's collateral. Many deals then became structured using both secured and unsecured debt. The unsecured component received a higher return to compensate for assuming the greater risk. Most of the larger LBOs that attract so much media attention are largely unsecured deals.

The main advantage of mezzanine layer financing is the profit potential that is provided by either a direct equity interest or warrants convertible into equity to go along with the debt position of the lender. This added return potential offsets the lack of security that secured debt has. There are often several types of mezzanine layer financing in a leveraged buyout. The debt is structured in several layers with each subordinate to another layer. Each layer that is subordinate to the layer before it in order of liquidation priority generally contains additional compensation for the lender to offset this lower degree of security. This source of LBO financing, which was often funded through the issuance of junk bonds, declined dramatically when the high-yield bond market collapsed towards the end of the 1980s. LBOs continued in the 1990s at a much slower pace and often without the aid of this type of financing.

THE CAPITAL STRUCTURE OF UNSECURED LBO FIRMS

The capital structure of LBO firms is usually quite different following the completion of the deal than it was before the buyout.[16] Leonard Caronia has outlined the capital structure for a typical unsecured leveraged buyout (see Table 7.1).

The capital structure of companies that have been taken private through a leveraged buyout does not remain constant following the buyout. The goal of both the company and the lender is to have the company reduce its total debt through debt retirements. Following the buyout, the firm is very heavily leveraged. In effect, the changes in capital structure caused by the buyout has transformed an otherwise healthy company into a sick company. As time passes, the firm's goal should be to retire the debt and return to a more normal capital structure. Usually, the firm aims to retire most of the LBO debt within five to seven years.

The costs of different components of the firm's capital structure vary. Generally, short-term debt costs are lower than long-term debt because of the additional risk imposed by longer term debt. The longer the term, the greater the probability that something can go wrong. Long-term debt is generally less costly than preferred stock which, in turn, is cheaper to the issuer than common stock. These cost differences

---

[16] Leonard Caronia, "Seeking Financing: The Unsecured Leveraged Buyout," in Stephen Diamond, *Leveraged Buyouts* (Homewood, Ill.: Dow Jones Irwin, 1985), pp. 58–70.

Table 7.1   LEVERAGED BUYOUT CAPITAL STRUCTURE

Securities	Percent of Capitalization	Source
Short or intermediate senior debt	5–20	Commercial banks
Long-term senior or subordinated debt	40–80	Life insurance companies, some banks, LBO funds
Preferred stock	10–20	Life insurance companies and venture capital firms
Common stock	1–20	Life insurance companies, venture capital firms, and managers

are in direct relation to the high degree of risk associated with equity versus debt.

Desirable Characteristics of Unsecured LBO Candidates   Unsecured firms share many of the same desirable characteristics of the secured LBO candidates. The lack of sufficient collateral increases the importance of other forms of lender protection, such as larger, dependable cash flows.

1. *Stable cash flows.*   The most important characteristic of cash flow LBO candidates is the existence of regular cash flows as determined by examining the pattern of historical cash flows for the company. Statistical measures such as the standard deviation of cash flows can be derived to measure this variability. The greater the variability, the riskier the LBO. Even in cases where the average cash flows exceed the loan payments by a comfortable margin the existence of high variability can worry a lender. The statistical analysis of cash flows is discussed later in this chapter. The existence of dependable cash flows alone is not sufficient to guarantee the success of an LBO. The financial difficulties of the Southland Corporation following its $4.9 billion buyout in 1987 is a case in point. The company's main business was the "cash cow" 7-Eleven convenience chain. Southland's problems emerged when part of the 7-Eleven cash flow was directed to noncore real estate ventures instead of paying off the buyout debt. This misadventure left the post-buyout Southland on the verge of bankruptcy in spite of the firm's sizable cash flows. Historical cash flows are used as a guide to projected future cash flows, but the past may be an imperfect guide to the future. Market conditions change, and the future business environment can be less favorable than what the company's historical data reflect. The lender has to make a judgment as to

whether the past is going to be a reliable indication of what the future will hold. Lenders and borrowers usually construct cash flow projections based on restrictive budgets and new cost structures. Such budget planning takes place for both secured and unsecured LBOs, but it is even more critical for cash flow LBOs. These budgets may include lower research and development expenditures and lower labor costs. The target attempts to find areas where costs can be cut—at least temporarily. These cost savings can be used to meet the loan payments on the LBO debt. That cash flows are important to sellers is underscored by a recent study by Lehn and Poulson.[17] They showed that buyout premiums were positively related to the firm's free cash flow.

2. *Ability to cut costs.*   Many LBO firms are inefficient and need cost restructuring. LBO firms, such as Kohlberg, Kravis and Roberts, have mastered the art of finding areas where cost can be cut. When these cost cuts come in areas where there was waste or excess expenditures, they can be of great benefit to the LBO target. The target can suffer, however, when the cuts are made in areas that will hurt the company in the future. Cuts in research and development, for example, can cause the company to fall behind its competitors and eventually lose market share. Whether or not research and product development expenditures can be cut may depend on the nature of the industry. Reductions are often difficult to make in rapidly evolving, high tech industries such as the computer industry. The firm may survive the LBO and pay off the debt only to be left behind by its competitors. A good example of a high tech LBO that should not have been conducted was the 1987 $866 million buyout of defense contractor Tracor, Inc. The company found itself with an unpredictable cash flow following defense industry cutbacks, but the capital demands of this high tech industry left the firm struggling to meet the LBO debt payments.

3. *Managerial experience.*   Managerial experience and expertise may be even more critical to the success of a cash flow LBO than a secured deal. Lenders do not have the protection of marketable collateral and, therefore, look to the security of a management team that will steer the course of the target to survive the added pressures of the high LBO debt service.

4. *Other factors.*   Each LBO candidate has a different product or

---

[17] K. Lehn and A. Poulson, "Sources of Value in Corporate Going Private Transactions," University of Washington Working Paper, February 1987.

service and a different history. The existence of unique or intangible factors can provide the impetus for a lender to provide financing when some ambivalence exists. A dynamic, growing, and innovative company can provide lenders with sufficient incentive to overlook some shortcomings. However, these factors, which are sometimes referred to as "the story," can only go so far to make up for deficiencies.

5. *Limited debt on the firm's balance sheet.*   The lower the amount of debt on the firm's balance sheet relative to the collateral value of the firm's assets, the greater the borrowing capacity of the firm. If the firm's balance sheet already reflects significant financial leverage, then it is more difficult to finance the leveraged buyout. Financing an LBO with a previously leveraged firm uses up all of the firm's borrowing capacity, which limits its ability to raise capital in the future. While this is clearly undesirable, most LBOs exhaust the firm's borrowing capacity anyway.

6. *Separable, noncore businesses.*   If the LBO candidate comprises certain core businesses plus other noncore businesses, the noncore businesses can be sold off to quickly pay off a significant part of the firm's post-LBO debt. This may be important for both secured and unsecured LBOs. Problems can occur when debt is incurred based on an unrealistic sales price for noncore divisions. The inability to sell component parts of the firm on a timely basis at prices similar to what its investment bankers anticipated they would sell for was one of the main factors that caused the bankruptcy of the Campean Corporation in 1989. Deals that are dependent on the large-scale selloff of most of the firm's businesses are referred to as *breakup LBOs*.

Statistical Analysis of Cash Flows

The statistical analysis of cash flows for leveraged buyouts and mergers and acquisitions is similar to the type of statistical cash flow analysis that is done in capital budgeting.[18] Two statistical measures are utilized: expected value and the standard deviation.

Expected Value   The expected value of the expected cash flows which a company would generate after a leveraged buyout can be developed by constructing a probability distribution. The probability distribution

---

[18] Robert W. Kolb, *Principles of Finance* (Glenview, Ill.: Scott, Foresman & Co., 1988), Chapter 15, pp. 466–511.

is constructed by considering most of the possible cash flow values which the firm could realize for each time period following the leveraged buyout. Different time horizons, such as five-year or ten-year, are often adopted.

A probability is assigned to each cash flow possibility and is often subjectively derived by analysts who assign probabilities based on their judgment of the likelihood of each alternative. Such a probability distribution is a *discrete probability distribution* since it considers only a limited number of outcomes as opposed to a *continuous probability distribution* which considers all possibilities between two values. It is also a *subjective probability distribution* since the probabilities are assigned by the analyst rather than being derived in a more objective manner. Normally, a more objective probability distribution could be developed by using the firm's historical cash flow data. In the case of a LBO, however, this may not be better than a subjective distribution since the post-LBO firm may be very different from the pre-buyout company.

The hypothetical cash flows of Company X are shown in Table 7.2.

This discrete probability distribution is depicted in Figure 7.7. The distribution looks similar to a normal distribution with its bell-shaped appearance and high degree of central tendency. Normal distributions, which are symmetric, have equal areas on the right or left of the mean. Such distributions are often used as a simplification of reality. The cash flows of each firm differ, and a normal distribution may not be appropriate. If the historical data show otherwise or if there is some other compelling reason to believe that the cash flow distribution should be skewed toward one direction, a different distribution should be developed. In the absence of such information, the normal distribution assumption may be adopted for simplicity's sake.

The expected value of a company's cash flows in a given period is given by the following expression:

Table 7.2   DISCRETE PROBABILITY
            DISTRIBUTION OF CASH FLOWS

Cash Flow	Probability
$20,000,000	0.10
$30,000,000	0.20
$40,000,000	0.50
$50,000,000	0.20
$60,000,000	0.10

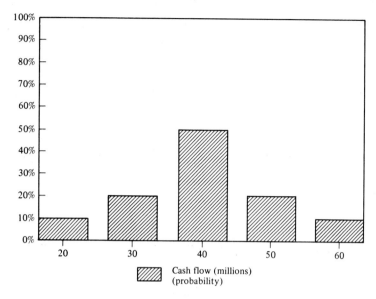

Figure 7.7 Hypothetical cash flows.

$$\text{Expected value} = \sum_{i=1}^{n} p_i(CF_i) \qquad (7.1)$$

where: p_i = the probability of ith cash flow
CF_i = the dollar value of the ith cash flow
n = the number of cash flow possibilities

The expected value indicates what cash flow would be expected to occur given the assigned probabilities. For the example above, this value is determined as follows:

Expected value = 0.10 ($20,000,000) + 0.20 ($30,000,000) +
0.40 ($40,000,000) + 0.20 ($50,000,000)
0.10 ($60,000,000)
= $40,000,000

Standard Deviation   The expected value only indicates an average cash flow value that may occur. It does not indicate how risky or variable the cash flows will be. This consideration is most important in a leveraged buyout since the company will be taking on a large amount of debt with high interest payments. This higher degree of financial leverage will make it more likely that the firm's regular cash flows will drop below the amount needed to service the debt. In this case, the firm could become *technically insolvent*, that is, unable to meet its regular payments.

The standard deviation can measure the variability of the company's cash flows. In doing so it can indicate how likely it is that the firm will become technically insolvent. The standard deviation is the square root of the variance. The variance is the weighted sum of the square differences between each cash flow possibility and the expected value. The weights are the individual probabilities.

The variance, denoted by Σ^2, is computed below:

$$\Sigma^2 = p_1(CF_1 - EV)^2 + p_2(CF_2 - EV)^2 + p_3(CF_3 - EV)^2 + \\ p_4(CF_4 - EV)^2 + p_5(CF_5 - EV)^2 \tag{7.2}$$

or more generally:

$$\Sigma^2 = \sum_{i=1}^{n} p_i(CF_i - EV)^2 \tag{7.2a}$$

In the example above, the variance of the cash flows is computed as follows:

$$
\begin{aligned}
\Sigma^2 = \ & 0.10(\$20,000,000 - \$40,000,000)^2 + \\
& 0.20(\$30,000,000 - \$40,000,000)^2 + \\
& 0.40(\$40,000,000 - \$40,000,000)^2 + \\
& 0.20(\$50,000,000 - \$40,000,000)^2 + \\
& 0.10(\$60,000,000 - \$40,000,000)^2
\end{aligned}
$$

$$
\begin{aligned}
\Sigma^2 = \ & \$40,000,000,000,000 + \\
& \$20,000,000,000,000 + \\
& \$0 \\
& \$20,000,000,000,000 \\
& \$40,000,000,000,000
\end{aligned}
$$

$$\Sigma^2 \text{ (cash flows)} = \$12,000,000,000,000$$

The standard deviation, denoted by Σ, is the square root of the variance and is often used in place of the variance since the variance shows dollars squared. Since squared dollars are sometimes difficult to interpret, the standard deviation is used instead.

Standard deviation $= \sqrt{\text{Variance}}$
Standard deviation $= \$34,641$

It is difficult to make sense out of the standard deviation by itself. It is more useful as a comparative measure where an analyst can compare the standard deviation of two sets of cash flows. Such a comparison can be made when we are examining the riskiness of two alternative acquisition targets. The one with the higher standard deviation is, all other factors constant, more risky. When the size of the two targets differs significantly, the standard deviation can be expressed in percentage terms by utilizing the *coefficient of variation*, which is the standard deviation divided by the expected value.

$$\text{Coefficient of variation} \frac{\text{Standard deviation}}{\text{Expected value}}$$

We can also use the standard deviation when we are attempting to measure the impact of alternative scenarios on the riskiness of the target. These scenarios might include the sale of particular assets or divisions of the firm. We use the standard deviation to ascertain whether these transactions lower the risk that the LBO candidate will not be able to meet its debt service payments.

Sensitivity Analysis   Leveraged buyout candidates often have to make several cost-cutting changes in the company in order to be able to sustain the debt service payments. These changes may involve laying off employees, shrinking departments, or cutting back on certain expenditures such as research and development.

Sensitivity analysis is a technique that measures the change in a dependent variable resulting from a certain change in an independent variable. It is often used in capital budgeting when a financial manager tries to estimate the impact of a change in certain factors on the financial performance of a project. It allows the financial manager to ask "what if" questions. For example, an analyst might want to see how sensitive a product development project is to changes in the price of the product itself as well as to changes in the prices of both labor and raw materials. Sensitivity analysis can also be most useful in leveraged buyouts. Here the problem is to focus on the key factors that will influence the success and failure of the LBO. Some of these factors might be the level of interest rates or total sales. Each is projected into the future based on the most reliable forecast possible. Sensitivity analysis is then used to see what the financial performance of the company will be for a given change in sales, interest rates, or any other major factor determined to be crucial.

Tables 7.3 and 7.4 construct a sensitivity analysis in which two crucial variables control the success of the leveraged buyout of the Link Computer Manufacturing Corporation: the level of sales and the rate of interest. This shows the influence of business risk versus the interest rate effects associated with increased financial leverage. Business risk refers to the variability in the firm's earnings before interest and taxes (EBIT). Financial leverage refers to the increased use of debt, which means increased susceptibility to interest rate fluctuations.

The key to a successful sensitivity analysis is to choose the right

Table 7.3 LINK COMPUTER MANUFACTURING CORPORATION SENSITIVITY ANALYSIS—FOCUS ON SALES

Sales	$400,000,000
Variable costs (50% of sales)	200,000,000
Fixed costs	100,000,000
Earnings before interest and taxes	$100,000,000
Interest payments (10.0% rate)	50,000,000
Earnings before taxes	$ 50,000,000

Earnings Projection Assuming 10% Reduction in Sales

Sales	$360,000,000
Variable costs (50% of sales)	180,000,000
Fixed costs	100,000,000
Earnings before interest and taxes	$ 80,000,000
Interest payments	50,000,000
Earnings before taxes	$ 30,000,000

variables which are crucial to the LBO's success. These are often sales and interest rates. Different rates of change are used for these and any other relevant variables. These different rates are then used to determine the critical level of change that would force the LBO candidate from a condition of profitability to a loss. A sensitivity analysis graph

Table 7.4 LINK COMPUTER MANUFACTURING CORPORATION SENSITIVITY ANALYSIS—FOCUS ON INTEREST RATES

Sales	$400,000,000
Variable costs (50% of sales)	200,000,000
Fixed costs	100,000,000
Earnings before interest and taxes	$100,000,000
Interest payments (10.0% rate)	50,000,000
Earnings before taxes	$ 50,000,000

Earnings Projection Assuming Interest Rates Rise to 20%

Sales	$400,000,000
Variable costs (50% of sales)	200,000,000
Fixed costs	100,000,000
Earnings before interest and taxes	$100,000,000
Interest payments (20%[a])	100,000,000
Earnings before taxes	$0

[a] For simplicity of exposition, an increase in interest rates from 10 to 20% is used. However, this would be a high increase to occur during the first five or even ten years of a leveraged buyout. Although it certainly is not impossible, it might be improbable.

From the above data, we can see that a 10% reduction in total sales still leaves the company in the black. However, an increase in interest rates from 10 to 20% would cause the firms to move into the red.

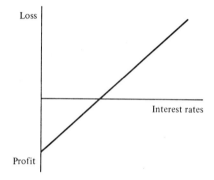

Figure 7.8 Sensitivity analysis diagrams.

can be constructed for each deterministic factor, which shows the critical levels for each. These are shown in Figure 7.8. Once these critical levels are determined, the likelihood of such a change needs to be assessed. If there is a relatively high probability that the change could occur, then the LBO needs to be reconsidered as it appears to be a risky endeavor.

Scenario Analysis

One disadvantage of sensitivity analysis is that it only allows for a change in one deterministic factor at a time. However, if the deterministic factors are interrelated, sensitivity analysis fails to show the interactions among these factors. *Scenario analysis* allows the financial analyst to see these interactions. The analyst specifies a certain scenario which he or she feels is likely to prevail, and the profitability of the LBO candidate is projected given the particular set of circumstances that prevail in this scenario. Another scenario can be projected with changes in several factors at the same time. Thus, the analyst can see the impact of the firm's profitability that results from several changes.

Let's consider the example of a computer manufacturer contemplating a leveraged buyout. This firm might want to consider the impact of an interest rate rise along with a slump in the computer market. It is possible that a modest rise in interest rates alone would not cause the firm's profitability to fall. However, a modest rise in interest rates coupled with a decline in sales could cause the firm to show a loss and be unable to service its debt. Given the volatility of sales in parts of the computer industry combined with the high degree of obsolescence that tends to characterize these products, it is not surprising that computer firms do not make good LBO conductors.

Scenario analysis is often conducted using three possible scenarios: an optimistic, a most likely, and a pessimistic scenario. The optimistic scenario might assume that sales are at a high level while interest rates and other costs are well within controlled levels. The most likely scenario would be the best forecast the firm can make. If profitability is barely achieved in this scenario, the LBO must be questioned. The pessimistic scenario assumes the worst. If the LBO is still profitable in the pessimistic case, then it may merit serious consideration.

RISKINESS OF LEVERAGED BUYOUTS

The riskiness of a leveraged buyout can be broken down into two main categories: business risk and interest rate risk.

Business risk refers to the risk that the firm that has been taken private in the LBO transaction will not generate sufficient earnings to meet the interest payments and other current obligations of the firm. This risk category takes into account factors such as cyclical downturns in the economy as well as competitive factors within the industry, such as greater price and nonprice competition. Firms with very cyclical sales patterns or companies in very competitive industries do not tend to be good LBO candidates.

Interest rate risk is the risk that interest rates will rise, thus increasing the firm's current obligations. This is quite important to firms that have more variable rate debt. Interest rate increases could force a firm into Chapter 11 even when it experienced greater than anticipated demand and held nonfinancial costs within reasonable bounds. The level of interest rates at the time of the LBO can be a guide to the probability that rates may rise in the future. For example, if interest rates are low at the time of the buyout, then interest rate increases may be more likely than if interest rates were at peak levels.

SOURCES OF LEVERAGED BUYOUT FINANCING

Table 7.1 points out the participation of the noncommercial bank sources of financing. These sources have grown dramatically in recent years. They have participated in both secured and unsecured financing, and they include different categories of institutional investors such as life insurance companies and pension funds. These institutional investors participate either directly in the LBO funding or indirectly through a leveraged buyout fund. These pools of funds are developed to invest in leveraged buyouts. By investing in LBOs, they realize higher returns than those available from other forms of lending, and by pooling the funds, they realize broad diversification and the resulting risk reduction. Diversification allows the investor to limit exposure to default by any one borrower.

While some institutional investors, such as insurance companies, tend to be unsecured investors, most participate in more than one type of LBO financing. It is common, for example, for institutions to participate in *vertical strips* of financing. This is where investors may participate in several layers of financing within the same deal. For example, they may hold some secured and more than one form of unsecured debt as well as some equity.

LBO FUNDS

One of the financial innovations of the 1980s was the appearance of LBO funds. These investment funds are established to invest in leveraged buyout transactions. They contain the invested capital of a variety of investors who seek to enjoy the high returns that can be achieved through leveraged buyouts. Like most funds, such as common stock mutual funds, LBO funds provide the investor with broad diversification that lowers the risk level of the investment. LBOs offer great opportunities for significant gains. However, because of the high debt levels generally associated with these types of transactions, the risk of default can be high. Through the diversification that LBO funds provide, investors can achieve high gains while having a lower degree of risk.

A broad range of investors allocate capital to LBO funds. These generally include conservative, institutional investors such as pension funds. In recent years the use of pension fund capital to fund leveraged buyout transactions has been widely criticized. Some feel that LBOs are not good for America because they result in a higher degree of debt than what would otherwise be advisable. Further criticism has also arisen regarding the fact that some LBOs are hostile transactions. These critics believe that hostile bids are not in the interest of corporate America.

During 1987 and 1988, the size of the commitments of capital to these funds rose dramatically. Foreign investors were particularly attracted to LBO fund investments, which is a type of investment that is not readily available outside the United States. For example, in 1988, the Nippon Life Insurance Company committed several hundred million dollars to Shearson's LBO fund, while Yamaichi Securities committed $100 million to the Lodestar Corporation Company which is a boutique LBO fund.[19] The pace of foreign investment in LBOs slowed dramatically as the 1980s came to an end.

Many of the LBO funds are established by LBO firms. These firms assemble capital and invest it mainly in leveraged buyouts.

LBO FIRMS

Several investment firms specialize in leveraged buyouts. These LBO specialists raise capital by offering investors an opportunity to enjoy the high returns attainable through investing in LBOs. Many of them assemble an LBO fund which they manage and use to invest in LBOs of their choosing. Investors are usually promised a certain percentage of the return which the fund will earn. Some of the more well-known LBO firms are Kohlberg, Kravis and Roberts, Forstmann, Little and Co., the Blackstone Group, Gibbons, Green and van Amerongen, Wasserstein and Perilla, and Wesray Capital. By far the largest of these firms is Kohlberg, Kravis and Roberts. This is the LBO firm that took RJR Nabisco and Co. private in the largest LBO ever ($22.88 billion) and that put together the 1984 LBO of Beatrice.

Most LBO firms are not interested in becoming day-to-day managers of the target company. Firms like Kohlberg, Kravis and Roberts usually select a management team to run the daily operations. The LBO firms' expertise is in selecting the right LBO target, raising capital, and overseeing cost reductions that will ensure the repayment of debt and a sufficient return for investors. It may be possible to accomplish this by keeping the management that was in place at the time of the LBO. On the other hand, this management may not look kindly on the sale of complete divisions in order to repay the debt. When the current managers are not agreeable to the changes the LBO firm has in mind, they are usually replaced by other managers.

---

[19] *New York Times*, August 7, 1988.

Some critics of LBO firms allege that they amass a large supply of capital and complete deals merely for the sake of completing transactions and enjoying high returns. It is asserted that LBO firms do not sufficiently consider whether an LBO is right for each firm or whether or not the firm will be viable in the years after the LBO firm has liquidated its investment and moved on to another LBO candidate. The validity of this criticism continues to be a point of debate within the financial community.

A shining example of the expertise at LBO firms occurred when the Wesray Corporation, led by former Treasury Secretary William Simon, experienced windfall gains when Wesray bought Gibson Greeting Cards from RCA in 1982. Wesray purchased Gibson Greeting Cards for $58 million in cash and the assumption of $22.6 million in liabilities. In May 1983, Wesray took Gibson public through a 3.5 million share offering at $27.5 per share. Simon and his partner, Raymond Chambers, retained 45 percent of the Gibson stock. Simon's profit on the stock sale was $14 million. Based on gains such as these, it is not surprising that LBO firms are so eager to complete deals.

The case of the buyout of Gibson Greeting Cards and the subsequent public offering of stock is an example of a *reverse LBO*. The reverse LBO works best when the going private transaction takes place when the stock market is down and the public offering occurs in a bull market.[20] Recent research has shown that firms involved in reverse LBOs tend to have above average profitability due to management's ability to lower costs and increase revenues.[21]

Why Creditors Support Leveraged Buyouts

Lenders participate in LBOs primarily to take advantage of the significantly higher returns offered through this type of investing. The return can be several points above the returns available from other types of investments.

Although leveraged buyouts are riskier than other forms of investing, this risk exposure can be significantly reduced through diversification. One way this diversification can be achieved for lenders is to pool LBO loans. Pooling is a risk-reduction technique that bankers and other large investors have used to reduce risk exposure. It involves

---

[20] Leslie Wayne, "Reverse LBO's Bring Riches," *New York Times*, April 23, 1987, p. D1.

[21] Chris J. Muscarella and Michael R. Vetsuypens, "Efficiency and Organizational Structure: A Study of Reverse LBOs." *Journal of Finance*, 45, no. 5 (December 1990): 1389–1414.

pooling several LBO loans and reselling them to other investors who desire to enjoy the returns available from LBO deals. The pooling reduces risk through diversification. Shares in these pools can be sold to large investors such as institutions. Many of the deals within the pool will provide a high return. Therefore, the pool as a whole probably yields a high average return even if all the LBOs do not do as well as expected. The advantage of pooling is that the risk exposure to one firm or industry can be reduced.

THE LEVERAGED BUYOUT NEGOTIATION PROCESS

Business Plan

Although leveraged buyouts are often initiated by management, they can also be put into motion by leveraged buyout agents. These agents are, dealmakers who may lack the requisite capital to put the deal together. Their role is to raise the capital and negotiate with the sellers to complete the transaction. This negotiation process focuses on several characteristics of the target which helps determine the sale price and the terms of the deal.

The desirable characteristics of good LBO candidates (already described above) will often be presented to lenders either by management or by an LBO agent in the form of a business plan. A good business plan is an invaluable ingredient of a successful business. It is not surprising that lenders carefully scrutinize a potential borrower's business plan to indicate their future ability to repay borrowed capital.

Marketing Strategy

One important part of a business plan is the firm's marketing strategy. Although most finance textbooks do not tend to consider marketing factors, buyers and sellers need to devote great attention to them. The financial aspects of a deal can be so structured that financially the deal looks positive. In spite of excellent financial terms and conditions, however, a leveraged buyout can easily fail owing to the LBO candidate's marketing deficiencies.

A firm's marketing strategy should take at least the following factors into account:

1. *Product*. The product or services that the target hopes to sell should be clearly defined. The position of this product or service relative to its competitors needs to be firmly established. In industries such as computers, which are continuously evolving,

product development for the future is an important consideration. This is especially important for LBO candidates since the debt service payments may make it difficult to fund the necessary research and development to make the company's product line competitive in the future. In service-oriented businesses, the ability to provide quality service is often determined by whether key personnel remain with the firm after the buyout. Employment contracts can help alleviate this concern. Another source of stability can be equity options offered to the more important employees to ensure they will remain with the company.

2. *Price*. The company's pricing strategy needs to be examined and compared to that of the competition. Product categories are often segmented into premium, high-priced products, middle-market priced, and discounted products. To evaluate whether the firm can realize greater revenues from a different pricing strategy, the price elasticity of demand needs to be considered. The intensity of price competition is an important consideration for buyers. The greater the degree of price competition, the greater the risk for buyers. On the other hand, if the product is premium priced with little chance of significant price competition, then there will be less downward pressure on the firm's profit margins and less risk for LBO participants.

3. *Distribution*. The stability of the distribution system can be an important consideration for manufacturing or retail firms. If the firm utilizes distributors to market its products, for example, the stability of this network has to be assessed. The existence of long-standing relationships with established distributors can be a valuable asset to the firm. If the firm does not use distributors, but rather utilizes manufacturer's representatives that serve as the company's sales force, then their strengths and limitations need to be considered. A weak distributor or manufacturer's representatives network can be an additional risk to the firm. If the distributors or "reps" service several other manufacturers, the company may not be able to rely on this network to promote and sell its products if times get difficult. If territories are overlapping rather than exclusive, the distributors may lack incentives to invest in marketing. With a lower investment, they may be more inclined to abandon ship if the firm hits a downturn. When the firm uses its own sales force, their quality and commitment to the firm also needs to be examined. Their experience and track record should be considered. When the firm has "proven stars," there needs to be some assurance that they will stay with the firm after the buyout.

4. *Market size*. Market size indicates the sales potential of the LBO candidate. Firms with larger, established market shares in growing markets tend to be good LBO candidates. If, however, the market is mature, or worse, declining, and the target has an uncertain share, this is a clear indicator of risk. Market size is difficult to judge when the product line is new. Newly developed products, which have not withstood the test of time, are considered risky.

FINANCIAL ANALYSIS OF LBO CANDIDATES

A careful financial analysis of an LBO candidate is critically important. The most basic question which the participants in a leveraged buyout must consider is whether or not the company will be able to service the debt following the leveraged buyout. The second, but equally important, consideration is whether the changes necessary to enable the firm to service the debt will cause it to lose market position and be unable to be viable after the debt has been retired. The heated pace of leveraged buyouts in the late 1980s has focused increasing criticism on LBO dealmakers for forsaking this second objective while focusing solely on debt service. Many LBO dealmakers, such as Ted Forstmann of the LBO firm Forstmann, Little, contend that they never go forward with a deal unless it fulfills both criteria. This firm has been known to turn down many deals that do not make economic sense.

A financial analysis of an LBO candidate begins with financial statement analysis. This often starts off with the construction of pro forma financial statements that project the firm's financial condition and income from several years into the future. A rule of thumb in an LBO financial analysis is to construct pro forma statements that depict the firm five years or more into the future. It is at this time that LBO debt pressures are usually the highest since most of the debt is still outstanding. Although financial statement analysis is covered in most corporate finance textbooks, this book will review the basic concepts as they apply to mergers and LBOs. This review is presented in Chapter 13.[22]

---

[22] See Charles Moyer, James R. McGuigan, and William Kretlow, *Contemporary Financial Management*, 3rd ed. (St. Paul, Minn.: West Publishing Co., 1987), pp. 156–204; J. Fred Weston and Thomas E. Copeland, *Managerial Finance*, 8th ed. (Chicago: Dryden Press, 1986), pp. 173–205; and Eugene F. Brigham and Louis C. Gapinski, *Intermediate Financial Management*, 2nd ed. (Chicago: Dryden Press, 1987), pp. 650–682.

Financial Ratio Analysis for Leveraged Buyouts

Financial ratio analysis is quite important to both leveraged buyouts and unleveraged acquisitions. It can be used to establish the financial well-being of the LBO candidate as well as to put this condition into an industry perspective. Ratios can be used to determine whether the financial condition of the firm is improving, staying the same, or deteriorating. They can be used to determine the firm's strengths or to detect problem areas.

The more important financial ratios are described in Chapter 13. The categories of ratios that should be part of a thorough leveraged buyout financial analysis are briefly highlighted as follows.

1. *Liquidity ratio.* These ratios measure the ability of the firm to meet its current obligations. The higher the degree of liquidity, the more debt the firm can service.

2. *Leverage ratios.* These ratios reflect the extent to which the firm's activities have been financed by debt. A leveraged buyout is usually followed by a dramatic increase in leverage. The lower the pre-LBO leverage ratios, the more likely the firm can sustain the post–buyout debt levels.

3. *Activity ratios.* These ratios measure the firm's efficiency in using its assets to generate sales. A downward trend in these ratios is an adverse development.

4. *Profitability ratios.* These ratios reflect the effectiveness with which management is able to generate profits and a return on the firm's investment. These ratios can be used as an indicator of the value of the firm to those contemplating the buyout.

Financial Analysis of LBOs from the Equity Holders' Viewpoint

One of the most basic factors which LBO investors have to consider is: what rate of return does my investment earn? To evaluate this question we must apply the techniques of financial analysis such as net present value and internal rate of return. These concepts, standard to most corporate finance textbooks, are reviewed in detail in Chapter 15.

To see how a lender might assess a leveraged buyout, let's consider the case of a management buyout of ABC Manufacturing Corporation.

Purchase Price   The purchase price of ABC Manufacturing in 1988 was $150 million. This price was 10 times the operating cash flow of the company.

Financing   The financing of the buyout was as follows:

Senior debt: $100 million
   15 percent rate of interest

Subordinated debt: $40 million
   12 percent interest rate convertible into 30 percent equity with
   deferred interest payments.

Equity: $10 million
   50 percent required rate of return. This high rate of return
   reflects the business, interest, and illiquidity risks.

Cash Flow Projections   Based upon the company's financial records,
the analysis of the industry, and future costs projections, the investors
assembled the following cash flow projections:

CASH FLOW PROJECTIONS 10% RATE OF GROWTH
(THOUSAND $)

Year	1989	1990	1991	1992	1993	1994	1995
$	15,000	16,500	18,150	19,995	21,962	24,158	26,573

Projected Future Value of the Company   Based on the fact that
the buyout price was 10 times operating cash flow, it is conservatively
assumed that the company could be sold after seven years for 7.5 times
the operating cash flow. That is:

($26,573,000) × 7.5 = $1,999,298,000

Position of Equity Holders   If we assume that there are no cash
distributions and that by 1990 the senior debt will be repaid and that
the equity will be held by the original equity holders and the subordinated debt holders (subordinated debt holders will have converted
the debt into equity), then the equity will be held in the following
proportions:

Original equity holders   70%
Subordinated debt holders   30%

Evaluation of Equity Holders Claims   The original equity holder's
investment and the return achieved by the subordinated debt holders
can be evaluated by calculating the net present value (NPV) and the
internal rate of return. These relationships are shown as follows:

$$NPV = \frac{CF_1}{(1 + r)^1} + \frac{CF_2}{(1 + r)^2} + \cdots + \frac{CF_n}{(1 + r)^n} - I_o \qquad (7.3)$$

where: I = initial investment
CF_i = ith period's cash flows
r = discount rate

$$\text{or NPV} = \sum_{i=1}^{n} \frac{CF_i}{(1 + r)^i} - I_o$$

The internal rate of return is the discount rate which will equate the value of I_o and the cash flow stream. In other words, given the cash flow stream $(CF_1 \ldots CF_n)$ and the investment I_o, the IRR is the rate of return that equates the two.

Original Equity Holders   To evaluate the position of the original equity holders, we need to calculate the net present value of this investment. This is done as follows:

Year	1988	1995
$ (thousands)	−$10,000	$1,399,508

(Note: The $1,399,508 is 70 percent of the $1,999,298.)

$$NPV = \frac{-\$10,000}{(1.50)^0} + \frac{\$1,399,508}{(1.50)^7}$$
$$= \$81,910$$

The positive NPV ($81,910) indicates that this would be a good investment for the original equity holders.

Subordinated Debt Holders

1988	1989	1990	1991	1992	1993	1994	1995
−40,000	4,800	4,800	4,800	4,800	4,800	4,800	4,800 + $599,789

(Note: The $599,789 is 30 percent of the $1,999,298.)

The above cash flow stream provides the subordinated debt holders with an internal rate of return of 52.5 percent, which is greater than the 50 percent required rate of return for equity holders. Therefore, it is also a good deal for the subordinated debt holders.

CASE STUDY: *FINANCIAL STATEMENT OF AN LBO CANDIDATE: BEFORE AND AFTER*

The following example presents hypothetical financial statements for an LBO firm: before and after the buyout.* In the example, Simple Deal Company is divested by its parent company for $2.5 million. The deal is financed by $1.25 million of bank financing and $750,000 in subordinated debt. Venture capital accounts for $200,000, while management contributes $300,000 in equity, for total equity of $500,000.

Table 7.5   SIMPLE DEAL BALANCE SHEETS ($ THOUSANDS)

	Before	After
Assets		
Current assets	$1,200	$1,200
Property, plant, & equipment	700	1,800[a]
	1,900	3,000
Liability and equity		
Current liabilities	500	500
Bank financing (long-term note)		1,250[b]
Mezzanine financing (subordinated note)		750[c]
Equity		
Parent company equity	1,400	
Management		300[d]
Venture capital company		200[e]
Total equity	$1,400	$ 500
Total equity and liabilities	$1,900	$3,000

[a] Assets are recorded at appraised value. The additional depreciation expense will decrease Simple Deal's income taxes. Parent Company realizes a $1.1 million gain on the sale of the assets. Also, the sale probably triggers recapture provisions of the tax laws (e.g., investment tax credits and depreciation).

[b] Note from bank with fixed assets as collateral. Interest rate is 2 percent over prime which is assumed to be 13 percent; annual principal payments are $250,000.

[c] Subordinated note from Venture Capital Company. Interest rate is 5 percent over prime which is assumed to be 13 percent, with a maximum of 20 percent. Principal payments of $150,000 per year begin six years after purchase. Such a note frequently incorporates warrants or a conversion feature.

[d] Management invests $300,000 or 12 percent of the purchase price. Management members own 60 percent of the voting common stock.

[e] Venture Capital Company obtains 40 percent of the stock for $200,000. The agreement gives management the option of acquiring this stock after five years at its value based on a professional valuation at that time. However, exercising this option accelerates the maturity of the subordinated note, which has to be repaid at the same time.

Source: The table is copied with modifications, from: Ernst & Whinney, *Management Buyouts* (New York: 1979), p. 19.

* Several sources were used to develop this example: Carolyn Brancato and Kevin Winch, "Merger Activity and Leveraged Buyouts: Sound Corporate Restructuring or Wall Street Alchemy," Report Prepared for the Committee on Energy and Commerce, U.S. House of Representatives, November 1984, pp. 18–21. The tables presented below are modified versions of those that were included in: Albert F. Gargiulo and Steven J. Levine, *The Leveraged Buyout* (New York: American Management Association, 1982); Ernst & Whinney, *Management Buyouts* (New York: 1979).

The liability section of Table 7.5 presents a breakdown of the financing under Liability and Equity. Table 7.6 shows that the firm is projected to have five years of successful operating results. This example projects that the interest of the venture capitalists will be bought out at a substantial premium (five times their original equity investment). This is shown in Table 7.7. Following the buyout of the venture capitalists, management will own 100 percent of the company. The value of this investment is shown to be $736,000 (Table 7.8). This is a 19.7 percent rate of return on the $300,000 investment of management.

Table 7.6   SIMPLE DEAL INCOME STATEMENTS: HISTORICAL AND PRO FORMA

	Historical	Pro Forma				
	base year					
	Year 0	Year 1	Year 2	Year 3	Year 4	Year 5
Net sales	$4,000	$4,203	$4,790	$5,478	$6,265	$7,253
Cost and expenses:						
Cost and expenses excluding depreciation and interest	3,200[a]	3,280	3,760	4,320	4,960	5,760
Depreciation[b]	100	300	270	240	210	180
Interest[c]	0	323	285	248	210	173
	3,300	3,903	4,315	4,808	5,380	6,113
Income before income taxes	700	300	475	670	885	1,140
Income taxes (50%)[d]	350	150	237	335	442	570
Net income	350	150	238	335	443	570
Return on equity[e]	25%	30%	37%	38%	36%	32%

[a] A review of Simple Deal's financial records indicates that no significant pro forma adjustments need to be made for the organizational changes. Amounts incurred for salaries and for legal, accounting, data processing, and other services will be approximately the same after purchase.

[b] Depreciation expense increases due to writing up the accounting and tax basis of the assets to the purchase price and adopting accelerated depreciation methods for book and tax purposes.

[c] Interest expense assumes a 13 percent prime rate throughout the period. This assumption is unrealistic in view of the history of interest rate fluctuations.

[d] The assumption that the income tax rate is 50 percent is made to simplify the example; the maximum corporate income tax rate is 46 percent, with the effective income tax rate usually below the maximum. See U.S. Congress, Joint Committee on Taxation, Study of 1982 Effective Tax Rates of Selected Large U.S. Corporations (Washington, D.C.: U.S. Government Printing Office, 1983), 28 p. (Joint Committee Print)

[e] Each year the equity base is increased by the previous year's net income.

Source: The table is copied, with modifications, from: Ernst & Whinney, *Management Buyouts* (New York: 1979), p. 20.

Table 7.7   SIMPLE DEAL CASH FLOW: HISTORICAL AND PRO FORMA
($ THOUSANDS)

	Historical	Pro Forma				
	base year					
	Year 0	Year 1	Year 2	Year 3	Year 4	Year 5
Cash provided by:						
Net Income	$350	$150	$238	$335	$443	$570
Depreciation	100	300	270	240	210	180
New bank loan	0	0	0	0	0	2,000
	450	450	508	575	653	2,750[a]
Cash applied to:						
Additions to fixed assets	0	100	100	100	100	100
Debt principal payments:						
Bank loan	0	250	250	250	250	250
Subordinated note payment	0		0	0	0	750[a]
Repurchase Venture Capital Company Equity interest	0	0	0	0	0	1,500[a]
	0	350	350	350	350	2,600
Cash available for crown and dividends	450	100	158	225	303	150

[a] Assumed prepayment of the Venture Capital Company $750,000 subordinated note and repurchase of its 40 percent equity interest at a negotiated price of $1.5 million. Simple Deal finances this principally through a new loan.

Source: The table is copied, with modifications, from: Ernst & Whinney, *Management Buyouts* (New York: 1979), p. 20.

Table 7.8   SIMPLE DEAL FIVE YEARS IN THE FUTURE: PRO FORMA BALANCE
SHEET[a] ($ THOUSANDS)

Current assets	$2,436
Property, plant & equipment:	
Original purchase	1,800
Subsequent additions	500
Less depreciation	(1,200)
	$1,100
Total	$3,536
Current liabilities	$ 800
Long-term note	2,000
Subordinated note	0

Table 7.8   SIMPLE DEAL FIVE YEARS IN THE FUTURE: PRO FORMA BALANCE
SHEET^a ($ THOUSANDS) (*continued*)

Equity:	
Stock outstanding	500
Retained earnings	1,736
Less treasury stock	(1,500)
	$ 736
Total	$3,536

^{a} The original bank note of $1,250,000 has been repaid, and the new bank loan of $2,000,000 was used to help finance the early retirement of the $750,000 subordinated note and the $1,500,000 repurchase of the Venture Capital Company stock interest. The company is now 100-percent owned by the executives.

Source: The table is copied, with modifications, from: Ernst & Whinney, *Management Buyouts* (New York, 1979), p. 21.

RETURNS TO STOCKHOLDERS FROM LBOs

The issue of stockholder gains from leveraged buyout transactions became an important issue in the late 1980s in the light of the fact that several legislative proposals were brought forward to regulate LBOs. These proposals, which would limit some of the LBO practices, could have an effect on the ability of LBO target shareholders to enjoy the high premiums associated with these leveraged bids.

DeAngelo, DeAngelo, and Rice analyzed the gains to both stockholders and management from management buyouts of 72 companies that proposed to go private during the period 1973–1980.[23] These researchers found average premiums above the market value of the LBO target's stock price equal to 56 percent. They concluded that managers are willing to offer a premium to public stockholders because they can achieve other productivity gains following the buyout. The fact that they are willing to offer a 56 percent average premium indicates that managers anticipate gains in excess of this premium. The DeAngelo, DeAngelo, and Rice results have been confirmed by other research studies. In a study of 28 management buyout proposals between 1979 and 1984, the average premium above the market value of the firm 30

---

[23] DeAngelo, DeAngelo, and Rice, "Going Private: Minority Freezeouts and Stockholder Wealth." Similar results are found in L. Marais, K. Schipper, and A. Smith, "Wealth Effects of Going Private on Senior Securities," Working Paper, University of Chicago, June 1988.

days before the announcement of the offer was 48 percent.[24] This premium was as high as 79 percent when there were three or more offers. (This common-sense result also supports the arguments for mandated auctions in leveraged buyouts.)

A study by Travlos and Cornett shows a statistically significant negative correlation between abnormal returns to shareholders and the P/E ratio of the firm relative to the industry.[25] This implies that the lower the P/E ratio, compared to similar firms, the greater probability that the firm is poorly managed. Travlos and Cornett interpret the low P/E ratios as reflecting greater room for improvement through changes such as the reduction of agency costs. Some of these efficiency gains can then be realized through going private. These gains become the source of the buyout premium.

The mere fact that public stockholders receive high premiums does not necessarily mitigate the need for regulation. If an auction was mandated, would the average premium be higher? Critics of leveraged buyouts would contend that higher premiums would result from a mandated auction. Proponents of the current unregulated LBO structure claim that many of these LBOs would not have been attempted in a more regulated environment and stockholders would be deprived of the available gains.

RETURNS TO STOCKHOLDERS FROM DIVISIONAL BUYOUTS

Many management buyouts result from a management group buying a division from the parent company. Many of these transactions are criticized for not being "arms-length" transactions. Managers of the parent company are often accused of giving preferential treatment to a management bid. The parent company may forsake the auction process and accept the management's offer without soliciting other, higher offers.

In 1989, Gailen Hite and Michael Vetsuypens conducted a study designed to show whether divisional buyouts had adverse effects on the wealth of parent stockholders.[26] Many feel that divisional buyouts may

---

[24] Louis Lowenstein, *What's Wrong with Wall Street* (Reading, Mass.: Addison–Wesley, 1988), pp. 183–184.

[25] Nicholas G. Travlos and M. M. Cornett, "Going Private Buyouts and Determinants of Shareholder Returns," *Journal of Accounting, Auditing and Finance*. forthcoming 1990.

[26] Gailen L. Hite and Michael R. Vetsuypens, "Management Buyouts of Divisions and Stockholder Wealth," *Journal of Finance* 44, no. 4 (September 1989): 953–970.

present opportunities for efficiency-related gains as the division becomes removed from the parent company's layers of bureaucracy.[27] This may be a source of value to the managers of the buying group but does not negate the often cited possibility that a fair price, which reflects an "auction-like" price, was not paid for the division.

Hite and Vetsuypens failed to find any evidence of a reduction in shareholder wealth following divisional buyouts by management. Their results show small, but statistically significant, wealth gains for a two-day period surrounding the buyout announcement. They interpret these results to indicate that division buyouts result in a more efficient allocation of assets. The existence of small wealth gains indicates that shareholders in the parent company shared in some of these gains.

EFFICIENCY GAINS FROM LEVERAGED BUYOUTS

Before considering regulation of leveraged buyouts, we need to investigate whether any efficiency gains result from LBOs. That is, do leveraged buyouts result in a more efficient post-buyout firm? Some critics contend that financial dealmakers facilitate the buyout process for the purpose of their personal enrichment. They contend that the end product is a heavily leveraged firm that has a much higher probability of falling into bankruptcy, with little offsetting gains in profitability or efficiency. In the interest of presenting an unbiased approach to this hotly debated issue, this discussion examines some of the leading academic studies on LBO efficiency effects and contrasts their results with the research conducted by Kohlberg, Kravis and Roberts.

A study by Steven Kaplan at the University of Chicago contradicts some of the critics' arguments.[28] His study finds additional value in post-LBO firms. This result seems to justify the high premiums associated with the buyout. Kaplan cites two main sources of value of leveraged buyouts: efficiency gains and tax benefits. He shows that, compared to industry median values, post-buyout companies experienced positive increases in operating income and operating margins for the first two years after the buyout. These same companies were shown to reduce inventories and capital expenditures relative to industry medians. All of these are clearly positive except for capital expenditures, which could also be considered a sacrifice of the company's future.

---

[27] Fama and Jensen, "Separation of Ownership Control."

[28] Steven Kaplan, "Management Buyouts: Efficiency Gains or Value Transfers," University of Chicago Working Paper No. 244, October 1988, Chicago.

In another study, Kaplan quantified the tax benefits that post-buyout firms enjoy.[29] "A comparison of the excess returns earned by pre-buyout and post-buyout investors to several measures of tax benefits is consistent with pre-buyout shareholders receiving most of the potential tax benefits. The returns to post-buyout investors are not related to the tax benefits created by the buyout. This is consistent with a market for corporate control that forces the buyout companies to pay public stockholders tax benefits that are ex-post predictable and obtainable by other bidders."[30]

The second Kaplan study shows that the tax benefits of LBOs are largely predictable and are incorporated in the premium that pre-LBO stockholders receive. This implies that the post-LBO investors need to find other sources of value. Both Kaplan studies show that any sweeping criticism of LBOs may be unwarranted. Clearly, the buyout process may create value. Therefore, an evaluation must be made on a case-by-case basis.

THE KOHLBERG, KRAVIS AND ROBERTS STUDY

The study most favorable to the LBO process was the one conducted by the buyout firm Kohlberg, Kravis and Roberts.[31] It is not surprising that a study sponsored by the leading LBO firm should disseminate results supportive of leveraged buyouts. While there is a strong potential for bias, the study should not be dismissed without a review of its methods and findings. A listing of companies in the study is shown in Table 7.9.

IMPACT OF LBOs ON EMPLOYMENT

It is a commonly held belief that LBOs, and mergers and acquisitions in general, cause unemployment and a displacement of employees as firms seek to lower costs so as to be able to service the increased debt created by the buyout. Not surprisingly, the KKR study failed to detect an adverse employment effect. The total number of employees at the KKR companies increased from 276,000 in the LBO year to 313,000 three years after the LBO. These results were adjusted for economy-wide increases in employment.

---

[29] Steven Kaplan, "Management Buyouts: Evidence on Taxes As a Source of Value," University of Chicago Working Paper No. 245, September 1988, Chicago.

[30] Kaplan, "Management Buyouts," Working Paper No. 245, p. 44.

[31] "Presentation on Leveraged Buyouts," Kohlberg, Kravis and Roberts, January 1989.

Table 7.9   COMPANIES IN THE KKR 1989 STUDY
DATA BASE

A. J. Industries
L. B. Foster Company
Houdaille Industries, Inc.
The Marley Company
Fred Meyer, Inc.
Pacific Realty Trust
Malone & Hyde, Inc.
Pace Industries, Inc.
Motel 6, Inc.
M & T, Inc.
Beatrice Companies, Inc.
Safeway Stores, Inc.
Owens-Illinois, Inc.
Jim Walter Corporation
Seaman Furniture Company
Stop & Shop Companies
Duracell, Inc.

IMPACT OF LBOs ON CAPITAL SPENDING

Consistent with its other favorable findings KKR found that aggregate capital spending increased from $1.054 billion in the year of the LBOs to 1.264 three years following the buyouts. KKR states that this amounted to a 14 percent increase above the capital spending level prior to the buyout.

This result is somewhat misleading, however. If we take into account a 4 to 5 percent rate of annual inflation, the gains quickly disappear. If we consider the year prior to the LBO, there is a significant decline in the year of the LBO and another significant decline in the year after the LBO.

IMPACT OF LBOs ON RESEARCH AND DEVELOPMENT EXPENDITURES

The KKR companies showed an increase in R&D expenditures following the LBOs. This increase sharply reversed a downward trend in these expenditures for the years prior to the LBOs. The KKR companies showed an increase of 19 percent in R&D expenditures immediately following the buyouts.

The KKR study did not adjust for either inflation or industry effects. As a result of these drawbacks, we have to be cautious about adopting their findings.

Table 7.10   KKR COMPANIES' CAPITAL STRUCTURE

Debt	
Senior commercial bank debt with required payment within 7 to 8 years	40%
Senior subordinated debt with repayment required in 9 to 12 years	15%
Subordinated debt with repayment required in 9 to 12 years	20%
Equity	
Preferred stock	15%
Common equity	10%
Total capital	100%

THE CAPITAL STRUCTURE OF KKR COMPANIES

The capital structure of the KKR companies was 75 percent debt and 25 percent equity (see Table 7.10). If one groups the preferred stock with debt, in light of its similarity to debt in the somewhat fixed nature of its dividends payments, the debt and preferred stock account for 90 percent of the KKR companies' capital structure. This is a highly leveraged and risky capital structure.

LBO PERFORMANCE RECORD: RECENT RESEARCH

Not surprisingly, the Kohlberg, Kravis and Roberts study presented a very favorable picture of leveraged buyouts. William Long and David Ravenscraft compared the results of the KKR study with other research in the field and concluded that the KKR results were not consistent with those of other major research studies.[32] The fact that the other

---

[32] Long and Ravenscraft compare the major conclusions of the KKR research with the following studies:

William F. Long and David J. Ravenscraft, "The Record of LBO Performance," Paper presented at the New York University Conference on Corporate Governance, May 17, 1989; Steven Kaplan, "A Summary of Sources of Value in Mangement Buyouts," Paper presented at the New York University Conference on Management Buyouts, May 20, 1988; Ivan Bull, "Management Performance in Leveraged Buyouts," Paper presented at the New York University Conference on Management Buyouts, May 20, 1988; Chris J. Muscarella and Michael R. Vesuypens, "Efficiency and Organizational Structure: A Study of Reverse LBOs," Manuscript, January 1989; National Science Foundation, "An Assessment of the Impact of Recent Leveraged Buyouts and Other Restructurings on Industrial research and Development Expenditures," Prepared for the House of Representatives Committee on Energy and Commerce, 1989; James Kitching, "Early Returns on LBOs," *Harvard Business Review* (November/December 1989): 74–81. (The Kitching study was not included in the Long and Ravenscraft review.)

studies they cite were conducted by researchers who did not earn income from leveraged buyouts may give their conclusions further credence.

In the next section we compare the multinational study of leveraged buyouts to the studies reviewed by Long and Ravenscraft. The comparative findings are broken down by topic categories.

Comparison Between the KKR Study and Other Research

Employment Effects   The KKR study found that average annual employment at the 17 companies in their sample was 13 percent higher than the pre-LBO employment levels. In their critique of the KKR findings, Long and Ravenscraft point out that the Kaplan and Muscarella and Vesuypens studies found either negative or no employment effects. The Kitching data base also showed that the employment effects were neutral.

Research and Development   The KKR study found that post-LBO research and development expenditures were 19 percent higher after the LBO. The issue of research and development is not well considered in any of the four studies Long and Ravenscraft used as the basis for their critique of KKR's research. They do point out, however, that the National Science Foundation (NSF) did note "that R&D declined between 1986 and 1987 by 12.8% for 8 out of the 200 leading U.S. R&D performing companies which had undergone LBO, buybacks, or other restructuring."[33] A total of 176 firms that were not involved in mergers, LBOs, or other restructurings increased the R&D by an average of 5.4 percent.

The NSF study does not refute the KKR findings, however, since neither study adjusted for industry changes that might have an effect on R&D expenditures. As pointed out above, the KKR study did not adjust for either inflation or industry effects. Therefore, the impact of LBOs on R&D must remain an open question.

Capital Spending   The KKR study purports to show an average 14 percent increase in capital expenditures three years following the LBOs. Kaplan's research, however, reveals small declines in capital expenditures, whereas the Bull study shows a 24.7 percent industry-adjusted decline (21.9 percent unadjusted) between one year before

---

[33] Long and Ravenscraft, "The Record of LBO Performance," p. 2.

the LBO and two years after. One must be careful about drawing conclusions from these results since they refer to different time periods. The longer the time after the buyout, the lower the debt pressures should be. If the LBO requires that capital expenditures or R&D be curtailed, this policy should be abandoned as the interest payment pressures subside. The longer the time period, the lower the capital expenditures effects.

Sample Size   All the studies considered above are compiled from small samples. Long and Ravenscraft point out that 1,473 LBOs occurred between 1983 and the second quarter of 1988. The largest sample of LBOs in the research they reviewed was in the Muscarella and Vesuypens study which focused on 35 buyouts. The KKR study examined only 17 LBOs. We have to be very careful in interpreting the results of studies based on such a small percentage of the population. The problem is further compounded by the fact that the samples of the various studies were not compiled in a way designed to draw on a representative cross section of the total LBO population. Therefore, concerns about the basis of the sample are also relevant.

The only study that reviewed a larger sample was the Kitching study which covered 320 transactions in the United States and Great Britain worth more than $50 million or £10 million. All the deals in the Kitching data base were completed prior to 1987.

The various research studies considered above provide evidence that partially contradicts the KKR findings. The academic studies do not lend much support to the view that LBOs have great beneficial effects. The KKR study has many methodological drawbacks that make it difficult to adopt its pro-LBO conclusions. For example, since the study was published, two of the firms in the KKR sample, Jim Walter Corporation (now renamed Hillsborough Holdings) and Seaman's furniture, have defaulted on their LBO debt. All analysts do agree, however, that LBOs do provide significant financial benefits for the shareholders of the firm that are bought out. The gains therefore have to be weighed against the various direct and indirect costs associated with the buyout.

RISK TO THE BANKING SYSTEM

Many analysts have expressed concern that many banks have invested too much capital in LBO loans. Because these business ventures are perceived to be inherently risky, many have become anxious about

Table 7.11   MAJOR BANK LENDERS TO LBOS

Bank	LBO Portfolio	Remarks
Citicorp	$4.0 billion	137 transactions in 27 countries; average loan: $30 million. Figure doesn't include $1 billion of senior subordinated debt in U.S. debt for borrowers in other countries and debt held by its venture capital unit.
Wells Fargo	$3.0 billion	76 deals; individual loans typically $40 to $60 million; 20% in consumer nondurable manufacturers.
Bankers Trust	$2.7 billion	112 borrowers; 33 industries, 66% of portfolio consists of loans less than $50 million.
Security Pacific	$2.4 billion	200 borrowers; 16 industries, average loan less than $50 million.
Manufacturers Hanover	$1.5–$2.0 billion	108 borrowers; average loan $21 million.
Bank America	$1.3 billion	50 borrowers; average loan outstanding: $25 million.
Chase Manhattan	$1.25 billion	Declined to elaborate.
First Chicago	$1.2 billion	Declined to elaborate.
Continental Illinois	$927 million	52 borrowers; originated $3.5 billion in buyout loans.
J. P. Morgan	$700–$800 million	Portfolio never exceeded $1 billion.

Source: "Big Banks Disclose Some Details of Leveraged Buyout Portfolios," Wall Street Journal, December 13, 1988, p. A14. Reprinted by permission of the Wall Street Journal, copyright © 1988, Dow Jones & Company, Inc. All Rights Reserved Worldwide.

their effect on raising the risk level of bank portfolios.[34] Not uncommonly, banks provide up to 85 percent of the total financing of leveraged buyouts. However, a *Wall Street Journal* survey of 10 major banks (see Table 7.11) failed to reveal that these investments had any adverse impact.

> The survey found that these banks held a total of $19 billion in senior debt of LBOs and had sold many times that amount to foreign and domestic institutional investors such as insurance companies, thrift institutions, and pension funds. The LBO component of the banks loan porfolios, therefore, was less significant than other risky areas such as Third World loans.[35]

Other surveys of executives at several major banks indicated that many of the money center banks do have an active LBO business. The survey indicates that, although the loans do not represent a large

---

[34] "Perils of Leveraged Buyouts: Large Loans Worry Banks," *New York Times*, May 14, 1984.

[35] *Wall Street Journal*, December 13, 1988, p. A3.

percentage of each bank's total portfolio, the investment is nonetheless significant. It is important also to bear in mind that this part of the bank's portfolio would be more susceptible to cyclical fluctuation in the economy than other bank investments. Fortunately, these banks which have invested approximately $50 billion in highly leveraged transactions (HLTs) appeared to have diversified their HLT loans more than their real estate portfolio.

Since large LBOs are a relatively new phenomenon, the impact on the banking system may not be fully apparent until the economy hits a major economic downturn. One factor that does lower the banks' exposure is the practice of reselling the LBO loans. The process of selling these LBO loans reduces the bank's total exposure to the riskiness of these investments.

Interestingly, commercial banks, which are known for relatively conservative investments, increased the sale of LBO debt when the number of defaults rose in 1989. The defaults, coupled with uncertainties about the economy, caused, for example, Continental Capital Markets, a subsidiary of Continental Bank, to sell more than $400 million in senior leveraged buyout debt in private placement in Europe during 1989. "The most recent transaction took place on Friday, when BNP Capital Markets Ltd. and Credit National offered $625 million of floating-rate notes, due in 1998, to investors in the Eurobond market. The notes are secured by senior, secured term loans made by about 20 banks in leveraged buyouts and recapitalization plans."[36]

Riskiness of Corporate America

LBOs have also been criticized for transforming companies that may have had a relatively low debt to equity ratio to companies that are highly leveraged. This high degree of leverage increases the riskiness of these firms while, at the same time, increasing the profit potential for the equity holders. "As early as mid-1984, the chairman of the Securities and Exchange Commission predicted that the more leveraged takeovers and buyouts now, the more bankruptcies tomorrow."[37] Well-known investment banker Felix Rohatyn had the following comments on the impact of LBOs on corporate America:

> A transaction called "leveraged buy-out" has swept corporate America. This transaction essentially turns public companies into private companies mostly by borrowing against their own assets and shrinking their equity dramatically. Thus a public company with, say $100 million of debt and

---

[36] "Banks' Sales of Buyout Debt Rising," *New York Times*, December 18, 1989, p. D1.

[37] Bryan Burrough and John Helyar, *Barbarians at the Gate: The Fall of Nabisco* (New York: Harper & Row, 1988), p. 141.

$900 million of equity is turned into a private company with $900 million of debt and $100 million of capital.

This has two consequences, both highly speculative. First, it bets the company on a combination of continued growth and lower interest rates, with no margin for error. Second, it substitutes debt for permanent capital, which is exactly the opposite of what our national investment objectives should be.[38]

The post-LBO firm is very vulnerable because the increased debt load eliminates the margin for error or "cushion" in the firm's cash flows. A good example of this risk was the 1986 leveraged buyout of Fruehauf, the tractor trailer and brake manufacturer. Fruehauf assumed $1.7 billion in high-yield debt to complete the buyout. The firm found that its pre-LBO planning had not anticipated the difficulties it encountered in the sale of its leasing and financing units. Nor did it anticipate that Fruehauf's market share of the domestic trailer market would fall from 25 percent before the buyout to 18 percent one year later. While a nonleveraged Fruehauf would be able to sustain the loss of market share, the post-buyout Fruehauf was left on the verge of bankruptcy.[39]

While corporate indebtedness has risen at an annual rate of approximately 12 percent since 1982, nearly one-third faster than the pace in the 1970s, the bulk of this debt is concentrated in a narrow segment of the economy that is less vulnerable to cyclical fluctuations. Stephen Roach of Morgan Stanley showed that much of the increase in corporate debt has occurred in the service sector and the utility industry, two business segments that tend to be not as vulnerable to economic downturns.[40] This debate will not be resolved until leveraged buyouts have withstood the test of time and business cycles.

Other critics feel that the LBO buyout boom has led to what is tantamount to an "asset shell game" rather than a beneficial restructuring of corporate assets.[41] They maintain that the redeployment of assets reaps large gains for "dealmakers" but does little for corporate growth.

---

[38] Felix G. Rohatyn, "On a Buyout Binge and a Takeover Tear," *Wall Street Journal,* May 18, 1984.

[39] "How Fruehauf Leveraged Itself into a Corner," *Business Week*, September 12, 1988, p. 38.

[40] Stephen S. Roach, "Living with Corporate Debt," *Journal of Applied Corporate Finance* 2, no. 1 (Spring, 1989): 19–29.

[41] Carolyn Brancato and Kevin Winch, "Leveraged Buyouts and the Pot of Gold: Trends, Public Policy, and Case Studies," Congressional Research Service, Library of Congress, September 15, 1987.

Part of what some see as the increased risk to corporate America is related not just to the quantity but to the *quality* of the LBO debt. Much of the debt that firms assume during a leveraged buyout is of short-term duration, and it usually has a high dollar value. Thus, the firm is forced to take drastic steps to pay off the total within this time period, placing great pressures on the firm which may cause some companies to fail. Of those that do not fail, many may be seriously damaged by the restrictive actions that may have to be taken to pay off the debt. The short-term debt may hamper long-term planning. This would not necessarily be the case if the debt was long term.

CONFLICTS OF INTEREST IN MANAGEMENT BUYOUTS

A clear conflict of interest exists in many management buyouts. Managers are responsible for managing the corporation so as to maximize the value of stockholders' investment and provide them with the highest return possible. These same managers take on a very different role when they are required to present an offer to stockholders to buy the company. This was the case when the management of RJR Nabisco presented an offer to stockholders to take Nabisco private in an MBO. This offer was quickly superseded by another offer from Kohlberg, Kravis and Roberts as well as other offers from management.[42] If management truly attempts to maximize the value of stockholders' investments, why does it choose to advocate an offer that it knows is clearly not in the stockholders' best interests? Many believe that managers cannot serve this dual, and sometimes conflicting, role—as agent for both the buyer and the seller.

One proposed solution to this conflict is *neutralized voting* whereby the proponents of a deal do not participate in the approval process. If the proponents are stockholders, their votes are not included in the approval process. They may have to participate in the voting process since, under some state laws, a quorum may not be possible without their participation if they hold a certain number of shares.[43] The appointment of an independent financial adviser to render a fairness opinion is a usual second step in this process, which is meant to help reduce the conflicts of interest.

Even if these precautionary measures are adopted, certain practical

---

[42] See Burrough and Helyar, *Barbarians at the Gate: The Fall of RJR Nabisco*.

[43] Arthur M. Borden, *Going Private* (New York: Law Journal Seminar Press, 1987), pp. 1–6.

considerations may limit their effectiveness. While those members of the board of directors who may profit from the LBO may not vote for its approval, other members of the board may have a close relationship to them and consider themselves obliged to support the deal. The use of lawsuits by stockholders suing directors for breach of fiduciary duty has placed limits on this tendency. Fairness opinions put forward by investment bankers who have done much business with management or who may have a financial interest in the deal may be of questionable value.

Although these steps are an important attempt to try to reduce some of the conflicts inherent in the MBO process, they still do not address the issue of the manager being both the buyer's and the seller's agent. This issue will probably not be resolved without further legislation. One solution that has been proposed is to have mandated auctions of corporations presented with a management buyout. Louis Lowenstein, director of the Columbia University Center for Law and Economics Studies, believes there is too great a temptation for management to act in advance of their offer to cause the stock price to decline.

> Unless there is an auction, the risks to stockholders are limited in substantial measure only by the imagination of the management group and its lack of scruples. It is easy to depress stock prices artificially so that the public can be offered a "premium" price—at a discount. The insiders can cut the dividend or increase it less than expected. The officers of a power company, Alamito, declined to meet with security analysts, thus withholding the type of access on which analysts and investment advisors depend. On a more manipulative level, it is not difficult to accelerate investments in long term projects or maintenance expenditures, both of which will reduce reported earnings in ways that do not diminish the company's intrinsic value. Since accountants are concerned primarily with the possibility that earnings may be overstated, it is easy enough to calculate reserves, inventories and expenses on a "conservative" basis. Even if the stock market were as smart as financial economists would have us believe, it would still mark down the company's stock to reflect the increasingly obvious possibility of corrupt intent.[44]

According to current case law, directors are not allowed to favor their own bid over another once the bidding process has begun. There is no requirement, however, that they actively seek out alternative bids or that an auction be conducted. When faced with more than one bidder, however, they may not favor one bidder over another.

---

[44] Louis Lowenstein, *What's Wrong with Wall Street?* (Reading, Mass.: Addison-Wesley Publishing Co., 1987), p. 184.

The prohibition on an unfair bidding process was set out by a number of important court decisions. In *Revlon, Inc. v. MacAndrews & Forbes Holdings, Inc.*, the Delaware Supreme Court ruled that Revlon's directors breached their fiduciary duty in granting a lockup option to "white knight" Forstmann, Little.[45] The court ruled that this constituted an unfair bidding process that favored Forstmann, Little over hostile bidder Pantry Pride.

In *Hanson Trust PLC v. SCM Corporation*, the Second Circuit Court took a similar position on the use of lockup options to favor a leveraged buyout by Merrill Lynch instead of a hostile bid by Hanson Trust PLC.[46] Hanson Trust had initially made a tender offer for SCM at $60 per share. In response to Merrill Lynch's LBO offer at $70 per share, Hanson Trust upped its bid to $72. The court ruled that SCM gave preferential treatment to Merrill Lynch by granting lockup options on two SCM divisions to Merrill Lynch.

In *Edelman v. Fruehauf*, the circuit court concluded that the board of directors had decided to conclude a deal with management and did not properly consider other bids such as the all-cash tender offer by Asher Edelman.[47] The court held that the Fruehauf board of directors did not conduct a fair auction for the company.[48]

Although the above decisions establish a precedent that an auction for a firm must be conducted fairly, the courts stop short of spelling out the rules for conducting or ending the bidding process. These decisions fall within the purview of the Business Judgment Rule. The law is also unclear regarding when or even if an auction is required. Further court decisions will help clarify the requirements of directors.

The formation of an independent directors committee can facilitate the auction process.[49] This process is often used when management has proposed a buyout. When faced with a management proposal to take the firm private, the board of directors will usually respond by creating a special committee of independent, nonmanagement directors to ensure that shareholders receive fair, if not maximal, value for their

---

[45] *Revlon, Inc. v. MacAndrews & Forbes Holdings, Inc.*, 506 A. 2d. 173 (Del. Sup. 1986).

[46] *Hanson Trust PLC v. SCM Corporation*, 781 F. 2d. 264 (2d. Cir. 1986).

[47] *Edelman v. Fruehauf*, 798 F. 2d. 882, 886–87 (6th Cir. 1986).

[48] Lawrence Lederman and Barry A. Bryer, "Representing a Public Company in a Leveraged Transaction," in Yakov Amihud, ed., *Leveraged Management Buyouts* (Homewood, Ill.: Dow Jones Irwin, 1989), pp. 111–174.

[49] Joseph Grunfest, "Management Buyouts and Leveraged Buyouts: Are the Critics Right?" in Yakov Amihud, ed., *Leveraged Management Buyouts* (Homewood, Ill.: Dow Jones Irwin, 1989), pp. 241–261.

investment. The committee may then decide to have its own valuation formulated, hire independent counsel, and conduct an auction.

SEC Rule 13e-3

SEC Rule 13e-3, which attempted to regulate some of the problems of management self-dealing associated with going private, is an amendment of the Securities and Exchange Act of 1934. The rule governs repurchases in going private transactions, and it applies to share repurchases that result in fewer than 300 shareholders or where the previously public company would no longer be listed on public stock exchanges or would no longer be quoted in an inter-dealer quotation system. The rule requires that the firm going private file a Schedule 13E-3 on which it discloses information similar to that disclosed on a 13D or a 14D-1. This information must be disseminated to stockholders and includes the following:

1. Disclosure of offers by unaffiliated parties within the previous 18 months.
2. Detailed discussion of the fairness of the transaction.
3. Inclusion of any fairness opinions.
4. Alternatives to the management buyout that was considered.
5. Disclosure of the position of the outside directors.

Rule 13e-1 provides valuable information that stockholders can consider when evaluating a going private proposal. Although it provides useful information, it does not eliminate an opportunity for management self-dealing.

Leveraged Buyouts As White Knights

Managers in target firms have used LBOs as an antitakeover defense, providing stockholders an offer they will accept instead of the hostile bid. More LBOs fell into the white knight category during the 1980s than in previous years.

In a study of 11 management buyouts between 1980 and 1984, Andrei Shleifer and Robert Vishny found that 6 of the 11 were responses to hostile threats. These threats came in the form of an outright hostile tender offer or the acquisition of shares with the intention to make a bid for control of the firm.[50]

---

[50] Andrei Shleifer and Robert W. Vishny, "Management's Buyouts As a Response to Market Pressure," *Mergers and Acquisitions* (Chicago: University of Chicago Press, 1988), pp. 87–103.

LBOs and the Position of Other Debt Holders

One area of interest to many critics in recent years has been the potential impact of the assumption of high amounts of LBO debt, and the associated issuance of junk bonds, on the value of the investment of current bondholders. (This issue is discussed in detail in Chapter 8.) The fact that bondholders are not part of the approval process when an LBO is approved has attracted much attention. The additional debt increases the fixed payments which the firm has to make after the buyout, and in doing so it increases the likelihood that the firm will be unable to meet these payments and then be forced into receivership.

This problem came to fore in the RJR Nabisco leveraged buyout of November 1988. The value of current bonds dropped sharply following the announcement of the LBO. Some bonds fell as much as 15 points, or $150 for each $1,000 face value amount in the week when the buyout was announced. Although the losses incurred to bondholders drew widespread attention in the RJR Nabisco buyout, bondholders have recognized it as a problem for some time. When the R. H. Macy and Company $3.6 billion buyout proposal was announced in 1985, the stock price rose $16 per share while the price of Macy notes fell over three points.

Investors who are holding bonds in a corporation that is involved in an LBO see the value and rating of their bonds deteriorate rapidly following the LBO announcement. This has alienated bondholders, particularly institutional investors who are becoming increasingly vocal. "High credit bonds are converted into junk bonds overnight," fumed John J. Creedon, chief executive officer of Metropolitan Life Insurance Company. 'We think management has a duty to all constituents of the company, including bondholders'."[51] Metropolitan Life saw its $340 million worth of A rated RJR bonds downgraded to junk-level BB for a $40 million loss.

The impact of takeover and leveraged buyout activity has become so pronounced that the rating agencies often lower the rating of a firm if it becomes a takeover or leveraged buyout candidate. "At the rating agencies, analysts are busy lowering the grades on securities of takeover targets [see Table 7.12]. So far this year, 27% of Moody's 134 downgrades resulted from takeover activity. The bond market's new vulnerability to takeovers is a far cry from the genteel days when a company's

---

[51] "Bondholders Are As Mad As Hell—And No Wonder," *Business Week*, December 5, 1988, p. 28.

Table 7.12   UNSECURED LONG-TERM BONDS

Company	Initial Rating	New Rating
CBS	AA	A
Unocal	AA+	BBB
Cheesebrough-Ponds	AA	BBB
Phillips Petroleum	AA	BBB
Diamond Shamrock	A	A−
Scott Paper Company	A−	BBB
Monsanto	A	A−

debt rating was mainly tied to company fundamentals and the business cycle."[52]

The state of acrimony between bondholders and RJR Nabisco following the announcement of the LBO led Metropolitan Life Insurance Company to sue Nabisco in a New York State court. Their suit alleged that a small group of Nabisco's management sought to enrich themselves at the expense of bondholders who had invested capital in Nabisco in good faith. Opponents of the bondholders contended that the bondholders were seeking to control the operations and decisions of the corporation in a manner that should only be reserved for stockholders. They felt that if bondholders wanted such control they should have taken the risk of buying stock, not the relativley lower risk bonds.

The conflict between bondholders and stockholders can be seen in Figure 7.9. As the takeover battle for RJR Nabisco heated up during October and November 1988, the value of Nabisco stock rose as is typical during a takeover battle. However, the value of Nabisco's outstanding bonds declined in response to the market's perception of the added risk and the increased probability of default that the post-buyout Nabisco would have. Figure 7.10 indicates that the fallout in the bond market went beyond Nabisco bonds. The value of new issues of corporate bonds declined following the erosion of the values of bonds related to LBO debt sales (see Figure 7.11).

Bondholders contend that buyouts involve a transferral or misappropriation of wealth from bondholders to stockholders; they believe that the board of directors has a fiduciary obligation to bondholders as well as to stockholders. Others believe that bondholders have to bear

---

[52] "Takeovers and Buyouts Clobber Blue Chip Bondholders," *Business Week*, November 11, 1985, pp. 113–114.

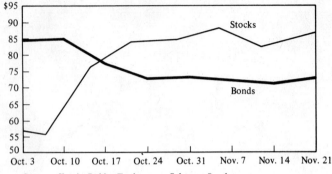

Source: *Knight-Ridder Tradecenter, Salomon Brothers*

Figure 7.9 RJR Nabisco bonds slip as stock soars: Price of the 8⅜ bond due in 2017 and the closing price of RJR Nabisco stock. (*Source:* "Battle Erupts Over Bonds," *New York Times,* November 27, 1988, p. 21. Copyright © 1988 by the New York Times Company. Reprinted by permission.)

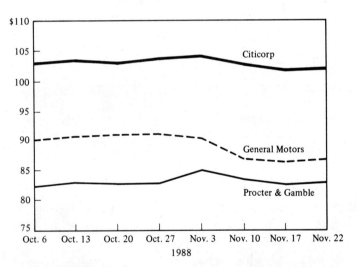

Source: *Salomon Brothers*

Figure 7.10 How other bonds have fared: Weekly closing prices for bonds of three leading companies: Proctor & Gamble, 8⅜ due 2016; General Motors, 8⅛ due 2016; Citicorp, 10¾ due 2015. (*Source:* "Battle Erupts Over Bonds," *New York Times,* November 27, 1988, p. 21. Copyright © 1988 by the New York Times Company. Reprinted by permission.)

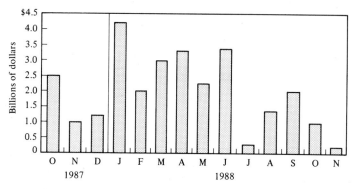

Source: IDD Information Services

Figure 7.11 A drought of new industrial bonds. New investment-grade industrial corporate bonds, excluding privately held issues. (*Source:* Reprinted by permission of the *Wall Street Journal*, December 14, 1988. Dow Jones & Company, Inc. All Rights Reserved Worldwide.)

"event risk" just like stockholders. They believe that the occurrence of an LBO is another form of event risk that a bondholder must assume when purchasing corporate debt. This debate may result in further legal decisions and legislation which will attempt to resolve this conflict between stockholders and bondholders.

On May 31, 1989, a federal judge ruled that an "implied covenant" did not exist between the corporation and the RJR Nabisco bondholders which would prevent the corporation from engaging in actions, such as a leveraged buyout, that would dramatically lower the value of the bonds. The court ruled, that, to be binding, such agreements had to be in writing.

EMPIRICAL RESEARCH ON WEALTH TRANSFER EFFECTS

There has been much public outcry in the media regarding the losses that bondholders have incurred following going private transactions. Such media coverage implies that there is a general wealth transfer effect from bondholders to equity holders in these types of transactions. A study by Ken Lehn and Annette Poulson failed to confirm the existence of such an effect.[53] They found no decrease in value of preferred

---

[53] Ken Lehn and Annette Poulson, "Leveraged Buyouts: Wealth Created or Wealth Distributed," in M. Weidenbaum and K. Chilton, eds., *Public Policy Towards Corporate Takeovers* (New Brunswick, N.J.: Transaction Publishers, 1988).

stock and bonds associated with LBOs. This result was contradicted by another study by Travlos and Cornett.[54] Although their analysis did reveal a decline in the value of bonds and preferred stock following the announcement of going private proposals, the decline they reported was relatively small.

Based on the limited research in this area, we can conclude that there is little support for a large wealth transfer effect. The empirical research indicates that if such an effect exists, it is not very significant. On the other hand, the reality of the Nabisco transaction contradicts this conclusion. This seems to imply that these results may not be relevant to very large transactions, such as the Nabisco buyout, in which there is a dramatic change in the bond rating and the financial leverage of the firm. Given the decline in the junk bond market, the supply of such large transactions has been limited. This will reduce the supply of data for additional research on this issue.

PROTECTION FOR BONDHOLDERS

Following the unfavorable federal court decision in the Metropolitan Life Insurance case, bond purchasers began to demand greater protection against the financial losses resulting from "event risk." In response, they received from bond issuers agreements that would allow them to get back their full principal in the event of a buyout that would lower the value of their debt holdings. The covenants are usually triggered by actions such as the purchase of a block of stock by a hostile bidder or other actions such as a management-led buyout. In return for the added protection, bond buyers pay a somewhat higher interest rate that is dependent on the issuer's financial condition. The rate can be structured to vary according to the magnitude of the rating change.

Much of the protection provided by the covenant agreements is in the form of a poison put allowing the bondholders to sell the bonds back to the issuer at an agreed upon price. Before the Nabisco case, poison puts were usually confined to privately held company bonds or new issue junk bonds. After the Nabisco bond downgradings, buyers of higher quality public issues demanded some of the same protection once they saw that their bonds could quickly fall into the same categories as the other higher risk issues. (See Table 7.13 for examples of poison put bond insurance.) Poison puts had also been used as a form of "shark repellent"; companies would issue poison puts as a means of creating a financial obstacle to hostile bidders (see Chapter 5).

---

[54] Travlos and Cornett, "Going Private Buyouts and Determinants of Shareholder Returns."

Table 7.13   EXAMPLES OF POST–NABISCO POISON PUT BOND INSURANCE

Company	Issue Date	Issue Amount (mil $)	Bondholder Gets Principal Back If—
Becton Dickinson	3/13/89	$100	20% of stock bought and ratings downgraded
Federal Express	4/18/89	$100	30% of stock bought and ratings downgraded
Long Island Lighting	4/10/89	$375	Acquired by a government body
RJR Nabisco	5/12/89	$4,110	KKR's state reduced to less than 40%
Vons Companies	4/25/89	$100	50% stock bought and ratings downgraded

Source: "Investors Are Developing a Taste for This Poison," Business Week, July 10, 1989, p. 78. Reprinted from July 10, 1989 issue of Business Week by special permission, copyright © 1989 by McGraw-Hill, Inc.

SUMMARY

A leveraged buyout is a financing technique in which the equity of a usually public corporation is purchased mostly with debt. Following the purchase, the public company is taken private. The 1980s witnessed the large-scale development of this technique and the widespread participation in the financing of LBOs by many groups of institutional investors. The deals grew larger and larger and were structured by many different layers of secured and unsecured debt as well as equity. LBOs were first known as asset-based lending deals that usually involved firms with significant fixed assets and much unused borrowing capacity. As the major LBO deal makers heavily promoted the financing technique in the 1980s, cash flow LBOs of firms that did not have significant assets to be used as collateral but had sizable and steady cash flows became popular. Stockholders of firms that were taken private reaped large gains, but some of these gains came at the expense of the firms' debtholders who saw the value of the debt they held in their now heavily leveraged firm decline dramatically.

Concerns about the potentially damaging effects of LBOs have surfaced at the congressional level where the Senate Finance Committee, as well as the House Ways and Means Committee, agreed to take up the issue of the effects of leveraged buyouts on the U.S. economy. Some of this criticism has focused on the fact that, because of the tax deductibility of interest payments, the government is, in effect, subsidizing the cost of LBOs. As a result, some analysts have called for an elimination of the tax deductibility of interest payments associated with LBOs as well as an elimination of the tax deductibility of junk bond interest payments for junk bonds used in mergers and acquisitions and LBOs. This issue has been discussed for some time at the congressional level. While the debate has at times appeared to result in new reform legislation, such reforms have yet to occur. The decline in the junk bond market at the end of the 1980s reduced some of the need for major reforms since market conditions dramatically slowed the pace of LBO deals.

As of the start of the 1990s, large-scale failures of LBOs such as those which took place in the 1980s have not occurred. There have been a few outright failures, and several other cases of failures were prevented by major debt restructuring. Critics of LBOs contend that the stage is set for a series of LBO failures. The pace of LBOs heated up in the mid-1980s when the U.S. economy was doing well. These critics feel that a true test for these highly leveraged firms will come if the economy slows down. In a slower economy, sales and cash flows of many companies will decline. When highly leveraged firms experience this reduction in their revenues, some may be forced into bankruptcy. If such an economic decline does not occur in the early 1990s, most of the firms that went private in the late 1980s will have paid off much of their debt and will be less vulnerable to a cyclical downturn.

REFERENCES

Anderson, Gary B. "Defining the Board Game." In Stephen C. Diamond, ed., *Leveraged Buyouts*. Homewood, Ill.: Dow Jones Irwin, 1985, pp. 11–39.

"Banks Sales of Buyout Debt Rising." *New York Times*, December 18, 1989, p. D1.

Blasi, Joseph. *Employee Ownership*. Cambridge, Mass.: Ballinger Publishing Co., 1988, p. 70.

Borden, Arthur M. *Going Private*. New York: Law Journal Seminar Press, 1987, pp. 1–6.

Brancato, Carolyn, and Kevin Winch. "Merger Activity and Leveraged Buyouts: Sound Corporate Restructuring or Wall Street Alchemy." Report Prepared for the Committee on Energy and Commerce, U.S. House of Representatives, November 1984, pp. 18–21.

Brancato, Carolyn, and Kevin Winch. "Leveraged Buyouts and the Pot of Gold: Trends, Public Policy, and Case Studies." Congressional Research Service, Library of Congress, September 15, 1987.

Brigham, Eugene F., and Louis C. Gapinski. *Intermediate Financial Management*. 2nd ed. Chicago: Dryden Press, 1987, pp. 650–682.

Brudney, Victor, and Marvin A. Chirelstein. "A Restatement of Corporate Freezeouts." *Yale Law Journal* 87 (June 1978):1136–1137.

Bull, Ivan. "Management Performance in Leveraged Buyouts." Paper presented at the New York University Conference on Management Buyouts, May 20, 1988.

Burrough, Bryan, and John Helyar. *Barbarians at the Gate: The Fall of RJR Nabisco*. New York: Harper & Row, 1988.

Business Week. "Takeovers and Buyouts Clobber Blue Chip Bondholders." November 11, 1985, pp. 113–114.

Business Week. "Bondholders Are As Mad As Hell—And No Wonder." December 5, 1988, p. 28.

Business Week. "Investors Are Developing a Taste for This Poison." July 10, 1989, p. 78.

Caronia, Leonard. "Seeking Financing: The Unsecured Leveraged Buyout." In Stephen Diamond, ed., *Leveraged Buyouts*. Homewood, Ill.: Dow Jones Irwin, 1985, pp. 58–70.

Dabney, Michael R. "Asset Based Financing." In Milton Rock, ed., *Mergers and Acquisitions*. New York: McGraw-Hill, 1987, pp. 393–399.

DeAngelo, Harry, Linda DeAngelo, and Edward Rice. "Going Private: Minority Freezeouts and Stockholder Wealth." *Journal of Law and Economics* (October 1984):367–402.

Diamond, Stephen C., ed. *Leveraged Buyouts*. Homewood, Ill.: Dow Jones Irwin, 1985.

Ernst & Whinney. *Management Buyouts*. 1979.

Fama, Eugene. "Agency Problems and the Theory of the Firm." *Journal of Political Economy* (April 1980):288–307.

Fama, Eugene, and Michael Jensen. "Separation of Ownership Control." *Journal of Law and Economics* 26 (1983):323–329.

Frisch, Robert A. *The Magic of ESOP's and LBO's*. New York: Farnsworth Publishing, 1985, p. 12.

Gargiulo, Albert F., and Steven J. Levine. *The Leveraged Buyout*. New York: American Management Association, 1982.

Graham, Benjamin. *The Interpretation of Financial Statements*. New York: Harper & Row, 1987, p. 17.

Greve, J. Terrance. "Management Buyouts and LBO's." In Milton Rock, ed., *Mergers and Acquisitions*. New York: McGraw-Hill, 1987, pp. 345–355.

Hite, Gailen L., and Michael R. Vetsuypens. "Management Buyouts of Divisions and Stockholder Wealth." *Journal of Finance* 44, (September 1989):953–970.

Industry Norms and Key Business Ratios. Murray Hill, N.J.: Dun & Bradstreet.

Jensen, Michael, and William Meckling. "Theory of the Firm: Mangerial Behavior, Agency Costs and Ownership Structure." *Journal of Financial Economics* 3 (October 1976):305–360.

Kaplan, Steven. "Management Buyouts: Efficiency Gains or Value Transfers." University of Chicago Working Paper No. 244. October 1988.

Kaplan, Steven. "Management Buyouts: Evidence on Taxes As a Source of Value." University of Chicago Working Paper No. 245, September 1988.

Kaplan, Steven. "A Summary of Sources of Value in Management Buyouts." Paper presented at the New York University Conference on Management Buyouts, May 20, 1988.

Kolb, Robert W. *Principles of Finance*. Glenview, Ill.: Scott, Foresman and Co., 1988, Chapter 15, pp. 466–511.

Lehn, K., and A. Poulson. "Sources of Value in Corporate Going Private Transactions." University of Washington Working Paper, February 1987.

Lichtenberg, Frank, and Donald Siegel. "The Effects of Takeovers on Employment and Wages of Central Office and Other Personnel," Columbia Graduate School Working Paper No. FB-89-05, 1989.

Long, William F., and David J. Ravenscraft. "The Record of LBO Performance." Paper presented at the New York University Conference on Corporate Governance, May 17, 1989.

Lowenstein, Louis. *What's Wrong with Wall Street*. Reading, Mass.: Addison-Wesley, 1988, pp. 183–184.

Marais, L., K. Schipper, and A. Smith. "Wealth Effects of Going Private on Senior Securities." Working Paper, University of Chicago, June 1988.

Moyer, R. Charles, James R. McGuigan, and William Kretlow. *Contemporary Financial Management*. 3rd ed. St. Paul: West Publishing Co., 1987, pp. 156–204.

Mueller, Dennis. "A Theory of Conglomerate Mergers." *Quarterly Journal of Economics* 83 (1969): 643–659.

Muscarella, Chris J., and Michael R. Vesuypens. "Efficiency and Organizational Structure: A Study of Reverse LBOs." *Journal of Finance*, 45, no. 5 (December 1990): 1389–1414.

National Science Foundation. "An Assessment of the Impact of Recent Leveraged Buyouts and Other Restructurings on Industrial Research and Development Expenditures." Prepared for the House of Representatives Committee on Energy and Commerce, 1989.

"Perils of Leveraged Buyouts: Large Loans Worry Banks." *New York Times*, May 14, 1984.

Prentice-Hall's Almanac of Business and Financial Ratios. Englewood Cliffs, N.J.: Prentice-Hall Publishing Co., 1989.

"Presentation on Leveraged Buyouts." Kohlberg, Kravis, & Roberts, January 1989.

Rohatyn, Felix G. "On a Buyout Binge and a Takeover Tear." *Wall Street Journal*, May 18, 1984.

Schuchert, Joseph S. "The Art of the ESOP Leveraged Buyout." In Stephen C. Diamond, ed., *Leveraged Buyouts*. Homewood, Ill.: Dow Jones Irwin, 1985, p. 94.

Shleifer, Andrei, and Robert W. Vishny. "Management's Buyouts As a Response to Market Pressure." *Mergers and Acquisitions*. Chicago: University of Chicago Press, 1988, pp. 87–103.

Travlos, Nicholas, and M. M. Cornett. "Going Private Buyouts and Determinants of Shareholder Returns." *Journal of Auditing and Finance*, 1990.

Waite, S., and M. Fridson, "The Credit Quality of Leveraged Buyouts," *High Performance*, Morgan Stanley, January, 1989, New York.

Chapter
8

Junk Bonds

*T*he junk bond market and the use of junk bonds as a financing tool for mergers and acquisitions and leveraged buyouts represent one of the most influential innovations in the field. The availability of very large amounts of capital through the junk bond market made possible the participation of many who would never have considered participating otherwise. The access to such large amounts of capital also made even the largest and most established firms potentially vulnerable to a takeover by much smaller suitors. The collapse of the junk bond market in the late 1980s was one of the main features responsible for the slowdown in the pace of mergers in the fourth merger wave.

HISTORY OF JUNK BONDS

Contrary to popular belief, junk bonds are not a recent innovation. Junk bonds, or high-yield bonds, as many of their proponents would prefer to have them called, have been around for decades. What is new is that takeover specialists helped pioneer their use as a financing source for mergers and LBOs.

One reason why many people think they are an innovation is that these bonds have had many different names in the past. They went under the name of low-grade bonds for decades. In the 1930s and 1940s, many of them were called "Fallen Angels." In the 1960s, some of the lower grade debt that was issued to help finance conglomerate acquisitions were referred to as "Chinese Paper." Financier Meshulam Riklis, CEO of Rapid American Corporation, states that the term *junk bonds* first originated in a conversation he had with Michael Milken, the former head of Drexel Burnham Lambert's junk bond operation. Riklis claims that when Milken surveyed some of the bonds that Riklis had issued, he exclaimed: "Rik, these are junk!"[1]

In the 1920s and 1930s, approximately 17 percent of all new corporate bond offerings were low-grade/high-yield bonds. A broader range of firms used these securities to finance their growth. The ranks of the high-yield bonds swelled during the 1930s as the Great Depression took its toll on many of America's companies. In 1928, 13 percent of all outstanding corporate bonds were low grade; in 1940, this percentage had risen to 42 percent.[2] Many of the bonds had entered the low-grade class through downgradings from rating agencies. (The rating process is discussed later in this chapter.) As the economy fell deeper and deeper into the depression and firms suffered the impact of declining demand for their goods and services, their ability to service the payments on their outstanding bonds was called into question. This led to a downgrading of the debt. As the overall level of economic demand fell, the revenues of some firms declined so much that they could no longer service the interest and principal payments on the outstanding bonds. As a result, the default rate on these bonds rose to 10 percent. Investors became disappointed by the rising default rate in a category of securities that they felt was generally low risk. Investors were previously attracted to the bond market by investment characteristics such as dependability of income coupled with low risk of default. As the risk of default rose, low-grade bonds became quite unpopular.

By the 1940s, the low-grade bond market started to decline as old issues were retired or the issuing corporations entered into some form of bankruptcy. The declining popularity of the low-grade bond market made new issues difficult to market. Between 1944 and 1965, high-yield bonds accounted for only 6.5 percent of total corporate bond issues. This percentage declined even further as the 1970s began; by the beginning of the decade, only 4 percent of all corporate bonds were low grade.

The low-grade/high-yield bond market's declining popularity preempted access to one form of debt financing to certain groups of borrowers. Many corporations that would have preferred to issue long-term bonds were now forced to borrow from banks in the form of term loans that were generally of shorter maturity than 20- and 30-year

---

[1] Connie Bruck, *The Predators Ball* (New York: Simon & Schuster, 1988), p. 39.

[2] Kevin J. Perry, "The Growing Role of Junk Bonds," *Journal of Applied Corporate Finance* 1, no. 1 (Spring 1988):37–45.

corporate bonds. Those that could not borrow on acceptable terms from a bank were forced to forsake expansion or to issue more equity, which had the adverse effect of diluting the shares of ownership for outstanding equity holders. In addition, the rate of return on equity is generally higher than debt. Therefore, equity is a more costly source of capital.

The high-yield/low-grade market began to change in the late 1970s. Lehman Brothers, an investment bank that was itself acquired in the 1980s by Shearson, underwrote a series of *new* issues of high-yield corporate debt. These bonds were offered by LTV ($75 million), Zapata Corporation ($75 million), Fuqua Industries ($60 million), and Pan American World Airways ($53 million).[3] This was followed by the entrance of a relatively smaller investment bank, Drexel Burnham Lambert, which started to underwrite issues of low-grade/high-yield debt on a larger scale. Drexel Burnham Lambert's role in the development was the key to the growth of the low-grade/high-yield bond market. Its role as a market maker for junk bonds, as they had began to be called, was crucial to the dramatic growth of the market.

By 1982, junk bond issuance had grown to $2.8 billion per year, accounting for 6 percent of all corporate bond issues. By 1985, this total had risen to $15 billion or 15 percent of total issues. In the first half of 1986 alone, this total had risen to $16 billion.

Why the Junk Bond Market Grew

The junk bond market experienced dramatic and rapid growth for several reasons, none of which by itself accounted for the precipitous increase that this market experienced. Some of these factors are as follows:

1. *Private placed bonds*—bonds that are sold not publicly but to a small group of investors—had become less popular. In such private sales the investment banker serves as an intermediary rather than as an underwriter, which is a riskier role. There were two reasons for this declining popularity. First, restrictive covenants associated with the indenture contract placed uncomfortable restrictions on the issuing firm. The *indenture contract* is the agreement between the bond issuer and the bond purchasers. *Restrictive covenants* are those restrictions that the purchasers require from the issuer before they purchase the securities. These restrictions limit the actions that the issuing firm can take in the course of its business activities. The restrictions

---

[3] Ibid., p. 44.

are designed to lower the risk to the lender. An example of such restrictions would be a limitation on the additional debt the firm could assume in the future.

Second, there was no standardization in the contracts for the bonds, thereby making sales in a secondary market more difficult. Buyers have to investigate the terms of each contract more carefully before purchasing, an additional time cost that many investors believe is not worth the added return. The lack of standardization meant that this market had limited liquidity which is an added element or risk that makes privately placed low-grade/high-yield bonds more difficult to market. The declining popularity of the privately placed market for low-grade/high-yield bonds created an opportunity for public issues of these bonds. This opportunity was not lost on investment bankers like Drexel Burnham Lambert.

2. A major factor leading to the growth of this market was the existence of an active market maker—a person who serves as an agent of liquidity in facilitating sales between buyers and sellers. Drexel Burnham Lambert was a very active market maker in the junk bond market. Rather than have an issue lose its marketability by not having buyers in times when the issuing firm is experiencing more difficulty, Drexel had been known to become a buyer of last resort. It had also been known to provide financial assistance in the form of refinancing when an issuer appears on the verge of default. This assistance, of course, comes at a price such as an equity interest in the issuing firm. Drexel's growth in the 1980s was attributable largely to its involvement in the junk bond market. Therefore, the firm went to great lengths to ensure the growth and vitality of the market.

3. Another factor has been the changing risk perceptions of investors toward junk bonds. Investors began to believe that the risks associated with junk bond investments were less than what they once believed. The altered risk perceptions came as a result of active promotion of this financing vehicle by interested parties such as Drexel Burnham Lambert and through academic research. Certain research studies examined the riskiness of junk bonds and reported that the risk of default was far less than what was popularly believed. Some of these findings would later be refuted by other studies.

4. Yet another factor was the expansion of the whole field of mergers and acquisitions. As the targets of mergers and acquisitions as well as leveraged buyouts became increasingly larger, the demand for capital to fund these purchases grew. Investors increas-

ingly relied on the junk bond market to provide a large part of this funding.

RATING SYSTEM FOR BONDS

A rating system for bonds was first published by John Moody in 1909. Since then, several services have also published ratings, the more well-known being Standard and Poor's and Moody's. Ratings are also provided by Fitch Investors Service and Duff and Phelps. In addition to bonds, ratings of other types of securities like preferred stock are also published. Ratings provide a gauge whereby an investor can judge the degree of default risk associated with the bond. Default risk refers to the likelihood that the issuer will not pay the periodic interest or principal payments. A breakdown of the ratings offered by the ratings services is provided in Table 8.1.

The investment community widely accepts the idea that ratings are

Table 8.1 MEANING OF BOND RATINGS

Moody's Rating	S & P Rating	Interpretation
Aaa	AAA	Highest rating. Extremely strong ability to pay interest and principal.
Aa	AA	Almost as high quality as the triple A firms. Strong capacity to pay interest and principal.
A	A	Good capacity to pay interest and principal. These bonds possess many favorable attributes but may be susceptible to economic downturns.
Baa	BBB	Interest and principal protection is adequate, but adverse economic conditions could weaken ability to pay interest and principal.
Ba	BB	Only moderate protection for principal and interest payments in good economic conditions and even worse in economic downturns.
B	B	Limited long-term assurance of principal and interest payments. Default risk is considered moderate.
Caa	CCC	High default risk. These bonds may be currently near default.
Ca	CC	These bonds are considered highly speculative investments. They are often already in default.
C		This is Moody's lowest rating. This rating is generally given to bonds that are paying no interest.
	C	S & P generally gives this rating when the issuer is in bankruptcy but is making interest payments on the issue.
	D	These bonds are in default. The interest or principal payments, or both, are in arrears.

Source: Standard & Poor's *Bond Guide* and Moody's *Bond Record,* Moody's Investor's Service.

a useful predictor of default risk. This concept originated in a well-known study by W. B. Hickman entitled *Corporate Bond Quality and Investor Experience* (1958) and showed that a significantly higher rate of default occurred among those securities that received lower quality ratings. The Hickman study used nine rating categories. Table 8.2 shows the comparable Standard and Poor's ratings using five categories.

Determinants of Bond Ratings

Bond rating agencies examine a broad range of information when they are preparing a rating for a firm, especially financial ratios. (In August 1990 Moody's acknowledged the market's concern about the quality of junk bonds by forming a separate unit within its industrials group to focus on the day-to-day analysis of junk bond companies. See "Moodys Establishes Unit for Junk Bond Companies," *New York Times*, August 16, 1990, p. D16.) A set of financial ratios are generally used which give the analyst an overall picture of the risk of default for the issuer of the bonds. These ratios are described in detail in Chapter 13. Some of the more important ratios used in ratings are concerned with the ability of the firm's income to cover the interest charges associated with the bonds. The higher the income relative to the interest and other fixed charges, the greater the security for the lender.

A simple interest coverage ratio might be:

$$\text{Interest coverage} = \frac{\text{Earnings before interest and taxes}}{\text{Interest charges on the bonds}}$$

If earnings are $100 million and interest charges are $20 million, then this gives us an interest coverage ratio of five times. The higher this ratio, the greater the probability that a higher rating will be given. As noted in Chapter 13, broader ratios can provide a fuller picture of

Table 8.2   BOND RATINGS AND DEFAULT

Rating Category	Comparable S&P Rating	Percent of Par Value Defaulting Prior to Maturity
I	AAA	6.0
II	AA	6.0
III	A	13.0
IV	BBB	19.0
V–IX	Below BBB	42.0

Sources: Robert C. Radcliffe, *Investments* (Glenview, Ill.: Scott, Foresman & Co., 1982), p. 384; W. B. Hickman, *Corporate Bond Quality and Investor Experience* (Princeton, N.J.: Princeton University Press, 1958).

the firm's ability to meet its mixed charges. The other ratios that could be used include:

Fixed charges coverage ratio* =

$$\frac{\text{Earnings before interest and taxes} + \text{lease payments}}{\text{Interest charges} + \text{lease payments} + \text{dividend}}$$
$$\text{payments} + \text{sinking fund payments}$$

Cash flow coverage ratio =

$$\frac{\text{Cash inflows}}{\text{Fixed charges} + \dfrac{\text{Preferred stock dividends}}{(1-t)} + \dfrac{\text{Debt repayments}}{(1-t)}}$$

The relationship between cash flow and total debt is a basic consideration in evaluating default risk. The greater the cash flow, the less likely the firm will default on its interest payments (Figure 8.1). A study by William Beaver on the use of financial ratios to predict default showed a very good predictive relationship between cash flow relative to debt and the probability of default.[4]

Consistency of Ratings

The consistency of bond ratings among the different rating services is a reliable indicator of default risk. If, for example, the two major rating services, Standard and Poor's and Moody's, were to give consistently different ratings for the same bonds, confusion would reign as to which service was the most reliable. Fortunately, this does not occur very often, and when it does, the difference often tends to be insignificant.

When the same bond receives a different rating from two rating agencies, it is referred to as a *split rating*. This would be the case if, for example, Moody's gave a particular corporate bond an AA rating while Standard and Poor's gave it an A rating. "Louis Brand, former head of Standard and Poors' bond department, indicates that the two agencies disagreed on about 1 in 20 utility bonds and 1 in 10 industrial bonds."[5] It would be most unlikely, however, for one service to give a radically different rating from that of another service. Services tend to

---

* Some components of this ratio, such as lease payments, may be expressed on a pretax basis by dividing by $(1 - t)$.

[4] William H. Beaver, "Financial Ratios As Predictors of Failure," *Empirical Research in Accounting, Selected Studies* (Chicago: Graduate School of Business, University of Chicago, 1966), pp. 71–127.

[5] H. C. Sherwood, "How They Rate Your Company's Bonds," *Business Management* 29 (March 1966):38–42.

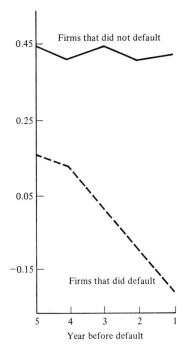

Figure 8.1 Ratio of cash flows to total debt. (*Source:* William H. Beaver, "Financial Ratios as Predictors of Failure," *Empirical Research in Accounting, Selected Studies* (Graduate School of Business, University of Chicago, 1966), pp. 71–127.

be consistent in their ratings because they use the same financial information and apply similar financial analysis techniques.

Triple A Rating

As of 1988, only 13 U.S. corporations had bonds earning a triple A rating. This group includes some of the larger corporations, with assets of $250 billion, a total market capitalization of $295 billion, and total annual earnings of $20 billion. These firms, grouped by industry, are as follows.[6]

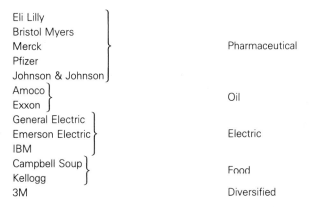

――――――――

[6] Corporate Finance Magazine data.

CASE STUDY: *W. T. GRANT'S: AN EXAMPLE OF THE PREDICTIVE POWER OF FINANCIAL RATIOS*

An example of how financial ratios can be used to predict default is the bankruptcy of W. T. Grant's, a large retail chain more commonly known as a 5 & 10 cent store. Quite popular at one time, these stores have been superseded in the retail world by more modern retail chains such as Wallmart and K-Mart. At its peak, W. T. Grant's had over 1,000 stores throughout the United States. Figure 8.2 traces the pattern of financial performance ratios from a steady dcline in the mid-1960s through October 1975 when the firm went bankrupt. Profitability ratios, such as the return on stockholders' equity and the return on assets, consistently declined until they began a precipitous drop in 1973. Activity ratios such as the inventory turnover, accounts receivable turnover, and the total assets turnover ratio also showed a downslide, indicating that the firm was losing its ability to move its inventory. W. T. Grant's liquidity decreased, indicating that its current liabilities were increasing faster than its current assets. The firm tried to take on debt to survive, as shown by

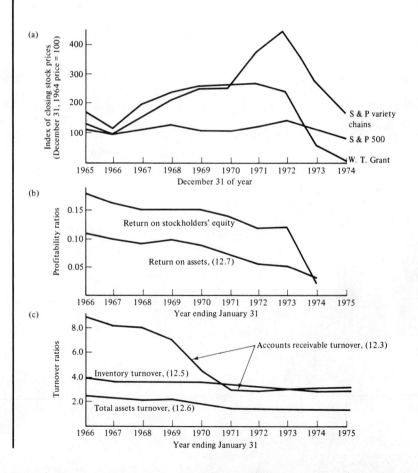

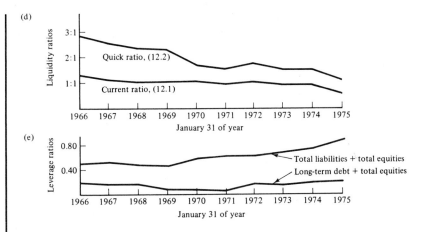

Figure 8.2 W. T. Grant's financial ratios. [*Source:* James A. Langay, III and Clyde P. Stickney, "Cashflows, Ratio Analysis and the W.T. Grant Company Bankruptcy," *Financial Analysts Journal* (July–August 1980): 52, exhibit 1.)]

the rise in the ratio of total liabilities to total equity or the ratio of long-term debt to total equity.

In the case of W. T. Grant's, the financial ratios provided a useful indication of the company's deteriorating financial condition. It, therefore, should have come as no surprise to stockholders and bondholders when the firm defaulted on its obligations. The market perceived the company's declining financial condition as reflected in the declining trend of its stock price. The price of W. T. Grant stock fell significantly more than the decline in the market as a whole or the other firms in that industry.[a]

[a] "Cashflows, Ratio Analysis and the W. T. Grant Bankruptcy," *Financial Analysts Journal* (July-August 1980):52. Jack Clark Francis, *Investments* (New York: McGraw-Hill, 1986), p. 334.

The triple A-rated corporation seems to be a dying species in corporate America. In 1981, there were 18 such firms compared to 13 by 1988. Many of the firms voluntarily fell out of the triple A group by 1988 because they were no longer willing to pay the price of achieving this rating: a lower amount of debt than it considered desirable. By having a lower amount of debt, firms cannot take advantage of the fact that debt has a lower cost than equity capital. In part, debt has lower cost because the interest payments on it are tax deductible, whereas dividends are not tax deductible. When a firm increases its leverage, its rate of return on equity often rises.

Another disadvantage of the higher rating is that the costs they incur are not worth the benefits. An A rating, for example, may mean the firm has to pay 25 basis points (¼ of 1 percent) more in interest for a bond issue than the lower rated firm. The firm may feel that paying 12½ percent as opposed to 12¼ percent is not a great price to pay to have access to a certain amount of debt capital, which it can then put to use to earn an even higher return for the corporation. For $200 million over 20 years, the added interest costs amount to $500,000 per year before taxes. Based on a 50 percent tax bracket, the undiscounted, after-tax cost of this lower rating is $250,000 per year. These costs may not seem so high for Fortune 500 firms if they can be assured that the returns from the investment of this debt capital will outweigh these costs.

In recent years the trend in the debt to total capital ratios for firms in the double A and single A category has been upward, which apparently shows that firms are taking advantage of investment opportunities for debt capital (see Table 8.3).

It would be short-sighted to conclude that all triple A firms are captives of a conservative, unimaginative financial management unwilling to have enough debt in their capital structure. Many triple A firms do not have to rely on external capital because their internal cash flows are extremely large. Pharmaceutical firms tend to be good examples. Many triple A firms have found ways other than the tax deductibility of interest payments on debt to lower their taxes and do not pay high taxes.

ZETA: A CREDIT EVALUATION ALTERNATIVE TO BOND RATINGS

The Zeta credit evaluation tool or the Altman Z, so-named after one of its developers, was developed in the late 1970s.[7] It utilizes a statistical technique known as discriminant analysis, a multivariate technique similar to regression analysis.[8] In this type of application, it allows the user to rate the bankruptcy risk of a corporation as a function of several indicator variables such as financial ratios. The relationship can be expressed as follows:

$$\text{Zeta} = a_0 + a_1X_1 + a_2X_2 + \cdots + a_6X_6 \qquad (8.1)$$

---

[7] Edward Altman, R. Haldeman, and P. Narayanan, "Zeta Analysis: A Model to Identify Bankruptcy Risk of Corporations," *Journal of Banking and Finance* (June 1977).

[8] Edward I. Altman, "Financial Ratios, Discriminant Analysis and the Prediction of Corporate Bankruptcy," *Journal of Finance* 23 (September 1968); 568–609.

Table 8.3   TRENDS IN DEBT/CAPITAL RATIOS,
            1973 AND 1988 (PERCENT)

Rating	1973	1988
Triple A	21.4	20.3
Double A	27.0	35.0
Single A	38.0	46.0

Source: Corporate Finance Magazine, New York, 1988.

where: Zeta = a firm's credit score
         X_1 = a profitability measure such as operating profits (earnings before interest and taxes)
         X_2 = stability of earnings measure (standard deviation of earnings)
         X_3 = ability to service debt measure such as times interest earned or fixed charge coverage ratio
         X_4 = working capital measure to reflect liquidity
         X_5 = cumulative retained earnings to total assets
         X_6 = market value of equity to the book value of total liabilities which will reflect financial leverage
    $a_1 \cdots a_n$ = coefficients or weights for each indicator variable

The more the firm is "in distress," the more likely it will receive a lower Zeta. The more creditworthy the company, the more likely it will receive a higher Zeta.

Both the founders of the Zeta technique and Zeta's marketers, Zeta Services, Inc., in Hoboken, New Jersey, claim a high degree of accuracy for the tool in predicting which firms may fall into bankruptcy. According to Altman and Namacher, 96 percent of bankrupt firms got a negative Zeta score one annual statement prior to bankruptcy, whereas 70 percent of bankrupt firms received a negative Zeta score five annual statements prior to bankruptcy.[9]

An evaluation of junk bonds reveals a good correlation between Zeta scores and the Standard & Poor's and Moody's bond ratings. Figure 8.3 shows that bonds rated BB received a Zeta rating between 1.75 and 1 between 1978 and 1985. Bonds with ratings below BB consistently received a negative Zeta rating. In contrast, the average single A company received a 5.6 Zeta score during the same time period.

---

[9] Edward Altman and Scott Namacher, *Investing in Junk Bonds* (New York: John Wiley & Sons, 1987), p. 148.

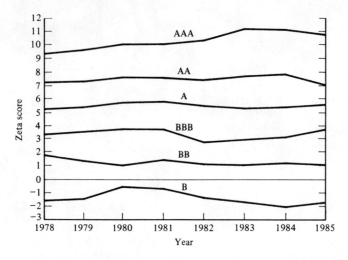

Figure 8.3 Zeta score vesus time. [*Source:* Edward Altman and Scott Namacher, *Investing in Junk Bonds* (New York: John Wiley & Sons, Inc., 1987.)]

THE DEFAULT RISK OF JUNK BONDS

Until the late 1970s, conservative investors saw no place for junk bonds in their portfolios, maintaining that the default risk of these bonds was too high. A major study by Edward I. Altman and Scott A. Namacher changed that thinking among investment banks and brokerage firms. Their comprehensive study provided evidence that the default rates of low-rated firms were much lower than was believed (Table 8.4).[10]

The Altman–Namacher study showed that the average default rate for junk bonds was 2.1 percent, which was not significantly higher than the default rate on investment grade securities which was almost 0 percent. On an annual basis the default rate has been declining, as shown in the following figures.

1970–1984	2.1%
1974–1984	2.0%
1978–1984	1.8%

Altman and Namacher also analyzed the number of firms that were originally given high ratings but that subsequently defaulted. Of the 112 issues they examined, only 8 percent (9 of the 112 issues) were originally rated A. Over 30 percent (34), however, were originally rated investment grade. This shows that a firm can achieve a high investment

---

[10] Edward I. Altman and Scott A. Namacher, "The Default Rate Experience on High Yield Corporate Debt" (New York: Morgan Stanley & Co., 1985).

Table 8.4   PERCENTAGE OF LOW-RATED FIRMS IN DEFAULT, 1970–1984

Year	Number of Low-Rated Firms	Number of Firms in Default	Percent in Default
1970	145	5	3.4
1971	150	1	0.7
1972	160	2	1.2
1973	180	3	1.7
1974	190	5	2.6
1975	190	4	2.1
1976	195	2	1.0
1977	185	8	4.3
1978	190	2	1.0
1979	230	1	0.1
1980	255	3	1.2
1981	280	2	0.7
1982	270	12	4.4
1983	305	9	2.9
1984	335	6	1.8

Source: Edward I. Altman and Scott A. Namacher, "The Default Rate Experience on High Yield Corporate Debt" (New York: Morgan Stanley & Co., 1985).

rating and later fall into bankruptcy. At first, this finding would seem to imply that the ratings are not a valuable guide to the future performance of the bonds. As Altman and Namacher point out, however, a trail of declining ratings usually precedes the point of default.

Altman and Namacher's default figures are consistent with those reported in previous studies. Fitzpatrick and Severiens, for example, showed that the default rate on BB/Ba and B rated bonds for the period 1965–1975 was 0.8 percent.[11] Another study, using a somewhat different methodology, by Fridson and Monaghan found a 1.07 percent default rate for a similar time period.[12]

Table 8.5 reveals that, as the time of default approaches, the rating declines. "We observe that 13 or 130 (10.0) were rated investment grade one year prior to default while only 4 out of 130 (3.0%) just six months prior to default."[13] This implies that the bond rating can be used as a reliable indicator of the likelihood of default.

---

[11] J. D. Fitzpatrick and J. T. Severiens, "Hickman Revisited: The Case for Junk Bonds," New York, Saloman Brothers, March 1984.

[12] Martin Fridson and Monaghan, "Default Experience of Corporate Bonds," New York, Saloman Brothers, March 1984.

[13] Altman and Namacher, "The Default Rate Experience on High Yield Corproate Debt."

In recent decades large bankruptcies have affected the junk bond market. For example, Penn Central's bankruptcy had a great impact on the 3.4 percent default rate for low-grade bonds in 1970. More recently, LTV's bankruptcy on June 17, 1986, had a profound impact on the bond market as a whole and the junk bond market in particular. LTV, the giant steel and oil firm, was the largest industrial corporation to declare bankruptcy. It was also one of the largest issuers of junk bonds at the time it filed Chapter 11. Not surprisingly, in response, LTV bonds fell 50 percent in value. The impact of the LTV bankruptcy on the junk bond market is discussed later in this chapter.

Criticism of the Altman–Namacher Methodology

The Altman–Namacher study had been one of the dominant pieces of research on the default risk of junk bonds. Their results, as well as those of other studies,[14] imply that the marketplace is inefficient and pays a return in excess of the risk on these securities. (The return on junk bonds is discussed later in this chapter.) Their methodology is subject to a number of criticisms, however. First, the results are biased in that the junk bond market was growing very rapidly during the time period in which their data were gathered, and the defaults were calculated based on the ratio of the number of defaults in a given year divided by the par value of junk bonds outstanding.

$$\text{Altman's default rate} = \frac{\text{Number of defaults in a given year}}{\text{Par value of junk bonds outstanding}}$$

The riskiness of a junk bond generally does not materialize until the junk bond has been on the market for several years. The firm is generally not going to default in the years immediately following the issuance. After several years, however, the risk factors affecting these junk bond issuers may take their toll, and some may default. The impact of these defaults may not be noticed in the Altman index because the junk bond market was growing so rapidly. During the 1980s, the denominator was growing more rapidly than the numerator! When the growth of the junk bond market slows and some of the firms with greater risk begin to default, the Altman index should rise significantly.

Another criticism of the Altman–Namacher study is that it does not follow junk bonds over the course of their lifetime. It does not, for example, take a group of junk bonds that were issued in a given year

---

[14] Mark I. Weinstein, "A Curmudgeon View of Junk Bonds," *Journal of Portfolio Management* (Spring 1987):76–80.

and trace the number of defaults year after year. It merely aggregates new and old issues together. It is the older issues, however, that have the higher degree of default risk and are a greater course of concern to investors.

Yet another criticism of the Altman–Namacher study is one that permeates much of scientific research. Morgan Stanley, the investment bank that financed the Altman and Namacher study, has a vested interest in the growth of the junk bond market. When the findings of a research study are found to support the funding entity's position, additional care must be taken to ensure the accuracy of the study and to rule out bias. There is no evidence, however, that the Altman study was biased as a result of this factor.

The Asquith, Mullins, and Wolff Study

Many of the purported shortcomings of the Altman–Namacher study have been rectified by the Asquith study.[15] Asquith considered the aging effect of junk bonds; he and his co-researchers followed the junk bonds that were issued in 1977 and 1978 until 1988. In doing so, they offset the effect of the rapidly growing junk bond market that pervaded the Altman–Namacher study.

Exchanges   The Asquith study also factored in the impact of exchanges on the default of junk bonds. When firms are in danger of defaulting, the creditors (including the junk bondholders) often engage in a voluntary reorganization agreement. Drexel Burnham Lambert was particularly skillful in this area. Through these agreements, new securities can be issued. These exchanges may involve the issuance of new bonds which have lower coupon payments, or they may involve the retirement of the original issue of junk bonds in exchange for a new combination of bonds and stocks. In extreme cases, where the firm's cash flows are very limited, the bonds are exchanged for common stock which carry no guarantee of regular dividend payments. When bondholders agree to such an exchange in advance of a formal default or declaration of bankruptcy, then these securities are not normally counted in bond default statistics.

Calls   Investors in junk bonds experience an additional element of call-related risks. Many firms that issued junk bonds with relatively

---

[15] Paul Asquith, David Mullins, and Eric Wolff, "Original Issue High Yield Bonds: Aging Analysis of Defaults, Exchanges and Call," Unpublished Harvard University Working Paper, March 1989.

higher interest rates took advantage of the decline in interest rates after they were issued. Many junk bonds have call protection for a limited period of time; during that period of time the bonds can't be called in. At the end of that period, the bonds may be called in, as a result of which the bondholders may be deprived of a rate of return superior to other rates available in the market.

Asquith and his co-workers reported that 23 to 43 percent of the bonds issued during 1977–1982 were called by November 1, 1988. These calls were a result of the decline in interest rates that started in 1982.

Defaults The Asquith study defined defaults to be either a declaration of default by the bond trustee, a bankruptcy filing by the issuer, or the assignment of a D rating by Standard and Poor's. If the bonds were exchanged for other securities that eventually defaulted, this too was considered a default of the original issue. This study showed that, as expected, default rates were higher for "older" issues. "An investor who bought and held all high yield bonds issued in 1977 and 1978 would experience by November 1, 1988 a cumulative default rate in excess of 34%."[16] (See Figure 8.4.)

Defaults and Aging The Asquith study also measured the relationship between defaults and aging. As noted above, it showed that default rates were low in the early years following the issuance of a junk bond.

> In fact for 7 of the 10 issue years, there are no defaults in the first year after issue and for four of the issue years there are no defaults in the first two years. Cumulative default rates three years after issue range from 0%–8%, with the majority in the 3%–6% range. Seven years after issue, cumulative default rates rise to 18%–26% for the issue years 1978–1982 although no 1977 issues had defaulted seven years after issue. Eleven and twelve years after issue date cumulative default rates exceed 34% for the only two relevant years, 1977 and 1978.[17]

The Asquith study raises serious questions regarding the riskiness of junk bonds. It contradicts the Altman and Namacher study, and others, which seem to imply that junk bonds are relatively low risk. It also confirms one's general intuition that the debt obligations of risky firms are a significantly riskier investment than those of investment grade firms. The true test of the difference in the risk levels of these two classes of debt securities may not come until we have a downturn

---

[16] Ibid., p. 11.

[17] Ibid., p. 12.

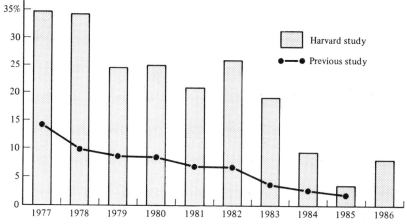

Source: Harvard data copyright 1989 Harvard Gradulate School of Business Administration

Figure 8.4 A new view of junk bond defaults: Harvard default rate equals the dollar amount in default as a percentage of amount issued, grouped by year of issue and cumulated through November 1, 1988. Default rate based on previous study is a cumulative annual default rate calculated from data presented in *Investing in Junk Bonds* by Edward I. Altman and Scott A. Namacher (New York: John Wiley & Sons, Inc., 1987).

in the economy. Both the Altman–Namacher and the Asquith studies were conducted during the longest postwar economic recovery that the U.S. economy has ever experienced. The impact of a mild recession may create a dramatic difference in the default rates of different classes of corporate debt. A recession would take its toll, for example, on the value of the large junk bond issues of department store chains like Allied Stores and Federated Stores, now owned by the Campeau Corporation following two highly leveraged transactions. With the downturn in consumer spending, these chains might not be able to meet their high interest obligations. This was underscored by the 1989 Chapter 11 filing of the Campeau Corporation which collapsed under its mountain of post-buyout junk bonds. The collapse came despite the otherwise sound conditions of many of its component divisions such as Bloomingdale's.

The Goldman Sachs–Barrie Wigmore Study

A more recent study than the Asquith study, one by Barrie Wigmore, a limited partner at the investment bank of Goldman Sachs, exposed further problems in the junk bond market.[18] Although the Asquith

---

[18] Barrie Wigmore, "The Decline in Credit Quality of Junk Bond Issues: 1980–1988," Study conducted by Goldman Sachs, November 7, 1989.

study pointed out the risk effects of junk bond aging, calls, and exchanges, it did not consider changes in the *quality* of bonds that were
being issued as the junk bond market grew. Asquith focused on bonds
that were originally issued in 1977 and 1978. Nonetheless, the consideration of these factors resulted in a high default rate of 34 percent.
Many junk bond critics maintain that, as the number of deals financed
by junk bonds grew, the quality of junk bonds being issued deteriorated.
This criticism was supported by Barrie Wigmore.

Wigmore examined a data base of 694 publicly underwritten junk
bonds issued between 1980 and 1988 (excluding financial institution
issues). He measured the quality of the issues by considering ratios
such as interest coverage, debt/net tangible assets, and cash flow as a
percentage of debt. He found that earnings before interest and taxes
(EBIT) coverage of interest charges fell from 1.99 in 1980 to 0.71 in
1988 (see Figure 8.5). Debt as a percentage of net tangible assets
presented a similar picture of deterioration. This ratio rose from 60
percent in 1980 to 202 percent in 1988 (see Figure 8.6). Cash flow as
a percentage of debt fell from 17 percent in 1980 to 3 percent in 1988
(see Figure 8.7).

Wigmore's financial ratios show that the quality of junk bonds issued
during the 1980s deteriorated steadily. It is not surprising, therefore,
that the junk bond market fell as we approached the late 1980s. The
decline of the junk bond market (discussed later in this chapter) would
be expected as the market rationally responded to a steadily lower
quality of issues being offered.

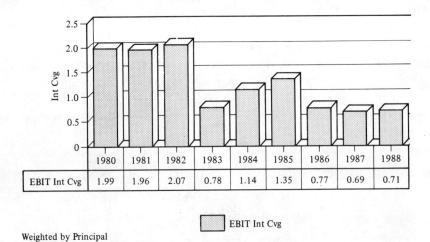

	1980	1981	1982	1983	1984	1985	1986	1987	1988
EBIT Int Cvg	1.99	1.96	2.07	0.78	1.14	1.35	0.77	0.69	0.71

EBIT Int Cvg

Weighted by Principal

Figure 8.5 Pro forma credit ratios for junk bond EBIT coverage of interest, 1980–
1988.

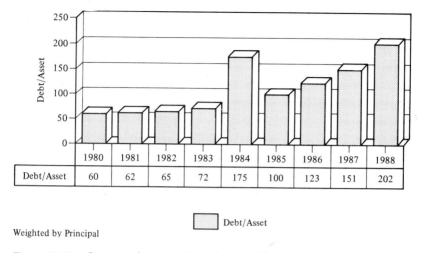

	1980	1981	1982	1983	1984	1985	1986	1987	1988
Debt/Asset	60	62	65	72	175	100	123	151	202

☐ Debt/Asset

Weighted by Principal

Figure 8.6 Pro forma credit ratios for junk bond debt as a percent of net tangible assets, 1980–1988.

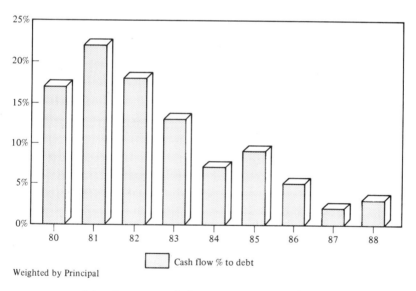

☐ Cash flow % to debt

Weighted by Principal

Figure 8.7 Junk bond issues: Cash flow as a percentage of debt.

RATE OF RETURN ON JUNK BONDS

One of the most well-established propositions in finance is the relationship between risk and return. With all other factors constant, investors will demand a higher return before they purchase a riskier asset while less risky, but otherwise identical, assets are available. Therefore, if firms are going to be able to market junk bonds, they must offer higher returns. This higher return is known as the *risk premium*. The risk premium associated with junk bonds is designed to compensate investors for two main categories of risk: default risk and liquidity risk. (Default risk was discussed at length in the previous section.) Liquidity risk means that junk bonds are not as liquid as other types of securities. An added element of risk to the investor is that there is no active secondary market for junk bonds as there is for other, lower risk securities such as U.S. Treasury bonds. Thus, if it became necessary to liquidate their junk bond investments, investors might not be able to do so or might only be able to sell them at a significant loss. For these reasons, junk bond yields have a distinct risk premium above the yields of higher quality and more liquid debt securities.

Marshall E. Blume and Donald E. Keim analyzed the returns on high-yield bonds for the time period of January 1982 through December 1987.[19] During this period they found that high-yield bonds paid an average monthly return of 1.26 percent, which translates into an average annual return of 16.2 percent (see Table 8.5). They also discovered that low-grade bonds had a lower volatility than high-grade corporates or equities as reflected by the standard deviation of monthly returns. The authors felt that this lower volatility could be explained by the fact that lower-grade bonds had higher coupons and lower durations than their high-grade counterparts. Low-grade bonds would, therefore, be less sensitive to interest rate fluctuations and theoretically exhibit less price variability. Blume and Keim also believed that since much of the risk of lower-grade bonds was firm specific, this risk could be reduced through diversification of bond portfolios. They noted that a comparison of the correlation coefficients between the returns of low-grade bonds, high-grade bonds, and equities showed a low correlation. This would mean that low-grade bonds might be effective diversification vehicles for a portfolio containing these different securities.

Drexel Burnham Lambert conducted an independent analysis of the performance of high-yield bonds (as Drexel calls junk bonds) as compared to Treasury securities between 1980 and February 1985. During that period junk bonds showed a compounded total return of 86.93

---

[19] Marshall E. Blume and Donald E. Keim, "Risk and Return Characteristics of Lower-Grade Bonds: 1977–1987," Rodney L. White Center for Financial Research, The Wharton School of the University of Pennsylvania, Philadelphia, August 1989.

Table 8.5   MONTHLY RETURNS
(January 1982 to December 1987)

Portfolio	Geometric Mean (percent)	Arithmetic Mean (percent)	Standard Deviation (percent)
B-K Lower-Grade Bonds	1.26	1.29	2.32
High-Grade Bonds	1.41	1.46	3.23
Long-Term Government	1.33	1.39	3.64
Treasury Bills	0.65	0.65	—
S&P 500	1.34	1.47	5.20

Source: Marshall E. Blume and Donald E. Keim, "Risk and Return Characteristics of Lower-Grade Bonds: 1977–1987," Rodney L. White Center for Financial Research, The Wharton School of the University of Pennsylvania, Philadelphia, August 1989.

percent versus a 54.02 percent return for comparable Treasury securities. These rates are shown in Table 8.6.

Recent Junk Bond Yield Data

The comparative rate of return of junk bonds is dependent on the time period used to make this measurement. During the late 1980s, the junk bond market suffered serious setbacks, including the following:

November 1986   Conviction of arbitrager Ivan Boesky. Boesky was a leading participant in the mergers and acquisition market which is a major user of junk bonds.

Table 8.6   DREXEL BURNHAM LAMBERT JUNK BOND YIELD, COMPARATIVE ANALYSIS, 1980–1985 (PERCENT)

Year	DBL 100	Tr. 8⅜% '00
1980	+ 0.93	− 4.11
1981	+ 2.73	− 1.98
1982	+32.48	+44.18
1983	+19.73	+ 0.45
1984	+ 8.50	+13.67
1985 (to 2/28)	+ 4.76	− 0.46
	+86.93	+54.02

Source: Drexel Burnham Lambert, "The Case for High Yield Bonds," 1985.

October 1987   Stock market crash. This resulted in a flight to quality and dampened the growth of the market.

February 1989   Indictment of Michael Milken and Drexel Burnham Lambert. Drexel Burnham Lambert is, by far, the leading underwriter of junk bonds.

These major events, coupled with several large defaults such as the Integrated Resources default (these defaults and the junk bond market crash of 1989 are discussed later in this chapter), caused a decline in the junk bond market. Measurements made at this time portray a very different picture of the comparative rate of return of junk bonds than that indicated by the Blume and Keim and Drexel Burnham Lambert studies. This difference can be seen by comparing the Merrill Lynch High Yield Master Index to the Merrill Lynch U.S. Treasury Index in early 1989. During this period, Treasury yields were higher than junk bond yields. Figure 8.8 shows that if different periods of time are selected, such as early 1989, a quite different picture of comparative junk bond yields emerges than the one seen in earlier studies.

Components of Junk Bond Risk Premiums

The rate of return on junk bonds can be analyzed by breaking it down into its component parts: risk-free rate; nondefault risk; and default risk. The Treasury bill rate can be used to measure the risk-free rate.

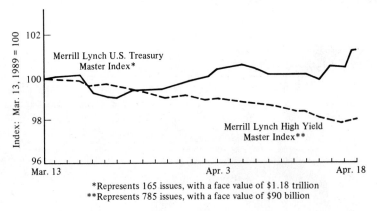

*Represents 165 issues, with a face value of $1.18 trillion
**Represents 785 issues, with a face value of $90 billion

Data: Merrill Lynch & Co.

Figure 8.8 Junk bonds slip as treasuries show strength. (*Source:* Reprinted from May 1, 1989 issue of *Business Week* by special permission, copyright © 1989 by McGraw-Hill, Inc.)

T-bills are said to be risk free because they are virtually free of default risk and have no reinvestment risk. The risk premium of junk bonds is, therefore, composed of these two elements. Nondefault risk includes factors such as *reinvestment risk* and *illiquidity risk*. Reinvestment risk is the risk that interest rates may rise and the coupons will be invested at lower rates than the rate of the junk bond.

Default risk is the risk that the issuer will default on the payments it is obliged to make. It is important to understand what this risk entails, for just considering the default rates shown above will present a misleading picture of the default risk of a junk bond. Defaulted bonds do not usually become valueless. They usually continue to trade in the marketplace but at values well below par. Investors purchase them and gamble that the firm will be able to survive the troubles that caused it to default on its obligations. Some aggressive investors purchase them with the intention of using their role as creditors to pressure the firm into eventually giving them an equity position in the firm.[20] In their sample of firms, Altman and Namacher showed that the defaulted bonds traded for an average of 41 percent of par value shortly after default. This figure translated into a reduction of 100 to 106 basis points in the average annual return.[21]

MEASURING THE DEFAULT RISK PREMIUM

In the 1970s Gordon Pye developed a methodology that attempted to measure what *yield to maturity* would fully compensate for the probability of default.[22] Yield to maturity refers to an investor's yield if the security is held to maturity. Pye's methodology is as follows. Let P_d = probability that the bond will default. Then the payment that the bondholder receives in the event of default equals: $(1 - X)$ times price of the bond a year earlier. X is determined by factors such as the liquidation value of assets.

The yield to maturity, Y, will be

$$Y = \frac{r + XP_d}{1 - P_d} \tag{8.2}$$

---

[20] "The None-Too-Gentle Art of the Bankruptcy Boys," *New York Times*, July 1988.

[21] Altman and Namacher, *Investing in Junk Bonds*, p. 1.

[22] Gordon Pye, "Gauging the Default Risk Premium," *Financial Analysts Journal* 30, no. 1 (January–February 1974):49–52.

where: Y = promised yield to maturity

r = bond's expected return in each year where it has not defaulted. This does not include a default risk premium.

The default premium (D) would then equal:

$$D = Y - r = \frac{r + XP_d}{1 - P_d} - r \qquad (8.3)$$

The following example is adapted from an example developed by William F. Sharpe, but it can be applied to the results of the Altman and Namacher study and will demonstrate how Pye's default premium can be calculated.[23]

EXAMPLE OF PYE'S DEFAULT PREMIUM

The average default rate for junk bonds, according to the results of the Altman and Namacher study, was 2.1 percent.

Then: P_d = 0.021

r = 0.09

X = 0.50

$$D = Y - r = \frac{r + XP_d}{1 - P_d} - r$$

$$= \frac{(0.09) + (0.5)(0.021)}{1 - 0.021} - 0.09$$

$$= \frac{0.09 + 0.0105}{1 - 0.021} - 0.09$$

$$= \frac{0.1005}{0.979} - 0.09$$

$$= 0.0127 \text{ or } 127 \text{ basis points}$$

So the yield to maturity, including default risk, as measured by Altman and Namacher's low 2.1 percent default rate, should be 0.1027 or 10.27 percent. Pye's methodology provides us with a means of computing the risk-inclusive yield for different default rates. It can be seen that if the default rate from the Asquith study were used here the yield would be far higher. The reader should verify this.

---

[23] William F. Sharpe, *Investments* (Englewood Cliffs, N.J.: Prentice–Hall, 1985), p. 336.

BOND YIELDS AND BOND RATINGS

The positive relationship between the degree of risk associated with a security and its return was shown above. We have also seen that bond ratings are a reasonable measure of the default risk component of total risk. The relationship between default risk and bond yields can be seen from Figure 8.9. The lower the rating, the higher the bond yield.

Correlation Between Ratings and Return: Investment Grade Versus Junk Bonds

Martin Fridson has tested the extent to which the correlation between risk and return applies to junk bonds in the same way that it applies to

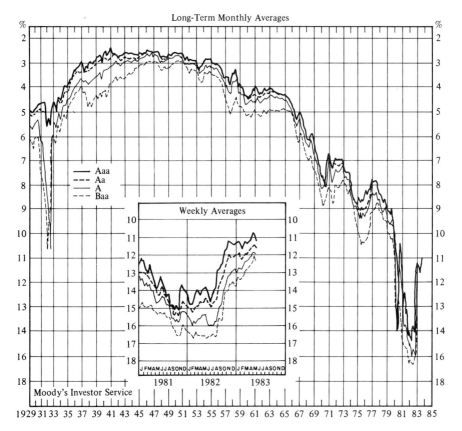

Figure 8.9 Industrial bond yields by ratings. (*Source:* Moody's Industrial Manual, 1983.)

investment grade securities.[24] In a comparison of a sample of invest-ment grade securities with high-yield bonds, he found that the corre-lation between ratings and yields proved to be higher in the investment grade sector than in the high-yield sector. For investment grade issues the R^2 factor was 0.891 versus 0.573 for the high-yield bonds. These results were significant at the 98.1 and 85.4 percent levels, respectively.

The Fridson study raises questions regarding the reliance on bond ratings when investing in junk bonds. The R^2 in his study showed a much looser relationship between the ratings and yields for high-yield securities than for investment grade bonds. These results indicate that, although ratings are a useful guide to the risk and require rates of return for bonds, the high-yield bond investor cannot blindly rely on the information content of bond ratings to determine the appropriate yield. Junk bond investors must carefully assess the issuer in order to determine whether the expected yield is consistent with the investor's perceived level of risk.

Response to an Increase in Default Risk

When the default risk of a security rises, the rate of return on the bond should also rise. Let's assume that a corporation has to pay a 11.5 percent coupon rate to be able to market $100 million of its corporate bonds. This rate was established in a discussion between the firm and its investment banker. The investment banker advised the firm that 11.5 percent would be attractive enough to enable the bank to sell the entire issue. Let's also assume, however, that certain unexpected news developed which showed that the company is riskier than originally perceived. Such news might be the discovery of significant, unexpected liabilities associated with employee on-the-job illnesses caused by toxic compounds used in the company's manufacturing processes. This news would increase the perception of risk on the part of the marketplace and elevate the risk premium that must be offered to sell the $100 million worth of bonds.

The reaction of the market to the higher risk perception is shown in Figure 8.10 where the slope of the supply and demand curves is opposite that of the traditional supply and demand curves. Interest rates are on the vertical axis, and corporate bond quality is on the horizontal. The supply curve is downward sloping since lower rates are associated with higher quality bonds, whereas the demand curve is

---

[24] Martin S. Fridson, *High Yield Bonds* (Chicago: Probus Publishing Co., 1989), pp. 37–38.

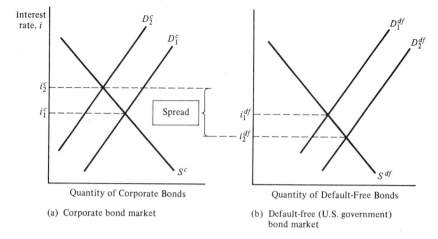

Figure 8.10 Response to an increase in default risk on corporate bonds. An increase in default risk on corporate bonds lowers the demand from D_1^c in to D_2^c. Simultaneously, it raises the demand for default-free bonds from D_1^{df} to D_2^{df}. The equilibrium rate for corporate bonds rises from i_1^c to i_2^c, while it falls from i_1^{df} to i_2^{df} in the default-free bond market. [*Source:* Frederic S. Mishkin, *The Economics of Money, Banking and Financial Markets*, 2nd ed. (Glenview, Ill.: Scott, Foresman & Co., 1989), p. 141.]

upward sloping since investors are willing to pay more for higher quality bonds. Figure 8.11(a) shows the supply and demand for the issuing corporation's bonds. The right-hand supply and demand curves show the market for default-free government bonds. The interest rate on corporate bonds is r_c whereas the rate of government bonds of similar maturity is r_g. The difference between $(r_c - r_g)$ is the default-risk premium (premium). As the risk perceptions of the market rise, the demand curve for the issuing corporation's bonds shifts to the left and the demand curve for the default-free bonds (or other lower risk bonds) shifts to the right. This causes the rate of return on the corporate bonds to rise at the same time that the rate on default-free bonds declines. The issuing corporation must offer high rates while the government would be able to offer lower rates to sell the same quantity of bonds.[25]

Term to Maturity and Bond Yields

Generally, the longer the term to maturity, the higher the yield. The basic reason is that the longer the term to maturity, the greater the risk

---

[25] This example is deliberately oversimplified to demonstrate what effect an increase in the issuer's risk has on the risk premium. The government issues should not be significantly affected by one offer of corporate bonds unless they are far above average size.

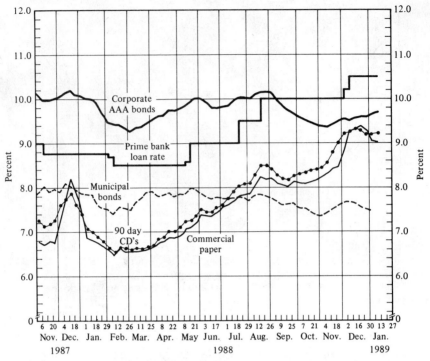

Latest data plotted are averages of rates available for the week ending, January 13, 1989.

Figure 8.11 Yields on selected securities averages of daily rates. (*Source:* U.S. Financial Data, January 12, 1989. Federal Reserve Bank of St. Louis.)

the creditor assumes that something unforeseen will occur to reduce the borrower's ability to repay the monies borrowed. This is usually depicted by a *yield curve*. (A typical yield curve is shown in Figure 8.11.)

The relationship between term to maturity and the rate offered on the bond is reasonable, but it is not always exact. The yield curve sometimes demonstrates a downward slope. While this is not commonplace, it does occur often enough to be more than just an academic issue. Various theories have been advanced to explain what is known as the term structure of interest rates.[26] Most such theories, however, do not explain the empirical facts of the marketplace very well. The yields on the bonds in the junk bond market normally bear the expected positive relationship to maturity, with longer maturity bonds providing a higher return.

---

[26] See Frederic Mishkin, *The Economics of Money, Banking and Financial Markets*. (Glenview, Ill.: Scott, Foresman and Co., 1988), pp. 139–160.

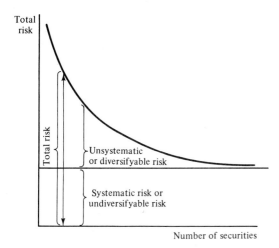

Figure 8.12

DIVERSIFICATION OF JUNK BOND INVESTMENTS

Diversifying junk bond investments enables investors to enjoy the higher average returns provided by junk bond yields without the higher degree of risk normally associated with individual junk bond issues. The risk-reduction benefits of diversification and the formation of portfolios has attracted much attention in the financial arena. Many studies have shown that, as the number of securities in a portfolio increases, the total risk declines and approaches the level of systematic risk, which is the undiversifiable risk that results from broad market-based movements (Figure 8.12). As the number of securities rises, there are few, if any, risk-reduction benefits.[27] As the other junk bonds are added to the portfolio, the exposure to the unsystematic risk of any one issue is reduced.

Wagner and Lau analyzed the risk-reduction effects of diversifying across randomly selected securities.[28] Table 8.7 indicates the lower risk as reflected by the lower standard deviation of monthly stock returns as the number of securities in a portfolio increased from 1 to 20.

---

[27] J. H. Evans and S. H. Archer, "Diversification and the Reduction of Dispersion: An Empirical Analysis," *Journal of Finance* (December 1968):761–767.

[28] W. H. Wagner and S. C. Lau, "The Effects of Diversification on Risk," *Financial Analysts Journal* (November–December 1971):49–51.

Table 8.7 PORTFOLIO RISK AND RETURNS

Number of Randomly Selected Stocks	Standard Deviation of Monthly Returns	Portfolio's Correlation with the Market
1	.70	.54
2	.50	.63
3	.48	.75
4	.46	.77
5	.46	.79
10	.42	.85
15	.40	.88
20	.39	.90

Source: Jack Clark Francis, *Investments* (New York: McGraw-Hill, 1986), p. 750. Reprinted by permission of McGraw-Hill, Inc.

Wagner and Lau expanded their study to focus on the addition of securities within the same risk classification. Their results showed a significant reduction in risk even when the securities were within the same quality rating level. For all categories of rated securities examined, Wagner and Lau showed steadily declining risk levels when more securities were added to the portfolio. The greatest risk-reduction benefits were achieved before the tenth security was added to the portfolio (see Figure 8.13).

The bulk of the empirical research was originally conducted on stocks and was later applied to bond portfolios. Investors discovered that a diversified portfolio of bonds would allow them to have a lower exposure to risk while still allowing them a relatively high return. The return of a junk bond portfolio is the weighted average of the returns of the individual bonds within the portfolio. The weights are the amounts the investor has invested in each type of bond. For example, let's assume that an investor has invested in the bonds of three companies: Corp. A ($10 million), Corp. B ($20 million), and Corp. C ($15 million). Then the weights will be:

Corp. A	$w_A = 0.22$	$r_A = 0.13$	(8.4)
Corp. B	$w_B = 0.44$	$r_B = 0.12$	
Corp. C	$w_C = 0.33$	$r_C = 0.135$	

where: w_i = the percent of the portfolio's capital invested in the ith security

r_i = the rate of return provided by the ith security

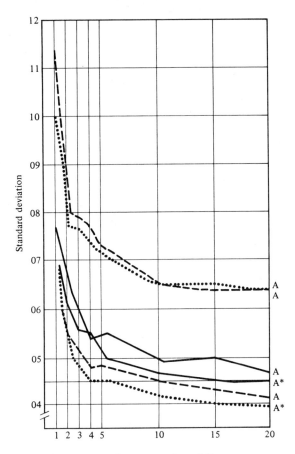

Figure 8.13 Diversification within different categories of stocks with identical quality ratings. [*Source:*
W. H. Wagner and S. Lau, "The Effects of Diversification on Risk," *Financial Analysts Journal* (November–December 1971): exhibit 1.]

The portfolio's return can be computed as follows:

$$r_P = w_A r_A + w_B r_B + w_C r_C \tag{8.5}$$
$$= 0.22(0.13) + 0.44(0.12) + 0.33(0.135)$$
$$= 0.0286 + 0.0528 + 0.04455$$
$$= 0.126$$

RISK OF A JUNK BOND PORTFOLIO

We cannot measure the risk of a junk bond portfolio simply by considering the variance of each junk bond's return. The problem is com-

pounded by the need to consider the covariability of the returns of each junk bond issue included in the portfolio.

An investor will gain little risk reduction by choosing securities whose returns all vary similarly. For example, the return on investments in the stock or junk bonds of steel companies might have a strong common element in that each is greatly affected by the performance of the steel market and the related factors that affect steel demand such as automobile sales. Therefore, to achieve greater risk-reduction benefits, an investor should select securities that do not vary so closely with those of the steel industry. This can be measured by the covariance of a security's return.

The covariance measures the extent to which two variables move together. The mathematical representations of both the standard deviation, which is the square root of the variance, and the covariance of a portfolio are shown below:

$$\text{Standard } \sigma_p \text{ deviation } = \sum_{j=1}^{n} \sum_{k=1}^{n} A_j A_k \, \sigma_{jk} \tag{8.6}$$

where: n = total number of securities in the portfolio
A_j = proportion of total funds invested in security j
A_k = proportion of total funds invested in security k
σ_{jk} = the covariable between the returns of securities j and k

$$\sigma_{jk} = r_{jk} \, \Sigma_j \Sigma_k \tag{8.7}$$

where: r = the correlation coefficient of the returns for securities j and k
σj = the standard deviation of the returns for security j
σk = the standard deviation of the returns for security k

The above computations are relatively simple to utilize for the basic two-security portfolio model. The calculations become more tedious when securities are added to the portfolio and the various correlations between the returns of each security have to be calculated. Sharpe and Lintner simplified the problem in the 1960s when they developed the capital asset pricing model.[29] The model reduces the number of calculations needed to measure a portfolio's risk by just focusing on a security's return relative to the market. Betas provide a measure of a

---

[29] William F. Sharpe, "Capital Asset Prices: A Theory of Market Equilibrium Under Conditions of Risk," *Journal of Finance* 19 (September 1964):425–442. John Lintner, "The Valuation of Risk Assets and the Selection of Risky Investments in Stock Portfolio and Capital Budgets," *Review of Economics and Statistics* 47 (February 1965):13–37.

security's variability relative to one common element—the market. This eliminates the need to compute the various correlations shown above since one Beta for each security captures the variability in return.[30]

Portfolios and the Transmutation of Junk Bonds

During the late 1980s, portfolios were used to transform junk bonds into high-grade debt. The process involved the securitization of debt, which is the pooling of debt securities and the issuance of new securities whose return is tied to the return of the overall pool of securities. The securitization of debt has taken place on a large scale in the mortgage-backed securities market where mortgages are packed into a pool that is used as collateral for the securities that are then issued. The market greatly expanded in the 1980s as it was extended to other forms of debt such as credit card receivables.

> Thus far, most securitizations have calculated collateral on the basis of market value. In the first deal, $100 million of 9.357 percent AAA collateralized notes issued by Imperial Savings and Loan Association in mid-1987, the rating agencies demanded 220 percent collateralization in order to offset the risks of price volatility and questionable liquidity—that is, the debt raters wanted $2.20 worth of CCC bonds in the portfolio for every dollar of investment grade bonds that were issued. And to preserve a 170 to 200 percent collateralization ratio, the bonds are marked to market every two weeks; if the value of the portfolio falls too far, Imperial must pledge new collateral. In addition, to qualify for a high grade rating, the portfolio must have no more than 8% in any industry or 3% of an issuer.[31]

Credit Research

The marketplace has responded to investor needs for a better evaluation of the default risk of junk bonds. Standard and Poor's now dedicates a separate department to junk bonds. Moody's issues special reports on the junk bond market. "Investment banks also moved aggressively into this area, with many establishing special credit and research areas, internally, to evaluate and report on potential offerings, trading opportunities and market trends. Morgan Stanley and Company publishes a monthly magazine, High Performance, and Drexel Burnham published High Yield Newsletter on a bimonthly basis prior to its bankruptcy."[32]

---

[30] See James Van Horne, *Financial Management and Policy* (Englewood Cliffs, N.J.: Prentice-Hall, 1989), pp. 61–73.

[31] Hilary Rosenberg, "The Unsinkable Junk Bond," *Institutional Investor* (January 1989):43–50.

[32] Altman and Namacher, *Investing in Junk Bonds*, p. 7.

Table 8.8 HIGH-YIELD BOND FUNDS

Name of Mutual Fund	Date Fund Established	Minimum Investment	Total Assets (millions)
AIM-High-Yield Securities	1977	$1,000	$ 74.4
Bull & Bear High-Yield Securities	1983	1,000	91.1
Cigna High-Yield Fund	1978	500	264.2
Colonial High-Yield Securities Trust	1969	250	456.9
Dean Witter High Yield	1979	1,000	2,101.2
Delchester Bond Fund	1970	25	663.9
Fidelity High Income	1977	2,500	1,832.4
Financial Bond Shares–High Yield	1984	250	62.4
Franklin AGE High Income	1969	100	2,200.0
GIT	1979	1,000	173.0
IDS Extra Income Fund	1983	2,000	1,279.9
Investment Trust of Boston High-Yield Plus	1984	1,000	11.0

Junk Bond Funds

Diversification can be easily accomplished through the use of junk bond funds. Several funds, which operate like the more common stock mutual funds, pool investment capital and invest in a portfolio of junk bonds. As noted above, these funds provide the appeal of the higher yields of junk bonds while reducing risk through the process of diversification. Diversification lowers the impact on the fund's portfolio of any single junk bond issue's default risk. During the first half of 1988, these funds accounted for a total asset investment of $28.6 billion. Some of the more popular funds are shown in Table 8.8

ROLE OF DREXEL BURNHAM LAMBERT AS A MARKET MAKER FOR JUNK BONDS

Drexel Burnham Lambert was one of the first investment banks to underwrite new issue junk bonds and was unique in its efforts to promote the junk bond market as an attractive investment alternative. These efforts were spearheaded by the former manager of Drexel's Beverly Hills office, Michael Milken. Drexel's unique role as a market maker became most apparent in 1986 when bondholders accused Morgan Stanley of failing to make a market for the junk bonds of People's Express which it had previously underwritten. When the price of the bonds fell significantly, Morgan Stanley did little to support them.

Morgan Stanley's passive stance contrasts strongly with Drexel's aggressive market making in the 1980s.

As a result of its involvement in the junk bond market, Drexel progressed from a second-tier to a major first-tier investment banking firm. The firm's dominance in the junk bond field during the 1980s made Drexel second only to Saloman Brothers as an underwriting firm.

Drexel made a market for the junk bonds it had underwritten by cultivating a number of buyers who could be depended on to purchase a new offering of junk bonds. The network of buyers for new issues usually consisted of previous issuers whose junk bonds were underwritten by Drexel Burnham. Drexel and Michael Milken used this network to guarantee a demand for new issues of junk bonds. This guarantee often came in the form of a *commitment letter* indicating that the buyer would buy a specific amount of a given issue of junk bonds when they were issued. The commitment fees which the investor might receive were usually less than 1 percent (i.e., three quarters of 1 percent) of the total capital committed. In riskier deals, however, it can range as high as 2 percent. The network of committed buyers is illustrated in Connie Bruck's *The Predators Ball*, in which she describes how Norman Peltz and his company, Triangle Industries, provided demand for new junk bonds that Drexel would issue.

> Moreover, Peltz had already shown himself as pliant, someone who understood how to play the Drexel game. A dues-paying member of the club, he had put up his Drexel-raised cash for each of the new junk bond financed takeovers as it came down the pike: $20 million for Phillips, $25 million for Coastal. Indeed, in the next month, even after his own deal had closed and he no longer had over $100 million burning a hole in his pocket, he would still find $35 million to commit to Unocal. And he knew he had to give up equity, both to Milken and to those buyers who took the riskiest pieces of his paper. Drexel already owned 12% of Triangle from the warrants it had received as part of its earlier financing, and it would cut another 4% piece of the pie for itself here.[33]

Drexel commanded a dominant 57 percent of the total market share of new public issues of junk bonds in 1983 and 40 to 50 percent from 1984 through the beginning of 1987 when its market share began to steadily decline. This was mainly the result of the energetic efforts of other large investment banks, especially Goldman Sachs, Merrill Lynch, First Boston, and Morgan Stanley, to capture part of the lucrative junk bond market (Figure 8.14). They increased their junk bond resources

---

[33] Bruck, *The Predators Ball*, p. 127.

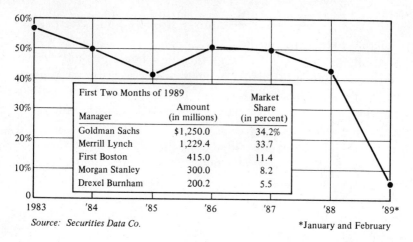

| First Two Months of 1989 | | Market |
Manager	Amount (in millions)	Share (in percent)
Goldman Sachs	$1,250.0	34.2%
Merrill Lynch	1,229.4	33.7
First Boston	415.0	11.4
Morgan Stanley	300.0	8.2
Drexel Burnham	200.2	5.5

Source: Securities Data Co.   *January and February

Figure 8.14 Drexel's share of public junk bond issues. First quarter share of new public issues of junk bonds with full credit to book manager. (*Source:* Reprinted by permission of the *Wall Street Journal*, copyright © 1989, Dow Jones & Company, Inc. All Rights Reserved Worldwide.)

by expanding their trading, research, and sales staffs. The investment apparently paid off, for by the late 1980s each of these banks had captured a significant part of the new public issue junk bond market. Drexel's dominant role in the junk bond market appeared to loosen in 1989, following Milken's indictment. Some firms, hesitant to do business with Drexel, turned to other underwriters. Drexel's end came ingloriously with its Chapter 11 filing in February 1990. (Drexel's bankruptcy is discussed later in this chapter in the context of major developments affecting the junk bond market.)

INVESTMENT BANKERS AND THE JUNK BOND MARKET

The investment banker assists the issuer in picking the most opportune time to put the newly issued junk bonds on the market. This is facilitated by a *shelf registration* of the bonds with the SEC. Shelf registration allows the issuer to register the securities it may want to issue in advance and to wait for the most favorable time to bring the securities to the market. The investment banker is attuned to the market and will advise the issuer when it will receive the highest price for the securities. The investment banker often provides *bridge financing* to the issuer which allows the issuing firm the time to select the best moment to bring the junk bonds to market. For example, First Boston

Corporation, a leading investment bank in mergers and acquisitions, committed $900 million to the Campeau Corporation, enabling Campeau to buy Allied Stores in 1986. The combination of bridge financing and advisory services was reported to have earned First Boston $100 million in fees.[34]

The riskiness of some of these bridge loans became apparent when some investment bankers, such as First Boston, were unable to arrange refinancing in the junk bond market when it declined in the late 1980s. In November, 1990, First Boston was eventually forced to sell some of its troubled "bridges," such as the $247 million bridge loan to Federated Stores and the $230 million bridge loan to Ohio Mattress Company to its owners, the Credit Suisse Bank and Metropolitan Life Insurance Company.[35]

Investment bankers have preserved the liquidity of the junk bond market by assisting in refinancing the issue if the issuer is unable to make the interest or principal payments. The resulting securities issued to replace the original junk bonds tend to be even riskier than the first set, for the new securities are the debt obligations of a company that cannot meet its current obligations.

Investment Bankers and Highly Confident Letters

As the size and complexity of the financing packages associated with the deals of the four merger wave increased, the need to demonstrate an ability to raise the requisite capital became more important, particularly for bidders who were significantly smaller than their targets. This process was facilitated by the use of a *Highly Confident Letter* in which the bidder's investment bank states that, based on market conditions and its analysis of the deal, it is highly confident that it can raise the necessary capital to complete the deal. This letter is often attached to tender offer filing documents such as the Schedule 14D-1.

The genesis of the Highly Confident Letter can be traced to Carl Icahn's $4.5 billion bid for Phillips Petroleum in 1985. Icahn's investment banker, Drexel Burnham Lambert, issued a Highly Confident Letter in which it stated, "We are highly confident we can arrange the financing."[36] The letter gave Icahn instant credibility and was a major contributing factor in his success in selling the shares he had acquired

[34] Miller, "Wall Street Money Wars," *Institutional Investor* (March 1987):169.

[35] Michael Siconolfi, "First Boston to Sell Bridges to Its Owners," *Wall Street Journal*, November 6, 1990, p. C1.

[36] Moira Johnson, *Takeover* (New York: Penguin Books, 1987), p. 147.

back to Phillips without testing the strength of Drexel's letter. Thereafter the Highly Confident Letter became an important part of the takeover business.

Icahn later used the Highly Confident Letter as an essential part of his "takeover tool kit." Armed with the letter and the resulting increased credibility produced by this investment banker's ability to marshall the vast financial resources of the then strong junk bond market, Icahn had to be taken more seriously. Many targets responded to threats from hostile bidders armed with their letters with an increased willingness to pay greenmail, and bidders quite willingly unveiled the position of their highly confident bankers. This was the case in Icahn's August 1986 bid for USX Corporation. In his letter to the board of directors of USX Icahn included references to the high degree of confidence of his investment banker Drexel Burnham Lambert and outlined his plans to make a $31 per share offer for the steel company.

> As holders of 25,349,800 shares of the common stock of USX, constituting approximately 9.83% of the outstanding shares, we share your belief [made public by the board in a statement it issued dated September 22, 1986] that USX has been undervalued in the market place. After reflecting on your additional statements that USX's pension fund is not significantly overfunded and noting USX's larger debt burden, it appears that an alternative to a restructuring might be the optimal way to "enhance shareholder value." We are prepared to offer just such an alternative and hereby propose a "friendly" cash merger transaction of USX with a corporation to be formed by our group for that purpose. . . .

> Of the approximately $8 million of cash required to fund the acquisition of the USX common stock, ACF Industries, Incorporated and other of my affiliates would be prepared to contribute approximately $1 billion in cash and USX stock for this purpose. Our financial advisor, Drexel Burnham Lambert Incorporated, has advised us that, based upon current market conditions, it is highly confident that it can obtain commitments for the placement of the new corporation's debt and equity securities sufficient for the balance of the acquisition. [37]

An example of a Highly Confident Letter (taken from Brancato's CRS report) is presented on the following page. It is a letter issued by Merrill Lynch Capital Markets to Smith-Vasiliou Management Company, Inc. for the bid for the Revere Copper and Brass, Inc., on May 13, 1986.

---

[37] Letter from Carl Icahn to the Board of Directors, USX Corporation, October 6, 1986, contained in the Schedule 13d filing to the Securities and Exchange Commission. As cited in Carolyn Brancato, "Takeover Bids and Highly Confident Letters," Congressional Research Service, Library of Congress, Report 87–724 E, August 28, 1987.

Merrill Lynch Capital Markets
Investment Banking

One Liberty Plaza
165 Broadway
New York, New York 10080
212 637 7455

 **Merrill Lynch**

May 13, 1986

Smith-Vasilou Management Co., Inc.
19 Rector Street
New York, NY   10006

Gentlemen:

You have advised us of your intention to acquire Revere Copper and Brass Incorporated ("Revere"), a Maryland corporation, in a negotiated cash merger transaction pursuant to which one of your subsidiaries will be merged with Revere and Revere's shareholders will receive $23.00 per share in cash for each share of common stock owned by them (the "Acquisition Transaction"). You have retained us to assist you in raising the funds required to consummate the Acquisition Transaction.

We are highly confident of our ability to finance the Acquisition Transaction subject to (i) no material adverse change in the financial condition, results of operations or business of Revere since March 31, 1986, (ii) market conditions similar to those currently existing, (iii) execution of customary underwriting or placement agreements, (iv) the execution of an acquisition agreement and approval of the Acquisition Transaction by the board of directors and shareholders of Revere, (v) completion of the divestiture of Revere's 34% equity interest in Ormet Corporation on terms similar to those contained in draft agreements relating to such divestiture and furnished to Merrill Lynch Capital Markets prior to the date hereof, (vi) the arrangement of a revolving credit facility and a senior term loan, both on terms and conditions reasonably similar to those contained in a letter to Smith-Vasiliou Management Co., Inc. from Bankers Trust Company dated May 13, 1986 and appended hereto, and (vii) placement of $7.0 million of common stock in Newco, a corporation to be formed for the purpose of acquiring the stock of Revere.

In the last four years, Merrill Lynch has acted as book-running manager or placement agent in completing over $8.0 billion of debt and preferred stock financings rated BB or below.

Very truly yours,

MERRILL LYNCH CAPITAL MARKETS
Merrill Lynch, Pierce, Fenner & Smith
  Incorporated

By

Managing Director

UNDERWRITING SPREADS

Underwriters receive higher spreads from *underwriting* junk bond offerings than from offerings of other less risky securities. Underwriting is the process whereby an investment bank guarantees an issuer of securities a given percentage of the value of the offering. The underwriter then bears the risk that the issue will be sold for a certain expected price.

The average gross underwriting spread is approximately 1 percent.[38] Gross underwriting spreads for junk bonds, however, average approximately 3 percent, with some as high as 4 or 5 percent. Altman and Namacher conducted a study of the determinants of underwriting spreads for junk bonds based on a regression analysis that had the following specification:[39]

$$GS = f(IS, TA, S\&P, Z) \tag{8.8}$$

where: GS = gross underwriting spread
IS = issue size
TA = total assets
$S\&P$ = Standard & Poor's rating
Z = Zeta score

They reported the following results for the 1983–1984 period:

$$GS = 1.6193 - 0.00016(IS) - 0.000044(TA) + 0.2640(SP)$$
$$\{5.22\} \quad \{-0.30\} \quad \{-0.89\} \quad \{4.63\}$$
$$- 0.0691(Z)$$
$$\{-2.34\}$$
$$R^2 = 38.1\%, \ N = 109$$

Durban Watson Statistic 1.72

Thus, we see an inverse relationship between the size of the issue and the underwriting spread. The terms in the brackets under each coefficient are t-statistics and indicate the level of statistical significance. Values greater than 1.96 indicate that there is a 95 percent probability that the true value of the coefficient is within a confidence interval that is constructed around the coefficient itself. In other words, the higher the t-statistics, the more confident we can feel about the coefficient.

The signs of the coefficients are consistent with other studies of underwriting commissions. The signs of the S & P and Zeta variables

---

[38] Ernest Bloch, *Inside Investment Banking* (Homewood, Ill.: Dow Jones Irwin, 1989), p. 323.

[39] Altman and Namacher, *Investing in Junk Bonds*, p. 47.

show that the higher the risk of the issue, the greater the underwriting spread. Similarly, as the size of the firm increases, the gross underwriting spreads decline, revealing that underwriters generally consider the larger firms to be less risky.

JUNK BOND YIELDS: THE LATE 1980s

During 1988, junk bonds averaged a yield of approximately 13.03 percent. This was a significant premium above the other, lower risk categories of bonds such as AAA and AA corporate bonds which averaged a yield of 7.93 percent or U.S. Treasury bonds which yielded only 6.33 percent. Total returns on junk bonds fell sharply in 1989, reflecting the troubles of the high-yield bond market. As of the first three quarters of 1989, junk bond returns averaged only 5.24 percent compared to 11.09 percent for U.S. Treasury and 12.56 percent for investment grade securities.[40] By October 1990, the average yield on 20 widely held

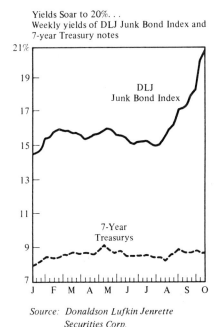

Yields Soar to 20%. . .
Weekly yields of DLJ Junk Bond Index and
7-year Treasury notes

Source: Donaldson Lufkin Jenrette Securities Corp.

Bond Prices Collapse

	PRICE/Cents on dollar	
	AUG.3	YESTERDAY
Amer. Standard 12 7/8% of 2000	84	65
Burlington 13 7/8% of 1996	89	54
Fort Howard 14 5/8% of 2004	91	76
Macy 14 1/2% of 2001	60	27
McCaw Cellular 14% of 1998	92½	70
Owens Illinois 12 3/4% of 1999	92½	75
Quantum Chemical 13% of 2004	84¼	48
Stone Container 11 1/2% of 1999	93¾	64

Source: Citicorp; Telerate

Figure 8.15 (*Source:* George Anders and Constance Mitchell, "Junk Bond Yields Go Through the Roof," *Wall Street Journal,* October 11, 1990, p. C1. Reprinted by permission of the *Wall Street Journal,* copyright © 1990, Dow Jones & Company, Inc. All Rights Reserved Worldwide.)

---

[40] "Mounting Losses Are Watershed Event for Era of Junk Bonds," *Wall Street Journal,* September 18, 1989, p. C1.

issues tracked by Donaldson Lufkin Jenrette Securities hit 20.5 percent.[41] (See Figure 8.15.) The increased yields offered to buyers came as a result of the decline in the price of these bonds compared to their face value and interest payments. These higher yields are necessary when buyers need extra encouragement to buy these securities. This encouragement comes in the form of lower and lower prices.

THE JUNK BOND MARKET

Figure 8.16, using data provided by Drexel Burnham Lambert, shows dramatic growth in the new-issue junk bond market during the 1980s. The market peaked in 1986 with new issues reaching almost $50 billion. The market declined in the wake of the 1987 stock market crash when investors flocked to the higher quality issues in order to lower risk. However, the large numbers of megamerger deals caused the market to rebound in 1988. The recovery of the junk bond market came to a halt with the sharp decline in the high-yield bond market in 1989. Nonetheless, the total size of the junk bond market is in excess of $200 billion.

The largest categories of junk bond buyers are insurance companies and mutual funds, each of which accounts for 30 percent of total junk bond demand. Mutual funds have found that junk bonds can significantly enhance the return of their securities portfolio. Separate funds, which invest exclusively in junk bonds, have been established and successfully marketed.

Insurance companies initially found junk bonds to be a rewarding avenue for the large investment capital they attracted from policyholders. When the market turned down in the late 1980s, however, many came to regret their high-yield investments. It became an even greater source of concern when the value of junk bond investments rose; for some insurers they rose two to four times the firm's capital. For example, Ohio Casualty held $169 million worth of junk bonds, which accounted for 481 percent of its statutory surplus capital, and Trans-America held $780 in junk bond investments which represented 223 percent of its statutory surplus capital.[42]

Pension funds account for 15 percent of total junk bond demand.

---

[41] George Anders and Constance Mitchell, "Junk Bond Yields Go Through the Roof," *Wall Street Journal*, October 11, 1990, p. C1.

[42] Linda Sandler, "Insurers Getting Queasy Over Junk Bond Holdings," *Wall Street Journal*, February 12, 1990, p. C1.

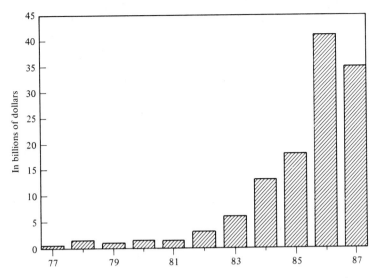

Figure 8.16 Junk bond's new issue. (*Source:* Drexel Burnham Lambert.)

The investment of pension funds, particularly state and local government pension funds, in junk bonds became a controversial issue in the late 1980s. Many analysts argue that these investments are too risky and may endanger the value of the retirees' capital in the event of a major economic downturn. Opponents of this view contend that, even though they fell in value, junk bonds withstood the great stock market crash in 1987 and give every sign of being a stable, high-yielding investment.

Another controversial group of investors has been the savings and loan associations (S & L's) whose investment strategies came under intense criticism following the failure of a large number of them. Many economists blame these failures on overall mismanagement and poor investments. Other S & L's, such as the Columbia Savings and Loan of Beverly Hills, California, which is referred to as the thirft institution that junk bonds built, appeared to be quite healthy before the junk bond market crash of the late 1980s.[43] At that time Columbia Savings held $3.8 billion worth of junk bonds, which amounted to nearly 40 percent of its assets. After the junk bond market decline, its high-yield portfolio declined $320 million in the months of October and November alone.[44] Given the intense regulatory scrutiny which S & L's will be

---

[43] "Columbia S & L Charts Two-Way Course," *Wall Street Journal*, February 9, 1989, p. A8.

[44] "A Savings Resignation over 'Junk'," *New York Times*, December 12, 1989, p. D1.

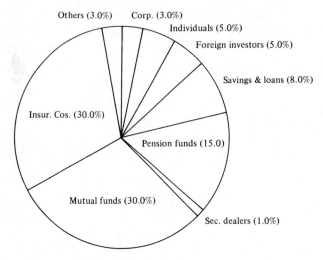

Source: GAO. Drexel Burnham Lambert.

Figure 8.17 Who buys junk bonds. (*Source: New York Times,* November 17, 1988, p. D5. Copyright © 1988 by The New York Times Company. Reprinted by permission.)

under in the future, clearly S & L's like Columbia Savings and Loan will be greatly limited in their ability to invest in risky securities such as junk bonds. Indeed, Columbia Savings & Loan on March 14, 1990, answered that it planned to sell its entire junk bond portfolio as part of its program to adhere to new federal regulatory requirements for thrifts and prevent a federal takeover of the bank.[45]

Foreign investors are the fastest growing group of investors in junk bonds. As of 1988, they constituted 5 percent of the total junk bond market. Many foreign investors, taking advantage of the falling dollar combined with their new awareness of the risk–return characteristics of high-yield bonds, have discovered them to be an attractive investment alternative (Figure 8.17). The appetite of foreign investors also decreased, however, when the market turned down in the late 1980s.

RECENT INNOVATIONS IN THE JUNK BOND MARKET

As the world of merger and acquisitions and leveraged buyouts awoke to the financial power of high-yield securities as a financing vehicle, dealmakers started to develop more innovative junk bonds that would

---

[45] Frederick Rose and Randall Smith, "Columbia S & L Intends to Sell All Junk Bonds," *Wall Street Journal*, March 15, 1990, p. A3.

be used to finance deals that might not otherwise have been possible. Carolyn Brancato has described some of these innovations.[46]

A Congressional Research Service (CRS) study notes the growth in variant types of high yield issues, some of which clearly begin to take on attributes more of equity than debt, and increasingly contain a series of innovative, highly specialized provisions "irreverently" referred to by market participants as "belles and whistles."[47] The permutations and combinations of these "variants" are virtually endless, and are limited only by the creativity of the financial dealmakers. Among the more prominent types are those with deferred interest payments and those with "pay-in-kind" (PIK) provisions which provide for non-cash compensation, including the following:

(a) *Zero Coupon or Zero-Slash Bonds* are bonds that are generally sold at a deep discount from par (or face value) and pay no cash interest for an initial period and then "jump up" to a current cash coupon; these are generally floated in connection with leveraged buyouts or recapitalizations to provide the issuer a partial respite from paying cash interest during which time the issuer can divest assets to improve cash flow. If, as is usually the case, the bond is callable at par right from the issue date, the "first economical call" is the date on which the cash coupon kicks in; prior to that time, it is presumed that the bond will trade at a discount, making a par call unattractive to the issuer.[48]

(b) *Pay-In-Kind (PIK) Bonds* are relatively new. According to industry sources cited by CRS, the first public issues were offered in the second half of 1986 as

"A component of the non-cash compensation provided to shareholders of acquired companies—so called 'cram down' securities . . . they are also novel—they offer the possibility of adding a stock option feature to a debt instrument. For an initial period which may range from three to ten years.

"A component of the non-cash compensation provided to shareholders of acquired companies—so called 'cram down' securities . . . they are also novel—they offer the possibility of adding a stock option feature to a debt instrument. For an initial period which may range from three to ten years the issuer of PIK debt can choose to make periodic payments to the bondholder either

---

[46] Carolyn Brancato, "Leveraged Buyouts and the Pot of Gold: 1989 Update," A Report Prepared for the Committee on Energy and Commerce, U.S. House of Representatives, July 1989.

[47] Kevin Winch, "Junk Bonds: 1988 Status Report," Congressional Research Service, Library of Congress, Report 89–22, December 30, 1988.

[48] Ibid. Martin S. Fridson, Fritz Wahl, and Steven Jones, "The Anatomy of the High Yield Debt Market: 1987 Update," Morgan Stanley, Fixed Income Credit Research Department, March 1988, pp. 14–16.

in cash or in additional securities. If the bondholders receive only cash, the PIK bond is no different than a conventional straight coupon bond; if the bondholders are paid only in additional securities, the PIK bonds are the same as a deferred coupon bond.[49]

(c) *Pay-in-Kind (PIK) Preferred Stock* are hybrid securities, according to CRS, sharing some of the characteristics of bonds (fixed income, no voting rights) and some of the charactertistics of common stock (no maturity date, no dividend if the company has no earnings). PIK stock would not be included in totals for the high yield bond market; thus the reduction in the proportion of high yield debt used in LBOs noted above is probably due to the advent of these types of issues to replace high yield debt.

Junk Bonds As a Source of Merger and Acquisition Financing

The growth of the junk bond market has added a highly combustible fuel to the fires of the mergers and acquisition movement. As described earlier, one of the first hostile takeover attempts financed by junk bonds was the attempted bid for Gulf Oil by the celebrated raider Boone Pickens. Pickens was president of the relatively small Mesa Petroleum. Being a small oil company, by seven sisters standards, Mesa was not a serious threat. When Pickens arranged a $2 billion commitment from Drexel Burnham Lambert, however, the smaller oil company gained instant credibility. Drexel issued the commitment in the form of a letter stating that the firm was highly confident it could raise the necessary $2 billion. The monies were ultimately to be raised by an offering of junk bonds. The access to such large amounts of financing instantly made Mesa a credible threat. Gulf took the offer seriously and finally agreed to be bought out by a white knight—Chevron. Ironically, Chevron's acquisition of Gulf appeared to have overextended Chevron's resources and caused its stock price to fall, making it vulnerable to a takeover.

The Typical Junk Bond Takeover Process

Step 1. The takeover process involving junk bonds usually begins with the acquirer establishing a shell corporation as a subsidiary. This shell serves as the acquisition vehicle for the target's takeover.

Step 2. The shell company makes a tender offer for the target. The

---

[49] Winch, "Junk Bonds," pp. 12–13.

offer is usually conditional on the arrangement of financing. The acquiring firm's investment bank issues a Highly Confident Letter indicating that the bank believes it can raise the requisite financing. The fall of the junk bond market made it more difficult for investment banks to be highly confident.

Step 3. At this point the investment bank secures commitments from investors who will buy the junks bonds when the shell corporation eventually issues them. Investors receive a guaranteed amount of money or commitment fee for agreeing to the commitment of their funds. This fee is not usually refundable even if the takeover is aborted.

Step 4. The investment bank may also arrange bridge financing to provide the necessary capital to complete the deal. The bridge loan will be refinanced following the sale of the junk bonds issued by the shell corporation. The advantage in using bridge financing is that the investment bank is able to choose the most opportune time to issue the junk bonds. If the junk bond market is temporarily depressed, such as immediately after several other large junk bond offerings, the investment bank may choose to wait until the rates decline. Investment banks consider the following factors:

    a. Recent and future junk bond offerings.

    b. Recent performance of the junk bond market.

    c. The current level of interest rates.

Many bridge financing commitments were left in suspended animation when the junk bond market collapsed and investment bankers couldn't refinance the bridge loans through an offering of junk bonds.

Step 5. Once the financing is arranged, the bonds are sold and the cash is used to buy the stock tendered. If the offer is a two tiered bid the cash is used to purchase the stock tendered in the first tier. The purchase of the first tier, which may amount to 51 percent of the target's outstanding common stock, gives the acquirer control of the target.

Step 6. Assuming a two tiered transaction, once the acquirer attains control of the first tier, another set of junk bonds is issued to purchase remaining stock in the second tier. It should be pointed out, however, that the double issue of junk bonds is not always necessary. Indeed, many takeovers financed by junk bonds involve just one junk bond offering.

Step 7. At this point, the acquiring firm and its shell subsidiary are beset with large interest payments associated with the junk bonds offered. The acquirer seeks to reduce these debt payments as soon as possible. This process usually involves the sale of the target's assets. The proceeds are used to retire the debt assumed in the takeover. This is why many heavily levered takeovers and leveraged buyouts have been referred to as bust-up takeovers.

The above takeover process was common in the mid-1980s but became increasingly less common toward the end of the 1980s as it became more and more difficult to find buyers for junk bonds.

Small Versus Large Hostile Raiders

The growth of the junk bond market has strengthened the credibility of small companies as raiders. Smaller companies do not usually have as much access to bank financing as larger, more creditworthy companies do. Before the junk bond market developed, these small companies would not be taken seriously if they made an offer to take over a much larger target.

As noted earlier in this chapter, when an investment bank provides a smaller bidder with a highly confident letter, it gives the bidder instant credibility. The investment bank knows the bonds will be marketable inasmuch as the substantial assets of the target will serve as collateral for the junk bonds that will be offered. A classic example of such instant credibility was Triangle Industries' offer for the National Can Company. In April 1985, Triangle Industries, led by CEO Nelson Peltz, made a $430 million, all-cash offer for National Can. In terms of sales, National Can (1.9 billion) was over six times larger than Triangle ($291 million). Triangle's investment bankers arranged the financing through agreements with 36 different large investors.[50] This was made possible through Triangle's investment banker, Drexel Burnham Lambert.

BANK LOAN FINANCING VERSUS JUNK BOND FINANCING

As noted above, smaller companies may have access to large-scale bank financing. Their size and the lesser credit standing do not make them attractive candidates for bank loans of the magnitude often necessary in the takeovers of the 1980s. Banks look for lower debt to equity ratios and other financial measures more stringent than those offered by smaller companies. The junk bond investor is not as demanding as the

---

[50] *New York Times*, April 14, 1985, p. 8.

bank lender, not because he does not care about the risk of the borrower, but because he is better able to lower risk through diversification. A buyer can purchase a diversified portfolio of junk bonds that will have lower risk because of diversification. Owing to the limited amount of capital (relative to the junk bond market as a whole), banks invest in loans to a limited number of borrowers. Therefore, a bank cannot easily maintain a well-diversified portfolio and thereby assume a higher degree of *event risk*.

Bank loan financing terms are generally inferior to junk bond financing terms. Bank loans typically have a term of less than 7 years, whereas junk bonds can have 10- to 20-year maturities. Junk bonds also have call options that allow the issuer to retire the issue more quickly if the opportunity arises.

JUNK BONDS AND GREENMAIL

That smaller, less well-financed raiders can become credible raiders has opened new opportunities for greenmail. Because less substantial bidders must now be taken seriously, more bidders can extract greenmail from targets. Targets, fearing they might eventually be taken over, are now more willing to pay greenmail. Until the development of the junk bond market, less well-capitalized raiders were not taken seriously. For example, in 1984 Saul Steinberg and his company Reliance sought to acquire the relatively larger Walt Disney. Steinberg needed $2.4 billion for the acquisition, some of which would come from Reliance's own resources and the banks it controlled. But Reliance was depending on Drexel Burnham Lambert to provide $1.5 billion in mezzanine layer financing, most of which would be raised through the sale of junk bonds. The greenmail offer to Steinberg was as follows:

> Disney would pay Reliance $325.5 million ($77.5 per share) for its 4.2 million shares. That included $297.3 million ($70.83 a share) for the Steinberg stock, plus $28 million ($6.67 a share) to cover Steinberg's expenses, including his legal bills and commitment fees he would have to pay Kirk Kerkorian, the Fishers, Irwin Jacobs, and the rest of the investors. Excluding those expenses, Steinberg would make a profit of $31.7 million on the buyback, the difference between the price he had paid for his stock over the last ninety days and the price Disney would pay for it.[51]

Without the credibility of the junk bond financing and Drexel's ability to raise this capital in the junk bond market, the greenmail offer might not have been made as quickly. Disney might have tried to wait out

---

[51] John Taylor, *Storming the Magic Kingdom* (New York: Ballantine Bools, 1987), pp. 128–129.

the offer in the hope that it could get away without having to incur the expense of greenmail. Given Steinberg's access to junk bond financing, the target had to take him seriously.

REGULATIONS AFFECTING JUNK BOND FINANCING

On December 6, 1985, the Federal Reserve through Regulation G, established margin requirements that affect the use of junk bonds to finance takeovers. In the 1930s, the Federal Reserve was empowered to establish margin requirements for the purchase of stock. The maximum value of a loan that uses stock as collateral is set at 50 percent. If the stock of a target corporation is used as collateral for a loan, this transaction is governed by the Federal Reserve's margin requirements.

As noted earlier, the acquisition process financed by junk bonds usually features the shell corporation, which is a wholly owned subsidiary of the original acquiring corporation. The shell issues the junk bonds and uses the proceeds to purchase the stock in the target. The target is then acquired by the shell. As of January 1986, however, shell corporations set up as acquisition vehicles were prohibited from purchasing more than 50 percent of a target corporation's stock with financing secured by junk bonds. At the time, the Federal Reserve felt that this regulation would limit takeovers financed by junk bonds. This reasoning proved to be quite short-sighted and underestimated the innovativeness of an investment banking community motivated by the desire to continue earning great profits.

The following exceptions to Regulation G apply:

1. Operating companies with substantial assets are not governed by this regulation, but shell corporations used as acquisition vehicles are.
2. A shell corporation may still issue an unrestricted amount of junk bonds if a corporation with substantial assets and cash flows, such as the shell's parent company, guarantees the junk bond issue.
3. If the target agrees to the merger, then Regulation G does not apply. The regulation is designed to limit *hostile* takeovers financed by junk bonds.
4. If the sources of financing are foreign leaders, Regulation G may not apply. This is another grey area of the law.[52] A legal decision

---

[52] Martin Lipton and Erica H. Steinberger, *Takeovers and Freezeouts* (New York: Law Journal Seminar Press, 1987), pp. 2.12(3)–2.12(4).

in the *Metro-Goldwyn-Mayer* v. *Transamerica Corporation* case held that foreign financing was not governed by Regulation G.[53]

Takeovers financed by junk bonds slowed down during the first nine months of 1986. Late that year, however, the number of such takeovers increased. The marketplace discovered an easy way around Regulation G. The regulation placed limits on the total financing that could be raised by shell corporations issuing junk bonds and using the stock of the target as collateral. The rule did not restrict the acquiring corporation itself from issuing the junk bonds directly rather than relying on the shell to issue the bonds.

The market also circumvented the restriction imposed by Regulation G by issuing *rising rate preferred stock* instead of junk bonds. This stock was used in the 1988 attempted takeover of Interco by the Rales Brothers. Although rising rate preferred stock is technically equity, it is actually more like junk bonds in disguise. The disadvantage of using these securities instead of junk bonds is that the investment criteria of some high-yield bond funds preclude their investing in these securities. This tends to reduce their marketability.

In the latter part of 1986 and the years that followed, corporations issued large amounts of junk bonds, using the capital as a "war chest" that could later be used to take over a suitable target. For example, in 1986 the Wickes Companies raised over $1 billion in the junk bond market for "acquisition purposes." At the time of the sale of the junk bonds, the Wickes Companies did not have any specific target in mind. This situation underscored the fact that the increased regulation did not place any permanent and meaningful limits on the growth of the junk bond market.

Institutional Investor Regulations

Certain regulations limit the ability of institutional investors to invest in junk bonds. These regulations are usually specific to the type of institution and do not transcend institutional boundaries.

Corporate pension funds.   Certain pension funds may by policy not invest in junk bonds that are used to finance hostile takeovers. Corporations which, for selfish reasons, are concerned about the growth of hostile takeovers may limit access to capital by refusing to invest in junk bonds that would be used for such purposes.

---

[53] *Metro-Goldwyn-Mayer, Inc.* v. *Transamerica Corporation*, 303 F. Supp. 1354 (S.D.N.Y. 1969).

Public pension funds.   Some states have established regulations limiting the fund's managers from investing in junk bonds used to finance takeovers. These regulations vary by state.

Insurance companies.   Some state laws limit the amount of junk bonds that an insurance company can purchase. These regulations are motivated by the belief that junk bonds are riskier securities and by the desire to reduce the risk to policyholders.

Savings and loan associations.   Savings and loan associations, seeking high returns, have tended to invest significant parts of their investment portfolio in junk bonds. These institutions have come under great criticism following the massive failures within the S & L loan industry. Under new guidelines enacted in the wake of this crisis, insolvent S & L's are prohibited from investing in junk bonds and must divest their holdings of these securities. The ability of thrifts to invest in junk bonds would, in part, be determined by the thrift's capitalization, with undercapitalized thrifts being restricted from purchasing junk bonds. As of March 1989, thrifts may not hold more than 11 percent of their investments in junk bonds, and only 5 percent of the S & L's total assets may be invested in one junk bond mutual fund.[54] The expanding S & L led some critics to call for further regulations completely prohibiting thrifts from holding junk bonds.

ARE JUNK BONDS MAKING AMERICAN COMPANIES TOO DEBT LADEN?

There has been much recent criticism that American companies are becoming less competitive because they have assumed so much debt as a result of a larger number of leveraged transactions. The debt of corporate America rose dramatically in the 1980s. "The outstanding debt of nonfinancial corporations rose 70 percent between 1983 and 1988, more than two-thirds faster than growth of nominal GNP."[55] As of 1989, the total corporate sector had liabilities amounting to 54 percent of gross national product, up from 45 percent in 1980.[56]

---

[54] "New Thrift Rule Curbs Involvement in Junk Bonds," *Wall Street Journal*, February 1, 1989.

[55] Ben Bernanke, "Is There Too Much Corporate Debt," *Federal Reserve Bank of Philadelphia Business Review* (September/October 1989):3.

[56] "Will Corporate Debt Force Fed to Scrap Zero Inflation," *Business Week*, October 23, 1989, p. 22.

We should place this higher debt level in perspective, however, by comparing it to foreign firms. This comparison can be facilitated by comparing the relative debt to equity ratios of American firms to those of Japanese and German firms. In 1988, debt as a percentage of equity was an average of 90 percent for American firms. This was the highest level in the postwar economy. Japanese and European firms tend to have significantly higher levels of debt than American firms. In fact, foreign firms have traditionally been willing to assume much higher levels of debt than their American counterparts. Up to 1985, the average debt level in Japan and Germany was three times greater than equity.

Some critics maintain that the comparison is not valid, for it may be less risky for a German or Japanese firm to assume more debt than for an American firm. The reason is that banks tend to hold substantial equity positions in corporations in Germany and Japan, and are able and willing to provide assistance to firms should the need arise. For example, Deutsche Bank stepped in to bail out and restructure Kloeckner and Company when the large trading company ran into trouble in November 1988.[57] Another reason why the comparison may not be valid is that the trend in the debt to equity ratios of European and Japanese firms has been declining while the ratios of American firms have been rising. European and Japanese firms have apparently decided that they do not want to maintain the previously higher debt to equity ratios. This raises questions as to the appropriateness of using this comparison to justify American firms increasing their debt levels.

Can Debt Promote Efficiency?

Some economists argue that the pressures of increased financial leverage can promote efficiency by eliminating the margin for engaging in less profitable activities. Michael Jensen and other advocates state that, without the need to service debt payments, firms would be tempted to invest their free cash flow into areas of low profitability such as expansion beyond the profit-maximizing size.[58] Increased financial leverage limits these activities by absorbing the otherwise discretionary free cash flow. Clearly, benefits are to be gained from increased leverage, such as a higher rate of return for equity holders. The benefits come at the expense of increased risk, however. It is premature to make a conclusive judgment as to what costs a more risky corporate America will produce.

---

[57] *Business Week*, November 14, 1988.

[58] Michael C. Jensen, "Takeovers: Their Causes and Consequences," *Journal of Economic Perspectives* 2 (Winter 1988):21–48.

MAJOR EVENTS AFFECTING THE JUNK BOND MARKET

Two major events have rocked the junk bond market: the bankruptcy of the LTV Corporation and the junk bond market crash of 1989.

The LTV Bankruptcy

The resiliency of the junk bond market was called into question in 1986 when the LTV Corporation defaulted on the high-yield bonds it had issued. The LTV bankruptcy was the largest corporate bankruptcy at that time and represented 56 percent of the total debt defaulting in 1986.[59] Ma et al. showed a temporary six-month revision in the market's probabilities for default, as reflected by the risk premium yields on junk bonds. This effect proved transitory, and the market more than fully rebounded afterward. The Ma study indicates that the junk bond market was at that time quite resilient and more than capable of withstanding the shock of a major default.

The Junk Bond Market Crash of 1989

The junk bond market, which had grown from $2 billion at the start of the 1980s to $200 billion by 1989, peaked in 1989 and turned sharply downward at the beginning of the year. Two main causal factors can be cited for the junk bond market decline. The first was the overall deterioration of the quality of the junk bonds being offered to the market. This is borne out by the data from the Barrie Wigmore–Goldman Sachs study showing how the deteriorating quality of the junk bonds being offered was reflected in several key debt and coverage ratios. The growing number of defaults, which were often masked by exchanges in which other securities were offered in exchange for the almost defaulting junk bonds, caused investors to look to lower risk securities.

The junk market was jolted by several critical events. Large offerings by issuers, such as Campeau Corporation, swelled the market with increased supply. In the first half of 1989, $20 billion worth of junk bonds were offered compared to $9.2 billion for the same period in 1988. Issuers had to offer higher and higher rates to attract investors to buy the risky securities. Campeau Corporation's offering of junk bonds in 1988, led by the investment bank First Boston Corporation,

---

[59] Christopher K. Ma, Ramesh P. Rao, and Richard L. Peterson, "The Resiliency of the High Yield Bond Market," *Journal of Finance* 44, no. 4 (September 1989):1085–1097.

was poorly received even though it provided 16 percent coupon payments on 12-year bonds and 17¾ percent coupons on 16-year bonds.[60] In October 1988, First Boston had to withdraw a $1.15 billion junk bond offering as investor demand for the debt-laden concern's securities failed to materialize. The investment bank responded with a smaller, $750 million offering that provided higher yields.

The secondary market also responded with decreased demand reflecting the fall-off that was occurring in the primary market. "Bonds of Resorts International declined by 40% this year, for example, and securities issued by Tracor and Interco are down by 38 percent."[61] The lack of a strong, reliable secondary market made it even more difficult to offer new high-yield bonds. This was a contributing factor to the unraveling of the financing for the buyout of United Airlines in October 1989. Even when reputable issuers, such as Ohio Mattress, maker of Sealy, Stearns, and Foster mattresses, offered 15 percent interest rates for a proposed $475 million issue in 1989, the market refused to respond.

In addition to increased supply, the junk bond market was rocked by a series of defaults, chief among which was the Integrated Resources default in June 1989 (see Case Study), followed by the liquidity crisis of the Campeau Corporation in September 1989. The number of defaulted issues continued to rise in the late 1980s. Many junk bonds that were issued during 1984 and 1986, for example, were added to the default list and rated single D by Standard and Poor's. These include such issues as AP Industries, Columbia Savings (Colorado), First Texas Savings Association, Gibraltar Financial Corporation, Integrated Resources, Metropolitan Broadcasting Corporation, Resorts International, Inc., Southmark Corporation, and Veyquest, Inc.[62]

The Bankruptcy of Drexel Burnham Lambert

In its heyday in 1986, Drexel reported pre-tax profits of $1 billion. Only two years later, in late 1988, it pleaded guilty to criminal charges and paid more than $40 million in fines. In 1989, Drexel showed a loss of $40 million.[63]

---

[60] "Campeau Retail Chains Are Heavily in Debt, Face Rising Troubles," *Wall Street Journal*, December 14, 1988, p. A1.

[61] Wallace, "Time for the Jitters in Junk Bonds."

[62] "Campeau Retail Chains Are Heavily in Debt," p. A1.

[63] "Junk Bond King Files for Bankruptcy," *Newark Star Ledger*, February 14, 1990, p. 39.

CASE STUDY: *INTEGRATED RESOURCES' BANKRUPTCY*

Integrated Resources sought bankruptcy protection under Chapter 11 of the Federal Bankruptcy Code on February 13, 1990. The once high-flying real estate syndicator had suffered serious financial setbacks during the late 1980s. The firm's chief difficulty had been in marketing its tax shelter programs after the Tax Reform Act of 1986.

Integrated Resources tried to diversify out of real estate syndications and into other areas of financial services such as mutual funds and aircraft leasing.[a] These diversification efforts proved to be quite costly and eroded Integrated's profitability. The failure of Integrated's diversification and subsequent cost-cutting efforts were reflected in its 17 cents per share stock price just prior to bankruptcy. The pressure of $1.6 billion worth of debt forced Integrated Resources to default in June 1989.[b] The company attempted to negotiate a settlement with its creditors. Some creditors, including First Fidelity Bank, N.A. of New Jersey, were reported to have gone to New York State Supreme Court to recover $11.6 million that the bank had lent to certain partnerships guaranteed by Integrated Resources. Because some creditors were unwilling to work out a negotiated settlement, Integrated was forced to seek bankruptcy protection.

Drexel Burnham Lambert was assisting Integrated Resources in raising finances to pursue its activities. When other Drexel clients were in a similar financial crisis, Drexel provided additional financing and liquidity. When Integrated's situation worsened, however, Drexel, immersed in its own financial troubles, was unable to provide financial assistance. Ironically, both Integrated Resources and Drexel Burnham Lambert filed for bankruptcy protection on the same day.

[a] Alison Leigh Cowan, "Integrated Resources Files for Chapter 11 Protection," *New York Times,* February 14, 1990, p. D2.
[b] Alison Leigh Cowan, "No-Frills Bankruptcy Planned for Integrated," *New York Times,* February 15, 1990, p. D6.

The immediate cause of Drexel's Chapter 11 bankruptcy filing was a liquidity crisis resulting from the firm's inability to pay short-term loans and commercial paper financing that came due. Securities firms generally rely on short-term capital to finance their securities holdings. Drexel had been the issuer of over $700 million in commercial paper. When the commercial paper market contracted in 1989, Drexel was forced to pay off over $575 million which could not be refinanced through the issues of new commercial paper.[64] Closing the commercial paper market effectively wiped out Drexel's liquidity. With the prior

---

[64] Affidavit Filed by Frederick H. Joseph in Drexel Bankruptcy Filing, printed by the *New York Times,* February 15, 1990, p. D5.

CASE STUDY: *REPACKAGING JUNK BONDS*

As the junk bond market turned downward in the late 1980s, market participants utilized certain innovations to rekindle the dwindling demand. Principal
among these was the *collateralization* of junk bonds which allows junk bondholders to package their junk bond portflio and reissue new, higher rated
securities backed by the low-rated junk bond debt. The technique, first applied
to junk bonds in November 1988, is an adaptation of a technique used in the
mortgage-backed securities market.

As noted earlier in this chapter, a diversified portfolio of high-yield debt
can provide a high average yield with a reduced degree of risk. The reduced
risk allows the securities to receive a higher quality debt rating.

The way in which the transactions are structured can be complicated. A
typical transaction process for a collateralized deal is structured through a
combination of sections called *tranches.*

> *The first tranche, usually about three quarters of the issue, is senior to
> the others. The so-called class A investors receive their interest payments
> before any other creditors, and the yield is typically about two percentage
> points higher than other A-rated bonds. For instance, a recent $300 million
> collateralized obligation offered by Duff & Phelps, an investment firm in
> Chicago, included a senior tranche of $240 million with a 10.05 yield,
> according to Timothy P. Norman, a vice-president of the firm. Investors in
> the second and third tranches—known as Class B and C holders—receive
> a much higher interest rate, but their securities have a lower rating. In
> the Duff & Phelps issue, the $45 million Class B tranche is a zero coupon
> yielding 15.29 percent. The yield on these units is much higher than the
> Class A tranche because of the risk that a higher-than-expected default
> rate will wipe out these investors' expected interest payments—but this
> tranche also has a great opportunity for appreciation.*
>
> *The capital structure of the collateralized obligation also includes a group
> of equity holders. In many cases, the issuing companies put their own
> capital into the equity and the third tranche. In exchange, they will receive
> whatever interest is left over when all of the bondholders have received
> their principal and interest. Their goals are to realize cash flow from the
> sale of the top tranches and to profit from the unusually wide yield spread
> between the average interest rate of the underlying bonds and the interest
> rate on the new bonds.[a]*

Institutions that have larger junk bond portfolios but that want to divest
themselves of these high-risk investments use the collateralization technique.
Large savings and loans have larger high-yield investments and want to reduce
their exposure to this risky market. Buyers of these securities also tend to be
institutions, particularly European institutional investors.

[a] Anise Wallace, "Making Junk Bonds Respectable," *New York Times,* December 15,
1989, p. D1.

Table 8.9   PRICE DECLINE OF SOME ACTIVELY TRADED JUNK BOND ISSUES

Issue	Coupon	Price per $1,000 Bond	
		2/16/90	8/11/89
American Standard	12.875	$940	$1,035
Burlington Industries	14.250	$870	$1,052
Caesars World	13.500	$1,030	$1,052
Colt Industries	12.500	$1,020	$1,045
Duracell	13.500	$1,025	$1,050
Fort Howard	12.265	$927	$1,025
Harcourt Brace	13.750	$650	$1,040
Kroger	13.125	$1,015	$1,057
Macy	14.500	$680	$1,017
Owens Illinois	12.750	$910	$1,002
Quantum Chemical	13.000	$810	$1,000
RJR Nabisco	13.500	$910	$1,077
Safeway	11.750	$1,005	$1,022
Viacom	11.800	$987	$1,012

Sources: Wall Street Journal, February 20, 1990, p. C1; Donaldson Lufkin and Jenrette Securities Corporation. Reprinted by permission of the Wall Street Journal, copyright © 1990 Dow Jones & Company, Inc. All Rights Reserved Worldwide.

collapse of the junk bond market, Drexel could not seek long-term financing as a substitute. The firm had no other recourse but to file for Chapter 11 protection.

DECLINE OF THE JUNK BONDS: A BUYBACK OPPORTUNITY

As is characteristic of many of the fluctuations in securities markets, a loss for one investor may be an opportunity for another. When the junk bond market declined in 1989 and 1990, many issuers of junk bonds seized this opportunity to buy back their high interest rate debt. Among these junk bond issuers were Revlon, Inc., Rexene Corporation, Mark IV Holdings, Conair Acquisition Corporation, Intermark Corporation, and Banner Industries. The lower the quality of the junk bonds, the greater the decline in the bond's price. Higher quality junk bonds tended not to decline as much as their low-quality counterparts. Although some of the better quality high-yield issues only declined as much as 2 percent, other poor-quality, high-yield issues declined as much as 40 percent.[65]

---

[65] Mitchell, "Junk Bond Buy-Backs Increasing," p. C1.

Table 8.10   PRICES OF TROUBLED JUNK BOND ISSUES

Issuer	Coupon	Maturity	Price per $100 of Face Value (September 1989)
Companies in default by September 1990			
Cannon Group	12.87%	2001	$52.00
Dart Drug Stores	12.70%	2001	$20.00
General Homes	12.75%	1998	$10.75
LTV	14.00%	2004	$34.50
Maxicare Health	11.75%	1996	$7.50
PS New Hampshire	17.50%	2004	$21.00
Republic Health	13.00%	2003	$22.50
Revco	13.12%	1994	$49.75
Southmark	11.87%	1993	$49.75
Companies about to default in September 1989			
Griffin Resorts	13.87%	1998	$65.00
Integrated Resources	12.25%	1998	$10.50
Resorts International	16.62%	2004	$30.00
Seaman Furniture	15.00%	1999	$7.00

Sources: "The Bills Are Coming Due," Business Week, September 11, 1989, pp. 84–86; Donaldson Lufkin and Jenrette Securities Corporation, Investment Dealers Digest, R. D. Smith & Co.

The extent of the decline is shown in the lower prices that prevailed in February 1989 compared to August 1989 (Table 8.9). The situation was even worse for some troubled issues. The value of these issues fell dramatically toward the end of 1989 (see Table 8.10).

SUMMARY

The junk bond market grew dramatically during the fourth merger wave and fell precipitously by the end of the 1980s. Its growth enabled the fourth wave to be fundamentally different from any of the previous merger periods. Using the junk bond market, relatively smaller firms were able to make hostile bids for far larger companies. Investors came to regard the junk bond debt used to finance these takeovers as a means to enjoy high returns while they diversified their junk bondholdings to try to lower their risk. The high returns provided by these securities made them quite popular among a variety of investors including large institutions such as pension funds, insurance companies, and savings and loan associations.

The market's view of junk bonds turned downward toward the end of the 1980s. Research studies conducted at the end of that decade contradicted the view of earlier studies which implied that junk bonds were a relatively safe investment vehicle that provided relatively high yields. These later studies showed that high-yield bonds had high default risk and were of questionable quality. The junk bond market was also rocked by several large defaults and the eventual collapse of its leading market maker, Drexel Burnham Lambert. The absence of Drexel's aggressive market making reduced the liquidity of these securities. In addition, regulatory changes forced some institutions to decrease or eliminate their holdings of high-yield bonds. The big buyouts of the 1980s left a large supply of junk bonds on a market that showed falling demand.

The fall of the junk bond market slowed the pace of mergers and leveraged buyouts. While it is too early to definitely state that the fourth merger wave ended in 1989, all signs point to this conclusion. To the extent that the wave continues, it will have great difficulty reaching the heights achieved in the middle of the 1980s with the fuel of the junk bond machine. The deals that occurred in 1990 relied much more on equity and less on debt. The M & A business was increasingly conducted by well-financed bidders and less by junk bond raiders.

REFERENCES

Altman, Edward I. "Financial Ratios, Discriminant Analysis and the Prediction of Corporate Bankruptcy." *Journal of Finance* 23 (September 1968):568–609.

Altman, Edward I. "Setting the Record Straight in Junk Bonds," *Journal of Applied Corporate Finance*, 3(2) Summer 1990.

Altman, Edward I., R. Haldeman, and P. Narayanan. "Zeta Analysis: A Model to Identify Bankruptcy Risk of Corporations." *Journal of Banking and Finance* (June 1977).

Altman, Edward I., and Scott A. Namacher. "The Default Rate Experience on High Yield Corporate Debt." New York: Morgan Stanley & Co., 1985.

Altman, Edward I., and Scott A. Namacher. *Investing in Junk Bonds: Inside the High Yield Debt Market*. New York: John Wiley & Sons, 1987.

Asquith, Paul, David Mullins, and Eric Wolff. "Original Issue High Yield Bonds: Aging Analysis of Defaults, Exchanges and Call." Unpublished Harvard University Working Paper, March 1989.

Beaver, William H. "Financial Ratios As Predictors of Failure." *Empirical Research in Accounting, Selected Studies*. Graduate School of Business, University of Chicago, 1966, pp. 71–127.

Blume, Marshall E., and Donald E. Keim. "Risk and Return Characteristics of Lower Grade Bonds." Working Paper, Rodney L. White
Center for Financial Research, Wharton School, University of Pennsylvania.

Brancato, Carolyn Kay. *Takeover Bids and Highly Confident Letters*.
Congressional Research Service, August 28, 1987, p. CRS–24.

Bruck, Connie. *The Predators Ball*. New York: Simon & Schuster, 1988.

Drexel Burnham Lambert. "The Case for High Yield Bonds." 1985.

Evans, J. H., and S. H. Archer. "Diversification and the Reduction of
Dispersion: An Empirical Analysis." *Journal of Finance* (December
1968):761–767.

Fitzpatrick and Severiens. "Hickman Revisited: The Case for Junk
Bonds." Saloman Brothers, March 1984.

Francis, Jack Clark. *Investments*. New York: McGraw-Hill, 1986.

Fridson and Monaghan. "Default Experience of Corporate Bonds."
Saloman Brothers, March 1984.

Fridson, Martin S. *High Yield Bonds*. Chicago: Probus Publishing Co.,
1989, pp. 37–38.

Hickman, W. B. *Corporate Bond Quality and Investor Experience*.
Princeton, N.J.: Princeton University Press, 1958.

Lintner, John. "The Valuation of Risk Assets and the Selection of Risky
Investments in Stock Portfolio and Capital Budget." *Review of Economics and Statistics* 47 (February 1965):13–37.

Lipton, Martin, and Erica H. Steinberger. *Takeovers and Freezeouts*.
New York: Law Journal Seminar Press, 1987, pp. 2.12(3)–2.12(4).

Mishkin, Frederic. *The Economics of Money, Banking and Financial
Markets*. Glenview, Ill.: Scott Foresman & Co., 1988, pp. 139–160.

"Nabisco Sued Over Bond Drop." *New York Times*, November 18,
1988.

"New Thrift Rule Curbs Involvement in Junk Bonds." *Wall Street
Journal*, February 1, 1989.

"The None-Too-Gentle Art of the Bankruptcy Boys." *New York Times*,
July 1988.

Perry, Kevin J. *Journal of Applied Corporate Finance* 1, no. 1 (Spring
1988):37–45.

Pye, Gordon. "Gauging the Default Risk Premium." *Financial Analysts
Journal* 30, no. 1 (January–February 1974):49–52.

Radcliffe, Robert C. *Investments*. Glenview, Ill.: Scott Foresman &
Co., 1982.

Rosenberg, Hilary. "The Unsinkable Junk Bond." *Institutional Investor*
(January 1989):43–50.

Sharpe, William F. "Capital Asset Prices: A Theory of Market Equilibrium Under Conditions of Risk." *Journal of Finance* 19 (September 1964):425–442.

Sharpe, William F. *Investments*. Englewood Cliffs, N.J.: Prentice-Hall, 1985.

Sherwood, H. C. "How They Rate Your Company's Bonds." *Business Management* 29 (March 1966):38–42.

Sinconolfi, Michael. "First Boston to Sell Bridges to Its Owners." *Wall Street Journal*, November 6, 1990, p. C1.

"Swiss Court Seeks to Halt Takeover of RJR Nabisco." *Wall Street Journal*, March 23, 1989, p. A19.

Taylor, John. *Storming the Magic Kingdom*. New York: Ballantine Books, 1987.

Van Horne, James. *Financial Management and Policy*. Englewood Cliffs, N.J.: Prentice-Hall, 1989, pp. 61–73.

Wagner, W. H., and S. C. Lau. "The Effects of Diversification on Risk." *Financial Analysts Journal* (November-December 1971):49–51.

Weinstein, Mark I. "A Curmudgeon View of Junk Bonds." *Journal of Portfolio Management* (Spring 1987):76–80.

Wigmore, Barrie. "The Decline in Credit Quality of Junk Bond Issues: 1980." Study Conducted by Goldman Sachs, November 7, 1989.

Yugo, Glenn. *Junk Bonds* (New York: Oxford University Press, 1991).

Chapter
9

Employee Stock Ownership Plans

Much of the dramatic growth of employee stock ownership plans (ESOPs) in the United States in the 1980s can be attributed to their role in mergers, acquisitions, and leveraged buyouts. Bidders and employees discovered that they could make a bid for a firm through an ESOP and realize significant tax benefits that would help lower the cost of the buyout. For their part targets discovered that ESOPs could provide them with an effective antitakeover defense.

Employee stock ownership plans are allowable under the Employee Retirement Income Security Act of 1974 (ERISA), a law that governs the administration and structure of corporate pension plans. ERISA specified how corporations could utilize ESOPs to provide employee benefits. An ESOP provides a vehicle whereby the employer corporation can make tax deductible contributions of cash or stock into a trust. These trust assets are then allocated in some predetermined manner to the employee participants in the trust. The corporation's contributions to the ESOP are tax deductible. Moreover, the employees are not taxed on the contributions they are entitled to receive until they withdraw them from the ESOP.

ESOPs are required to invest in the employer's stock. They can buy stock in subsidiaries of the employer's corporation if the employer corporation owns more than 50 percent of the subsidiary's stock. Unlike pension plans, ESOPs do not try to lower the risk level of their assets by diversifying. Although pension plans seek to invest their assets in a variety of assets, so as to lower risk, ESOPs are designed to hold only cash, cash equivalents, or the stock of the employer corporation.

ESOPs were very popular in the United States during the 1920s at a time when the stock market was rising and Americans widely owned stock. The stock market crash of 1929 and the economic downturn that followed caused the stockholdings of employees to decline dramatically. After the decline in the value of the firm's stock, employees were less willing to take shares in the company as compensation, given the added risk that this form of compensation brought. ESOPs remained less popular through the 1970s.

ESOPs became popular in the 1980s, especially toward the end of the decade. Table 9.1 lists some of the larger ESOPs that have been established in recent years, and Table 9.2 focuses on the growth in the number of ESOP plans from 1978 to 1988. "During the first six months of 1989, U.S. Corporations acquired over $19 billion of their own stock to establish employee stock ownership plans (ESOPs). This compares to only $5.6 billion for all of 1988 and less than $1.5 billion per year from the passage of the Employee Retirement Security Act in 1974 through 1987."[1]

TYPES OF PENSION PLANS

The ESOP is an alternative to a corporate pension plan.[2] The three main types of pension plans are defined benefit plans, defined contribution plans, and profit-sharing plans.

Defined Benefit Plans

In a defined benefit plan, an employer agrees to pay employees specific benefits upon retirement. These benefits may be defined in terms of a dollar amount per month or a percentage of the last year's salary or several years' salary according to a pre-set formula.

---

[1] Myron Scholes and Mark Wolfson, "Employee Stock Ownership Plans and Corporate Restructuring: Myths and Realities," *Financial Management* 19, no. 1 (Spring 1990):12–28.

[2] For a review of pension plan management, see Eugene F. Brigham and Louis C. Gapenski, *Intermediate Financial Management*, 2nd ed. (Chicago: Dryden Press, 1987), pp. 759–784.

Table 9.1   ELEVEN LARGE ESOPS

Employee Ownership
The majority-owned ESOP companies with the greatest number of employees and the year the ESOP began.

Company	Business	Year	Employees
Health Trust Nashville	Hospital management	1987	30,000
Avis Garden City, N.Y.	Car rental	1987	12,500
EPIC Healthcare Group Dallas	Hospital management	1988	10,000
Charter Medical Macon, G.A.	Hospital management	1987	9,000
Parsons Pasadena, Calif.	Engineering & construction	1974	8,600
Amstead Industries Chicago	Diversified machinery	1986	8,300
Weirton Steel Weirton, W. Va.	Steel manufacturing	1984	8,200
Avondale Industries New Orleans	Shipbuilding	1985	7,500
Dan River Danville, Va.	Textiles	1983	7,000
Austin Industries Austin, Texas	Construction	1987	6,500
Wyatt Cafeterias Dallas	Cafeterias	1988	6,500

Source: Leslie Wayne, "Some Lessons from Avis for UAL Buyout," *New York Times,* September 24, 1989, p. 4. Copyright © 1989 by The New York Times Company. Reprinted by permission.

Table 9.2   GROWTH IN THE NUMBER OF ESOP PLANS AND NUMBER OF EMPLOYEES COVERED, 1978–1988

Year	Number of Plans	Number of Employees Covered
1978	4,028	2,800,000
1984	6,904	6,576,000
1986	8,046	7,800,000
1988	9,500	9,500,000

Sources: National Center for Employee Ownership; Myron Scholes and Mark Wolfson, "Employee Stock Ownership Plans and Corporate Restructuring: Myths and Realities." *Financial Management* 19, no. 1 (Spring 1990):12–28.

Defined Contribution Plans

Employers guarantee a specific contribution, rather than a specific benefit, in a defined contribution plan. The employee's pension payments are dependent on the investment performance of the benefit fund. These funds may be managed by a union which oversees investment of the funds. Defined contribution plans are riskier for employees since their pension payments will be dependent on the investment performance of the fund, which is not guaranteed by the employer. ESOPs are a defined contribution plan in which the contributions are the employer's stock as opposed to cash.

Profit-Sharing Plans

A profit-sharing plan is even riskier for employees than a defined contribution plan. Here the contributions made by the employer are a function of the company's profitability. The contributions are usually specified as a percentage of the firm's pre-tax profits.

CHARACTERISTICS OF ESOPs

In 1986, the General Accounting Office (GAO) conducted a survey of firms that had ESOPs in place. They found that 91 percent of the respondents indicated that the primary reason for starting an ESOP was to provide benefits to employees; 74 percent cited tax incentives; and 70 percent mentioned improved productivity.[3]

Using data derived from the GAO as well as other sources, Corey Rosen found that half the plans were used to buy the company. In approximately one-third of ESOPs, employees owned a majority of the company, and in almost another one-third they owned less than 25 percent of the firm.[4]

Average Contribution

Employers with ESOPs contribute approximately 8 to 10 percent of their payroll to the ESOP each year. This is less than the maximum contribution allowable as a tax deduction under the law.[5]

---

[3] U.S. General Accounting Office, "Employee Stock Ownership Plans: Benefits and Costs of ESOP Tax Incentives for Broadening Stock Ownership," Washington, D.C., 1987.

[4] Corey Rosen, "The Record of Employee Ownership," *Financial Management* 19, no. 1 (Spring 1990):39–47.

[5] Ibid.

LEVERAGED VERSUS UNLEVERAGED ESOPs

ESOPs can be divided into two groups: leveraged and unleveraged. Leveraged ESOPs, called LESOPs, are those that borrow, whereas unleveraged ESOPs do not borrow. Leveraged ESOPs are of more interest to us as a vehicle for leveraged buyouts.

The size of the contributions which the corporation can make to the ESOP depends on whether or not it is a leveraged ESOP. Unleveraged ESOPs can make annual contributions up to 15 percent of the payroll. If the contributions are less than the full 15 percent, the corporation receives a credit carryover for the difference, which can then be contributed in later years up to a maximum in any one year of 25 percent.

With leveraged ESOPs, the corporation borrows to buy stock in the corporation. The corporation makes a contribution to the ESOP which is used to pay the principal and interest on the loan.

CORPORATE FINANCE USES OF ESOPs

The world of corporate finance has developed several innovative uses for ESOPs. Some of these uses are outlined below.[6]

Buyouts

ESOPs have been widely used as a vehicle to purchase companies. This technique has been used for both private and public firms. Robert Bruner reports that 59 percent of leveraged ESOPs have been used to buy out owners of private companies.

Divestitures

ESOPs have also been widely used as divestiture and selloff vehicles. Bruner reports that 37 percent of the leveraged ESOPs have been used as divestiture vehicles. As an example, he cites the Hospitals Corporation of America which sold off 104 of its 180 hospitals to a new corporation, HealthTrust, which was owned by its employees through a leveraged ESOP.

Rescue of Failing Companies

The employees of a failing company can use an ESOP as an alternative to bankruptcy. There have been several examples of this in the troubled

---

[6] This outline is based partially on: Robert F. Bruner, "Leveraged ESOPs and Corporate Restructuring," *Journal of Applied Corporate Finance* 1, no. 1 (Spring 1988):54–66.

steel industry. The employees of McLouth Steel, for example, exchanged wage concessions for stock in the company in an effort to avoid bankruptcy proceedings. Weirton Steel's 1983 rescue is another example.

Raising Capital

An ESOP can also be used to raise new capital for the corporation. The use of an ESOP as an alternative to a public offering of stock is discussed later in this chapter. Bruner reports that 11 percent of ESOPs have been used for this purpose.

VOTING OF ESOP SHARES

Voting the ESOP shares can be an important issue when the ESOP is used as a tool in mergers and leveraged acquisitions. As noted in Chapter 5, a target corporation can try to use the ESOP as a white squire by placing stock in the plan. It then hopes that the ESOP shares will vote with management on major decisions such as approving mergers and other major transactions. Use of ESOPs as an antitakeover defense is discussed in greater detail later in this chapter. We will see that the voting rights of the shares is an important determinant of the use of the ESOP as an antitakeover defense.

In public corporations, employee shareholders in an ESOP hold shares that have voting rights. This may not be the case, however, for private corporations. Whether or not the ESOP employee participants in private corporations retain the right to vote their shares depends on the prevailing state laws which vary from state to state. Some states provide for *limited voting rights* which do not allow full voting privileges for the individual employee shareholders.

Approval for the Establishment of an ESOP

Shareholder approval may not always be necessary to establish an ESOP. However, companies traded on the New York Stock Exchange are required to receive stockholder approval when an ESOP that will acquire more than 18.5 percent of the firm's stock is established.

CASH FLOW IMPLICATIONS

As noted above, cash flows are critically important to the success of a leveraged buyout. ESOP stock contributions positively affect the cash flow of all corporations whether or not they are involved in a leveraged buyout.

Let us assume that a corporation makes a $1,000 stock contribution to an ESOP. Since the contribution is in the form of stock, there is no cash outlay. Tax laws allow the corporation a $500 tax deduction, which improves the firm's cash flow by the same amount. We should not conclude, however, that these cash flow benefits are costless. The benefits may be partially or completely offset by a dilution in the equity holdings of the non-ESOP stockholders. This may be reflected in lower earnings per share.

VALUATION OF STOCK CONTRIBUTED INTO THE ESOP

The cash flow of the corporation can be significantly improved by the tax benefits of the ESOP contribution. In deciding the size of the stock contribution, the company must first determine its value. For public corporations this is clear as there is a readily available market value to use. The problem is less clear for private corporations. It becomes necessary to rely on the various techniques of securities valuation for privately held companies. These methods are discussed in Chapter 15. The services of a business appraiser or an expert in business valuations may be utilized to determine the securities value.

ELIGIBILITY OF ESOPs

The ESOP must fulfill certain requirements in order to qualify for tax deductibility benefits. It must include all employees 21 years old and over with one year of service during which they have worked 1,000 hours.[7] One exception to this requirement is seasonal industries. The plan should include at least 80 percent of the eligible employees.

PUT OPTIONS OF ESOPs

Employees may receive a put option to sell their stock back to the employer corporation within 60 days of receiving it. If they do not

---

[7] Robert Frisch, *The Magic of ESOPs and LBOs* (New York: Farnsworth Publishing, 1985).

choose to exercise this option in 60 days, they may receive another 60-day option in the following year. Put options may even have a life of up to five years. The put option may be waived if the corporation does not have sufficient retained earnings to purchase the stock. If retained earnings are not sufficient, the company can defer the put option to a year in which it does have sufficient retained earnings.

If a private company with an ESOP decides to go public in the future, the put option may be terminated. This is the case when the ESOP shares are included in the registration statement for going public.

DIVIDENDS PAID TO ESOPs

Dividends paid by the employer corporation on the ESOP shares are charged against retained earnings. These dividend payments are a tax deductible expense if they are paid in the following manner:

1. Dividends are paid directly to ESOP participants.
2. Dividends are paid directly to the ESOP, which distributes them to the ESOP participants within 90 days of the close of the plan year.
3. Dividends on the ESOP are used to make payments on an ESOP loan.[8]

ESOPs VERSUS A PUBLIC OFFERING OF STOCK

Let us compare the relative benefit of an ESOP to a public offering of stock. Consider the example of a public offering of stock of $1 million brings in $1 million less investment banking fees, legal charges, and other costs associated with the issuance and sale of equity. These costs are often referred to as *floatation costs*. Employee compensation and benefits are generally not affected by such a transaction.

A sale of stock to an ESOP can bring in $1 million without the normal floatation costs of a public offering. However, employee compensation and benefits usually decline as the contributed stock takes the place of some of the compensation and benefits. For example, pension plan contributions could be eliminated. The firm receives a tax deduction on the ESOP contribution, although the pension plan contributions and wages that were paid before the ESOP was established

---

[8] Scholes and Wolfson, "Employee Stock Ownership Plans and Corporate Restructuring," pp. 23–24.

were already tax deductible. If the ESOP incurs interest costs for borrowing the capital needed to purchase the stock, the tax deduction should more than offset the interest payments.

The substitution of an ESOP for parts of the employee benefits package that was in effect before the ESOP was established may present an employee relations problem for the firm. If the pension plan is eliminated, employees may not be eligible to receive the same defined benefits at the time of retirement. With the ESOP, their post-retirement income will be a function of the company's financial performance. Employees may not prefer this increase in the uncertainty of their retirement compensation. The employer may have to convince the employees that they will make substantial contributions to the ESOP. The size of the proposed contributions plus a favorable track record of financial performance may persuade employees that they will be better off with the ESOP. Employees may also be favorably impressed by the fact that when stock paid to an ESOP is substituted for wage income, employees enjoy the benefits of a tax shield.

Many privately held companies are reluctant to repurchase the ESOP shares. While they have a legal obligation to do so, they may openly declare that such sales are considered a sign of corporate disloyalty and may reflect badly on the employee seeking advancement within the company. This practice reduces the liquidity of part of this employee's compensation. The employee will then have to weigh the increased compensation against this reduced liquidity.

In addition to eliminating pension obligations, corporations such as Ralston Purina and Boise Cascade have substituted ESOPs for post-retirement health care plans. The corporation will then make contributions of stock into an ESOP. The ESOP, in turn, will fund the provision of health care benefits to employees. Given the rising cost of health care and the resulting uncertainty vis-à-vis the corporation's future cost structure, firms are eager to find ways to avoid these potential liabilities. ESOPs offer them one alternative.

EMPLOYEE RISK AND ESOPs

By accepting part of their compensation in the form of stock in the employer corporation, workers take on an increased risk. They are, in effect, "putting more of their eggs in one basket." If the company fails, they will not only lose their regular source of income but perhaps also the value of their pension. An example of this risk occurred in January 1990 when the South Bend Lathe Company was forced to file for bankruptcy under Chapter 7 of the bankruptcy law. Chapter 7 is the part of the law that regulates firms in liquidation. South Bend Lathe, a manufacturing firm established in 1906, was purchased in 1976 by its employees who owned 100 percent of the stock. The creditors, who initiated the bankruptcy filing, sought to seize 100 percent of the firm's stock which was used as collateral for a loan to one creditor.[9]

Corporations can offset some of this risk by contributing convertible preferred shares instead of shares of common stock. Convertible preferred shares have a higher priority in bankruptcy than common stock. If the value of the firm's stock increases, the employees will be able to participate in this growth by converting to shares of common stock.

SECURITIES LAWS AND ESOPs

Under federal securities laws, the sale of stock to an ESOP is not considered an issuance of securities to the public. When this stock is issued, it generally comes with a letter stating it is not subject to a sale to a third party. State corporation laws differ in their treatment of ESOPs. For example, New York laws do not require the registration of the donated securities, but they do require that the ESOP be registered as a securities dealer.

CORPORATION LOANS VERSUS LESOP LOANS

If a corporation borrows directly from a bank, only the interest payments are tax deductible. However, if the LESOP borrows from a bank, both the interest and the principal payments are tax deductible. This significantly lowers the costs of debt capital. In addition, a corporation may be able to get a low-interest rate on ESOP loans, perhaps even lower than the prime rate. This is possible because tax laws allow lenders to be taxed only on 50 percent of the interest income which they receive from ESOP loans. This interest exclusion applies solely to ESOP loans with a maximum term of seven years. Several legislative proposals have been made in Washington to repeal this interest exclusion.

Other Tax Benefits of ESOPs

If the target is not a public company, the target shareholders who tender their shares to an acquiring firm's leveraged ESOP may elect to defer

---

[9] The source of this report is Paul Dodson, "Creditors Seek Bankruptcy for S. B. Lathe," *Indiana Tribune*, January 18, 1990, p. 19.

the gain from the sale of the stock. Target shareholders are eligible for this deferment if certain conditions are met such as the ESOP holding at least 30 percent of the value of the outstanding shares after the sale.[10] A further tax benefit of ESOPs is that dividends paid to the ESOP shares are generally tax deductible.

THE BALANCE SHEET EFFECTS OF ESOPs

The debt that a leveraged ESOP incurs must be recorded on the firm's balance sheet. This corresponding reduction in shareholder equity must also be reflected on the firm's financial statements.[11] The shares issued to the ESOP must be counted as outstanding shares for the purpose of computing earnings per share. In doing so, the post-ESOP earnings per share measure captures the equity dilution effects.

DRAWBACKS OF LEVERAGED ESOPs

Equity Dilution Effects

The ability of ESOPs to borrow, while providing the borrower with attractive tax advantages that lower the ultimate borrowing costs, is a clear advantage. However, to compare the after-tax effects of borrowing directly from a bank with those of borrowing through an ESOP would be misleading. When a firm borrows through an ESOP, the employer firm is issuing equity while it is borrowing. From the original stockholders' viewpoint, the result is a dilution of equity. These new equity holders, the firm's employees, will share in any gains that the new debt capital can generate. These equity holders will still be there expecting to receive returns on their stock even after the loan is repaid. Therefore, a true analysis of the costs of borrowing through an ESOP will be accurate only if the equity dilution effects are considered. This is difficult to do since the equity dilution costs are dependent on the firm's future performance, which may be difficult to predict. The true equity dilution effects are based on the productivity of the new "capital" which derive from the ESOP's cost savings effects.

To reverse the equity dilution effects, the firm must repurchase the newly issued shares at a later date. When it does so, the discounted

---

[10] Coopers & Lybrand, *Business Acquisitions and Leveraged Buyouts* (1989), pp. 181–183.

[11] Ibid.

value of this expenditure can be used to derive a measure of the true costs of borrowing.

> Leveraged ESOP financing will be most advantageous for a publicly held company that can easily repurchase the shares. It will also be useful in a privately held firm where the repurchase liability can be passed on to a new set of owners. If the present users of the leveraged ESOP plan to be non-owners of the company (as in the case of a leveraged buyout by management, perhaps in combination with a takeover defense), the company usually will not issue new shares—leveraging will be used simply to replace one set of owners with another. When it does not result in new equity, the leveraged ESOP has more advantages.

> It is also conceivable that management may decide to use a leveraged ESOP instead of debt financing for the short-term advantages of cheaper credit or lower interest rates or because a specific lender may decide that the ESOP ameliorates an otherwise unacceptable credit scenario.[12]

The Distributional Effects of ESOPs

Depending on the price the ESOP pays for the firm's shares, the distributional effects may be associated with the ESOP. If employees receive shares in the company at a below-market price, a redistribution of wealth may occur. Employees gain wealth at the expense of nonemployee shareholders. If employees make other sacrifices, such as lower wages or benefits, which offset the gain on the below-market price shares, there will not be any redistributional effects.

In a survey of 192 publicly held firms with ESOPs, Susan Chaplinsky and Greg Niehaus found that 48.2 percent of the firms reported an increase in employee compensation as a result of the ESOP and that 39.3 percent did not change their compensation. Only 6 percent reported a decline in employee compensation when the ESOP was adopted.[13]

Since almost half the cases in the Chaplinsky–Niehaus sample reported increases in employee compensation, there may be a redistribution of wealth from nonemployee shareholders to employees. It would be short-sighted, however, to conclude that the total net effect is that nonemployee shareholders lose. Some of the higher employee compensation may be necessary to offset the increased risk of their total compensation package. In addition, productivity gains may be associ-

---

[12] Joseph Blasi, *Employee Ownership* (Cambridge, Mass.: Ballinger Publishing Co., 1988), p. 70.

[13] Susan Chaplinsky and Greg Niehaus, "The Tax and Distributional Effects of Leveraged ESOPs," *Financial Management* 19, no. 1 (Spring 1990):29–38.

ated with the fact that employees are now owners of shares in the company.

Loss of Control

Another disadvantage of ESOPs, which is related to the equity dilution effects, is the loss of control by the non-ESOP stockholders. After shares have been issued to the ESOP, the non-ESOP stockholders experience reduced ownership and control of the corporation.

It is more difficult for management to expand its control when an ESOP owns much of the firm's stock. The Tax Reform Act of 1986 contained antidiscrimination provisions requiring that an ESOP's benefits cannot be controlled by a small group of managers. This law requires that the percentage of employees who are not highly compensated must comprise at least 70 percent of the shareholdings controlled by highly compensated employees. Highly compensated employees are defined as those who earn more than $75,000 or those who earn more than $50,000 and who are in the top 20 percent employee compensation bracket for that company. Given this restriction, it is more difficult for management to control a larger number of shares directly. This drawback may be partially offset by the workers' tendency to vote with management on most issues.

ESOPs AND CORPORATE PERFORMANCE

Some proponents of ESOPs contend that ESOPs are beneficial for corporations because, as discussed above, they help finance capital expenditures and facilitate improvements in labor productivity. ESOPs may also enhance worker productivity if the workers view their ownership position as a reason to take a greater interest in their performance. With sufficient financial incentives, workers may be less resistant to productivity-enhancing changes such as mechanization or more efficient work procedures.

In a report to the chairman of the U.S. Senate Finance Committee, the General Accounting Office (GAO) found little evidence of such benefits.[14] The study failed to find a perceptible difference in profitability between firms that had ESOPs and those that did not. Apparently,

---

[14] "Employee Stock Ownership Effects: Little Evidence of Effects on Corporate Performance," U.S. General Accounting Office, Report to the Committee on Finance, U.S. Senate, October 1987.

CASE STUDY: *DAN RIVER, INC.: CASE OF A FAILED ESOP*

Dan River, Inc., a textile manufacturer in Danville, Virginia, went private in 1983 in order to prevent being taken over by corporate raider, Carl Icahn.[a] As part of the going private transaction, workers agreed to give up their pensions in return for an employee stock ownership plan. The ESOP gave workers 70 percent of the stock in the company. The company adopted the ESOP, in part, to achieve the tax advantages associated with this type of benefit package while avoiding being taken over.

Media reports soon documented worker disenchantment with their failure to achieve greater voice in the company's affairs even though they were majority owners of the firm.

The company did not perform well following the buyout. It incurred the following losses in the three years after the buyout:

Year	Losses
1984	$8.4 million
1985	$32.9 million
1986	$8.1 million

Dan River, Inc., had planned to offer the public 34 percent of total equity in the company in an effort to reduce the $181 million debt the firm had accumulated. The offering of stock would lower the employees' percentage of ownership. Management, however, owned a separate class of stock, Class B, which, according to a formula designed at the time of the buyout, appreciated faster than the employees' shares. Employees, owning Class A shares, would sacrifice the potential to achieve greater appreciation while retaining higher priority in the event of liquidation.

Gains in worker productivity are often cited as one of the potential benefits of ESOPs. Dan River's workers, however, did not reportedly experience any increase in their involvement in determining the company's direction. The public stock offering, for example, did not require the employees' approval, even though it would affect their ownership shares. The Dan River case illustrates that employee ownership is not necessarily synonymous with increases in employee morale.

[a] This account is partially based on Dean Foust, "How Dan River Misses the Boat," *Business Week*, October 26, 1987, pp. 34–35.

in the first year after adopting an ESOP, firms experienced a temporary increase in profitability; there were no noticeable long-term increases in profitability. The GAO study also compared labor productivity, as measured by the ratio of real value added to real compensation of ESOP firms, with non-ESOP firms. An examination of the productivity trend for ESOP firms appears to show an increase following the adoption of the ESOP. A statistical analysis of this relationship fails to reveal a significant relationship, however.

ESOPs AS AN ANTITAKEOVER DEFENSE

Much of the rising popularity of ESOPs is related to the use of this compensation vehicle as an antitakeover defense rather than because of its tax advantages. Although the antitakeover implications of ESOPs have already been discussed in Chapter 5, in the interest of completeness they are reviewed and expanded on here.

A larger percentage of American corporations are incorporated in Delaware where an antitakeover law became effective December 27, 1987 (see Chapter 3). As noted earlier, this law provided that if a bidder purchases more than 15 percent of a firm's stock, the bidder cannot complete the takeover for three years unless:

1. The bidder purchases as much as 85 percent of the target's shares.
2. Two-thirds of the shareholders approve the acquisition (excluding the bidder's shares).
3. The board of directors and the shareholders decide to exempt themselves from the provisions of the law.

A Delaware corporation can establish an ESOP, which can act as its own white squire. The combined holdings of stock in the ESOP plus other "loyal" blocks of stock may prevent a bidder from ever reaching the 85 percent level necessary to complete the takeover. This defense was used most effectively in the Polaroid-Shamrock Holdings takeover battle in 1988.

ESOPs AND SHAREHOLDER WEALTH

Theoretically, ESOPs can have an impact on shareholder wealth in two opposing ways. On the one hand, ESOPs may provide tax benefits to corporations which can lower their tax liabilities. If tax liabilities are lowered, then after-tax profitability is greater and larger distributions can be made to shareholders. On the other hand, if the ESOP is used as an antitakeover defense, the probability that shareholders might receive a takeover premium may be reduced as the firm's stock price could decline.

In a study of 165 announcements of the formation of an ESOP, Saeyoung Chang found that 65 percent of the firms showed positive abnormal returns for a two-day period around the announcement. The average abnormal two-day return was 3.66 percent.[15] Chang then ana-

---

[15] Saeyoung Chang, "Employee Stock Ownership Plans and Shareholder Wealth: An Empirical Investigation," *Financial Management* 19, no. 1 (Spring 1990):48–58.

CASE STUDY: *POLAROID: AN ESOP AS AN ANTITAKEOVER DEFENSE*

Polaroid made the first use of an ESOP as an antitakeover defense in response to an unsolicited $40 per share bid from Shamrock Holdings on July 20, 1988. The ESOP did not provide additional compensation to Polaroid employees. The ESOP was funded through a 5 percent pay cut and a reduction in certain other employee benefits. The ESOP was structured so that all employees would participate.

> The ESOP borrowed a total of $285 million and received a total of $15 million in cash form Polaroid to purchase 9.7166 million new shares at $30.875. . . . The share price to the ESOP was determined more by legal reference rather than from financial analysis. Legal precedent suggested three possible pricing rules: (i) closing price on the date of the plan approval by the board (July 12), (ii) average between the high and low price on July 12, and (iii) the average share price over a longer time period. Polaroid adopted the lowest price consistent with these rules, rule (ii).[a]

The sale of shares to the ESOP was followed by a share repurchase program that was implemented through a self-tender. A total of 24.5 million shares were repurchased at an average price of $45.918 per share, resulting in a decline in the number of Polaroid shares outstanding and leaving the ESOP holding approximately 20 percent of the firm's stock.[b]

Shamrock Holdings attempted to dismantle the ESOP defense through legal action in the Delaware courts. They took the position that the ESOP was discriminatory in that it was established to prevent Shamrock from purchasing Polaroid. As noted earlier, however, the court found that Polaroid's board of directors had considered establishing an ESOP as early as 1985. The court failed to agree with Shamrock's position that the ESOP shares not be considered in computing total shares according to Delaware's antitakeover law. The court felt that because the Polaroid ESOP plan allowed the employees holding shares through the ESOP to vote those shares in the tender offer, these shares should be considered with the other outstanding shares in computing the 85 percent. Judge Berger stated that the ESOP was "fundamentally fair" and did not advance management's interest over those of the employees.[c] This made it almost impossible for Shamrock to acquire the 85 percent of total shares necessary to complete the takeover under this law.

Many corporations realized that the cost of establishing a defensive ESOP might be far less than the 14 percent shareholding that Polaroid used for its ESOP. Many firms already have shares in various pension, savings, and employee benefit plans. These shares may be used as part, if not all, of the necessary 15 percent to achieve protection under the Delaware law. Chevron, for example, only had to place 5 percent of its shares in an ESOP because it

[a] Robert F. Bruner and E. Richard Brownlee II, "Leveraged ESOPs, Wealth Transfers and 'Shareholder Neutrality': The Case of Polaroid," *Financial Management* 19, no. 1 (Spring 1990):63.

[b] Ibid., p. 64

[c] Keith Hammonds, John Hoerr, and Zachary Schiller, "A New Way to Keep Raiders at Bay," *Business Week,* January 23, 1989, p. 39.

already had 11 percent of its stock in company employee benefit plans.[d] Some firms already have 15 percent of their shares in employee benefit plans, which means that an ESOP can be established without the usual dilution of equity. The firm may be required to alter the voting rights of the shares already in employee benefit plans to allow for the shares to have voting rights if they do not already possess these rights.

Shamrock Holdings was forced to drop its bid and entered into a 10-year standstill agreement with Polaroid. Shamrock, in turn, was compensated by Polaroid for some of the expenses it incurred through the bidding process. Polaroid also paid Shamrock Holdings for advertising time on some of the radio stations owned by Shamrock as part of the reimbursement agreement.

[d] Aaron Bernstein, "How to Keep Raiders at Bay—On the Cheap," *Business Week*, January 29, 1990, p. 59.

lyzed the different motives for adopting an ESOP, such as financing an LBO or adopting an antitakeover defense. He considered the impact on shareholder wealth for each of these separate subsamples of ESOP adoptions. For firms that adopted an ESOP to facilitate the financing of a leveraged buyout, the average abnormal two-day return was 11.45 percent. Firms that adopted an ESOP to achieve wage concessions from employees and thereby improve cash flows showed an abnormal two-day return of 4.19 percent. When an ESOP was adopted as an antitakeover defense, a −2.34 percent average abnormal return was shown.

Chang's results imply that ESOPs may increase shareholder wealth except when they are used as an antitakeover defense. The negative effect of the antitakeover defense on shareholder wealth might not be apparent if a longer time period than the two-day window around the announcement was used. If the ESOP results in a better negotiating position for a target, which, in turn, results in a higher takeover premium, this might not be apparent in the short two-day window. Therefore, although ESOPs that are used as an antitakeover defense may reduce shareholder wealth, further analysis is necessary to prove it.

ESOPs AND LEVERAGED BUYOUTS

One of the more dynamic ways in which LBOs can be structured involves the innovative use of ESOPs.[16] Louis Kelso of Kelso and

---

[16] Frisch, *The Magic of ESOPs and LBOs*, p. 12. This book provides a comprehensive treatment of the use of ESOPs to finance LBOs.

Company pioneered the use of this technique to purchase firms. (Kelso was also active in convincing legislators, such as Senator Russell Long, former chairman of the Senate Finance Committee, to support provisions of ERISA which would enhance the powers of ESOPs.) Using an ESOP as a corporate finance tool, he helped the employees of a small newspaper chain in Palo Alto, California, Peninsula Newspapers, to buy this business from the retiring owner of the chain.[17] The plan enabled them to buy the company while enjoying significant tax benefits that lowered the cost of the purchase.

With regard to the use of ESOPs for leveraged buyouts, the ESOP, or more appropriately the LESOP, arranges to borrow funds that will be used to finance the leveraged buyout. This can be done through a bank or a group of lenders. The larger the amount of funds required, the more likely the capital will come from a group of lenders. The LESOP borrows a certain amount of money from a bank (or group of lenders). The collateral for this loan will be the stock in the borrowing corporation. The loan may also be guaranteed by the parent corporation in the case of a leveraged buyout of a division of a company. The employer corporation makes tax deductible contributions to the LESOP for the payment of the loan and principal.

The LESOP–LBO Process

All LBOs are somewhat different but tend to share many common characteristics. For the purposes of exposition, let's consider the case of a selloff of a division in which the management of the parent company seeks to buy the division through a leveraged buyout. The steps by which this transaction could take place, using a LESOP, are as follows:

Step 1. A new company is formed which will be the division in an independent form.

Step 2. The management of the division, which will constitute the new owners of that part of the parent company, may make an equity investment in the division. At this point, the division may be a corporate shell without assets.

Step 3. An ESOP for the new company is established. The ESOP negotiates with a bank or other lenders for a loan and then becomes a LESOP. The new company agrees to make periodic payments to service the loan interest and principal.

---

[17] Joseph S. Schuchert, "The Art of the ESOP Leveraged Buyout," in Stephen C. Diamond, ed., *Leveraged Buyouts* (Homewood, Ill.: Dow Jones Irwin 1985), p. 94.

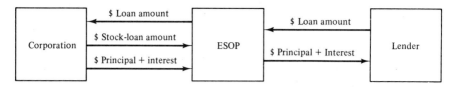

Figure 9.1

This loan can also be guaranteed by the original corporation if that becomes a condition of the lenders. When the risk level of the new company is perceived to be high, a guarantee is often required.

Step 4. The LESOP uses the proceeds of the loan to purchase the assets that will be put into the new company. These assets were allocated to the divested division when it was part of the parent company. After this transaction, the LESOP owns them.

Step 5. The LESOP then sells the acquired assets to the new corporation for stock in the new company.

Step 6. The new company makes periodic contributions to the LESOP, which the LESOP uses to repay the loan. These contributions have the great advantage of being tax deductible.

The above process is diagramatically depicted in Figure 9.1. The deal can also be structured so that the LESOP uses the loan proceeds to purchase stock in the new corporation rather than to purchase assets. Under this scenario, the new corporation uses the proceeds of the sale to buy the assets of the parent corporation.

ESOPs can be used to lower the cost of the LBO by taking advantage of the tax deductions allowable under the law. In this way they are an innovative means of completing a leveraged buyout. In a leveraged ESOP, the securities that are purchased are placed in a *suspense account*. These securities are allocated to the participants in the ESOP as the loan is repaid. The allocation is based on the compensation relevant to each participating employee.

SUMMARY

Employee stock ownership plans were originally developed to provide benefits to employees. Finance practitioners have discovered, however, that they can also be a highly innovative corporate finance tool. When used as borrowing vehicles by corporations, they can provide the company with significant tax benefits. These cash flow benefits can be enhanced when the company combines the tax benefits with a reduction in outstanding contributions to other benefits programs. Buyers of corporations have realized that these financing tools could be used to provide bidders with cost advantages in raising the debt capital necessary to finance leveraged acquisitions. ESOPs, therefore, can be used by hostile bidders as well as by employee groups interested in acquiring their company. While ESOPs can be of great benefit to buyers of companies, they have also proved to be instrumental in creating a potent antitakeover defense for corporations chartered in Delaware. The value of this antitakeover defense has been underscored by the fact that it has successfully withstood a serious legal challenge. The result is that ESOPs have become an important tool in the arsenal of both bidders and targets.

REFERENCES

Bernstein, Aaron. "How to Keep Raiders at Bay—On the Cheap." *Business Week*, January 29, 1990, p. 59.

Blasi, Joseph. *Employee Ownership*. Cambridge, Mass.: Ballinger Publishing Co., 1988.

Brigham, Eugene F., and Louis C. Gapenski. *Intermediate Financial Management*. 2nd ed. Chicago: Dryden Press, 1987, pp. 759–784.

Bruner, Robert F. "Leveraged ESOPs and Corporate Restructuring." *Journal of Applied Corporate Finance* 1, no. 1 (Spring 1988):54–66.

Bruner, Robert F., and E. Richard Brownlee II. "Leveraged ESOPs, Wealth Transfers and 'Shareholder Neutrality': The Case of Polaroid." *Financial Management* 19, no. 1 (Spring 1990):59–74.

Chang, Saeyoung. "Employee Stock Ownership Plans and Shareholder Wealth: An Empirical Investigation." *Financial Management* 19, no. 1 (Spring 1990):48–58.

Chen, Andrew H. "Beyond the Tax Benefits of ESOPs." *Journal of Applied Corporate Finance* 1, no. 1 (Spring 1988):67–75.

Coopers & Lybrand. *Business Acquisitions and Leveraged Buyouts*. New York: 1989.

Foust, Dean. "How Dan River Misses the Boat." *Business Week*, October 26, 1987, pp. 34–35.

Frisch, Robert A. *The Magic of ESOPs and LBOs*. New York: Farnsworth Publishing, 1985, p. 12.

Hammonds, Keith, John Hoerr, and Zachary Schiller. "A New Way to Keep Raiders at Bay." *Business Week*, January 23, 1989, p. 29.

Rosen, Corey. "The Record of Employee Ownership." *Financial Management* 19, no. 1 (Spring 1990):39–47.

Scholes, Myron, and Mark Wolfson. "Employee Stock Ownership Plans and Corporate Restructuring: Myths and Realities." *Financial Management* 19, no. 1 (Spring 1990):12–28.

Schuchert, Joseph S. "The Art of the ESOP Leveraged Buyout." In Stephen C. Diamond, ed., *Leveraged Buyouts*. Homewood, Ill.: Dow Jones Irwin, 1985.

U.S. General Accounting Office. "Employee Stock Ownership Plans: Benefits and Costs of ESOP Tax Incentives for Broadening Stock Ownership." Washington, D.C., 1987.

Chapter
10

Case Studies in Leveraged Buyouts

INTRODUCTION

The previous three chapters presented a framework for understanding leveraged buyouts. The reader can now apply this information to an examination of some of the more notable leveraged buyouts. The RJR Nabisco buyout will be discussed first since it is the largest single transaction of any type of merger, acquisition, or leveraged buyout. It is useful to examine since it appears that this buyout will perform well even though a record amount of debt was sold to finance it. As with the other case studies discussed in this section, a basic financial analysis of the firm prior to the buyout will be presented to put the valuation by the investors in perspective. The financial structure of the buyout package is also explained. In addition, unique aspects of the LBO as well as the overall background of the transaction are discussed.

The LBO of the Revco drug store chain is a classic example of a buyout that failed. The firm's failure can be attributed to many reasons, including too much debt and poor marketing. It is a highly instructive case study since it shows why LBOs can fail. This case study is then contrasted with the Safeway leveraged buyout which has performed quite well. Where Revco succumbed to the pressures of the LBO debt, Safeway made the necessary changes in its operations to provide good returns to its LBO investors. Safeway, therefore, is an excellent case study showing how a leveraged buyout should be structured and what the beneficial effects of a good LBO should be. The Safeway case study, which is often cited by proponents of LBOs, will be critically examined in light of some of the adverse effects such as reductions in workforce. It will be seen that even good LBOs may have some negative aspects.

THE RJR NABISCO LEVERAGED BUYOUT

The RJR Nabisco LBO is by far the largest merger, acquisition, or leveraged buyout in U.S. history ($25.1 billion). It is almost double the size of the previously largest acquisition, the Chevron acquisition of Gulf ($13.3 billion). Table 10.1 shows the size of the previous ten largest LBOs.

Firm and Industry Background

The RJR Nabisco buyout is more difficult to categorize than other LBOs such as Revco and Safeway because it is not exclusively in one industry category. Rather, its revenues are derived from two principal areas of operation: tobacco product sales and food product sales. In 1987, approximately 40 percent of the firm's revenues were tobacco sales and 60 percent were food related. Although the majority of the firm's revenues came from food products, 67 percent of the firm's operating income derived from tobacco products, whereas only 33 percent came from food (see Table 10.2).

There has been a clear downward trend in the domestic consumption of tobacco products, primarily because of the public's increasing awareness of the health hazards associated with tobacco consumption.

Table 10.1   THE TEN LARGEST LBOs PRECEDING THE RJR NABISCO BUYOUT

Date	Target Name	Acquirer's Name	Amount (billion $)
4/17/86	Beatrice	Kohlberg, Kravis	$6.2
7/30/87	Borg Warner	Merrill Lynch	4.7
12/15/87	Southland	Thompson	4.6
11/24/86	Safeway Stores	Kohlberg, Kravis	4.3
6/23/88	Montgomery Ward	Bernard Brennan	3.8
7/15/86	R. H. Macy	Macy Acquiring Co.	3.7
3/24/87	Owens-Illinois	Kohlberg, Kravis	3.7
12/31/86	Allied Stores	Campeau	3.6
6/9/87	Viacom	National Amusement	3.4
12/5/85	Storer Comm.	Kohlberg, Kravis	2.5

Table 10.2   RJR NABISCO SALES AND INCOME, 1983–1987 (PCT.)

Net sales	1987	1986	1985	1984	1983
Tobacco	40	39	47	63	64
Food	60	61	53	37	36

Operating income	1987	1986	1985	1984	1983
Tobacco	67	67	73	88	90
Food	33	33	27	12	10

The government's tendency to raise taxes on tobacco products has accelerated this downward trend. In 1987, total cigarette consumption declined approximately 2 percent. However, the company's total tobacco sales, including other tobacco products such as cigars and chewing tobacco, rose $480 million, bringing Nabisco's market share up to 32.5 percent. The rise in sales, at a time when domestic consumption was waning, came as a result of higher prices, record international volume, and favorable currency variations.

The long-term outlook for the tobacco business in the United States may not be as bright as it once was. Although tobacco sales and income have been steadily rising, owing partly to the solid performance of RJR's major international brands such as Camel, Salem, and Winston, future sales and income are projected to level off. On the other hand, the addictive nature of the product results in it being a steady producer of cash flows. The company will increasingly have to look to other areas for growth. Aware of this pessimistic outlook for tobacco product sales, the firm began using its prodigious tobacco income to diversify. In 1985, for example, it purchased Nabisco Brands and Planters Life Savers. The major product lines associated with these two divisions provide RJR with a broad-based, recession-resistant product line that will likely fuel its future growth.

The food industry grew at a rate of approximately 1.7 percent in 1987 and 1988. RJR's food sales grew $184 million to a total of $9.4 billion in 1987. The company experienced strong results from certain product categories, such as cookies, crackers, and cereal.

The Auction Process

The RJR buyout started with an initial bid from the then chairman, F. Ross Johnson. His group included Shearson Lehman Brothers and other members of senior management. Some considered his initial offer of $75 a share "lowballing." This low bid, however, put the company in play and resulted in a bidding contest between the Johnson lead group and Kohlberg, Kravis & Roberts (KKR). Johnson later increased his bid to $112, which was roughly equivalent to KKR's final offer of $109 after the risk levels of the securities in the two packages were considered. Since the two offers were roughly equivalent, the board of directors considered other nonfinancial factors when awarding their decision to KKR. Many analysts contend that the board of directors was disappointed in Johnson's handling of the process. According to one report, "He lowballed his bid, offering $75 per share, and he negotiated an overly generous compensation package for himself and a few colleagues."[1]

The RJR deal raised serious questions as to whether CEOs should mount leveraged buyouts. Clearly, the potential of a conflict of interest exists: On the one hand, the CEO has the fiduciary obligation to maximize shareholder value, but on the other, it is in his interest to minimize his offer. The RJR case illustrates how the auction process took care of the conflict of interest. Johnson offered a low bid that inspired an auction for the firm in which the value of the stockholder's investment was increased.

Nabisco's Pre-LBO Financial Condition

Liquidity   RJR's current ratio has been steadily declining since 1983. The current ratio, reflecting the ratio of current assets of current liabilities, was as high as 3.30 in 1983 but declined to 1.36 in 1986. The average for all manufacturing firms is approximately 2. Food manufacturing firms have an average current ratio of 1.85, whereas tobacco manufacturers have an average current ratio of 2.12. The lower than average liquidity indicates a greater risk that the firm will not be able to meet its short-term liabilities. The lower the current ratio, the lower the amount of working capital (current assets − current liabilities). Although this is a negative characteristic of the firm, Nabisco's size and its short-term borrowing capacity and ability to establish lines of credit provide protection against this eventuality. However, liquidity is still an important consideration for an LBO candidate since further deterioration in the firm's liquidity might make it more difficult for the firm to meet its higher interest obligations. Therefore, although the firm's liquidity is below average, it could maintain such a position, assuming there was not a major deterioration in other financial characteristics. The ratios of current assets to current liabilities for 1978–1988 were as follows:

---

[1] Judith H. Dobrzynski, "The Lessons of the RJR Free-for-All," *Business Week*, December 19, 1988, p. 30.

RJR NABISCO'S CURRENT RATIOS

1978	1979	1980	1981	1982	1983	1984	1985	1986	1987	1988
3.30	2.50	2.30	2.40	2.20	3.30	2.50	1.40	1.33	1.42	1.47

Ratios for the 1977–1988 period are shown in Figure 10.1.

Leverage   RJR Nabisco substantially increased its leverage in the 1980s as a result of its acquisition of Nabisco in 1985. Long-term debt rose dramatically that year. This is important since the more debt the firm already has, the less additional debt it can comfortably assume. It is also important since the higher debt will increase the risk that the firm will not be able to meet its debt and other fixed payments. The higher leverage is reflected in a rising debt to total assets ratio. This ratio has been rising steadily since 1978 (see Figures 10.2 and 10.3). The debt to assets ratios for 1978–1988 were as follows:

RJR NABISCO'S DEBT TO ASSETS RATIO

1978	1979	1980	1981	1982	1983	1984	1985	1986	1987	1988
0.15	0.39	0.40	0.38	0.45	0.40	0.43	0.61	0.66	0.63	0.68

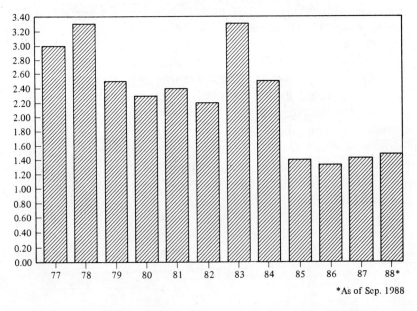

*As of Sep. 1988

Figure 10.1 Current ratio, Nabisco.

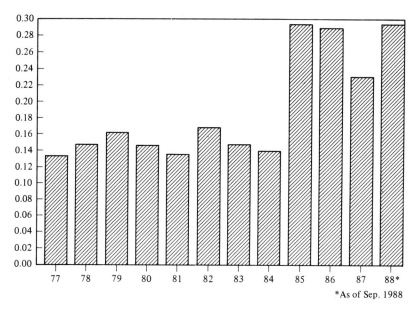

Figure 10.2 Long-term debt to asset, Nabisco.

We can evaluate the firm's ability to service higher debt levels by examining the trends in the times interest earned ratio. This trend turned sharply downward from as high as 13.77 in 1978 to 4.44 in 1988. The 13.77 figure is quite good, but 4.44 is still in the acceptable range,

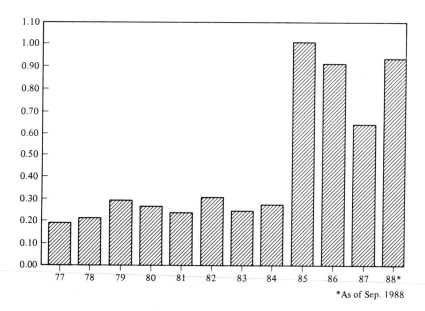

Figure 10.3 Long-term debt to equity, Nabisco.

which is usually considered to lie between 3 and 5. This ratio fell sharply when the LBO debt payments started.

Earnings before interest and taxes/interest changes for 1978–1988 were as follows. (See also Figure 10.4.)

RJR NABISCO'S INTEREST COVERAGE RATIOS

1978	1979	1980	1981	1982	1983	1984	1985	1986	1987	1988
0.15	0.39	0.40	0.38	0.45	0.40	0.43	0.61	0.66	0.63	0.68

Profitability   RJR Nabisco remained fairly profitable during the 1980s, maintaining a high return on equity which reached 24 percent in 1988 compared to an average of 8.5 percent for all manufacturing firms. This performance was quite good, although it is not unusual for firms that have added income-generating assets financed by debt, not equity, to experience such returns. The return on total assets of 8 percent was satisfactory, although it was down from 13 percent in 1984. The average for manufacturing firms was 4.1 percent that year.

Nabisco appears to have above-average profitability, which helps explain why it was such a desirable target and why it attracted such a high winning bid. The preliminary view of the profitability of the post-

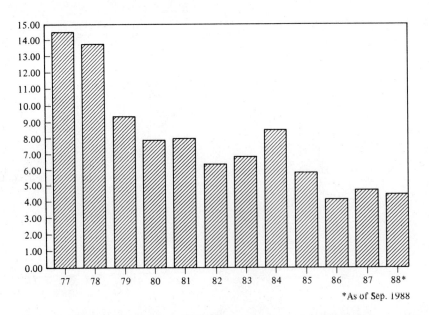

*As of Sep. 1988

Figure 10.4 Times interest earned, Nabisco.

LBO RJR Nabisco appears to be promising. Fourth-quarter 1988 earnings were strong and in line with analysts' expectations. The earnings boosted the note offering by Drexel Burnham Lambert following the buyout. These expectations were somewhat dampened by a less than optimistic first-quarter earnings report that showed a 62 percent drop in first-quarter earnings. These pessimistic results were primarily the result of the expenses associated with the buyout and the failure of RJR Nabisco's Premier smokeless cigarettes. These losses and payments are one-time charges, however, and should not affect RJR Nabisco's long-term performance. For a view of Nabisco's operating and net income for 1977–1988, see Figures 10.5 and 10.6.

Price of the LBO   The final compensation package for RJR Nabisco provided for a total compensation of $25.08 billion, or $109 per share, as follows:

Cash: $81 per share

Exchangeable preferred stock: $18 per share

Convertible debentures: $10 per share

It should be noted that $28 of the $34 increase above the Ross Johnson/Shearson initial offer of $75 came in the form of noncash compensation such as preferred stock and debentures.

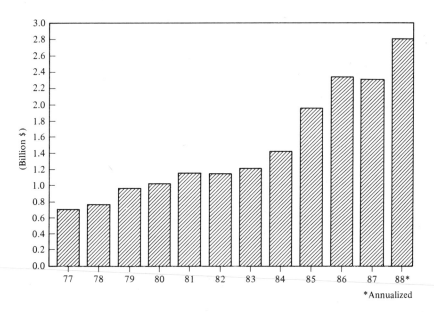

Figure 10.5 Operating income, Nabisco.

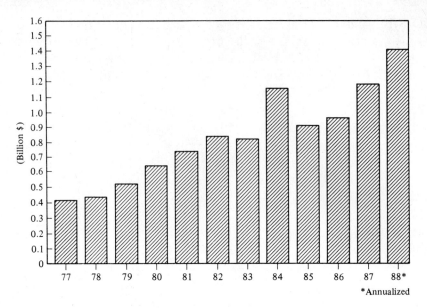

Figure 10.6 Net income, Nabisco.

Kohlberg, Kravis & Roberts also agreed to keep the tobacco business and most of the food businesses intact, thereby alleviating many of the concerns of the board of directors that the company would be broken up to pay for the costs of debt. KKR also agreed to guarantee severance payments and other benefits to employees who might lose their jobs as a result of the change in control.[2]

Apparently, the bidding war between KKR and the RJR Nabisco management group led by Johnson extracted a maximum value for the firm. A valuation of the different divisions of the firm conducted by Smith Barney, Harris Upham & Co. shows a total valuation in the range $24.6 to $26.1 billion. The breakdown of this valuation is shown in Table 10.3.

Financing the RJR Nabisco LBO   The offer from Kohlberg, Kravis & Roberts was financed largely by the sales of senior subordinated debentures and subordinated debentures. The deal was put together utilizing bridge loan financing. In this method of financing, the bidding firm arranges a loan from various lenders which will be used to consummate the offer as well as to pay off certain indebtedness and fees associated with the merger. The bridge financing in the RJR deal was

---

[2] *Wall Street Journal*, December 2, 1988, p. A10.

Table 10.3 PRE-LBO VALUATION OF RJR NABISCO DIVISIONS

Division	Value
Tobacco (i.e., Camel, Winston, Salem, and Vantage cigarettes)	$12.5–$13.0 billion
Food operations	$12.1–$13.1 billion
Nabisco cookies and crackers (i.e., Oreo and Ritz)	$5 billion
Canned vegetables (i.e., Del Monte)	$500 million
Canned fruits (i.e., Del Monte)	$300 million
Cereals (i.e., Shredded wheat and cream of wheat)	$750–$1 billion
Planters peanuts	$800–$900 million
Life Savers	$400–$500 million
Candy bars (i.e., Baby Ruth, Butterfinger)	$300 million
Bubble gum (i.e., Carefree Bubble Yum)	$200 million
Margarine (Fleischmann's, Blue Bonnet)	$200–$300 million
Fresh fruit (i.e., Del Monte)	$700 million
Ortega Mexican food	$150 million
A-1 Steak Sauce	$100–$150 million
Milkbone dog biscuits	$200 million
International food	$2.5–$3 billion

Sources: Smith Barney, Harris Upham & Co., Wall Street Journal, December 2, 1988, p. A10. Reprinted by permission of the Wall Street Journal, copyright © 1988 Dow Jones & Company, Inc. All Rights Reserved Worldwide.

scheduled to mature six months after the deal was completed. At that time, the bridge financing was refinanced with permanent debt securities. The market's positive response to the deal was underscored by the fact that the initial offering of junk bonds by Drexel Burnham Lambert was oversubscribed.[3]

Sources of Financing The original financing plan proposed by Kohlberg, Kravis & Roberts in the Schedule 14D1 filed with the SEC called for funding from the following sources:

Borrowing from a syndicate of banks	65.0%
Subordinated bridge financing from Drexel Burnham and Merrill Lynch	24.6%
Equity capital supplied by Kohlberg, Kravis	7.5%
Other permanent debt securities	2.5%

The note offering following the LBO proved to be more popular than Drexel Burnham Lambert had anticipated. For example, Drexel had originally planned to offer $3 billion worth of notes, but in the face

[3] Wall Street Journal, January 26, 1989.

of strong demand, this total was increased to $5 billion. The popularity of the notes reduced the need for bridge financing from Drexel and Merrill Lynch. In effect, the higher than anticipated note sale took the place of the bridge financing. The notes were refinanced in the spring of 1989 through the sale of junk bonds. The magnitude of the deal can be seen through the sheer size of the capital flows that took place. On one day, $18.9 billion of the total $25.08 billion changed hands, the largest commercial financing in history. The transfer of funds was so large that it taxed the ability of the Federal Reserve's wire transfer system. The Federal Reserve interbank wire transfer system can transfer a maximum of $999 in a single transaction. RJR's bankers had to engage in several individual transfers of $900 million each.[4] The transfer of funds is outlined in Figure 10.7.

Interest Rate Risk on Buyout Debt and Hedging Strategies

Firms often assume variable rate debt obligations in a leveraged buyout. Therefore, companies incur great interest rate risk associated with the possibility of adverse movements in interest rates. This risk becomes especially pronounced in a deal the size of the RJR Nabisco transaction. In an effort to minimize the interest rate risk, Kohlberg, Kravis & Roberts arranged a series of hedges referred to as an "interest rate cap." KKR paid a fee to a bank which, in turn, promised to pay any excess interest payments above a ceiling established in the interest rate cap agreement. The bank accomplished this by investing the proceeds of the cap agreement in the Eurodollar futures market as well as in Treasury securities. These monies were invested in ways that would allow the bank to earn profits if rates rose. The use of interest rate hedges reduced RJR Nabisco's vulnerability to unexpected increases in interest rates and made it easier for the buyout firm to raise the necessary financing since it lowers the risk of the LBO. According to the *New York Times*, "Kohlberg, Kravis & Roberts is required to keep an interest rate hedge on half of its outstanding bank debt until the total outstanding falls below $5 billion."[5] The cap agreement cost KKR $500,000 per $100 million of debt. This agreement would provide payment to KKR if interest rates rose above 11 percent.

---

[4] George Anders, "RJR Finale Will Send Money Coursing," *Wall Street Journal*, p. C1.

[5] Michael Quint, "Cutting Rate Risk on Buyout Debt," *New York Times*, February 16, 1989, p. D2.

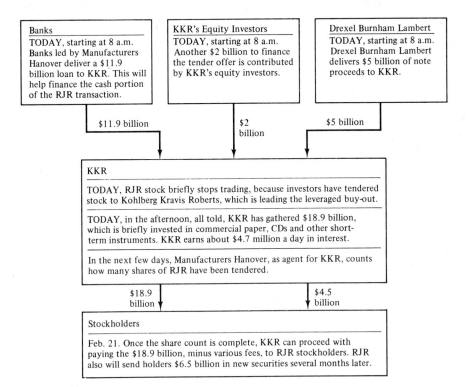

Banks	KKR's Equity Investors	Drexel Burnham Lambert
TODAY, starting at 8 a.m. Banks led by Manufacturers Hanover deliver a $11.9 billion loan to KKR. This will help finance the cash portion of the RJR transaction.	TODAY, starting at 8 a.m. Another $2 billion to finance the tender offer is contributed by KKR's equity investors.	TODAY, starting at 8 a.m. Drexel Burnham Lambert delivers $5 billion of note proceeds to KKR.

$11.9 billion $2 billion $5 billion

KKR

TODAY, RJR stock briefly stops trading, because investors have tendered stock to Kohlberg Kravis Roberts, which is leading the leveraged buy-out.

TODAY, in the afternoon, all told, KKR has gathered $18.9 billion, which is briefly invested in commercial paper, CDs and other short-term instruments. KKR earns about $4.7 million a day in interest.

In the next few days, Manufacturers Hanover, as agent for KKR, counts how many shares of RJR have been tendered.

$18.9 billion $4.5 billion

Stockholders

Feb. 21. Once the share count is complete, KKR can proceed with paying the $18.9 billion, minus various fees, to RJR stockholders. RJR also will send holders $6.5 billion in new securities several months later.

Figure 10.7 How $18.9 billion moves today in RJR deal. Reprinted by permission of the Wall Street Journal, copyright © Dow Jones & Company, Inc. All Rights Reserved Worldwide.

Asset Sales and Capital Expenditures After the LBO

The post-LBO RJR Nabisco is run by a new CEO—Leo V. Gerstner, the former president of American Express. Gerstner oversees the asset sales that are used to pay on the debt the firm assumed in the buyout. The asset sales plan formulated following the buyout called for the sale of assets and a reduction in expenditures in several areas.

> Selling roughly $8 billion of profitable assets, about 27% of RJR's revenue base, within a year. The likeliest divestiture candidates are the Del Monte Foods, International Nabisco Brands and Planters Life Savers units, plus the company's 20% stake in ESPN, the cable TV sports channel.

> Cutting back about $33 million, some 10% of the Nabisco unit's marketing budget and an additional $57 million in overhead. That could require layoffs of about 1,000 employees, 14% of the workforce, according to a former senior executive. Maintaining RJR's operating profit next year at 1989 levels despite the asset sales. To meet that rosy assumption, the memorandum projects that Nabisco's operating profit will grow 40% this

year and an additional 14% next year, a breathless pace for a food company.[6]

After a leveraged buyout, firms tend to cut back in capital expenditures. This is a potential problem area for RJR Nabisco. Prior to the buyout, it had been lagging behind its competitors in the use of advanced technology in the bakery business. The firm had planned to invest $2.8 billion in capital expenditures to upgrade the firm's facilities. The new technology would enable the firm to be more efficient by lowering the "overweight quotient" in a package of cookies. Other technology would reduce the amount of breakage. The implementation of this technology would make RJR more efficient. The post-LBO RJR Nabisco plans to invest significantly less in capital expenditures. Figure 10.8 shows a markedly lower level of capital outlays after the buyout. Given the firm's dominant position in both the tobacco and food businesses, it is unlikely that this alone will mean the downfall of the company. However, the lower level of capital outlays might mean an erosion in the firm's market share.

Fees Paid in the Buyout

The large amount of compensation paid to upper management and other dealmakers has come under considerable criticism. Many stockholders feel that such compensation is excessive and constitutes both a misappropriation of stockholder assets and a breach of the board of directors' fiduciary responsibilities. The RJR Nabisco buyout is a clear example of this excessively high compensation. RJR Nabisco paid $13.7 million to former chief executive, F. Ross Johnson, to cancel certain restricted stock Johnson owned. The company also paid the former head of the tobacco unit, Edward Horrigan, $13.6 million for his restricted stock.[7] In addition, the company reported payments of $247 million in severance payments to workers who left the firm after the buyout.

Kohlberg, Kravis & Roberts' one-time fee of $75 million for arranging the buyout was the largest single fee to date in a leveraged buyout.[8] "Kohlberg Kravis and Roberts earned $60 million each for the buyouts of Safeway Stores and Owens-Illinois Corp., whose price tags were $4.5 billion and $3.8 billion, respectively, and $45 million for its $6.2 billion

[6] Peter Waldman, "A New RJR Chief Faces a Daunting Challenge at Debt Heavy Firm," *Wall Street Journal*, March 14, 1989, p. 1.

[7] RJR Prospectus, *Wall Street Journal*, April 6, 1989, p. A11.

[8] Schedule 14D1 filed by Kohlberg, Kravis & Roberts, *Wall Street Journal*, February 1, 1989, p. A6.

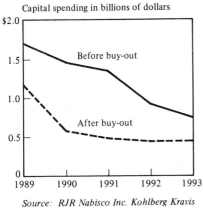

Capital spending in billions of dollars

Source: RJR Nabisco Inc. Kohlberg Kravis Roberts & Co.

Figure 10.8 RJR's planned outlays. (*Source:* "Change of Pace: RJR's New Chief, Long Known for Building Companies, Faces Tough Pruning Job," *Wall Street Journal*, March 14, 1989, p. A16. Reprinted by permission of the Wall Street Journal, copyright © Dow Jones & Company, Inc. All Rights Reserved Worldwide.)

buyout of Beatrice."[9] KKR and other dealmakers would contend that they create value through their ability to raise the requisite financing as well as through their efficiency-enhancing alterations of the post-buyout firm. Critics counter that their activities are mere financial sleight of hand and do not create value.

Shareholder Wealth Effects

Shareholders enjoyed very significant gains as a result of the RJR buyout. Total shareholder returns were close to 100 percent.[10] These larger than average returns to shareholders can be attributed to the auction process where Kohlberg Kravis and Roberts was forced to significantly increase the buyout package in order to outbid the Ross Johnson-Shearson group. Some say, however, that these gains to share-holders came at the expense of bondholders who saw the value of the debt securities decline dramatically after the firm assumed the large amounts of additional debt necessary to pay shareholders the high price for their shares.

RJR Nabisco's Post-Buyout Performance

RJR Nabisco's post-buyout performance, as of the middle of 1990, has been mixed. The firm posted losses, such as the $222 million loss for

---

[9] Ibid.

[10] Nancy Mohan and Carl Chen, "A Review of the RJR Nabisco Buyout," *Journal of Applied Corporate Finance*, 3(2), pp. 102–108.

the first quarter of 1990.[11] This loss was caused primarily by the massive debt expenses the firm had to service as a result of the buyout. The firm's bonds sold at a significant discount (some at 60 cents on the dollar), which was exacerbated when some of the RJR senior convertible debentures and payment in kind debt that was issued during the buyout was modestly downgraded by Moody's from B-2 to B-3.[12] The poor price of RJR debts was, in large part, a result of the overall decline in the junk bond market following the buyout.

The firm's post-buyout performance had many positive aspects, including the continued generation of strong cash flows from tobacco sales and an increase in food sales of 3.9 percent for 1989. Kohlberg, Kravis and Roberts continued its gradual asset sales program while looking for optimal prices for these assets. The strong cash flows of the firm enabled KKR to seek out the best prices rather to enter into quick sales at fire sales prices. In addition, KKR raised $1.7 billion in cash from its investors in 1990 which helped improve the performance of the firm's bonds.[13]

The outlook for RJR Nabisco appears quite positive today. The firm will likely be able to retire much of the post-buyout debt with asset sales. The firm's sizable cash flows prevent it from experiencing many of the problems of other debt-financing acquisition such as the Campeau buyout of Federated Stores which resulted in Campeau filing for bankruptcy. If there is one important lesson to be learned from the RJR Nabisco buyout, it is the value of a cash flow and the existence of significant marketable noncore assets. The firm with these two characteristics has greater ability to survive a leveraged buyout and to pay investors sizable returns.

THE REVCO LEVERAGED BUYOUT

On March 11, 1986, Revco received a buyout bid from a management group led by the then chief executive officer Sidney Dworkin. The bid offered $1.16 billion for the drug store chain which at that time was the second largest LBO in this industry. Following the LBO, however, the firm performed below expectations and became one of the first

---

[11] Peter Waldman, "R.J.R. Reports 1st-Period Loss of $222 Million," *Wall Street Journal*, April 25, 1990, p. A3.

[12] Kenneth Gilpin, "R.J.R. Bonds Off Sharply for 2nd Day," *New York Times*, January 10, 1990, p. A1.

[13] James White and David Hilder, "KKR Said to Raise $1.7 Billion for RJR in Bid to Bolster Firm's Sagging Bonds," *Wall Street Journal*, June 13, 1990, p. A3.

major LBOs to fail. For this reason the Revco LBO merits further study.

Industry Background

Drug store sales had been growing rapidly during the ten-year period before the buyout, increasing at an average annual rate of 11.6 percent between 1976 and 1986.[14] Sales for the 1987–1988 period ran close to the 7.5–8.0 percent range that was projected during the buyout negotiations. In response to the growing consumer demand, many drug store chains opened new outlets. Others expanded by buying other chains. One example was the Rite Aid Corporation's acquisition of the Grey Drug Fair chain, which was owned by the Sherwin Williams Paint Company.

The pharmaceutical industry has instituted many other innovations designed to improve productivity, including the increased use of computers to track and enhance inventory control. However, competitive forces require that the industry be even more efficient. This competition is in the form of combination food and drug stores chains as well as discount drug chains. Pharmaceuticals are considered one of the two recession-proof industries in the U.S. economy. (The other is the food industry.) A noncyclical firm is a better candidate for a leveraged buyout, all other factors being constant, since there is a lower probability that the cash flows will suffer a sudden, unpredictable fall-off owing to a cyclical reduction in demand.

The drug store industry continued to do well in the two-year period following the buyout. Sales continued to rise without a significant reduction in profit margins. The increased use of private labels provided firms with higher margin products that could be sold to consumers at competitive prices. The Revco buyout may have been inspired by the October 1985 LBO of Eckerd Drug Stores which went private for $1.184 billion. The rise in the number of large LBO offers in the drug store industry can be attributed to the general well-being of the industry, combined with the decline in interest rates as well as the cash-flow-generating ability of these firms.

Revco's Position in the Industry

As of August 23, 1986, Revco was the largest drug store chain in the United States with 2,049 stores in 30 states. Most of the company's stores were concentrated in Michigan, Ohio, Pennsylvania, North Car-

---

[14] U.S. Department of Commerce, *U.S. Industrial Outlook, 1989*.

olina, South Carolina, Georgia, Virginia, Tennessee, Arizona, and Texas. Although Revco had diversified into other areas, the majority of its income came from traditional drug store products. Revco's Odd Lot and Tangible Industries subsidiaries accounted for approximately 5 percent of its 1986 sales. These subsidiaries are wholesalers of closeout merchandise. Another 5 percent of its 1986 sales came from generic and private label drugs and vitamins.

Background of the Revco LBO

Revco was formerly Regal D. S., Inc., a Detroit-based drug store chain. In 1966, the company went public under the name Revco and moved its headquarters to Cleveland, Ohio. The company expanded and purchased Carter–Glogau Laboratories, a vitamin manufacturer. Revco also bought the Stanton Corporation which administered lie detector tests. Revco's CEO, Sidney Dworkin, had been with the firm since 1956 when he joined the company as an accountant. He oversaw Revco's development into one of the largest drug store chains in the country. By 1983, the company had 1,700 stores in 28 states. Its sales were almost $2 billion, with profits increasing at an impressive 37 percent per year.

Tragically, in 1983 vitamins made by Carter–Glogau were blamed for the deaths of 38 infants. As a result, the price of Revco stock fell, and Dworkin feared that the now undervalued Revco would be taken over. His defense was to place a large block of stock in what he believed would be friendly hands. In May 1984, Revco bought Odd Lot Trading Company, which had a chain of 70 discount stores, for $113 million in stock. This amounted to 12 percent of Revco's outstanding shares.

There have been numerous reports of personal conflicts between Dworkin and his new larger stockholders, the previous owners of Odd Lot Trading—Bernard Marden and Issac Perlmutter.[15] According to these reports, Dworkin favored the close involvement of his two sons in Revco's business operations, a move opposed by Marden and Perlmutter. It is further reported that Marden and Perlmutter threatened to take over Revco. Revco eventually bought back their shares for $98.2 million. The conflict between Dworkin and Marden and Perlmutter, together with the resulting stock buyback, marked the decline of Dworkin's role in Revco. When the board of directors opposed the involve-

---

[15] "Revco: Anatomy of a Failed Buyout," *Business Week*, October 3, 1988, pp. 58–59.

ment of Dworkin's sons, he was forced to hire a new president from the outside—William Edwards.

The stock buyback put financial pressure on Revco because it was financed by debt. The increased fixed charges associated with the interest payments came at a time when Revco was having trouble keeping the Odd Lot Trading business profitable. By 1985, Revco experienced a loss of $35 million—mainly as a result of a large supply of unsold video cartridges. Dworkin's solution to Revco's financial problems and his declining role in the company was to arrange a leveraged buyout. He retained Salomon Brothers and Transcontinental Services Group, which was a European investment group, to arrange a leveraged buyout. Dworkin offered the stockholders $36 per share, which was $6 per share higher than what the stock price was trading for four months earlier when the news of the leveraged buyout was first announced. However, the LBO offer attracted the interest of the Haft family who, through their company, the Dart Group, made a higher offer. Dworkin responded by raising his offer to $38.50 per share or $1.25 billion. The bidding process took seven months to complete before Dworkin's bid was accepted.

The LBO increased Revco's debt four times to $1.3 billion. Revco had planned to pay the debt by selling off the nondrug businesses. Curiously, Revco also planned to expand at the same time, its goal being to open 100 new stores. This was an unusual move since most LBOs require downsizing and asset sales to "pay down" the debt. Increasingly concerned about Revco's financial condition, the board of directors favored a new marketing approach which William Edwards, Revco's president, implemented. This marketing strategy abandoned the everyday low prices, which Revco had been known for, in favor of weekend specials and promotions. However, a major thrust of this marketing strategy was to expand Revco's product line to include televisions, furniture, and VCRs. Customers became confused when they saw furniture for sale in stores they had previously known as pharmacies. Revco's profits fell, reflecting the public's negative reaction.

In March 1987, Dworkin was removed as CEO. Edwards made various other attempts to turn the failing company around. For example, he cut prices to clear out inventories, and he rearranged the stores to promote better store traffic. The result was yet more customer confusion, and the company continued to decline. In October 1987 Boake Sells, a former Dayton Hudson president, was appointed new CEO and charged with turning Revco around. But this was too little, too late. The 1987 Christmas season was a disaster with Revco in short supply of many essential and basic products such as toothpaste but with stockpiles of televisions and furniture. Cash flow problems became acute as revenues declined while fixed charges remained high.

Revco's Financial Condition

Sixteen months after going private through a leveraged buyout, Revco became the first of the big LBOs to fail when it missed a $46 million interest payment. In the 1980s, prior to the LBO, it had shown consistent profitability (see Figure 10.9). Net income remained positive until 1987 when the firm was unable to generate sufficient revenues to meet its higher fixed expenses. To say that sales were not sufficient would be misleading, however. Sales rose in each year prior to 1987 when they declined to their 1985 levels (see Figure 10.10). However, Revco relied on pre-LBO forecasts which projected a continually higher sales volume. The 1987 decline in sales should not have forced a nonhighly leveraged firm into bankruptcy, but the pressures of the LBO debt left little room for error. Indeed, the report of the examiner confirmed that the pre-LBO predictions were unrealistically optimistic. This characteristic proved to be symptomatic of other troubled LBOs.

Liquidity Even before entering the leveraged buyout, Revco was not in a very liquid position. Simply looking at the firm's current ratio (current assets/current liabilities) does not provide a true indication of the firm's liquidity problems. Although the current ratio did decline somewhat in 1986, it recovered to a more than acceptable 2.52 in 1987 and a minimally acceptable 1.97 in 1988.

One of Revco's problems was its large holdings of nonmarketable

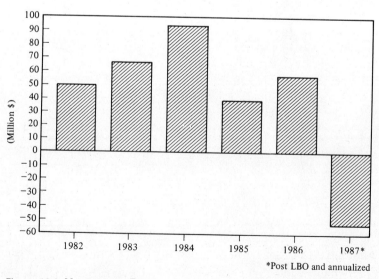

Figure 10.9 Net income, Revco.

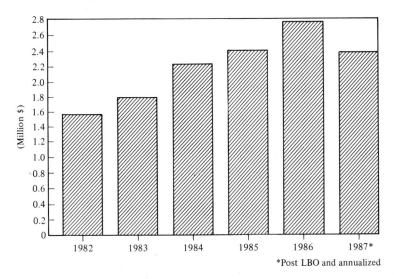

Figure 10.10 Sales, Revco.

inventories. Inventories are included in current assets. If they are not marketable, the current ratio will present a misleading impression of the company's actual liquidity. In such cases, one should rely on the quick ratio, which is also called the *acid test ratio*. The quick ratio is the ratio of current assets minus inventories divided by current liabilities. It is a more stringent measure of liquidity than the current ratio. A quick ratio of 1 is generally considered acceptable. However, Revco had consistently had a very low quick ratio. A low quick ratio combined with an acceptable current ratio means that a firm is relying on its inventories to be marketable. The unsold stockpiles of inventories, combined with shortages in critical, marketable inventories, proved to be a major problem for Revco. The values of Revco's for the current ratio and quick ratio for 1982–1987 are as follows.

CURRENT RATIO (Current assets/Current liabilities)					
1982	1983	1984	1985	1986	1987
2.42	2.49	2.10	1.74	2.52	1.97

QUICK RATIO (Current assets − Inventories/Current liabilities)					
1982	1983	1984	1985	1986	1987
0.48	0.63	0.34	0.32	0.54	0.94

Activity   As noted above, Revco's investment in inventories was a problem for the firm. Many of the company's inventories were not liquid and, therefore, the firm was forced into an illiquid position in 1987. The firm made an effort to reduce its levels of unproductive inventories by a program called Operation Clean Sweep, but the program worsened the firm's fortunes when Revco failed to have sufficient inventories to meet the increased seasonal demand associated with the upcoming Christmas season.

The problems with these and other assets can be measured by activity ratios. Activity ratios measure the speed with which various accounts are converted into cash. The company's inability to convert its assets into cash can be seen in the trend of the total asset turnover ratio (see the accompanying tabulation for 1982–1987). This measure represents the ratio of sales to total assets. It measures the effectiveness with which the firm uses its assets to generate sales. This ratio headed steadily downward in the 1980s, showing that the firm's assets were not being translated into sales and that, therefore, the firm's investments in inventories and other assets were unproductive.

TOTAL ASSET TURNOVER
(Sales/Total assets)

1982	1983	1984	1985	1986	1987
3.10	3.00	2.87	2.74	2.78	1.26

Leverage   Revco's financial condition was weakened by the increased interest payments associated with the rise in long-term debt which it had assumed to buy back stock and to take the firm private. The firm increased its debt in 1985 when it bought back the 12 percent interest held by Bernard Marden and Issac Perlmutter owing to conflicts associated with the firm's management. This made Revco a more heavily leveraged firm even before it entered into the LBO. This leverage was dramatically increased with the buyout (see Figures 10.11 and 10.12).

The debt to equity ratio rose from 0.09 in 1984 to 0.78 in 1986.

DEBT TO EQUITY
(Long-term debt/Stockholder equity)

1982	1983	1984	1985	1986
0.23	0.12	0.09	0.10	0.78

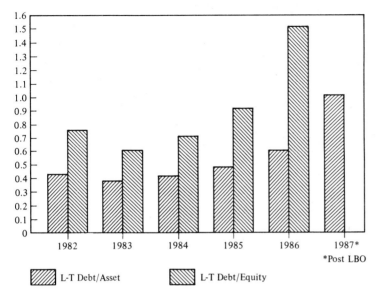

Figure 10.11 Debt-asset and debt-equity ratios, Revco.

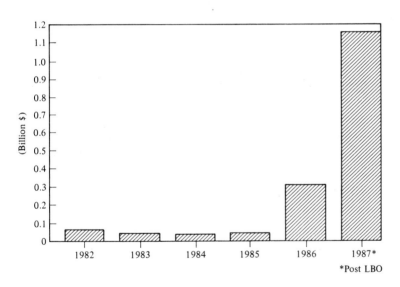

Figure 10.12 Long-term debts, Revco.

The company's ability to meet its interest payments declined dramatically in 1985 and degenerated even more in 1986. We can see this fall-off by examining the times interest earned ratio (sometimes called the total interest coverage ratio) which declined from a high of 58.43 in 1984 to 6.23 in 1985 and 4.83 in 1986. This ratio fell even further to 0.66 in 1987. (See Figure 10.13.)

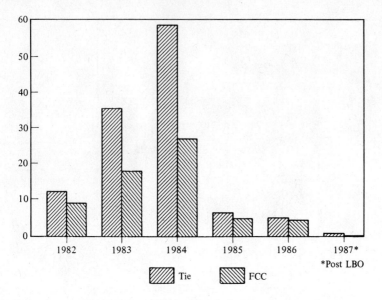

Figure 10.13 Times interest earned fixed charge coverage, Revco.

TIMES INTEREST EARNED (Earnings before interest and taxes)					
1982	1983	1984	1985	1986	1987
12.12	35.36	58.43	6.23	4.83	0.66

The reduced ability to service debt, owing to the increased interest expense (see Figure 10.14), made it imperative that Revco's sales increase. When sales declined, Revco's fate was sealed.

FIXED CHARGE COVERAGE (Includes all fixed charges including interest)					
1982	1983	1984	1985	1986	1987
8.86	17.80	26.85	4.73	4.13	0.20

Profitability   An analysis of Revco's pre-LBO profitability provides additional insight into Revco's value as a leveraged buyout candidate. Revco's return on equity declined from a high of 21 percent in 1984 to 9 percent in 1985.

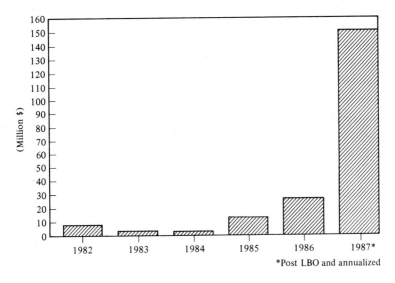

Figure 10.14 Interest expense, Revco.

RETURN ON EQUITY (Net profits after taxes/Stockholder equity)				
1982	1983	1984	1985	1986
0.17	0.18	0.21	0.09	0.15

The company's basic earning power, as reflected in the ratio of earnings before interest and taxes (see Figure 10.15) to total assets, declined from 23 percent in 1984 to 9 percent in 1985 and 5 percent in 1987.

BASIC EARNING POWER (Earnings before interest and taxes/Total assets)					
1982	1983	1984	1985	1986	1987
0.20	0.21	0.23	0.09	0.13	0.05

These results and others imply that Revco's recent history does not indicate that this firm would be a highly desirable candidate. Other factors, such as management's desire to become a private company and have greater independence, apparently motivated the LBO. On the other hand, optimistic forecasts made before the LBO showed that the

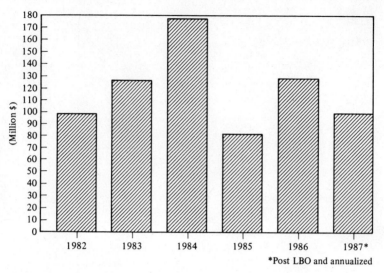

Figure 10.15 Operating income, Revco.

firm would be quite profitable in the future. Revco's profitability preceding the LBO, however, failed to provide much support for these projections.

Characteristics of the LBO

Pricing The buyout provided $38.50 per share in cash for each outstanding share of Revco common stock. The management group, led by Chairman Dworkin, originally offered $33 a share in cash and a share of preferred stock that had a face value of $3 per share. The examiner appointed in the bankruptcy process concluded that Revco's main financial adviser, Salomon Brothers, made overly optimistic LBO projections. During the LBO negotiations Revco missed its own profit projections. In response, Salomon lowered its projections for the current quarter but did not adjust its future projections.[16]

Financing the LBO The total financing package amounted to $1.438 billion (see Table 10.4).

Analysis of the Financing

The three principal components of the financing of the buyout were senior debt ($445 million), subordinated debt ($700 million) and equity (preferred and common stock—$280,000). The financing package placed significantly greater stress on Revco's revenues. Between 1982 and

---

[16] "Revco Can Sue Its Ex-Advisors Over Buyout," *Wall Street Journal,* January 3, 1991, p. A3.

Table 10.4   SOURCES AND USES TO FINANCING IN THE REVCO LBO

Sources	(Thousands)
Cash in Revco	$ 13,904
Term loans	445,000
Issuance of subodinated debt	700,000
Issuance of convertible preferred stock	85,000
Issuance of exchangeable preferred stock	130,000
Issuance of junior preferred stock	30,098
Issuance of holding common stock	34,902
Total sources	$1,438,904
Uses of funds	
Payment of cash for shares of Revco common stock and cancellation of stock options	$1,253,420
Repayment of certain indebtedness of Revco	117,484
Payment of fees and expenses associated with the LBO	78,000
	$1,448,904

1986, Revco's revenues were rising at a 11.5 percent annual rate. Profitability in 1986 was just under $150 million. The company's financial advisers predicted that profits would rise 42 percent to $103.6 million.[17]

Bankruptcy

Revco's bankruptcy was instigated by the holders of the firm's high-yield bonds, not the bank lenders. The company had missed an interest payment, leading to negotiations with the bondholders to restructure the firm's debt. But a settlement agreeable to the bondholders could not be arranged. Revco had hoped to restructure the firm's debt in a debt for equity swap,[18] and when the proposed swap was not satisfactory to the bondholders, Revco was forced into bankruptcy.

The failure of post-LBO Revco to be as profitable as the investment bankers had optimistically projected has caused investors to be even more skeptical of the projections of interested parties.

Many Revco bondholders regretted forcing the firm into bankruptcy. According to a *New York Times* report, "The bonds of bankrupt companies can often be bought for a fraction of their value. Bonds of Revco D.S., Inc., the large drugstore chain that filed for bankruptcy protection last summer, have sold for as little as 16 cents on the dollar."[19]

---

[17] *Wall Street Journal,* June 14, 1988, p. 6.

[18] "A Painful Reminder of Risk," *Mergers and Acquisitions,* November/December 1988, pp. 8–12.

[19] "Investors Await a Rash of Defaults," *New York Times,* November 5, 1988, p. D1.

All is not lost for the Revco bondholders, however. Buyers of these bonds can profit handsomely if the bankrupt firm can reverse its financial condition. Indeed, the buyers in the market for Revco's bonds are hoping to profit from an eventual turnaround that will provide them with a high return on their risky investment.

The LBO market will never be the same after the Revco bankruptcy. The Revco LBO was just the first of a series of troubled LBOs that defaulted on their debt payments.

THE SAFEWAY LEVERAGED BUYOUT

In November 1986, Safeway Stores was taken private in a leveraged buyout by Kohlberg, Kravis & Roberts. The food retailer was purchased for $4.25 billion. This LBO is often cited as a classic example of an LBO that performed well. Much of this post-LBO-enhanced performance is attributed to increased efficiencies instituted under the direction of KKR.

Industry

The food retailing industry is composed of several large retail chains that account for a significant part of the total retail food market. Industry sales have been rising at a 4.9 percent annual rate from 1983 through 1988.[20] Industry profitability is based on high volume, not high markup. According to the U.S. Bureau of the Census's quarterly financial report, retail food store profits averaged just 1.3 percent of sales in 1987.

The low-profit margin does not leave much room for error; miscalculation can quickly cause a once profitable firm to go into bankruptcy. This fact has important ramifications for a leveraged buyout since the increased debt associated with financing the buyout places greater financial pressures on the firm. A low-profit margin is an undesirable characteristic for an LBO candidate, but balancing this drawback is the food industry's noncyclical nature which makes it somewhat recession-proof. As a result, it reduces the probability of a sudden drop in the firm's cash flows in reaction to an economywide downturn in demand.

Safeway's Position in the Industry

Safeway Stores is a food retail chain that was founded in 1926 in Oakland, California, by the Magowan family. As of 1986, it had 2,326

---

[20] U.S. Department of Commerce, U.S. Industrial Outlook, 1989.

grocery stores in 29 states as well as England, Australia, Canada, and Mexico, which made it the nation's largest supermarket chain. The firm had a consistently good record of earnings in the 1980s. In addition, it had spent over $5 billion on capital improvements during the five years prior to the LBO. These improvements included the creation of several upscale "superstores" which have proved to be most successful in recent years. The firm has already taken steps to have a more efficient work-force through some layoffs and attrition. The fact that earnings had more than doubled in the first four years of the 1980s to a record $321 million in 1985 did not go unnoticed by the stock market. The firm's stock price tripled over the three years prior to the LBO, while dividends increased for four years in a row. Safeway's position within the industry, combined with its overall profitability and increased capital expenditures, increased its appeal as a takeover candidate.

When Kohlberg, Kravis & Roberts acquired Safeway, KKR became the largest food retailer in the United States. The buyout firm had previously acquired the Seattle-based chain, Fred Myer and Company, as well as Boston's Stop & Shop chain.

Background of the Safeway LBO

During most of 1985, Safeway's common stock had traded in the $30 to $35 range. Although the stock market had been rallying in 1985 through 1986, Safeway's stock did not participate in the bull market. The market did not look on Safeway favorably, and the firm began to be considered a takeover candidate.

In July 1986, the Dart Group, a Landover, Maryland, retailer led by Herbert and Robert Haft, made a hostile bid for Safeway Stores. They bought 5.9 percent of Safeway and made a tender offer for the remainder of its 61.6 million shares outstanding at $58 per share. The Dart Group was basically a corporate shell that resulted from the buyout of the Dart Drug Store Company in the summer of 1984. Dart Drugs went private in a management buyout that still left its founding chair-man Herbert Haft in the position of running the firm.[21]

Much of Safeway's stock quickly fell into the hands of arbitragers. Arbitragers, who profit by investing in the stock of companies that become takeover candidates, are normally not loyal to the management of the companies they invest in. They will sell to the highest bidder. When arbitragers gain ownership of a significant percentage of the stock of a firm, the company becomes vulnerable to a takeover. The break-

---

[21] Carl Shrager, "LBO Case Study: Safeway Stores," *Buyouts and Acquisitions*, March/April 1987, pp. 34–38.

down of the company's stock ownership following the announcement of the bid is shown below:[22]

Insiders	1.0%
Dart Group	5.9%
Institutions	44.7%

In an effort to escape the clutches of the Hafts, Safeway agreed to be taken private in a leveraged buyout by KKR.[23] The deal was consummated in November 1986 and resulted in a purchase price of $4.25 billion. Shareholders received $67.50 per share, which was an 82 percent premium over the stock price three months prior to the buyout. This premium was further enhanced by warrants that gave them a 5.6 percent stake in the post-buyout firm. These gains were also enjoyed by employees, who held 10 percent of the pre-buyout firm, as well as Chairman Magowan who made $5.7 million on the shares he owned. Other management employees made $19.3 million on their shareholdings. In addition, Magowan and 60 other managers received options to buy a total of 10 percent of the new Safeway at a bargain price of only $2 per share. By the second quarter of 1989, those options were worth approximately $100 million based on an estimated share price of $12.125. The Hafts, even though they had lost the bidding, made $100 million when they liquidated their holdings in addition to receiving options to purchase 20 percent of the post-buyout firm.[24]

The process whereby Safeway Stores was able to successfully reduce its debt load is the real lesson of this LBO. In July 1986, Safeway had 2,326 stores; by October 1986 the number was only 1,161. Following the buyout, Safeway underwent a major restructuring that included many other changes in addition to asset sales. It reduced its labor costs by selling the stores with higher labor costs. This was made possible through an agreement with the United Food and Commercial Workers Union. The union agreed to the cuts only after Safeway guaranteed it would increase the number of union members at the remaining stores.

Safeway's Pre-LBO Financial Condition

Liquidity   Safeway had below-average liquidity before the LBO, but its other positive attributes more than offset this drawback. Its below-

---

[22] Ibid.

[23] Ibid.

[24] Susan Faludi, "Safeway LBO Yields Vast Profits But Exacts a Heavy Human Toll," *Wall Street Journal*, May 1990, p. A1.

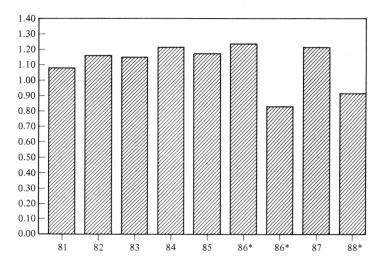

Figure 10.16 Current ratio, Safeway Stores.

average liquidity is reflected in a current ratio of 1.21 and 1.17 (1984 and 1985, respectively). (See Figure 10.16.)

CURRENT RATIO (Current assets/Current liabilities)					
1981	1982	1983	1984	1985	1986*
1.08	1.16	1.15	1.21	1.17	1.23

* First 36 weeks of 1986.

Because of the company's short-term inventories and their overall liquidity, the quick ratio (current ratio − inventories/current liabilities) may not be more useful than the current ratio. The quick ratio was in the 0.2 to 0.27 range in the years preceding the LBO. The average current and quick ratios for firms in the same industry as Safeway are 1.8 and 0.8, respectively.

Leverage   Safeway was not heavily leveraged before the buyout. The firm's long-term debt to equity reflected a debt level that was not excessively high (Figure 10.17). These ratios are consistent with the averages for this industry, which normally does not carry the high levels of debt one might find in a more capital-intensive industry. Safeway did, however, have below-average interest coverage leading up to the

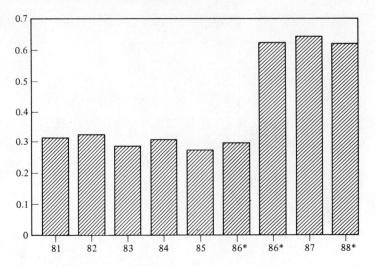

Figure 10.17 Long-term debts to equity, Safeway Stores.

LBO. The times interest earned ratio was approximately 2.42 before the LBO (Figure 10.18).

TIMES INTEREST EARNED (Earnings before interest and taxes/Interest charges)					
1981	1982	1983	1984	1985	1986*
2.25	2.71	3.08	2.80	2.47	2.42

* First 36 weeks of 1986.

(A range between 3 and 5 is normally considered acceptable.) Further increases in the level of Safeway's debt might be difficult to sustain unless Safeway quickly reduced this debt level through the sales of assets and underperforming divisions of the company. These indicators imply that Safeway would need careful asset management following the LBO—a need that most firms share following the increase in debt that is normally associated with an LBO.

Following the buyout, Safeway quickly took actions to lower its debt level and the associated interest charges, as shown in Figures 10.19 and 10.20. As is clear from these figures the firm accomplished this reduction in part through asset sales. As noted earlier, Safeway's total assets declined significantly in 1987 and even more in 1988 (see Figure 10.21).

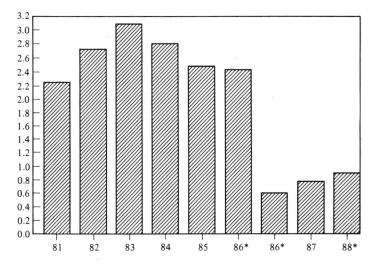

Figure 10.18 Times interest earned, Safeway Stores.

Profitability   Safeway's annualized pre-LBO and post-LBO operating income was somewhat lower in 1986 than in 1985. However, operating income rose sharply in 1987, even after asset sales such as the sale of certain chains of stores (Figure 10.22). The lower 1988 income figures do not lend themselves to a comparison to the earlier years since the post-LBO Safeway is a smaller company.

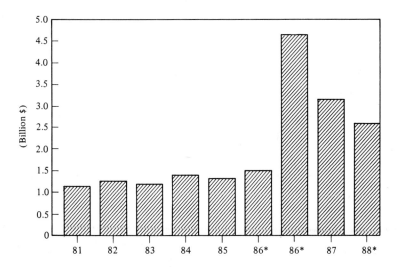

Figure 10.19 Long-term debts, Safeway Stores.

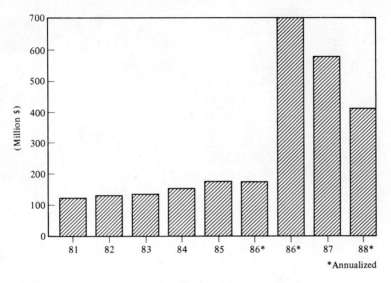

Figure 10.20 Interest expenses, actual and annualized, Safeway Stores.

Characteristics of the Safeway LBO

Price   Kohlberg, Kravis, & Roberts bought Safeway by means of a two-tiered offer whereby the price and the terms differed between the two tiers. Kohlberg gave $69 per share for the first 73 percent of Safeway's outstanding shares. In the second step of the tender offer, Kohlberg swapped debentures, which, at the time of the offer, were

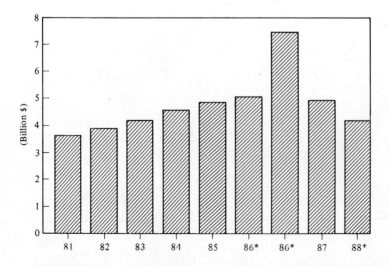

Figure 10.21 Total assets, Safeway Stores.

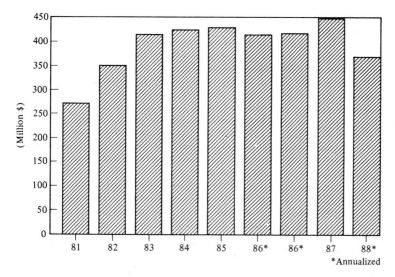

Figure 10.22 Operating income, actual and annualized, Safeway Stores.

estimated to have a value of $61.60, as well as a warrant entitling the holder to buy stock in a new closely held corporation that would own Safeway Stores. At the time of the buyout, each warrant was valued at $7.40.

Financing the LBO   A financing package worth over $4.9 billion was put together to finance the Safeway LBO. The sources and uses of the financing package are shown in Table 10.5.

Outcome of the Safeway LBO

There are numerous indications that the Safeway LBO has performed well. A Securities and Exchange Commission filing covering the period beginning in 1988 showed that Safeway had reduced its total debt from $5.01 billion to $3.36 billion. This 33 percent reduction in total debt helped relieve the food retailer of significant interest payment pressures. Total debt declined further to $3.12 billion in 1989 which was still substantially above the 1985 debt level of $1.49 billion. At the point of the buyout, long-term debt was as high as $4 billion. By the beginning of 1988, long-term debt had fallen to $2.8 billion.

The debt reduction and improvement in the firm's financial condition were part of a planned asset sale and divestiture program.

The planned sales are part of a massive and uncompleted divestiture program the company undertook after going private. In the buyout, Safe-

Table 10.5 SOURCES AND USES OF FUNDS IN THE
SAFEWAY LBO

Sources of Funds	Thousands
Bank Financing	$2,605
Senior subordinated notes	750
Subordinated debentures	250
Merger debentures	1,025
Holdings note	59
Holdings preferred stock	45
Holdings common stock	130
Safeway cash	43
Total	$4,907

Uses of Funds	
Cash payments for Safeway common stock	$3,105
Issuance of merger debentures	1,025
Repayment of certain existing debt	500
Merger fees and expenses	277
	$4,907

way started out with $45 of debt for each dollar of equity, one of the highest such ratios ever in a large deal. Asset sales in 1987 total $1.5 billion, according to the filing, and the current sales agreement calls for the company to receive an estimated additional $525 million for the current year.

Safeway has shed, among other things, its Liquor Barn discount liquor operation, its supermarket operations in Britain and some Midwest states, and substantial holdings in an Australian concern. It also has closed a significant number of grocery stores, and agreed to sell its grocery operations in Southern California and Arkansas. As of January 2, 1988, assets stood at $4.94 billion, down from $7.44 a year earlier.[25]

The asset sales continued as planned in 1988. In June 1988, Safeway announced that it was selling a 99-store chain based in Houston to a management group. These asset sales were the last of the original planned asset sale and divestiture program. At the same time that the company was shedding assets, it continued to generate impressive sales. Its 1989 revenues were $14.3 billion, which represented 72 percent of the firm's pre-LBO sales (see Figure 10.23). This is impressive since it was accomplished with only half as many stores as the pre-LBO firm.

---

[25] *Wall Street Journal*, April 25, 1988.

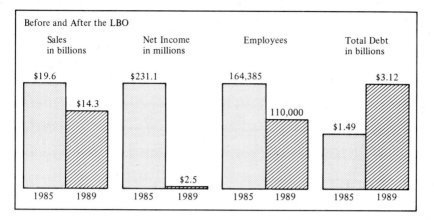

Figure 10.23 Before and after the LBO, Safeway Stores. (*Source:* Susan Faludi, "Safeway LBO Yields Vast Profits But Exacts a Heavy Human Toll," *Wall Street Journal*, May 16, 1990, p. A9. Reprinted by permission of the Wall Street Journal, copyright © Dow Jones & Company, Inc., 1990. All Rights Reserved Worldwide.)

Like most firms that have gone through a leveraged buyout, Safeway significantly reduced capital expenditures, cutting back to $300,000 annually after the buyout. The firm did not, however, neglect to keep its stores up. It remodeled over 100 stores every year at an average price of $750,000 each. As a result, sales went up 20 to 100 percent or more.

Impact on Employees

The success of the Safeway LBO has not been without controversy. Some complain that Safeway's improved financial condition came at the expense of jobs. At the time of the buyout, Safeway Stores employed approximately 164,385 people; in 1989, that figure was down to approximately 110,000 (see Figure 10.23), representing a 49 percent reduction in the firm's workforce. This was one reason why the United Food and Commercial Workers International Union sued to block KKR's takeover of Safeway. In defense of the firm, it can be pointed out that the reduction in workforce does not mean that all these jobs were lost. Most of the job reductions were accomplished through sales of groups of stores to new owners. A *Wall Street Journal* report in May 1990, however, pointed out that, while some of these employees have retained their jobs with the new owners, others have lost their positions.[26] There is no clear evidence to show how many workers have

---

[26] Faludi, "Safeway LBO Yields Vast Profits," p. A1.

been unable to find similar employment after being terminated by Safeway.

LBO Versus Recapitalization Plan: Safeway Versus Kroger's

Safeway's response to the threat to its independence brought on by the Hafts' offer can be contrasted with that of its rival, Kroger's, which faced a similar threat two years later. In September 1988, Kroger's, a Cincinnati-based food retail chain, incurred $4.1 billion in debt in order to institute a recapitalization plan that would pay shareholders a large dividend while exhausting much of the firm's debt capacity. This defense combined with an employee stock ownership plan enabled the firm to defeat the hostile $55 bid by the Haft brothers. The board of directors approved the Kroger recapitalization plan which provided for a cash dividend of $40 plus a junior subordinated debenture valued at $8, combined with a stub that had an initial offering value of approximately $9. The board approval of the package came despite the fact that a final bid by KKR, which had been attracted to the fray in a similar manner as in the Safeway deal, reached as high as $64 per share. The board appeared to respond favorably to Kroger's offer which provided for an increased employee ownership potential. While Kroger's didn't choose to go the LBO route, the increased debt it assumed to finance the recapitalization plan forced it to engage in the same painful cost cutting that is more often attributed to LBOs. Kroger's laid off employees, cut salaries, and sold off 100 of its stores in order to be able to pay down its debt.[27] Although the firm showed a loss one year after the recapitalization plan, owing to the increased debt, its losses are declining amid strong cash flows. Combined with asset sales that include 10 percent of the firm's stores, these cash flows have significantly reduced the firm's financial leverage.

SUMMARY

The three case studies described in this chapter present marked contrasts. The RJR Nabisco buyout was far larger than any other merger, acquisition, or leveraged buyout in U.S. history. The fact that a deal of that size could have been constructed testifies to the frenzy of the fourth merger wave. The financing for the deal proved to be most

---

[27] Ibid.

complicated and involved many different layers of debt and equity financing. The investor participation was widespread and included many different types of investors, including the larger institutional investors. Other institutions, such as life insurance companies, that held RJR Nabisco's high-quality debt prior to the LBO have vehemently opposed the deal that converted their debt holdings into junk bonds. They attribute the large gains that stockholders received in the buyout to losses they incurred. The RJR deal also featured a glaring conflict of interest by a management group that recommended a buyout offer to shareholders which proved to be well below the market value of the firm.

RJR Nabisco's apparent ability to have survived its leveraged buyout demonstrates that larger scale leveraged buyouts can be financially viable. Although LBOs may never reach the heights they did during the fourth merger wave, they have become a permanent part of the world of corporate finance. One reason why they may never reach their late-1980s peak is the risk exemplified by the Revco LBO. Revco was a firm that possessed some of the desirable characteristics of successful LBO candidates. However, positive factors, such as noncyclical cash flow, proved to have been offset by more important factors such as too much pre-LBO debt and managerial errors. Future LBO investors will always be aware that their investments could suffer the fate of Revco's investors who saw the firm's debt sell for larger discounts as the firm entered bankruptcy, succumbing to its burdensome holdings of debt. Unfortunately, Revco proved to be the first in a series of trouble LBOs.

LBO proponents always cite the successful Safeway deal, which featured sizable gains enjoyed by a broad group including shareholders, management, some employees, as well as LBO investors. Although other LBOs were unable to meet their interest obligations, Safeway lowered its debt through asset sales while instituting various efficiency enhancements that decreased nondebt-related costs. The financial success of the Safeway deal was underscored by a 1990 public offering of 10 million shares which represented approximately 10 percent of the firm. This equity offering provided KKR with a return that was reported to be as high as seven times its investment.[28] The Safeway buyout has become the classic example of how to structure and manage a leveraged buyout. The fact that Safeway was already becoming a well-managed and more efficient firm prior to the buyout seems to have been a factor

---

[28] Ken Wells and Randall Smith, "Safeway Stores Plans to Go Public Again in Possible Financial Windfall for KKR," *Wall Street Journal*, February 13, 1990.

in the LBO's success. Its pre-buyout condition of relatively low-debt, noncyclical cash flows, and good management, combined with quick assets sales at prices that allowed significant debt reduction, has become a formula for LBO success.

REFERENCES

Dobrzynski, Judith H. "The Lessons of the RJR Free-for All." *Business Week*, December 19, 1988.

"How Two Big Grocers Are Bringing Home the Bacon." *Business Week*, April 24, 1989, p. 141.

"Investors Await a Rash of Defaults." *New York Times*, November 5, 1988, p. D1.

"A Painful Reminder of Risk." *Mergers and Acquisitions*, November/December 1988.

Quint, Michael. "Cutting Rate Risk on Buyout Debt." *New York Times*, February 16, 1989.

"Revco: Anatomy of a Failed Buyout." *Business Week*, October 3, 1988, pp. 58–59.

"RJR Finale Will Send Money Coursing." *Wall Street Journal*, p. C1.

RJR Prospectus.

Schedule 14D1 filed by Kohlberg, Kravis & Roberts.

Shrager, Carl. "LBO Case Study: Safeway Stores." *Buyouts and Acquisitions*, March/April 1987, pp. 34–38.

Smith Barney, Harris Upham & Co.

U.S. Department of Commerce, *U.S. Industrial Outlook*, 1989.

Waldman, Peter. "A New RJR Chief Faces a Daunting Challenge at Debt Heavy Firm." *Wall Street Journal*, March 14, 1989, p. 1.

Chapter
11

Corporate Restructuring

*A*lthough the field of mergers and acquisitions tends to focus on corporate expansion, companies often have to contract and downsize their operations. This need may arise because a division of the company is performing poorly or simply because it no longer fits into the firm's plans. Restructuring may also be necessary to undo a previous merger or acquisition that proved unsuccessful. As the pace of the fourth merger wave slowed toward the end of the 1980s, the need for divestitures and selloffs increased as firms began to reconsider prior expansionary plans. The pressures of large interest payment obligations that were incurred to expand through acquisitions or to go private in a leveraged buyout began to take their toll. Divestitures and selloffs were among the few alternatives available to corporations to help pay down debt.

In this chapter we consider the different types of corporate contraction and develop a decision-making methodology for reaching the divestiture decision. The methods used to value acquisition targets are also used by companies to determine whether a particular component of the firm is worth retaining. Both the divesting and the acquiring firm commonly go through a similar type of analysis as they view the transaction from opposite sides. Even though the methods are similar, the two parties may come up with different values because they use different assumptions or have different needs.

This chapter considers the shareholder wealth effects of several forms of corporate restructuring. Corporate contraction can have positive stock price effects when the divested component fails to yield a value to the corporation that is commensurate with its market value. In such instances the corporation may be able to enhance the value of shareholder investments by pursuing a policy of corporate restructuring.

Corporate restructuring can take several different forms: divestitures, equity carve-outs, spinoffs, splitoffs, and splitups. A divestiture is a sale of a portion of the firm to an outside party. The selling firm is usually paid in cash, marketable securities, or a combination of the two. An equity carve-out is a variation of a divestiture that involves the sale of an equity interest in a subsidiary to outsiders. The sale may not necessarily leave the parent company in control of the subsidiary. The new equity gives the investors shares of ownership in the portion of the selling company that is being divested. In an equity carve-out, a new legal entity is created with a stockholder base that may be different from that of the parent selling company. The divested company has a different management team and is run as a separate firm.

A new legal entity is also created in a standard spinoff. Once again, new shares are issued and distributed to stockholders on a pro rata basis. As a result of the proportional distribution of shares, the stockholder base in the new company is the same as that of the old company. Although the stockholders are initially the same, the spunoff firm has its own management and is run as a separate company. One difference between a spinoff and a divestiture is that a divestiture involves an infusion of funds into the parent corporation whereas a spinoff normally does not provide the parent with a cash infusion.[1]

In a splitoff, some of the stockholders in the parent company are given shares in the company which are split off *in exchange for* their shares in the parent company. A variation on a splitoff occurred in 1981 when Dome Petroleum, which had purchased an equity interest in Conoco, exchanged its shares in Conoco for Conoco's Hudson Bay oil and gas fields.

Finally, in a splitup the entire firm is broken up into a series of spinoffs. The end result of this process is that the parent company no longer exists, leaving only the newly formed companies. The stockholders in the companies may be different since stockholders exchange their shares in the parent company for shares in one or more of the units that are spun off.

Sometimes a combination of a divestiture and a spinoff may occur.

---

[1] Joel Stern, "A Discussion of Corporate Restructuring," Comments of Galen Hite, *Midland Corporate Finance Journal* 2, no. 2 (Summer 1984):69.

For example, Trans World Corporation (TWA) sold shares in TWA to the public equal to approximately 20 percent of the ownership of the airline. This is also referred to as a *partial public offering*. The remaining shares were distributed to existing TWA stockholders.

DIVESTITURES

The most common form of divestiture involves the sale of a division of the parent company to another firm. The process is a form of contraction for the selling company but a means of expansion for the purchasing corporation. The number of divestitures that took place during the 1965–1989 period is listed in Table 11.1.

Table 11.1   DIVESTITURES, 1965–1989

Year	Number	Percent of All Transactions
1965	191	9
1966	264	11
1967	328	11
1968	557	12
1969	801	13
1970	1,401	27
1971	1,920	42
1972	1,770	37
1973	1,557	39
1974	1,331	47
1975	1,236	54
1976	1,204	53
1977	1,002	45
1978	820	39
1979	752	35
1980	666	35
1981	830	35
1982	875	37
1983	932	37
1984	900	36
1985	1,218	41
1986	1,259	38
1987	807	40
1988	894	40
1989	1,055	45

Source: Merrill Lynch Business Brokerage and Valuation, *Mergerstat Review,* 1989.

Historical Trends

In the late 1960s, during the third merger wave, the number of divestitures and selloffs was relatively small as a percentage of the total number of transactions. Companies were engaging in major expansions at this time, widely using the acquisition of other firms as a method of increasing the acquiring company's stock price. This expansion came to an abrupt end following changes in the tax laws and other regulatory measures and the stock market decline. Companies then began to reconsider some of the acquisitions that had proved to be poor combinations—a need intensified by the 1974–1975 recession. Under the pressure of falling economic demand, companies were forced to sell off divisions in order to raise funds and improve cash flow. International competition also pressured some of the 1960s conglomerates to become more efficient by selling off prior acquisitions that were not competitive in a world market.

This reversal of the acquisition trend was visible as early as 1971 when divestitures jumped to 42 percent of total transactions. The trend peaked in 1975, a period of economic recession, when the number of divestitures constituted 54 percent of all transactions. They remained between 35 and 40 percent throughout the 1980s.

Many divestitures are the result of selloffs of previous acquisitions. The relationship between acquisitions and subsequent divestitures is shown in Figure 11.1. The belief that many divestitures are the undoing

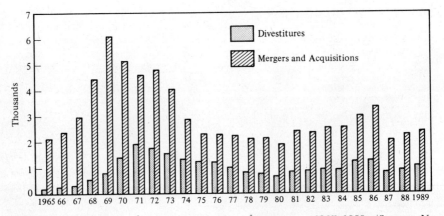

Figure 11.1 Mergers and acquisitions versus divestitures, 1965–1989. (*Source:* New York: *Mergerstat Review,* Merrill Lynch Business Brokerage and Valuation.)

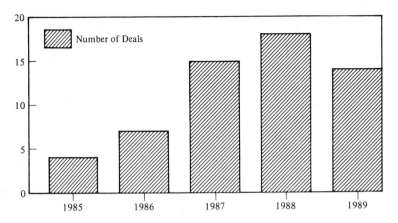

Figure 11.2 Spin-offs, 1985–1989. (*Source:* IDD Information Services.)

of previous acquisitions is seen in the leading trend in the acquisitions curve relative to the divestiture curve. The intense period of merger activity of the late 1960s is reflected in a pronounced peak at this time, followed by a peak in the divestiture curve in the early 1970s. The stock market performance seemed to play a determining role in the volume of divestitures: "Using regression analysis, we found that in years when the stock market fell—such as 1966, 1969 and 1973–1974— the rate of divestiture fell below what one would have predicted given the previous merger rates; and when stocks performed well there was a tendency for more divestitures to occur."[2] Figures 11.2 and 11.3 show that when merger and acquisition activity slowed in the late 1980s, the pace of spin-offs and divestitures increased.

Many critics of corporate acquisitions use the record of the divestitures following poor acquisitions as evidence of ill-conceived expansion planning. Using a sample of 33 companies during the 1950–1986 period, Michael Porter shows that these firms divested 53 percent of the acquisitions that brought the acquiring companies into new industries.[3] Based on this evidence he concludes that the corporate acquisition record is "dismal." Others take a less harsh view of the divesting

[2] Scott C. Linn and Michael S. Rozeff, "The Corporate Selloff," *Midland Corporate Finance Journal* 2, no. 2 (Summer 1984):24.

[3] Michael Porter, "From Competitive Advantage to Corporate Strategy," *Harvard Business Review* (May-June 1987):43–59.

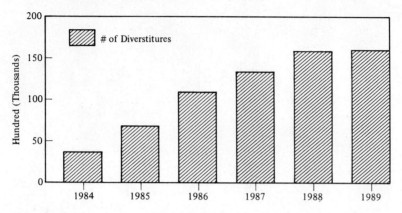

Figure 11.3 Divestitures, 1985–1989. (*Source:* IDD Information Services.)

companies. Fred Weston, for example, points out that divestitures tend to increase shareholder value and thus have wealth-increasing effects for shareholders.[4] He observes that divestitures occur for a variety of reasons and not just to remedy poor acquisitions. For instance, divestitures can be motivated by the firm's desire to pursue a new strategy made possible by the development of recent new opporunities in the marketplace that did not exist at the time of the original acquisition.

Involuntary Versus Voluntary Divestitures

A divestiture can be either voluntary or involuntary. An involuntary divestiture may occur when a company receives an unfavorable review by the Justice Department or the Federal Trade Commission, requiring the company to divest itself of a particular division. For example, in June 1987 in a 4 to 1 vote the Interstate Commerce Commission (ICC) ruled that the merger of the Santa Fe and Southern Pacific railway systems might reduce competition.[5] Sante Fe had merged with Southern Pacific in 1983 in one of the biggest mergers in railway history. The combined railway was operated together while awaiting an antitrust analysis and ruling from the ICC that had antitrust jurisdiction for this type of merger. Following the ruling, the ICC required Santa Fe–

---

[4] J. Fred Weston, "Divestitures: Mistakes or Learnings," *Journal of Applied Corporate Finance* 2, no. 2 (Summer 1989):68–76.

[5] Laurie McGinley, Judith Valente, and Daniel Machalaba, "ICC Reaffirms Its Rejection of Merger of Santa Fe, Southern Pacific Railroads," *Wall Street Journal*, July 1, 1987, p. 1.

Southern Pacific to submit a divestiture plan within 90 days. The adverse ruling had a depressing effect on Santa Fe's stock price and made the firm a target of a bid by the Henley Group.

Voluntary divestitures are more common than involuntary divestitures and are motivated by a variety of reasons. For example, the parent company may want to move out of a particular line of business which it feels no longer fits into its plans or in which it is unable to operate profitably. This does not mean that another firm, with greater expertise in this line of business, could not profitably manage the division's assets. Divestitures then become part of an efficient market process that reallocates assets to those that will allow them to reach their greatest gain.

Reverse Synergy

One motive that is often ascribed to mergers and acquisitions is synergy. As described in Chapter 4, synergy refers to the additional gains that can be derived when two forms combine. When synergy exists, the combined entity is worth more than the sum of the parts valued separately. In other words, $2 + 2 = 5$. *Reverse synergy* means that the parts are worth more separately than they are within the parent company's corporate structure. In other words, $4 - 1 = 5$. In such cases, an outside bidder might be able to pay more for a division than what the division is worth to the parent company. For instance, a large parent company is not able to operate a division profitably, whereas a smaller firm, or even the division by itself, might operate more efficiently and, therefore, earn a higher rate of return. Reverse synergy occurred in the late 1980s when the Allegis Corporation was forced to sell off its previously acquired companies, Hertz Car Rental and Weston and Hilton International Hotels. Allegis had paid a high price for these acquisitions based on the belief that synergistic benefits would more than justify the high prices. When the synergistic benefits failed to materialize, the stock price fell, setting the stage for a hostile bid from the New York investment firm, Coniston Partners. Coniston made a bid based on its analysis that the separate parts of Allegis were worth more than the combined entity.

Other Reasons for Voluntary Divestitures As mentioned earlier, a firm may decide to divest a division simply because it no longer fits into the parent company's plans. This may occur with a division that is no longer generating sufficient profit. The division could fail to pay a rate of return that exceeds the parent company's *hurdle rate*—the minimum threshold that a company will use to evaluate projects or the performance of parts of the overall company. A typical hurdle rate could be the firm's cost of capital.

A division could decline for many reasons. The industry as a whole might be in a state of decline. For example, high labor costs, caused by a unionized labor force may make the division uncompetitive in the world market. This occurred when Swift and Company decided that it would have to sell the fresh meats division. (See Case Study later in this chapter.) Beset with a high-cost, unionized labor force, this division could not compete with its nonunionzed competitors, and Swift and Company decided to sell it off.

Capital Market Factors

A divestiture may also take place because the post-divestiture firm, as well as the divested division, has greater access to capital markets. The combined corporate structure may be more difficult for investors to categorize. Certain providers of capital might be looking to invest in steel companies but not in pharmaceutical firms. Other investors might seek to invest capital in pharmaceutical companies but may feel that the steel industry is too cyclical and has low-growth potential. These two groups of investors might not want to invest in a combined steel-pharmaceutical company, but each group might separately invest in a standalone steel or pharmaceutical firm. Divestiture might provide greater access to capital markets for the two firms as separate companies than as a combined corporation.

Similarly, divestitures can create companies in which investors would like to invest but which do not exist in the marketplace. Such companies are sometimes referred to as *pure plays*. Many analysts argue that the market is incomplete and there is a demand for certain types of firms which is not matched by a supply of securities in the market. The sale of those parts of the parent company that are pure plays helps complete the market.

The separation of divisions facilitates clearer identification and market segmentation for the investment community. New investment dollars can then be attracted. Ronald Kudla and Thomas McInish give the following example of enhanced capital access:

> An example of a capital market induced spin-off involves Koger Properties, Inc. which historically consisted of two distinct businesses. These two businesses were development and construction and property ownership and management. The development and construction business traditionally had provided investors with relatively volatile, high risk opportunities. As a result, earnings were quite sensitive to the availability and cost of capital for real estate development, and to the strength of the national and local economies. But the ownership and management of the rental office

properties, while also involving risks to the investor, was not as sensitive to those factors because completed, leased properties have established rental income and generally are financed through long term mortgage indebtedness having fixed equal monthly payments of principal and interest. Koger Properties, Inc.'s management felt that the development aspect of the company was never fully reflected in the marketplace. Accordingly, management believed that it was in the interest of stockholders for the firm's two business activities to be conducted by separate and independent companies.[6]

Cash Flow Factors

A selloff produces the immediate benefits of an infusion of cash from the sale. The selling firm is selling a long-term asset, which generated a certain cash flow per period, in exchange for a larger payment in the short run. Companies that are under financial duress are often forced to sell off valuable assets in order to enhance cash flows. Chrysler Corporation was forced to sell off its prized tank division in an effort to stave off bankruptcy. International Harvester (now known as Navistar) sold its profitable Solar Turbines International Division to Caterpillar Tractor Company in order to realize the immediate proceeds of $505 million. These funds actually cut Harvester's short-term debt in half.

Abandoning the Core Business

The sale of a company's core business is a less common reason for a selloff. An example of the sale of a core business was the 1987 sale by Greyhound of its bus business. The sale of a core business is often motivated by management's desire to leave an area which it believes has matured and presents few growth opportunities. Usually, the firm has already diversified into other, more profitable areas, and the sale of the core business can help finance the expansion of these more productive activities.

Involuntary Spinoffs

When faced with an adverse regulatory ruling, a firm may decide that a spinoff is the only viable manner of complying. The classic example of such an involuntary spinoff was the mammoth spinoff of AT&T's operating companies in 1984. As a result of an antitrust suit originally

---

[6] Ronald J. Kudla and Thomas H. McInish, *Corporate Spin-Offs: Strategy for the 1980s* (Westport, Conn.: Quorum Books, 1984), p. 18.

CASE STUDY: *SWIFT AND COMPANY*

Swift and Company was a food products concern with nearly a 10-year record of success.[a] Its profitability began declining in the 1960s as a result of competition from more efficient producers. Of particular concern was the fresh meats division. The meatpacking business was characterized by low-profit margins and high labor cost for those companies, like Swift, that had a unionized workforce. The union steadfastly objected to wage concessions that would have helped make Swift's fresh meats division more competitive and threatened to strike if Swift tried to force the concessions on the union. A strike would mean that Swift would be unable to deliver its meat products to the supermarkets. Their shelf space would then be taken by other aggressive competitors who might not relinquish it easily after the strike was over.

Through broad acquisitions of firms like Playtex, Jensen Stereos, STP Oil, and Danskin leotards, Swift, under the leadership of CEO Donald Kelly, had been shifting toward a diversified consumer products concern. During the early 1980s Swift and Company was just one part of Kelly's growing conglomerate that traded under the name Esmark. Kelly believed that the strategy of continued acquisitions of consumer products companies would strengthen the company. He simply considered the fresh meats division a thorn in the parent company's side. The newly acquired companies were generally performing up to expectations whereas the Swift and Company part of Esmark was subject to erratic income swings and low profitability.

The union contract made Swift and Company an unattractive target. Although Kelly through his investment bank, Salomon Brothers, tried to sell the division, no takers could be found. The situation was troubling for Kelly because Swift's poor performance was hurting Esmark's stock price, making the parent company vulnerable to a takeover. Next, Esmark, in association with Salomon Brothers, conducted a valuation analysis of each Esmark subsidiary. Such an analysis is a standard first step when a divestiture is being contemplated. The firm determined the value of each division of the parent company as though it were a separate company and then compared it to the market value of each division. The profits of each division were used to compute the going concern's value and to compare this value to each division's liquidation value. (See the following table.)

ESMARK'S DIVISIONAL VALUATION ANALYSIS

Division	Value
Estech	$350–$400 million
International Jensen	$125–$150
International Playtex	$500–$600
Vickers Petroleum Corporation	$610–$700
STP Corporation	$50–$75 million
Swift and Company	$300 million

Source: Lambert, *Behind Closed Doors,* pp. 293–294.

[a] The discussion of this case is based on several sources, especially Hope Lambert, *Behind Closed Doors* (New York: Atheneum Publishers, 1986), pp. 277–324.

The final tabulation of the combined firm showed Esmark's total value as $1,220 to $1,580 million, or $55 to $71 per share.

The focus of the analysis was the poorly performing Swift division. The weakest component of Swift, the fresh meats division was burdened with noncompetitive wage rates enforced by an inflexible union. Esmark reevaluated the fresh meats component based on the assumption of wage concessions from the unions. It tried to sell the fresh meats division to the union but to no avail, at which point Esmark decided to sell the division to the public in an equity carve-out. A total of 2.75 million shares were sold for $15 per share,[b] and Esmark raised $41.25 million from the sale. This was greater than the sales projection by Salomon Brothers.

The post-divestiture Swift proved to be economically viable. The scaled-down company was able to wrest wage concessions from the union, something Esmark couldn't do. Some plants were renovated and others were sold. In addition, the price of Esmark's stock rose as the stock market signaled that the post-divestiture Esmark was more valuable than its pre-divestiture form.

[b] Lambert, *Behind Closed Doors,* p. 322.

filed in 1974 by the Justice Department, the government and AT&T reached an agreement providing for the breakup of the large telecommunications company. The agreement, which became effective January 1, 1984, provided for the reorganization of the 22 operating companies within AT&T into seven regional holding companies. These holding companies would be responsible for local telecommunications service, while the new AT&T would maintain responsibility for long distance communications.

The spinoff of the 22 operating companies would still allow AT&T shareholders to have the same number of shares in the post-spinoff company. These shares would represent ownership rights in a much smaller telecommunications company. For every ten shares that each shareholder had in the original AT&T, shareholders would receive one share in each of the seven regional holding companies.[7] Those shareholders who had fewer than ten shares would receive a cash value for their shares rather than shares in the regional holding companies. They would still be shareholders in the post-spinoff AT&T. The spinoff created a major administrative problem. Thousands of workers were hired to process the stock transfers and to handle recordkeeping. A special administrative center was established in Jacksonville, Florida, to coordinate the paperwork and share distribution.[8]

[7] *AT&T Shareholders Newsletter,* Fourth Quarter, 1982.
[8] Kudla and McInish, *Corporate Spin-Offs,* p. 8.

The AT&T spinoff is an extreme form of an involuntary spinoff given the sheer size of the transaction. The spinoff resulted in a dramatic change in the nature of the telecommunications industry in the United States. Most spinoffs, however, are not on this scale and are not a response to a regulatory mandate.

Tax Consequences of Spinoffs   The shares in the regional Bells which stockholders received did not represent any additional tax liability for those shareholders. The IRS treated the distribution of shares in the AT&T spinoff as neither a gain nor a loss. Voluntary spinoffs are also often treated as nontaxable transactions. If the spinoff occurs for valid business reasons, rather than for the purpose of tax avoidance, Section 355 of the tax code allows for the transaction to be nontaxable. The code requires that both the parent company and the spunoff entity be in business for at least five years prior to the restructuring. The subsidiary must also be at least 80 percent owned by the parent company in order for the transaction to qualify for tax-free status.

THE DIVESTITURE AND SPINOFF PROCESS

Step 1.   Divestitures or the Spinoff Decision.   The management of the parent company must decide whether a divestiture is the appropriate course of action. This decision can be made only after a thorough financial analysis of the various alternatives has been completed. The method of conducting the financial analysis for a divestiture or spinoff will be discussed later in this chapter.

Step 2.   Formulation of a Restructuring Plan.   A restructuring or reorganization plan must be formulated, and so an agreement between the parent and the subsidiary may be negotiated. This plan is necessary in the case of a spinoff that will feature a continuing relationship between the parent and the subsidiary. The plan should cover such details as the disposition of the subsidiary's assets and liabilities. In cases where the subsidiary is to keep certain of its assets while others are to be transferred back to the parent company, the plan may provide a detailed breakdown of the asset disposition. Other issues, such as the retention of employees and the funding of their pension liabilities, should also be addressed.

Step 3.   Approval of the Plan by Shareholders.   The extent to which approval of the plan is necessary depends on the significance of the transaction and the relevant state laws. In cases such as a spinoff of a major division of the parent company, stockholder approval may be required. If so, the plan is submitted to the stockholders at a stockholders' meeting which may be the normally scheduled stockholders' meeting or a special meeting called just to consider this issue. A proxy statement requesting approval of the spinoff is also sent to stockholders. The materials submitted to stockholders may address other issues related to the meeting, such as the amendment of the articles of incorporation.

Step 4. Registration of Shares.   Shares issued in a spinoff must be registered with the SEC. As part of the normal registration process, a prospectus, which is part of the registration statement, must be produced. The prospectus must be distributed to all shareholders who receive stock in the spunoff entity.

Step 5. Completion of the Deal.   After all these preliminary steps have been taken, the deal can be consummated. Consideration is exchanged, and the division is separated from the parent company according to a prearranged timetable.

Treatment of Warrants and Convertible Securities

When the parent company has issued warrants or convertible securities, such as convertible debentures, the conversion ratio may have to be adjusted when shares are issued in a spinoff. The spinoff may cause the common stock in the parent company to be less valuable. If the deal is so structured that current common stockholders gain through the distribution of proceeds in the form of a special dividend, warrant holders and convertible security holders may not participate in this gain. After the distribution, the stock price of the parent company *may* fall, making the expected conversion more difficult since it will be less likely that the price will rise high enough to enable the securities to be converted. If this is the case, the conversion prices may need to be adjusted as part of the terms of the deal.

Employee Stock Option Plans

For employees holding shares under an employee stock option plan (ESOP), the number of shares obtainable by option holders may also need to be adjusted following a spinoff. The adjustment is designed to leave the market value of shares that could be obtained following the spinoff at the same level. This is usually done by increasing the number of shares that can be obtained with a given option. Those option-holding employees in the parent company who become employees in the spun-off entity have their stock options changed to become options in the new company. Here again, the goal is to maintain the market value of the shares that can be obtained through conversion of the employee stock options.

Financial Evaluation of Divestitures

Financial evaluation techniques are discussed in Chapters 14 and 15. The financial evaluation of a subsidiary by a parent company contemplating divestiture should proceed in a logical fashion. The steps outlined below form a basis for a general process of evaluation.

Step 1. Estimation of After-Tax Cash Flows. The parent company needs to estimate the after-tax cash flows of the division. This analysis should consider the interrelationship between the subsidiary's and the parent company's respective capabilities to generate cash flow. If, for example, the subsidiary's operations are closely related to the parent company's activities, the parent company's cash flows may be positively or negatively affected after the divestiture. This needs to be factored into the analysis at the start of the evaluation process.

Step 2. Determination of the Division's Discount Rate. The present value of the division's after-tax cash flows needs to be calculated. In order to do so, a division-specific discount rate must be derived, taking into account the risk characteristics of the division on a standalone basis. The cost of capital of other firms that are in the same business and approximately the same size would be a good proxy for this discount rate.

Step 3. Present Value Calculation. Using the discount rate derived in Step 2, we can calculate the present value of each projected after-tax cash flow. The sum of these terms will represent the present value of the income generation capability of the division by itself.

Step 4. Deduction of the Market Value of the Division's Liabilities. Step 3 of this process did not take into account the division's liabilities. The market value of these liabilities needs to be deducted from the present value of the after-tax cash flows. The market value is used since the market has, in effect, already completed the present value calculation in its determination of the current value of these obligations. This results in a net of liability value of the division, which is the value of the division based on the parent company, assuming it maintains ownership of the division.

$$NOL = \sum_{i=1}^{n} \frac{ATCF_i}{(1 + k)^i} - MVL$$

where: NOL = the net of liabilities value of the present value of the after-tax cash flows

   ATCF = the after-tax cash flows

   k = the division-specific discount rate

   MVL = the market value of the liabilities

Step 5. Deduction of the Divestiture Proceeds. The proceeds that the parent can derive from a sale of the division are then compared to the value developed in Step 4. If the divestiture proceeds are higher than the value of keeping the division, the unit should be sold.

DP > NOL   Sell division.

DP = NOL   Other factors will control decision.

DP < NOL   Keep division.

ECONOMIC ANALYSIS AND THE WEALTH EFFECTS OF SELLOFFS

A major motivating factor for divestitures and spinoffs is the belief that reverse synergy may exist. Divestitures and spinoffs are basically a "downsizing" of the parent firm; therefore, the smaller firm must be economically more viable than the larger company. Several research studies have analyzed the impact of spinoffs by examining the effect on the stock prices of both the parent company and the spunoff entity. This effect is then compared to a market index to determine whether the stocks experience extranormal performance that cannot be explained by market movements alone. Spinoffs are a unique opportunity to analyze the effects of the separation since a market exists for both the stock of the parent and the spunoff entity.

The Oppenheimer Study

In 1981, Oppenheimer and Company conducted a study of 19 major spinoffs in the 1970s.[9] It was reported that the combined value of the

---

[9] "The Sum of the Parts," New York, Oppenheimer and Co., January 14, 1981.

Table 11.2 THE KUDLA AND MCINISH SAMPLE CHARACTERISTICS

Parent Firm	Spunoff Firm	Size of Spinoff (pct.)
Browning–Ferris Industries	Consolidated Fibres	22
Easco Corporation	Eastmet Corporation	47
Olin Corporation	Olinkraft Corporation	12
Tandy Corporation	Tandycraft Corporation	18
Tandy Corporation	Tandy Brands	6
Valmac Corporation	Distribuco, Inc.	10

Source: Ronald Kudla and Thomas McInish, "Valuation Consequences of Corporate Spin-Offs," *Review of Business and Economic Research* (March 1983):71–77.

parent company and the spunoff entity was greater than the market value of the parent company prior to the spinoff in the majority of cases considered. Fourteen of the nineteen spunoff companies outperformed the Standard and Poor's 400 index for a period of six months after the spinoff. In addition, a portfolio of these spinoff firms yielded a 440 percent return during the 1970s.

The Kudla–McInish Study

Kudla and McInish, in a study of six major spinoffs in the 1970s, used residuals as the measure of market-adjusted returns (Table 11.2).[10] This measure, developed by Fama, Fisher, Jensen, and Roll, is standard to much of the research in this area. Their results showed a positive reaction to the spinoffs. Interestingly, Kudla and McInish showed that the pronounced positive reaction occurred between 15 and 40 weeks **prior to** the spinoff (Figure 11.4). This indicates that the market correctly anticipated the spinoffs long before the actual event. Since the performance of a division can be actively debated in the media or the market well in advance of a decision to sever the division from the parent company, it is not surprising that the market would anticipate the parent company's reaction.

The Miles–Rosenfeld Study

James Miles and James Rosenfeld conducted a study of 59 spinoffs between 1963 and 1980, focusing on the impact of the spinoff on the

---

[10] Ronald Kudla and Thomas McInish, "Valuation Consequences of Corporate Spin-Offs," *Review of Economics and Business Research* (March 1983):71–77.

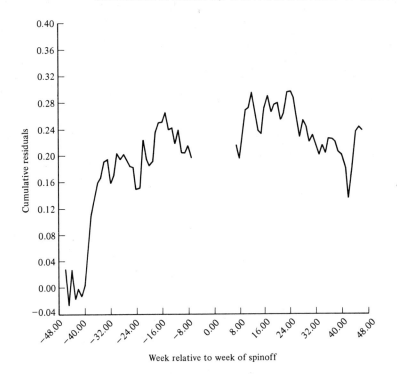

Figure 11.4 Plot of cumulative residuals for six voluntary corporate spin-offs. (*Source:* Ronald Kudla and Thomas McInish, "Valuation Consequences of Corporate Spin-offs," *Review of Economics and Business and Research* (March 1983): 71–77.)

difference between predicted and actual returns.[11] Using this method, they filtered out the influence of the market. As did Kudla and McInish, Miles and Rosenfeld found that the effect of the spinoff was positive and internalized in the stock price prior to the actual spinoff date.

The Miles–Rosenfeld study also revealed that the positive stock price reaction was accompanied by a negative price reaction by the parent company's bonds. In effect, it seems that the wealth-increasing effects for stockholders comes at the expense of the bondholders. Some have interpreted this to be the result of the fact that the cash flow from the spunoff entity can no longer be relied on to meet the debt service payments. Another explanation is that, all other factors being constant, larger firms tend to receive higher bond ratings.

---

[11] James Miles and James Rosenfeld, "An Empirical Analysis of the Effects of Spin-Off Announcements on Shareholder Wealth," *Journal of Finance* 38, no. 5 (December 1983):1597–1606.

The Price Effects of Voluntary Selloffs

The Kudla–McInish and the Miles–Rosenfeld studies demonstrate the positive stock price reaction of corporate selloffs. This reaction is supported in an abundance of other research studies. The research findings of other notable studies in this field have been summarized by Linn and Rozeff (see Table 11.3). The table shows an increase in stockholder wealth resulting from corporate selloffs, the positive impact on equity values ranging from 0.17 to 2.33 percent. The equity market clearly concludes that the voluntary selling of a division is a positive development that will result in an increase in the value of the firm's stock.

Rationale for a Positive Stock Price Reaction to Selloffs

When a firm decides to sell off a poorly performing division, this asset goes to another owner who presumably will value it more highly because he or she can utilize this asset more advantageously than the seller. The seller receives cash (or sometimes other compensation) in place of the asset. When the market responds positively to this asset reallocation, it is expressing a belief that the firm will use this cash more efficiently than it was utilizing the asset that was sold. Moreover, the asset that was sold may have attracted a premium above market value, which should also cause the market to respond positively.

The selling firm has a few options at its disposal when contemplating the disposition of the newly acquired cash. The firm can pay the cash to stockholders in the form of a dividend, or it may repurchase its own shares at a premium. Either option is a way the selling corporation can give its stockhodlers an immediate payout. If the seller retains the cash, it will be used for internal investment to expand in one of its current

Table 11.3   THE AVERAGE STOCK PRICE EFFECTS OF VOLUNTARY SELLOFFS

Study	Days	Average Abnormal Returns (pct.)	Period Sampled	Sample Size
Alexander, Benson, and Kampmeyer (1984)	−1 through 0	0.17	1964–1973	53
Hite and Owens (1984)	−1 through 0	1.5	1963–1979	56
Klein (1983)	−2 through 0	1.12	1970–1979	202
Linn and Rozeff (1984)	−1 through 0	1.45	1977–1982	77
Rosenfeld	−1 through 0	2.33	1963–1981	62

areas of activity or for an acquisition. The choice of another acquisition may give stockholders cause for concern. The fact that acquisitions can have a dampening effect on stock prices has been documented in financial research. (See Chapter 4.)

Another argument in favor of the value-increasing effects of selloffs is that the market might find it difficult to evaluate highly diversified companies. The validity of this argument is a matter of considerable debate since it implies that the market is somewhat inefficient. If the market is inefficient in evaluating these types of firms, then the sale of one or more divisions might facilitate categorization of the parent company. The greater ease of categorization and evaluation would encourage investors looking to invest in certain types of companies.

The Wealth Effects of Involuntary Selloffs

Most research studies on the effects of selloffs on stockholder wealth conclude that selloffs increase the wealth of parent company stockholders and that the market is somewhat efficient in anticipating the event. Therefore, the stock price reaction occurs in advance of the actual selloff date. The wealth-increasing effects of a selloff of an unwanted or poorly performing subsidiary should be different from those of a parent company being forced to divest itself of a profitable division. This was the case when Santa Fe–Southern Pacific received its unfavorable ruling requiring it to divest itself of the Southern Pacific Railway. As noted earlier, the stock price decined, and Santa Fe became a takeover target.

In 1981, Kudla and McInish conducted a case study of the effects of the required spinoff of the Louisiana-Pacific Corporation by Georgia-Pacific, the parent company.[12] The spinoff was required by the Federal Trade Commission which concluded that the acquisition of 16 companies in the southern part of the United States, which accounted for a total of 673,000 acres of pine trees, would result in an anticompetitive concentration in the plywood industry. Using cumulative residuals to adjust for market effects, Kudla and McInish showed that the price of Georgia-Pacific stock had been declining prior to the formal filing of the FTC complaint. Louisiana-Pacific was spun off in 1972. Figure 11.5 shows that the downward movement of the stock price ended with the spinoff, after which the stock price rebounded. Although the stock price rebound was significant, the cumulative residuals did not fully recover to the start of the 1971 level even as late as March 1974.

---

[12] Ronald Kudla and Thomas McInish, "The Microeconomic Consequences of an Involuntary Corporate Spin-Off," *Sloan Management Review* 22, no. 4 (1981).

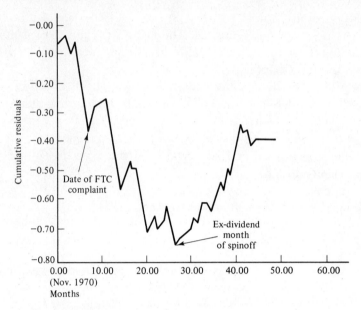

Figure 11.5 Georgia-Pacific Corporation's cumulative residuals versus time. (*Source:* Reprinted from "The Microeconomic Consequences of an Involuntary Corporate Spin-off," Ronald J. Kudla and Thomas H. McInish, *Sloan Management Review*, vol. 22, no. 4, p. 45. By permission of the publisher. Copyright © 1981 by The Sloan Management Review Association. All rights reserved.)

The Miles–Rosenfeld study showed that the wealth of bondholders declined after the spinoff even while the wealth of stockholders increased. This was believed to have been attributed to the lower cash flows after the spinoff and the resulting increase in risk to bondholders. Kudla and McInish attempted to measure the risk effects of the involuntary Louisiana-Pacific spinoff by examining the betas of Georgia-Pacific before and after the spinoff. The betas would then reflect any change in the systematic or undiversifiable risk associated with Georgia-Pacific stock. Kudla and McInish found a large, statistically significant increase in the betas of Georgia-Pacific after the spinoff. They attributed this increase to the market's perception that Georgia-Pacific incurred a decrease in monopoly power after the spinoff and that this caused the firm to be riskier.

The finance research community seems to have reached a consensus that a divestiture that is forced by government mandate, as opposed to a voluntary selloff, will have an adverse effect on the divesting firm's stock price. James Ellert's review of 205 defendants in antitrust merger lawsuits showed a −1.86 percent decline in the value of the equity of these firms during the month the complaint was filed.[13] The issue that the Kudla–McInish study addresses is the timing of that impact and of the reversal of the declining trend.

If the antitrust enforcement is effective in reducing the selling firm's monopoly power, then this should be reflected in an *increase* in the value of the equity of that firm's competitors. Unfortunately, the antitrust authorities can find little support for their actions in the stock prices of the competitors of divesting firms.[14] The value of the equity of competitors of divesting firms failed to show a significant positive response to mandated selloffs.

EQUITY CARVE-OUTS

Equity carve-outs became a popular financing technique in the late 1980s, even though the market for public offerings was poor. Companies such as Enron Corporation, W. R. Grace, Hanson Trust, and Macmillan decided that equity carve-outs provided significant financial advantages over other forms of restructuring. Between 1987 and 1989, the 10 largest equity carve-outs totaled $13.92 billion, even though the initial public offering market was depressed.[15]

The parent company may sell a 100 percent interest in the subsidiary, or it may choose to remain in the subsidiary's line of business by selling only a partial interest and keeping the remaining percentage of ownership. This was the case when the Neoax Corporation chose to sell a 53 percent ownership in a trucking business that it had acquired in March 1988 in a highly leveraged transaction.[16] Neoax sold 51 percent of the trucking company, which it had renamed Landstar, for $94 million. The transaction enabled Neoax to maintain a reduced total debt load while providing the firm with the option to regain control of the trucking company in the future. Neoax also received a value for the division that was consistent with its internal valuation analysis, which

---

[13] James C. Ellert, "Mergers, Antitrust Law Enforcement and the Behavior of Stock Prices," *Journal of Finance* 31 (1976):715–732.

[14] Robert Stillman, "Examining Antitrust Policy Towards Horizontal Mergers," *Journal of Financial Economics* 11 (1983):225–240; Bjorn E. Eckbo, "Horizontal Mergers, Collusion and Stockholder Wealth," *Journal of Financial Economics* 11 (1983):241–274.

[15] Susan Jarzombek, "A Way to Put a Spotlight on Unseen Value," *Corporate Finance* (December 1989):62–64.

[16] Ibid.

showed that the entire division was worth $200 million. Efforts to sell the division outright failed to attract offers near this value.

Many firms have looked to equity carve-outs as a means of reducing their exposure to a riskier line of business. For example, American Express bought the brokerage firm, Shearson, in 1981. It later acquired the investment bank, Lehman Brothers, to form Shearson Lehman. This is a riskier line of business than American Express's traditional charge card operations. Later, American Express decided that, although it still liked the synergy that came with being a diversified financial services company, it wanted to reduce its exposure to the risks of the securities business. In 1987, Amexco, its holding company, sold off a 39 percent interest in Shearson Lehman. This proved to be fortuitous since the sale preceded the stock market crash, an event that securities firms still had not recovered from by the end of the 1980s.

Equity Carve-Outs Versus Public Offerings

An equity carve-out, as opposed to a spinoff, brings in new capital to the parent company. Since the acquisition of capital is obviously a motivating factor for this type of selloff, we must investigate why the equity carve-out option may be chosen over a public offering of stock. Katherine Schipper and Abbie Smith conducted a major study of the equity carve-out, examining the share price reactions to 76 carve-out announcements. They compared these reactions to previous studies documenting the stock price reactions to public equity offerings.[17] Previous studies have shown that the announcement of seasoned equity offerings results in an abnormal stock return of between -2 and -3 percent in the time periods around the equity offering.[18] In contrast to other equity financing arrangements, Schipper and Smith found that equity carve-outs *increase* shareholder wealth. Schipper and Smith found that the shareholders of the parent firms experienced average gains of 1.8 percent. They compared this positive stock price effect with a -3 percent shareholder loss for a subset of parent firms that engaged in public offerings of common stock or debt.

Schipper and Smith propose that the positive stock price reactions

---

[17] Katherine Schipper and Abbie Smith, "A Comparison of Equity Carve-Outs and Seasonized Equity Offerings," *Journal of Financial Economics* 15 (January–February 1986):153–186.

[18] For a review of some of this literature as well as additional research showing that the effects of stock offerings are more negative for industrial firms than for public utilities, see Ronald W. Masulis and Ashok N. Korwar, "Seasonized Equity Offerings," *Journal of Financial Economics* 15, no. 11 (January–February 1986):91–118.

are due to a combination of effects, including better and more defined information available on both the parent and the subsidiary. This fact is clear to those who have attempted to evaluate the subsidiaries of a publicly held company. The annual reports and other publicly available documents can be very brief and yield little of the data necessary to value the component parts of a company. When the subsidiary becomes a standalone public company, it publishes more detailed information on its operations since its activities are its only line of business as opposed to merely being a part of a larger parent company.

Schipper and Smith also point out other possible factors responsible for the positive stock price reaction to equity carve-outs—for instance, the restructuring and asset management that tends to be associated with equity carve-outs. In addition, divisions can be consolidated into a more efficient form, and managers can work with new compensation incentives. The combination of these and other changes may make the subsidiary a more viable entity as a separate public company. The market may perceive this value which may be a source of a premium for the selling company. The parent company, no longer encumbered by a subsidiary that it could not manage as well as another owner might, becomes more valuable when it converts this asset into cash which it can, hopefully, invest in more productive areas.

VOLUNTARY LIQUIDATIONS OR BUST-UPS

Voluntary liquidations or bust-ups are the most extreme form of corporate restructuring. Corporate liquidations are more often associated with bankruptcy. A company may be liquidated in bankruptcy when all parties concerned recognize that the continuation of the firm in a reorganized form will not enhance its value. The outlook, however, is not as negative for voluntary liquidations. The general criterion applied is as follows: if the market value of the firm's assets significantly exceeds the value of the firm's equity, then a liquidation may need to be seriously considered. This is not to imply that liquidation should be an alternative in instances of a temporary downturn of the firm's stock. The liquidation option becomes viable only when the firm's stock has been depressed for an extended time period. The liquidation option becomes even more likely when the stock prices of other firms in the same industry are not also depressed. In addition, low P/E ratios can sometimes point to a need to consider the liquidation option. Managers are often reluctant to consider such a drastic step, which would result in their losing their positions. They may prefer to sell the entire firm to a single acquirer rather than pursue liquidation. Stockholders sometimes try to force management's hand by threatening a proxy battle to decide the issue.

Voluntary liquidations can be contrasted with divestitures. A divestiture is generally a single transaction in which a certain part of the firm is sold, whereas a voluntary liquidation is a series of transactions in which all the firm's assets are sold in separate parcels.

Tax motives may make a liquidation more attractive than a divestiture. Divestitures can be subject to capital gains taxes, whereas voluntary liquidations can often be structured to receive more preferential tax treatment. As noted above, spinoffs involving only 20 percent of the parent company can also be a tax-free transaction. However, the 20 percent threshold may not be comparable to the more drastic downsizing that is necessary for firms contemplating liquidation. Therefore, a liquidation may enhance shareholder wealth more than a divestiture.

The Shareholder Wealth Effects of Voluntary Spinoffs

Skantz and Marchesini's study of liquidation announcements made by 37 firms during 1970–1982 showed an average excess return of 21.4 percent during the month of the announcement.[19] Hite, Owens, and Rogers found similar positive shareholder wealth effects during the month of the announcement of voluntary liquidations made by the 49 firms in their sample covering the years 1966–1975.[20] They showed positive abnormal return in the announcement month equal to 13.62 percent. Almost half the firms in their sample had been the object of bids for control within two years of the announcement of the liquidation plan. These bids included a wide range of actions including leveraged buyouts, tender offers, and proxy contests. Moreover, more than 80 percent of the firms in their sample showed positive abnormal returns. This implies the stock market's agreement that continued operation of the firm under its prior operating policy will reduce shareholder wealth.

The positive stock market reaction was affirmed by yet another study. Kim and Schatzberg found 14 percent positive return for 73 liquidating firms during a three-day time period associated with the liquidation announcement.[21] They revealed that a 3 percent return was

[19] Terence Skantz and Roberto Marchesini, "The Effect of Voluntary Corporate Liquidation on Shareholder Wealth," *Journal of Financial Research* 10 (Spring 1987): 65–75.

[20] Gailen Hite, James Owens, and Ronald Rogers, "The Market for Interfirm Asset Sales: Partial Selloffs and Total Liquidations," *Journal of Financial Economics* 18 (June 1987):229–252.

[21] E. Han Kim and John Schatzberg, "Voluntary Corporate Liquidations," *Journal of Financial Economics* 19, no. 2 (December 1987):311–328.

added when shareholders confirmed the transaction. Kim and Schatzberg failed to detect any significant wealth effect, either positive or negative, for the shareholders of the acquiring firms.

As suggested earlier, these research studies imply that the stock market often agrees that the continued operation of the firm under its prior operating policy will reduce shareholder wealth. This is not surprising since most firms considering liquidation are suffering serious problems. Liquidation then releases the firm's assets to other companies that might be able to realize a higher return on them.

MASTER LIMITED PARTNERSHIPS

Master limited partnerships (MLPs) are limited partnerships in which the shares are publicly traded. A limited partnership consists of a general partner and one or more limited partners. The general partner runs the business and bears unlimited liability. This is one of the major disadvantages of this form of business organization compared to a corporation. In a corporation, the owners, the stockholders, are insulated from the company's liabilities. The limited partners in the MLP, however, do not incur the liability exposure of the general partner.

The key advantage of the MLP is its elimination of the corporate layer of taxation. Stockholders in a corporation are taxed twice on their investments: first at the corporate level and second, as distributions in the form of dividends, at the individual level. MLPs are not taxed as a separate business entity, and the returns to the business flow through to the owners just as they do in other partnerships. This advantage was strengthened by the 1986 Tax Reform Act which lowered the highest personal income tax bracket to 28 percent (which is less than the top corporate rate of 34 percent). This advantage may be reduced when the tax law is changed once again to raise the rate charged in the upper tax bracket in 1991.

Corporations have used MLPs to redistribute assets so that their returns will not be subject to double taxation. In a *roll-out* MLP, corporations can transfer assets or divisions in separate MLPs.[22] Stockholders in the corporation are then given units of ownership in the MLP while still maintaining their shares in the corporation. The income distributed by the MLP is not subject to double taxation.

MLPs have been popular in the petroleum industry. Oil companies have distributed oil and gas assets into MLPs, allowing the returns to

---

[22] J. Fred Weston, Kwang S. Chung, and Susan E. Hoag, *Mergers, Restructuring and Corporate Control* (Englewood Cliffs, N.J.: Prentice Hall, 1990), pp. 384–385.

flow through directly to stockholders without double taxation. Initially, start-up businesses can also be structured as MLPs. The MLP can be run by a general partner who receives an income from managing the business. The general partner may or may not own a unit in the MLP. Capital is raised through an initial sales of MLP units to investors.

SUMMARY

Corporate restructuring is often warranted when the current structure of the corporation is not yielding values that are consistent with market or management expectations. It may occur when a given part of a company no longer fits into management plans. Other restructuring may prove necessary when a prior acquisition has not performed up to management's expectations. The decision to sell may be difficult because it requires management to admit that the firm made a mistake when it acquired the asset that is being sold. Once the decision to sell has been made, management must then decide how the firm will sell the division or asset. Managers may consider several of the different options discussed in this chapter such as a straightforward sale or divestiture or the sale of an equity interest in a subsidiary to outsiders which is an equity carve-out. In both cases a separate legal entity is created, and the divested entity is run by a new management team as a separate company. An alternative that also results in the creation of a separate legal entity is a spinoff. Here shares are issued on a pro rata basis and are distributed to the parent company's shareholders also on a pro rata basis. When the transaction is structured so that shares in the original company are exchanged for shares in the parent firm, the deal is called a splitoff. A splitup occurs when the entire firm is broken up and shareholders exchange their shares in the parent company according to a predetermined formula.

Empirical research has found that a significant amount of selloffs are associated with positive shareholder wealth effects. This implies that the market agrees that the sale of part of the company will yield a higher return than the continued operation of the division under current operating policies. The market is indicating that the proceeds of the sale of the firm can be utilized more advantageously than the division that is being sold.

REFERENCES

AT&T Shareholders Newsletter, Fourth Quarter, 1982.

Eckbo, Bjorn E. "Horizontal Mergers, Collusion and Stockholders Wealth." *Journal of Financial Economics* 11 (1983):241–274.

Ellert, James C. "Mergers, Antitrust Law Enforcement and the Behavior of Stock Prices." *Journal of Finance* 31 (1976):715–732.

Hite, Gailen, and James Owens. "Security Price Reactions Around Corporate Spinoff Announcements." *Journal of Financial Economics* 12, no. 4 (December 1983):409–436.

Hite, Gailen, James Owens, and Ronald Rogers. "The Market for Interfirm Asset Sales: Partial Selloffs and Total Liquidations." *Journal of Financial Economics* 18 (June 1987):229–252.

Jarzombek, Susan. "A Way to Put a Spotlight on Unseen Value." *Corporate Finance* (December 1989):62–64.

Kim, E. Han, and John Schatzberg. "Voluntary Corporate Liquidations." *Journal of Financial Economics* 19, no. 2 (December 1987):311–328.

Kudla, Ronald J., and Thomas H. McInish. *Corporate Spin-Offs: Strategy for the 1980s.* Westport, Conn.: Quorum Books, 1984, p. 18.

Kudla, Ronald J., and Thomas H. McInish. "The Microeconomic Consequences of an Involuntary Corporate Spin-Off." *Sloan Management Review* 22, no. 4 (1981).

Kudla, Ronald J., and Thomas H. McInish. "Valuation Consequences of Corporate Spin-Offs." *Review of Economics and Business Research* (March 1983):71–77.

Lambert, Hope. *Behind Closed Doors.* New York: Atheneum Publishers, 1986.

Linn, Scott C., and Michael S. Rozeff. "The Corporate Selloff." *Midland Corporate Finance Journal* 2, no. 2 (Summer 1984).

McGinley, Laurie, Judith Valente, and Daniel Machalaba. "ICC Reaffirms Its Rejection of Merger of Santa Fe, Southern Pacific Railroads." *Wall Street Journal,* July 1, 1987.

Masulis, Ronald W., and Ashok N. Korwar. "Seasonized Equity Offerings." *Journal of Financial Economics* 15, no. 1/2 (January/February 1986):91–118.

Miles, James, and James Rosenfeld. "An Empirical Analysis of the Effects of Spin-Off Announcements on Shareholder Wealth." *Journal of Finance* 38, no. 5 (December 1983):1597–1606.

Porter, Michael. "From Competitive Advantage to Corporate Strategy." *Harvard Business Review* (May-June 1987).

Schipper, Katherine, and Abbie Smith. "A Comparison of Equity Carve-Outs and Seasonized Equity Offerings." *Journal of Financial Economics* 15 (January-February 1986):153–186.

Skantz, Terrence, and Roberto Marchesini. "The Effect of Voluntary Corporate Liquidation on Shareholder Wealth." *Journal of Financial Research* 10 (Spring 1987):65–75.

Stern, Joel. "A Discussion of Corporate Restructuring." Comments of Gailen Hite. *Midland Corporate Finance Journal* 2, no. 2 (Summer 1984):69.

Stillman, Robert. "Examining Antitrust Policy Towards Horizontal Mergers." *Journal of Financial Economics* 11 (1983):225–240.

"The Sum of the Parts." Oppenheimer and Company, New York, January 14, 1981.

Weston, J. Fred. "Divestitures: Mistakes or Learnings." *Journal of Applied Corporate Finance* 2, no. 2 (Summer 1989):68–76.

Weston, J. Fred, Kwang S. Chung, and Susan E. Hoag. *Mergers, Restructuring and Corporate Control*. Englewood Cliffs, N.J.: Prentice Hall, 1990, pp. 384–385.

Chapter
12

Tax Issues in Mergers and Acquisitions

*D*epending on the method used to finance the transaction, certain mergers and acquisitions can be tax free. Some firms may use their tax benefits as assets in establishing the correct price that they might command in the marketplace. For this reason, tax considerations are important as both the motivation for a transaction and the valuation of a company. Part of the tax benefits from a transaction may derive from *tax synergy*, whereby one of the firms involved in a merger may not be able to fully utilize its tax shields. When combined with the merger partner, however, the tax shields may offset income. Some of these gains may come from unused net operating losses which can be utilized by a more profitable merger partner. Tax reform, however, has limited the ability of firms to sell these net operating losses through mergers. Other sources of tax benefits in mergers may arise from a market value of depreciable assets, which is greater than the value that these assets are kept on the target's books. The acquiring firm able to step up the basis of these assets in accordance with the purchase price may finally realize tax savings.

This chapter discusses the mechanics of realizing some of the tax benefits through mergers. It also reviews the research studies that attempt to determine the importance of tax effects as a motivating factor for mergers and leveraged buyouts, and examines the different accounting treatments that can be applied to a merger or acquisition. These methods, which are regulated by tax laws, affect the importance of taxes in the overall merger valuation. It will be seen that various reforms in tax laws have diminished the role that taxes play in mergers and acquisitions. However, taxes can still be an important consideration that both the seller and buyer must carefully weigh before completing a transaction.

FINANCIAL ACCOUNTING FOR MERGERS AND ACQUISITIONS

The two principal accounting methods used in mergers and acquisitions are (1) the pooling of interests method and (2) the purchase method. The main difference between them is the value that the combined firm's balance sheet places on the assets of the acquired firm, as well as the depreciation allowances and charges against income following the merger.

The Pooling of Interests Method

In order for a transaction to qualify for the pooling of interests accounting treatment, it must satisfy certain accounting critieria, the most important being the following.[1]

1. The acquiring company must finance the acquisition with common stock that is the same as the outstanding common stock of the acquiring firm. This common stock must be used to purchase at least 90 percent of the common stock of the target corporation.
2. The common stock used to finance the acquisition may not be retired or repurchased later.
3. The target company's shareholders must retain an ownership position in the acquiring company.
4. The two firms must be autonomous for at least two years prior to pooling and independent of other firms as reflected by the fact that no more than 10 percent of the stock in either firm can be owned by another firm.
5. The transaction must be completed in a single transaction or according to a specific plan that is completed within a one-year time period.

In a pooling of interests, the individual items on the two firms' balance sheets are added together. Assets are recorded at the values

---

[1] James Van Horne, *Financial Management and Policy* (Englewood Cliffs, N.J.: Prentice Hall, 1989), pp. 647–648. *Opinions of the Accounting Principles Board*, No. 16, American Institute of Certified Public Accountants, New York, August 1970.

they held on the acquired firm's books. The end result of a pooling of interests transaction is that the total assets of the combined firm are equal to the sum of the assets of the individual firms. No goodwill is generated, and there are no charges against earnings. In effect, the stockholders in the two companies combine to form an entirely new entity. Each group of stockholders will share in the profits of the combined company according to the terms of exchange. No additional capital is involved in a pooling of interests transaction. Moreover, there is no change in the "basis" in such a transaction. Therefore, the assets, liabilities, and retainer earnings are combined at their recorded amounts.[2]

The Purchase Method

In the purchase method, the acquired assets are carried on the firm's books at the price that was paid plus any liabilities acquired in the transaction. The total liabilities of the combined firm equals the sum of the two firms' individual liabilities.[3] The equity of the acquiring firm is increased by the amount of the purchase price. The purchase method allows the acquiring company to increase the value of the target firm's assets by the fair market value. These assets are presumably greater than the values that they have carried on the target firm's books. Goodwill is created when the total assets are less than the total liabilities and equity. (The difference between these values is goodwill.)

Although goodwill is an asset and entered on the firm's balance sheet, it is not treated in the same way as other assets for accounting purposes. Physical assets, for example, are depreciated for tax purposes, whereas goodwill is not. Nonetheless, the goodwill is charged against income and amortized over a period that cannot exceed 40 years. In other words, earnings are reduced by the amount of the charge in each year of this writeoff period. This is a disadvantage to the acquiring firm since these writeoffs are not tax deductible.

In the event that the purchase price of the target firm exceeds the value of the target firm's equity, the combined firm's equity is greater than the sum of the individual common equity of the two merged firms. For a comparison of the pooling and purchase methods, see Table 12.1.

---

[2] Robert Levine and Richard P. Miller, "Accounting for Business Combinations," in Steven James Lee and Robert Douglas Coleman, eds., *Handbook of Mergers and Acquisitions* (Englewood Cliffs, N.J.: Prentice–Hall, 1981), pp. 251–292.

[3] Robert Neveau, *Managerial Finance* (Cincinnati, Ohio: South Western Publishing Co., 1985), pp. 663–666.

Table 12.1   EXAMPLE OF THE POOLING VERSUS PURCHASE METHOD

	Balance Sheet Before Merger		Balance Sheet After Merger	
	Company A	Company B	Purchase	Pooling
		(Thousands $)		
Assets net of depreciation	$20,000	$3,000	$24,000	$23,000
Goodwill	0	0	$500	0
Total assets	$20,000	$3,000	$24,500	$23,000
Total liabilities	$10,000	$1,500	$11,500	$11,500
Equity	$10,000	$1,500	$13,000	$11,500
Total liabilities and equity	$20,000	$3,000	$24,500	$23,000

In the transaction shown in Table 12.1, Company A has acquired Company B. Company B, the target, has assets, net of depreciation, equal to $3 million and total liabilities and total equity each at $1.5 million. (The numbers shown in the table are in thousands.) Company A, the acquirer, has assets of $20 million, with total liabilities and net worth equal to $10 million each. The transaction is financed by the issuance of $3 million worth of common stock by Company A. Note that before the merger Company B had a net worth of $1.5 million. Under the purchase method, the assets of Company B are written up as $1 million. This amount is the premium above book value that is paid for Company B.

The assets of Company B are revalued at $4 million after the merger instead of $3 million before the merger. The amount that is then entered as goodwill, $500,000, is a result of the process of asset balancing where goodwill is the difference between the final value of the total assets, $4.5 million, and the new values on the firm's books, $4 million.

Advantages and Disadvantages of Each Method

With pooling of interests the acquiring firm does not face the problem of valuing goodwill. As noted above, this goodwill must be amortized over a period of time less than 40 years and charged off against income. Although it is a charge against income, goodwill does not consitute a tax deduction. It reflects negatively against income without a compensating tax advantage. With the purchase method of accounting, the cost basis of the assets of the acquired firm can be adjusted upward. This creates an opportunity for the acquiring firm to have a higher depreciation expense that reflects positively on taxable income.

Another difference between the two methods is that purchase accounting only allows the inclusion on the financial statements of the combined firm that income which was recorded on the target's books as of the date of the transaction.[4] So if Company X acquires Company Y on July 1, 1990, and X has current earnings of $5 million while Y has earnings of $2.5 million, with purchase accounting the financial statements of Company X, after the merger, will show $6.5 million of earnings. This is the earnings of X plus the earnings of Y for half a year. Y's earnings for the period prior to the merger are not included on X's post-merger financial statements. Pooling accounting would allow Company X to report earnings equal to $7.5 million for the years before and after the transaction. This is the combined income of both firms. When reporting the income for previous time periods, the income of the two firms is simply added together, thereby making Company X's historical earnings look higher than they would if the purchase method were used.

The choice of accounting treatment will then affect the acquisition year's reported income. A company with weak earnings can use the pooling of interests method to try to cover up its own weak earnings.[5] This advantage is one reason why the pooling of interests accounting treatment is often preferred. On the other hand, restrictions on the use of pooling of interests may prevent its use in mergers.

Effect of Accounting Treatment on Stock Prices

Although the purchase method does permit the creation of tax deductible expenses, the choice of method does not itself create any value. The accounting treatment does not produce synergistic effects or other benefits that would affect the combined firm's cash flows. Therefore, if the securities markets are efficient with regard to accounting methods, these paper changes should not affect security prices. Hong, Mandelker, and Kaplan found that stock prices were unaffected by the choice of acquisition accounting.[6]

---

[4] Laurence D. Schall and Charles D. Haley, *Introduction to Financial Management* (New York: McGraw–Hill, 1986), 4th ed., pp. 690–691.

[5] Neil E. Seiz, *Capital Budgeting and Long Term Capital Decisions* (Orlando, Fla.: Dryden Press, 1990), p. 532.

[6] H. Hong, G. Mandelker, and R. S. Kaplan, "Pooling vs. Purchase: The Effects of Accounting for Mergers on Stock Prices," *Accounting Review* 53 (January 1978):31–47.

TAXABLE VERSUS TAX-FREE TRANSACTIONS

A merger or an acquisition may be either a taxable or a tax-free transaction. The tax status of a transaction may affect the value of the transaction from both the buyer's and the seller's viewpoint. A tax-free transaction is known as a tax-free reorganization.

Tax-Free Reorganization

Type A Reorganization   In order for a transaction to qualify as a tax-free reorganization, it must be structured in certain ways.[7] One of these ways is a Type A reorganization, which is considered a more flexible tax-free reorganization technique than some of the others that will be discussed below. In contrast to a Type B reorganization, the Type A allows the buyer to use either voting or nonvoting stock. It also permits the buyer to use more cash in the total consideration since the law does not stipulate a maximum amount of cash that can be used. At least 50 percent of the consideration, however, must be stock in the acquiring corporation. In addition, in a Type A reorganization, the acquiring corporation may choose not to purchase all the target's assets. For example, the deal could be structured in a manner that would allow the target to sell off certain assets separately and exclude them from this transaction.

In cases where at least 50 percent of the bidder's stock is used as the consideration, but other considerations are used, such as cash, debt, or nonequity securities, the transaction may be partially taxable. Capital gains taxes must be paid on those shares that were exchanged for nonequity consideration, while taxes are deferred for those shares that were exchanged for stock. Rights and warrants that are convertible into the bidding firm's equity securities are generally classified as taxable.[8]

Type B Reorganization   A Type B merger or reorganization requires that the acquiring corporation use mainly its own voting common stock as the consideration for purchase of the target corporation's common

---

[7] The description of the tax-free reorganizations draws heavily on George Rodoff's fine article: George Rodoff, "Tax Consequences to Shareholders in an Acquisitive Reorganization," in Steven James Lee and Robert Douglas Coleman, eds., *Handbook of Merger, Acquisitions and Buyouts* (Englewood Cliffs, N.J.: Prentice-Hall, 1981), pp. 359–379.

[8] Cathy M. Niden, "Acquisition Premia: Further Evidence on the Effects of Payment Method and Acquisition Method," Paper presented at the American Economics Association Annual Meeting, December 1989.

stock. Cash must constitute no more than 20 percent of the total consideration, and at least 80 percent of the target's stock must be paid for by voting stock in the acquirer. In this type of transaction, the acquiring corporation must buy at least 80 percent of the stock of the target, although the purchase of 100 percent is more common. Following the purchase of the target's stock, the target becomes a subsidiary of the acquiring corporation.

In both Type A and Type B reorganizations the transactions are viewed, from a tax regulatory point of view, as merely a continuation of the original corporate entities but in a reorganized form. Therefore, these transactions are not taxed since they are not considered true sales.

Type C Reorganization   In a Type C reorganization, the acquiring corporation must purchase 80 percent of the fair market value of the target's assets. Cash can be used only if at least 80 percent of the fair market value of the target's assets have been purchased using the voting stock of the acquiring corporation.

Subsidiary Merger   A subsidiary merger is similar to a Type A reorganization. With this type of transaction, the shares of the target corporation are exchanged for the stock or cash of the acquiring corporation. The acquiring corporation can use either voting or nonvoting stock. With a subsidiary merger, the acquiring corporation must purchase most of the target's assets. In contrast to a Type A reorganization, only those parts of the target that the acquirer desires can be purchased.

THE TAX CONSEQUENCES OF A STOCK-FOR-STOCK EXCHANGE

Target stockholders who receive the stock of the acquiring corporation in exchange for their common stock are not immediately taxed on the consideration they receive. Taxes will have to be paid only if the stock is eventually sold. Given the time value of money, this postponement of tax payments clearly has value. If cash is included in the transaction, this cash may be taxed to the extent that it represents a gain on the sale of stock.

Taxable Purchases of Stock

As noted above, consideration other than stock, such as cash or debt securities, may result in a tax liability for the target shareholders. This tax liability applies only to a gain that might be realized from sale of the stock. If the stock is sold at a loss, something that is less common in the fourth merger wave, then no tax liability will result.

Taxable Purchases of Assets

A tax liability can also result when the acquiring corporation purchases the assets of the target using consideration other than stock in the acquiring corporation. The potential tax liability is measured by comparing the purchase price of the assets with the adjusted basis of these assets.

Tax Loss Carry-Forwards

The tax losses of target corporations can be used to offset a limited amount of the acquiring corporation's future income. These tax losses can be used to offset income for a maximum of 15 years or until the tax loss is exhausted. Before 1981, the maximum period was five years. Only tax losses for the previous three years can be utilized to offset future income.

Tax loss carry-forwards can motivate mergers and acquisitions in two ways. A company that has earned profits may find value in the tax losses of a target corporation which can be used to offset the income it plans to earn. On the other hand, the tax losses realized by a company that has lost money can be utilized in the purchase of a profitable company. Although tax benefits may be an important factor in determining whether or not a merger will take place, they cannot be the sole motivating one. A merger may not, however, be structured solely for tax purposes. The goal of the merger must be to maximize the acquiring corporation's profitability.

An acquiring corporation cannot make unrestricted use of the tax loss carry-forwards which it receives through an acquisition. "The main restrictions are the following: the acquirer must continue to operate the pre-acquisition business of the company in a net loss position; and the acquirer must give up any tax savings from a change in the asset basis of the 'loss company' that might otherwise have resulted from a taxable acquisition."[9] For an example of tax loss carry-forwards, see Table 12.2.

In Table 12.2, the acquiring corporation expects to earn $500 million in each of the next two years. (All dollar amounts shown in the table

---

[9] Mark J. Warshawsky, "Determinants of Corporate Merger Activity: A Review of the Literature," Staff Study No. 152, Board of Governors of the Federal Reserve System, April 1987, p. 5.

Table 12.2 EXAMPLE OF TAX LOSS CARRY-FORWARDS

	Taxes and Income Without the Merger (thousand $)	
	Year I	Year II
Taxable income	$500,000	$500,000
Taxes (40%)	$200,000	$200,000
Income after taxes	$300,000	$300,000

	Taxes and Income with the Merger (thousand $)	
	Year I	Year II
Income before tax loss	$500,000	$500,000
Tax loss carry-forward	$500,000	$100,000
Taxable income	$0	$400,000
Taxes (40%)	$0	$160,000
Income after taxes	$500,000	$340,000

are in thousands of dollars.) It has acquired a company that has a tax loss of $600 million. The acquirer can use this tax loss to offset all the projected income for the year following the acquisition. In addition, $100 million is still available to offset income earned in the following year. The value of this tax loss is seen by the income after taxes in the first year of $500 million with the merger as opposed to $300 million without the merger. In addition, income after taxes is $40 million higher after the merger in the second year. This income must be discounted to reflect the present value of these amounts. They are then used in the valuation process when the purchase price of the target is determined.

Tax Loss Carry-Forward Research A number of research studies have sought to estimate the present value of the tax loss carry-forwards. These tax benefits may be less than their "face value," not only because of the time value of money, but also because they might expire without being fully utilized. Estimates of these values have been developed by Alan Auerbach and James Poterba (1987) and by Roseanne Altshuler and Alan Auerbach (1987).[10] These research studies indicate that the

[10] Alan Auerbach and James Poterba, "Tax Loss Carry Forwards and Corporate Tax Incentives," in Martin Feldstein, ed., *The Effect of Taxation on Capital Accumulation* (Chicago: University of Chicago Press, 1987). Roseanne Altshuler and Alan Auerbach, "The Importance of Tax Law Asymmetries: An Economic Analysis," National Bureau of Economic Research Working Paper No. 2279, National Bureau of Economic Research, Cambridge, Mass., 1987.

two offsetting factors of deferral and expiration reduce the tax benefits to half their face value.

The General Utilities Doctrine

Until its repeal with the Tax Reform Act of 1986, the General Utilities Doctrine allowed preferential treatment for "disincorporating" or liquidating corporations.[11] According to this doctrine, the sale of corporate assets and a liquidating distribution to shareholders were exempt from capital gains taxation. These distributions could occur, for example, following the acquisition of one corporation by another. The acquiring corporation could then sell off the assets of the acquired corporation and distribute the proceeds to shareholders without incurring capital gains tax liability to the corporation. These tax-free liquidating distributions could also occur without an acquisition such as when a firm would choose to sell off certain assets and distribute the proceeds to shareholders.

Assets sales were often structured by establishing separate subsidiary corporations. An acquired corporation could be purchased and its assets distributed into one or more subsidiaries. These subsidiaries would contain the assets that the acquiring corporation was not interested in keeping.[12] The assets that would be retained would be put into the parent corporation or in a separate subsidiary. The stock of the subsidiaries containing the unwanted assets could then be sold without incurring a significant tax liability. With the repeal of the General Utilities Doctrine, the gains or losses from an acquisition must be attributed to the acquiring corporation. The opportunities to avoid such tax liabilities have been narrowed with passage of the Tax Reform Act of 1986.

ASSET BASIS STEP-UP

Tax advantages can arise in an acquisition when a target corporation carries assets on its books with a basis, for tax purposes, which are a fraction of their replacement cost or market value. These assets could be more valuable, for tax purposes, if they were owned by another

---

[11] *General Utilities* v. *Helvering*, 296 U.S. 200 (1935).

[12] John S. Karls, "Federal Income Tax Considerations," in Richard S. Bibler, ed., *The Arthur Young Management Guide to Mergers and Acquisitions* (New York: John Wiley & Sons, 1989), pp. 212–213.

corporation which could increase their tax basis following the acquisition and gain additional depreciation benefits. The tax basis for the acquiring corporation is the cost or purchase price of the assets. The acquiring corporation can use this higher asset basis to shelter income.

The Tax Reform Act of 1986 has also reduced some of these tax benefits. The selling corporation now incurs a greater tax liability on assets sales, which reduces the seller's incentive to participate in the transaction. Moreover, research seeking to find the existence of asset basis step-up as a motivating factor for mergers and acquisitions, prior to the Tax Reform Act of 1986, did not find asset basis step-up to be a significant motivating factor.[13]

TAX TREATMENT OF SPINOFFS AND SPLITOFFS

Spinoffs and splitoffs can qualify for tax-free treatment if the transaction qualifies under the strict guidelines set forth in the tax law. As noted earlier, both the distributing company and the subsidiary must have been actively involved in business for at least five years before the transaction. Neither must have been acquired during that five-year period. In addition, the transaction must transfer at least 80 percent control of the subsidiary to the shareholders.

The drawback to being able to achieve the tax savings from this type of reorganization is that the divesting company cannot sell the subsidiary to a third party. Sales to a third party, however, are the major source of acquisition premiums. Thus, although the tax-free option may be available for spinoffs and splitoffs, it may only come at the expense of a significant premium.

THE ROLE OF TAXES IN THE MERGER DECISION

Recently, Auerbach and Reishus examined a sample of 318 mergers and acquisitions that occurred between 1968 and 1983. Approximately two-thirds of these mergers were in the manufacturing sector, with the average acquiring firm approximately ten times larger than the acquired company.

> A substantial fraction of the sample companies entered the mergers with some constraints on their ability to use tax benefits. About a fifth of all

---

[13] Alan J. Auerbach and David Reishus, "The Impact of Taxation on Mergers and Acquisitions," *Mergers and Acquisitions* (National Bureau of Economic Research, University of Chicago Press, 1988), pp. 69–88.

mergers in the sample involved cases where one firm faced such constraints (indicated by the presence of tax credits or losses carried forward), while the other had positive current federal taxes and no such constraints. Such firms may have reduced their combined federal taxes by merging. Our estimates suggest, however, that the magnitude of such gains, though averaging 10.5% of the acquired firm's market value, exceeded 10% in only a third of the cases, or about 6.5% of the sample. When expressed as a fraction of equity, rather than total market value, gains this large area are of similar order of magnitude as the average stock price premium paid for target firm's in successful tender offers (Jensen & Ruback, 1983). Thus for a small fraction of the mergers, the transfer of tax benefits could have played a significant role.[14]

The Effects of Increased Leverage

Interest payments on debt are a tax deductible expense, whereas dividend payments from equity ownership are not. The existence of a tax advantage for debt is an incentive to have greater use of debt, as opposed to equity, as the means of exchange in mergers and acquisitions.

The leverage argument implies that the acquiring firm has a suboptimal debt/equity ratio and has not sufficiently utilized debt in its capital mix. The argument goes on to put forward mergers and acquisitions as a means whereby companies can achieve greater utilization of debt. An overly simplistic "test" of this hypothesis would be to look at the debt/equity ratios before and after various mergers and acquisitions. This test is considered overly simplistic because the acquiring corporation might retain earnings for one or more years prior to an acquisition in anticipation of the takeover. Following the takeover, which might be financed with internal funds and borrowed capital, there would be a sudden increase in the debt/equity ratio. This jump in the debt/equity ratio may be offset by a gradual reduction over the years following the acquisition as the firm moves to a long-term debt/equity ratio which it considers optimal.

The tax deductibility of interest payments is not an incentive to merger; rather, it is an incentive to increase the potential acquiring firm's borrowing. This can be done in a much more cost-effective manner by issuing bonds or directly borrowing from a lender than through the costly process of engaging in an acquisition.

---

[14] Alan J. Auerbach and David Reishus, "Taxes and the Merger Decision," in John C. Coffee, Jr., Louis Lowenstein, and Susan Rose Ackerman, eds., *Knights, Raiders and Targets* (New York: Oxford University Press, 1988), pp. 300–313.

It is interesting to note that Auerbach and Reishus found, contrary to popular belief, that firms that merge more frequently do not borrow more than firms that have exhibited less tendency to merger.[15] They also discovered that the long-term debt/equity ratios of firms in their sample increased from 25.4 to only 26.7 percent following the mergers that took place at a time when debt/equity ratios were increasing throughout the economy.

TAXES AS A SOURCE OF VALUE IN MANAGEMENT BUYOUTS

Taxes have quite a different role in management buyouts than they do in mergers and acquisitions. Steven Kaplan measured the value of tax benefits for 76 management buyouts between 1980 and 1986.[16] In this sample of MBOs, the average premium was 42.3 percent above the market price two months before the initial announcement of the buyout. The median ratio of debt to total capital rose from 18.8 percent before the buyouts to 87.8 percent afterward. Kaplan found that the value of increased interest and depreciation deductions ranged between 21.0 and 142.6 percent of the premium paid to pre-buyout shareholders. A regression analysis relating the total tax deductions generated by the buyout to the premium available to pre-buyout shareholders implied that total tax deductions is an important deterministic variable. T-statistics equal to 5.9 indicated that total tax deductions were a highly significant explanatory variable. Kaplan's regression results were as follows.

$$\text{Buyout premiums} = f(\text{Total tax deductions})$$
$$\text{MAP} = -0.13 + 0.76 \times \text{Total tax deductions}$$
$$\quad\quad (1.5) \quad\quad\quad\quad\quad (5.9)$$

where: MAP = Market adjusted premium
  (*t*-statistics are in parentheses)
  R^2 = 0.31
  N = 75
  (number of observations)

---

[15] Ibid., p. 80.

[16] Steven Kaplan, "Management Buyouts: Evidence on Taxes as Source of Value," *Journal of Finance* 44, no. 3 (July 1989):611–632.

SUMMARY

This chapter has discussed the various ways in which taxes can play a role in mergers and acquisitions. It was seen that the tax impact of a transaction is a function of the accounting treatment applied to the deal, which, in turn, is regulated by tax laws. Tax law changes, such as those that occurred in 1986, have reduced the initiative to merge and acquire companies simply to realize tax gains.

Clearly, taxes must be carefully examined in any merger, acquisition, or leveraged buyout, for they are important in evaluating the target firm and the overall cost of the acquisition. There is little evidence, however, that taxes are a principal motivating factor in mergers and acquisitions. This result is important because there has been much debate in Washington with regard to passing new tax legislation that would limit the tax advantages associated with using debt in mergers, acquisitions, and leveraged buyouts. The research results imply that such legislation may not have a pronounced impact on the number and size of transactions. These studies do not go so far as to say that taxes can be ignored when evaluating a merger target. Rather, they show that taxes are not a primary deterministic, explanatory variable but may play a secondary role in both the incidence of mergers and acquisitions and in the returns derived from these transactions. The evidence on the importance of taxes is somewhat greater for leveraged buyouts. Given that the pace of LBOs has slowed owing to the decline in the junk bond market, the pressure to adopt new tax-related regulations may decline.

REFERENCES

Altshuler, Roseanne, and Alan Auerbach. "The Importance of Tax Law Asymmetries: An Economic Analysis." National Bureau of Economic Research Working Paper No. 2279, National Bureau of Economic Research, Cambridge, Mass.

Auerbach, Alan, and James Poterba. "Tax Loss Carry Forwards and Corporate Tax Incentives." In Martin Feldstein, ed., *The Effect of Taxation on Capital Accumulation*. Chicago: University of Chicago Press, 1987.

Auerbach, Alan J., and David Reishus. "The Impact of Taxation on Mergers and Acquisitions." *Mergers and Acquisitions*. National Bureau of Economic Research, University of Chicago Press, 1988, pp. 69–88.

Auerbach, Alan J., and David Reishus. "Taxes and the Merger Decision." In John C. Coffee, Jr., Louis Lowenstein, and Susan Rose Ackerman, eds. *Knights, Raiders and Targets*. New York: Oxford University Press, 1988, pp. 300–313.

Collins, J. Markham, and Roger P. Bey. "The Master Limited Partnership: An Alternative to the Corporation." *Financial Management*, 15(4), Winter 1986, pp. 5–9.

General Utilities v. *Helvering*, 296 U.S. 200 (1935).

Hong, H., G. Mandelker, and R. S. Kaplan. "Pooling vs. Purchase: The Effects of Accounting for Mergers on Stock Prices." *Accounting Review* 53 (January 1978): 31–47.

Karls, John S. "Federal Income Tax Considerations." In Richard S. Bibler, ed. *The Arthur Young Management Guide to Mergers and Acquisitions*. New York: John Wiley & Sons, 1989, pp. 212–213.

Levine, Robert, and Richard P. Miller. "Accounting for Business Combinations." In Steven James Lee and Robert Douglas Coleman, eds., *Handbook of Mergers and Acquisitions*. Englewood Cliffs, N.J.: Prentice-Hall, 1981, pp. 251–292.

Neveau, Robert. *Managerial Finance*. Cincinnati, Ohio: South Western Publishing Co., 1985, pp. 663–666.

Opinions of the Accounting Principles Board, No. 16. American Institute of Certified Public Accountants, New York, August 1970.

Rodoff, George. "Tax Consequences to Shareholders in an Acquisitive Reorganization." In Steven James Lee and Robert Douglas Coleman, eds., *Acquisitions and Buyouts*. Englewood Cliffs, N.J.: Prentice–Hall, 1981, pp. 359–379.

Schall, Laurence D., and Charles D. Haley. *Introduction to Financial Management*, 4th ed. New York: McGraw-Hill, 1986, pp. 690–691.

Van Horne, James. *Financial Management and Policy*. Englewood Cliffs, N.J.: Prentice–Hall, 1989, pp. 647–648.

Warshawsky, Mark J. "Determinants of Corporate Merger Activity: A Review of the Literature." Staff Study No. 152, Board of Governors of the Federal Reserve System, April 1987, p. 5.

Chapter
13

Financial Analysis for Mergers and Acquisitions

*M*any financial documents should be analyzed as part of conducting a thorough study of a potential target. The analysis should be conducted by both the acquirer and the target. The acquirer needs to ascertain the value of the target in order to determine the proper offering price or whether the target meets the acquirer's financial standards. The target, in turn, needs to know what its value is. Presumably, this will tell the acquirer's management and board of directors if the offer is in the stockholders' best interest. As part of this analysis, we will examine a series of key financial statements. Each acquisition will present its own unique characteristics that make it different from other acquisitions. These novel aspects will often be in the form of other documents that need to be examined. Therefore, the framework of financial statement analysis presented in this chapter is a basic model that may be followed in an analysis of a merger or an acquisition. It is a minimum and should be supplemented by the additional analysis that is required due to the unique aspects of each transaction.

This chapter provides a review of financial statements and financial ratio analysis. The discussion of financial statement analysis is not meant to be comprehensive. Rather, it is designed to highlight some of the basic financial issues that need to be considered when conducting a financial evaluation of a merger candidate. A more thorough and detailed discussion can be found in most good corporate finance textbooks. Suggested references are provided at the end of the chapter.

The three most basic financial statements are the balance sheet, the income statement, and the statement of cash flows. Publicly held companies prepare these statements on a quarterly and annual basis. The quarterly statements are available in the 10Q quarterly reports that are filed with the Securities and Exchange Commission. The annual statements are available in the firm's 10K and Annual Report.

THE BALANCE SHEET

The balance sheet, sometimes called the statement of financial position, is basically a snapshot of the firm's financial position at a given moment in time. The statement constructed on a different date may present a very different picture of the firm's financial position. This may be important for an analyst to bear in mind if he or she suspects that the seller is attempting to present an inaccurate picture of value in order to inflate the purchase price. The seller may attempt temporarily to alter the makeup of the balance sheet so as to try to receive a higher purchase price for the firm. In such instances, buyers must critically scrutinize the balance sheet to detect inaccuracies. The balance sheet reflects information on the resources and assets owned by the company along with the firm's various obligations. The name "balance sheet" comes from the equality between assets and liabilities and stockholder equity. These two parts of the balance sheet are, by definition, always in balance since the difference between assets and liabilities is the value of stockholders' equity.

Assets = liabilities + stockholders' equity

The balance sheet is constructed so that current items appear before noncurrent items. A review of the items that normally appear in a balance sheet is provided in the following outline.

Assets
   Current Assets.   Current assets can be converted into cash within a
      year. Among the assets incuded here are cash, marketable se-
      curities, accounts receivable, inventories, and prepaid expenses.
   Cash.   Obviously, this is the seller's most liquid asset. Firms con-
      cerned about being the object of a hostile bid may attempt to
      keep their cash reserves as low as the normal operations of the
      business will allow so as to prevent the cash from being used to
      finance the offer. The value of cash (as opposed to securities) to
      the success of a tender offer was emphasized in Chapter 6.

Marketable Securities. These are short-term investments of excess cash. Typical investments are Treasury securities, certificates of deposit (CDs), or other money market securities.

Accounts Receivable. These items reflect the amount of money the company expects to collect from sales. It includes an allowance for bad debts based on the firm's historical collection efforts. The accounts receivable and the allowance for bad debts are usually shown separately, with the net accounts receivable shown in the rightmost column of the balance sheet.

Inventories. Inventories include items such as work in progress, raw materials, and finished goods. Inventories are typically the least liquid asset of the firm. Goods that are finished are naturally considered more liquid than work in progress.

Prepaid Expenses. These items have already been paid in advance. Examples are insurance premiums or rent.

Other Assets. This category comprises items such as long-term investments, including the stock or bonds of other companies. For firms that are active in takeovers, this category may be an important one. The value of these investments will depend on their liquidity and the size of the holdings. The greater the liquidity, the more valuable the asset. If the company holds a larger amount of the available stock of a company that is traded on the over-the-counter market with a relatively small daily trading volume, then the value of this asset may be questionable.

Plant and Equipment. Plant and equipment consist of the tangible, capital assets of the firm. They are usually valued at cost minus accumulated depreciation and include land, buildings, machinery, and other tangible assets the firm may own such as computer equipment, vehicles, and furniture. A buyer may attempt to revalue these assets at market prices rather than the book values that the balance sheet reflects. Quick sales of some of these assets may enable a buyer to pay down some of the debt assumed in a leveraged transaction. An inaccurate valuation of the market value of such assets may cause a buyer to assume more debt than the combined firms can handle. Some investment banks were the object of criticism in the late 1980s for presenting an overly optimistic picture of the market value of the assets of merger partners and LBO candidates.

Liabilities

Current Liabilities. Current liabilities consist of those obligations that the firm has to pay within one year. Among the liabilities included here are accounts payable, notes payable, and accrued expenses.

Accounts Payable.   These are the amounts owed by the firm to suppliers for credit purchases. For each accounts payable there should be a corresponding accounts receivable on the supplier's balance.

Notes Payable.   Notes payable are outstanding obligations such as loans to commercial banks or obligations to other creditors.

Accrued Expenses.   These are expenses for items that have been used to generate sales for which the firm has not been paid. They may or may not have been billed for these goods or services.

Long-term Debt.   Long-term debts are debt obligations for which payment does not have to be made within one year. This might be, for example, the value of the bonds that the firm may have issued or term loans from financial institutions. The balance sheet should include, where relevant, the long-term obligations of the company such as capital lease obligations, pension liabilities, and estimated liabilities under warranty agreements. Some explanation of these items may be contained in footnotes.

Depending on the company's accounting practices, there may also be a description of deferred federal income taxes. This will be affected by tax law changes that will determine the firm's ability to shelter income through accelerated depreciation write-offs and other tax-avoidance methods. Buyers have to be careful to detect the presence of hidden liabilities. These are the potential obligations of the seller that may not be explicitly highlighted on the firm's balance sheet. Such liabilities might include future environmental liabilities or losses from pending litigation. These hidden liabilities have become a greater cause for concern in certain industries such as the chemicals industry.

Stockholders' Equity.   This part of the balance sheet shows the owner's claims on the firm's assets after taking into account the obligations to creditors who have a prior claim before equity holders. It includes the ownership interests of both preferred and common stockholders.

Preferred Stock.   The company may or may not have issued preferred stock. Preferred stock is more like debt than equity in that it usually pays a fixed dividend that must be paid before dividends are paid to common stockholders. As noted in Chapter 5, preferred stock has been used as a poison pill defense. One reason why this defense is not used as much as poison pill warrants is that preferred stock issued by the firm has to be clearly displayed on the balance sheet. Given its debt-like characteristics, this does not enhance the company's financial appearance.

Common Stock.   Common stock represents the claims of ownership of the corporation. In the event of bankruptcy, common stockholders have the last claim on the corporation's assets. Several different classes of common stock can exist. The issuance of different classes of common stock with different voting rights is another antitakeover defense. The common stock is listed on the balance sheet at par value, which is an arbitrarily assigned value for the common stock used primarily for accounting purposes. It may also be used as an indicator of the value of the stock in the event of liquidation. It does not, however, have a useful relationship to the market price of the stock of a publicly held company.

Paid in Capital in Excess of Par.   This is the amount of money received for the sale of the common stock that was in excess of the par value.

Retained Earnings.   Retained earnings represents the earnings of the corporation not paid out in dividends. The retained earnings on the balance sheet are not a supply of available cash that is put into a bank account and used to pay bills. These are monies that may be used to finance fixed assets such as plant and equipment.

Issues Related to Understanding Balance Sheets

1. *Time element.*   As noted above, balance sheets reflect the company's position at an instant in time. The time period chosen will therefore affect the value reflected on the balance sheet.
2. *Cash versus noncash assets.*   The only item on the balance sheet that is actual cash is the one listed as cash. Although the other assets are denoted in dollars, they are not cash. They may be, for example, receivables or inventories, but they cannot be used at the moment to directly pay bills. (It is possible, however, to factor receivables or inventories and receive cash to pay bills.)
3. *Inventory accounting.*   The value of the inventory will be affected by the type of accounting method used—FIFO (first-in, first-out) or LIFO (last-in, first out). The FIFO method assumes that the items the firm uses from its inventory are the oldest items in the inventory, whereas LIFO assumes that the items used are the newest. In a world of rising prices, FIFO will show lower costs and higher profits and will also result in a higher tax bill.

Areas to Consider in Analyzing Balance Sheets

1. *Understated liabilities.* Beware when the firm has the discretion to estimate its own liabilities. Firms that are offering themselves for sale may want to understate liabilities to increase the value of the firm. Firms may estimate the potential liabilities in various areas such as litigation, health care, and pension liabilities. The bad debt policy of the firm should be examined, particularly if the firm has increased its sales by selling to a riskier category of customers while not increasing the allowances for bad debts.

2. *Low-quality assets.* It should be determined that the valuation of all major assets on the balance sheet accurately reflects the value these assets might command in the marketplace or their value to an acquirer. Assets that can be affected by changing government policies, such as pollution control equipment, or assets that are related to the sale of products that may become obsolete have to be examined more closely. Unfortunately, publicly available documents, such as annual reports, lack the detail necessary to determine the market value of some assets. This may be a problem for hostile bidders who may have to rely solely on public documents.

3. *Overstated receivables.* A receivable is only as good as its likelihood of being paid. Receivables to firms that are in financial difficulty or that are subject to return policies may have to be revalued. Receivables from firms that are affiliated with the parent company may have been "manufactured" to overstate the parent's value.

4. *Inventory.* Changes in the level of inventory from period to period need to be considered. A rapid buildup of inventory may signal a decreased marketability for the product. This is often the case, for example, in the toy business.

5. *Valuation of securities.* For firms that have substantial assets in marketable securities, an analysis of the portfolio of the firm needs to be conducted. The marketability of each security in the portfolio should be determined. The increased volatility of securities has heightened the need to be cautious in valuing such assets. Substantial holdings of the debt or common stock of firms that are traded in thin markets may be of questionable value unless ownership in these firms is one of the acquirer's goals. The riskiness of the securities portfolio should comport with that of the acquirer. The more marketable the securities and the smaller the holdings, the more likely the acquirer can sell them if he or she chooses without incurring a significant cost.

6. *Intangible assets.* Intangible assets, such as goodwill, though difficult to value, may be quite valuable. The name of an established business with a sound reputation in the marketplace may be valuable, even though it is intangible. Assets such as patents may only be as valuable as the company's ability and will to defend them through costly litigation. Patents can often be copied without incurring significant legal liability. When this is likely, careful consideration must be given before paying a high price for these assets.

7. *Real estate assets.* Real estate assets have been a motivation for many takeover battles such as the recent Campeau takeover of Federated Stores and Olympia and York's attempted takeover of Santa Fe–Southern Pacific. The valuation of these assets is subject to the vicissitudes of the real estate market. The importance of an accurate valuation of these assets is one reason why the real estate expert became more important in the fourth merger wave. The dramatic decline in the real estate market in the late 1980s diminished the importance of real estate assets in takeovers.

8. *Valuation of divisions.* The valuation of divisions of companies became crucial in the highly leveraged takeovers of the 1980s. The value that a division, subsidiary, or major asset might bring the market will only be known after it has actually been sold. This problem can be prevented if the sale of certain assets can be prearranged in advance with a third party. One problem with working with public documents such as annual reports is that it is difficult to get a detailed breakdown of the performance of separate divisions. Such information is hard to acquire in a hostile takeover. Sometimes an acquirer will resist increasing its bid unless the target provides the detailed information necessary to do a full evaluation.

THE INCOME STATEMENT

The income statement measures the net results of the firm's operations over a specific time interval such as a calendar year or a fiscal year. A fiscal year is an accounting year that ends on a day other than December 31. The balance sheet and income statement are usually presented together. Most large companies typically prepare monthly statements for management and quarterly statements for stockholders. The balance sheet is usually prepared for the last date of the time period covered by the income statement. The income statement is sometimes referred to as the profit and loss statement.

Net Sales.   Net sales are usually the first item listed on the income statement. By net is meant the sales after returns on goods shipped and other factors such as breakage. Cost of goods sold is deducted from net sales to determine the net operating profit.

Cost of Goods Sold.   Cost of goods sold refers to the company's cost for the goods and services sold. For manufacturing firms this includes labor, materials, and other items such as overhead.

Gross Profits.   Gross profits are the difference between sales revenues and the cost of goods sold. Gross profit divided by sales revenues is the gross profit margin or gross margin.

Operating Expenses.   Operating expenses are deducted from gross profits to determine *operating profit*. The main categories of operating expenses are: selling expense; general and administrative expense; and depreciation expense.

Operating Profit.   Operating profit is also called *earnings before interest* and *taxes* (EBIT). This important definition of income will be used in the valuation of businesses in Chapter 14. Operating profit is often considered a good measure of managerial success. It reflects the profit derived from management's operating activities, not financing decisions or governmental tax obligations. This measure may be used as an indicator of the target management's performance. Operating profit can be placed in perspective by considering it as a percentage of sales and comparing it to similarly sized firms in the same industry.

Interest Expense.   Interest expense is deducted from operating profit to determine *earnings before taxes (EBT)*.

Taxes.   Taxes are deducted from the EBT at the relevant tax rate for the corporation. A 40 percent rate is typical. The result is *earnings after taxes*.

Earnings Available for Stockholders.   Preferred stock dividends are deducted from earnings after taxes to determine the income available for distribution to common stockholders as dividends.

Earnings per Share (EPS).   EPS is calculated by dividing the earnings available to common stockholders by the number of shares of common stock outstanding.

Issues Related to Understanding Income Statements

1. *Depreciation.*   Depreciation refers to the charging of a portion of the cost of certain capital assets against revenues. Different methods of depreciation will result in different levels of taxable income for the same revenue stream. More rapid depreciation will show a lower taxable income. The Generally Acceptable Accounting Principles (GAAP) set forth the accepted methods of

writing off an asset. The two primary methods are straight-line depreciation and accelerated depreciation. The same amount of depreciation is allowed under each method, but the timing of the writeoff is different.

2. *Valuing inventory.* The valuation of inventory will affect the value of cost of goods sold in the income statement. This factor, already discussed in the context of balance sheet analysis, will affect profitability on the balance sheet. If a firm wants to appear to be more profitable, it may do so by using FIFO rather than LIFO inventory accounting.

Areas to Consider in Analyzing Income Statements

1. *Quality of earnings.* The quality of earnings may be suspect for a wide variety of reasons. Some firms in industries that have been experiencing hard times have resorted to accounting manipulations to generate income. An example of this occurred in the thrift industry in 1984. Savings and loan associations treated as income a stock dividend paid to them by the Federal Home Loan Mortgage Association (Freddie Mac), an institution owned by the thrifts, as income. The Financial Accounting Standards Board (FASB) stated that this was like paying yourself money. In 1984, the total profits of the S & L industry were $2.1 billion, but the stock dividend accounted for $600 million of this amount. The financial difficulties of the thrift industry motivated many mergers as the industry sought to consolidate. The acquiring and merging firms had to examine the earnings and expected earnings of their merger partners to ascertain if they were truly of high quality.

2. *Revenue recognition.* Firms can alter the income that appears on their income statement through various accounting manipulations. For example, companies can recognize revenues for services that have not been performed and, in fact, may be performed in later time periods. This has the effect of increasing the profits in the current time period.[1]

STATEMENT OF CASH FLOWS

In November 1987, the FASB issued Financial Accounting Standard 95 (FAS 95) which required that, effective for all fiscal years subsequent

---

[1] Joel G. Siegel, *How to Analyze Businesses, Financial Statements and the Quality of Earnings* (Englewood Cliffs, N.J.: Prentice-Hall, 1982), pp. 101–103.

to July 15, 1988, firms issue a statement of cash flows instead of a statement of changes in financial position. This statement would provide analysts and investors with valuable information on the cash receipts and cash payments of the firm. It shows the impact of the firm's operations, investment, and financial decisions on its cash position. (This is depicted in Table 13.1.) Analyzing the statement of cash flows enables the merger analyst to assess the firm's ability to generate future cash flows that can be used to service the debt that might result from a merger or LBO. The ability to generate sufficient cash flows may determine whether the firm can survive a leveraged transaction. More basically, firms have been forced into bankruptcy when their cash position deteriorated, even though their net income remained positive. The highly leveraged deals that occurred in the fourth merger wave made cash flows even more important for firms that assumed the pressure of high debt service to finance the transactions. These high interest payments heightened the need to accurately predict the firm's ability to generate stable cash flows. One example was W. T. Grant and Company which filed for bankruptcy in 1975. The firm had been profitable for the years prior to the bankruptcy filing and showed a positive net income in those years.[2] The statement of cash flows adjusts net income to remove the noncash effects such as accruals of future cash receipts, gains and losses on sales of assets, and depreciation. In doing so, the statement of cash flows becomes a valuable measure of a firm's ability to generate cash after taking into account the firm's cash needs. The difference between cash flows and net income can indicate the quality of earnings. The smaller this difference, the higher the quality of earnings. The ratio of cash flow to net income is ofen used as an indicator of earnings quality across different firms in the same industry.[3]

Depreciation and Cash Flows.   The income statement and the statement of cash flows differ in how they treat depreciation. All noncash charges, those that do not involve a cash outlay, are added back to the net after-tax income to determine the cash flow. One of the major categories of noncash charges is depreciation. These charges are tax shields that minimize taxes but distort the firm's true cash flow. More basically, depreciation is neither a source nor a use of funds. In its simplest form, cash flow can be expressed as follows:

Cash flow from operations = Net after-tax profits + Noncash charges

---

[2] Dennis E. Logue, *Handbook of Modern Finance* (Boston: Warren, Gorham and Lamont, 1984), p. 15–19.

[3] Joel Siegel and Anthony Akel, "A Financial Analysis and Evaluation of the Statement of Cash Flows," *The Practical Accounting* (June 1989):71–73.

Table 13.1 INVESTING, FINANCING, AND OPERATING ACTIVITIES

Investing Activities

Inflows

Receipts from collections or sales of loans made by the enterprise and of other entities' debt instruments (other than cash equivalents) that were purchased by the enterprise

Receipts from sales of equity instruments of other enterprises and from returns of investment in those instruments

Receipts from sales of property, plant, and equipment and other productive assets

Outflows

Disbursements for loans made by the enterprise and payments to acquire debt instruments of other entities (other than cash equivalents)

Payments to acquire equity instruments of other enterprises

Payments at the time of purchase or soon before or after purchase to acquire property, plant, and equipment and other productive assets

Financing Activities

Inflows

Proceeds from issuing equity instruments

Proceeds from issuing bonds, mortgages, notes, and from other short- or long-term borrowing

Outflows

Payments of dividends or other distributions to owners, including outlays to reacquire the enterprise's equity instruments

Repayments of amounts borrowed

Other principal payments to creditors who have extended long-term credit

Operating Activities

Inflows

Cash receipts from sales of goods or services, including receipts from collection or sale of accounts and both short- and long-term notes receivable from customers arising from those sales

Cash receipts from returns on loans, other debt instruments of other entities, and equity securities—interest and dividends

All other cash receipts that do not stem from transactions defined as investing or financing activites, such as amounts received to settle lawsuits; proceeds of insurance settlements except for those that are directly related to investing or financing activities, such as from destruction of a building; and refunds from suppliers

Outflows

Cash payments to acquire materials for manufacture or goods for resale, including principal payments on accounts and both short- and long-term notes payable to suppliers for those materials or goods

Cash payments to other suppliers and employees for other goods or services

Cash payments to governments for taxes, duties, fines, and other fees or penalties

Cash payments to lenders and other creditors for interest

All other cash payments that do not stem from transactions defined as investing or financing activities, such as payments to settle lawsuits, cash contributions to charities, and cash refunds to customers

Adapted: FASB, 1987

Source: James Thompson and Thomas Buttross, "Return to Cash Flow," *CPA Journal* (March 1988):37.

Free Cash Flows.   Free cash flows became a "buzz word" in the fourth merger wave. It is defined differently by different users. However, in one of its more common forms, it is the cash per period minus the amount the firm has allowed for capital expenditures during that period. This provides a useful measure of the firm's available cash resources after allocations have been made to maintain capital equipment. Free cash flows can be projected into the future after taking into consideration the firm's future capital investment needs. Including capital investment enables free cash flow to be more than a short-term measure of the firm's health. One criticism of cash flow is that it is too short term oriented.[4] Using free cash flow, as it is defined above, the analyst can measure both the quality of the firm's future earnings and the firm's ability to maintain its future competitive position.

THE FREE CASH FLOW THEORY OF MERGERS AND ACQUISITIONS

Some researchers believe that a firm's amount of free cash flow may determine whether or not it is going to engage in takeovers.[5] The theory implies that managers of firms that have unused borrowing capacity and ample free cash flows are more likely to engage in takeovers. Managers use the cash resources to acquire other firms instead of paying the monies to stockholders in the form of higher dividends.

Michael Jensen contends that many of these mergers result in "low benefits or even value destroying mergers. Diversification programs generally fit this cateogry and the theory predicts that they will generate lower total gains."[6] According to Jensen, these mergers are more likely to occur in industries that are in a period of retrenchment but that nonetheless have large cash flows. When the mergers are horizontal, they may create value because the payment of cash to the stockholders of the target firm is a way in which cash is leaving the industry. On the other hand, mergers outside the industry, in Jensen's view, can have low or even negative returns since the managers will be running a company in an industry that may be outside their area of managerial expertise.

As an example, Jensen cites tobacco firms that are experiencing a

---

[4] Ellen Benoit, "Real Money," *Financial World*, September 20, 1988, pp. 46–47.

[5] Michael Jensen, "The Takeover Controversy: Analysis and Evidence," in John C. Coffee, Jr., Louis Lowenstein, and Susan Rose Ackerman, eds., *Knights, Raiders and Targets* (New York: Oxford University Press, 1988), pp. 333–337.

[6] Ibid.

gradual decline in demand as society becomes more aware of the link between disease and tobacco consumption. The gradual decline in demand notwithstanding, tobacco companies still have large free cash flows to invest. Jensen's theory would then imply that the diversifying acquisitions, such as Philip Morris's acquisition of General Foods and R. J. Reynolds' acquisition of Nabisco, are more likely to have negative productivity effects. A different point of view is expressed in the Philip Morris case study in Chapter 16.

Another characteristic of industries that have high free cash flows and limited opportunities for growth is the increased amount of leveraged buyouts that occur. The LBOs occur because of the high free cash flows that can be used to service the debt. This was the case in the RJR Nabisco LBO as well as in the various leveraged buyouts in supermarkets and food-related industries such as Supermarkets General and Beatrice.

ANALYSIS OF FINANCIAL STATEMENTS AND COMPUTER PROGRAMS

Having discussed the basics of financial statements, we will now analyze them to determine the firm's financial condition. The analysts' main tool is a spreadsheet program such as LOTUS which allows the user to perform a great number of financial calculations very rapidly. It also permits a complete set of calculations to be redone instantly after certain changes have been enacted. A good guide to LOTUS is *Using 123*.[7]

The various other software packages available are really large macro programs that use LOTUS. The user loads LOTUS into his or her computer and then asks LOTUS to use the programs written on this software package. One software package that provides good summary data for financial analysis is *Financial Calculator*.[8] Among its many other functions, this package instantly provides a large array of financial ratios after the user inputs the balance sheet and income statements. This package and others lack the flexibility to alter the framework to deal with the unique aspects of each merger. In effect, the user is locked into a standard framework that may not be that appropriate to the case at hand. Other software packages do even more intricate analysis, but they are less user friendly.[9]

---

[7] *Using 123* (Carmel, Ind.: Que Corporation, 1987), Special Edition.

[8] Sidney R. Finkel, *Financial Calculator* (Cincinnati, Ohio: South Western Publishing Co., 1987).

[9] LBO Plan II, Venture Economics (San Diego, Calif.: Business Publications, 1987).

FINANCIAL RATIO ANALYSIS

Financial ratio analysis, one of the main tools of financial analysis, permits an easy comparison with similar firms, such as those in the same industry and of a similar size. Ratio analysis standardizes the financial data that help reduce the effect of factors such as sheer size. In doing so, we can better compare the financial performance of acquisition candidates in the same industry that are of very different sizes.

Financial ratios can be divided into the following categories:

1. Liquidity ratios.
2. Activity ratios.
3. Financial leverage ratios.
4. Profitability ratios.

Liquidity Ratios

Liquidity ratios measure the firm's ability to satisfy its current obligations as they come due. The two principal liquidity ratios are the current ratio and the quick ratio.

$$\text{Current ratio} = \frac{\text{Current assets}}{\text{Current liabilities}}$$

$$\text{Quick ratio} = \frac{\text{Current assets} - \text{Inventories}}{\text{Current liabilities}}$$

Current assets = cash plus all assets that can be converted into cash within a year. These include short-term marketable securities, accounts receivable, and inventories.

Current liabilities = all the financial obligations that are expected to be paid within a year. These include accounts payable, notes payable, and the current part of the long-term debt.

Working capital = Current assets − Current liabilities

The current ratio measures the firm's ability to meet its short-term obligations using assets that are expected to be converted into cash within a year. The quick ratio removes inventories from current assets because they may not be as liquid as some of the other current assets. The more liquid a firm is, the higher the current and quick ratios. The greater the liquidity of a firm, the lower the probability it can become *technically insolvent*, which means that the firm cannot meet its current obligations as they come due. The more liquid the firm, in advance of a takeover, the more likely it will not face liquidity problems if it assumes additional post-merger costs such as higher interest payments. If, on the other hand, the firm is only marginally liquid at the time of the merger, it may experience liquidity problems following the merger unless it can rely on the other merger partner for additional liquidity.

Generally, the more illiquid part of the current assets are the inventories. If the analyst would like to have a more stringent measure of liquidity, the quick ratio can be used. When there are questions about the liquidity of the company's inventories, greater reliance is placed on the quick ratio than on the current ratio and other ratios, such as the activity ratios, need to be carefully examined.

Activity Ratios

Activity ratios measure the speed with which various accounts are converted into cash. Activity ratios are an important supplement to liquidity ratios because liquidity ratios do not provide information on the composition of the firm's various assets.

$$\text{Average collection period} = \frac{\text{Accounts receivable}}{\text{Annual credit sales}/360}$$

The average collection period indicates the number of days an account remains outstanding. For example, if the average collection period is 60 days, this means that it takes the firm an average of 60 days to collect an account receivable.

As with all financial ratios, they make sense only in relation to the firm's collection policy. If the firm requires customers to pay within 30 days and the average collection period is 60 days, this is a negative indicator. On the other hand, if the firm allows customers to pay within 90 days, and the average collection period is 60 days, this looks good. Further analysis would still have to be done to see if the early payment was a result of cash discounts for early payment which would cut into the company's profitability.

In a merger it is important to determine whether the collection and credit policies of the two firms are similar. If they are not, and if the acquirer plans to institute stricter payment and credit policies, then the impact of the policies on the target's sales needs to be projected. If the target has large sales only because it is extending credit to those customers with weaker credit ratings, then the compatibility of the two firms and their credit policies needs to be examined further. Moreover, the profitability of the target, after the acquirer's credit policies are instituted, may be below what might be necessary to meet the cost of capital associated with the acquisition.

Inventory Turnover

$$\text{Inventory turnover} = \frac{\text{Cost of goods sold}}{\text{Average inventory}}$$

The inventory turnover ratio reveals how often the inventory of the firm turns over in a year. The cost of goods sold is derived from the income statement, whereas the average inventory is taken from the balance sheet. Given that the balance sheet reflects the firm's position on a given day, it might be useful to derive the average inventory by taking the beginning year inventory from the previous year's balance sheet and averaging that with this year's amount. A better way would be to determine the inventory levels on a monthly basis and average these amounts. This would help reduce the impact of seasonal influences. The more seasonal the business, the more care needs to be exercised in interpreting the inventory turnover ratio.

The appropriate amount of inventory turnover is highly dependent on industry norms. A ratio of 30 may be normal for a retail food store, whereas an aircraft manufacturer may be quite pleased with a value of 1.

Although the inventory turnover value should be compared with industry averages, care should be exercised not to place too much weight on the pure number without further analysis. A high inventory turnover is normally a good sign, but this need not always be the case. For example, a firm could have a very high inventory turnover level by holding a smaller than appropriate inventory level. A high inventory turnover could be a result of shortages, or it could be related to the firm's credit policies whereby the firm is lowering its profit margins and is, in effect, "giving the product away" to move inventory. Therefore, inventory levels need to be placed in perspective with the firm's average inventory levels and the average for the industry.

Generally, a low inventory turnover is a bad sign for a potential target, for it may be indicative of illiquid or inactive inventories. If the acquirer believes that the inventories are indeed marketable, then it must also have an answer to the question, why was the manufacturer of the inventory unable to sell these goods in a manner that was comparable with competitors? If the answer is mismanagement and if the acquirer believes it can solve this problem, then the low inventory turnover should not be of as great concern.

Fixed Asset Turnover

$$\text{Fixed asset turnover} = \frac{\text{Sales}}{\text{Net fixed assets}}$$

Fixed asset turnover reflects the extent to which a firm is utilizing its fixed assets to generate sales. This ratio is important to an acquirer who is contemplating acquiring a capital-intensive firm. However, the analyst should take great care when comparing this ratio to industry averages. The fixed asset turnover value derived from the ratio shown above is very sensitive to several factors that may vary from firm to firm.

The fixed asset ratio is based on the historical cost of assets. Firms that have acquired their assets more recently may show a lower fixed asset turnover because the dollar value of their fixed assets is higher and this value enters into the denominator of the ratio. The greater the rate of inflation over the period of asset acquisition, the more this ratio can lead to deceptive results.

Other factors that can affect the fixed asset turnover are the firm's depreciation policies and the use of leased rather than purchased assets. If the assets were recently acquired, there may be a lag between the acquisition of the assets and the resulting generation of sales from the use of these assets. Therefore, a recent acquisition may increase the denominator of the ratio but have little immediate effect on the numerator. Consideration of the industry norms relating to the investment–sales lag should be given before any judgment is made with regard to a target's use of fixed assets. A fixed asset turnover of 1.90 means that a firm turns over its fixed assets 1.9 times a year.

Total Asset Turnover

$$\text{Total asset turnover} = \frac{\text{Sales}}{\text{Total assets}}$$

This ratio shows how effectively a firm uses its total resources. The caveats that apply to the use of the fixed asset turnover also apply here. A total asset turnover ratio of 1.60 means that the firm turns over its assets 1.60 times a year.

Financial Leverage Ratios

Given the large amounts of debt frequently associated with takeovers in the fourth merger wave, financial leverage ratios become a most useful financial analysis tool for the merger analyst. The financial leverage or debt ratios indicate the degree of financial leverage that the firm has assumed. Financial leverage refers to the amount of debt the firm has used relative to the equity in its total capitalization.

In takeovers, the analyst must compute the financial leverage ratios based on different assumptions regarding the total debt used to finance the acquisition. These resulting debt levels are then compared to industry norms and standards to reveal how the merged firm compares to other firms in the industry. A takeover often results in a firm being well above the industry average.

When the acquirer has plans to "pay down" the debt following the acquisition by assets sales, the financial leverage ratios should be projected for several years to determine the impact of the debt retirement. In this case, the analyst would like to determine how long it takes until the debt ratios return to industry norms.

$$\text{Debt ratio} = \frac{\text{Total debt}}{\text{Total assets}}$$

The debt ratio is usually computed by adding together short-term and long-term debt. It is also sometimes computed by using total liabilities rather than just formal debt. The debt ratio indicates the firm's ability to service its debt. Obviously, creditors want this ratio to be low. An acquirer may consider a target firm with a relatively larger amount of marketable fixed assets and a low debt ratio to be an ideal takeover target. Such a firm may have much unused borrowing capacity and may be vulnerable to a takeover. Companies with low-debt ratios relative to the industry sometimes feel they are vulnerable and load up on debt.

A debt ratio of 0.65 means that the firm has financed 65 percent of its assets by using debt.

Debt to Equity Ratio

$$\text{Debt to equity ratio} = \frac{\text{Long-term debt}}{\text{Total equity}}$$

The debt to equity ratio is one of the more often quoted financial leveraged ratios. Preferred stock is commonly added to long-term debt in the computation because preferred stock payments are somewhat fixed. A firm cannot be forced into receivership if preferred stock payments are not made. It is usually assumed that the firm has every intention of making these payments when the debt is issued. Therefore, they should be treated as fixed. This is why preferred stock is more like debt than equity and is usually categorized with fixed income securities.

It is difficult to judge a good debt to equity ratio without analyzing the firm's cash flows. Firms with very stable cash flows can more predictably handle higher debt levels. If an acquirer is considering taking over a target and financing the acquisition primarily with debt, a cash flow analysis needs to be conducted. If the cash flows are volatile, an added element of risk is introduced. A debt to equity ratio of 0.67, for example, shows that the firm's long-term debt is only 67 percent as large as its equity.

Debt to Total Capitalization Ratio

$$\frac{\text{Debt to total}}{\text{capitalization ratio}} = \frac{\text{Long-term debt}}{\text{Long-term debt} + \text{Stockholders' equity}}$$

This ratio determines the proportion of total capitalization, which is the firm's permanent financing, that long-term debt represents. A low debt to total capitalization ratio is usually taken to be a desirable attribute in a target. Generally, firms with lower debt to total capitalization ratios are considered better credit risks because a larger equity cushion exists to protect creditors. Such firms can become takeover targets because of a greater, unused borrowing capacity.

In addition to the leverage ratios discussed above, coverage ratios are often used to measure the firm's ability to meet its interest payments and other fixed payments. These ratios are the times interest earned ratio and the fixed charge coverage ratio.

Times Interest Earned

$$\text{Times interest earned} = \frac{\text{EBIT}}{\text{Interest charges}}$$

As noted earlier, earnings before interest and taxes (EBIT) is also called operating profit. The times interest earned ratio is a good measure of the firm's ability to meet its debt obligations. It is a particularly important measure for creditors since it tells them how much operating profit can shrink and the firm still be able to meet its debt obligations. For this reason, it has great relevance to firms that are planning to finance an acquisition through debt.

The pre-merger and the post-merger times interest earned ratios are calculated to determine whether earnings are sufficient to meet the expected debt payments. Generally, a ratio between 3 and 5 is considered good. Firms in more volatile or cyclical industries may need to have higher ratios.

Fixed Charge Coverage

$$\text{Fixed charge coverage} = \frac{\text{EBIT}}{\begin{array}{c} \text{Interest payments} + \text{Lease payments} + \\ \text{Preferred stock dividends before tax} + \\ \text{Before-tax sinking fund payments} \end{array}}$$

This ratio, along with variations, is used when there are other significant fixed payments in addition to interest payments. Since the inability to meet other fixed obligations could easily force the firm into receivership, the fixed charge coverage may be a better way to measure this type of risk.

Profitability Ratios

These ratios allow the firm to measure profit in relation to sales volume. The purpose of an acquisition should be to generate profits. For profit-minded acquirers, a given amount of capital is invested to secure the right to an expected future stream of profits. These profitability ratios allow the acquirer to determine the target's profitability relative to that of its competitors and other firms.

$$\text{Gross profit margin} = \frac{\text{Sales} - \text{Cost of goods sold}}{\text{Sales}}$$

$$= \frac{\text{Gross profit}}{\text{Sales}}$$

$$\text{Operating profit margin} = \frac{\text{EBIT}}{\text{Sales}}$$

$$\text{Net profit margin} = \frac{\text{Earnings after taxes}}{\text{Sales}}$$

The gross profit indicates how much is left, on a percentage basis, after payments are expended for goods. The operating profit margin measures what is left before the impact of the financing decisions and governmental tax liabilities. The net profit margin is an after-tax measure of the firm's profitability. It measures what is left after all payments, including taxes, are made. There is no standard net profit margin; there are great differences across industries. While the net profit margin is often cited as a measure of a corporation's success, good net margins differ considerably across industries. A net margin of 1 or less may be acceptable for a high-volume business like a retail food store, while a net profit margin of 10 percent would be low for a jewelry store.

The merger analyst should review the historical trend in the firm's gross, operating, and net profit margins. An upward trend is usually a sign of financial strength, whereas a decline generally signifies weakness. A decline in those margins may make a firm vulnerable to a hostile takeover if it causes the stock price to sag. Falling stock prices combined with highly marketable assets can present an opportunity to leveraged buyers who may be able to sell assets quickly to pay off the debt while keeping the remaining assets that they acquired at bargain prices.

Return on Investment

$$\text{Return on investment} = \frac{\text{Earnings after taxes}}{\text{Total assets}}$$

The return on investment ratio is sometimes also called the total asset ratio. This ratio measures how effectively management can generate after-tax profits by using the firm's available assets. It has a number of drawbacks, including the fact that it is a book value ratio. If the assets are not carried on the books at accurate values, then the ratio may not be very meaningful. This was the same drawback of the total asset turnover ratio. Merger analysts are more concerned with market values than with book values. Therefore, this ratio may serve as a rough guide to the true return that the firm is receiving on its assets. If the market value of the assets is significantly greater than the book value, then the return on investment may overstate the effectiveness of the firm's management. Buyers should understand that this high return does not mean that they could buy the target's assets and achieve a similar return. A low return on investment, however, does not mean that the target's assets could not be better utilized by the buyer.

Return on Equity

$$\text{Return on equity} = \frac{\text{Earnings after taxes}}{\text{Stockholders' equity}}$$

This ratio is usually calculated by including both preferred stock and common stock in the denominator. It is a measure of the kind of return the company's owners are earning. The return on equity is an often-cited measure of performance used by both investors and management. Since equity, like total assets, is a balance sheet item, it may not accurately reflect the value of equity during the full year. An average of quarterly values can help offset this drawback. The return on equity also suffers from the fact that it is a book value, not a market value. Ironically, a high return on equity does not mean that shareholders will receive a high return on their investment. This problem is greater when there is a larger divergence between the market value of the equity and the book value. One solution to this problem is for the analyst to reconstruct the return on equity by substituting the market value for the book value of equity.

The return on equity is greatly influenced by the degree of financial leverage the firm employs. For example, if a firm is willing to increase its level of debt by borrowing to purchase income-generating assets, then it can increase after-tax earnings while stockholders' equity remains constant. A naive analyst might interpret this as an up-and-coming company and a good takeover target. The higher return on equity, however, does not come without a price. The cost of this higher return on equity is the additional risk the firm assumes when it increases its financial leverage.

Market-Based Ratios

If securities markets are relatively efficient, adverse information contained in the financial statements should be reflected in the market-based ratios. These ratios contain the market's assessment of the financial well-being of the firm as well as the market's projection of the company's future ability to provide stockholders a profitable return on their investment.

P/E Ratio

$$\text{P/E ratio} = \frac{\text{Market price per share}}{\text{Current earnings per share}} = \frac{\text{P}}{\text{EPS}}$$

$$\text{EPS} = \frac{\text{Total earnings available to common stockholders}}{\text{Number of common shares outstanding}}$$

The P/E ratio will be discussed in greater detail in Chapter 14. This ratio is useful in determining the appropriate capitalization rate that can be used to value the firm's projected income stream. Generally, a higher P/E ratio indicates that investors have a greater degree of confidence in the firm's future prospects. The P/E ratio, however, can also be deeply affected by the performance of the market as a whole. For example, the P/E ratios of most firms fell dramatically following the October 1987 stock market crash. Some believe that the very high pre-crash P/E ratios created a situation whereby investors believed a correction that would bring the P/E ratios of many firms back in line with their intrinsic earning power was necessary. To offset short-term market fluctuations, the P/E ratio can be adjusted. One such adjustment would be to convert the numerator to a moving average of the past 30 days' stock prices. In cases of high-growth firms, where analysts want to measure the future prospects of the firm, the last quarter's earnings, as opposed to the past year's earnings, can be annualized by multiplying by four and inserting into the denominator of the ratio.

The P/E ratio will also be affected by whether the firm has been subject to rumors of its eventual takeover. The P/E ratio of potential takeover targets normally rises as the market anticipates the possibility of receiving a takeover premium. The more likely the takeover seems, the greater the increase in the stock prices and the P/E ratio. If news is released that reduces the probability of a takeover, such as a likely antitrust conflict, the P/E ratio should decline.

Payout Ratio

$$\text{Payout ratio} = \frac{\text{Dividends}}{\text{EPS}}$$

The dividend payout ratio reflects the percentage of earnings that are paid to stockholders as dividends. This measure, though important for investors, is not as relevant to potential acquirers since the buyer can set the dividend policy. Therefore, the payout ratio, while an often cited ratio in financial analysis, does not play a role in mergers and acquisition analysis.

SUMMARY

The analysis in this chapter is based on financial statements that are normally available publicly to the merger analyst by virtue of legal filing requirements for publicly held companies. In addition, various financial ratios commonly used to measure the financial well-being of a company were discussed. The value of much of this financial analysis depends on the quality of the available financial data. Friendly transactions tend to feature greater disclosure between the two parties. In a hostile takeover, however, the target will only disclose the minimum as required by federal disclosure laws and any other disclosure requirements imposed by litigation.

Exclusive reliance on public data is a disadvantage for the bidder. The bidder must then depend on the accuracy of financial statements, which may not be sufficiently detailed to give an accurate picture of the company's financial condition. This problem of relying on public data was highlighted in the takeover battle between Merv Griffin and Donald Trump over Resorts International, Inc.[10] Merv Griffin took over Resorts in November 1988. As of July 1989, Resorts' $925 million worth of bonds had fallen 42 percent in value as the market responded to the declining fortunes of the gambling and hotel concern. The 1989 debt service amounted to $133.6 million, while net income plus depreciation were estimated to be between $55 million and $68 million. Part of the

---

[10] Pauline Yoshihasi and Neil Barsky, "Merv Griffin's Plunge into Casino Gambling Could Prove a Loser," *Wall Street Journal*, July 5, 1989, pp. A1 and A7. This example draws on data supplied by the authors of this article.

problem resulted from an inaccurate estimate of the cash flows of Resorts as well as the underestimated cost of maintaining some of Resorts' assets. For example, renovation costs for the hotel-casino in Atlantic City and the company's facilities on Paradise Island in the Bahamas proved to be higher than anticipated. Griffin estimated that the renovations costs would run to $50 million but after the takeover he discovered that at least $100 million would be necessary.

According to the *Wall Street Journal*, Griffin's projection of the sale prices of Resorts' land assets proved to be unreasonably optimistic. In a New Jersey Casino Control Commission hearing in October 1988, Griffin's real estate appraiser valued the Atlantic City land at between $145 and $161 million. Market conditions brought the value well below that following the merger. Given the competitive nature of the Atlantic City casino business, Resorts needed to upgrade its facilities to remain on a par with the competition. This placed added pressure on the firm's cash flows, which were already stretched thin with the high debt service payments. Part of the problem was the limited data available to Griffin. Resorts' president, David P. Hanlon, reportedly stated, "We found a surprising number of things about the company that were different than what we anticipated."[11] Apparently, the value of Resorts' assets had been overestimated. Moreover, other assets proved to need greater maintenance investments than they were thought to have needed.

REFERENCES

Bowlin, Oswald, John Martin, and David Scott. *Guide to Financial Analysis*. New York: McGraw–Hill, 1980.

Brealey, Richard, and Stewart Myers. *Principles of Corporate Finance*, 3rd ed. New York: McGraw–Hill, 1988.

Brigham, Eugene, and Louis Gapinski. *Intermediate Financial Management*, 2nd ed. Chicago: Dryden Press, 1987.

Finkel, Sidney R. *Financial Calculator*. Cincinnati, Ohio: South Western Publishing Co., 1987.

Gitman, Lawrence J. *Principles of Managerial Finance*. 5th ed. New York: Harper & Row, 1988.

Helfert, Erich. *Techniques of Financial Analysis*. 6th ed. New York: Irwin Publications, 1987.

Higgens, Robert. *Analysis for Financial Management*. 2nd ed. Homewood, Ill.: Irwin Publications, 1989.

---

[11] Yoshihasi and Barsky, "Merv Griffin's Plunge into Casino Gambling," p. A7.

Jensen, Michael. "The Takeover Controversy: Analysis and Evidence." In John C. Coffee, Jr., Louis Lowenstein, and Susan Rose Ackerman, eds. *Knights, Raiders, and Targets*. New York: Oxford University Press, 1988.

LBO Plan II. Venture Economics. San Diego, Calif.: Business Publications, 1987.

Logue, Dennis E. *Handbook of Modern Finance*. Boston: Warren, Gorham and Lamont, 1984.

Ross, Stephen, Randolph Westerfield, and Jeffrey Jaffe. *Corporate Finance*, 2nd ed. Homewood, Ill.: Irwin Publishing Company, 1988.

Siegel, Joel G. *How to Analyze Businesses, Financial Statements and the Quality of Earnings*. Englewood Cliffs, N.J.: Prentice–Hall, 1982.

Using 123. Special Edition. Carmel, Ind.: Que Corporation, 1987.

Weston, J. Fred, and Thomas Copeland. *Managerial Finance*, 8th ed. Chicago: Dryden Press, 1989.

Yoshihasi, Pauline, and Neil Barsky. "Merv Griffin's Plunge into Casino Gambling Could Prove a Loser." *Wall Street Journal*, July 5, 1989, pp. A1 and A7.

Chapter 14

Valuation of a Publicly Held Company

INTRODUCTION

The need for a systematic valuation process became more pronounced for corporate America during the fourth merger wave when many companies found themselves the target of friendly or unfriendly offers. Even companies that had not been targets had to determine their proper value in the event such a bid might materialize. In order to exercise due diligence, the board of directors must fully and properly evaluate an offer and compare this price to its own internal valuation of the firm. The need to perform this evaluation as diligently as possible was emphasized in the 1980 bid for the Trans Union Corporation by Jay Pritzker and the Marmon Corporation.

In September 1980, Jerome Van Gorkom, chairman and chief executive of Trans Union, suggested to Jay Pritzker that Pritzker make a $55 a share merger bid for Trans Union which would be merged with the Marmon Group, a company controlled by Pritzker. Van Gorkom called a board of directors meeting on September 20, 1980 on a one-day notice. Most of the directors had not been advised of the purpose of the meeting. The meeting featured a 20-minute presentation on the Pritzker bid and the terms of the offer. The offer allowed Trans Union to accept competing bids for 90 days. Some directors felt that the $55 offer would only be considered the beginning of the range of the value of the company. Following a two-hour discussion, the directors agreed to the terms of the offer and a merger agreement was executed.

When the offer was announced, only the merger agreement was mentioned, and not an intent to accept other bids.

The Trans Union directors were sued by the stockholders who felt that the offer was inadequate. A Delaware court found that the decision to sell the company for $55 was not an informed business judgment.

> The directors (1) did not adequately inform themselves as to Van Gorkom's role in forcing the "sale" of the Company and in the per share purchase price; (2) were uninformed as to the intrinsic value of the Company; and (3) given these circumstances, at a minimum, were grossly negligent in approving the "sale" of the Company upon two hours consideration, without prior notice, and without the exigency of a crisis or emergency.[1]

Based on these facts, the case seems to be one of clear negligence on the part of the directors. However, there is evidence that the directors had conducted an analysis of the value of the firm before the meeting in which they approved the offer. Actually, the directors had been monitoring the firm's financial condition for several years before the Pritzker bid. Their defense also included the following factors:

> The directors' key defense was the "substantial" premium in Pritzker's $55 offer over Trans Union's market price of $38 per share. The merger price offered to the shareholders . . . represented a premium of 62 percent over the average of the high and low prices at which Trans Union had traded in 1980, a premium of 48 percent over the last closing price, and a premium of 39 percent over the highest price at which the stock . . . had traded at any time during the prior six years. They offered several other defenses as well. First, the market test period provided opportunity for other offers. Second, the board's collective experience was adequate to determine the reasonableness of the Pritzker offer. Third, their attorney, Brennan, advised them that they might be sued if they rejected the Pritzker proposal. Lastly, there was the stockholder's overwhelming vote approving the merger.[2]

There was some merit in the directors' defense, as reflected in the opinions of the two dissenting justices who saw adequate evidence that the directors had studied the value of Trans Union for an extended period of time prior to the directors' meeting and were in a position to determine whether the offer was inadequate.

The board of directors also considered the comments of Donald

---

[1] *Smith* v. *Van Gorkom*, 488 A.2d 858 (Del. 1985). As cited in Dennis J. Block, Nancy E. Barton, and Stephen A. Radin, *The Business Judgment Rule* (Englewood Cliffs, N.J.: Prentice–Hall Law & Business, 1987), p. 37.

[2] Arthur Fleisher, Geoffrey C. Hazard, Jr., and Miriam Z. Klipper, *Board Games* (Boston: Little, Brown, 1988), pp. 31–32.

Romans, Trans Union's chief financial officer, who had stated that the $55 offer was at the beginning of the range within which an adequate value of Trans Union lay. Romans' analysis was prepared in order to determine whether Trans Union could service the necessary debt to fund the leveraged buyout he was contemplating. The court had not, however, considered his analysis to represent a sufficient basis for the board to consider since it was not a valuation study. This ruling is significant, for it affirms the need for a formal valuation analysis in all mergers, acquisitions, and leveraged buyouts. Ultimately, then, the *Smith* v. *Van Gorkom* decision is important because it set forth, under the Business Judgment Rule, the responsibilities of directors of public companies to have a thorough and complete valuation analysis conducted by an objective party, such as an investment bank or valuation firm.

VALUATION METHODS: SCIENCE OR ART?

The methods and data considered in the valuation of businesses vary widely. In some respects, business valuation is more of an art than a science. It is exact and scientific in the sense that there are standard methods and hard data to consider in the formulation of valuation. On the other hand, several different methods can be employed in a given evaluation. The methods may provide different valuations and thus give the impression that the general methodology may lack systematic rigor.

The naive reader may infer that the valuation of businesses may lack a scientific basis. A closer examination of the methodology, however, will reveal that objective valuations can be achieved. The variability of values is natural given that we are considering the market for a business in which different participants may place different values on the same business or collection of assets because the anticipated uses of these businesses or assets may be different in different hands.

This chapter and Chapter 15 discuss the methods of business valuation. Here we will focus on the valuation of public companies, and in the following chapter we consider the methods of valuation of closely held businesses. The methods and relevant issues differ considerably.

MANAGING VALUE AS AN ANTITAKEOVER DEFENSE

The intensified takeover pressures that managers experienced in the fourth merger gave them a great incentive to increase the value of their firm so as to reduce their vulnerability to a takeover. Firms with a falling stock price but with marketable assets are vulnerable to a take-over. Managers have found that adopting a management strategy that will boost the stock price makes the firm a more expensive target. With an increased stock price, raiders have trouble convincing stockholders that management is doing a bad job and that there are more value-enhancing ways to run the company.

An increase in stock price reduces the effectiveness of several take-over tactics. It makes a tender offer more difficult by raising the cost of control, and it decreases the effectiveness of a proxy fight because it will be harder to garner the requisite number of votes from other shareholders when management has increased the value of their investment. Some supporters of takeovers maintain that the pressures placed on management have benefited shareholders by forcing management to take actions that will maximize the value of their investment. The stock price has become a report card of management performance. Managers now have to regularly monitor the market's valuation of their actions. This marks a significant change in the way corporations were run in earlier years when managers kept the stock price in mind but did not make it a factor in most of their major decisions. For this reason among others, valuation has been placed in the forefront of corporation management.

STOCK VALUATION METHODS

The most basic difference between the valuation of public and private corporations is that an active market exists for publicly held companies, whereas the stock of privately held corporations is not traded. The value of a public company's stock can be more readily discerned by considering the value for which the security trades in the market. Even this price, however, may not accurately reflect the value that would arise in a takeover. To fully understand this concept, it is necessary for us to consider the traditional stock valuation methods.

The Gordon Stock Valuation Model

One of the most often cited models is the *Gordon Stock Dividend Valuation Model*. This model determines the value of common stock by considering the present value of the dividends that would be derived from the ownership of the security. The Gordon model can determine different values, depending on the assumptions about the expected growth of the dividends.

One method of stock valuation is to express the value of a share of common stock as the present value of the future dividends. The value of a share of common stock in a given company at time 0 can be expressed as follows:

$$P_O = \frac{D_1}{(1 + k_s)^1} + \frac{D_2}{(1 + k_s)^2} + \cdots + \frac{D_\infty}{(1 + k_s)^\infty} \qquad (14.1)$$

where: P_O = the stock price at time 0
D_i = the dividend at time i
k_s = the capitalization rate for this firm's common stock

One of the first questions that arises from Equation 14.1 is, what will dividends D_1 through D_n equal? Presumably, the dividends would grow as a result of the effects of inflation and the growth of the company. Therefore, a more accurate stock-dividend valuation model should reflect this growth. One assumption that would simplify this process would be to have dividends growing at a constant rate. This assumption can be rationalized if the historical evidence indicates a certain rate of growth in dividends which is apparent from the company's recent history. The constant growth rate model is often simply referred to as the Gordon model.[3]

This growth rate can be incorporated as follows:

$$P_O = \frac{D_0(1 + g)^1}{(1 + k_s)^1} + \frac{D_0(1 + g)^2}{(1 + k_s)^2} + \cdots + \frac{D_0(1 + g)^\infty}{(1 + k_s)^\infty} \qquad (14.2)$$

Equation 14.2 can be simplified as follows:

$$P_O = \frac{D_i}{k_s - g} \qquad (14.3)$$

Equation 14.3 will yield accurate values for P_O assuming that the capitalization rate, k_s, is greater than the growth rate, g. The growth rate of dividends can be determined by considering a reasonable historical period such as the past 10 years. The average annual growth rate can be determined by applying the following expression:

$$D_{11} = D_1 (1 + g)^{11} \qquad (14.4)$$

Solving for G, we get

$$g = \sqrt[10]{\frac{D_{11}}{D_1}} - 1 \qquad (14.5)$$

---

[3] Myron Gordon, *The Investment, Financing and Valuation of the Modern Corporation* (Homewood, Ill.: Irwin, 1962).

Let us assume, for simplicity's sake, that dividends are paid annually. For the 10-year period shown in the accompanying tabulation, we can apply Equation 14.5 to determine the growth rate.

Year	Dividend
1	$1.00
2	1.10
3	1.20
4	1.35
5	1.45
6	1.60
7	1.90
8	1.90
9	2.00
10	2.10
11	2.15

$$G = \sqrt[10]{\frac{2.15}{1.00}} - 1 \qquad (14.6)$$

$$G = 7.95\%$$

The 10-year time period is somewhat arbitrary and is assumed to be a period for which there has been a stable dividends flow and one that will be indicative of future dividends flow. We have derived an average annual compounded rate of growth and have made the assumption that this average rate will apply in the future. Having derived the growth rate, we can apply it in an example. Let's assume that the capitalization rate for the company in question is 15 percent or 0.15. Then, substituting this into Equation 14.3, we get a valuation as of the eleventh period.

$$P = \frac{\$2.15}{0.15 - 0.0795} \qquad (14.7)$$

$$P = \$30.50$$

Higher growth rates will yield higher stock valuations; lower growth rates will have the opposite effect. For example, if we were valuing the stock of a newer, growing company, a higher rate of growth might be anticipated for an initial period. As the firm matured and established itself in the marketplace, the growth rate would stabilize at some level. If we blindly applied the high initial growth rate, unrealistic stock prices would result.

Equation 14.3 can be adjusted to reflect a high initial rate of growth in dividends followed by a stable growth rate. This calculation can be conducted in two steps:

1. Calculate the present value of the dividends for the initial high-growth period. This can be done as follows:

$$P_O = \sum_{t=1}^{m} \frac{D_O(1 + g_1)^t}{(1 + k_s)^t} \tag{14.8}$$

   where: g_1 = the high initial growth rate
   m = the initial high-growth rate period

2. Calculate the present value of stock after the initial growth period. This is simply the value of the stock using Equation 14.3, which is its value at that time, and discounting the result back to time O. The undiscounted part of this expression is the price that the stock should sell for at that time.

$$P_m = \frac{1}{(1 + k_s)^m} + \frac{D_{m+1}}{(k_s - g_2)} \tag{14.9}$$

   where: g_2 = the stabilized rate of growth

3. The value of the firm's stock is then calculated by adding the results of steps 1 and 2.

An obvious question arises, How do we determine what g_1 and g_2 should be equal to? One rule of thumb would be to use the recent historical growth of dividends for the firm as an estimate of g_i. g_2 can be approximated by using the industry growth rate of dividends.

Let's consider the following example, GrowMax Computer Technologies, a manufacturer of computer components for large computer companies which has been in existence for five years. Unlike many other high-growth companies, GrowMax has paid annual dividends that have been rising as fast as its earnings. Let's assume that these dividends have been paid in all five years of its brief existence. This would be unusual since many high-growth companies decide to put the earnings back into the company where they can earn a higher return than the stockholders' could earn on alternative investments, particularly after the double corporation tax.

GrowMax's annual dividends for the years 1984–1988 are as follows:

1984	$1.50
1985	1.80
1986	2.30
1987	2.90
1988	3.65

The annual rate of growth in dividends is approximately 25 percent. Let's assume that this rate of growth is projected to continue for the next five years. After this period, it is assumed that the firm will pay the industry growth rate of dividends which we assume to be 5 percent.

The valuation of GrowMax stock encompasses three steps.

Step 1. The 1990 dividend amount of $3.65 is used as the base. The discount rate is 17 percent. See Table 14.1 for the valuations figures during 1991–1995.

Step 2. The value of the stock at the end of five years, 1995, is calculated by determining the dividend amount at the end of the sixth year, 1996. This value is:

$$\$3.65(1.25)^5(1.05) = \$11.70 \tag{14.10}$$

Applying Equation 14.3,

$$P_5 = \frac{\$11.70}{(0.17 - 0.05)} = \$97.50 \tag{14.11}$$

$$(\$97.50)(0.456) = \$44.46$$

Step 3. Add steps 1 and 2.

$$P_O = \$22.31 + \$44.46 = \$66.77 \tag{14.12}$$

As is true of all financial analysis, we would need to give the analysis and results a "sensibility check." The analysis was based on the assumption of a continued 25 percent growth in dividends for five years based on the historical growth rate between 1984 and 1989. Is this realistic? The analysis then makes the assumption that the firm would approach the industry growth rate in dividends of 5 percent. This is a simplifying assumption because it would be more reasonable to have an intermediate period with a different growth rate between 25 and 5 percent. A gradual reduction approaching the industry growth rate might be more realistic.

Table 14.1   VALUATION OF GROWMAX STOCK, 1991–1995

Year	Dividend	Growth Factor	Discount Factor	Value
1991	$3.65	1.25	0.850	$ 3.87
1992	3.65	1.56	0.730	4.16
1993	3.65	1.95	0.624	4.44
1994	3.65	2.44	0.534	4.76
1995	3.65	3.05	0.456	5.08
				$22.31

Step 3 shows a stock value of $66.77. The question that arises is, what are similar firms selling for? This, of course, assumes that you can find other firms with the impressive rate of annual dividend growth exhibited by GrowMax. If these other firms are selling for a fraction of what your analysis indicates GrowMax is worth, then your assessment of the value of GrowMax differs dramatically from the market's assessment of similar firms. On the other hand, GrowMax's historical rate of growth in dividends is so high that comparable firms may not exist. In this case the company could possibly be worth the $66.77 value.

One obvious problem that arises from a consideration of this methodology concerns what we do for firms that do not pay out dividends. It might be more reasonable that such a high-growth firm like GrowMax would not pay out earnings in the form of dividends, but rather would retain these earnings and reinvest them in the firm. Firms like Digital Equipment and the Tandy Corporation have been examples of such companies. This is one of the major drawbacks of the dividend stock valuation method.

Another major disadvantage of the Gordon model is that it considers only a small number of factors. It may be necessary to go beyond the historical growth rate of dividends and to examine many of the relevant factors that will affect the future dividend growth. The riskiness of the firm would need to be assessed in determining the appropriate discount rate. The risk of the company may be determined by a broad set of factors. Such important deterministic factors may be one reason why the market arrives at a very different assessment of the appropriate value of the stock.

Another consideration in applying the Gordon model is that the analysis considers the flow of dividends for a given number of shares of stock outstanding. This valuation would be affected by a change in the number of shares that might result from the future issuance of equity and the earnings generated by this additional equity capital.

In sum, the Gordon stock dividend valuation formula is a convenient rule of thumb, but its requisite simplifying assumptions limit its use. It is a mainstay of most corporate finance textbooks, but the mergers and acquisition analyst cannot put it to great use by itself.

MARKETABILITY OF THE STOCK

The marketability of common stock varies considerably. The equity of publicly held companies is traded on organized exchanges and on the over-the-counter market. The major organized exchanges, in order of size, are the New York Stock Exchange (the Big Board); the Midwest

Stock Exchange; the American Stock Exchange; the Pacific Stock Exchange; and the Philadelphia Stock Exchange. Other regional exchanges, such as the Boston Stock Exchange and the Cincinnati Stock Exchange, trade smaller securities of companies that may lack national awareness. They also trade securities that are listed on both the New York Stock Exchange and the regional exchange. These types of securities are called *dually listed securities*.

Most smaller companies trade on the *over-the-counter market (OTC)*. This market is a trading system wherein securities are bought and sold through a network of brokers and dealers who trade through the National Association of Security Dealers' Automated Quotations (NASDAQ) computerized network. OTC securities that are seldom traded are not kept on the NASDAQ computer network. Prices on these securities are available through the *pink sheets*. Their prices appear on the pink sheets daily and are made available through the National Quotation Bureau. The OTC market accounts for only about a third of all stock trading in the United States.[4]

Figure 14.1 compares the trading volume of the OTC market with that of the New York Stock Exchange (NYSE) and the American Stock Exchange (AMEX).

The market where the security is traded is an important consideration in the valuation process. The broader the market and the greater the daily trading volume, the more liquid the security. This means that if you want to sell the stock you have a better opportunity to sell a larger amount of stock without depressing the price significantly when it is actively traded on an organized exchange. On the other hand, if the stock is a seldom traded security on the OTC market, the price quoted may be less reliable. A seller may not be able to sell a large block of stock for anywhere near the last price quoted on the pink sheets. The exact value of the stock may not be determinable until offers for the block have been made.

The "thinness" of the market is a major determinant of the liquidity of the security. Lack of liquidity is another element of risk that has to be factored into the stock price. This can be accomplished by adjusting the discount rate used to bring the dividends to present value. The greater the risk, the higher the discount rate and the lower the stock price. We will return to the issue of adjusting the discount rate later in this and the following chapter.

We can judge the thinness of the market by looking at the number of *float shares*—the number of shares available for trading. Small companies on the OTC market may have only a small percentage of their

---

[4] Jack Clark Francis, *Investments* (New York: McGraw–Hill, 1988), p. 91.

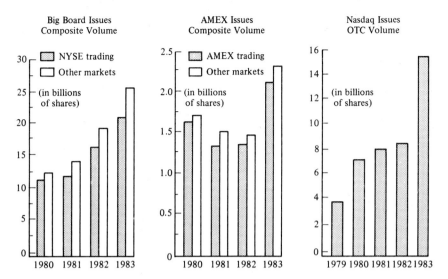

Figure 14.1 NYSE, AMEX, and NASDAQ volume. (*Source: Wall Street Journal.* Reprinted by permission of the Wall Street Journal, copyright © Dow Jones & Company, Inc., 1983. All Rights Reserved Worldwide.)

shares traded, whereas most of the shares may be rarely traded. When the number of float shares is small, compared to the total shares outstanding, the valuation provided by the market may not be that useful. Moreover, when the number of float shares is small, any sudden increase in trading volume can greatly affect the stock price. This is another element of risk that needs to be considered.

A related influence on the price a buyer may be willing to pay for an OTC-traded security is the concentration of securities in the hands of certain groups. The companies traded on the OTC market frequently have large blocks of stock concentrated in the hands of a small group of individuals. Some of these companies may be firms that have recently gone public and have large blocks of stock owned by family members. Such a concentration makes the likelihood of a successful takeover by an outside party less probable unless it is a friendly transaction. The greater the concentration of securities in the hands of parties opposed to a takeover, the less valuable the securities are to a bidder—unless the bidder is convinced that the holders of these concentrated shares will be amenable to a deal.

CONTROL PREMIUM

A major difference exists between the price of a single share quoted on an organized exchange and the price of a 51 percent block of stock that will give the buyer effective control of the company. When a buyer buys a controlling interest in a target company, he or she receives a combined package of two "goods" in one: the investment features normally associated with ownership of a share of stock and the right to control and change the company's direction. Control allows the buyer to use the target's assets in a manner that will maximize the value of the acquirer's stock. This additional control characteristic commands its own price. Therefore, the buyer of a controlling block of stock must pay a control premium.

The comparative value of a controlling interest relative to a minority interest can be seen by examining the data in Table 14.2. In each of the years shown (1982–1988), the controlling interest commanded a higher value.

The basis for the premium can also be found in the factors affecting supply and demand for the firm's stock. The amount of the target's stock is fixed at any moment in time. This assumes that the target is not going to take actions that will increase or decrease its outstanding shares in an effort to thwart an unwelcome bid. When a new bidder seeks to buy a large block of stock, the price of the target's stock may go up (see Figure 14.2). Since the supply of the target's stock outstanding is fixed, at any moment in time, the supply curve for those shares is vertical at the quantity denoting that number of shares. D_B represents the market demand for the target's shares prior to the acquirer's bid. The impact of the additional demand by the acquirer is shown by the shift of the demand curve to the right to D_A.

The analysis demonstrated in Figure 14.2 is not the complete story. In addition to the control feature, which will by itself add value to the target's share price, there may be some offsetting effects. These offset-

Table 14.2   AVERAGE PERCENT PREMIUM PAID THE CONTROLLING VERSUS MINORITY INTEREST, 1982–1988

Year	Controlling Interest (pct.)	Base[a]	Minority Interest (pct.)	Base[a]
1982	42.5	165	29.6	11
1983	37.8	160	35.9	8
1984	39.0	191	16.8	8
1985	37.3	310	34.2	21
1986	39.1	308	27.2	25
1987	38.2	228	39.8	9
1988	41.9	402	58.9	8

[a] Base: The number of transactions in which a price was reported and a premium over market was paid.

Source: Merrill Lynch Business Brokerage and Valuation, *Mergerstat Review, 1988*, p. 96.

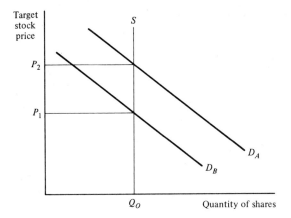

Figure 14.2 Demand-price effects of control bids. Assuming a fixed supply of shares, the increase in demand $(D_B \rightarrow D_A)$ bids the share price up.

ting effects may come in the form of quantity-purchased discounts that often accompany large block purchases. When institutional investors purchase larger blocks of stock, they are often able to negotiate a quantity discount from the seller who may be another institution, such as an insurance company or a pension fund.

Robert Holthausen, Richard Leftwich, and David Mayers found that for seller-initiated transactions, buyers receive temporary price concessions that are related to the size of the block.[5] For buyer-initiated transactions, the buyer is given a premium that is also a function of the size of the block. For cases when the acquirer initiates the bid, the Holthausen, Leftwich, and Mayers study supports the demand-driven price adjustment shown in Figure 14.2. The offsetting effects discussed earlier may come into play in cases where the target is putting itself up for sale. Even when it exists, this effect may not be observable because the control premium may more than totally offset it.

The Holthausen study does not focus on large blocks bought for the purposes of mergers. Its focus is on normal block trading that is a normal part of securities markets. It is useful, however, because it indicates how the size of the block itself affects the purchase price.

Several studies have been conducted on measuring the size of the control premium. Naturally, these studies vary in the size of the pre-

---

[5] Robert W. Holthausen, Richard W. Leftwich, and David Mayers, "The Effect of Larger Block Transactions on Security Prices," *Journal of Financial Economics* 19 (1987):237–267.

mium since they cover different mergers and acquisitions that occur in different time periods. The average premium was greater for tender offers than for merger agreements. The average premium for tender offers was 30 percent higher than the pre-offer price of the target's stock. For merger agreements the price was approximately 15 to 20 percent higher.[6] Other studies, using different data bases drawn from different time periods, have found higher premiums.

Some studies have measured the impact of takeover bids on shareholder returns. They found that stock prices tended to rise in advance of the announcement date. This occurred before both successful and unsuccessful takeovers.[7] Although the cumulative excess returns for successful takeovers were positive, as expected, they were also positive for unsuccessful takeovers, though significantly less so. This presumably reflected the market's anticipation of another bid. The size of the average premium that occurs in takeovers will be discussed in further detail later in this chapter. The difference in returns for successful and unsuccessful bids is depicted in Figure 14.3.

The Asquith results were supported by a later study by Debra Dennis and John McConnell who found a cumulative market-adjusted return of 18.63 percent for the time period 19 days prior to and 20 days following the announcement date.[8] Their study focused on the common stock of 26 acquired firms.

Historical Trends in Merger Premiums

Contrary to popular belief, the magnitude of merger premiums did not rise dramatically through the fourth merger wave. Indeed, the average merger premium hit a high of 50.1 percent in 1974 (Table 14.3, p. 542). It fell to 37.1 percent in 1985 and rose to 41.9 percent in 1988. This does not mean, however, that offer prices did not rise. Merger offer premiums were greatly influenced by the level of stock market activity. Mergers and acquisitions, in turn, also lifted the stock market in the 1980s.

Stock Market Activity and Merger Premiums

The normal ups and downs of the stock market cause stock prices to rise and fall more than can be explained by variations in their earnings

---

[6] Michael Jensen and Richard Ruback, "The Market for Corporate Control: The Scientific Evidence," *Journal of Financial Economics* (April 1983):5–50.

[7] Paul Asquith, "Merger Bids and Stockholder Returns," *Journal of Financial Economics* (April 1983):51–83.

[8] Debra K. Dennis and John J. McConnell, "Corporate Mergers and Security Returns," *Journal of Financial Economics* 16, no. 2 (June 1986):143–187.

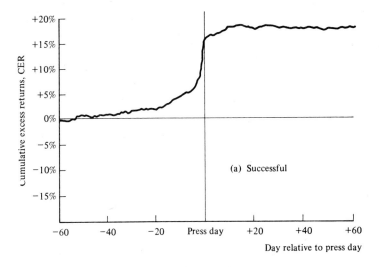

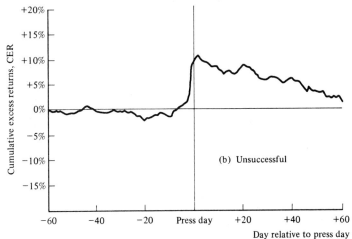

Figure 14.3 Average cumulative excess returns for 211 successful and 91 unsuccessful target firms from 60 days before until 60 days after the press day in the period 1962–1976. [*Source: Journal of Economics* (April 1983): 62.)]

or dividends.[9] This causes some stock to be overpriced at times and underpriced at other times. Managers know that in a bear market their stock prices may be below the long-term value of the firm. Believing that their stock price is only temporarily undervalued, managers are

---

[9] Robert Shiller used this relationship to show that security markets are not perpetually efficient as some researchers would like to believe. See Robert Shiller, "Do Stock Prices Move Too Much to Be Explained by Subsequent Changes in Dividends," *American Economic Review* 71 (1981):421–426.

Table 14.3   PERCENT PREMIUM PAID OVER MARKET PRICE, 1968–1989

Year	DJIA High	DJIA Low	Average Premium (pct.)	Base
1968	985.21	825.13	25.1	271
1969	968.85	769.93	25.7	191
1970	842.00	631.16	33.4	80
1971	950.82	797.97	33.1	74
1972	1036.27	889.15	33.8	93
1973	1051.70	788.31	44.5	145
1974	891.66	577.60	50.1	147
1975	881.81	632.04	41.4	129
1976	1014.79	858.71	40.4	168
1977	999.75	800.85	40.9	218
1978	907.74	742.12	46.2	240
1979	897.61	796.67	49.9	229
1980	1000.17	759.13	49.9	169
1981	1024.05	824.01	48.0	166
1982	1070.55	776.92	47.4	176
1983	1287.20	1027.04	37.7	168
1984	1286.64	1086.57	37.9	199
1985	1553.10	1184.96	37.1	331
1986	1955.60	1502.30	38.2	333
1987	2722.42	1738.74	38.3	237
1988	2183.50	1879.14	41.9	410
1989	2791.41	2144.64	41.0	303

Source: Merrill Lynch Business Brokerage and Valuation, *Mergerstat Review, 1989,* p. 84.

inclined to resist selling in bear markets unless a higher than average premium is forthcoming. Similarly, in bull markets, bidders are less inclined to pay the same average premium knowing that the market has overpriced most stock already.

This relationship can be seen by comparing the trend in the Dow Jones Industrial Average (DJIA) and the average premium percentage shown in Table 14.3. During the conglomerate merger wave of the late 1960s, which featured a bull market, the average premium ranged between 13 and 25 percent. When the market turned down in the 1970s, the average premium rose to between 33.1 and 50.1 percent. The highest premium, 50.1 percent, occurred in 1974 when the Dow Jones Industrial Average fell to 577.60, which was its lowest level in a decade.[10]

Having cited the abundant evidence supporting the existence of a

---

[10] *Mergerstat Review: 1988,* Merrill Lynch.

control premium in takeovers, we should determine whether control provides a premium in the absence of takeovers. In a study designed to measure the premium paid for control, Ronald Lease, John McConnell, and Wayne Mikkelson found evidence contradicting the belief that a premium should automatically be associated with control.[11] Their study specifically sought to determine whether capital markets place a separate value on control.

The Lease study examined the market prices of common stocks of 30 companies with classes of common stock that pay identical dividends but that differ significantly in their voting rights. One group had substantially greater voting rights on issues related to the control of the firm such as the election of directors. The two groups of securities provided the same opportunities for financial gain and differed only in their voting rights and the opportunities to control the company's future. Their results showed that for 26 firms that had no voting preferred stock outstanding, the superior voting common stock graded at a premium relative to the other classes of common stock. The average premium they found was 5.44 percent. It is important to remember that this is not inconsistent with the premiums cited above since these other premiums are found in takeovers. (The Lease study did not focus on takeovers.)

Four of the 30 firms considered in the study showed that the superior voting rights common stock traded at a discount relative to the other class of common stock. These firms differed, however, from the other 26 in that they had a more complex capital structure that featured preferred stock with voting rights. Given the existence of this type of voting preferred stock, these four are not as comparable to the other 26 clear-cut cases. Another study that focused on specific industries, such as the banking industry, found control premiums in the range of 50 to 70 percent.[12]

DIVIDENDS VERSUS EARNINGS

The stock dividend valuation methodologies are usually applied from an investor's point of view. They consider the value of a security in the investor's portfolio. This valuation is affected by the firm's dividend

---

[11] Ronald C. Lease, John J. McConnell, and Wayne H. Mikkelson, "The Market Value of Control in Publicly Traded Corporations," *Journal of Financial Economics* 11 (April 1983):439–471.

[12] Larry G. Meeker and O. Maurice Joy, "Price Premiums for Controlling Shares of Closely Held Bank Stock," *Journal of Business* 53 (1980):297–314.

policy. It is important to note, however, that such leading figures in economics and finance as Nobel prize laureate Franco Modigliani and Morton Miller state that dividend policy should not affect securities prices. They believe that the market will correctly offset any changes in the dividend policy to reflect an accurate valuation of the security. The dividend policy is irrelevant to the acquirer who is considering buying 100 percent of the target. The acquirer can set the dividend policy to be whatever the acquirer chooses within the limits of the firm's earnings. Earnings, not dividends, are what the acquirer is seeking. (This discussion uses the term *earnings* in the general sense. Later in this chapter, we will differentiate between accounting earnings, which the acquirer is less interested in, and free cash flow, which is a better measure of value.) A firm that has a low dividend payout ratio, the percentage of earnings that are paid out in the form of dividends, would not be valued differently by an acquirer than a firm that was similar in all other respects but that had a high dividend payout ratio. For this reason, stock valuation for mergers and acquisitions should focus on some measure of earnings rather than dividends. The dividend flow is not irrelevant. It helps determine what the *market* is willing to pay for the stock. Earnings reflect what the *acquirer* is willing to pay. If the market valuation, based on dividends, is higher than the acquirer's own subjective valuation, based on earnings, the acquirer may have to bypass the company since it is too costly relative to its earning power from the acquirer's viewpoint.

DEFINING THE EARNINGS BASE

Four commonly used ways to define earnings for the purposes of valuation of publicly held companies are:

EBDIT	Earnings before depreciation, interest, and taxes
EBIT	Earnings before interest or taxes
EBT	Earnings before taxes
Net income	Earnings after all operating expenses, depreciation, interest, taxes, and owners' compenation

The choice of the appropriate definition is a matter of the analyst's judgment based on his or her experience and the type of company being valued. EBIT, or operating income, and net income are the more common of the four definitions. If the target is very similar to the acquiring firm, in terms of taxes, interest payments, and other expenses, it might seem reasonable to consider net income. On the other hand, if the target's taxes paid, as a percentage of income, are not

CASE STUDY: *TIME–WARNER–PARAMOUNT: CASH FLOW VERSUS EARNINGS VALUATIONS*

In June 1989, Time made a bid for Warner Communications, Inc. which was followed by a bid by Paramount Communications, Inc., for Time, Inc. Both combinations—Time–Warner and Paramount–Time—would result in a highly leveraged company that would generate few earnings. Paramount took on $8 billion in debt to complete a $14 billion acquisition of Warner. This, however, did not make the company valueless in the eyes of its bidders. Paramount offered $12.2 billion or $200 per share for Time, Inc. The key to the target's value was the cash-flow-generating capacity of the media assets that these communications giants commanded.

"What's significant is that Time, one of America's leading companies, is putting a stamp of approval on cash flow valuations as opposed to earnings valuations," said Bernard Gallagher, vice-president and treasurer of the Philadelphia-based Comcast Corporation, the nation's third largest cable company. "Paramount, Time and Warner, all traditional earnings oriented companies, are now saying that earnings aren't nearly as important as combining and building assets that will generate cash in the future."

"The cash flow method of analyzing companies gained credence more than a decade ago with Denver-based cable giant Tele-Communications, Inc. Drexel Burnham Lambert analyst John Reidy says the company "made a decision years ago that it was foolish to generate a lot of earnings and pay taxes, when, by adding leverage, they could reduce taxes and add value by buying new cable systems." Adds Mr. Reidy, "everyone else in the cable industry took a page out of their book."[a]

The presence of high cash flows is not enough to ensure profitability. The $8 billion Time borrowed to finance the merger with Warner left the combined firm, which became the world's largest media company, with $11 billion of debt. As with many of the leveraged transactions of the fourth merger wave, the pressure of interest payments on this debt took its toll on the firm's profitability. Time–Warner posted a $432 million loss for 1989.

It is ironic that Time turned down a substantial offer from Paramount based on the belief of Time's management that the price of Time–Warner stock would eventually rise to $200 per share. As of February 1990, Time–Warner's stock was trading as low as $96.125 per share, less than half management's projections.[b] The cause can be traced to the debt pressures as well as proposals for additional regulation of the cable industry which would limit the size of some of the cable companies.

[a] "Time's Warner Bid Reflects Emphasis on Value of Cash Flow, Not Earnings," *Wall Street Journal*, June 27, 1989, p. A2.

[b] David Hilder, "Time Warner Holders Fret As Stock Sinks," *Wall Street Journal*, February 7, 1990, p. 21.

comparable to the acquirer's tax bracket, then a pre-tax definition of income should be used.

Earnings Versus Cash Flow

Many merger analysts do not choose to use earnings. Rather, they rely on free cash flow as a more dependable measure of the target's value. This is particularly important since earnings can be greatly influenced by the accounting methods used by the target. With different accounting methods, two otherwise identical firms can have very different earnings. An example of the importance of cash flows, as opposed to earnings, was shown in the 1989 Paramount bid for Time, Inc. (see Case Study). The bids made in this takeover contest were based on multiples of cash flow, not earnings. This is typical of buyout offers for these highly leveraged media companies.

Free cash flow, which is defined as after-tax income with various adjustments and addbacks included, such as depreciation, deferred taxes, as well as certain necessary expenditures, such as increases in net working capital or capital investment deducted, is considered a more reliable measure of the value of a target corporation to a potential acquirer. An alternative statement of the definition of cash flow comes from Mike Jensen: "Free cash flow is cash flow in excess of that required to fund all projects that have positive net present values when discounted at the relevant cost of capital."[13]

Many investors and stock analysts pay little attention to reported income. Recognizing that reported earnings present a limited picture of a company's ability to generate cash, they focus on cash flows instead. Some utilize a ratio of stock price to free cash flow as opposed to the often used price/earnings ratio. This measure can present a very different picture of a given company's investment value.

Measuring Free Cash Flows

The basic measurement of free cash flow is as follows:

```
+ Adjusted net income
- Depreciation
- Planned capital expenditures
- Changes in working capital
= Free cash flow
```

---

[13] Michael C. Jensen, "The Takeover Controversy: Analysis and Evidence," in John C. Coffee, Louis Lowenstein, and Susan Rose Ackerman, eds., *Knights, Raiders and Targets* (New York: Oxford University Press, 1988), p. 321.

The adjustments to net income will vary depending on the particular circumstances of each merger. These adjustments might include cost reductions in the target owing to reductions in the labor force or duplicate facilities. Other adjustments might be various "belt-tightening" measures that can be instituted by the acquiring company's management.

If a corporation is constructing an estimate of its own free cash flows, it may want to consider the dividends it pays to its own stockholders. If a certain level of dividend payments is considered sacrosanct, then it should be deducted from revenues in the free cash flow calculation process. If, on the other hand, the firm has flexibility in its dividend payments, it may not want to make this deduction. When analyzing the target's free cash flows, however, the acquiring firm may not want to consider the target's dividend payments directly since it may be acquiring 100 percent of the target's stock and will not have to be concerned about paying dividends to these stockholders. On the other hand, if investors are used to receiving a stable percentage of earnings as dividends, then the buyer may need to allocate a certain percentage of the target's expected earnings to dividends which will be paid to the buyer's stockholders.

Bottom-Up Versus Top-Down Free Cash Flow Calculations

The above method of calculating free cash flows, which starts with earnings, is a commonly used way of deriving free cash flow. It is sometimes referred to as the *bottom-up method*. Since earnings are so commonly used and referred to, it is logical that we should start with earnings and make the appropriate adjustments to arrive at the more useful measure—free cash flow. An alternative method of arriving at free cash flow is the *top-down method* which starts with revenues and deducts expenses items such as operating costs. Both methods can be used to derive the same free cash flow value.

The use of the top-down method raises some interesting accounting issues. For example, conventional accounting practices call for the expensing of advertising and promotion.[14] These monies are invested in the development of the name and reputation of the firm's products, which is similar to a capital good. The treatment of research and development expenditures presents similar issues. One way of adapting

---

[14] Joel Stern, "Why Earnings Do Not Measure Value," *Corporate Finance* (September 1989):59–60.

the top-down calculation of cash flow to the economic realities of these types of expenditures is to allocate the expenditures across a longer time period that is similar to the life of the effects generated by the expenditures. While this may make sense, it is a nonstandard process and would raise issues of compatibility with other free cash flow measures used by those that are in greater accord with standard accounting methods. The issue disappears if we use the bottom-up method and start with earnings that are defined according to standard accounting practices.

Forecasting Future Free Cash Flows

Techniques used to forecast future free cash flows vary widely in degree of sophistication. The simplest method is to look at the historical rate of growth and extrapolate this growth into the future. For example, if revenues have been growing at an annual compounded rate of 10 percent, then a 10 percent growth factor could be applied to the most recent year's revenues and a five- or ten-year projection could be constructed. If we assume that the various direct costs (i.e., materials) and general and administrative (G&A) costs will continue to maintain their historical proportions to revenues, they can also be projected out annually. In the example shown in Table 14.4, direct costs are assumed to be 50 percent of revenues while G&A is 15 percent.

The construction of cash flows does not consider depreciation expense as a deduction from revenues. This is one of the major areas of difference between this type of projection and an earnings projection.

Table 14.4   FREE CASH FLOW VALUATION ANALYSIS (THOUSAND $)

		0	1
Discount rate		0.17	
Acquisition price		$1,500	
	Year		
Revenues		$4,000	$4,400
Direct costs (50% of revenues)		$2,000	$2,200
G&A (15% of revenues)		$600	$660
Capital expenditures		$400	$400
Working capital		$800	$880
Free cash flow		$200	$260
Net present value	264.02	($1,500)	$260
Net present value (Scl)	2,303.17		
Present value	1,809.03		
Present value (Scl)	4,194.71		

Further deductions, however, must be made for other cost factors such as capital expenditures and working capital expenditures. In the example below, we assume that higher capital expenditures will be necessary for the first two years owing to various improvements in capital equipment that might be necessary to bring the target up to competitive industry standards. It is also assumed that for every increase in revenues, working capital needs to increase by 20 percent.

The above analysis demonstrates how cash flows can be derived from revenues and used instead of earnings. In addition to assuming that direct costs are 50 percent of revenues and G&A expenses are 15 percent, it is further assumed that the acquirer would have to make an initial infusion of capital to improve the physical assets of the target. This is shown by assuming that $400,000 (in thousands $) would be invested in the first two years and $150,000 each year thereafter to maintain this capital base. Working capital needs are $800,000 in the first year and are assumed to grow at the same rate as revenues.

In this example, the revenues of the firm are projected to grow at 10 percent per year. This projection is based on the five-year historical growth rate. (The use of forecasting methods will be discussed further shortly.) The point of this exercise is to see how free cash flows, which are shown below the expenses, are derived. These free cash flows, not accounting earnings, are what the acquirer focuses on when evaluating the target. They are then evaluated using methods, such as the net present value.

Accounting Valuation Versus Free Cash Flow: The Stock Market's View

The use of net income as it appears on a firm's income statement to value a business is sometimes termed the *accounting method of valuation*. The alternative which we recommend can be called the *free cash flow method of valuation*. The merits of the accounting approach can be examined by seeing how the stock market values changes in accounting income that are not reflected in corresponding changes in the company's cash flow.

Many studies have considered the impact of accounting changes on stock prices. T. Ross Archibald, for example, examined the market's reaction to changing the depreciation method of accounting from accelerated depreciation to straight-line depreciation.[15] The reported in-

---

[15] T. Ross Archibald, "Stock Market Reaction to the Depreciation Switch-Back," *Accounting Review* 47, no. 1 (January 1972):22–30.

come of the 65 firms in Archibald's sample increased without affecting their cash position. Stock prices, however, failed to increase in response to the increases in accounting income, demonstrating that the market does not react to accounting changes that are not reflected in corresponding changes in cash flow.

Other studies have confirmed Archibald's findings. Robert Kaplan and Richard Roll found negative price reactions to similar depreciation policy changes which caused reported income to rise while not affecting cash flow.[16] They indicate that the firms that engaged in accounting changes tended to be the firms that were preforming poorly and were attempting to mask this performance through artificial means. Instead of ignoring these changes, the market seemed to interpret the accounting changes as confirmation of the firm's poor performance and lowered its valuation.

Accounting changes that do affect the cash flow of firms are shown in other studies to have a positive impact on stock prices. Shyam Sunder examined 126 firms that switched from FIFO to LIFO accounting methods.[17] These changes lowered reported earnings but improved the cash flow through lower tax payments. Sunder showed that the stock price reaction to these changes was positive prior to the announcement of the accounting change.

These research studies provide evidence that securities markets value cash flow and not mere accounting changes that are not also reflected in cash flow. While some analysts often cite earnings per share as an indicator of value, it should be clear from this discussion that it has major shortcomings.[18] Cash flow per share is a much more revealing measure of value.

Further Evidence That the Market Values Cash Flow

McKinsey and Company studied the relationship between earnings per share growth and P/E ratios of Standard and Poor's 400.[19] The P/E ratios were used as an indicator of the market's valuation of earnings growth. Their analysis showed a low correlation as reflected in a correlation coefficient $R^2 = 0.024$. Their analysis showed that many of the

---

[16] Robert S. Kaplan and Richard Roll, "Investor Evaluation of Accounting Information: Some Empirical Information," *Journal of Business* 45, no. 2 (April 1972):225–257.

[17] Shyam Sunder, "Stock Price and Risk Related to Accounting Changes in Valuation Inventory Valuation," *The Accounting Review* 50, no. 2 (April 1975):305–315.

[18] Tom Copeland, Tim Koller, and Jack Murrin, *Valuation: Managing the Value of Companies* (New York: John Wiley & Co., 1990), pp. 73–94.

[19] Ibid.

companies that had high earnings growth also had low P/E ratios. The McKinsey study then examined the correlation between the market value/book value ratio for 30 companies in their sample with the discounted cash flow/book value ratio. This analysis, though not a thorough and scientific study, did show a high correlation of $R^2 = 0.94$. This result seems to imply that discounted cash flow explained the market's value of the firms in this small sample.

FORECASTING METHODS

Forecasting methods vary from the most simple and straightforward to the highly sophisticated and complex econometric forecasting techniques. Econometrics is the highly specialized field of economics that utilizes statistical tools to analyze economic and financial variables. With regard to choosing between the simple and the more sophisticated techniques, the general guiding principle is to use the simplest and least costly tools to develop a forecast. The problem often becomes moot when the analyst is not knowledgeable in sophisticated methodologies. The gains to be derived from employing these methods may also not be clear. The following discussion reviews some of the basic forecasting methods.

Extrapolating Historical Growth Rates

This method involves determining the historical growth rate for a selected time period and projecting it into the future. This calculation usually involves measuring the compounded annual rate of growth as opposed to using a simple average of the different annual growth rates. This can be derived using the same formula we used to derive the dividend compound growth rate (Eq. 14.4).

$$Y = (1 + g)^n X \qquad\qquad (14.13)$$

where: Y = the last cash flow value
$\qquad\quad X$ = the first cash flow value
$\qquad\quad n$ = the number of historical years or periods chosen
$\qquad\quad g$ = the compounded annual growth rate

We have the values for Y, X, and n, and we have to solve for g. Rearranging the above equation to do that, we get the same type of equation as Equation 14.5.

$$g = \sqrt[n]{\frac{Y}{X}} - 1 \qquad\qquad (14.14)$$

The compounded annual rate of cash flows or earnings growth is then applied to the last value the firm recorded. This rate of annual growth is used to project the future annual sales growth. In its simplest form of application, costs are assumed to maintain their historical relationship with revenues. In this way, a balance sheet can be projected for each year into the future that the analyst is interested in. When specific information is available which would alter the level of a particular cost category, this information can be selectively applied to make a more accurate projection.

If the last time period used as the base in the projection is atypical, then an average of several other years might have to be used. This process will help reduce the biased influence of the last year in formulating the base. When there is an upward trend in the cash flows or earnings, the averaging process will reduce the influence of the firm's own growth. The analyst has to consider both factors and make a judgment on the costs and benefits of this tradeoff.

The Weighted Average Method

The analyst may feel that there have been significant changes in either the firm being analyzed or the market, as a whole, or both, which make the revenues earned in later years more relevant to the firm's future performance than revenues earned in earlier years. The difference, however, may not be so great that the analyst will want to discard the earlier years. The analyst can accommodate the difference in the importance attributed to the various years by using a weighting process that places greater emphasis on more recent data. The choice of weights depends on the importance the analyst attributes to the different time periods. Larger weights are applied to more recent years when the analyst wants these years to play a greater role in the resulting forecasted values.

Table 14.5 presents an example of a weighted average forecasting process based on seven years of historical revenue data.

Weighted average method   Simple average method

$$\frac{\$54.25}{28.00} = \$1.94 \qquad\qquad \frac{\$11.40}{7} = \$1.63$$

The weighted average method gives greater importance to recent years when revenues rose more quickly. In doing so, the sharp revenue increases in 1985 and 1986 play a greater role in the final projected value of $1.94. This is why the weighted average value of $1.94 is

Table 14.5   WEIGHTED AVERAGE METHOD FOR 1980–1986 (MILLION $)

Year	Revenues	Weight	Weighted Revenues
1980	$ 1.05	1	$ 1.05
1981	1.10	2	2.20
1982	1.20	3	3.60
1983	1.25	4	5.00
1984	1.50	5	7.50
1985	2.20	6	13.20
1986	3.10	7	21.70
	$11.40	28	$54.25

greater than the simple average value of $1.63, which is derived from a process that places equal value on each year's revenues.

Both the weighted average and the simple average methods have serious drawbacks. In an inflationary environment, revenues tend to rise through the influence of inflation. Although the compounded average annual rate of growth takes this factor into account, the weighted and simple average methods fail to fully incorporate the upward annual increase brought on by inflation and other variables such as industry- and firm-specific growth. These methods are clearly inappropriate for newer and more rapidly growing businesses. They are somewhat more appropriate for mature firms in low-growth industries. If these industries have been keeping pace with inflation, however, the application of the relevant inflation factor to the most recent year's revenues may be a better forecasting method than either the weighted or the simple average method.

Linear Trend Analysis

A more sophisticated method of projecting future sales is to approximate the trend in the firm's revenues using a straight line. Although the firm's historical revenues vary in a nonlinear manner, the trend can be approximated by assuming that the trend is approximately linear. The simplest way of accomplishing this is to plot the linear trend equation:

$$\overline{R} = a + bT \qquad (14.15)$$

where: $\overline{R}$ = the projected value of revenues for a selected time T
a = the revenue intercept
b = the slope of the line. This slope tells us how much revenues increase when T changes by one unit.
T = time

Time	Revenues
1	$1.05
2	1.10
3	1.20
4	1.25
5	1.50
6	2.20
7	3.10

The slope of the curve can be derived by the simple relationship:

$$b = \frac{R_7 - R_1}{T_7 - T_1} = \frac{\$3.10 - \$1.05}{7 - 1} = \$0.29 \qquad (14.16)$$

The value of b, the slope, tells us that the average annual increase in sales was $0.29 million. The straight line in Figure 14.4 has a slope of 0.29.

This analysis provides us with the following general equation:

$$\overline{Y} = 0.76 + 0.29 \times \qquad (14.17)$$

Y is the dependent variable (revenues in this example) and X is the independent variable (time in this example). This equation can be used to project revenues for future years. It is sometimes done by a crude "eyeball" placement within the set of available revenue points on a piece of graph paper. This involves subjective judgment by the analyst and can be very imprecise.

Regression Analysis

The curve-fitting procedure can be made more precise through use of the least squares method, a method that allows us to find the line that will exactly fit in the "middle" of the different points we have. It does so through a formula that minimizes the sum of the squared deviations from the actual data points for the variable that will be forecast and the values given by the line. Squaring the deviations prevents negative deviations from offsetting positive deviations. Moreover, through this method, the larger deviations receive greater weight in the forecasting process than smaller deviations. The reason is that when small numbers become squared they become bigger, but when larger numbers become squared they become dramatically larger.

This method provides us with more precise estimates of the two parameters a and b. These two parameters, the intercept and the slope, define and place the curve on the graph. They can be determined,

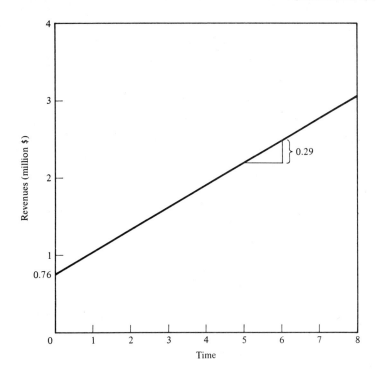

Figure 14.4

using the least squares method, by means of the following general formula:

$$b = \frac{N(\Sigma XY) - (\Sigma X)(\Sigma Y)}{N(\Sigma X^2) - (\Sigma X)^2}$$

$$a = \frac{\Sigma Y - b(\Sigma X)}{N}$$

(14.18)

In the example we have been using regarding the annual revenues of the corporation, the years are denoted by X and Y represents annual revenues (Table 14.6). Calculating the components of the intercept and slope terms, we get the following values:

$$b = \frac{7(54.25) - (28)(11.4)}{7(140) - (28^2)} = \frac{379.75 - 319.2}{980 - 784} = \frac{60.55}{196} = 0.30$$

$$a = \frac{11.40 - 0.30(28)}{7} = \frac{11.40 - 8.4}{7} = \frac{3}{7} = 0.42$$

$$Y = 0.42 + 0.30 X$$

(14.19)

The regression equation derived above can be used to forecast the firm's revenues for a given number of years into the future. For ex-

Table 14.6   REGRESSION ANALYSIS OF REVENUES

Years X	Revenues Y	X^2	XY	N = 7
1	1.05	1	1.05	
2	1.10	4	2.20	
3	1.20	9	3.60	
4	1.25	16	5.00	
5	1.50	25	7.50	
6	2.20	36	13.20	
7	3.10	49	21.70	
28	11.40	140	54.25	

ample, we can project revenues for years 8 and 9 by substituting 8 and 9 for X in the least squares equation, and we get:

$$0.42 + 0.30(8) = 2.82 \quad \text{Year 8}$$
$$0.42 + 0.30(9) = 3.12 \quad \text{Year 9}$$

The forecasted value of revenues for year 7 (2.52) is less than the actual value of 3.10 because, compared to previous years, the last year of data was atypical. It is not surprising, however, that the forecasted value for year 8 (2.82) is less the actual value for year 7. Revenues for year 9 (3.12) are slightly higher than the actual value for year 7.

If the factors that caused the marked increases in revenues for years 6 and 7 are expected to prevail in the future, then our least squares line will underestimate the revenues. On the other hand, if the variations experienced in years 6 and 7 are normal cyclical variations in the industry, then the least squares equation will provide more accurate forecasts.

Simple regression analysis utilizing the least squares principle can provide fairly accurate projections of future revenues based on historical sales data. The disadvantage of this type of approach is that it does not consider the functional relationship between revenues and other deterministic variables such as the overall level of economic activity or the price of inputs. These factors can be incorporated into the projection process through use of multiple regression analysis. Multiple regression analysis allows the analyst to incorporate information on the principal deterministic factors that influence sales. The analyst then derives a multiple regression equation of the form:

$$R = a_0 + a_1X_1 + a_2X_2 + a_3X_3 \tag{14.20}$$

This equation implies that three principal factors determine revenues. The methodology necessary to calculate this regression and the resulting parameters are more intricate than simple linear regression. The process can be tedious without the aid of a computer. The major complication, however, is not access to a computer, since PCs and the econometric software necessary to compute the regression equation are readily available. (One of the most user friendly, yet high-quality, econometric software packages is TSP which is published by the McGraw-Hill Publishing Company.) The complications can arise in the exact specification of the multiple regression equation: the determination of the appropriate functional form (i.e., linear or nonlinear) and the selection of the independent variables that best determine the dependent variable. This task can be very time consuming and can lead to misleading or even erroneous results if the analyst does not know how to conduct the necessary econometric tests. Most merger analysts use simple trend-fitting techniques.

FINANCIAL VALUATION METHODOLOGIES

The field of corporate finance employs various valuation techniques to determine the current value of an investment that will provide cash flows for different future time periods. These techniques are traditionally discussed in the framework of capital budgeting decisions. This is where a firm is investing a certain amount of capital in a project which will generate net cash flows in the future. The analysis of an acquisition of a company is a similar type of analytical process. Instead of investing capital in a project, such as a new plant, the acquiring firm is investing capital in a complete company. The principal analytical techniques employed are net present value and internal rate of return. The net present value of a proposed acquisition is the present value of the future cash flows of the target, discounted at the appropriate discount rate, minus the acquisition price. The internal rate of return is the discount rate that equates the present value of the cash flows with the cost of the acquisition. This is the discount rate that gives the acquisition a net present value of zero.

Present Value and Discounting

The value of money varies over time; that is, a dollar next year is worth less than a dollar this year. This is because a dollar today can be invested and earn a return over the coming year and be worth more than a dollar by next year. How much less a dollar is worth next year depends on the rate of return that a dollar today could have earned. The longer funds are invested, the more income will be earned. This income-earning process is enhanced by the fact that the investor would earn interest on interest. This process is called *compounding*. The relationship below indicates how the future value of a sum of money will grow if it is invested at an interest rate of r and invested for n time periods:

$$FV = PV (1 + r)^n \qquad (14.21)$$

where: FV = future value
PV = present value
r = discount rate
n = number of periods

From this equation we can see that if we wanted to determine what a certain value in the future is worth today, we could simply manipulate the above relationship to see that

$$PV = \frac{FV}{(1 + r)^n} \qquad (14.22)$$

The process that allows us to determine the value today of a sum of money in the future is called *discounting*. This method can be applied not only to a single sum of money in the future, but also to a stream of income generated at different time periods. Such a process is described in the following equation:

$$PV = \frac{FV_1}{(1 + r)} + \frac{FV_2}{(1 + r)^2} + \cdots + \frac{FV_n}{(1 + r)^n} \qquad (14.23)$$

Net Present Value

The functional representation of net present value applied to free cash flows is shown below:

$$NPV = \frac{FCF_1}{(1 + r)} + \frac{FCF_2}{(1 + r)^2} + \cdots + \frac{FCF_n}{(1 + r)^n} - P_A \qquad (14.24)$$

where: FCF_i = free cash flows generated in period i
P_A = acquisition price
r = discount rate
n = number of periods the acquisition is projected to generate cash flows

The prevent value of each projected cash flow can be calculated by multiplying the cash flow by the appropriate present value factor that will bring this term to current dollars. These present value factors, which are referred to as PVIF factors, can be found in present value tables which are readily available. For each discount rate chosen, there is a PVIF factor for each period that will convert the projected cash flows to current terms.

The calculation of the net present value of an acquisition was shown earlier. A discount rate of 17 percent was used to bring the future cash flows to present value. The determination of the appropriate discount rate will be discussed later in this chapter. The net present value was computed by performing the following calculation:

$$\text{NPV} = \frac{\text{FCF}_1}{(1 + 0.17)} + \frac{\text{FCF}_2}{(1 + 0.17)^2} + \cdots + \frac{\text{FCF}_5}{(1 + 0.17)^5}$$

$$+ \frac{\text{SP}_6}{(1 + 0.17)^6} - AP_0$$

$$\text{NPV} = \frac{\$260}{(1.17)} + \frac{\$576}{(1.17)^2} + \frac{\$649}{(1.17)^3} + \frac{\$728}{(1.17)^4} + \frac{\$816}{(1.17)^5}$$

$$+ \frac{\$6,120}{(1.17)^6} - \$1,500 \tag{14.25}$$

In this example, it is assumed that the acquiring firm can confidently project the target's free cash flows for at least a five-year period. We can sidestep the problem of constructing longer projections by assuming that the target can be sold in the sixth year for the same multiple of its free cash flows as it was acquired for. It is therefore assumed that the target can be sold in the sixth year after the acquisition for 7.5 times its fifth year's cash flows, or $6,120,000 (SP = sales price).

$$\text{NPV} = \$260 \ (\text{PVIF})_{1,17} + \$576 \ (\text{PVIF}_{2,17}) + \$649 \ (\text{PVIF}_{3,17})$$
$$+ \$728 \ (\text{PVIF}_{4,17}) + \$816 \ (\text{PVIF}_{5,17}) + \$6,120 \ (\text{PVIF}_{6,17})$$
$$- \$1,500$$

$$\text{NPV} = \$260(0.8547) + \$576(0.7305) + \$649(0.6244)$$
$$+ \$728(0.5337) + \$816(0.4561) + \$6,120(0.3898)$$
$$- \$1,500$$

$$= \$2,303 \tag{14.26}$$

The general rule of capital budgeting is that if the net present value for a project or, in our case, an acquisition, is greater than zero, then the project should be accepted. This assumes that the acquisition is advisable based on all the other relevant criteria. If the acquiring firm is considering a choice among several potential acquisition candidates, then the one with the highest net present value should be selected.

Internal Rate of Return

The internal rate of return is the discount rate that will equate the discounted free cash flows of the target to the acquisition price. In other words, it is the discount rate that equates the acquisition's net present value to zero.

$$P_A = \frac{FCF_1}{(1 + r)} + \frac{FCF_2}{(1 + r)^2} + \cdots + \frac{FCF_n}{(1 + r)^n} \tag{14.27}$$

In the above analysis, we have the values of the free cash flows of the target, the potential sale value in the sixth year, as well as the acquisition price. The internal rate of return can be computed by solving for the discount rate r.

$$\$1,500 = \frac{\$260}{(1 + r)} + \frac{\$576}{(1 + r)^2} + \frac{\$649}{(1 + r)^3} + \frac{\$728}{(1 + r)^4}$$

$$+ \frac{\$816}{(1 + r)^5} + \frac{\$6,120}{(1 + r)^6}$$

$$IRR = 47.7\% \tag{14.28}$$

The analysis for the internal rate of return can be computed by hand through trial and error. The analyst simply tries different discount rates, starting with the best estimate of what the right rate might be. The correct rate is selected when the right side of the above expression equals the left side.

Although it is not too difficult to compute the internal rate of return (IRR) by trial and error, it is much easier to use one of the many calculators that compute IRR. Many analysts use LOTUS to compute both the internal rate of return and the net present value. LOTUS has a convenient function that allows both to be computed using one command. LOTUS also allows the analyst to perform many other necessary calculations on one spreadsheet.

Choice of the Discount Rate

The choice of the appropriate discount rate to calculate the net present value of the target requires that the riskiness of the target be determined. As is true of other forms of capital investment, an acquisition is a risky endeavor. The discounting process gives us a means of internalizing our judgments about the risk of a capital project or acquisition within the discount rate.

If a project were judged to be without risk, then the appropriate discount rate would be the rate offered on Treasury bills, which are short-term government securities with a maturity of up to one year. Treasury bonds, the longer term version of U.S. government securities, may also have zero default risk but they carry interest rate risk. This is the risk that interest rates may rise above the rate that the investor receives from the Treasury bond. Although the investor is guaranteed the predetermined coupon payments, these coupon payments will not necessarily be invested at the same rate of interest. If they cannot, then the investment's proceeds will not be compounded at the rate of interest offered on the Treasury bond.

The riskier the investment, the higher the discount rate that should be used; the higher the discount rate, the lower the present value of the projected cash flows. However, a firm methodology for matching the risk with the discount rate needs to be established.

Cost of Capital and the Discount Rate

One of the basic rules regarding the choice of the discount rate is to use the firm's cost of capital. This measure is useful in capital budgeting because only one firm is involved. The cost of capital for a given company can be generally derived through the following expression:

$$CC = \sum_{i=1}^{n} w_i k_i \qquad (14.29)$$

where: CC = the firm's cost of capital

w_i = is the weight assigned to the particular k_i. This weight is the percent of the total capital mix of the firm which this source of capital accounts for.

k_i = the rate for this source of capital

Let's consider a simple example of a firm whose capital structure is composed of 50 percent debt and 50 percent equity. The weights for each source are 0.50. If the debt rate is 9 percent and the rate of return on equity is 15 percent, then the cost of capital can be computed as follows:

$$
\begin{aligned}
CC &= 0.50(0.09) + 0.50(0.15) \\
&= 0\ 045 + 0.075 \qquad (14.30) \\
&= 0.12
\end{aligned}
$$

The cost of capital can then be used as the discount rate for the firm when evaluating the net present value of an investment or acquisition. As we expand the analysis to make the cost of capital reflect the true capital costs of the firm, we must consider all the various components of the capital mix. Therefore, if the firm has preferred stock outstanding as well as different forms of debt, such as secured bonds, unsecured debentures, and bank loans, then each needs to be considered separately in the new expanded version of Equation (14.30)

Cost of Debt

The after-tax debt rate reflects the true cost of debt, given the fact that debt is a tax deductible expense. The after-tax rate of debt can be determined as follows:

$$k_d^t = k_d(1 - t) \tag{14.31}$$

where: k_d^t = the after-tax cost of debt
k_d = the pre-tax cost of debt
t = the actual corporate tax rate for the firm

THE COST OF PREFERRED STOCK

Because preferred stock dividends are usually fixed, preferred stock shares some of the same characteristics as debt securities. Therefore, preferred stock is also known as a fixed income security.

The cost of preferred stock to the issuer can be determined by considering the dividends that have to be paid each period relative to the proceeds derived by the issuer. These proceeds should be net of flotation costs. Let's consider a firm that has issued 8 percent preferred stock with a par value of $100. Let's further assume that flotation costs are 2.0 percent of the par value. This implies a net of proceeds value of $98. The annual dividends are $8 or 8 percent of the $100 par value. (Dividends are annualized for simplicity.) The cost can be determined as follows:

$$\text{Cost of preferred stock} = \frac{D_p}{P_n} = \frac{\$8}{\$98} = 8.16\%$$

The consideration of flotation costs should also be applied to all publicly issued securities. For the sake of brevity, we will only consider flotation costs for preferred stock.

THE COST OF COMMON STOCK

Many rules determine the cost to the corporation of the common stock it has issued. One of the simplest is to calculate the historical rate of return on equity for the stock over a given time period. A five- to ten-year historical period is often chosen. The time period selected would have to be placed in perspective by considering the corporation's growth to see if it is representative of the company's current and expected condition.

If the company is a start-up company with little available history, proxy firms should be used. Proxy firms are similar to the firm being analyzed but have more historical rate of return data available. The rate of return on equity for proxy firms is used in place of the company being analyzed.

Another method that is a favorite of academicians but is used less in day-to-day corporate finance is the Beta risk measure derived from the capital asset pricing model. This measure allows us to consider the riskiness of the company and to use this risk level to determine the appropriate rate of return on the company's equity. The Beta can be derived from the following expression:

$$R_i = R_{RF} + B_i(R_M - R_{RF}) \tag{14.32}$$

where: R_i = the rate of return on equity for security i
R_{RF} = the risk-free rate. The Treasury bill rate is typically used as the risk-free rate of interest.
B_i = the Beta for security i
R_M = the rate of return for the market
$(R_M - R_{RF})$ = the market risk premium

The Beta measure is derived from a regression analysis in which the variability of the market's return is compared to the variability of the security's return. From this analysis, we derive a Beta for the firm which can be used to weigh the risk premium. This weighted risk premium is then specific to the firm being analyzed. This method of measuring the cost of capital makes good conceptual sense but is not commonly used in daily merger analysis.

The rate of return on equity can also be measured by directly projecting the dividend flow. This calculation is easy in the case of preferred stock because the dividends are generally fixed. The following equation, derived from the Gordon model discussed earlier, demonstrates the relationship between the stock price and dividends.

$$P_s = \frac{D_1}{k_e - g} \tag{14.33}$$

where: P_s = the price of the firm's stock
D_1 = the dividend paid in period 1 (i.e., the next quarter)
k_e = the capitalization rate for this stock
g = the growth rate of dividends

We can manipulate the above expression to solve for k_e:

$$k_e = \frac{D_1}{P_o} + g \tag{14.34}$$

Consider the example of a firm whose common stock is currently selling for $40 per share. Annual dividends are $3, and the expected growth in dividends is 7 percent per year. (For simplicity's sake, dividends are considered annually, even though they may be paid quarterly.) The capitalization rate can be calculated as follows:

$$k_e = \frac{\$3\,(1.07)}{\$40} + 0.07$$

$$= 15\% \tag{14.35}$$

The capitalization rate can be used as a measure of the firm's cost of capital.

A simple guideline in deriving the cost of equity is to consider that the rate on equity is generally 4 to 6 percent higher than the rate on debt. The rate of debt may be clear if the firm does not have many different types of debt. In this case, the debt rate is given, and 4 to 6 percent can simply be added to derive the rate for equity.

HOW THE MARKET DETERMINES DISCOUNT RATES

As should now be clear, no set discount rate exists; many different interest rates are available. The overall market for capital consists of many submarkets. The rate within each market is determined by that market's supply and demand for capital. Markets are differentiated on the basis of risk level. For example, the market for debt capital contains many different gradations of debt that vary according to their risk level. The market for secured debt offers a lower rate of return than the market for unsecured debt. Within each of the secured and unsecured categories we have other gradations, each of which has its own interest rate. The historical relationship between the broad categories of capital can be seen in Tables 14.7 and 14.8.

Table 14.7   RATES OF RETURN AND INFLATION, 1926–1989

Category	Rate (pct.)
Inflation	3.1
Treasury bills	3.6
Long-term Treasury bonds	4.6
Long-term corporate bonds	5.2
Common stock	10.2
Common stock of small corporations	12.2

Source: © Ibbotson, Roger G., and Rex A. Sinquefield, *Stocks, Bonds, Bills, and Inflation* (SBBI), updated in *Stocks, Bonds, Bills, and Inflation 1990 Yearbook.* Ibbotson Associates, Chicago. All rights reserved.

Table 14.8   RATES OF RETURN AND INFLATION, 1968–1990

Category	Rate (pct.)
Inflation	6.2
Treasury bills	7.4[a]
Long-term Treasury bonds	7.9
Long-term corporate bonds	8.4
Common stock	10.6
Common stock of small corporations	12.4

[a] We would normally expect the rate of return on Treasury bills to be less than that on long-term Treasury bonds. This would give use the normal upward-sloping yield curve. This is not always the case, however, and the years 1968–1987 are an example. In this time period, long-term Treasuries yielded a 7.3% rate of return, whereas T-bills earned 7.4%.

Source: © Ibbotson, Roger G., and Rex A. Sinquefield, Stocks, Bonds, Bills, and Inflation (SBBI), updated in Stocks, Bonds, Bills, and Inflation 1990 Yearbook. Ibbotson Associates, Chicago. All rights reserved.

VALUATION OF STOCK-FOR-STOCK EXCHANGES

Most of the major acquisitions and hostile takeovers of the fourth merger wave were cash for stock exchanges. The acquirer generally determined the value of the target and offered a negotiated amount of cash for the target. Although the cash was raised through a variety of means, there was heavy reliance on debt.

The stock-for-stock swaps which were the modus operandi of the third merger wave were less common in the 1980s. As hostile mergers became more prevalent, managers became concerned that they might become targets of hostile bids. As a consequence, many managers became reluctant to make an offer for another firm lest their own firm be "put in play." It was felt that an offer for another firm might force both firms to be auctioned to the highest bidder. The mere announcement of an offer might bring other hostile bidders onto the scene with a demand for an auction in which they would attempt to offer the highest bid. Stock-for-stock mergers sometimes take a longer time to complete, and during this interval the participants in the merger are vulnerable to a takeover.

This was the case in the 1989 Time, Inc., offer for Warner Communications discussed earlier. The announcement of a friendly stock-for-stock swap merger between Time, Inc., and Warner Communications brought an unwanted bid by Paramount, Inc. Paramount demanded that the companies be put for sale to the highest bidder. Paramount's position was that the announcement of the bid by Time and Warner required an auction. The Delaware court ruling, however, failed to agree. The court's position was that an auction was not required. The Delaware decision has great significance for the future of friendly stock-for-stock mergers. Management and directors now have more leeway in agreeing to such transactions by relying on the Business Judgment Rule. Managers and directors can take the position that they have a long-term plan for the corporation that is in the best interests of stockholders, and they may choose not to accept a hostile bid from another firm. This paves the way for more stock-financed friendly mergers and acquisitions.

Tax Incentives for Stock Versus Cash Transactions

The tax laws provide that stock-for-stock exchanges may be treated as tax-free reorganizations.[20] This means that the stock which target stockholders receive will not be taxed until the shares are sold. The stockholder in the target is thus able to postpone being taxed on the consideration that is received for the shares in the target company until the new shares in the acquirer are sold.

One tax disadvantage of a reorganization is that the acquirer cannot utilize other tax benefits that would be allowable if the transaction were not a reorganization, such as if it was financed by cash. If the transaction were not a reorganization, then other tax advantages, such as the ability to step up the asset base or utilize unused tax credits that the target might possess, would be available. It is also possible to receive debt in exchange for the target's shares. For example, the target stockholders could receive debt as part of an installment sale of the target. In this case, the deferred payments are not taxed until they are actually received.[21] The seller can accumulate interest, tax-free, on the unreceived portions of the sale price.

EXCHANGE RATIO

The exchange ratio is the number of the acquirer's shares that are offered for each share of the target. The number of shares offered depends on the valuation of the target by the acquirer. Both the acquirer

---

[20] Alan J. Auerbach and David Reishus, "The Impact of Taxation on Mergers and Acquisitions," in Alan J. Auerbach, ed., *Mergers and Acquisitions* (Chicago: National Bureau of Economic Research, 1987), pp. 69–85.

[21] Alan J. Auerbach and David Reishus, "Taxes and the Merger Decision," in John C. Coffee, Jr., Louis Lowenstein, and Susan Rose Ackerman, eds., *Knights, Raiders, and Targets* (New York: Oxford University Press, 1988), pp. 300–313.

and the target conduct a valuation of the target, and from this process, the acquirer determines the maximum price it is willing to pay and the target determines the minimum it is willing to accept. Within this range, the actual agreement price will depend on each party's other investment opportunities and relative bargaining abilities. Based on a valuation of the target, the acquirer determines the per share price it is offering to pay. The exchange ratio is determined by dividing the per share offer price by the market price of the acquirer's shares. Let's consider the example of United Communications which has made an offer for Dynamic Entertainment. (See Table 14.9.) Let's assume that, based on its valuation of Dynamic, United Communications has determined that it is willing to offer $65 per share for Dynamic. This is a 30 percent premium above the pre-merger market price of Dynamic. In terms of United's shares, the $65 offer is equivalent to United's $65/$150 share.

$$\text{Exchange ratio} = \frac{\text{Offer price}}{\text{Share price of acquirer}}$$

$$= \frac{\$65}{\$150} = 0.43 \text{ shares}$$

Based on the above data, United Communications can calculate the total number of shares that it will have to offer to complete a bid for 100 percent of Dynamic Entertainment.

Total shares that United Communications will have to issue

$$= \frac{(\text{Offer price})(\text{Total outstanding shares of target})}{\text{Price of acquirer}}$$

$$= \frac{(\$65)(2,000,000)}{\$150} = 866,666.67 \text{ shares}$$

Table 14.9   UNITED COMMUNICATIONS AND DYNAMIC ENTERTAINMENT: COMPARATIVE FINANCIAL CONDITION

	United Communications	Dynamic Entertainment
Present earnings	$50,000,000	$10,000,000
Shares outstanding	5,000,000	2,000,000
Earnings per share	$10	$5
Stock price	$150	$50
P/E ratio	15	10

EPS of the Surviving Company

Calculating the earnings per share (EPS) of the surviving company reveals the impact of the merger on the acquirer's EPS.

Combined earnings = \$50,000,000 + \$10,000,000
Total shares outstanding = 5,000,000 + 866,666.67

$$\text{Post-merger EPS} = \frac{\$60,000,000}{5,866,666.67} = \$10.23$$

**United Communications' Impact
on EPS—\$65 Offer**

Pre-merger EPS	Post-merger EPS
\$10	\$10.23

United Communications will experience an increase in its EPS if the deal is completed. Let's see the impact on earnings per share if a higher price is offered for Dynamic Entertainment.

Let's assume that Dynamic Entertainment rejects the first offer of \$65 per share. Let's further assume that this rejection is based partly on Dynamic's own internal analysis showing the value of Dynamic to be at least \$75. Dynamic also feels that its value to United is well in excess of \$75. Based on some hard bargaining, United brings a \$90 offer to the table.

To see the impact on the surviving company's earnings per share, we will have to redo the above analysis using this higher offer price.

$$\text{Exchange ratio} = \frac{\text{Offer price}}{\text{Share price of acquirer}}$$

$$= \frac{\$90}{\$150} = 0.60 \text{ shares}$$

Total shares that United Communications will have to issue

$$= \frac{(\text{Offer price}) \, (\text{Total outstanding shares of target})}{\text{Price of acquirer}}$$

$$= \frac{(\$90)(2,000,000)}{\$150} = 1,200,000 \text{ shares}$$

Combined earnings = \$50,000,000 + \$10,000,000
Total shares outstanding = 5,000,000 + 1,200,000

$$\text{Post-merger EPS} = \frac{\$60,000,000}{6,200,000} = \$9.68$$

United Communications' Impact on EPS—$90 Offer	
Pre-merger EPS	Post-merger EPS
$10	$9.68

United Communications' EPS declined following the higher offer of $90. This is an example of dilution in earnings per share.

Criteria for Dilution in EPS

Dilution in EPS will occur any time the P/E ratio paid for the target exceeds the P/E ratio of the company doing the acquiring (Table 14.10). The P/E ratio paid is calculated by dividing the EPS of the target into the per share offer price. This is as follows:

Offer price $65

$$\text{P/E ratio paid} = \frac{\$65}{\$5} = \$13 < \$15$$

In the case of the $65 offer, the P/E ratio paid was less than the P/E ratio of the acquirer, and there was no dilution in EPS.

Offer price $90

$$\text{P/E ratio paid} = \frac{\$90}{\$5} = \$18$$

No Dollar sign

In the case of the $90 offer, the P/E ratio paid was greater than the P/E ratio of the acquirer, and there was a dilution in EPS.

Table 14.10   MEDIAN P/E PAID, 1980–1989

Year	Acquisition of Public Companies	Base	Acquisition of Private Companies	Base
1980	11.5	162	10.3	81
1981	14.0	160	11.5	70
1982	12.8	150	10.1	43
1983	15.5	141	11.5	48
1984	15.1	183	11.4	63
1985	16.4	240	12.3	187
1986	24.3	259	16.5	105
1987	21.7	191	15.2	25
1988	18.3	309	12.8	50
1989	18.4	222	12.7	42

Source: Merrill Lynch Business Brokerage and Valuation, *Mergerstat Review, 1989,* p. 93.

Highest Offer Price Without Dilution in EPS

We can determine the maximum offer price that will not result in a dilution in EPS by solving for P' in the following expression:

Maximum nondilution offer price (P')

$$\$15 = \frac{P'}{\$5}$$

$$P' = \$75$$

Solving for P', we see that the maximum offer price that will not result in a dilution in earnings per share is \$75. This does not mean that the acquirer will not offer a price in excess of \$75 per share. A firm might be willing to incur an initial dilution in EPS to achieve certain benefits, such as synergies, which will result in an eventual increase in per share earnings. This can be seen in the trend in earning per share in Table 14.11.

An examination of Table 14.11 reveals that, while United Communications would incur an initial \$0.32 dilution in EPS, United would quickly surpass its pre-merger EPS level. Let's assume that United had a historical 4 percent growth in earnings per share prior to the merger. In other words, United's rate of growth in EPS was only equal to the rate of inflation. Presumably, United was interested in Dynamic Entertainment in order to achieve a higher rate of growth. Let's also assume that a pre-merger analysis convinced United that it would be able to achieve a 5 percent rate of growth after it had acquired Dynamic Entertainment.

Based on a 5 percent rate of growth, it is clear that United Communications would achieve a higher EPS level by the fourth year. A

Table 14.11   EPS WITH AND WITHOUT MERGER, UNITED COMMUNICATIONS

Years	Without Merger (4% growth)	With Merger (5% growth)
0	$10.00	$ 9.68
1	$10.40	$10.16
2	$10.82	$10.67
3	$11.25	$11.21
4	$11.70	$11.77
5	$12.17	$12.35
6	$12.66	$12.97
7	$13.16	$13.62
8	$13.69	$14.30

more precise estimate of the breakeven point can be determined as follows:

$$\$10 \, (1.04)^t = \$9.68 \, (1.05)^t \qquad\qquad (14.36)$$

where: t = the breakeven time period

Solving for t, we get

$$\frac{\$10.00}{\$9.68} = \frac{(1.05)^t}{(1.04)^t}$$

$$
\begin{aligned}
0.033 &= (1.05/1.04)^t \\
\log(1.033) &= t \log(1.05/1.04) \\
0.01412 &= t\,(0.004156) \\
t &= 3.397 \text{ years}
\end{aligned}
$$

The firm may have a ceiling on the maximum amount of time it may be willing to wait until it breaks even with respect to EPS. If United Communications is willing to wait approximately 3⅓ years to break even, then it may agree to the merger at the higher price of $90. If United feels that this time period is too long to wait, it may only agree at a lower price or it may look for other merger candidates.

Factors That Influence Initial Changes in EPS

The amount of change in EPS is a function of two main factors:[22]

1. *Differential in P/E Ratios*
   Rule: The higher the P/E ratio of the acquirer relative to the target, the greater the increase in EPS of the acquirer.
2. *Relative Size of the Two Firms as Measured by Earnings*
   Rule: The larger the earnings of the target relative to the acquirer, the greater the increase in the acquirer's EPS.

The first factor has already been explained, but the role of the relative size of the two firms needs to be explored. For the sake of this discussion, let's assume that earnings are an acceptable measure of value. Since EPS is the ratio of earnings divided by the number of outstanding shares, the greater the addition to the earnings of the surviving firm that is accounted for by the addition of the target's earnings, the greater the EPS of the surviving firm. This is a common-sense proposition.

We can combine the effect of both factors to say that the higher the

---

[22] For an excellent discussion of these factors, see James C. Van Horne, *Financial Management and Policy*, 8th ed. (Englewood Cliffs, N.J.: Prentice Hall, 1989).

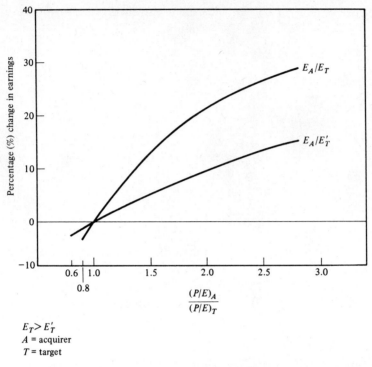

$E_T > E'_T$
A = acquirer
T = target

Figure 14.5

P/E ratio of the acquirer relative to the target and the greater the earnings of the target relative to the acquirer, the greater the increase in the combined company's EPS. The opposite also follows. The combined effect of the P/E ratio differential and the relative earnings of the two firms can be seen in Figure 14.5.

Bootstrapping Earnings per Share

Bootstrapping earnings per share refers to the corporation's ability to increase its EPS through the purchase of other companies. These earnings were prevalent during the third merger wave of the late 1960s. During this time period, the market was not efficient in its valuation of conglomerates. These conglomerates were able to experience an increase in earnings per share and stock prices simply by acquiring other firms.

In the case of United Communications' acquisition of Dynamic Entertainment, United issued 866,666.67 shares of stock based on a $65 offer price. This results in 5,866,667.67 total shares of United Commmunications outstanding (see Table 14.12).

Table 14.12   UNITED COMMUNICATIONS' POST-
MERGER FINANCIAL CONDITION

Earnings	$60,000,000.00
Shares outstanding	5,866,666.67
EPS	$10.23
P/E ratio	15.00
Stock price	$153.45

With the offer price of $65 per share, United Communications can offer Dynamic Entertainment a 30 percent premium above its pre-merger price of $50 and still experience an increase in EPS. If we assume that the market will still apply the same EPS to United before and after the merger, then the stock price has to rise. This can be seen from the following expression:

$$\text{P/E} = \frac{P}{\text{EPS}}$$

$$15 = \frac{P}{\$10.23}$$

$$P = \$153.45$$

United Communications' post-merger stock price has risen to $153.45 as a result of bootstrapping earnings per share. Two conditions are necessary for bootstrapping EPS to occur:

1. *The P/E ratio must not decline following the merger.* This implies that the market must be willing to apply at least the pre-merger P/E ratio following the merger. If the market decides that the combined firm is not as valuable, per dollar of earnings, there may be a market correction and the P/E ratio may fall. In the third merger wave, the market was slow to reevaluate the growing conglomerates and apply a lower P/E ratio.
2. *The acquirer must have a higher P/E ratio than the target.* If these two conditions prevail, companies with higher P/E ratios can acquire companies with lower P/E ratios and experience growth in EPS. This gives the acquiring company an incentive to continue with further acquisitions and have even greater increase in EPS. The process will continue to work as long as the stock market continues to value the acquiring company with the same P/E ratio. This occurred during the late 1960s. The movement came to an end when the market corrected itself as it questioned many of the acquisitions that appeared to lack synergistic benefits.

The Post-Merger P/E Ratio

If the market is efficient, then bookstrapping EPS will not be possible. The post-merger P/E ratio will be a weighted average of the pre-merger P/E ratios. This can be calculated using the expression below.

$$P/E_{A+B} = \frac{(P_A \times S_A) + (P_B \times S_B)}{E_A + E_B} \tag{14.37}$$

where: P/E_{A+B} = the post-merger P/E ratio
P_A = the pre-merger stock price of Company A
P_B = the pre-merger stock price of Company B
S_A = the number of outstanding shares of Company A
S_B = the number of outstanding shares of Company B
E_A = the earnings of Company A
E_B = the earnings of Company B

Using the above expression, we can calculate United Communication's post-merger P/E ratio after the stock-for-stock acquisition of Dynamic Entertainment. We will calculate this ratio based on the $65 initial offer that required the issuance of 866,666.67 shares.

$$P/E_{U+D} = \frac{(P_U \times S_U) + (P_D \times S_D)}{E_U + E_D}$$

$$P/E_{U+D} = \frac{[\$150 \times 5,000,000] + [\$50 \times 2,000,000]}{\$50,000,000 + \$10,000,000}$$

$$= \frac{\$750,000,000 + \$100,000,000}{\$60,000,000} = \frac{\$850,000,000}{\$60,000,000}$$

$$= 14.17 \tag{14.38}$$

Without the bootstrapping effect, the P/E ratio of the combined firm falls relative to United Communications' pre-merger P/E ratio. The resulting P/E ratio is a blended combination of United's P/E ratio (15) and Dynamic's lower P/E ratio (10).

STOCK PRICE VARIABILITY AND COLLAR AGREEMENTS

Stock-for-stock exchanges tend to take a longer time to complete than the all-cash acquisition. The value of the respective shares may change during the time between when an agreed on exchange ratio is determined and the acquisition date. One solution to this problem is to agree to a *collar arrangement*. This agreement usually stipulates that if the stock price goes above or below a certain value, there will be an adjustment in the exchange ratios. Such an arrangement protects the acquiring firm in the case where its stock price is higher or the target's is lower on the date of the merger than on the agreement date. If the merger were to be completed at the original exchange ratio, the acquirer would have overpaid. Similarly, the collar agreement protects the target when the acquirer's stock price has fallen since the agreement date or when the target's has risen.

The agreement may tolerate small movements in the stock price without causing changes in the exchange ratio. A certain threshold is established beyond which the exchange ratio has to be adjusted. The existence of a collar agreement in a merger is usually a point of negotiation.[23] It is more important if the stock of one or both of the participants tends to be volatile. If both firms are in the same industry, then *market* movements in each stock might offset each other.

BENCHMARKS OF VALUE

The analysis presented in this chapter provides several different methods of valuing a company. Their accuracy can be tested through a basic sensibility check which can be performed by comparing the resulting values with certain benchmarks that indicate the *floor value* of the company. The floor value is the normal minimum value that the company should command in the marketplace. Some of these benchmarks are described in the following sections.

Book Value

Book value is the per share dollar value that would be received if the assets were liquidated for the values that the assets are kept on the books minus the monies that must be paid to liquidate the liabilities and preferred stock. Book value is sometimes also called shareholders' equity or net worth. Book value tends not to be an accurate measure of a company's value. It tends merely to reflect the values for which the assets are held on the books. If these historical balance sheet values are not consistent with the true value of the company's assets, then book value will not be as relevant to the company's valuation.

---

[23] In the Diamond Shamrock–Natomas merger in 1983, the existence of a collar arrangement was an important point of negotiation between the two firms. See Dorman L. Commons, *Tender Offer* (New York: Penguin Books, 1986), pp. 103–104.

One use of book value is to provide a floor, with the true value of the company being some amount higher. The valuator's role is to determine how much higher the true value of the company is. In some cases, however, the company may be worth less than the book value. While this is not common, a company may have many uncertain liabilities, such as pending litigation, which may make its value less than the book value.

Most companies sell for a multiple of book value. These multiples tend to vary by industry. Depending on the current trends in the industry, there will be a certain average value that can be used to gauge the current market price of potential targets. If firms in the industry are priced at a certain average value, such as selling at six times the book value, and the firm in question is only selling for 1½ times the book value, then this might be an indicator of an undervalued situation. Book value is a preliminary indicator that takeover artists use to find undervalued firms.

Liquidation Value

Liquidation value is another benchmark of the company's floor value. It is a measure of the per share value that would be derived if the firm's assets were liquidated and all liabilities and preferred stock were paid. Liquidation value may be a more realistic measure than book value. If accurately computed, it may be a more accurate indicator of the true value of the firm's assets.

On the negative side, the liquidation value does not measure the earning power of the firm's assets. These assets may have different values depending on the user. If the firm is using its assets very efficiently, the company's value may be well in excess of the liquidation value.

DESIRABLE FINANCIAL CHARACTERISTICS OF TARGETS

Acquirers can use the following characteristics as financial screens.[24]

1. *P/E ratio less than or equal to the average highs for the last three years.* A low P/E ratio is generally considered a desirable

---

[24] This discussion is partly based on Garry S. Cunio and James J. Jenkins, *A Financial Approach to Mergers and Acquisitions*, 2nd ed. (Boston: American Management Association, 1987).

characteristic in a target. The lower the P/E ratio, the lower the price that will be paid to acquire the target's earning power. Because of market fluctuations, the P/E ratio of a firm or an industry category can go up and down. In addition, the market fluctuates up and down. A falling stock price that is not caused by a reduction in the potential target's earning power can present a temporary undervaluation and an acquisition opportunity. An acquirer can measure the extent of the undervaluation by comparing the P/E ratio with the previous level over the preceding three years. A low level can either mean undervaluation due to changes in investor preferences, or it can reflect a change in the firm's ability to generate income in the future. The lowest value in three years is an indicator of one of the two; it is the analyst's job to decide which it is.

2. *Stock price less than book value.*   Book value is a more reliable measure of value in certain industries. Industries that tend to have more liquid assets also tend to have more useful book values. Finance companies and banks are examples of firms with a large percentage of liquid assets. Even in industries where assets may be less liquid, such as firms that have large real estate holdings, however, book value can be put to use as a floor value. This was the case in Campeau's acquisition of Federated Stores in 1988. Both firms had large real estate holdings and marketable divisions and store chains. The combined market value of these assets and the estimated market value of the divisions on a per share basis made Federated a vulnerable target. In retrospect, the estimated value of the divisions proved to be greater than their market value when they were offered for sale.

3. *Current ratio greater than two.*   As described in Chapter 13, the current ratio is a measure of the firm's liquidity. The more liquid the target, the more desirable it becomes. This is even more applicable for debt-financed takeovers where the liquidity of the target may be an important factor in the target's ability to pay for its own financing after the merger. When inventories are of questionable liquidity, a quick ratio greater than one is desirable. As with the current ratio, the greater the value the better.

4. *Debt ratio less than one.*   The debt ratio is the ratio of total liabilities to stockholders' equity. The lower this ratio the better. The more cyclical the industry, the lower this ratio should be because industry volatility can cause revenues to rise and fall. The downturns in revenues may make the firm unable to meet its interest payments.

5. *Earnings per share rising at an annual rate of 10 percent for the past five to seven years.* A rising pattern of EPS is a most desirable characteristic. The analyst must make sure, however, that this is not the result of mere accounting manipulations. For this reason, the free cash flow pattern should also be considered to see if it mirrors the EPS trend. If not, the free cash flow per share should be calculated. Care should also be exercised to make sure that the average annual rate of EPS growth is not the result of a very low starting point. Higher growth can be the result of low earnings values caused by poor performance in the early years. The rate of inflation also needs to be considered. Rising earnings should be the result of real growth, not general inflation.

SUMMARY

This chapter discussed the variety of different financial techniques available to value publicly held companies. Some techniques that value the stock price of companies, such as the Gordon Stock Dividend Valuation Model, receive much attention in corporate finance textbooks but are of limited use in the valuation of a company. A number of other factors not addressed by this model, such as the control premium and the depth of the market, need to be considered in order to determine the appropriate acquisition value. This value is also dependent on whether the deal was friendly or hostile. Hostile deals were shown to have higher premiums than friendly transactions.

Valuation analysis requires that the buyer forecast the free cash flows of the target. A variety of forecasting methods can be used, ranging from simple techniques to more complex econometric forecasts. Many of the same techniques that are used in capital budgeting, such as the net present value and internal rate of return, are also applicable to the valuation of cash flows of public companies. This is reasonable since a merger valuation problem can be considered a capital budgeting exercise. The accuracy of the results of these methods is dependent on the discount rate selected. This rate can be adjusted to reflect the seller's risk characteristics. Higher risk firms tend to require a higher discount rate.

The analysis for stock-for-stock offers is different from that for cash offers. The relative value of the stock of both firms needs to be considered in stock-for-stock deals. Factors such as the dilution of earnings per share have to be factored in order to do a thorough analysis. The agreed upon relative stock values can then be "locked in" by a collar arrangement that would adjust the stock amounts on either side of the deal according to market fluctuations in the stock prices of both firms.

Valuation analysis can be an intricate process that requires a well-rounded knowledge of finance and other related fields. In order to construct a reliable analysis, much due diligence analysis needs to be done. The lessons of some of the merger failures of the fourth merger wave point to deficiencies in this type of analysis.

REFERENCES

Asquith, Paul. "Merger Bids and Stockholder Returns." *Journal of Financial Economics* (April 1983):51–83.

Auerbach, Alan J., and David Reishus. "The Impact of Taxation on Mergers and Acquisitions." In Alan J. Auerbach, ed. *Mergers and Acquisitions*. Chicago: National Bureau of Economic Research, 1987.

Auerbach, Alan J., and David Reishus. "Taxes and the Merger Decision." In John C. Coffee, Jr., Louis Lowenstein, and Susan Rose Ackerman, eds. *Knights, Raiders and Targets*. New York: Oxford University Press, 1988.

Bierman, Harold, and Seymore Smidt. *The Capital Investment Decision*, 6th ed. New York: Macmillan Publishing Company, 1984.

Commons, Dorman L. *Tender Offer*. New York: Penguin Books, 1986.

Cunio, Garry S., and James J. Jenkins. *A Financial Approach to Mergers and Acquisitions*, 2nd ed. Boston: American Management Association, 1987.

Dennis, Debra K., and John J. McConnell. "Corporate Mergers and Security Returns." *Journal of Financial Economics* 16, no. 2 (June 1986):143–187.

Francis, Jack Clark. *Investments*. New York: McGraw–Hill, 1988.

Gordon, Myron. *The Investment, Financing and Valuation of the Modern Corporation*. Homewood, Ill.: Irwin, 1962.

Hilder, David. "Time Warner Holders Fret As Stock Sinks." *Wall Street Journal*, February 7, 1990, p. 21.

Holthausen, Robert W., Richard W. Leftwich, and David Mayers. "The Effect of Larger Block Transactions on Security Prices." *Journal of Financial Economics* 19 (1987):237–267.

Jensen, Michael C. "The Takeover Controversy: Analysis and Evidence." In John C. Coffee, Louis Lowenstein, and Susan Rose

Ackerman, eds. *Knights, Raiders and Targets*. New York: Oxford University Press, 1988, p. 321.

Jensen, Michael, and Richard Ruback. "The Market for Corporate Control: The Scientific Evidence." *Journal of Financial Economics* (April 1983):5–50.

Lease, Ronald C., John J. McConnell, and Wayne H. Mikkelson. "The Market Value of Control in Publicly Traded Corporations." *Journal of Financial Economics* 11 (April 1983):439–471.

Levy, Haim, and Marshall Salnat. *Capital Investment and Financial Decisions*, 3rd ed. Englewood Cliffs, N.J.: Prentice Hall, 1986.

Meeker, Larry G., and O. Maurice Joy. "Price Premiums for Controlling Shares of Closely Held Bank Stock." *Journal of Business* 53 (1980):297–314.

Mergerstat Review 1988, Merrill Lynch.

Pratt, Shannon. *Valuing a Business*. 2nd ed. Homewood, Ill.: Dow Jones Irwin, 1990.

Shiller, Robert. "Do Stock Prices Move Too Much to Be Explained by Subsequent Changes in Dividends?" *American Economic Review* 71 (1981):421–426.

Stocks, Bills, Bonds and Inflation: 1988 Yearbook. Chicago: Ibbotson Associates.

"Time's Warner Bid Reflects Emphasis on Value of Cash Flow, Not Earnings." *Wall Street Journal*, June 27, 1989, p. A2.

Van Horne, James C. *Financial Management and Policy*. 8th ed. Englewood Cliffs, N.J.: Prentice Hall, 1989.

Chapter
15

Valuation of Privately Held Businesses

INTRODUCTION

Of the myriad methods employed in business valuation, some are more appropriate to public firms and others to privately held concerns. Public firms often tend to be larger than privately held firms, a factor that greatly influences the method chosen. This chapter discusses the differences in the valuation methods used for public and privately held firms, followed by techniques used in private business valuation.

The analyst of a privately held firm often faces a more difficult task in valuing a business, given the general lack of data for private firms and the broadly circulated opinions that exist for public companies. A wide range of securities analysts often study public firms in order to determine the investment value of the firm's equity. In addition, the various financial media publish a regular supply of articles about public firms. The analyst of a private firm, however, lacks the luxury of these information sources. He or she must rely on more original sources.

While the academic world places great emphasis on teaching the traditional methods of financial analysis as they apply to the large Fortune 500 public firms, they ignore the methods that are unique to valuing privately held concerns. These methods are found in only a small collection of specialized books that are designed for the practitioner in the field of valuation. This literature, rather than academic research studies, serves as the basis for much of the material in this chapter.

DIFFERENCES IN VALUATION OF PUBLIC AND PRIVATE BUSINESSES

Reported Taxable Income

A major difference between public and private business valuations centers on the availability and reliability of financial data.[1] Some of these differences are caused by the efforts of firms, particularly private businesses, to minimize taxable income. Another factor is the requirement that public firms disclose certain financial data in a specific manner while private firms do not face such requirements.

Public and private corporations are subject to different requirements with regard to the declaration of taxable income. Owners of closely held businesses take every opportunity to keep taxable income low and, therefore, have a lower tax obligation. Although public firms also want to minimize their taxes, privately held businesses have greater means available to do so than their public counterparts. As a result of these efforts to minimize taxable income, the financial data issued by private companies may be less reliable than the financial data given out by public firms. Therefore, analysts may not be able to rely on the reported income of privately held firms to reflect their true profitability and earning power.

With regard to declaring income, public and private corporations have dramatically different objectives. Public corporations have several outside constraints that provide strong incentives to declare a higher taxable income. One of these constraints is the pressure applied by stockholders, the true "owners" of the corporation, to have a regular flow of dividends. Since dividends are paid out of taxable income, the public corporation's ability to minimize taxable income is limited.

Public Corporations and the Reporting of Income

Like their private counterparts, public corporations want to minimize their taxable income, but in addition to the obligations toward stockholders, public corporations have fewer opportunities to do so. They do not have as much ability to manipulate their reported income, owing primarily to the accounting review requirements which the process of required reports to stockholders imposes on them.

---

[1] This section is drawn from the following paper: Patrick A. Gaughan and Henry Fuentes, "Taxable Income and Lost Profits Litigation," *Journal of Forensic Economics*, (1991), forthcoming.

In preparing financial statements, there are three levels of accounting reports: compilation, review, and audited statements. The compilation is the least rigorous of the three, whereas audited financial statements require an independent analysis of the company's financial records. Public corporations are required to prepare audited financial statements for their annual reports. These audit requirements are enforced by the SEC subject to the requirements of the Securities and Exchange Act of 1934.[2] The SEC does not accept a review or a compilation statement for a 10K report. A review is acceptable for a 10Q quarterly report. However, a compilation is not acceptable for use in preparing either of these types of published financial reports.

Because the reported income contained in published financial statements is subject to audit, the profit numbers tend to be more reliable than those that appear in the financial statements of private firms, which are generally not audited. The lack of required audit scrutiny is one reason why the reported profit levels may lack validity. The lack of an audit requirement allows private firms to manipulate their reported income levels to minimize taxable income. It is in this area that public and private corporations tend to have two very different agendas. Public firms may want to demonstrate higher reported profits to impress stockholders. Stockholders may become more impressed when these reported profits are translated into higher dividend payments or increased stock prices. The relationship between stock prices and dividends is discussed in Chapter 14.

The need for higher reported income and dividends became even more important for public companies with the advent of the fourth merger wave in the United States. This wave, unlike the three previous periods of intense merger activity, was characterized by an increased number of hostile bids and tender offers. Corporations that suffer a fall in profits or are forced to cut their dividends can become targets of unwanted hostile bids. An example of this trend was the June 1984 decrease in ITT's quarterly dividend from $2.76 to $1.00 per share. This cut, and the resulting decline in the stock price, was one reason why a group led by financier Jay Pritzger launched a hostile bid to take over the giant conglomerate.[3]

Higher reported dividends are the firm's signal to securities markets that the company's performance has improved. In February 1989, Gen-

---

[2] Paul J. Wendell, *Corporate Controllers Manual* (Boston: Warren, Gorham and Lamont, 1989), pp. C2-14–C2-23.

[3] Rand Araskog, *The ITT Wars* (New York: Henry Holt Co., 1989).

eral Motors announced a 2 for 1 stock split, a 20 percent increase in the quarterly dividend (on pre-split shares) for its main class of shares, as well as increases in the dividends for its Class E and Class H shares. GM chairman Roger Smith stated: "This sends a message to our stockholders that we got a fundamental improvement in our earning power."[4] The stock price rose prior to and following the GM announcement in anticipation of the dividend increase.

Private corporations are subject neither to the government's public disclosure requirements nor to the constraints and pressures of public securities markets. Freer to utilize every opportunity to show a smaller taxable income, they therefore have a lower tax bill.

A private corporation can reduce taxable income in two ways. The first is to have lower reported revenues, and the second is to show higher costs. The first approach is more common for small businesses, particularly cash businesses such as restaurants or certain retail establishments, which sometimes show a smaller than actual level of reported income. Forensic economists and accountants have encountered instances where businesses have kept two sets of books—one for the IRS and another for their own monitoring and compensation needs. This practice, in addition to being illegal, creates obvious problems for the evaluators.

If there is a reason to believe that a business's revenues have been underreported, an estimate of the actual revenues can be reconstructed. This sometimes occurs in litigation involving minority stockholders who are suing for their share in a business. The actual revenue levels can be reconstructed from activity and volume measures such as materials and inputs purchased, which can be translated into sales of final outputs.

The most common form of income manipulation for purposes of minimizing taxes is giving higher than normal compensation, benefits, and prerequisites for officers. The entrepreneurs of closely held companies may withdraw a disproportionate amount of income from the company relative to total revenues. Furthermore, entrepreneur-owners may list a variety of extraordinary personal benefits on the corporation's books as expenses. Although these expenses may be legitimate tax deductions, they are really another form of compensation to the owner. Any measure of the closely held corporation's profitability that does not take into account these other, less overt, forms of return to the owners will fall short of measuring the business's real profitability.

---

[4] "GM Splits Its Basic Stock 2 for 1," *Wall Street Journal*, February 7, 1989, p. A3.

DIFFERENCES IN REPORTING OF INCOME

Understating Income

One example of underreported income comes from the food retail industry.[5] The client was a food broker—a business that arranges for the placement of name brand food products in major food retail chains. The broker is compensated through a commission on food shipments to the stores. The commission is a negotiated rate that varies between 1.5 and 4.0 percent. It is difficult for the food broker to know the level of current revenues, at any one time. Orders are continually placed, but many are never actually shipped. Payment is usually made within 30 days of the actual shipments.

In the last month of the fiscal year, this particular food broker would tell his customers not to pay until the next month, which was another reporting year. The purpose was to minimize the current year's taxable income. The end result was a continual 30-day float on tax payments. For a business with monthly revenues of $2 million per month and a 12 percent cost of capital, this equals an annual value of $240,000. In a growing business, each year's profits are lower than the actual profits for that year. The float, which is clearly a benefit to the business, becomes larger every year.

Overstating Income

Understating income is more common, but overstating can also occur. Specifically, companies tend to overstate their true income when the company is trying to give a more profitable appearance to prospective buyers of the company. One such case, encountered by Economatrix Research Associates, Inc., a consulting firm specializing in forensic economics and business valuations, involved a paint manufacturer that would increase its sales and profits at the end of the fiscal year through an agreement with customers to accept higher than needed shipments during the last month of the fiscal year. Year-end sales and profits would be higher as a result of the last month's surge in sales. The higher sales, however, would be reversed by returns that occurred in the first month of the next fiscal year. The customers would simply return the paint and be issued credit memos.

This practice illustrates the difference between the reporting and

---

[5] Gaughan and Fuentes, "Taxable Income and Lost Profits Litigation."

audit requirements of public and private companies. A private company may prepare its financial statements through a noncertified review process. Accounting review or compilation standards and practices do not normally require that credit memos in the following period be examined.[6] Therefore, this practice would not be detected in the formation of the typical private firm's financial statements. Public companies, adhering to stricter certified financial statement standards and normal audit procedures, would hopefully be confronted by a diligent auditor. Public firms should not be able to manipulate income in this manner.

Costs of the Private Corporation

Inflating the private company's costs is the most often used approach to minimizing taxable income. The increase in costs tends to come through discretionary expenses. The most common areas of overstatement are Compensation, Travel and entertainment (T&E), pension, Automobile expenses, Personal insurance, and Excess rent paid.

The area of greatest inflation is compensation. Principals in closely held businesses generally enjoy far higher compensation relative to the firm's sales volume than the management of public companies. For example, a case study provided by Economatrix Research Associates, Inc., involves a company with annual revenues of $5.7 million. The company's five principals had a combined annual compensation of $1.8 to $2 million when all forms of compensation including salary and pension are considered. (This business is a service business with little overhead and fixed expenses.)

A tell-tale sign of this type of extraordinary compensation is to compare the growth in sales to the growth in officer's compensation. If, for example, the firm experiences a one-year increase in sales of $1 million in a service-oriented business and officer's compensation increases by $400,000, then the officer's compensation needs to be more closely examined.

Travel and entertainment is another area in which considerable forms of personal compensation are hidden in seemingly legitimate expenses. Another instance reported by Economatrix Research Associates, Inc. is a company that lists as expenses two condominiums in Florida. A vast array of similar personal expenses, ranging from business/personal travel to season tickets to sporting events, may be sources

---

[6] SSARS No. 1.

of income to a buyer. This area of expenses may contain many "costs" that are actually forms of compensation to the business owners. They are truly discretionary expenditures that would be available to a buyer as profits. For this reason, an evaluator may treat them as income.

Reconstruction of True Profitability

This analysis reconstructs the true profitability of the privately held concern by means of addbacks to the taxable income. It is similar to the types of adjustments that are regularly done in the valuation of closely held businesses.

> Of course, in most closely held businesses there are expense accounts, compensation, and other special arrangements accorded owners and others they may designate, not found in public companies. To some extent, these special arrangements can be taken into consideration in the valuation by appropriate adjustments to the earnings base.[7]

The primary adjustment usually takes place in employee compensation. The analyst must differentiate between the appropriate compensation for the actual duties which the principal/manager performs and the excessive compensation which the manager withdraws from the company because the manager has the discretion to set his or her compensation at an inordinately high level. Here it is necessary to critically examine what the principal/manager really does. Is he or she a truly innovative owner who would be very difficult to replace? The importance of a key individual was recently underscored when Eddie Antar, CEO of Crazie Eddie, an East Coast electronics chain, resigned because of illness. (Crazie Eddie declared bankruptcy in 1989.) In response, the stock price of this public company dropped dramatically.

Whether agents rather than an active owner should manage the business is not an issue that can be ignored.[8] Agents cannot be expected to maximize income in the same way an owner would. On the other hand, does the owner manage a business that runs itself through the direction of several departmental managers who report to him while he may spend the bulk of his day on the golf course? In this case, from the potential buyer's viewpoint, the true compensation for the work

---

[7] Shannon Pratt, *Valuing a Business* (Homewood, Ill.: Dow Jones Irwin, 1981), p. 36.

[8] Michael Jensen and William Meckling, "Theory of the Firm: Managerial Behavior, Agency Costs and Ownership Structure," *Journal of Financial Economics* 3 (October 1976): 305–360; Eugene Fama, "Agency Problems and the Theory of the Firm," *Journal of Political Economy* (April 1980):288–307.

done by the owner/manager should be minimal, with the excess compensation being put back in the company's bottom line.

RECASTING THE INCOME STATEMENT: AN EXAMPLE OF THE ADDBACK PROCESS

The example presented here is that of a service-oriented business and is taken from a case history provided by Economatrix Research Associates, Inc. A variety of addbacks are used to reconstruct the true profitability of this closely held company. The company, whose name is listed as XYZ Corporation, is a construction industry service company. The primary adjustments take place in the following areas: compensation, travel and entertainment, pension contributions, compensation of family members, and excessive rent payments to a family-run business.

A pro forma income statement for the past five years is shown in Table 15.1. The top half lists the main income and cost items as they appeared on financial statements prepared for tax purposes. The bottom half shows the reconstruction of profitability.

Table 15.1   XYZ SERVICE CORPORATION: PRO FORMA INCOME STATEMENT, 1984–1988

	1984	1985	1986	1987	1988
Sales	$3,590,000	$4,150,000	$4,750,000	$5,980,000	$7,220,000
Cost of sales	$2,270,700	$2,540,000	$3,060,000	$3,827,000	$4,421,000
Gross profit	$1,319,300	$1,610,000	$1,690,000	$2,153,000	$2,799,000
Other expenses	$1,289,140	$1,522,500	$1,588,400	$2,039,000	$2,679,500
Net profit	$30,160	$87,500	$101,600	$114,000	$119,500
Addbacks					
Officers' salaries	$225,000	$250,000	$325,000	$375,000	$425,000
Pension contributions	$18,750	$18,750	$18,750	$18,750	$18,750
T&E	$20,000	$30,000	$35,000	$38,000	$41,000
Auto	$20,000	$20,000	$25,000	$25,000	$35,000
Personal insurance	$5,000	$7,000	$8,000	$8,000	$9,000
Family relations	$30,000	$45,000	$50,000	$50,000	$50,000
Excess rent	$60,000	$60,000	$60,000	$75,000	$75,000
True profits	$408,910	$518,250	$623,350	$703,750	$773,250

Explanation of Addback Items

Officers' salaries   This adjustment was made after it was determined that the owner was performing the basic functions of a manager. After a consultation with a personnel specialist, it was determined that the market salary for such a manager was $75,000. This amount was then subtracted from the compensation which the owner was receiving to determine the appropriate addback. In the interests of accuracy, this replacement salary should be adjusted for inflation each year.[9]

Pension contributions

Travel and entertainment

Automobile expenses

Personal insurance

The reasoning for these adjustments is similar to that for officers' salaries.

Family relations   This is the compensation of a family member who did not really play a role in the business. The demonstration of this nonrole, however, may present IRS problems.

Rent in excess of fair market rent   This was the excess rent paid by the business as rent to a family-owned business that owned the building which the business was renting. The difference was computed by determining the market rental rates, per square foot, for similar commercial properties and deducting this total from the actual rent paid.

Examples of Other Individualistic Addbacks

In order to make a full and accurate adjustment of true profitability, the analyst must usually learn more about the business and the industry. A more detailed review of the industry norms will allow the analyst to spot unusual practices. Listed below are examples of some unusual forms of indirect compensation that have appeared as costs in financial statements.

Excessive Professional Fees   When professionals are principals or owners of a business, while still maintaining a professional practice as a separate business, two forms of compensation are available: direct compensation from the firm and indirect compensation derived from

---

[9] See also Executive Compensation Service, American Management Association, Karen Tracy, *Executive Compensation: Selected References* (Cambridge, Mass.: Harvard University Press, 1990).

fees paid to the other firm. These fees can occur in many different ways. They can occur, for example, in a construction contracting company that pays fees to an engineering firm owned by one or more of the owners of the construction firm. Another example would be a computer hardware firm that uses the services of a software company that is owned by the principals of the hardware company.

Excessive Legal Fees   One relevant case of a business valuation, also reported by Economatrix Research Associates, Inc., involved an attorney who was a partner in a law firm in addition to maintaining his position as managing partner in a medical research company. One unusual aspect of this medical research business was the large amount of legal fees it paid to the law firm. This was an indirect form of compensation to the attorney since his compensation at the law firm was proportionate to his billings. The true profitability of the medical research company had to be estimated without these legal fees when the nonattorney owner of the medical research company sued for the 50 percent value of the firm in a dispute with the attorney over the buyout purchase price that the attorney had previously paid.

Other Areas

Numerous other factors help determine the true profitability of the privately held firm. Depreciation policies, for example, can be used to understate or overstate profitability.[10] Ideally, the most appropriate depreciation schedule, for the purposes of lost profit analysis, should be one that best reflects the matching of revenue and expense. Depreciation, is in effect, a cost allocation.[11]

Accounting policies can greatly affect the profitability of the closely held firm. For example, a switch from a FIFO to a LIFO accounting method, in order to reduce taxable income, can result in understated reported income.[12] These and other accounting practices may need to be considered before the true profitability of the firm can be determined. It is required that the income effects of changes in accounting practices be specifically disclosed on the firm's income statement.[13]

---

[10] Joel Siegel, *How to Analyze Businesses, Financial Statements and the Quality of Earnings* (Englewood Cliffs, N.J.: Prentice-Hall, 1982), pp. 67–68.

[11] Donald Kieso and Jerry Weygandt, *Intermediate Accounting* (New York: John Wiley & Sons, 1986).

[12] Charles Moyer, James McGuigan, and William Kretlow, *Contemporary Financial Management* (St. Paul, Minn.: West Publishing Co., 1984), p. 199.

[13] "Accounting Changes," *Accounting Principles Board Opinion*, No. 20 (July 1971).

MOST COMMONLY USED VALUATION METHODS

1. *Discounted future earnings.* This method, discussed in Chapter 14, requires a projection of future income and the selection of a discount rate. The method is also dependent on the particular definition of income chosen.

2. *Capitalization of earnings.* This valuation technique is similar to the discounted future earnings approach. Capitalization of future earnings also requires the calculation of the present value of a future income stream. The acquirer is considered to obtain the right to a future income stream of indefinite length. The usefulness of this method also hinges on the definition of income and the selection of the capitalization rate.

3. *Earnings multiples.* This is a very common approach to valuing a privately held firm or a small business. Many business brokers, for example, simply use standard multiples of income or revenues as their basis for establishing the purchase price. Our discussion of the process of capitalization of earnings later in this chapter shows how the use of earnings multiples is tantamount to capitalizing earnings.

4. *Assets-oriented approaches.* There are several asset-oriented approaches, some of which are relevant to the valuation of both public and private businesses, and others are applied more frequently to privately held businesses. These approaches are fair market value, fair value, book value, and liquidation value. (Some of these methods were already discussed in Chapters 13 and 14. Therefore they will only be briefly highlighted here.)

Fair market value is the market value of the business. It is easier to obtain a value of a public company because a market exists for such a firm's stock. If there is an active market, for similar private businesses, this method can be used. Generally, however, fair market value is difficult to obtain since data on the sales of similar businesses tend to be limited. For this reason evaluators place more reliance on *fair value*, a method used when there is no market for the business. It is a dollar value that is derived through appraising the value of the tangible assets and determining the value of the intangible assets. These values are added together to determine the fair value of the business.

Book value is an accounting concept and is not a good measure of value. As discussed in Chapter 14, book value reflects the value of the assets as they are valued on the firm's books. It may or may not bear a close relationship to the market value of the firm's assets.

Finally, *liquidation value* is the estimated value of the firm's assets if they were sold off in liquidation. As discussed in Chapter 14, it may not be a good measure of a firm's value in an acquisition, but it may serve as a *floor value* for the valuation process.

Having provided an overview of the different valuation approaches, we will now detail some of the important issues related to these methods.

The Discounted Future Earnings or Net Present Value Approach

When the investment that is required to purchase the target firm is incorporated into the discounted future earnings, this method becomes the net present value. Therefore, the mechanics of using this approach will not be developed from the beginning. The methodology is the same as the net present value approach discussed in Chapter 14. However, its application and applicability to the valuation of a privately held firm may differ.

The discounted future earnings approach to valuing a business is based on the value of the future benefits that it will generate. These annual benefits, which may be defined in terms of earnings or cash flows, are then discounted back to present value to determine the current value of the future benefits. The purchase price, (I_0), is then subtracted from the discounted future benefits to determine net present value.

$$\text{NPV} = I_0 - \sum_{i=1}^{n} \frac{\text{FB}_1}{(1 + r)} + \cdots + \frac{\text{FB}_n}{(1 + r)^n} \qquad (15.1)$$

The discounted future earnings is not as widely used for privately held businesses as it is for publicly held companies. This is particularly the case for small and medium-sized, privately held companies. One reason why is that, in order to use this approach, we must construct a reliable projection of future earnings. This task may not be easily done with a smaller firm that may have more volatile sales. The revenues of privately held firms, especially small and medium-sized firms, are closely related to the activity and efforts of the owners of the business. They may have the ability to work harder and to influence the performance of the business. In contrast, larger companies may be less influenced by the actions of single individuals or groups.

An acquiring company cannot easily predict the level of effort that the owners of a business will exercise. They may reach an agreement that specifies that the previous owners will continue to work with the firm, but that does not mean that the previous owners will exercise the same level of effort as they did before the acquisition. Typically, the acquiring firm endeavors to create incentives, such as profit sharing, to ensure that they will exercise a full effort.

If the acquisition agreement specifies that the previous owners will not stay with the firm, then the acquirer has to make a judgment of what level of performance can be generated following the acquisition using a management team that the acquirer will put in place. This is difficult to do. On the other hand, if the acquiring company has had significant experience in this industry, then it may be more easily achieved.

The acquirer who chooses to use the discounted future earnings approach must select a discount rate. This choice is discussed in greater detail in the context of the capitalization of future earnings approach, which is more often used in the valuation of privately held businesses.

Discount Rate and Risk   The greater the risk associated with a given earnings stream, the higher the discount rate that will be used. If the projected income stream is thought to be a certainty, then a lower discount rate should be used. For high-risk income streams, a risk premium is added which will increase the discount rate. The use of a higher discount rate lowers the present value of each annual projected income amount.

Application of the Discounted Future Earnings Approach   Let's consider the case of a privately held company in which the owners are contemplating leaving the business and "cashing out" on their investment. Let's assume that the business is a family-owned company that has been in business for 15 years and has enjoyed a 5 percent average annual compounded rate of earnings growth for the last 10 years.

We begin the analysis by constructing optimistic, most likely, and pessimistic projection scenarios (Table 15.2). Based on the acquirer's knowledge of the industry and the 10-year track record of steady 5 percent earnings growth, a 5 percent annual rate of growth is assumed to be most likely. It is possible that the target could benefit from the improved management and enhanced technology that would be available when the acquirer took over the target and provided an infusion of capital. Therefore, a 7.5 percent rate of growth is judged to be optimistic but possible.

The acquiring firm did have concerns about losing key personnel after the acquisition. There was also a concern that, although there was an agreement that some of the previous management would continue to work with the firm for at least two years following the takeover, they might not apply the same level of effort as they did when they were

Table 15.2   OPTIMISTIC, MOST LIKELY, AND PESSIMISTIC PROJECTION SCENARIOS, 1990–1996

Year	Projected Earnings (thousand $)	Optimistic Scenario (7.5% growth) Discount Rates			
		20%	25%	30%	35%
1990	$10,750,000	$8,958,333	$8,600,000	$8,269,231	$7,962,963
1991	$11,556,250	$7,465,278	$6,880,000	$6,360,947	$5,898,491
1992	$12,422,969	$6,221,065	$5,504,000	$4,893,036	$4,369,253
1993	$13,354,691	$5,184,221	$4,403,200	$3,763,874	$3,236,483
1994	$14,356,293	$4,320,184	$3,522,560	$2,895,288	$2,397,395
1995	$15,433,015	$3,600,153	$2,818,048	$2,227,144	$1,775,848
1996	$16,590,491	$3,000,128	$2,254,438	$1,713,188	$1,315,443
Total		$38,749,361	$33,982,246	$30,122,707	$26,955,877
		Most Likely Scenario (5% growth)			
1990	$10,500,000	$8,750,000	$8,400,000	$8,076,923	$7,777,778
1991	$11,025,000	$7,291,667	$6,720,000	$6,213,018	$5,761,317
1992	$11,576,250	$6,076,389	$5,376,000	$4,779,244	$4,267,642
1993	$12,155,063	$5,063,657	$4,300,800	$3,676,342	$3,161,216
1994	$12,762,816	$4,219,715	$3,440,640	$2,827,955	$2,341,642
1995	$13,400,956	$3,516,429	$2,752,512	$2,175,350	$1,734,549
1996	$14,071,004	$2,930,357	$2,202,010	$1,673,346	$1,284,851
Total		$37,848,214	$33,191,962	$29,422,179	$25,702,651
		Pessimistic Scenario (2.5% growth)			
1990	$10,250,000	$8,541,667	$8,200,000	$7,884,615	$7,592,593
1991	$10,506,250	$7,118,056	$6,560,000	$6,065,089	$5,624,143
1992	$10,768,906	$5,931,713	$5,248,000	$4,665,453	$4,166,032
1993	$11,038,129	$4,943,094	$4,198,400	$3,588,810	$3,085,949
1994	$11,314,082	$4,119,245	$3,358,720	$2,760,623	$2,285,888
1995	$11,596,934	$3,432,704	$2,686,976	$2,123,556	$1,693,251
1996	$11,886,858	$2,860,587	$2,149,581	$1,633,505	$1,254,260
Total		$36,947,066	$32,401,677	$28,721,651	$25,702,115

owners. For this reason, the acquirer believed that a 2.5 percent rate of annual was possible. This rate is then taken to be the pessimistic alternative.

The last year's earnings of $10 million are taken as the base. The different rates of growth are applied to this dollar amount. See Table 15.2. Some obvious trends are apparent in the table. The higher the discount rate, the lower the future value of the earnings stream that is generated. The greater the rate of growth of earnings, the greater the present value of the future earnings stream.

In the optimistic scenario, a maximum purchase price between $26,955,877 and $38,749,361 could be paid for the firm, depending on the discount rate, and the acquisition would be advantageous. At a lower growth rate, such as 5 percent in the most likely scenario, the amount that could be paid, while still providing an acceptable rate of return, falls to between $25,702,651 and $37,848,214. At a 2.5 percent rate of growth, in the pessimistic case, the range falls still further to between $25,702,115 and $36,947,066.

As is easily discernible, there is considerable room for disagreement among evaluators of businesses. Depending on the analyst's assumptions regarding the growth rate and the discount rate, different conclusions as to the value of the business can be developed. It is, therefore, critical to develop sound estimates of both the growth rate and the level of risk of the business which, in turn, will provide guidance for selecting the appropriate discount rate. When the business has an extended earnings history in a mature industry, the growth rate assumptions may be relatively straightforward. If the earnings pattern has been stable, a low-risk discount rate should be chosen. On the other hand, when earnings have been high but volatile, the analyst may have less confidence in the earnings growth rate assumptions, and a higher, risk-adjusted, discount rate is in order. The selection of a "customized" discount rate will be discussed shortly.

Capitalization of Earnings

The capitalization process allows the business analyst to determine the present value of a business's future income. There is no specific ending period in the capitalization process, unlike the forecasting of future earnings where a forecast for a specific time period is used.

Some naive critics disparage the capitalization of earnings technique because, in their view, the process assumes that the business will be in existence for an infinite time period. This is not a valid criticism, inasmuch as monies that would be received an infinite number of years from now would be worth nothing given the time value of money. Moreover, the present value of income that is received further into the future is worth less and less. The more distant the income that will be received, the less valuable it is to an acquirer.

The terms *capitalization rate* and *discount rate* are sometimes used interchangeably. When a specific projection of income per period has been developed for a certain time period, then the term *discount rate* is used. When the task is to value a business that is capable of generating an income stream for an indefinite period of time, then the term *capitalization rate* is used.

Students of corporate finance are already familiar with capitalization when calculating the value of preferred and common stock. Consider a share of preferred stock that pays annual dividends of $4 per share. If the appropriate capitalization rate is 0.15, the value of a single share of preferred stock that pays a constant $4 annual dividend for an indefinite period of time is

$$P_s = \frac{\$4}{0.15} = \$26.67 \tag{15.1}$$

Thus, $26.67 is the present value of a perpetual income stream that yields $4 per year. (This does not take into account the possibility that the preferred stock might be retired.) The capitalization rate is 0.15. This rate, used to capitalize the $4 income stream, might be the company's rate of return on equity.

Choice of Income Definition   The choice of the specific definition of income to be capitalized is crucial to the capitalization process. As we have already seen, several alternative definitions of income can be used, including free cash flow, earnings before interest and taxes (EBIT), and earnings after taxes. The capitalized value of the business will vary depending on the definition chosen.

Selection of the Capitalization Rate   The capitalization rate should reflect the rate of return that is available in the marketplace on investments that are expected to produce a similar income stream. It therefore reflects the opportunity costs from investing the same amount of money (which is used to purchase the business) in a similar investment. The capitalization rate has to be "tailor made" for the type of income stream that the firm is expected to generate.

Two possible capitalization rates are the rate of return on investment (ROI) and the rate of return on equity.[14] ROI is the rate of return provided by the total invested capital in the business—including both debt and equity. It may include only long-term debt or both short- and long-term debt. If the firm's debt capital is composed of some long-term debt and some short-term debt that is "rolled over" each year, then the short-term debt is actually disguised long-term debt. It should therefore be considered part of the firm's permanent debt capital. Short-term debt that is clearly short term may be left out.

---

[14] Shannon Pratt, *Valuing Businesses and Professional Practices* (Homewood, Ill.: Dow Jones Irwin, 1986), pp. 125–127.

The rate of return on equity refers to the rate of return provided by the ownership interest in the business. This return measure considers a more narrow definition of capital than the rate of return on investment. Both ROI and the rate of return on equity can be computed on a pre-tax or post-tax basis. Given the problems with the reliability of post-tax income for privately held firms, pre-tax earnings should be used for closely held businesses and post-tax earnings for public companies.

Let's assume that a given privately held firm earns, on a pre-tax basis, $2 million. The total equity in the firm is $25 million, while the total borrowed capital is $20 million. The rate of return on investment and equity is computed as follows:

$$\text{Rate of return on investment} = \frac{\$2,000,000}{\$45,000,000} = 0.04\%$$

$$\text{Rate of return on equity} = \frac{\$2,000,000}{\$25,000,000} = 0.08\%$$

These two rates can then be used to capitalize the value of a business, which may yield a pre-tax income of $2 million:

The rate of return on investment as the capitalization rate is

$$\frac{\$2,000,000}{0.04} = \$5,000,000$$

The rate of return on equity as the capitalization rate is

$$\frac{\$2,000,000}{0.08} = \$2,500,000$$

Cost of Capital as the Capitalization Rate   In Chapter 14 we derived the cost of capital, which we then used to discount further income. The cost of capital is sometimes also used as the capitalization rate because it reflects the minimum acceptable rate of return for the firm. This includes a rate of return sufficient to meet the debt payments and to provide the expected rate of return on equity.

The Summation or Buildup Method   The capitalization rate can be determined by breaking the rate down into several component parts, a method termed the *summation* or *buildup method*. The three principal components are: (1) risk-free rate; (2) risk premium; (3) illiquidity premium.

  1. *Risk-free rate*. The risk-free rate is the rate of return that an investor would receive from a risk-free investment. In other

words, it is the rate of return provided when the investor parts with his or her invested capital but has complete assurance of receiving it back along with a return to compensate for forsaking consumption.

The rate of return on Treasury bills is considered the best proxy for a risk-free rate. T-bills have no default risk since the U.S. government is not expected to go out of business during the duration of this short-term investment. (They can have a maturity of up to one year.) The historical rate of return of Treasury bills is shown in Figure 15.1. T-bills are also somewhat free of interest rate risk. This is the risk that an adverse movement in interest rates will cause the value of the T-bill, which pays a fixed rate, to fall. In contrast, long-term Treasury securities are more influenced by interest rate movements.

2. *Risk premium.* At least two kinds of risk are relevant to acquiring a business: business risk and interest rate risk (see Chapter 10). Business risk is the risk that the company being acquired may not perform up to the level of expectation set forth at the time of acquisition. This expectation is built into the acquisition price. Failure to live up to it will cause the investment to pay lower returns. In the extreme case, business risk can mean the default of the business. With a default, the return is considerably less than the level of expectations but not necessarily a zero return.

Interest rate risk is the risk of adverse movements in interest rates. Specifically, it is the risk that other investments will provide a higher rate of return, while the investment in question, the acquisition of a business, pays a more or less constant return. The acquisition of a business does not present as great an interest rate risk as investments such as fixed income securities. Fixed income securities, such as government or corporate bonds, usually offer a fixed rate. Increases in interest rates or inflation will erode the value of the fixed payment stream.

The revenue and income of a business will normally adjust to increases in the rate of inflation unless the business is in an industry that tends to lag behind the movements in the inflationary process. Therefore, interest rate risk is a lesser concern to acquisitions of businesses than to investments in fixed income securities. It is relevant, however, to determining the appropriate risk premium since the analyst may use as benchmarks the rate of return on fixed income securities. The level of business and interest rate risk that is internalized into the market's de-

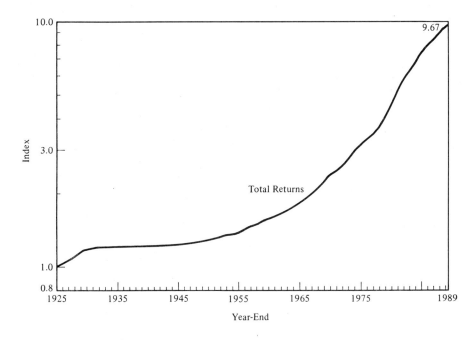

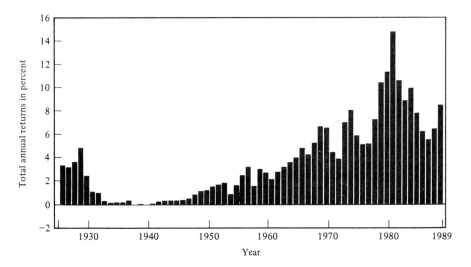

Figure 15.1 U.S. Treasury bills: return indices and returns, 1926–1989. (*Source:* ©
Ibbotson, Roger G., and Rex A. Sinquefield, *Stocks, Bonds, Bills, and Inflation* (SBBI),
updated in *Stocks, Bonds, Bills and Inflation 1990 Yearbook*™, Ibbotson Associates,
Chicago. All rights reserved.)

termination of the rate on the security being used as a proxy for the capitalization rate needs to be considerd.

A wide variety of benchmarks can be considered as guides for the appropriate risk premium. The risk premium is the difference between the rate offered on another investment that has a similar level of risk. Among these benchmarks, *long-term government bonds* can be considered first. They contain virtually the same level of default risk as their short-term counterparts, T-bills, but they carry greater interest rate risk. For this reason, it is not surprising that the normal shape of the Treasury securities' yield curve is upward sloping, reflecting the fact that longer term securities normally command higher rates of return (Figure 15.2). The level of risk associated with long-term government securities will be significantly less than that associated with the acquisition of a business. The historical rate of return of long-term government securities is shown in Figure 15.3.

The rates offered on *corporate bonds* reflect more business risk than those on government securities and are ranked according to default risk by the major rating agencies such as Standard and Poor's and Moody's. The historical rates of return on high-grade, long-term corporate bonds are shown in Figure 15.4. (For the relationship between these ratings and the rates offered on the rated securities, see Chapter 8.) The lower the security's rating, the higher the rate of return. Most privately held businesses will generally have significantly higher risk than the highly rated companies. Therefore, the rates offered on Triple AAA- or AA-rated companies may not encompass the level of risk associated with smaller, privately held firms. The rates of-

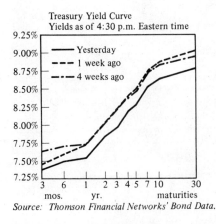

Treasury Yield Curve
Yields as of 4:30 p.m. Eastern time

— Yesterday
--- 1 week ago
—·— 4 weeks ago

Source: Thomson Financial Networks' Bond Data.

Figure 15.2 Treasury yield curve. (*Source: Wall Street Journal,* October 5, 1990, p. C5. Reprinted by permission of the Wall Street Journal, copyright © Dow Jones & Company, Inc., 1990. All Rights Reserved Worldwide.)

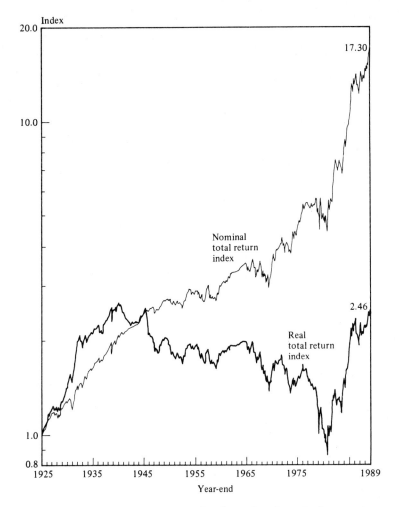

Figure 15.3 Long-term government bonds: real and nominal return indices, 1926–1989. (*Source:* © Ibbotson, Roger G., and Rex A. Sinquefield, *Stocks, Bonds, Bills, and Inflation* (SBBI), updated in *Stocks, Bonds, Bills and Inflation 1990 Yearbook*™, Ibbotson Associates, Chicago. All rights reserved.)

fered on high-yield junk bonds may be a more useful benchmark for the risk premium on private business acquisitions. These securities, rated BB or lower, may offer rates of almost 20 percent. They contain both business risk and liquidity risk since the secondary market for junk bonds is weak.

Numerous other securities can be used as benchmarks for the risk premium. Most of these will contain less risk than junk bonds and, therefore, will not be as useful. An example would

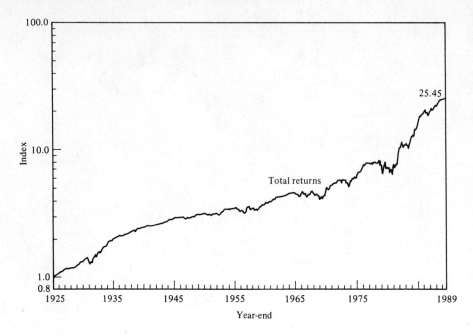

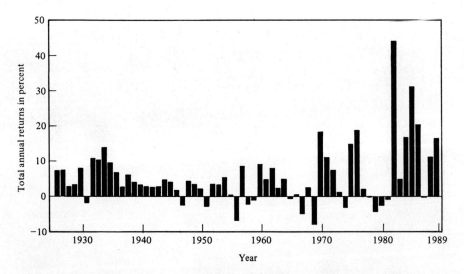

Figure 15.4 Long-term corporate bonds: return indices and returns, 1926–1989. (*Source:* © Ibbotson, Roger G., and Rex A. Sinquefield, *Stocks, Bonds, Bills, and Inflation* (SBBI), updated in *Stocks, Bonds, Bills and Inflation 1990 Yearbook*™, Ibbotson Associates, Chicago. All rights reserved.)

be municipal bonds. Given that the income stream generated by a privately held firm may be even more risky than the income stream derived from a junk bond investment which may carry municipal bond insurance, less risky investments such as many municipal bonds may not warrant consideration.

Bonds offer less default risk than equity investments, providing more protection for the investor in the event of default and bankruptcy since the bondholder will have access to the liquidation proceeds prior to equity investors. Equity investors will usually get a small percentage of their investment back, if anything. Equities contain greater risk and reward potential than debt securities offered by the same company. For this reason, the difference between the rates offered on equities of comparable companies and on T-bills may be used as a partial measure of the risk premium. The historical rates of return on common stock are shown in Figures 15.5 and 15.6.

Although the privately held company may be comparable to some companies that are traded on the New York Stock Exchange, comparable companies will more likely be found on other public exchanges such as the American Stock Exchange, the Pacific Stock Exchange, or the Philadelphia Stock Exchange. It may even be more likely that a comparable company will be found on the over-the-counter market. The OTC market contains companies that may not fulfill the requirements to be traded on an organized exchange. They are generally smaller with a lower total capitalization. These firms are usually considered riskier.

The most generally available data sources are the *Wall Street Journal* and the *New York Times*. These publications provide daily quotes on the current rates offered on a variety of categories of securities described here. For historical data on rates of return many sources are available, one of the more authoritative being the Ibbotson Associates' *Stocks, Bonds, Bills and Inflation*.

3. *Illiquidity premium.*   Small capitalization stocks that are traded on the New York Stock Exchange are relatively liquid investments. This liquidity is provided by the reputation of the New York Stock Exchange and the Exchange's efforts to facilitate, through a system of specialists in each security, a liquid market that is somewhat free from sudden, large swings in prices. The acquirer of a company does not have the advantage of having a liquid investment. Some businesses are more marketable than others. The acquirer who wants to liquidate his or her invest-

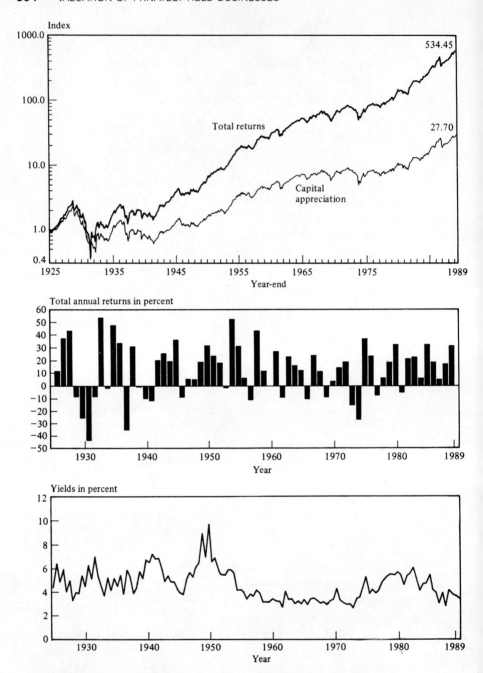

Figure 15.5 Common stocks: return indices, returns, and yields, 1926–1989. (*Source:* © Ibbotson, Roger G., and Rex A. Sinquefield, *Stocks, Bonds, Bills, and Inflation* (SBBI), updated in *Stocks, Bonds, Bills and Inflation 1990 Yearbook™*, Ibbotson Associates, Chicago. All rights reserved.)

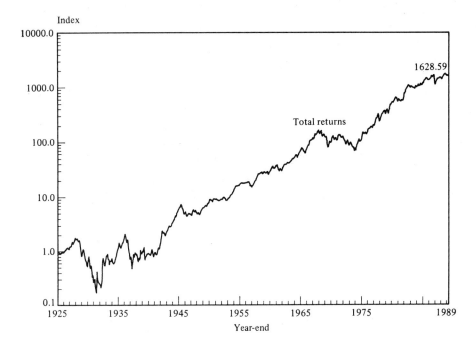

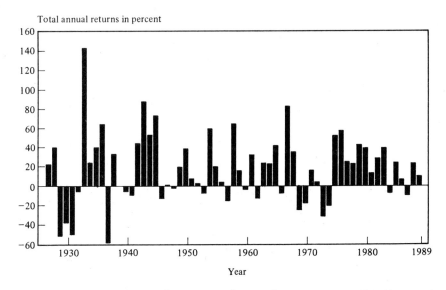

Figure 15.6 Small company stocks: return indices and returns, 1926–1989. (*Source:* ©
Ibbotson, Roger G., and Rex A. Sinquefield, *Stocks, Bonds, Bills, and Inflation* (SBBI),
updated in *Stocks, Bonds, Bills and Inflation 1990 Yearbook*™, Ibbotson Associates,
Chicago. All rights reserved.)

ment might have to wait an extended period of time before selling or suffer a large loss. For this reason, an illiquidity premium must be added to the risk premium derived above.

One proxy for the illiquidity premium might be the rates offered on OTC stocks. Many of the stocks traded on the OTC market have thin markets with low daily trading volume. Because they have a small number of market makers, there is less protection from larger price swings. The sale of a large block of a firm's outstanding equity can greatly depress the stock prices. For this reason, many OTC stocks are considered less liquid investments. Therefore, the rates of return provided by firms that are in the same industry and of similar size can be regarded as a guide to the illiquidity premium. This premium might be part of the difference in the rate of return between the OTC company and a comparable company on the New York Stock Exchange. Unfortunately, an investment in OTC equities may be more liquid than the acquisition of a privately held company. An even higher illiquidity premium, therefore, may need to be derived.

One benchmark that can be used is the rate of return demanded by venture capitalists who make equity investments in small, start-up companies. They usually demand a marked higher rate of return than that offered by the more conventional investments. These rates incorporate both risk and illiquidity premiums. Venture capitalists look for 25 to 50 percent (or sometimes more) compounded annual rates of return, depending on the stage of development of the company and the degree of risk. One business broker says that 30 to 40 percent is a typically required discount rate for a service business in his area of the country, and a slightly lower rate applies to manufacturing, wholesaling and product distribution businesses.[15]

Example of the Buildup Method   The summation or buildup method uses the risk-free rate as the base and adds various premiums that are determined by the risk characteristics of the company being evaluated. Consider the case of an athletic goods manufacturer that manufactures and markets under its own brand name. The firm has been in existence for six years and has experienced rapid growth during the past four years. Annual sales are $80 million. The industry is highly competitive but is also growing fairly rapidly. The company has received

---

[15] Ibid., p. 142.

overtures from its larger rivals to sell the firm. The CEO of this closely held company wants to know what value his company should command in the marketplace. Since there are no other comparable recent acquisitions, it is difficult to look to other recent transactions for guidance.

The appropriate capitalization rate can be determined as follows:

	T-bills as of August 30, 1989
Risk-free rate	8.2%
Rate recently offered on junk bonds of a publicly held company in the same industry	21%
Additional illiquidity and risk premium	10%

Based on market data at the time of the offer, the junk bonds of a publicly held company that is traded on the OTC market provides a 21 percent rate of return. This rate of return includes a risk premium represented by the fact that the proxy company is a medium-sized company and the securities are considered risky. There is also an illiquidity premium in the 21 percent rate of return, showing that the junk bond market is not a very liquid market.

An additional illiqudity and risk premium is necessary. The $80 million company that may be sold is smaller than the $1 billion company that is used as a proxy firm. The larger proxy firm is traded publicly and has been in business for 18 years. In addition, the junk bonds that were offering a 21 percent rate of return are more liquid than the $80 million private company as a whole. The exact additional risk and illiquidity premium chosen is a matter of judgment and experience. Since the rates of return required by venture capitalists were in the 40 to 50 percent range at the time of the offer, an additional 10 percent, which would make the capitalization rate 31 percent, might be a reasonable and conservative premium.

The Capitalization Rate and Earnings Growth   The capitalization rate derived from the summation method can be adjusted to reflect an expected high rate of growth in the target's earnings. This adjustment is made by subtracting the expected rate of growth from the capitalization rate.

Consider the example of a firm with $1 million in annual earnings. Let's assume that the summation method provided a capitalization rate of 45 percent. Let's also assume that the firm has exhibited a steady annual rate of growth in excess of 15 percent. A conservative evaluation might assume that a 10 percent rate of growth would be continued into the foreseeable future. The evaluation would be as follows:

$$\text{Value of the firm} = \frac{\$1,000,000}{0.45 - 0.10} = \$2,857,143$$

The adjusted capitalization rate was 33 percent.

Use of the P/E Ratio for the Capitalization Rate

The price-earnings ratio can be used as a guide to the capitalization rate. Since the capitalization rate is the reciprocal of the P/E ratio, the higher the P/E ratio, the lower the capitalization rate.

$$\text{Capitalization rate} = \frac{1}{\text{P/E ratio}}$$

The price-earnings ratio can be calculated by using the current or most recent year's earnings or by using projected earnings. It is more common to use current or the most recent year's earnings.[16]

The P/E ratio reflects the amount an investor is willing to pay for the firm's earnings on a per share basis. For example, on September 6, 1989, the fast-food chain, McDonald's, showed a P/E ratio of 16, which implies a low capitalization rate of 6.75 percent. In a valuation of privately held firms, the analyst determines the P/E ratio of comparable public companies or the industry average P/E ratio. We must use caution in applying the P/E-derived capitalization rate. Simply because a notable food chain sells for 16 times its current earnings does not mean that the buyer of a privately held food chain should seek only a 6.75 percent rate of return. This capitalization rate needs to be adjusted to reflect the relevant types of risk for the firm being evaluated.

It is necessary to examine other food chains and to compare their P/E ratios. An industry P/E average should also be considered. In addition, the trend in the market needs to be factored into the analysis. The P/E ratio of 16 for McDonald's came at a time when the market was reaching all-time highs. A more "average" market might show a lower P/E ratio and thus a higher capitalization rate.

The P/E ratio may not be useful if the expected rate of growth in earnings for the privately held company is very different from the P/Es of proxy firms. If the proxy firms, and the industry as a whole, are considered mature and have leveled off at a lower rate of growth, then their P/E ratios will not be comparable to those of the privately

---

[16] Sidney Cottle, Roger F. Murray, and Frank E. Block, *Graham and Dood's Security Analysis*, 5th ed. (New York: McGraw-Hill, 1988), p. 346.

held firm that might be growing at a rapid rate of growth. In this event, the analyst will have to look elsewhere, such as to the summation method, for the appropriate capitalization rate.

The use of the P/E ratio is a market-based method of determining the capitalization rate since the ratios that are used are determined by a market process. It is also an earnings rather than an asset-oriented approach. This attribute can be attractive when the firm being valued has many assets of questionable market value. The use of the P/E ratio is also a future-oriented approach since buyers of the firm's stock are concerned about the firm's future earning power and not just current earnings.

The P/E Ratio and the Payback Method   The payback method states that a project should not be accepted if the expected cumulative net cash flows do not equal the purchase price within a predetermined time period. The P/E ratio is roughly equal to the number of years an acquisition is expected to pay for itself. For example, a buyer who pays a sum that is equal to eight times the target's earnings shows that the buyer is willing to wait eight years to have the acquisition pay for itself.

The Capitalization Rate and the Payback Period   Since the P/E ratio can be equated with the payback period, the capitalization rate, which is the reciprocal of the P/E ratio, can also be equated with it. The capitalization rate must, therefore, also be equal to the reciprocal of the payback period.

$$\text{Capitalization rate} = \frac{1}{\text{Payback period}}$$

For example, an acquirer with a four-year payback period would value a firm with $500,000 in earnings as follows:

$$\text{Capitalization rate} = \frac{1}{4 \text{ years}} = 0.25$$

$$\text{Value of the company} = \frac{\$500,000}{0.25} = \$2,000,000$$

Using the assumptions about the buyer's payback period as a guide to the capitalization rate has certain disadvantages. The payback period does not take into account the time value of money. This method of evaluating projects would value two projects or acquisitions that have the same payback period as equally good purchases. One company, however, may return 65 percent of the total purchase price within the first three years, whereas the other might have paid only 20 percent of the total purchase price within this time period, even though the payback period was the same. Given the time value of money, the discounted future earnings approach might reach a very different conclusion about the relative merits of these two approaches.

EARNINGS MULTIPLES AND CAPITALIZATION RATES

The P/E ratio is an example of the use of earnings multiples in the valuation process. The capitalization rate is the reciprocal of the earnings multiple. Earnings multiples are frequently used in the valuation of privately held firms and small businesses.[17]

Some market multiples are unique to each industry. For example, a real estate agency might sell for between one and two times net operating profits, with 1.5 being the most typical.[18] The multiplier of 1.5 implies a capitalization rate of 0.67. It is ironic that, although the use of earnings multiples in small business valuation is quite common, many users are not familiar with capitalization rates, even though the use of the multiple is tantamount to using the capitalization of earnings method.

SUMMARY

This chapter discussed several of the more commonly used approaches to valuing a privately held business. In addition to the asset-oriented approaches highlighted in Chapter 14, the use of the discounted future earnings and capitalization of future earnings methods were explained. These techniques are quite sensitive to the choice of discount rate or capitalization rate. The rate chosen must reflect the risk characteristics of the firm being evaluated. A market-derived proxy rate that has similar risk characteristics and a similar built-in risk premium can then be selected to serve as the capitalization rate. Many proxy rates are available, including the rates offered on Treasury securities, corporate bonds, and the equities of larger and small firms.

Analysts must be careful in using market-derived measures as a proxy for the capitalization rate for a privately held firm that lacks a public market in its equities. The lack of a public market may mean that the equity of the private firm is less liquid. Therefore, an illiquidity

---

[17] Glenn Desmond and John Marcello, *Handbook of Small Business Valuation* (Marina Del Rey, Calif.: Valuation Press, 1988).

[18] Ibid., p. 233.

premium may have to be added to the proxy rate to derive a fuller risk adjustment. The use of the rate of return for junk bonds, which have equity characteristics and are less liquid than higher rated bonds and equities, can help account for some of this illiquidity.

It may be more difficult to value privately held businesses than public firms, primarily because the large supply of information and readily available reports that are available for the large public firms are not available for their privately held counterparts. The analyst of a private firm may have to conduct a more original study than the public firm analyst. The methods and data used in valuing private firms may differ more across analysts than is true for public firms. For this reason, we need to exercise more care when considering the results of these analyses.

REFERENCES

"Accounting Changes." *Accounting Principles Board Opinion,* no. 20, July 1971.

Araskog, Rand. *The ITT Wars.* New York: Henry Holt & Co., 1989.

Cottle, Sidney, Roger F. Murray, and Frank E. Block. *Graham and Dood's Security Analysis,* 5th ed. New York: McGraw-Hill, 1988.

Executive Compensation Service, American Management Association, Karen Tracy, *Executive Compensation: Selected References.* Cambridge, Mass.: Harvard University Press, 1990.

Fama, Eugene. "Agency Problems and the Theory of the Firm." *Journal of Political Economy* (April 1980):288–307.

Gaughan, Patrick A., and Henry Fuentes. "Taxable Income and Lost Profits Litigation." *Journal of Forensic Economics,* 1991 (forthcoming).

"GM Splits Its Basic Stock 2 for 1." *Wall Street Journal,* February 7, 1989, p. A3.

Jensen, Michael, and William Meckling. "Theory of the Firm: Managerial Behavior, Agency Costs and Ownership Structure." *Journal of Financial Economics* 3 (October 1976):305–360.

Kieso, Donald, and Jerry Weygandt. *Intermediate Accounting.* New York: John Wiley & Sons, 1986.

Moyer, Charles, James McGuigan, and William Kretlow. *Contemporary Financial Management.* St. Paul, Minn.: West Publishing Co., 1984.

Pratt, Shannon. *Valuing a Business*. 2nd ed. Homewood, Ill.: Dow Jones Irwin, 1989.

Pratt, Shannon. *Valuing Businesses and Professional Practices*. Homewood, Ill.: Dow Jones Irwin, 1986.

Siegel, Joel. *How to Analyze Businesses, Financial Statements and the Quality of Earnings*. Englewood Cliffs, N.J.: Prentice-Hall, 1982.

Wendell, Paul J. *Corporate Controllers Manual*. Boston: Warren, Gorham and Lamont, 1989.

Chapter
16

Case Studies in Mergers and Acquisitions

DUNKIN DONUTS CASE STUDY[1]

*D*unkin Donuts is the largest coffee and donut chain in the United States. As of 1989, the company has 1,764 shops throughout the world. The firm, founded in 1950 in Quincy, Massachusetts, has expanded its product line over the years to include sandwiches and a wider selection of beverages so that it can cater to the breakfast and luncheon trade. Much of the firm's growth came between 1968 and 1973. Nonetheless, the firm posted a loss of approximately $1.5 million in 1973. It responded to the loss by slowing its rate of expansion.

Following the fall-off in profitability, Dunkin Donuts changed its expansion emphasis from the number of units to sales at existing units. The company also began to make a more careful evaluation of individuals selected to own franchises, thereby enhancing the quality of its franchise network. In 1985, the firm expanded beyond its traditional coffee and donut business, entering into an agreement with Chili's, Inc. to develop Chili's Bar & Grill restaurants. By 1989, it had opened nine such restaurants.

---

[1] This case study is a joint effort by Patrick A. Gaughan, Janet Gabrielo, and Mona Shahad.

Table 16.1 DUNKIN DONUTS' REAL ESTATE
OPERATIONS

Status	Number of Units
Own land and building	215
Own building/lease land	345
Lease land and building	382
No real estate interest	727

VALUATION OF INCOME BY SOURCE

Dunkin Donuts' main sources of revenue are its rental and franchise fee income.[2] The business is so structured that the company owns a small number of units and franchises the remaining ones, giving the company franchise fee income for the use of the company's name and know-how. The company's other major source of income, rental income, comes from a number of major real estate holdings (Table 16.1).

The rental income provides stable cash flows that can be used to service debt. A breakdown of the excess cash flow from the real estate part of the business, as represented by the difference between rental income and cash rental expenses, is shown in Table 16.2. The table shows that Dunkin Donuts' ability to service debt rose in the late 1980s. Based on a valuation multiple of eight times cash flow, the real estate division of the company was worth $216 million in 1988, or $34 per share.

Dunkin Donuts' franchise fee income is approximately equal to 5 percent of sales. The company also receives between $20,000 and $40,000 for each new unit that is opened, resulting in the income stream shown in Table 16.3. Using the same eight times cash flow multiple that was used to value the real estate cash flow, we find that the franchise fee income equals $152 million, or approximately $24 per share.

In addition to rental and franchise fee income, Dunkin Donuts owned 29 shops in 1988, which produced approximately $4 million in cash flows. Using the cash flow multiple of 8, we observe that this is valued at $32 million or approximately $5 per share.

Combined Cash Flow Valuation

The three sources of cash flow as of 1988 are shown in Table 16.4 and Figure 16.1 (on page 616).

---

[2] Based on data provided by Arnon Deshe.

Table 16.2   REAL ESTATE CASH FLOWS, 1985–1988 (MILLION $)

Income/expenditures	1988 (est.)	1987	1986	1985
Rental income	$41.0	$38.5	$35.4	$32.8
Cash rental expenses[a]	14.0	12.8	11.7	11.5
Cash flow	$27.0	$25.7	$23.7	$21.3

[a] Includes roughly $2 debt service on $10 in mortgages.

Source: Data provided by Arnon Deshe.

Table 16.3   FRANCHISE FEE INCOME, 1985–1988 (MILLION $)

Income/expenditures	1988 (est.)	1987	1986	1985
Fee income	$35.0	$32.7	$28.8	$25.6
Cash rental expenses	16.0	15.0	11.2	10.1
Cash flow	$19.0	$17.7	$17.6	$15.5

Source: Data provided by Arnon Deshe.

Applying the cash flow multiple of 8 to the combined cash flow of $50, we see that Dunkin Donuts can be valued at $400 million, or approximately $63 per share. If the market were willing to apply a higher multiple, such as 10, the value would rise to $500 million or approximately $79.

MARKET VALUATION

During mid-1988, Dunkin Donuts stock traded in the mid-$20 range. Based on 8 to 10 cash flow multiples, Dunkin Donuts was significantly undervalued in the mid-1980s, making the firm vulnerable for a take-

Table 16.4   COMBINED CASH FLOWS, 1988 (MILLION $)

Source	Amount
Real estate	$27.0
Franchise fees	$19.0
Company-owned units	$ 4.0
Total	$50.0

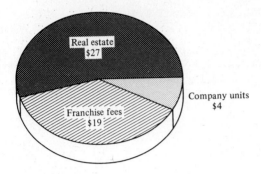

Figure 16.1 Cash flow breakdown, Dunkin Donuts, 1988 (million $).

over. The cash flows from the real estate assets could be used to service
debt that a bidder might assume to finance the takeover. Moreover,
the real estate assets could be used as security for creditors, thereby
enhancing a bidder's ability to raise the necessary debt capital to finance
the bid. It is important to note that the valuation year of 1988 precedes
the major downturn in the real estate market. If the valuation year was
1990 the same multiple might not apply given that the real estate
market was severely depressed and real estate assets lost much of their
marketability.

OFFSETTING FACTORS

Competition

Dunkin Donuts' primary business is fast food, a highly competitive
business characterized by intense price and promotional competition.
The industry appears to have reached maturity, as reflected in the small
rise in sales by fast-food restaurants in 1988 (only 1.7 percent). This
was the smallest increase in any five-year period prior to 1988.

Dunkin Donuts was somewhat insulated from most of this competition, which was directed mainly at hamburger chains such as Mc-
Donald's, Burger King, and Wendy's. Once these firms expanded their
product lines, however, and entered into the breakfast market, Dunkin
Donuts became more vulnerable to these competitive pressures in the
late 1980s.

Labor Costs

In the late 1980s, the labor market became increasingly tight for employers. The unemployment rate hovered around 5.3 percent. Fast-

food marketers were forced to raise wages to compete for workers. Moreover, the pool of young workers, which fast-food chains rely on for inexpensive labor, shrank in the 1980s. The U.S. Department of Labor showed that workers between 16 and 24 years of age represented only 16.3 percent of the civilian labor force in 1989, down from 19.8 percent in 1986. Much of Dunkin Donuts' business is concentrated in the northeastern United States where the labor shortage is even worse. This implies higher labor costs and lower profit margins if conditions remain the same or worsen in the 1990s.

Chili's Restaurant Division Loss

The Chili's restaurant division lost approximately $2 million in 1987. In addition, Dunkin Donuts had to invest $4 million in building two new Chili's restaurants. Seven more units were planned for 1988. This imposed a drain on the firm's capital and reduced its borrowing capacity.

ANTITAKEOVER MEASURES

During the late 1980s, Dunkin Donuts was undervalued by the market, making it vulnerable to a hostile takeover. As a preventative measure, the firm adopted various antitakeover measures. These measures, which were consistent with Delaware's corporation laws, included the super-majority provision, classified board, ESOP, convertible preferred stock, and poison pills.

Supermajority Provision

Dunkin Donuts amended its articles of incorporation so that a vote of 75 percent of the outstanding shares was required for approval of mergers.

Classified Board

Dunkin Donuts adopted a classified board voting structure whereby only one-third of the board can be replaced in any given election. According to this provision, a majority of the board could be achieved only after a second annual stockholders meeting following a takeover.

Employee Stock Ownership Plan (ESOP)

Dunkin Donuts adopted an ESOP on April 20, 1989, selling 1.1 million shares to the newly established ESOP for $35.25 per share. The ESOP was a leveraged employee stock ownership plan funded by a loan from the company in the amount of $38,702,633.

Convertible Preferred Stock

On May 30, 1989, Dunkin Donuts sold 28,000 shares of convertible preferred stock to General Electric Capital Corporation for $28 million. The preferred stock provided a 10 percent cash dividend that would increase semiannually up to a maximum of 11.5 percent. The preferred shares were convertible into common stock, at the holder's option, at $40 per share in the event the company was taken over. Dunkin Donuts could redeem these convertible preferred shares at any time at par plus at initially a 10 percent premium. The redemption premium was set to decline each year until December 1993 when it would remain at a minimum of 2.5 percent. This defense is similar to a combination of a white squire and a poison pill.

Poison Pills

In October 1987, the company distributed as a dividend one right for each share outstanding. The rights were a poison pill that would allow the right holders to purchase shares at half price if a bidder were to announce an offer to acquire 20 percent of the firm's outstanding stock or to make a tender offer for 30 percent of the firm's outstanding stock. The rights were convertible into either participating preferred stock or common stock depending on the occurrence of particular events. The poison pills could be redeemed by a two-thirds vote of the board of directors for $0.01 per right.

EFFECT OF THE ANTITAKEOVER MEASURES

As discussed in Chapter 5, antitakeover measures do not guarantee a firm's independence, but they may improve a target's bargaining position, in turn, increasing the premium offered by bidding firms.

STOCK OWNERSHIP

As of the end of 1988, institutional investors owned 52 percent of the outstanding stock of Dunkin Donuts, the five largest of these holdings accounting for 28 percent. This larger concentration of shares in the hands of institutions increases the firm's vulnerability to a takeover. At one point, insider holders accounted for as much as 13 percent of the outstanding stock. This declined to 9 percent toward the late 1980s.

As of October 1987, Dunkin Donuts had approximately 7.78 million shares outstanding, a total that also included 0.4 million shares of Treasury stock. The company later instituted a shares repurchase program at an average price of $25.44 per share. This reduced the total number of shares outstanding to 6.4 million shares. The large holdings by institutions, as well as the decline in insider holdings, increased the firm's vulnerability to a takeover.

FINANCIAL RATIO ANALYSIS

A financial ratio analysis of Dunkin Donuts is shown below. The ratios include liquidity, activity, leverage, and performance ratios. In addition to the firm and industry average for each ratio, Table 16.5 also shows the degree of dispersion of the industry ratios that make up the average through the variance and standard deviation. These variability measures provide information on the degree of central tendency of the components that make up the industry average, thereby providing an indication of the reliability of the industry averages.

Table 16.5 presents an analysis of various financial ratios for five years ending 1988.

Liquidity Ratios

Quick Ratio

	Actual	Industry
Ratio	0.7	0.4
Standard deviation	0.13	0.04

Current Ratio

	Firm	Industry
Ratio	1.0	0.5
Standard deviation	0.15	0.04

Table 16.5   STATISTICAL ANALYSIS OF ACTUAL VERSUS INDUSTRY RATIOS FOR
FIVE YEARS ENDED 1988

	Mean		Variance		Standard Deviation	
	Firm	Industry	Firm	Industry	Firm	Industry
Quick ratio	0.7	0.4	0.0176	0.0016	0.133	0.040
Current ratio	0.8	0.6	0.0234	0.0016	0.153	0.040
Debt to equity	0.9	4.4	0.0192	1.6064	0.138	1.267
Net fixed assets to equity	1.5	3.4	0.0087	0.5864	0.094	0.766
Sales to working capital	−321.5	−27.3	324299.5266	3.9904	569.473	1.998
Interest coverage	9.2	2.5	6.2654	0.0136	2.503	0.117
Inventory turnover	32.7	38.4	27.9955	6.2440	5.291	2.499
Return on equity (ROE)%	32.9	34.3	2.4707	10.7696	1.572	3.282
Return on assets (ROA)%	17.4	8.1	2.0420	1.2504	1.429	1.118

Since Dunkin Donuts was quite liquid as of 1988, this implies that the company should not have any difficulty meeting its current obligations as they become due.

Activity Ratios

The activity ratio selected here is inventory turnover.

Inventory Turnover

	Firm	Industry
Ratio	29.1	36.3
Standard deviation	5.29	2.50

Although this ratio is lower than the industry norm, this is not a source of concern given the nature of the firm's business.

Leverage Ratios

The debt to equity ratio is used as an indicator of the degree of financial leverage of Dunkin Donuts. The interest coverage ratio is then used to measure the firm's ability to service this debt.

Debt to Equity

	Firm	Industry
Ratio	1.0	6.7
Standard deviation	0.14	1.27

Interest Coverage

	Firm	Industry
Ratio	9.7	2.4
Standard deviation	2.5	0.12

Dunkin Donuts has a significantly lower level of debt than other firms in this industry. It also easily covers its interest charges. This implies that it has much unused debt capacity that could make it vulnerable to a takeover.

Profitability Ratios

The performance of the firm is partly reflected in the return on equity and return on assets.

Return on Equity

	Firm	Industry
Ratio	31.2	37.4
Standard deviation	1.57	3.28

Return on Assets

	Firm	Industry
Ratio	15.6	6.8
Standard deviation	1.43	1.12

Table 16.6 DUNKIN DONUTS CAPITALIZATION TABLE ($000's)

Percent Funded	Amount Funded	Method	Rate (%)	Derivation Rates as of 4/27/90
20%	$64,000	Revolver	12.06	3.50 + 8.56 Libor
34%	$110,000	Senior notes (floating)	12.55	3.50 + 9.50 5 yr. Treasury
29%	$95,000	Senior notes	12.55	3.50 + 9.50 5 yr. Treasury
7%	$23,500	Jr. subordinated	13.84	4.75 + 9.09 7 yr. Treasury
10%	$32,500	C.S. @ $50	N/A	
100%	$325,000			

Although the return on equity is somewhat below industry norms, the return on assets is higher than that in the industry generally. Both measures, however, are of limited value; therefore, an analyst should not place too much emphasis on them. The industry average for the return on equity is skewed, as are most of the industry norms used in this section, by the larger fast-food chains that are not very similar to Dunkin Donuts. The company's return on assets is also affected by the fact that the firm's real estate assets are not carried on its books at their appropriate market value.

FINANCING STRUCTURE AND CASH FLOW ANALYSIS

Based on the $50 per share or $325 million total price derived above, we can construct a capital structure of the buyout. The capital structure and the payout schedule are shown in Tables 16.6 and 16.7, respectively.

THE TAKEOVER PROCESS

Dunkin Donuts became the target of a hostile bid in May 1989. For the chronology of the bidding process, see the accompanying outline.

Chronological Order of Events

Dunkin Donuts ("Dunkin' ") and the Kingsbridge Group had discussions prior to April 1989.

4/89	Board of directors approves an ESOP plan. Dunkin's first takeover defense.
5/31/89	Kingsbridge purchases Dunkin's shares of 370,000 on the open market; owns 12% of the company and makes a $42 bid for Dunkin'.

5/31/89	Dunkin' finds a white squire. Sells 28,000 shares of preferred stock for $28MM to General Electric Capital which are convertible to 700,000 shares of common stock at $40 per share in 1990.
6/12/89	Dunkin' authorizes the buyback of 1.4 MM shares of stock on the open market to get the shares into friendly hands.
7/1/89	$43 bid: Value Line says the bid should be closer to $50.
7/10/89	Dunkin' rejects $43 bid. The $43 share offer is extended to 7/27.
7/26/89	Dunkin' obtains an injunction in the U.S. district court against the pending tender offer by Kingsbridge.
8/8/89	$43 share extended to 8/15.
8/22/89	DD acquisition is willing to increase its offer from $43 to $45 if takeover defenses are overturned.
8/29/89	DD acquisition's $45 bid is conditional on at least 50.1% shares being tendered and removal of Dunkin's poison pill which expires September 15.
9/11/89	Dunkin' rejects $45 offer saying it's inadequate.
9/12/89	Dunkin' will now explore the possibility of an LBO.
9/13/89	Dunkin' agrees to meet with DD acquiring executives (joint venture of Unicorp Canada and Cara Operations).
9/28/89	In an effort to explore possibilities, franchise owners offer to help finance the LBO.
9/29/89	$45 offer extended to 10/16.
10/16/89	$45 offer extended to 11/1.
10/24/89	Dunkin' is ready to accept proposals. November 10 is the last day for competing bids. DD acquisition is challenging Dunkin's takeover defenses in the Delaware court of chancery. They allege that Dunkin' has diverted a substantial portion of Dunkin's value to themselves in the form of "golden parachutes" contracts. DD acquisiton said these contracts will cost Dunkin' at least $16MM.
11/1/89	DD acquisition's $45 offer extended to November 20. At the close of business 38.5% of the outstanding shares are tendered.
11/10/89	Dunkin's board extends the deadline for proposals to November 15.
11/17/89	Allied–Lyons PLC, a major British drinks group, agrees to buy Dunkin' in a $325 million cash bid at $47.25 a share. Allied feels Dunkin' would be a good strategic fit. Allied–Lyons' proposal is subject to various conditions, including acquisition of at least 75% of Dunkin's outstanding shares. Their offer will expire December 20.
11/20/89	DD acquisition extends its offer of $45 a share to 12/4.
12/4/89	DD acquisition extends its offer of $45 a share to 12/21.

EPILOGUE

After an extended takeover battle, Dunkin Donuts agreed to a takeover by the British food and beverage company, Allied–Lyons PLC.[2] The

---

[2] "Dunkin Donuts Agrees to Sale," *New York Times*, November 18, 1989, p. 37.

Table 16.7 PROSPECTIVE DEBT SCHEDULES FOR DUNKIN DONUTS

Year	88	89	90	91	92	93	94	95	96	97	98	99	00	01	02	03
MAXIMUM FIXED CHARGES:																
REVOLVER:																
Balance (end of period)	$64,000	$64,000	$64,000	$64,000	$64,000	$64,000	$64,000	$64,000	$64,000	$64,000	$64,000	$64,000	$64,000	$64,000	$64,000	$64,000
Additional borrowings		$0	$0	$0	$0	$0	$0	$0	$0	$0	$0	$0	$0	$0	$0	$0
Principal repayments		$0	$0	$0	$0	$0	$0	$0	$0	$0	$0	$0	$0	$0	$0	$0
Interest expense		$7,718	$7,718	$7,718	$7,718	$7,718	$7,718	$7,718								
Interest expense based on outs balance at beginning of period.																
Balance-1/15th assmptn	$64,000	$59,733	$55,467	$51,200	$46,933	$42,667	$38,400	34,133	$29,867	$25,600	$21,333	$17,067	$12,800	$8,533	$4,267	$0
Amortization-1/15 assmptn		$4,267	$4,267	$4,267	$4,267	$4,267	$4,267	$4,267	$4,267	$4,267	$4,267	$4,267	$4,267	$4,267	$4,267	$4,267
Interest-1/15th assmptn		$7,461	$6,947	$6,432	$5,917	$5,403	$4,888	$4,374	$0							
TERM LOAN-FLOATING:																
Balance (end of period)	$110,000	$94,300	$78,600	$62,900	$47,200	$31,500	$15,800	$0								
Principal repayments		$15,700	$15,700	$15,700	$15,700	$15,700	$15,700	$15,800								
Interest expense		$0	$10,849	$8,879	$6,909	$4,938	$2,968	$991								
TERM LOAN-FIXED:																
Balance (end of period)	$95,000	$81,400	$67,800	$54,200	$40,600	$27,000	$13,400	$-3,400								
Principal repayments		$13,600	$13,600	$13,600	$13,600	$13,600	$13,600	$3,400								
Interest expense		$11,069	$9,362	$7,656	$5,949	$4,242	$2,535	$841								
SUBORDINATED-FLOATING:																
Balance (end of period)	$0	$0	$0	$0	$0	$0	$0	$0								
Principal repayments		$0	$0	$0	$0	$0	$0	$0								
Interest expense		$0	$0	$0	$0	$0	$0	$0								
SUBORDINATED-FIXED:																
Balance (end of period)	$23,500	$21,933	$20,367	$18,800	$17,233	$15,667	$14,100	$12,533	$10,967	$9,400	$7,833	$6,267	$4,700	$3,133	$1,567	$5
Principle repayments		$1,567	$1,567	$1,567	$1,567	$1,567	$1,567	$1,567	$1,567	$1,567	$1,567	$1,567	$1,567	$1,567	$1,567	$1,562
Interest expense		$3,144	$2,927	$2,710	$2,494	$2,277	$2,060	$1,843	$1,626	$1,409	$1,193	$976	$759	$542	$325	$109

THIRD PARTY DEBT: / ASSUMED (PFE-LBO EXISTING FINANCING) schedule

Line item	1	2	3	4	5	6	7	8	9	10	11	12	13	14	15
THIRD PARTY DEBT:															
Balance (end of period)	$0	$0	$0	$0	$0	$0	$0	$0	$0	$0	$0	$0	$0	$0	$0
Principal repayments	$0	$0	$0	$0	$0	$0	$0	$0	$0	$0	$0	$0	$0	$0	$0
Interest expense	$0	$0	$0	$0	$0	$0	$0	$0	$0	$0	$0	$0	$0	$0	$0
ASSUMED (PFE-LBO EXISTING FINANCING):															
Balance (end cf period)	$0	$0	$0	$0	$0	$0	$0	$0	$0	$0	$0	$0	$0	$0	$0
Principal payments	$0	$0	$0	$0	$0	$0	$0	$0	$0	$0	$0	$0	$0	$0	$0
Interest expense	$0	$0	$0	$0	$0	$0	$0	$0	$0	$0	$0	$0	$0	$0	$0
TOTAL FIXED CHARGES:	$292,500														
TOTAL BALANCE:	$261,633	$230,767	$199,900	$169,033	$138,167	$107,300	$76,533	$74,967	$73,400	$71,833	$70,267	$68,133	$67,133	$65,567	$64,005
Total principal repayments	$30,867	$30,867	$30,867	$30,867	$30,867	$30,867	$30,767	$1,567	$1,567	$1,567	$1,567	$1,567	$1,567	$1,567	$1,562
Total interest expense	$21,931	$26,963	$23,069	$19,175	$15,281	$11,394		$1,626	$1,409	$1,193	$976	$759	$542	$325	$109
Rents	$0	$0	$0	$0	$0	$0	$0	$0	$0	$0	$0	$0	$0	$0	$0
TOTAL FIXED CHARGES:	$52,798	$57,830	$53,936	$50,042	$46,148	$42,160		$3,193	$2,976	$2,759	$2,542	$2,326	$2,109	$1,892	$1,670
Reduction of Fixed Charges															
ADJ. TOTAL FIXED CHARGES (uses 1/15 assumption):	$56,808	$65,219	$60,810	$56,402	$51,993	$47,585	$43,082	$7,460	$7,243	$7,026	$6,809	$6,592	$6,375	$6,159	$5,937
MAX. FIXED CHARGES (ADJ.):	$65,219														
PREFERRED															
Balance	$0	$0	$0	$0	$0	$0	$0	$0	$0	$0	$0	$0	$0	$0	$0
Sinking fund	$0	$0	$0	$0	$0	$0	$0	$0	$0	$0	$0	$0	$0	$0	$0
Dividends	$0	$0	$0	$0	$0	$0	$0	$0	$0	$0	$0	$0	$0	$0	$0
THIRD PARTY PREFERRED:															
Balance	$0	$0	$0	$0	$0	$0	$0	$0	$0	$0	$0	$0	$0	$0	$0
Sinking fund	$0	$0	$0	$0	$0	$0	$0	$0	$0	$0	$0	$0	$0	$0	$0
Dividends	$0	$0	$0	$0	$0	$0	$0	$0	$0	$0	$0	$0	$0	$0	$0

AVERAGE LIFE:

Line item	(life)							
Term loan-floating	4.00	$15,700	$31,400	$47,100	$62,800	$78,500	$94,200	$110,600
Term loan-fixed	3.99	$13,600	$27,200	$40,800	$54,400	$68,000	$81,600	$93,800
Subordinated-floating	NA	$0	$0	$0	$0	$0	$0	$0
Subordinated-fixed	8.00	$1,567	$3,133	$4,700	$6,267	$7,833	$9,400	$10,967

purchase price was $325 million in cash, or $47.25 per share. The number of shares outstanding changed during 1988–1989. Based on the valuation cash flow analysis that showed a total value of $400 million, Allied–Lyons appeared to have received a good price.

CASE STUDY: PHILIP MORRIS CORPORATION GROWTH THROUGH ACQUISITIONS

The case of Philip Morris Companies, Inc., is a good example of how acquisitions can be used profitably to achieve growth. Prior to the acquisition of General Foods, Philip Morris' main lines of business were tobacco and beer. The company decided at the end of 1985 that the significant cash flows of the firm, generated by the tobacco business, could be used to diversify the company's operations into other growth areas. The company acquired General Foods in November 1985. This acquisition was the first in a series of three large acquisitions in the food industry during the period 1985–1990. The end result was a company that still had large and dependable cash flows but one which was not as dependent on the U.S. tobacco market, whose long-term outlook is not as optimistic as it once was. As of the beginning of 1990, the firm showed an impressive combination of economic strength and growth potential. Much of this can be attributed to major acquisitions it made during this time period.

THREE MAJOR FOOD MARKET ACQUISITIONS

Acquired Firm	Year	Price
General Foods	1985	$5.6 billion
Kraft	1988	$12.9 billion
Jacob Suchard[1]	1990	$3.8 billion

OVERVIEW OF THE PHILIP MORRIS COMPANIES, INC.

The Philip Morris Companies, Inc., is a diversified firm that produces products in the following industry categories:

Tobacco
Food
Beer
Financial services and real estate

---

[1] The acquisition of $3.8 billion reflected the acquisition of 80 percent of the firm's outstanding shares.

Tobacco

The Philip Morris Companies, Inc. is the largest cigarette company in the world. The firm has been highly successful in this area. This success is, in part, attributed to the popularity of its leading brands such as Marlboro, which is the best-selling packaged cigarette in the world. The firm also markets other leading brands such as Merit, Benson & Hedges, and Virginia Slims. While the growth of the U.S. tobacco business has slowed, Philip Morris still appears strong. In addition, the company's brands have performed well in international markets, thereby offsetting the slowdown in the U.S. market and reinforcing the firm's globalization strategy.

Food

The 1988 acquisition of Kraft by Philip Morris and the eventual merger of this business into the General Foods' operations resulted in the formation of one of the world's largest food manufacturers. Together, these two divisions market a large variety of notable brands that have enjoyed considerable financial success. The move into the food business was reinforced by the subsequent acquisition of the Swiss coffee and chocolate maker Jacob Suchard. This acquisition not only increased Philip Morris' emphasis on food businesses but also firmly established the company's presence in the European market. With this last acquisition, tobacco sales accounted for less than 50 percent of the firm's total revenues.

Beer

The Miller Brewing brand of the Philip Morris Companies, Inc., commands a rising 23.1 percent share of the U.S. market. This division markets several variations of the Miller brand name including Miller Lite, which is the second best-selling beer in the United States. The firm has maintained its position in this highly competitive industry category through aggressive marketing, costs containment, and the development of new brands.

Financial Services and Real Estate

This category is clearly the smallest of the four business segments discussed here. Its performance is mixed, with financial services showing a profit and real estate causing losses. The combined effects, however, were positive, particularly in 1988 when the real estate segment made a positive contribution to earnings.

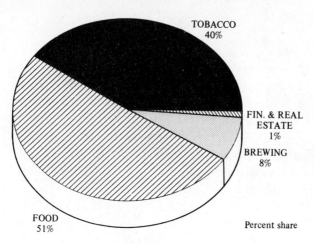

Figure 16.2 Revenues, Philip Morris Companies, Inc.

The contributions to revenues and profits for each of the above business segments are depicted in Figures 16.2 and 16.3. The high profitability of the tobacco segment is reflected by the fact that while 40 percent of the company's revenues are generated from tobacco, 72 percent of Philip Morris' profits in 1989 resulted from tobacco sales.

Leading Products of the Acquired Companies

A review of the list of a few of the major brands of the acquired companies shows that Philip Morris acquired established brands with leading market shares with each of the three acquisitions.

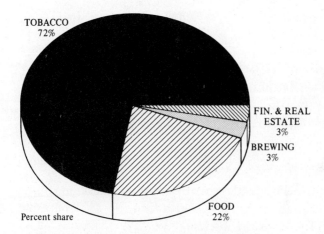

Figure 16.3 Profits, Philip Morris Companies, Inc.

General Foods

Kool Aid
Maxwell House Coffee
Yuban Coffee
Jello
Freihofer Baking Company
Entenmann's Baking Company

Kraft

Kraft Cheese
Velveeta
Miracle Whip
Philadelphia Brand Cream Cheese
Parkay Margarine
Seven Seas Salad Dressing

Jacob Suchard

Jacob's Cafe Brand Coffee
Toblerone Candy
Milka Chocolate

Acquisition Strategy

Philip Morris used a well-designed acquisition strategy to reduce the company's dependence on an uncertain tobacco industry. The strategy featured transition of the firm from a tobacco company into one of the world's leading food producers. The move into the food business was fundamentally sound, given the fact that there is an inelastic demand for food in general. While there is intense competition in many areas of the food business, the fact that Phillip Morris purchased leading brand names through its acquisitions helped insulate the company from some of these competitive pressures.

While many firms dramatically increased their financial leverage during the 1980s in order to finance acquisitions that proved to be poor investments, Philip Morris carefully avoided such pitfalls in the acquisition game. Using the dependable cash flows that Philip Morris derived from the tobacco business, the company helped finance the acquisitions without excessive reliance on debt financing. The fact that the acquisitions improved Philip Morris' financial well-being is underscored by the financial analysis shown on the following page.

Table 16.8   QUARTERLY FINANCIAL STATEMENTS, REVENUES AND INCOME
Philip Morris Companies, Inc.

Date	Sales (mil $)	Income (mil $)	Primary EPS	Dividends per share	Shares outstanding (000)
06/90	12,740	948	1.03	0.35	928,530
03/90	11,388	775	0.84	0.34	928,530
12/89	11,147	863	0.93	0.35	927,899
09/89	11,247	748	0.81	0.27	926,544
06/89	11,595	745	0.81	0.29	924,124
03/89	10,770	590	0.64	0.28	923,892
12/88	9,140	296	0.33	0.28	946,504
09/88	7,547	639	0.69	0.23	946,504
06/88	7,819	627	0.67	0.22	946,504
03/88	7,236	502	0.53	0.23	946,504
12/87	7,064	478	0.51	0.19	953,092
09/87	6,967	502	0.53	0.18	953,092
06/87	7,116	476	0.50	0.19	952,560
03/87	6,554	386	0.41	0.19	951,432
12/86	6,553	371	0.39	0.15	957,304
09/86	6,398	414	0.44	0.14	957,304

FIVE-YEAR GROWTH RATES
Sales Growth Rate:	32%
EPS Growth Rate:	26%
Dividend Growth Rate:	25%

Source: Media General Data Rule.

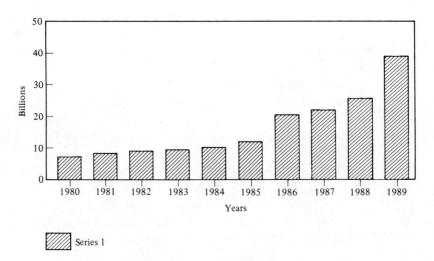

Figure 16.4 Revenues, Philip Morris Companies, Inc.

Table 16.8 and Figure 16.4 show a pattern of steadily increasing revenues. This trend was mirrored in the exponentially increasing operating and net income figures. (See Figures 16.5 and 16.6.) One should bear in mind, however, that a significant component of these increases came from the addition of the General Foods and Kraft revenues and profits.

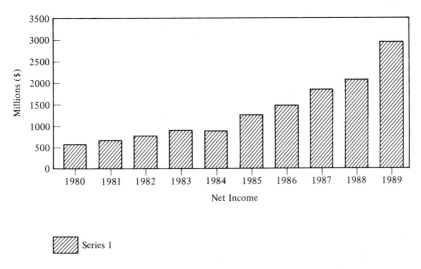

Figure 16.5 Net income, Philip Morris Companies, Inc.

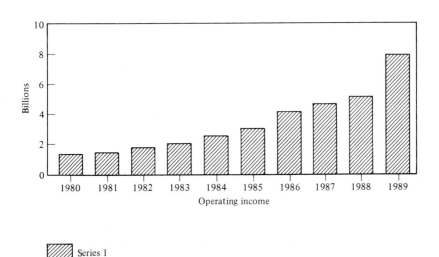

Figure 16.6 Operating income, Philip Morris Companies, Inc.

Financial Ratios

A review of selected financial ratios also depicts a growing company that maintained its financial well-being while aggressively pursuing a major acquisition strategy. (See Table 16.9.) Industry ratios were computed through a weighted average of the industry ratios for the food and tobacco industries. Since food sales account for 51 percent of revenues and tobacco 40 percent, a simple industry ratio is constructed by converting the industry ratios for each category into 100 percent equivalents using weights of .56 and .44, respectively.

Table 16.9   PHILIP MORRIS' FINANCIAL RATIOS

Financial Ratios	Weighted Average Industry	Philip Morris' Ratios				
		12/89	12/88	12/87	12/86	12/85
Profit margin, pretax (Percent of sales)	1.7	11.3	12.6	12.1	13.6	19.2
Current ratio	1.4	1.0	1.0	1.3	1.3	1.5
Quick ratio	0.8	0.3	0.3	0.4	0.4	0.5
Coverage ratio	3.3	2.7	4.5	3.7	3.0	4.6
Asset turnover	1.3	1.2	0.9	1.4	1.2	0.7
Total liabilities to net worth	1.0	1.6	2.1	0.8	1.1	1.5
Return on assets (%)	11.1	7.6	6.3	9.6	8.4	7.2
Return on equity (%)	8.8	30.8	30.4	27.0	26.1	26.5

Interpretation of Selected Ratios

Pretax Profit Margin   Philip Morris' profit margin is significantly higher than the industry average.

Current Ratio   The current ratio of Philip Morris is lower than the industry average.

Quick Ratio   The quick ratio is also lower than the industry average.

Comment on the Liquidity Ratios   The lower liquidity ratios of Philip Morris do not present a problem since the firm is not in danger of becoming so illiquid that it would not be able to pay its bills as they come due.

Asset Turnover   There is little difference between the industry asset turnover average and the Philip Morris value.

Total Liabilities to Net Worth   Philip Morris increased its leverage in 1988. This is not surprising for firms that engage in major acquisitions. The financial leverage, however, as measured by this ratio, declined from 2.1 to 1.6 from 1988 to 1989. An examination of the return on equity, however, shows that this additional leverage was used to generate a higher rate of return on equity. The additional leverage does not represent a significant increase in the riskiness of the firm given the great ability of the firm to generate cash flows.

Return on Assets   The return on assets for Philip Morris is less than the industry average.

Return on Equity   The return on equity for Philip Morris, in contrast to the return on assets, is significantly higher than the industry average.

Conclusion of Financial Ratio Analysis

The financial ratio analysis of the Philip Morris Companies, Inc., reflects a picture of financial health and high stockholder value relative to industry averages. This picture was reflected in the firm's stock market performance, which reflected a steady upward trend through the second half of the 1980s. (See Figure 16.7.)

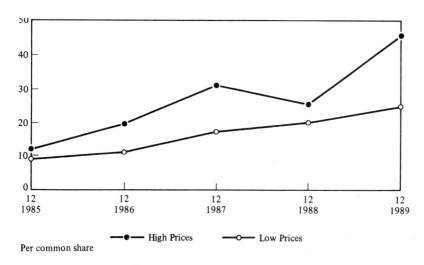

Per common share

Figure 16.7 High-low prices, Philip Morris Companies, Inc.

CONCLUSION OF PHILIP MORRIS CASE STUDY

Philip Morris is a good example of how a company can effectively utilize acquisitions to pursue a strategy of low-risk growth. Many of the acquisitions that took place during the fourth merger wave involved firms that financed poorly conceived acquisition strategies through an excessive reliance on high-yield debt. The pursuit of some of these acquisition strategies damaged some firms' financial well-being while adding little to the future growth of the firm. The Philip Morris movement into the food industry through three major strategic acquisitions during the period 1985–1990 transformed this tobacco company into one that does not rely excessively on a business segment that has an uncertain future. In doing so, Philip Morris has demonstrated that a well-designed series of diversification/acquisitions can lead to growth and increases in shareholder wealth. While many other firms have unsuccessfully attempted to diversify, Philip Morris pursued a series of strategic acquisitions in the food industry involving leading firms with larger market shares. The stock market confirmed its approval of this strategy by continually bidding up the company's stock price. As of the start of the 1990s, Philip Morris has not only become a firm with strong cash flows from its tobacco business but also a company that markets leading brands in both the food and tobacco business. The future of the company appears to have been significantly enhanced as a result of its strategic acquisitions.

Index